In Search of a Liberal Germany

In Search of a Liberal Germany

*Studies in the History of German Liberalism
from 1789 to the Present*

Edited by
Konrad H. Jarausch *and* **Larry Eugene Jones**

BERG
New York/Oxford/Munich
Distributed exclusively in the U.S. and Canada by
St. Martin's Press, New York

Published in 1990 by
Berg Publishers, Inc.
Editorial offices:
165 Taber Avenue, Providence, RI 02906, U.S.A.
150 Cowley Road, Oxford, OX4 1JJ, UK
Westermühlstraße 26, 8000 München, 5, FRG

Library of Congress Cataloging-in-Publication Data

In search of a liberal Germany: studies in the history of German
liberalism from 1789 to the present / edited by Konrad H. Jarausch
and Larry Eugene Jones
p. cm.
"Essays . . . dedicated to the honor of Theodore S. Hamerow"—Pref.
Includes bibliographical references.
ISBN 0–85496–614–5 : $60.00
1. Germany—Politics and government—1789–1900. 2. Germany—
Politics and government—20th century. 3. Liberalism—Germany.
4. Hamerow, Theodore S. I. Jarausch, Konrad Hugo. II. Jones,
Larry Eugene. III. Hamerow, Theodore S.
DD204.I5 1990
320.5'1'0943—dc20   89–39741

British Library Cataloguing in Publication Data

In search of a liberal Germany : studies in the history of
German liberalism from 1789 to the present.
1. Germany. Political ideologies: Liberalism, history
I. Jarausch, Konrad H. (Konrad Hugo), 1941–
II. Jones, Larry Eugene
320.5'1'0943

ISBN 0–85496–614–5

Printed in Great Britain by Billing & Sons Ltd, Worcester

Essays Presented in Honor of
Theodore S. Hamerow

Contents

Contents

Preface

The essays in this volume are dedicated to Theodore S. Hamerow. Of the fourteen contributors, exactly half received their doctorates at the University of Wisconsin under his direction. For them, this volume is a welcome opportunity to repay in small measure their personal and professional debt to their mentor. Instead of preparing a conventional festschrift that lacks coherence, it seemed more appropriate to honor Professor Hamerow with a collection of essays organized around a single theme. Since the problem of German liberalism has played a central role in Hamerow's work as well as in the writings of many of his students, this topic provided a natural focus for a book in his honor.

This collection seeks to present a cross section of recent Anglo-American scholarship on one of the most important facets of the much-discussed German problem. To demonstrate the maturity and liveliness of Anglo-American research on modern German history, the editors went beyond the circle of Hamerow's students to invite a number of well-established scholars in the field to take part in the project. A prominent German historian also agreed to collaborate so as to make current writing in the Federal Republic accessible to an English-speaking audience. Although the volume makes no claim to being all-inclusive, it spans the entire temporal range of liberal development over the past two centuries and explores not only the more traditional area of political history but its broader social and cultural dimensions as well.

The anthology addresses three distinct audiences. In the first place, it is designed to provide the specialist in modern German history with a survey of the most recent Anglo-American research on the topic of German liberalism and its development since the French Revolution. In this respect, the volume transcends traditional party history through a variety of innovative approaches that explore the interconnections between liberal currents in culture, society, and politics. At the same time, these essays offer the generalist in either German or European history fresh insight into the historiographical debates that are currently redefining the traditional notion of liberalism and its place in modern German history. By focusing on local and regional developments, this volume suggests that the failure of German liberalism was by no means as complete or as widespread as the traditional literature has tended to argue. Third, the collection seeks to provide comparative historians with the foundation from which they can draw meaningful conclusions about the relative strengths and weaknesses of the German liberal tradition. This, in turn, will make it possible to develop a more meaningful perspective from which the vexing problem of the German *Sonderweg* can be addressed.

The editors would like to take this opportunity to pay a brief tribute to the memory of one of their colleagues, Stanley Zucker. Stanley belonged to the circle of former Hamerow students who originally conceived of this project, and he was in the process of writing his own contribution on Marie Pinder and the revolution of 1848 when he passed away after a brief illness in the fall of 1988. In many respects Stanley is as much a part of this book as any of its present contributors.

The completion of this book was made possible through the cooperation of many colleagues and friends. The editors are especially indebted to the more than two dozen Hamerow students and other colleagues who lent their enthusiastic support to this project. We are particularly grateful to Gretchen Hollmer of Canisius College, without whose help much of the initial correspondence could not have been conducted in a timely and orderly fashion. We would also like to express our appreciation to the National Humanities Center in the Research Triangle Park, North Carolina, for providing indispensable library and clerical services as well as for having made our collaboration possible. And lastly, we would like to thank Marion Berghahn of Berg Publishers, both for her initial interest in this volume and for her patience in seeing it through to its fruition.

Chapel Hill, North Carolina, May 1989 K.H.J./L.E.J.

German Liberalism Reconsidered
Inevitable Decline, Bourgeois Hegemony, or Partial Achievement?

Konrad H. Jarausch and Larry Eugene Jones

The triumphs and travails of German liberalism have fascinated Anglo-American students of modern German history for more than a half century. This preoccupation stems in no small measure from the enormous and indeed tragic impact of German developments on the general course of European history since the middle of the nineteenth century. After all, did not the weakness of German liberalism contribute to the triumphs of Bismarck and Hitler and thus set the scene for nearly a century of European conflict? In a larger sense, however, the interest of American and British intellectuals in the failure of German liberalism also reflects their own anxiety about the implications of the Nazi experience for the viability of the liberal humanistic values at the heart of their own political culture. Time and time again, twentieth-century humanists have been forced to ask whether what happened in Germany might not occur elsewhere, whether it is still possible to sustain the liberal faith in human rationality in light of the holocaust, and whether free institutions can survive such massive social and economic crises. If the fate of liberalism has attracted considerable attention in Germany, it has been studied with no less intensity – and perhaps with an even greater sense of moral urgency – in Great Britain and the United States.

For English-speaking intellectuals, questions about German liberalism have served the further purpose of demarcating and validating their own political experience. From their perspective, the Germans seem to be first cousins whose political culture is both sufficiently similar and yet distinctive enough to yield meaningful conclusions about the viability of their own. Few scholars, for example, would seriously investigate Russian or Chinese liberalism as a way of developing better insight into

1

the strengths and weaknesses of Western political institutions. Anglo-American liberals have been fascinated by the failure in Central Europe of once-promising attempts to achieve goals similar to their own. The inability of German liberals to transform state and society in accordance with Anglo-American standards of liberty and equality has thus become a central feature of the so-called German problem. However, the uncritical application of their own yardstick to the German experience has produced a morality tale that all too frequently only reconfirms Western claims of political superiority. In using Central European failures to highlight their own success, Western liberals have unwittingly accepted German claims of distinctiveness without realizing the implications this holds for the accuracy of their understanding of the Central European experience or the validity of the conclusions they have drawn from it.

Ironically, postwar German historians have internalized the Anglo-American standard and used it to judge their own history in essentially negative terms. Since 1945 German scholars have frequently inverted the traditional German notion of a Central European *Sonderweg* as superior to Western decadence and addressed the problematic peculiarity of their own past in dramatically new and different terms. At the heart of this endeavor lay their desire to legitimate new political institutions and to create a democratic consensus through a critical understanding of liberalism's role in the German past. In doing so, however, they have produced a kaleidoscope of successive negative images of liberalism – including the failed idealism of 1848–49, the arrested parliamentarism of 1867, the misguided imperialism of 1900 to 1914, and the ill-fated constitutional republicanism of 1919 to 1933. This litany of failure, in turn, only served to reinforce the more general complaints that Anglo-American liberals had made about specific aspects of the Central European experience, such as the excessive nationalism of the Bismarckian Reich, the unbridled authoritarianism of the late Wilhelmine Empire, and the rampant expansionism of World War I. If historians on either side of the Atlantic are to develop a more accurate understanding of the strengths and weaknesses of the German tradition, they must free themselves from the contemporary political concerns that have informed, if not confused, their assessment of liberalism and its place in modern German history.

2

The Indictment of Liberal Failure

The literature on modern German history is marked by an ubiquity of interest in the fate of liberalism and a dearth of specific titles on the topic. To be sure, the "tragedy" of liberalism has been a mainstay of the standard histories of modern Germany that preeminent scholars such as Koppel Pinson, Hajo Holborn, and Gordon Craig have written for the benefit of the English-speaking public. Looking for some fundamental flaw in Central European evolution that might explain the Third Reich, these texts mingle sympathetic portrayals of liberal constitutional aspirations and economic achievements with caustic denunciations of ideological doctrinairism and inept parliamentary leadership. At the same time, relatively few scholars have undertaken specialized studies on the problems that have actually shaped the course of liberal development in modern German history. This deficit, in turn, has generated textbook generalizations that often assume a problematic life of their own. A case in point would be the perennial debate over the precise date at which the defeat of Central European liberalism became irreversible. Was it in the revolutions of 1848–49, during the constitutional conflict of the mid-1860s, with the unification of Germany from above in 1871, or at the time of Bismarck's break with the National Liberals in 1878–79? Whatever answer historians might provide, the notion of liberal decline became an idée fixe in the first wave of Anglo-American research in the 1950s and 1960s, an approach that made it difficult to appreciate the positive impact that liberalism had had on German social and political life.

As early as World War I, Thorstein Veblen pondered the paradox of Germany's advanced industrial economic development and relative political backwardness. As Anglo-American scholars tried to explain this discrepancy, they began by focusing their attention on constitutional history. In 1943, for example, John Hallowell published a thin volume entitled *The Decline of German Liberalism as an Ideology* in which he traced the decline of liberal constitutional theory from its origins in Kant and Hegel to twentieth-century apologists for the totalitarian state like Carl Schmitt. A more comprehensive historical analysis was Eugene N. Anderson's impressive volume on *The Social and Political Conflict in Prussia, 1858–1864*, published in 1954. Attempting to

3

understand the character of liberalism and conservatism on the eve of German unification, Anderson's work examined the social and institutional dimensions of the three-sided conflict – between the Crown, its liberal critics, and the conservative Junkers – that developed in Prussia during the New Era after 1858. In the final analysis, Anderson argued that the close relationship between nationalism and liberalism undercut the latter's potential for success and left it vulnerable to manipulation by the Iron Chancellor, Otto von Bismarck. In criticizing the Prussian liberals for having allowed their fascination with the successes of Bismarck's realpolitik to compromise their own principles, Anderson betrayed a moralistic tone that typified the first wave of Anglo-American scholarship on the history of German liberalism.

Other historians turned their attention to the intellectual shortcomings of the German liberal tradition. This line of inquiry was inspired by Guido de Ruggiero's *History of European Liberalism*, a philosophically imposing treatment that became influential after World War II. In 1951 R. Hinton Thomas followed this with a short study of liberal intellectuals from 1822 to 1847. Both of these works, however, were quickly superseded by the appearance of Leonard Krieger's grandiose work on *The German Idea of Freedom* in 1957. Using a typically Western definition of liberalism as "individual secular liberty" as his point of departure, Krieger traced the way in which the leading intellectuals of the German liberal tradition had wrestled with the vexatious problem of freedom throughout the nineteenth century. His conclusion regarding the impact of their ideas upon German society was characteristically ambivalent: "The liberal spirit did affect German institutions. . . . But this process was incomplete and unintegrated. Not only was the capstone of political rights left wanting, but spiritual and material liberties were never organized into a single system of rights, and consequently the half-finished structure crumbled under the strain of later social and international conflicts" (pp. 3–4). Krieger explained this vulnerability not as a deficit but as "a particular German tradition of liberty" that defined freedom as something attainable only within the framework of the state. This, along with the fragmentation of the liberal movement into reformers, constitutionalists, and radicals and the rise of conservative nationalism, meant that by 1871 the liberal challenge had essentially failed, particularly insofar as it had aspired to bring about the introduction of effective parliamentary government.

The echoes of Krieger's work reverberated in several different directions. In 1963 Donald Rohr produced a slim volume exploring the limits of the liberal vision as it pertained to the question of social reform in the period before the revolutions of 1848–49. Other studies traced the intellectual origins of the antiliberal reaction that was to become such a prominent feature of German political life in the last decades of the nineteenth century. In his *Politics of Cultural Despair* of 1961, Fritz Stern examined the role that three conservative theorists – Paul de Lagarde, Julius Langbehn, and Arthur Moeller van den Bruck – had played in eroding the foundations of cultural and political liberalism. Three years later, in his *Crisis of the German Ideology,* George Mosse examined the dissemination and institutionalization of the *völkisch* and racist counterideology throughout German society. Both works were predicated upon the assumption that there was a fundamental liberal deficit in Germany's development that helped to account for the success and pervasiveness of antiliberal, antimodern, and racist tendencies before 1933.

This preoccupation with the intellectual dimensions of the liberal failure found an important corrective in Theodore S. Hamerow's societal analysis of nineteenth-century German history. Initially influenced by Rudolf Stadelmann's classic study of the social and political causes for the failure of the German liberal movement in the revolution of 1848–49, Hamerow's *Restoration, Revolution, Reaction* treated liberalism more as a social than as a constitutional or intellectual movement. The mid-century revolution was "the expression not only of ideological forces like nationalism and liberalism, but also of deepseated popular dissatisfactions engendered by the transition from agrarian manorialism to industrial capitalism" (pp. viii–ix). The failure of the revolution's liberal leadership, therefore, was not so much a function of ideological deficiencies, national quarrels, or political incompetence as the consequence of a profound schism within the coalition of social forces that had brought about the upheaval in the first place. In championing the cause of constitutionalism and laissez-faire economics, the leaders of the liberal middle class abandoned the starving peasants and hard-pressed artisans, who had rallied to their support in spring of 1848, and left them prey to manipulation by the

5

conservative foes of liberal reform. As a result, the forces of German liberalism suffered a defeat from which they never recovered.

A decade later Hamerow returned to this theme in his two-volume study on *The Social Foundations of German Unification, 1858–1871*. Extending his interpretation of liberal failures from the revolution to unification, Hamerow devoted careful attention to the "social matrix of civic activity" as the point of departure for his analysis of the events that eventually culminated in the founding of the Second Empire. The critical step in the process of German unification was not so much Bismarck's appointment as Prussian minister president as the "decisive breakthrough" of the industrial mode of production in the late 1850s and 1860s. By concentrating wealth and economic power in the hands of a bourgeois elite that began to demand a measure of political influence commensurate with its burgeoning economic resources, the first wave of German industrialization not only served as a catalyst for the revival of liberal energies but also provided a solid economic foundation for unification. Yet as Germany's bourgeois elite began to press for a liberal reform of the Prussian political system, it was unable to come to terms with the social consequences of the industrial revolution and failed to find a solution to the social problem. The creation of the Second Empire, therefore, rested upon an "unwritten compromise" between Prussia's conservative aristocracy and Germany's industrial bourgeoisie, a compromise that provided for economic integration and the facade of parliamentary government at the expense of civic democracy, social justice, and control over the military. The historic weakness of German liberalism, therefore, was more social than ideological in nature.

Similar questions about the shortcomings of liberalism permeated the scholarly biographies of prominent nineteenth- and twentieth-century liberals. Two of Hamerow's own students, James F. Harris and Stanley Zucker, produced important biographies of influential nineteenth-century liberals, Eduard Lasker and Ludwig Bamberger. Equally significant were James Sheehan's study of the liberal economist Lujo Brentano and Lamar Cecil's life of shipping magnate Albert Ballin, published in 1966 and 1967, respectively.

No representative of the German liberal tradition, however,

has attracted more attention than Max Weber. Wolfgang Mommsen's *Max Weber and German Politics*, which was first published in German in 1959, revised extensively in 1974, and then translated into English ten years later, remains the most important historical contribution to the impressive body of English-language literature on Weber and his place in modern German history. Mommsen saw Weber as a "liberal in despair" whose conversion to Nietzschean vitalism did little to temper his congenital skepticism regarding the future of humanistic values in an increasingly rationalized and bureaucratized world. In a book provocatively entitled *The Iron Cage*, Arthur Mitzman employed a Freudian approach to explain Weber's pessimism as the product of an unresolved Oedipal conflict that was paradigmatic of Weber's entire generation. In contrast to the theoretical richness of the literature on Weber, studies of the other leading liberal, Gustav Stresemann, tended to be conceptually bland. Only Henry Turner's *Stresemann and the Politics of the Weimar Republic* made a major contribution to an understanding of the liberal problematic in German history, although without going beyond the terms in which it had been defined by Krieger, Hamerow, and their contemporaries.

Studies of liberal organizations and institutions, by contrast, have been sparse and disappointing. It was particularly unfortunate that John Snell died before he could complete his magnum opus on the German democratic movement from 1789 to 1914, although Hans Schmitt eventually edited, completed, and published this manuscript in 1976. By the same token, Lenore O'Boyle never succeeded in turning the impressive articles she wrote in the 1950s and 1960s on the German National Association (Deutscher Nationalverein) and other liberal organizations into a more comprehensive study of the social and political dimensions of nineteenth-century German liberalism. Among the more recent monographs, only James Hunt's study on the People's Party in Württemberg and Southwest Germany from 1890 to 1914 questioned the inherited wisdom of irreversible liberal decline by suggesting that in certain parts of the country the forces of political liberalism were still very much alive. Both Dan White's investigation of the dissolution of the National Liberal hegemony in Hesse and Modris Eksteins's analysis of the democratic press in the Weimar Republic were much too concerned with aspects of liberal decline to question the more general premises on which this work was based.

The theoretical assumptions that informed the first wave of research on the history of German liberalism received their classic formulation in Ralf Dahrendorf's *Society and Democracy in Germany*. Published in 1967 by a prominent German sociologist, this penetrating analysis of Germany's recent past drew heavily on the author's personal experiences in Great Britain and the United States and did much to confirm the Western indictment of German liberalism. From the perspective of a committed liberal, Dahrendorf set out to explain just "what it was in German society that continued to prevent the establishment of a democratic order": "There is a conception of liberty that holds that man can be free only where an experimental attitude to knowledge, the competition of social forces and liberal political institutions are combined. This conception has never really gained a hold in Germany. Why not? This is the German question" (pp. 15–16). In explaining the persistence of social inequality, the nostalgia for synthesis over conflict, "the cartel-ization of elites," and the preference for private over public virtues, Dahrendorf essentially reaffirmed the general outlines of the paradigm that historians had been using to explain the peculiar tragedy of German history. At the heart of the German problem lay the extremely rapid pace of economic moderniz-ation within a social and political system that was still essentially feudal. This temporal disjuncture produced such curious anom-alies as the "industrial feudal society" and the "authoritarian welfare state." The net effect of these tensions was to retard the social and political development of the German bourgeoisie and to prevent the Anglo-American idea of citizenship, with all its attendant rights and obligations, from being firmly established in Germany.

Stressing cultural as well as social determinants, Dahrendorf's masterful dissection of the German problem was as reassuring to Anglo-American scholars as it was unsettling to their German counterparts. The thesis of a fundamental liberal deficit in Ger-many's political development received immediate support from Anglo-American scholars like Fritz Stern. In the preface to a collection of essays on *The Failure of Illiberalism*, he argued that the key to understanding modern German history lay in the inherently illiberal character of Germany's political culture. The notion of "German illiberalism" both reassured Anglo-American liberals as to the superiority of their own political institutions and challenged West German liberals to abolish the social bases for the persistence of illiberal patterns in their own society. In spite of their wide currency, the twin notions of liberal deficit and German illiberalism perpetuated a somewhat distorted reading of the role of liberalism in modern German history. Motivated by the need to explain the German catastrophes of the twentieth century, the initial wave of research on the history of German liberalism was heavily teleological and moral. But in exposing the weaknesses of the German liberal tradition and the roots of German antiliberalism, postwar research also created a negative master plot that could explain neither the rise of liberal aspirations nor their positive impact on the course of Germany's development.

The Rediscovery of Bourgeois Success

Just when it seemed as if the Anglo-American understanding of German liberalism had received its definitive form, the terms of the debate were suddenly changed by renewed controversy over the Second Empire. Hans-Ulrich Wehler's immensely influential *Das deutsche Kaiserreich* of 1973 presented such a sweeping indictment of German illiberalism that it prompted a vigorous reaction against the entire negative consensus. Only recently translated into English, Wehler's brilliant neo-Weberian synthesis of German history from 1871 to 1918 seemed to establish the structural limitations of German liberalism beyond any shadow of academic doubt. By analyzing Bismarck's astute strategems, such as wars for hegemony and revolution from above, it demonstrated how liberal forces were pushed to the periphery of national politics through the Great Depression of 1873–95 and the emergence of organized capitalism. The evolution of the political system from a Bonapartist dictatorship to a state of permanent crisis left the liberals politically impotent and condemned them to "a constant process of disintegration" that permanently eroded their parliamentary efficacy. Based on "structural hostility towards democracy," the defeat of liberalism was in fact so decisive that its failure in the Weimar Republic, admittedly under radically different historical conditions, became a foregone conclusion. Wehler states: "The unbroken tradition of government by pre-industrial power-

9

elites, the prolongation of absolutism among the military, the weakness of liberalism and the very early appearance of deliberalizing measures suggest on the surface a depoliticizing of society, but one which deep down favored a continuation of the *status quo*" (p. 242). Wehler thus drew a direct line of continuity from the establishment of conservative elite hegemony in the Second Empire to the triumph of Nazism in the period from 1933 to 1945. Quickly acquiring the status of a "new orthodoxy," Wehler's self-critical reading of German peculiarity emerged as the cornerstone of what was soon to be known as the Bielefeld school.

Although Wehler's analysis of the Second Empire drew heavily on earlier American work, it elicited only muted, if not ambivalent, responses on this side of the Atlantic. Published in 1974 under the title of *From Bassermann to Bebel*, Beverly Heckart's study of the movement for democratic reform between 1900 and 1914 implicitly undercut the central thrust of Wehler's argument by offering an essentially optimistic assessment of the prospects for reform in the late Wilhelmine Empire. By contrast, James Sheehan's *German Liberalism in the Nineteenth Century* sought to work out the implications of the Wehler thesis for the development of liberalism in a more guarded fashion. Sheehan's complex analysis of "the relationship between liberalism and German society" emphasized "the way in which the historical situation narrowed liberals' choices and often precluded alternatives that might have enabled them to save themselves and their ideals." In balancing structural obstacles with contextual factors such as "parliamentary paralysis and ideological sterility," he recounted an all too familiar story of failure: "By the 1890s, their dreams emptied by frustration, dissension and defeat, the liberals receded to the fringes of political life, enhancing the Wilhelmine stalemate and the dangerous drift towards radical nationalism." In his work on *Students, Society, and Politics in Imperial Germany*, Konrad Jarausch addressed one of the major questions raised by Sheehan's book, namely, the survival of political liberalism in an inherently illiberal society. By tracing the rise of illiberalism and anti-Semitism among university students in the Second Empire, Jarausch analyzed the eclipse of liberal principles within a group that had served throughout much of the nineteenth century as one of the great vanguards of the liberal cause. At the same time, Jarausch modified and refined rather than rejected the prevailing negative views on the Second Empire. Jarausch identified promising neoliberal currents in successive student cohorts and explained the rise of the new nationalism as a result not of manipulation but of social or ideological pressures on young academics.

A far more direct challenge to Wehler's reading of modern German history came from two British social historians, David Blackbourn and Geoff Eley. In two essays published together in 1984 as *The Peculiarities of German History*, Blackbourn and Eley questioned many of the assumptions on which the entire historiographical tradition from Krieger and Hamerow to Wehler had been based. For although Blackbourn and Eley shared Wehler's commitment to a radical and progressive critique of the German past, they argued that the notion of Central European deviance that lay at the heart of the Bielefeld interpretation rested upon assumptions about the French and English experience that historians of those countries' political traditions were no longer prepared to accept. More important, they contended that the preoccupation with the notion of Germany's abortive bourgeois revolution had led to a serious misreading of German development, one that made it difficult to appreciate just how much liberals had achieved over the course of the nineteenth century. In spite of liberalism's conspicuous political failures in 1848–49, 1866–67, and 1878–79, the period of unification witnessed a silent bourgeois revolution in which the German middle class succeeded in realizing many of its most important goals, particularly in the realm of civil society. That this was not accompanied by the introduction of effective parliamentary institutions should not, Blackbourn and Eley maintained, diminish the significance of what the forces of bourgeois liberalism had in fact been able to accomplish. Much of what an earlier generation of German historians had decried as the ill-gotten fruits of liberalism's fateful compromise with the Bismarckian state was now seen as positive proof of liberal success. By no means was the defeat or failure of nineteenth-century German liberalism as final or as complete as those who viewed its achievements from the perspective of 1933 might be led to think.

The publication of *Peculiarities of German History* reinvigorated the debate on German liberalism on both sides of the Atlantic. Conceived independently of the Blackbourn–Eley challenge, Stanley Suval's *Electoral Politics in Wilhelmine Germany* revealed that an increasingly sophisticated voting public had emerged in the last years of the empire and exposed the cherished notion of the "unpolitical German" as a historical myth that needed to be modified if not altogether abandoned. Similarly, Dieter Langewiesche's *Liberalismus in Deutschland* argued that the history of liberalism was not a story of continuous decline but rather consisted of an uneven pattern of development with peaks and valleys of its own. In the first two decades of the twentieth century, for example, the progressive elements in the liberal movement experienced a remarkable revival that the secondary literature on the history of the Wilhelmine Empire has all but ignored. Finally, Larry Eugene Jones used the Black-bourn–Eley critique as the point of departure for his study of *German Liberalism and the Dissolution of the Weimar Party System*. Not only did Jones predicate his interpretation of Weimar liberalism upon a positive reassessment of political development during the last years of the Wilhelmine Empire, but he also insisted that the subsequent failure of liberalism could only be understood in terms of the specific factors that robbed it of vitality and promise between 1918 to 1933. No longer would it suffice to explain the defeat of Weimar democracy as a simple consequence of the repeated setbacks liberalism had supposedly suffered during the nineteenth century.

The historiography of liberalism – and with it much of the writing on modern German history – has undergone a remarkable transformation in the past decade. With greater emotional distance from World War II, the inherited wisdom of continuous decline has been challenged and in some cases decisively repudiated. But the demise of the classical explanation has not yet yielded a new paradigm that students of nineteenth- and twentieth-century German history can use in its place. While Blackbourn and Eley have played an important role in opening up new vistas of investigation and research and in freeing German historical thinking from "the tyranny of historical hindsight," it would be premature to suggest that they have succeeded in providing historians with a compelling alternative interpretation of the troubled German past. As comparative studies have questioned the notion of German exceptionality and pointed to the peculiarity of other national experiences, old questions have been suddenly reopened and new issues added to the agenda. Developing outside the field of research on liberalism, new historiographical currents such as quantification, feminist studies, and regional investigations have begun to pose fresh questions. Only further empirical research and new conceptual departures will resolve the increasingly vigorous debate over the extent to which the history of German liberalism can be read as a record of success or failure.

New Answers and Continuing Debates

This volume presents a critical reexamination of popular myths and prevalent academic assumptions about liberalism and its place in German history. In pursuing this goal, it employs a catholic definition of liberalism. For although liberalism functioned as an organized political movement operating within the traditional arena of parliamentary conflicts and partisan struggles, it also represented a set of cultural attitudes, social practices, and economic principles that resonated throughout German life. Liberalism, therefore, refers not merely to programs, institutions, and modes of political operation in the public realm, but also to patterns of social, economic, and cultural interaction that define the larger context in which the struggle for a liberal Germany has taken place. The multidimensionality of these liberal forces and currents, in turn, requires a diversity of conceptual approaches and a variety of methodologies that explore their interaction in the broadest possible way. This volume therefore seeks to address specific deficiencies in the secondary literature on the history of German liberalism, deficiencies that in some cases have become apparent only in the wake of the controversy over the German *Sonderweg*. As the lacunae in the history of German liberalism are both chronological and topical, the essays presented below seek to break new ground in several different directions.

The first cluster of contributions focuses on the articulation and limits of the liberal vision. Contrasting the writings of two prolific early nineteenth-century social theorists – Christian Friedrich Germershausen and Albrecht Daniel Thaer – Marion Gray traces the shift in German agricultural thought "from a preliberal conception of economic society to one in which liberalism was the formative ideological framework." Gray's essay explores the dynamic effects that redefinition of farming as a trade had on the emergence of rural capitalism, in making

13

"market freedom" an important dimension of conceptions of liberty. In her contribution on the thought of the 1840s feminist Louise Dittmar, Dagmar Herzog explores the limits of the liberal vision as it pertains to the constitution of gender relations in the first half of the nineteenth century. Although German liberals articulated their aspirations in universalist language, they continued to assert that women could not be equal because they were "naturally" different from men. In contesting the "naturalization" of gender difference that had become so prevalent in German liberal thought, Dittmar promoted a radical strand within liberalism that insisted on every individual's right to self-determination. In a similar vein, Richard J. Bazillion explores the tension between the liberating impulses of bourgeois capitalism and the blighting effect of market freedom on the industrial working class. Using the industrially advanced region of Saxony as a case study, Bazillion exposes the structural weaknesses of liberal solutions to proletarian suffering, such as cooperation and adult education. Together, these chapters on the history of liberal ideas demonstrate both the energizing force of liberal ideology in mobilizing German society and the problematic nature of the liberal vision as it related to the agrarian sector, women, and workers. The emergence of rival movements in the form of agrarian interest groups, modern feminism, and democratic socialism all represent responses to specific shortcomings in the liberal vision.

A second group of methodologically innovative essays deals with the popular or grass-roots basis of emerging liberal politics. In a preliminary examination of the liberal movement in Berlin in the first half of the nineteenth century, Jonathan Knudsen explores the obstacles that liberals had to confront in articulating their ideas and organizing their supporters. Although Restoration Berlin was hardly a hospitable environment for the emergence of political liberalism, Knudsen suggests that the evolution of an increasingly liberal culture in the decades immediately preceding the revolutions of 1848–49 may help explain why liberals were so surprisingly effective in challenging royal prerogative in March 1848. In a similar vein, James F. Harris investigates the relationship of the middle class to liberalism and to the revolutions of 1848–49 through an analysis of the Franconian civic guard (*Bürgerwehr*). Quantitative analysis of militia lists reveals that the *Bürgerwehr* was composed largely of

14

family heads from the "old" middle class of craftsmen, small tradesmen, lower officials, and modest landowners. Harris concludes that while the democratically structured *Bürgerwehr* facilitated political mobilization, it was directed toward the defense of private property rather than to specific liberal goals. In a similar study, Michael John investigates the gradual emergence of national liberalism in the province of Hanover on the eve of German unification. John suggests that during the era of reaction that followed the defeat of 1848–49, liberal activity relocated into unpolitical associations, thereby ensuring its survival but predisposing it toward apolitical nationalism in the New Era. The surprising strength of liberalism during the period of unification rested on the control of local politics by associations under the leadership of bourgeois notables. These three essays suggest that the liberal ascendancy of the 1860s and 1870s owed much to middle-class social networks that were dominated by notables of *Besitz und Bildung*. They also establish the way in which concerns for peace and order, local autonomy, and national unity left these elements predisposed to compromise with Bismarck's unification from above.

A third set of essays examines the crisis and dissolution of the liberal hegemony in Imperial Germany from four distinct perspectives. In his essay on the political realignment of the 1890s, Geoff Eley concentrates on the erosion of National Liberal power in the countryside, where the emergence of a new style of nationalist politics put liberals at the mercy of right-wing pressure groups. The decline of German liberalism between 1880 and 1900 thus stemmed in large part from the inability of liberal notables in predominantly agricultural regions like Hanover and Prussian Hesse to adapt their style of political leadership to the exigencies of mass politics as practiced by conservative rural populists. Representing the best of current West German scholarship on this topic, Dieter Langewiesche's wide-ranging essay on German liberalism from 1871 to 1914 views the decline in liberal Reichstag mandates as a process of normalization that was inevitable once unification had been achieved and other political forces had begun to emerge. With Bismarck's second *Reichsgründung* of 1878–79 and the fragmentation of the liberal electorate, urban liberals tried to arrest their electoral decline by embracing a program of progressive municipal reform. The rise of mass nationalist politics and the birth of cultural modernism in the early twentieth century so thoroughly shook the self-confidence of Germany's *Bildungsbürgertum* that it began to abandon the cause of political liberalism. Approaching the problem from a different perspective, Eleanor Turk demonstrates how German liberals struggled to create the legal preconditions for a more democratic political process with the passage of the Association Law of 1908. In seeking to retain provisions aimed at excluding farm workers, civil servants, and those who did not speak German from the benefits of a liberalized association law, however, German liberals only revealed their ambivalence towards the fruits of democracy. By suggesting that the development of German liberalism was uneven and that it differed from one part of the country to another, these essays provide a more nuanced interpretation of liberal decline and revival in the Second German Empire.

The fourth cluster of essays explores the disintegration of liberalism during the Weimar Republic from a sociopolitical perspective. In his study of the decline of liberal professionalism, Konrad H. Jarausch explores the erosion of support in one of the key constituent groups of bourgeois liberalism. Drawing on the experience of lawyers, doctors, teachers, and engineers, Jarausch argues that the liberal recasting of the professions encountered increasing difficulties during the empire. The ineffectiveness of liberal solutions, such as a more rigorous selection process or competition during the Great Depression, ultimately broke the bond between professionals and liberalism, rendering the former more susceptible to nationalist and *völkisch* appeals. In a similar vein, Larry Eugene Jones investigates the baffling alienation of the younger generation from the liberal parties of the Weimar Republic. In spite of vigorous organizational efforts by the German Democratic Party (Deutsche Demokratische Partei or DDP) and the German People's Party (Deutsche Volkspartei or DVP), the vast majority of youth rejected established bourgeois politics as compromised and preferred various kinds of nationalist Bünde. Generational protest intensified the legitimacy crisis of the Weimar party system and accelerated the dissolution of the German liberal parties. Liberal hegemony in the Weimar Republic, as Thomas Childers argues in a conceptually innovative essay on the language of liberal discourse in Weimar Germany, was further eroded through a situation in which the liberal parties were forced to compete for electoral support on linguistic terrain inimical to their own basic principles. By employing a social vocabulary inherited from the corporatist tradition of nineteenth-century German conservatism, the liberal parties placed themselves at a severe disadvantage vis-à-vis their major rivals for the political loyalties of the German middle class. German liberalism might have been strong enough to put its imprint upon the Weimar Constitution, but, as these three essays show, it was not powerful enough to prevent the erosion of its social base, to bridge the generational cleavages that cut through all strata of German society, or to overcome the handicap of a linguistic bias in Germany's political culture that worked in favor of its conservative and fascist rivals.

The final group of biographical articles reflects on the implications of the liberal legacy for the German Federal Republic. By comparing Wolfgang Haußmann and Hildegard Hamm-Brücher as representatives of two different generations of postwar German liberalism, Rebecca Boehling explores the secret of liberalism's survival after 1945 in the form of the Free Democratic Party (Freie Demokratische Partei or FDP). With its distinctive blend of laissez-faire economics and legal individualism, the FDP has continued the tradition of governmental liberalism by playing a pivotal role in Bonn coalition politics. With Haußmann serving as the symbol of continuity with pre-Nazi liberal traditions and Hamm-Brücher representing a new generation of reform-minded democrats concerned with education, women's issues, and social policy, the Free Democrats have succeeded in giving political liberalism a new lease on life in the postwar period. The concluding chapter by A.J. Nicholls illustrates the broader impact of liberalism on postwar German society. The restoration of economic neoliberalism was not due to liberal party power but to the influence of the dynamic and amiable Ludwig Erhard, a member of the Christian Democratic Union. Enshrined in the Basic Law (Grundgesetz) of the German Federal Republic and in the revival of a free market economy, liberalism achieved its greatest influence at precisely the point when it was at its organizational nadir. Liberalism, as these essays convincingly argue, not only survived the debacle of 1933–45 but left an indelible mark on the politics of the Federal Republic.

The evidence presented in this volume suggests that a partial resolution of the *Sonderweg* debate, especially if put into a comparative context, is now possible. By drawing on detailed

17

local studies, by extending the time frame into the twentieth century, and by connecting the dimensions of culture, society, and politics more systematically than before, recent research points to an intermediary position. As a result, it seems that both the Wehler critique and the Blackbourn-Eley challenge were somewhat overstated. Not only was German society less illiberal than Wehler had maintained, but bourgeois hegemony was never as complete as Blackbourn and Eley had claimed. Even the principals of the controversy have begun to admit not only that middle-class values and patterns of social interaction became dominant by the turn of the century but also that true parliamentary government continued to escape liberals in the Second Empire. To gain cognitive distance, it might help to set developments in Germany against the background of the even more dramatic decline of Austrian liberalism. John Boyer's probing study of the origins of the Christian Social movement in the second half of the nineteenth century provides a compelling analysis of the role that nationality conflict, anti-Semitism, and Catholic social concern played in the decline of Austrian liberalism and the emergence of illiberal mass politics. By the same token, Carl Schorske's imaginative set of essays on fin de siècle Vienna shows how the rise of cultural modernism was closely related to the crisis of Austrian liberalism, and how this in turn helped erode the ethical and cultural ideals of the Viennese *Bildungsbürgertum*. By underlining the speed and thoroughness of the liberal collapse in Vienna, these studies only highlight the relative strength and persistence of liberal traditions in the German states.

Resolving the Liberal Paradox

What new insights does the most recent research on the history of German liberalism have to offer? At the very least, it seems that the inherited wisdom of uninterrupted and irreversible liberal decline is in need of substantial modification. From its early nineteenth-century origins to the post-1945 period, the development of German liberalism has been characterized by at least three discrete peaks of success separated by corresponding valleys of disappointment and failure. The years from 1789 to 1848 witnessed the emergence of liberal ideas in specific sectors of German society and the growth of a network of progressive associations. The failure of German liberalism in the revolutions of 1848–49 represented a temporary setback from which liberal forces had recovered by the end of the following decade. The period from the beginning of the so-called liberal era in 1858 to the second *Reichsgründung* of 1878–80 marked the first heyday of German liberalism, in which liberals were able to place their decisive imprint on much of the major legislation of the Second Empire. Bismarck's break with the National Liberals at the end of the 1870s, however, initiated an era of decay and fragmentation that continued for the next twenty years.

The turn of the century initiated a second wave of liberal accomplishment. The revival of German liberalism in the late Wilhelmine period could be seen in the unification of the various left-liberal parties in the Progressive People's Party (Fortschrittliche Volkspartei or FVP), the emergence of the Hansa-Bund (Hansa-Bund für Gewerbe, Handel und Industrie) and the German Peasants' League (Deutscher Bauernbund), and the ability of progressive liberals to reach across class and religious lines to potential allies in the Social Democratic and Catholic camps. The passage of the Peace Resolution in the summer of 1917, the formation of the interparliamentary committee shortly thereafter, and the creation of the Weimar Coalition at the beginning of 1919 showed that German liberalism had managed to break out of the political isolation that had plagued its efforts during the last decades of the Second Empire. Challenged by the rise of Social Democracy and alerted to the possibilities that this created for a structural reform of Germany's political system, German liberals were once again in a position to exercise decisive influence on the course of German history. The ratification of the Weimar Constitution in August 1919 was a major liberal triumph, and the political order that emerged from the ruins of the November revolution was essentially a liberal achievement. The founding of the Weimar Republic thus marked the culmination of a liberal revival that had been under way since the turn of the century.

Liberal achievements of the early twentieth century soon turned to bitter ashes. Almost from the outset, the legitimacy of the new political order was compromised by the imposition of the Versailles Peace Treaty. As a result, Weimar became synonymous in the eyes of potential middle-class supporters with Germany's defeat and national humiliation. Liberal disenchantment with Wilsonian idealism was compounded by the need to cooperate with the Social Democrats under the auspices of the Weimar Coalition and by the compromises on social and economic policy this necessarily entailed. Moreover, the chaotic course of social and economic development during the Weimar Republic made it increasingly difficult for liberal politicians to integrate the diverse social groups that constituted the liberal electorate into a cohesive political force. The runaway inflation of the early 1920s had a devastating effect on the social bases of the German liberal parties, their local organizations, and their backing in the German business community. The fragmentation of the middle class in the second half of the 1920s rendered the decline of the liberal parties irreversible and provided the Nazi Party (Nationalsozialistische Deutsche Arbeiterpartei or NSDAP) with much of the raw material for its impressive string of electoral triumphs from 1929 to 1932. Even then, however, it would be a serious oversimplification to dismiss the collapse of Weimar liberalism as merely a consequence of liberalism's historic failures in the nineteenth century. Not only does this greatly exaggerate the extent of earlier liberal defeats, but, more important, it robs the history of liberalism in the first third of the twentieth century of much of its inherent drama and significance. It is therefore essential to understand the demise of Weimar liberalism in terms of the specific factors that effectively destroyed it between 1919 and 1933.

By the same token, liberalism has had a more positive impact on the political landscape of postwar Germany than might appear at first glance. It is indeed ironic that at a time when organized political liberalism had been reduced to a splinter party, many of its most important ideas on personal liberty and parliamentary government found their way into the Basic Law of the German Federal Republic. Moreover, the astute coalition politics of the Free Democratic Party – often denounced as mere opportunism – provided German liberals with a measure of influence that extended far beyond the number of votes the FDP had received in any given election. At the same time, important elements of the liberal agenda such as free market economics have been incorporated into the political programs of both the Christian Democratic Union (Christlich-Demokratische Union or CDU) and – to a lesser degree – the Social Democratic Party (Sozialdemokratische Partei Deutschlands or SPD). In spite of illiberal remnants such as the *Berufsverbot*, liberal ideas and practices have become firmly embedded in the social, economic, and political fabric of the German Federal Republic. If anything, the German experience after 1945 suggests that the single advance and long decline model of liberal development must be replaced with a more complex bimodal or trimodal conception. Even the recent upheaval in the German Democratic Republic displays echoes of liberalism in its insistence on civil rights, the return to a social market economy, and the revival of liberal parties. Therefore it is necessary to develop more useful standards for evaluating the success or failure of German liberalism than the electoral performance of any particular party or set of parties. This, in turn, requires broadening the definition of liberalism beyond the political arena, to include both a social and a cultural dimension.

In terms of its social dimension, liberalism functioned both as a principle of organization and as a web of relationships that bound together its various social constituencies. Recent work has begun to sketch the outlines of the associational infrastructure that propelled the process of liberal mobilization in the middle of the nineteenth century. By now the role that the notables of *Besitz und Bildung* and the lesser *Mittelstand* played in this process is well known. But the dynamics of the process by which constituent middle-class groups alternately supported and deserted the liberal parties need to be understood in greater depth. For much of the nineteenth century, general progress and bourgeois self-interest went hand in hand. But with the arrival of organized capitalism in the 1880s, traditional liberal nostrums about the values of free competition became increasingly problematic. Although the bourgeois associational model could be adapted to interest group formation, the socioeconomic demands of bourgeois organizations grew increasingly protectionist after the turn of the present century. As a regulator of the free play of market forces, politics played a crucial role in guaranteeing the economic health of Germany's liberal constituency. When contraction of the Weimar economy made it impossible for the liberal parties to provide their constituents with the protection they had come to expect, their middle-class support quickly evaporated. The very style of voluntary cooperation that characterized liberal political organizations inhibited the development of social cohesion and frustrated the achievement of compromise whenever external pressure made itself felt. As liberalism's political ascendancy had depended upon the emergence of a middle-class milieu, so its fall was precipitated by the erosion of its bourgeois infrastructure.

In terms of its cultural dimension, liberalism existed as a powerful cluster of related ideas and principles that helped legitimate bourgeois claims to social and political hegemony. At the heart of this cluster lay a cultural vision that placed primary emphasis on the emancipation of the individual from anything that might interfere with the free development of one's personality. Directed against the unholy trinity of feudalism, absolutism, and religious orthodoxy, this ideal posited the cultivation of human reason and the development of the human intellect as the highest goal of all cultural activity. As *Bildungsliberalismus*, this principle was institutionalized in the German educational system, where it proceeded to capture a considerable segment of the Protestant middle class and perhaps even more of the Jewish *Bürgertum*. The fact that liberalism's cultural and moral ethos permeated other intellectual movements such as Catholicism made it both ubiquitous and amorphous. Yet, in spite of its diffusion into the universities, the courts, and other institutions of nineteenth-century German life, liberal hegemony was never undisputed; it found itself repeatedly challenged by religious tradition as well as by irrational and racist countercurrents. The liberal revival of the early twentieth century was weakened not only by the internal contradictions of its own message and the restrictive application of its universalist principles to exclude the lower classes, women, and youth, but also by the disorienting effect of cultural modernism on Germany's educated elite. By the same token, the Weimar Republic's close association with Anglo-American liberalism gave its conservative opponents an opportunity to denounce it as "un-German" both during and after World War I. The Weimar Republic thus became the battleground on which the struggle for cultural hegemony between competing sectors of the German bourgeoisie was waged with such bitter intensity that it eventually consumed the republic itself.

The paradoxes of German liberalism will continue to challenge the historical imagination. From a postmodern perspective, its contradictions and ironies should perhaps not be explained away, but rather accepted as inherent in the subject.

Instead of reducing complex reality to a single formula, scholars dealing with the strange history of German liberalism might find it more fruitful to recognize the specific tensions that have existed within the German liberal tradition. Whoever wants to come to grips with the essence of German liberalism must account not only for demoralizing failures but also for surprising successes. While structural determinants such as territorial disunity played a major role in determining German liberalism's checkered and uncertain course, contingent developments such as the outbreak of the world economic crisis must be considered as well. Internal problems – the limits of the liberal vision for women, national minorities, or the proletariat, among others – were often compounded by external factors like Bismarck's personality. The result of these conflicting forces was a liberal movement that was strong enough in the 1860s, 1920s, and 1950s to challenge for power and even put its imprint on German political development but that was too weak to bring German politics under its permanent control. The apparently contradictory images of liberal victory or defeat, therefore, are not only equally correct, but causally interrelated. If anything, it is precisely this irreducible concatenation of shadow and light that will continue to inspire historians on both sides of the Atlantic in their search for a liberal Germany.

1

From the Household Economy to "Rational Agriculture"

The Establishment of Liberal Ideals in German Agricultural Thought

Marion W. Gray

Although liberalism, as a political movement and a system of economic thought, belongs to the industrial era, its underlying ideals circulated vibrantly in the late eighteenth and the early nineteenth centuries. In the form of Enlightenment thought and economic concepts of the market economy, the basic tenets of political and economic liberalism – though not the word itself – formed an undercurrent of protest against the absolutist and semifeudal institutions of the Germanies as early as the 1770s.[1] The experience of the French Revolution and the Napoleonic era provided an atmosphere in which these ideas could form a clear and vivid constellation.

Focusing on practical agricultural thought, this essay documents

1. J.J. Sheehan, *German Liberalism in the Nineteenth Century* (Chicago and London, 1978), pp. 7–48. On the origins and the early development of liberalism see also: J.J. Sheehan, "Partei, Volk und Staat: Some Reflections on the Relationship between Liberal Thought and Action in Vormärz," in H.-U. Wehler, ed., *Sozialgeschichte heute: Festschrift für Hans Rosenberg*, Kritische Studien zur Geschichtswissenschaft, vol. 11 (Göttingen, 1974), pp. 162–74; H. Rosenberg, "Theologischer Rationalismus und vormärzlicher Vulgärliberalismus," in *Politische Denkströmungen im deutschen Vormärz*, Kritische Studien zur Geschichtswissenschaft, vol. 3 (Göttingen, 1972), pp. 26–32; L. Gall, "Liberalismus und 'bürgerliche Gesellschaft': Zu Charakter und Entwicklung der liberalen Bewegung in Deutschland," *Historische Zeitschrift* 220 (1975): 324–56; G. de Bertier de Sauvigny, "Liberalism, Nationalism, Socialism: The Birth of Three Words," *Review of Politics* 36 (1974): 504–20; W.J. Mommsen, "Der deutsche Liberalismus zwischen 'klassenloser Bürgergesellschaft' und 'organisiertem Kapitalismus': Zu einigen neueren Liberalismusinterpretationen," *Geschichte und Gesellschaft: Zeitschrift für historische Sozialwissenschaft* 4 (1978): 77–90; R. Vierhaus, "Liberalismus," in O. Brunner, W. Conze, and R. Koselleck, eds., *Geschichtliche Grundbegriffe: Historisches Lexikon zur politisch-sozialen Sprache in Deutschland*, 5 vols. (Stuttgart, 1972–84), vol. 3, pp. 741–44.

a transition in the conceptualization of economic society in the era spanning the late Enlightenment and the early Vormärz. During this time the ideals of market capitalism took root in the minds of economic planners in Central Europe. Germany was an agrarian society. At least two of every three persons spent their lives coaxing products for human consumption from the soil.[2] The publicists who wrote to improve agriculture were therefore directly concerned with the structure of human society. Their descriptive and prescriptive works mirrored the realities and the ideals of the larger socioeconomic order.

In the 1780s, a decade in which the monarchs Maria Theresa and Frederick the Great were still on their thrones, many social theorists considered agricultural society, like the social order as a whole, to be a collection of households, each striving for self-sufficiency and each guided by a set of laws derived from divine authority. By the 1830s, after a half century of encounters with foreign ideas, encounters catalyzed in large part by the French Revolution, the leading writers had abandoned this concept, favoring instead an ideal vision of agriculture as a market-oriented enterprise. According to this concept, each estate was a part of a vast international network of labor and commodity-exchange systems. The belief that society was guided by impersonal laws of the marketplace had superseded the theocratic conceptualization of the balanced household economy.[3]

The contrasting ideals of two prolific writers in the field of agricultural economics, Christian Friedrich Germershausen (1725–1810) and Albrecht Daniel Thaer (1752–1828), illustrate this transition. Separated by a generation, these two economists epitomize Germany's shift from a preliberal conception of economic society to one in which liberalism was the formative ideological framework.

In 1778 Germershausen, pastor of the village Schlalach bei Treuenbrietzen in the Hohenzollern province of Brandenburg,

---

2. E. Klein, *Geschichte der deutschen Landwirtschaft: Ein Überblick* (Stuttgart, 1969), p. 72, and R. Rürup, *Deutschland im 19. Jahrhundert, 1815–1871*, Deutsche Geschichte, vol. 8 (Göttingen, 1984), p. 33.

3. This was but one of the many profound shifts in the sociopolitical vocabulary of the era from 1750 to 1850. See R. Koselleck's introduction to *Geschichtliche Grundbegriffe*, 1: xiii–xxxvii.

published the first installment of a five-volume agricultural handbook that was to bring him widespread recognition and a new identity as an economist. Within four years he had completed the reference work *Die Hausmutter in allen ihren Geschäfften*,[4] which the rapidly growing reading public of the late eighteenth century received with enthusiasm. There soon followed a companion work, *Der Hausvater in systematischer Ordnung*,[5] and numerous other publications for agriculturalists including the author's *Oekonomisches Reallexikon*.[6] Germershausen's economic literature was extremely popular. Publishers reprinted his books frequently, in complete as well as abridged editions, until as late as 1818, eight years after the author's death.[7] Offering advice of a practical nature and focusing on the techniques of running agricultural estates, Germershausen articulated a view of society whose essence was the preindustrial household. In his view, God had granted the estate as a sacred trust to be administered according to divinely sanctioned principles. Economically, it was a self-contained, inward-looking unit with goals of stability and balance. Socially, Germershausen's ideal household was a patriarchal hierarchy resting upon the principles of unequal but harmonious human relationships.

While Germershausen, a parish pastor, was enjoying widespread popularity as an agricultural expert, Albrecht Daniel Thaer, a young medical doctor in Celle, near Hanover, was similarly embarking upon a second career as an agricultural publicist. Like Germershausen, Thaer had originally followed his father's professional footsteps, in this case assuming the posts of town and court physician. Anxious to increase the yield of his own estate, he eagerly pursued the study of agriculture. Unlike Germershausen, who drew inspiration from the ancient German authorities, Thaer, twenty-seven years younger, turned to the writers of Great Britain who were witnessing and recording

---

4. C.F. Germershausen, *Die Hausmutter in allen ihren Geschäfften*, 5 vols. (Leipzig, 1778–81).

5. C.F. Germershausen, *Der Hausvater in systematischer Ordnung*, 5 vols. (Leipzig, 1783–86).

6. C.F. Germershausen, *Oekonomisches Reallexikon, worin alles was nach den Theorien und erprobten Erfahrungen der bewährtesten Oekonomen unsrer Zeit zu wissen nöthig ist*, 4 vol. (Leipzig, 1795–99).

7. *Gesamtverzeichnis des deutschsprachigen Schrifttums (GV), 1700–1910*, ed. P. Geils and W. Gorzny, 160 vols. (Munich, 1972–84), vol. 45, p. 367.

the results of their society's agrarian revolution. Thaer became a partisan of new techniques such as crop rotation and stall feeding. In 1791 he initiated his prolific publishing career with a practical manual on the cultivation of clover and on stall feeding,[8] and shortly thereafter he brought out his systematic *Einleitung zur Kenntniß der englischen Landwirthschaft*.[9] By 1799 he had founded a journal of agricultural science.[10] In 1804 Prussian *Staatskanzler* Hardenberg, a friend of Thaer from university days in Göttingen, served as an intermediary for King Frederick William III in requesting Thaer to enter the service of the Hohenzollern state as a privy councilor and to establish an agricultural institute, Möglin, near Berlin. Distressed by the French occupation of his home principality, Hanover, Thaer accepted. In 1810, the year of Germershausen's death, Thaer became professor of cameral sciences at Berlin's recently founded university. As an author, editor, and translator, Thaer published over sixty-five volumes and countless articles, establishing himself by a wide margin as Germany's most famous expert in agricultural affairs. Thaer's most well-known and systematic work, his five-volume *Grundsätze der rationellen Landwirthschaft* (1809–12), was reprinted throughout the nineteenth century and was translated widely.[11]

Like Germershausen, Thaer was very practical in his orientation. He sought to bring to agriculturalists the most up-to-date technical knowledge that would enable them to pursue their profession to the greatest profit. Thaer's view of the world led him to adopt a vocabulary that Germershausen and his readers would have hardly understood. Living in an era nurtured on the ideas of Adam Smith, Thaer conceptualized a society run by the invisible hand of the market. Movement, change, and progress were his objectives. Scientific methodology and freedom of

---

8. A. Thaer, *Unterricht über den Kleebau und Stallfütterung für den lüneburgischen Landmann* (Celle, 1791). See also W. Körte, *Albrecht Thaer: Sein Leben und Wirken, als Arzt und Landwirth* (Leipzig, 1839; repr. Hanover, 1975), p. 417.

9. A. Thaer, *Einleitung zur Kenntniß der englischen Landwirthschaft*, 3 vols. (Hanover, 1798–1800).

10. A. Thaer, ed., *Annalen der niedersächischen Landwirthschaft*, 6 vols. (Hanover, 1799–1804).

11. A. Thaer, *Grundsätze der rationellen Landwirthschaft*, 4 vols. (Berlin, 1804–12). Citations in this paper from 3d ed. (Stuttgart, 1837–39; reprinted until as late as 1880). See W. Simons, *Albrecht Thaer: Nach amtlichen und privaten Dokumentation aus einer großen Zeit* (Berlin, 1929), pp. 99–232.

trade were prerequisites for a healthy agricultural economy, according to Thaer. Competition, rather than a set of harmonious relationships, lent order to Thaer's world.

Thaer's memory is kept alive in history books and in the lecture halls of agricultural institutions, while Germershausen, popular in his own era, is all but forgotten today. This is because the Brandenburg pastor-economist spoke for an age in eclipse; the town doctor who became a professor of agriculture, on the other hand, articulated ideals that became foundation stones for the ideologies of the following two centuries. An abrupt break in intellectual tradition separated the writers who were, chronologically, a mere generation apart.

Neither of the two authors set out expressly to develop or defend a specific ideology. Neither thought of himself as representing principles of a philosophical nature. Living in an era in which agriculture was the primary human enterprise, both sought simply to help farmers do their best. Germershausen was certainly aware that the household economy he sought to buttress was under attack, but rather than responding with a theoretical defense of the old order, he published practical information on how to run an estate. And while it is true that Thaer saw himself as an innovator, it is significant that he chose to emphasize applied techniques rather than a philosophical defense of capitalism. This is typical because liberalism itself was, and has remained throughout its history, a largely unconscious ideology. Unlike the defenders of other modern political ideals, many partisans of liberalism have not viewed themselves as adherents of a particular party. They have believed their values – progress, freedom, justice, scientific methodology – to be inherent and universal rather than contingent and ideological. Thus, although it is accurate to characterize Germershausen as a defender of a preliberal conception of society and Thaer as an advocate of early liberalism, it is likely that neither would have recognized the labels as applying to himself. Each believed, simply, that he was contributing to the well-being of society.

The Household Economy

Germershausen wrote consciously in the tradition of the early modern school that is best known by the label *Hausväter-*

Marion W. Gray

literatur.[12] This genre flourished from the sixteenth through the eighteenth centuries in German-speaking Europe. Written for the aristocratic heads of estates, these handsomely bound volumes, referred to by contemporaries simply as *Hausbücher*, contained information of various sorts – scientific, technical, social, ethical, and religious. They were based on a conception of society drawn from antiquity, especially from Aristotle. Economics, or the "doctrine of the household," was one of Aristotle's three branches of practical philosophy alongside ethics, the doctrine of the individual, and politics, the doctrine of the polis.[13]

The *Hausbücher* prescribed the activities of the household and the relationships between its members. While household economic literature is not unique to Germany,[14] a significant characteristic of the genre in German cultural areas is its theological character. Drawing upon the tradition of the "sermons on the Christian household," established by Martin Luther and his contemporaries, the "economic" writers adhered to patriarchal religious views of the worldly household, which were thought to mirror the divine household. Luther's contemporary, Justus

12. W. Roscher gave currency to this term, which became fixed in the vocabulary of the historiography of the early modern era. See his *Geschichte der National-Oekonomik in Deutschland*, Geschichte der Wissenschaften in Deutschland. Neuere Zeit, vol. 14 (Munich, 1874), p. 137. See also O. Brunner, "Hausväterliteratur," in *Handwörterbuch der Sozialwissenschaften*, 12 vols. (Stuttgart, Tübingen, and Göttingen, 1956–66), vol. 5, pp. 92–93, and J. Brückner: *Staatswissenschaften, Kameralismus und Naturrecht: Ein Beitrag zur Geschichte der politischen Wissenschaft im Deutschland des späten 17. und frühen 18. Jahrhunderts*, Münchener Studien zur Politik, vol. 27 (Munich, 1977), pp. 51–56. G. Frühsorge points out that the term *Hausväterliteratur* is misleading, suggesting as an alternative *die alte Ökonomieliteratur*. See G. Frühsorge, "Die Begründung der 'väterlichen Gesellschaft' in der europäischen Oeconomia Christiana: Zur Rolle des Vaters in der 'Hausväterliteratur' des 16. bis 18. Jahrhunderts in Deutschland," in H. Tellenbach, ed., *Das Vaterbild im Abendland, I. Rom, frühes Christentum, Mittelalter, Neuzeit, Gegenwart* (Stuttgart, 1978), pp. 112–13.

13. O. Brunner, "Das 'ganze Haus' und die alteuropäische 'Ökonomik,'" in *Neue Wege der Verfassungs- und Sozialgeschichte*, 3d ed. (Göttingen, 1980), pp. 103–27. See also S. Krüger, "Zum Verständnis der Oeconomica Konrads von Megenberg: Griechische Ursprünge der spätmittelalterlichen Lehre vom Hause," *Deutsches Archiv für Erforschung des Mittelalters* 20 (1964): 475–561.

14. E. Fox-Genovese, "The Ideological Bases of Domestic Economy: The Representation of Women and the Family in the Age of Expansion," in E. Fox-Genovese and E. Genovese, *Fruits of Merchant Capital: Slavery and Bourgeois Property in the Rise and Expansion of Capitalism* (New York and Oxford, 1983), pp. 299–336. See also K. Tribe, *Land, Labour, and Economic Discourse* (London, 1978), pp. 53–79.

Menius, popularized the term "Christian economy," a phrase that embedded itself in household literature.[15] Significantly, the authors of the encyclopedic *Hausväterliteratur* were not concerned with trade or commerce, activities they considered to be external to the realm of "economics." Instead they focused on the ordering of all affairs of the estate, both inside and outside the house. "Oeconomie" dealt strictly with agriculture, as the concept in its German forms makes clear: *Haushaltung* or *Haus- und Feldwirtschaft*. For example, in 1744 the editor of the journal *Oeconomische Nachrichten* clarified the primary objective of economic publications "to demonstrate how one can use every product of nature the most advantageously."[16]

Authors of the *Hausväterliteratur* prescribed productive roles for all members of the household: adults and children as well as masters and servants. Because the science of economics belonged strictly to the household, it included spheres of life that later writers would consider to be noneconomic – medicine, education, religion, architecture, the furnishing of houses – in addition to more familiar activities such as farming, gardening, animal husbandry, fishing, and beekeeping.[17] According to this early modern doctrine, the estate was a fief placed by God under the care of a steward, the master of the household. It was his responsibility, working with his partner, the mistress of the household, to administer the estate wisely, according to divinely ordained principles.

For Germershausen, economics was a practical science. He filled the majority of the pages of his ten volumes of economic handbooks with concrete information on subjects such as the cultivation of crops, animal husbandry, food preparation and

15. J. Hoffmann, *Die "Hausväterliteratur" und die "Predigten über den christlichen Hausstand,"* Göttinger Studien zur Pädagogik, vol. 37 (Weinheim an der Bergstraße and Berlin, 1959). See also G. Frühsorge, "Begründung der 'väterlichen Gesellschaft,'" pp. 113–15.

16. J.H.C. Beutler and J.C.F. Guts-Muths, *Allgemeines Sachregister über die wichtigsten deutschen Zeit- und Wochenschriften*, 2 vols. (Leipzig, 1790), vol. 1, p. 32.

17. For a contextual definition of "Oeconomie," see F.K.G. Gericke, *Praktische Anleitung zur Führung der Wirthschafts-Geschäfte für angehende Landwirthe*, 2d ed. 4 vols. (Berlin, 1808–11), vol. 1, pp. 1–131. The title page alone of Enslin's "Economic Bibliography" indicates what is included in the old definition: *Bibliotheca Oeconomica, oder Verzeichnis . . . Bücher über die Haus- und Handwirthschaft und darin einzelne Zweige: den Wein- und Gartenbau, die Bienen-, Schaaf-, Rindvieh-, und Pferdezucht, die Kochkunst . . . Bierbrauen, Essigbrauen, Bleichen, etc.* (Berlin, 1825).

preservation, and the production of nonfood products, especially textiles. Two entire volumes of the *Hausvater* deal with the growing of crops, while three hundred pages of the *Hausmutter* pertain to the care of cattle and swine.[18] Like his predecessors in the genre of *Hausväterliteratur*, Germershausen believed that technical information was the essential tool that would enable master and mistress to fulfill their respective responsibilities. But the author was equally concerned with the human relationships of the household. He emphasized the collaborative roles of the two presiding figures:

> If both marriage partners do not share a single, unified goal with regard to the household, the effectiveness of [each] is restricted. . . . If the *Hausvater* and *Hausmutter* are in agreement, so that each and every endeavor aims . . . for the common good of the household or an increase of productivity, they can, with the support of the supreme *Hausvater*, who bestows . . . order and diligence upon humans, [be assured] that they will not be guarding, caring for, and working [their estate] in vain.[19]

Marriage was an economic partnership with two purposes: "the mutual support of the two spouses and the producing and rearing of children." The division of labor by gender was strict: fieldwork, construction, and the keeping of horses and dogs were masculine activities; the cultivation of vegetables, dairy operations, the care of swine and poultry, and the preparation of food, brewing, and textile production were feminine. The *Hausvater* was to oversee the male servants, while the *Hausmutter* supervised the women. Some responsibilities were shared – haying, for example, because it was a field activity, which was the province of males, yet at the same time a task done to support the dairy, a female realm.[20]

The household included a large number of workers (*Gesinde*). Otto von Münchhausen, a contemporary of Germershausen who also wrote in the *Hausväter* tradition, reported that on a

---

18. Germershausen, *Hausvater*, vols. 2–3, passim; *Hausmutter*, 4: 535–872.

19. Germershausen, *Hausvater*, 1: 166.

20. Germershausen, articles "Ehe" and "Ehestand" in *Oekonomisches Reallexikon*, 2: 359–60. See also his *Hausvater*, 1: 217–80, and *Hausmutter*, 5: 63–149. In addition see the articles by G.H. Zincken, "Ehe," "Ehe-Geld," and "Ehe-Mann," in *Allgemeines oeconomisches Lexicon*, 2 vols. (Leipzig, 1744), vol. 1, pp. 604–5.

normal day 48 to 50 people ate at least two meals at his table. Judicially, as well as in a socioeconomic sense, these people belonged to the household. The abiding nature of this patriarchal relationship was reconfirmed in Prussia with the codification of the General Law Code of 1794.[21] Germershausen stressed the economic nature of the master-servant relationship. Under the heading "Principles of Field Cultivation," he emphasized the importance of maintaining within the household just the right number of people, neither too many nor too few, so as to achieve "a certain order" in the affairs of the estate. There was a variety of categories of workers, depending on the tasks they performed and the relationships they had to the household. *Ackergesinde* were those housed and fed on the estate, or even within the house. *Cossäthen* and *Häuseler* occupied small cottages without land on the estate and were obligated to work without compensation certain days of the week – sometimes an unspecified number – for the master; in some localities they were called *Hofdiener* and *Fröhner*. Another class of people, the *Tagelöhner*, *Arbeitsleute*, and *Handarbeiter*, were, as their names implied, hired laborers who were also frequently contracted to the estate for certain periods of time. They differed in an essential way from the *Gesinde*, however, because they were not legally part of the household. "One may have one or all of these types of people; their number should accord with the actual or projected economic activities [*Geschäfften*] of the property so that [these affairs] are carried out according to their natural order."[22]

In the course of the 1780s the cost of keeping contractually bound laborers on estates rose appreciably. Indeed, to the

21. *Allgemeines Landrecht für die preußischen Staaten von 1794*, ed. H. Hattenhauer and G. Barth (Frankfurt a.M., 1970), I, title 1, §3–4, p. 55, and O. v. Münchhausen, *Der Hausvater*, 3d ed., 6 vols. bound in 13 (Hanover, 1771–73), vol. 1, p. 426. See R. Koselleck, *Preußen zwischen Reform und Revolution: Allgemeines Landrecht, Verwaltung und soziale Bewegung von 1791 bis 1848*, Industrielle Welt, vol. 7 (Stuttgart, 1967), p. 62, and D. Schwab, "Familie," in *Geschichtliche Grundbegriffe*, 2: 253–301.

22. Germershausen, *Hausvater*, 1: 280–83. For eighteenth-century definitions, see H. Zincken's articles on "Gesinde," "Gesinde-Lohn," and "Gesinde-Noth" in *Allgemeines oeconomisches Lexicon*, 1: 929–32; and G. Leonhardi, *Erdbeschreibung der preußischen Monarchie*, 5 vols. (Halle, 1791–98), vol. 1, pp. 347–48, 359. See also *Allgemeines Landrecht*, pt. 2, title 7, pt. 6, §308–471, pp. 443–49. On the meaning of the term "*Geschäft*" in eighteenth-century context, see G. Frühsorge, "Die Einheit aller Geschäffte: Tradition und Veränderung des 'Hausmutter'-Bildes in der deutschen Ökonomieliteratur des 18. Jahrhunderts," *Wolfenbüttler Studien zur Aufklärung* 3 (1976): 137–40.

puzzlement of many observers, the very rate of pay to *Ackerge-sinde* was increasing. There were complex causes for this phenomenon, including population growth, inflation in the price of consumer goods, expansion of the international grain market, proto-industrial development and land speculation.[23]

Germershausen's explanation of the rise in the wages of the house and field workers, however, did not include these factors, which are understood by modern economic historians to have been inflationary. It was based, rather, on the pastor-economist's concept of the economy as an ethical and social system. He reasoned that a decay in the traditional forms of household, school, and church authority over the serving classes was allowing them to become desirous of luxury: "For this reason the servants are forcing wages up year after year. Estate account books . . . provide visible proof that servants in most regions receive half as much again as they did thirty years ago." Moreover, the practice of giving "presents" such as money for fairs and for decorative apparel like straw hats and camisoles for the young women had become popular.[24] Even the age-old master-servant codes [*Gesindeordnungen*], designed to preserve predictability in household relations, were of no help, Germershausen complained. The ordinances in most provinces forbade increases in compensation, but landlords frequently met the demands of the workers anyway, fearing that they would become unpopular with the villagers if they failed to do so. What was to be done about this? The master should from time to time, at his own discretion, make presents to those servants who worked diligently. This would make them grateful and restore the proper order to the economy. Above all, managers should take a firm stand to reverse the inflationary trend, which was nothing

---

23. H. Schissler, *Preußische Agrargesellschaft im Wandel: Wirtschaftliche, gesellschaftliche und politische Transformationsprozesse von 1763 bis 1847*, Kritische Studien zur Geschichtswissenschaft, vol. 33 (Göttingen, 1978), pp. 59–104. See also W. Abel, *Agrarkrisen und Agrarkonjunktur: Eine Geschichte der Land- und Ernährungswirtschaft Mitteleuropas seit dem hohen Mittelalter*, 3d ed. (Hamburg and Berlin, 1978), pp. 196–219; and P. Kriedte, *Peasants, Landlords, and Merchant Capitalists: Europe and the World Economy, 1500–1800* (Leamington Spa, 1983), pp. 101–15.

24. Germershausen, *Hausvater*, 1: 223–26. Contemporaries perceived the deterioration of authority of the *Hausvater* to be very real. See Koselleck, *Preußen zwischen Reform und Revolution*, pp. 62–70, and H.-H. Müller, "Der agrarische Fortschritt und die Bauern in Brandenburg vor den Reformen von 1807," *Zeitschrift für Geschichtswissenschaft* 12 (1964): 636–48.

more than the result of human choice: "Every master and mistress must make a commitment neither to promise nor to pay higher wages to their servants than is customary in the region."[25]

Recognizing that economic circumstances were changing, Germershausen addressed the issue foremost in the minds of many of his contemporaries, the gradual transition to a wage-labor market. Many estate owners, he noted, were reducing the number of their *Gesinde* and relying increasingly on hired workers. On the surface this had advantages, the pastor observed. Wage-earners were often more motivated, more efficient, and thus more prosperous than their neighbors who were still bound by law to estates.[26] However, the trend toward free labor was emphatically not a solution to society's problems. If allowed to go unchecked, it would generate devastating, long-term consequences. The breakdown in the traditional household relationships, including, for example, those of the *Haus-, Schul- und Kirchenzucht*, was a result of the "increasing moral decay and irreligion" of the times. It could lead to a situation in which "the present generation of the common folk . . . [would] rise up [and] prefer to give orders rather than to obey." To counter this, one should work for the creation of a proper balance in which estate servants could meet their responsibilities without overwork, oppression, or arbitrary treatment. In the villages, what was needed was a revitalization of communal institutions, such as councils of elders who could look out for the inhabitants, discover misdeeds, and "bring the people back to a better path." This would induce the *Ackergesinde* to work diligently, loyally, and capably. The council of elders could keep rural folk up-to-date without letting change get out of hand. For example, they might establish small libraries of "economic books" to teach the people how to improve themselves.[27] Above all, however, it should never be forgotten that "the contract through which our present servant classes obligate themselves to serve a family for a certain period of time . . . naturally [includes] the unspoken condition that they subjugate themselves to household authority."[28]

25. Germershausen, *Hausmutter*, 5: 97–102; *Hausvater*, 1: 223–26.
26. Germershausen, *Hausvater*, 1: 298–301.
27. Ibid., pp. 301, 304–6.
28. Germershausen, *Hausmutter*, 5: 133–34.

The household, then, was to be maintained as an economic entity with a moral dimension. It was the basic unit of society and should be governed according to practices ordained by tradition. The mistress of the household, unlike her husband, who typically inherited an estate, often came to a household from a distant area by contractual marriage arrangement. For the sake of stability and continuity, it was her responsibility to familiarize herself with the local customs, including culinary tastes, cultural patterns, and norms of behavior. By incorporating these into her own routine she would contribute to the preservation of order.[29]

Germershausen liked to illustrate his prescriptive advice with concrete examples. To demonstrate the importance of tradition to the "economy," he described the situation of the hapless "Pastor Thorsander" who came to a rural household from the city and knew little about agriculture. Thorsander suffered the additional misfortune of having a spouse who was also of urban upbringing. "He would have been wise to marry either a daughter of his deceased predecessor or at least a girl from the country [who could] lead him [and compensate for] his total lack of experience." It was equally unfortunate that Thorsander employed servants unfamiliar with his particular estate. They lacked both knowledge of traditional local ways and loyalty to the household. They cheated Thorsander and mismanaged his property. Within seven years, the poor man's "economic circumstances" were in ruin. Even the Seven Years' War, "which aided so many household managers . . . to get on their feet, did not help him out of his problems." At Thorsander's death, the estate had sunk to a mere quarter of its original value. Thorsander was not a good economist. He did not administer his fief according to the rules of nature and tradition.[30]

Each estate was a unit unto itself, a small government (*Regierung*) that was to be administered according to a budget (*Wirthschaftsfuß*). The fiscal objective was the maintenance of equilibrium from year to year so that each household retained its status. There should always be a surplus at year's end, not for reinvestment, but for emergencies. Fiscal management was the joint responsibility of master and mistress. Each presided over a

29. Ibid., 1: 367–416.
30. Germershausen, *Hausvater*, 1: 293–96.

separate budget related to his or her respective responsibilities, although the budget of the *Hausmutter* was subordinate to that of her husband. By mutual agreement – not by arbitrary choice of the male, Germershausen stressed – they would decide on the appropriate proportion for the wife's budget. She, from her special vantage within the household, might have a better view of the whole estate than her husband. For this reason, and because she was to act in his stead during his absence, it was her responsibility to maintain an overview, despite the fact that her budget was but a "branch" of his. She was always to exercise the "female virtue" of thrift. But "the master must not expect that she alone practice frugality; he must do the same. . . . It is an error to expect this economic virtue from one partner more than from the other." Tradition, hard work, frugality, and piety were the "economic virtues" that would increase productivity and sustain the yearly rhythm of life.[31]

It is no wonder that the cameralists, the academic economists of Germershausen's day, greeted the new versions of the *Hausväterliteratur* enthusiastically. Johann Beckmann, professor of economics at Göttingen, welcomed Germershausen's *Hausmutter*, which "fill[ed] an important gap in the economic library in an excellent manner." Friedrich Benedict Weber, who held the title of cameral scientist at the university of Frankfurt an der Oder, gave Germershausen's publications special consideration in his *Handbuch der ökonomischen Literatur*.[32] Germershausen's rejuvenation of the *Hausväterliteratur* complemented the work of these professors of *Oeconomie, Policey, und Kammer-Sachen*, for he shared their ways of conceptualizing economic society. While they wrote for Germany's princes, who managed the royal households, Germershausen addressed his work to the household managers at the "middle level of society."[33] The term

31. Ibid., pp. 166–213, quotations from pp. 200, 209. See also Germershausen, *Hausmutter*, 5: 28–63. On the early modern concept of "economic virtues," see P. Münch, ed., *Ordnung, Fleiß und Sparsamkeit: Texte und Dokumente zur Entstehung der "bürgerlichen Tugenden"* (Munich, 1984), pp. 24–32.

32. J. Beckmann, *Physikalisch-Ökonomische Bibliothek*, 23 vols. (Göttingen, 1770–1805), vol. 9, p. 272. See also F.B. Weber, *Handbuch der ökonomischen Literatur*, 9 vols. (Berlin, 1803–42), vol. 2, pp. 263–82.

33. Germershausen used the term "Mittelmann" to describe the proprietary classes. See, for example, "Küche des Mittelmannes" in *Hausmutter*, vol. 2, pp. 1–490. For a discussion of the concept "Mittelmann," see W. Conze, "Mittelstand," in *Geschichtliche Grundbegriffe*, 4: 49–52.

Marion W. Gray

"cameralism" itself denotes the centrality of the household: *camera*, derived from the Greek and Latin, signified the "rooms" of the palace, or the household of the ruler, from which the domains were administered. The Prussian king Frederick William I had established the first chairs of cameralism in 1727 at the universities of Halle and Frankfurt an der Oder in order to assure himself of expert advice in the economic and social policies of his lands. Other German rulers had followed suit, and for the next century, the uniquely German school of cameralism had flourished.[34]

These sciences of political economics and domestic government, cameralism and *Polizei*, were inseparable in the eighteenth-century view of the world. Economics at the princely level was concerned with ordered productivity, and *Polizei* was aimed at establishing and preserving order through such diverse realms as education, charity, the guarding of moral principles, and transportation.[35] Whereas the cameralists outlined the ideals and the exercise of princely power, Germershausen prescribed the execution of the authority of the *Hausvater* on the estate. So parallel were these specializations that the cameralists themselves devised complete systems of *Hauspolizei* for agricultural estates just like the *Polizei* at the governmental level. *Hauspolizei* comprised "the principles and measures . . . through which . . . the household is insured and protected against all misfortunes . . . and dangers." Its goal was to effect the "correct utilization and management of private holdings [and to bring about] the contentment and well-being of families."[36]

The cameralists as well as the authors of the household books sought to communicate applied knowledge rather than theory. These writers shared the belief that agriculture was the primary source of wealth. They stressed frugality, order, balance, and

34. E. Dittrich, *Die deutschen und österreichischen Kameralisten*, Erträge der Forschung, vol. 23 (Darmstadt, 1974), pp. 31–32. See also K. Tribe, "Cameralism and the Science of Government," *Journal of Modern History* 56 (1984): 263–65; M. Walker, "Rights and Functions: The Social Categories of Eighteenth-Century German Jurists and Cameralists," *Journal of Modern History* 50 (1978): 234–51; and Brückner, *Staatswissenschaften*, pp. 292–93.

35. F.-L. Knemeyer, "Polizeibegriffe in den Gesetzen des 15. bis 18. Jahrhunderts: Kritische Bemerkungen zur Literatur über die Entwicklung des Polizeibegriffes," *Archiv des öffentlichen Rechts* 92 (1967): 165. See also Walker, "Rights and Functions," pp. 234–51.

36. F.B. Weber, *Systematisches Handbuch der Staatswirthschaft*, 2 vols. (Berlin, 1804–5), pp. 606–30.

the increase of yields, and they insisted on the need to keep surpluses at home or in treasuries. Both groups sought to improve "the happiness of the people."[37]

Although economists concerned with the state had a somewhat broader conception of the "economy" than authors in the *Hausbücher* tradition, they nevertheless affirmed that the household system was the real location of economic activity. Earlier in the century, Julius Bernhard von Rohr had outlined the relationship between public and private spheres. He described *Cameralwesen* as "the economy of rulers," parallel in many ways to the private economy. Of the two branches in the private sphere, urban and rural, he named the latter as the one of greatest interest to economists. Johann Gottlob von Justi, the most prominent cameralist of the second half of the eighteenth century, agreed: the concept of "economy" could be applied, on the one hand, broadly to the state and would actually encompass not only *Polizei* but also commerce and urban exchange of goods and services. But in its commonest usage it referred to "[private] estates and the production of food substances. . . . It is the science of employing our resources in order to foster our present well-being [*Glückseligkeit*]."[38] In other words, the household economy not only paralleled the economy of the ruler, it was also essential to the balance and operation of the state. Individual *Hausväter* and *Hausmütter* had to perform their roles well in order for society at large to function properly. Society was a compendium of households, each striving for its own order and each having as its ultimate goal contributing to the harmony of the whole.

For this reason Germershausen regarded his handbooks, which were designed strictly for private use, as important to political rulers. While he insisted that the state should not interfere in the affairs of the household,[39] he did expect that governments would be by nature interested in the "progress"

---

37. Tribe, "Cameralism and the Science of Government," pp. 266–67.
38. J.B. v. Rohr, *Compendieuse Haushaltungsbibliotheck* (Leipzig, 1716), pp. 1–3 and passim, on the categories of literature understood to belong to the field of *Haushaltungskunst*. See also J.H.G. v. Justi, *Staatswissenschaft, oder systematische Abhandlung aller oekonomischen und Cameralwissenschaften, die zur Regierung eines Landes erfordert werden*, 2d ed. (Leipzig, 1758), pp. 59, 437, 451–89.
39. Germershausen, *Hausmutter*, 15: 134.

his work was designed to foster. He defined progress in a typically eighteenth-century manner to be "increasing the yields of the soil." He argued for progress in "rural industry,"[40] by which he meant hard work and ingenuity. National policy (*Staatspolitik*) must aim at more than the maintenance of the status quo, he urged. Those concerned with the "private happiness and greatest welfare" must strive for improved production through industriousness (*Fleiß*), art (*Kunst*), and improvement of the soil in order to maintain the integrity and balance of the household economy.[41]

Scientific Agriculture and Liberal Ideals

The world of the household economy that Germershausen was seeking to preserve was shaken severely as the aftereffects of the French Revolution burst into Central Europe with Napoleon Bonaparte's imperial armies. Military defeat catalyzed the creation of new conceptualizations of society. Governments – both those directly established by Napoleon, such as in the Kingdom of Westphalia, and those that attempted to meet the challenges of the new era from within, such as the reform-oriented ministries in Austria and Prussia – sought to put new ideals into practice. A generation of reformers, frustrated by the relatively static nature of the old sociopolitical system, found seedbeds for their ideas in this new era. Representatives of the Enlightenment – the proponents of early and unnamed liberalism – could come out of the closet, for kings and princes, rather than suppressing critical thought as they had often done in the past, were beginning to recruit innovators into their planning councils. The ideas of Adam Smith, which had been published three decades earlier and were known but not widely accepted in the Germanies, suddenly found ready advocates and eager audiences in the lecture halls of German universities.[42]

40. On the history of word "Industrie," see D. Hilger and L. Hölscher, "Industrie, Gewerbe," in *Geschichtliche Grundbegriffe*, 3: 237–42.

41. Germershausen, *Hausvater*, vol. 1, "Vorrede," p. ix.

42. H. Berding, *Napoleonische Herrschafts- und Gesellschaftspolitik im Königreich Westfalen, 1807–1813*, Kritische Studien zur Geschichtswissenschaft, vol. 7 (Göttingen, 1973). See also E. Fehrenbach, *Traditionale Gesellschaft und revolutionäres Recht: Die Einführung des Code Napoléon in den Rheinbundstaaten*, Kritische Studien zur Geschichtswissenschaft, vol. 13, 2d ed. (Göttingen, 1978); E. Weis and E. Müller-Luckner, eds., *Reformen im rheinbündischen Deutschland*, Schriften des

In this context, Albrecht Thaer, who himself had worked quietly for a decade to promote the introduction of "scientific and rational agriculture," found not only a forum for his ideas, but also a compelling invitation to put them into practice in the service of the Prussian state, where the ministers of King Frederick William III were struggling to lay the foundation for a rejuvenated society after destructive blows from the French. Thaer moved to Prussia and took up residence on his new model farm and experimental institute, Möglin. He gave up his medical practice to accept governmental posts through which he could direct the transformation of Prussia's agriculture.[43]

A product of the age of Enlightenment, Thaer declared agriculture to be a "science" established on empirical principles and rational methodology. These consisted of the systematic collection of data, followed by use of hypothesis, experimentation, and observation. He spurned the idea that tradition – so important to Germershausen – could be an appropriate base for sound farming practices. On the other hand, farmers equipped with scientific methodology would become "rational agriculturalists" who, like navigators, would use charts and instruments to traverse the unknown. In contrast, the farmers whose knowledge was based solely on experience were mere "coastal travelers" who dared not venture out of sight of land and therefore could never progress far.[44]

Thaer had little use for the German agricultural experts. With verve he related how as a young man he had studied every

Historischen Kollegs. Kolloquien, vol. 4 (Munich, 1984); M.W. Gray, *Prussia in Transition: Society and Politics under the Stein Reform Ministry of 1808*, Transactions of the American Philosophical Society, vol. 76, pt. 1 (Philadelphia, 1986); M.-E. Vopelius, *Die altliberalen Ökonomen und die Reformzeit*, Sozialwissenschaftliche Studien 11 (Stuttgart, 1968); as well as Tribe, "Cameralism and the Science of Government," pp. 277–84; and W. Treue, "Adam Smith in Deutschland: Zum Problem des 'politischen Professors' zwischen 1776 und 1810," in W. Conze, ed., *Deutschland und Europa: Historische Studien zur Völker- und Staatenordnung des Abendlandes, Festschrift für Hans Rothfels* (Düsseldorf, 1951), pp. 101–33. For a concrete example of the way in which Smith's ideas made their way into Germany's university lecture halls, see T. v. Schön's notes from lectures by Professor C.J. Kraus, 1788–95, Königsberger Staatsarchiv: Geheimes Staatsarchiv Preußischer Kulturbesitz, Berlin-Dahlem, Rep. 300, Depositum Brünneck, I: Nachlaß Schön, Nos. 73–79, 91, passim.

43. Frederick William to Thaer, Berlin, 19 March 1804, in Körte, *Albrecht Thaer*, pp. 167–69. See also ibid., pp. 162–82, and Thaer, *Geschichte meiner Wirthschaft zu Möglin* (Berlin and Vienna, 1815).

44. Thaer, *Grundsätze*, pp. 4–14.

agricultural manual he could obtain from German libraries and bookstores, discovering that all were poor in quality and mired in petty debates. This experience caused him to "long more than ever" for "precise economic information." Turning to foreign authors, he finally encountered Arthur Young, whom he ecstatically credited with "uncountable services to the [British] empire and to human posterity." Young was England's foremost proponent of enclosure, crop rotation, and scientific fertilization. Thaer compared Young to the British philosophers Bacon, Newton, and Locke.[45]

In his two-volume handbook, *Grundsätze der rationellen Landwirthschaft*, which may have replaced on many estate-house bookshelves the nearly thirty-year-old works of Germershausen, Thaer described new realms of possibility. In this work, as in his other writings, he championed new technology, highly productive crops relatively unknown in Germany, and innovative methods of plowing, planting, cultivating, fertilizing, and threshing. Indeed, it is for his crusading work on behalf of experimental farming techniques that Thaer was best known to his contemporaries and is often cited in historical literature.[46]

Even more than inventions and scientific discoveries, however, Thaer's vision of the ideal socioeconomic system set him apart from his predecessors. He defined "economy" in a new way, declaring that it encompassed a wide variety of human enterprises rather than agriculture alone. It had been a mistake in German thinking and etymology, he maintained, that "economics" had been associated exclusively with farming. While it was true that ancient Greek authorities such as Xenophon and Aristotle had limited their concept of economics to the household and to agriculture, the Romans had understood the term to be universal: their meaning, which the Germans should have maintained, was simply "the relationship of the parts to the whole." This allowed them to think of economics as consisting

---

45. Thaer, *Einleitung zur englischen Landwirthschaft*, 1: 4–16. On Young, see H. Higgs, "Arthur Young," in *Dictionary of National Biography*, 2d ed., vol. 21 (1909), pp. 1272–78.

46. Thaer, *Grundsätze*, passim. See also Thaer's *Beschreibung der nutzbarsten neuen Ackergeräthe*, 3 vols. (Hanover, 1803–6). On Thaer's reputation as an innovator in agricultural technology see C. Leisewitz, "Albrecht Daniel Thaer," *Allgemeine deutsche Biographie*, vol. 37 (1894), pp. 636–41, and W. Abel, *Geschichte der deutschen Landwirtschaft vom frühen Mittelalter bis zum 19. Jahrhundert*, Deutsche Agrargeschichte, vol. 2 (Stuttgart, 1962), pp. 310, 320.

of many branches: natural production, animal production, state economics, and, above all, business (*Gewerbe*). The English and the French utilized this inclusive understanding of economic science, as demonstrated by their terminology. Agriculture in these countries was considered to be but a branch of the larger economic system, for unlike the Germans, for whom *Ökonomie* was synonymous with the rural household, they used modifiers to indicate farming, as in "rural economy" and *économie rurale*. Furthermore, the Germans had limited themselves unnecessarily in their equation of economics with the notion of frugality. This was unwarranted and could have stifling consequences. For those engaged in economic activities, thrift was comparable to miserliness and was a mentality that would lead to the exhaustion of business activity.[47]

But although it was only one facet of a complex economy, agriculture was the enterprise to which Thaer devoted himself with zeal. His vocabulary belonged to the nineteenth rather than to the eighteenth century: agricultural tasks included the hiring, supervision, and maintenance of the workforce; the keeping of livestock; the cultivation of the fields; and the fertilization of crops. The yield of products was, however, a means not an end, for "agriculture is a business [*ein Gewerbe*] that has the purpose . . . of producing a profit or earning money."[48]

Thaer's use of the term *Gewerbe* to signify a nonindustrial profit-making enterprise illustrates how transitional was the stage of economic thought in which he participated. Only a few decades earlier German writers had used the word in connection with the work of artisans to mean handwork and crafts. By the end of the eighteenth century, it had gained a wider application and was now associated with the production and exchange of a variety of products in a market setting. This was the sense in which Thaer applied it to agriculture as he sought to associate farming with the economic system of capitalism. Later in the nineteenth century the term *Gewerbe* would come to be identified with industrial production.[49]

Thaer viewed labor as the central aspect of the economy. Those who regarded land as the source of wealth were wrong, he declared. "It is through labor that humans gain . . . all that

47. Thaer, *Grundsätze*, 1: 101–2.
48. Ibid., p. 3.
49. Hilger and Hölscher, "Industrie, Gewerbe," pp. 242–49, 262–64.

they consume. . . . Labor [is] the source of all wealth."[50] In contrast to Germershausen, who warned against the transition to a free labor market, Thaer welcomed this development. But Thaer was no dogmatist; he recognized that the *Gesinde* system of landlord-servant relationships, still extant in many parts of Germany, had some advantages for workers, such as the security that membership in the household guaranteed them. Those villagers who were contractually bound to the estate could, in some cases, benefit proprietors when they did work that required constant attention, such as animal herding. Where the traditional household system still existed, Thaer recommended that local custom be followed rigorously, as, for example, in the housing and feeding of estate servants and in the acknowledgment of local festivals and celebrations. With regard to *Frohnen* – unpaid, obligatory labor by the workers bound to estates – Thaer urged proprietors to make the best of the situation. With advice reminiscent of the *Hausväterliteratur*, he suggested treating the people who served with kindness rather than with force. Positive treatment would cause them to work more diligently. In the long run, however, it was "urgent . . . for the master, the worker, and the general welfare that [forced labor] be abolished."[51]

Almost in direct answer to Germershausen's expressed alarm about rising labor costs, Thaer addressed the problem from the perspective of market economics:

> For some time there has been a general complaint among agrarian proprietors that the wages of workers and servants have risen, and this is viewed as a great evil. . . . In regions where obligatory labor has been partially abolished, the high wages are attributed to this. However, it is rather increased food prices, along with a higher level of production, [itself] stimulated by the high prices, that . . . pushed up the monetary rate of workers' pay. Furthermore, the productivity of the working people is stimulated by the abolition of obligatory labor, and therefore the amount of work performed has increased, which actually leads . . . to a lowering of the [real] cost of labor.

50. Thaer, *Grundsätze*, 1:103.
51. Ibid., 1: 148–60. Thaer's rejection of the theory that land was the source of wealth may have been a reaction to the influential French physiocratic school. See E. Fox-Genovese, *The Origins of Physiocracy: Economic Revolution and Social Order in Eighteenth-Century France* (Ithaca, N.Y., and London, 1976), pp. 11, 50, 125, 126, 218.

Thaer explained in detail that the level of wages was dependent on a variety of factors, including food prices, the pace of business activity, local customs, and calamities. Especially in agriculture, the cost of labor was a far more complex phenomenon than the nominal wage. Landlords should not equate the two. "Frequently [the] complaint [of wage inflation] is totally unfounded, and the rise in the cost of labor is in name only, and in no way real. Indeed, because [of general inflation] the cost of labor is [lower now] than [it was] previously."[52]

Thaer's ultimate vision was that of a new system in which none of the conditions of the old household economy would continue to exist. He left no doubt about the advantages of a free labor market. Wage labor was more profitable than compulsory service because free workers could be employed and dismissed according to proprietors' needs and workers' diligence. As to the latter: "They are more industrious because they must take care of themselves and their families and therefore must guard against being fired on account of poor work." As to the types of free workers, day laborers required relatively direct supervision, while pieceworkers and quota workers could be left to control their own pace. "Piecework is undeniably advantageous for the employer as well as for the worker."

Thaer acknowledged that under existing conditions it was still often necessary to provide housing for farm employees. He cautioned managers to anticipate and plan for this. He also urged them to distribute agricultural work throughout the year so that the laborers utilized during cultivation and harvest would not be left destitute in traditionally slack seasons.[53] Thaer tolerated the notion of unfree labor in the household economy until the system he held to be more efficient, fair, and profitable could be established. He believed in gradual change. In his vision of the future, however, the impersonal rules of the market would govern peoples' lives, not the traditional, paternalistic canons of the household economy.

52. Thaer, *Grundsätze*, 1: 106–17, quotation from 106–7. Thaer addressed this theme consistently throughout his career. As early as 1798 he had reached the same conclusion in an article published in *Annalen der niedersächischen Landwirthschaft* 6 (1804). On this, see Abel, *Geschichte der deutschen Landwirthschaft*, p. 335. See also the anonymous article with an introduction by Thaer, "Versuch zur Bestimmung des Werthes der Frohndienste," *Möglinsche Annalen der Landwirthschaft* 1 (1817): 174–99.

53. Thaer, *Grundsätze*, 1: 148–60.

Agriculturalists were business managers (*Wirthschafts-Direktoren*). Some were owners outright, administering the activities of their own estates, and others were employed by landowners and delegated to act on the latters' behalf. The former situation was preferable, because owner-managers possessed unlimited freedom of action. They might, for example, decide in particular years to reinvest their disposable income in the estate with the goal of deferring capital gains until the more distant future. Hired managers, on the other hand, were usually required to deliver profits each year. Along with free labor, absolute freedom of decision in the disposition of capital was essential to successful agricultural enterprise.[54]

As for capital, Thaer offered a lesson in market economics. There were three types: ground capital, or the worth of the estate itself; standing capital, or the buildings, livestock, and machinery; and operating capital, or liquid assets. Because "operating capital is the motivating force of the whole operation," the largest percentage of each enterprise's resources should be in this form. "The true yield of the business is determined less by the size of the estate than by the sum of the [investment]." Informed managers knew that it was best to plan for the long range rather than to attempt each year to produce huge earnings. For example, instead of planting strictly cash crops, one should use a part of the land for fertilizer production. Many rich estate owners did not follow this principle. "They think only about the yearly monetary profit and are poor managers."[55]

With regard to types of land management, Thaer preferred outright ownership over leased farms because "the owner delights in improving the estate, while the leaseholder [is interested] in filling a money chest. The estate is the beloved wife of an owner, [but it is] the mistress of the leaseholder, from whom he will separate." Moreover, Thaer predictably criticized semifeudal institutions such as milling and brewing monopolies, calling them "highly detrimental limitations of trade."[56]

Given his economic ideals, it is no surprise that he participated in the Prussian agrarian reforms initiated under Stein and

54. Ibid., pp. 189–90.
55. Ibid., pp. 24–31.
56. Ibid., pp. 82–3. See also the anonymously published article, "Zeitpacht, Erbpacht, und ganz freies Eigenthum," *Möglinsche Annalen* 3 (1819): 463–73.

carried forward during the ministries of Altenstein-Dohna and Hardenberg. Thaer's objective, and that of most of his colleagues, was to convert former semifeudal estates into modern private holdings and, concurrently, to abolish compulsory labor. He especially directed his energies toward devising plans for the transformation of the common lands of estates into private ownership. The reformers developed formulas that were turned into law through the governmental edicts of 1808, 1811, 1816, and 1821, which required prosperous peasants to divide their holdings, with part going to the master and the rest becoming their own. Those *Ackergesinde* with small farms were deprived, either by governmental action or by the pressures of the market, of their semifeudal rights to hold land or to remain part of the household.[57]

As a member of the reform bureaucracy, Thaer worked in close relationship with Theodor von Schön, the primary author of the October edict of 1807, which initiated the conversion of Prussian agriculture to a free enterprise system. Maintaining that he was interested solely in agriculture, Thaer nevertheless became involved in the wider objectives of the reform movement, with the intent of transforming all of society according to liberal principles. Never leaving Möglin, his estate, and tirelessly dedicating himself to empirical experimentation, to teaching, and to his publications, Thaer increasingly saw his work in agriculture as connected to the greater reform of society. He believed that the breakup of semifeudal conditions would ultimately lead to the transformation of former peasants into citizens, and, to this end, he advocated education of the rural lower classes by establishing "model farms for school teachers and peasants." Optimistically, he declared his trust in the positive outcome of combined agricultural, economic, and educational innovations. In 1810 he wrote Schön: "I am very pleased that you have faith in the nation, as I do. . . . I understand the

57. Thaer had little direct participation in the formulation of the well-known October Edict of 1807, although his work was highly respected by the reform leader, Baron vom Stein. In the administrations following that of Stein, Thaer played a more direct role. See E. Botzenhardt and W. Hubatsch, eds., *Freiherr vom Stein: Briefe und amtliche Schriften*, 10 vols. (Stuttgart, 1957–74), vol. 1, p. 501, and vol. 3, pp. 273–74; and H. Harnisch, "Die Bedeutung der kapitalistischen Agrarreformen für die Herausbildung des inneren Marktes und die industrielle Revolution in den östlichen Provinzen Preußens in der ersten Hälfte des 19. Jahrhunderts," *Jahrbuch für Wirtschaftsgeschichte* (1977/4): 63–82, esp. 71–72.

nation to be [comprised of those] who can read and write. The others must first become members of the civic community [*bürgerliche Menschen*]. This part of the population is naturally inclined to this, but under the conditions of its previous treatment things were *bound to* go badly."[58]

By 1815 Thaer had published a work that could genuinely be described as a handbook of agricultural economics, conceived for a modern, capitalist system, *Leitfaden zur allgemeinen landwirthschaftlichen Gewerbs-Lehre*. In this volume he attributed the origin of national economic theory (*National-Wirthschaftslehre*) to Adam Smith and intensified his insistence on the establishment of free markets in land and labor so that increased capital investment would flow into agriculture. He urged the abolition of landlord-servant relationships and emphasized the advantages of competition in agricultural enterprise. Thaer's specific affirmation of Smith's ideals demonstrated beyond doubt that agriculture and economics were on a new footing in Germany. The idea that the household was the primary location of economic activity had become outmoded. Economics had become a science whose locus was national rather than domestic. Furthermore, in spite of the theory of laissez-faire, economics was a sphere of life in which governments would play an increasingly directive role.[59]

As an agricultural innovator, an experimenter, and a governmental reformer, Thaer consciously sought the dissolution of the remnants of the household economy in Prussia, the very system that Germershausen had endeavored to undergird. Thaer did so with the optimism characteristic of early nineteenth-century liberalism, believing that the principles of individualism, private property, and the free market would lead to progress and prosperity.

---

58. See Thaer's correspondence to Schön, 3 May 1807, 17 January 1810, and 4 April 1810 in Königsberg-Staatsarchiv, Geheimes Staatsarchiv Preußischer Kulturbesitz, Berlin-Dahlem, Rep. 300 von Brünneck I: Nachlaß Schön, no. 6. See Körte, *Albrecht Thaer*, pp. 264–308.

59. A. Thaer, *Leitfaden zur allgemeinen landwirthschaftlichen Gewerbs-Lehre* (Berlin, 1815). See J.G. Gagliardo, *From Pariah to Patriot: The Changing Image of the German Peasant, 1770–1840* (Lexington, 1969), pp. 130–31, as well as Brunner, "Hausväterliteratur," pp. 92–93.

Implications

It is not the individual economists, Germershausen and Thaer, who are important for this study. The former has frequently been called a latecomer in the tradition of *Hausväterliteratur*,[60] and Thaer is but one of a myriad of contemporaries sharing the views of early economic liberalism.[61] What they personify, however, is a dramatic transformation, within a single generation, that included a redefinition of economics and a reconceptualization of society in German-speaking Europe.

While this study explores the history of ideas rather than the impact of ideas on practices or institutions, it is nevertheless appropriate to compare the transformation of economic thought with actual alterations in society, economy, and culture. An obvious example of such a change is the evolving structure of Prussian agriculture during the decades following Thaer's activity. Leaving aside the question of whether Thaer's work was actually responsible for these changes, one can easily see that many alterations occurred in the Vormärz that were entirely consistent with his ideals. Due to the series of reform edicts enacted in the first three decades of the nineteenth century, agricultural enterprise divested itself of many household-related institutions and replaced them with market freedoms. The process was gradual, and remnants of the old system, such as patrimonial jurisdiction and the master-servant laws, often continued in place until the revolutions of 1848, giving the Prussian rural labor market an authoritarian character. But the transition to agrarian capitalism was undeniable.[62]

During the first half of the century, middle-class entrepreneurs, permitted for the first time by governmental reforms to invest in agriculture, rushed into the countryside and established them-

60. Abel, *Geschichte der deutschen Landwirthschaft*, p. 201.
61. See, for example, A.F. Lueder, *Über Nationalindustrie und Staatswirthschaft nach Adam Smith bearbeitet*, 2 vols. (Berlin, 1800–1802); and L.H. Jakob, *Grundsätze der National-Oekonomie oder Wirthschaftslehre* (Halle, 1805).
62. H. Harnisch, "Vom Oktoberedikt des Jahres 1807 zur Deklaration von 1816: Problematik und Charakter der preußischen Agrarreformgesetzgebung zwischen 1807 und 1816," *Studien zu den Agrarreformen des 19. Jahrhunderts in Preußen und Rußland*, special edition of *Jahrbuch für Wirtschaftsgeschichte* (Berlin, 1978), pp. 229–93. See also R. Berthold, "Die Veränderungen im Bodeneigentum und in der Zahl der Bauernstellen, der Kleinstellen und der Ritter güter in den preußischen Provinzen Sachsen, Brandenburg und Pommern während der Durchführung der Agrarreformen des 19. Jahrhunderts," ibid., pp. 1–116.

selves as estate owners. At the same time, aristocratic landlords quickly adapted to the new conditions and profited by them. Both were able to benefit from the new ease of exchanging property and from the enclosure of peasant farms and common lands, all of which Thaer had advocated. As the economist August von Haxthausen observed in 1839: "Since 1805 . . . only a very few [noble estates] have been destroyed. . . . All of those which still exist have become significantly larger. . . . This is due in part to [government actions] and in part to the purchase and enclosure of peasant farms." In general, productivity and profit rose significantly in Prussian agriculture.[63]

On the other hand, the agrarian transition accelerated the dislocation of former *Gesinde* of the rural estates, fostering the growth of a large group of mobile, landless workers dependent on the vagaries of the market. Many were compelled to forfeit their homes and lands as a direct result of the dissolution of the household economy. Those who were not immediately forced off the land were hard-pressed to keep their farms viable without the use of common pastures and woodlands or other types of manorial support. During the decade of the 1820s, a serious agricultural depression dealt a severe blow to small proprietors of the eastern provinces. Lack of credit prevented small farmers from utilizing capital to their advantage, and many could not maintain their ownership of lands during these hard times. The process of agrarian reform increased agricultural output as villagers lost their properties to the owners of large estates. During the Vormärz, Prussia gained a rural proletariat, the fastest growing class in society.[64]

63. A. von Haxthausen, *Die ländliche Verfassung in den einzelnen Provinzen der preußischen Monarchie* (Königsberg, 1839), pp. 180–83. See also Koselleck, *Preußen zwischen Reform und Revolution*, pp. 498–518, and H. Bleiber, "Staat und bürgerliche Umwälzung in Deutschland: Zum Charakter besonders des preußischen Staates in der ersten Hälfte des 19. Jahrhunderts," *Universalhistorische Aspekte und Dimensionen des Jakobismus*, Sitzungsberichte der Akademie der Wissenschaften der DDR 10/G (Berlin, 1976), pp. 213–14.

64. Schissler, *Preußische Agrargesellschaft*, pp. 168–73. See also W.J. Orr, Jr., "East Prussia and the Revolutions of 1848," *Central European History* 13 (1980): 304–6; Engelsing, *Sozial- und Wirtschaftsgeschichte*, pp. 108–18; Conze, "Vom 'Pöbel' zum 'Proletariat': Sozialgeschichtliche Voraussetzungen für den Sozialismus in Deutschland," *Vierteljahrsschrift für Sozial- und Wirtschaftsgeschichte* 41 (1954): 334–38; and R.A. Dickler, "Organization and Change in Productivity in Eastern Prussia," in W.N. Parker and E.L. Jones, eds., *European Peasants and Their Markets: Essays in Agrarian Economic History* (Princeton, N.J., 1975), pp. 269–92.

Germany's acceptance of liberal economic ideals coincided with a significant cultural transformation, the development of new gender norms.[65] The old economic literature – and this is especially pronounced in the writings of Germershausen – described women and men as essential partners in the household economy. In his five-volume handbook for female estate managers, Germershausen placed the mistress of the household in charge of significant operations of the estate and made her coequal with her husband in others. Following the publication of the *Hausmutter*, there developed a short-lived but prolific genre of agricultural writings for females, the *Hausmütter-literatur*, which was popular perhaps in part because contemporaries saw that both new ideals of economic liberalism and actual changing economic conditions were threatening the long-accepted female role in the economy. Otto von Münchhausen warned in the 1770s against a *Hausvater* violating the gender division of labor by giving too much attention to the female realms. The household economy was based upon the notion that all members were vital contributors to the clocklike functioning of the estate. These ideals were central to the notion that the household was the primary economic institution of society.[66]

Albrecht Thaer's conception of a well-ordered society had no place for women in directive roles, and he envisioned increased managerial responsibilities for males. This may have been unconscious on his part. The new science of agricultural economics focused more on process, and less on people, than the eighteenth-century household books. Whereas Germershausen was highly concerned with the people and their relationships in the

65. On the transformation of gender norms in Germany during this era see K. Hausen, "Family and Role-Division: The Polarisation of Sexual Stereotypes in the Nineteenth Century – An Aspect of the Dissociation of Work and Family," in R.J. Evans and W.R. Lee, eds., *The German Family: Essays on the Social History of the Family in Nineteenth- and Twentieth-Century Germany* (London, 1981), pp. 51–83.

66. M.W. Gray, "Prescriptions for Productive Female Domesticity in a Transitional Era: Germany's *Hausmütterliteratur*, 1780–1840," *History of European Ideas* 8 (1987), special issue: Karen Offen, ed., "Women in European Culture and Society," pp. 413–26. Münchhausen, *Hausvater*, vol. 2, pt. 2, pp. 593, 612. In general on the economic role of the mistress of the household see H. Schmedlin, *Arbeit und Stellung der Frau in der Landgutswirtschaft der Hausväter* (Heidelberg, 1941). While this work romanticizes the role of women in preindustrial society, reflecting a National Socialist bias, it nevertheless is a very useful analysis.

household economy, frequently specifying explicit male and female activities, Thaer often used the impersonal, though not gender-neutral, German expression *"man"* to depict human roles. In a way characteristic of liberal economists, he believed that because the market determined people's place, it was not the economist's role to prescribe specific activities. Nevertheless, Thaer's language reflects a clear diminution of the female part and an expansion of the authority of the male.

He emphasized, for example, the importance of systematic, institutional schooling for estate managers, as opposed to the handed-down traditions that had been so important to the master and mistress of the household under the household system. It is clear that Thaer envisioned that the sons of estate managers would attend the new agricultural institutes. He employed masculine words to describe the students: *"der rationelle Landwirth," "der Jüngling," "Männer von entschiedenem Talent."* Occasionally he used the less explicit term *"man,"* but he never mentioned the schooling of daughters, wives, or *"Landwirthinnen."* The professionalization of agriculture was leading to its becoming a male-directed enterprise. Thaer was hoping to realize an ideal articulated a quarter of a century earlier by the Dresden economist August Fischer, who had advocated that economics, or agriculture, in Germany, although traditionally the realm of "women and servants," should be developed as an academic field that the sons of estate owners would study at the universities.[67]

It is not that gender roles had disappeared in Thaer's conception of agriculture, for he frequently described labor in the traditional terms. Dairy workers, for example, were still "milkmaids." In extensive tables delineating the amounts and types of labor needed for individual tasks on a typical estate, he listed jobs according to the number of days of work needed from four sources: horses, oxen teams, men, and "females and youths." In the harvest, as described by Thaer, men did the mowing and

67. Thaer, *Grundsätze*, 1: 16–24. See also H.A. Fischer, *Versuch einer historisch-programatischen Beschreibung der alten deutschen Ökonomie und des in der Folge der Zeit daraus erwachsenen deutschen fürstlichen Camerwesens* (Leipzig, 1775), pp. 1–2, 7, 27. On the discrepancies between male and female education, see U. Herrmann, "Erziehung und Schulunterricht für Mädchen im 18. Jahrhundert," *Wolfenbüttler Studien zur Aufklärung* 3 (1976): 101–35, and J. Zinnecker, *Sozialgeschichte der Mädchenbildung: Zur Kritik der Schulerziehung von Mädchen im bürgerlichen Patriarchalismus* (Weinheim and Basel, 1973), p. 27.

women and youths the raking and binding of grain stalks. Both sexes worked to load the sheaths on wagons and bring them to the barns.

What had vanished was the woman as supervisor. Whereas Germershausen had specified administrative roles for women in keeping animals and the production of fiber and garden products, one finds no mention of such in Thaer. One exception is the governance of female labor: "A female overseer is of great importance in . . . the dairy, the internal household, and in all . . . work that is done exclusively by women." But this was itself a subordinate employee position, not that of a managing partner, or mistress of the household: "If one finds a person who is qualified to do this and who combines knowledge, activity, love of order, and domesticity, she is invaluable."[68]

Germershausen's careful description of the sharing of budgetary and administrative responsibilities between the presiding marriage partners was absent in Thaer's writing. Thaer's conceptions of gender roles, in large part unarticulated, anticipated the developing bourgeois ideal of female domesticity, according to which middle-class women of the nineteenth century became housewives – consumers rather than producers, economic dependents rather than partners. The old "economic" virtues of order, hard work, and frugality were giving way to the middle-class virtues of domesticity, confining women to reproductive roles under the ideals of economic liberalism.[69]

Historians in search of liberalism in Germany have looked most often to politics and government. However, the triumph of Thaer's weltanschauung over that of Germershausen illustrates the centrality of economic thought and practice in the development of a liberal Germany. During the half century from 1780 to 1830, the ideals of individualism and freedom quietly took precedence over those of collective society in the new agricultural

---

68. Thaer, *Grundsätze*, 1: 149, 173–78, and 201; see also Thaer, *Leitfaden*, pp. 190–93.

69. B. Duden, "Das Schöne Eigentum: Zur Herausbildung des bürgerlichen Frauenbildes an der Wende vom 18. zum 19. Jahrhundert," *Kursbuch* 47 (1977): 125–140. See also Hausen, "Family and Role-Division," pp. 51–83, and Münch, *Ordnung, Fleiß und Sparsamkeit*, pp. 24–32. For comparison see B.G. Smith, *Ladies of the Leisure Class: The Bourgeoisies of Northern France in the Nineteenth Century* (Princeton, N.J., 1981). Describing a very different setting and a nonagricultural population, Smith documents women's transition from economically productive roles in the late eighteenth century to reproductive functions in the nineteenth.

institutes, in university lecture halls, in libraries and bookstores, and on the bookshelves of rural estates. In many facets of the society there occurred – sometimes with governmental encouragement, and sometimes more spontaneously – what one historian has called a "silent bourgeois revolution." The liberal ideal of "freedom," popularized in the transitional era spanning the late Enlightenment and the early Vormärz, in applied terms very often meant, simply, freedom of the market.[70]

The transition from the ideal of the household economy to that of capitalist agriculture demonstrates an endorsement of economic change on the part of the academic and the political leadership in Germany during the revolutionary and Napoleonic eras. Regardless of the ways in which political liberalism was accepted or rejected, economic liberalism changed Germans' views of the ideal relationships between property and people, estate owners and workers, males and females, and humans and the market, leaving the economic landscape of German-speaking Europe transformed forever.

70. D. Blackbourn and G. Eley, *The Peculiarities of German History: Bourgeois Society and Politics in Nineteenth-Century Germany* (Oxford, 1984), pp. 75–97, 176–89; and J. Schlumbohm, *Freiheit – Die Anfänge der bürgerlichen Emanzipationsbewegung in Deutschland im Spiegel ihres Leitwortes (ca. 1760–ca. 1800)*, Geschichte und Gesellschaft. Bochumer Historische Studien, vol. 12 (Düsseldorf, 1975), pp. 122–27.

2
Liberalism, Religious Dissent, and Women's Rights
Louise Dittmar's Writings from the 1840s

Dagmar Herzog

Historians of German liberalism have discussed at length the hesitancy of leading liberals in the Vormärz to advocate universal male suffrage and to challenge the authority of the monarchy. For many of these liberal leaders, parliamentarism was more important than democracy, national unity more important than civil liberties. Even in their theoretical attempts to reconcile *Staat* and *Volk* they displayed discomfort and uneasiness, and the solutions they ultimately profferred were vague.[1] Far more rarely do historians point out that one of the most stubbornly persistent philosophical problems facing liberals has concerned the tension between demands for equality and recognition of individual and group differences. This equality-versus-difference dilemma transcended national boundaries.[2] Born of the impulse to resist aristocratic privilege and feudal hierarchy, liberalism advanced an ideal of liberty and equality for all, at the same time seeking new demarcations around which to organize society. In the German situation, those most obviously excluded from equal political participation were women, Jews, and the emerging working class. Critics of women's emancipation

1. The author would like to thank the editors, as well as Volker Berghahn, Jane Caplan, Mary Gluck, Isabel Hull, Carola Lipp, Joan Scott, and, most especially, Michael Staub, for their thoughtful and thought-provoking readings of earlier drafts and their many helpful criticisms. See L. Krieger, *The German Idea of Freedom* (Boston, 1957), esp. pp. 278–340; J.J. Sheehan, *German Liberalism in the Nineteenth Century* (Chicago and London, 1978), especially pp. 35–76 and 105–7; and G. Birtsch, "Gemäßigter Liberalismus und Grundrechte: Zur Traditionsbestimmtheit des deutschen Liberalismus von 1848/49," in W. Schieder, ed., *Liberalismus in der Gesellschaft des deutschen Vormärz* (Göttingen, 1983).

2. For an overview of contemporary literature on the equality-versus-difference dilemma, see J.W. Scott, "The Sears Case," in *Gender and the Politics of History* (New York, 1988).

argued that women could not be equal because they were different from men. Critics of Jewish emancipation argued that Jews could not be equal because their religion and culture made them different from Christians. Opponents of working-class suffrage argued that the poor could not be equal because, lacking property, they did not have a stake in social stability. The liberals' demand for equality of all individuals before the law stood in tension with their insistence on differences in skill levels and individual achievement, and their resulting defense of social inequality.[3]

Defenders of equality among all individuals were thus left with a philosophical dilemma, which had distinctly different theoretical ramifications for the three excluded groups. For example, in the Vormärz many of those defending Jewish emancipation argued that given equality, Jews would assimilate – that is, become less different. Others argued that religious and cultural differences should be no obstacle to political equality. A radical minority argued that differences should be appreciated and celebrated, and advanced an ideal of pluralism as well as equality.[4] Liberalism's attitude toward class divisions was far more complicated and difficult for historians to pin down, as Vormärz society was not yet so sharply divided. Artisans as well as professionals were carriers of liberal ideology, and this social base to some extent modified the content of the ideology as well.[5] Yet, in the later nineteenth century, the organized

3. See. H. Haan, "Die Gesellschaftstheorie Georg Friedrich Kolbs zwischen Utopie und Ideologie," in Schieder, *Liberalismus,* esp. p. 81; and E. Fehrenbach, "Rheinischer Liberalismus und gesellschaftliche Verfassung," in Schieder, *Liberalismus,* esp. pp. 281 and 291.

4. For example, see the debates over Jewish emancipation in the Baden Landtag: *Verhandlungen der Stände-Versammlung des Großherzogthums Baden im Jahre 1843/45,* 12. Protokollheft, pp. 73–84 (18 February 1845); 13. Beilagenheft, pp. 353–66 (19 February 1845); *Verhandlungen der Stände-Versammlung des Großherzogthums Baden in den Jahren 1845 bis 1846,* 9. Protokollheft, pp. 46–74 (21 August 1846); 7. Beilagenheft, pp. 331–44 (7 August 1846). Compare also D. Sorkin, *The Transformation of German Jewry, 1780–1840* (New York and Oxford, 1987); and R. Rürup, *Emanzipation und Antisemitismus: Studien zur "Judenfrage" der bürgerlichen Gesellschaft* (Göttingen, 1975).

5. See, for example, H.-U. Thamer, "Emanzipation und Tradition: Zur Ideen- und Sozialgeschichte von Liberalismus und Handwerk in der ersten Hälfte des 19. Jahrhunderts," in Schieder, *Liberalismus.* Because of the Schieder collection, the liberal attitude toward class differences has been far more thoroughly integrated into the history of German liberal philosophy in general than liberal attitudes toward Jews and women.

working class was also caught in a tension between separatist revolutionary politics and assimilationist reformist politics.

Far from being marginal, debates over gender relations went to the heart of the liberal dilemma, for gender was the primary category around which bourgeois society organized itself.[6] Most German liberals agreed with conservatives in opposing women's equality with men on the basis of sexual difference. Advocates of women's rights were thus stymied by the seeming opposition that had been established between equality and difference. Even among those who demanded greater equality for women, most nevertheless made a virtue of sexual difference and emphasized women's special qualities, always tempering their demands for equality with demands that women remain "womanly" and different from men. Only a small minority argued that sexual difference was the product of social conditioning rather than biology, and that every individual should be able to develop according to his or her own inner impulses.

In discussing Richard Evans's groundbreaking book, *The Feminist Movement in Germany, 1894–1933*, David Blackbourn notes that "the failure [of the feminist movement] . . . is attributed to the absence in nineteenth-century Germany – by contrast with England, for example – of the sort of bourgeois political culture in which reformist movements like pacifism and feminism could take root."[7] Yet the analysis proposed by Blackbourn and Geoff Eley in *The Peculiarities of German History* suggests that although the bourgeoisie may have failed in political terms, it was highly successful in cultural terms. Although Blackbourn and Eley do not say so, this cultural influence was powerfully expressed in the realm of gender relations. As Jürgen Kocka put it recently, "There is much evidence that beside the social class differences between owners of the means of production and wage laborers, gender difference belongs to this foundation of inequality which constitutes bourgeois

---

6. As many historians now emphasize, gender relations are central to a society's self-understanding. For example, see U. Frevert, ed., *Bürgerinnen und Bürger: Geschlechterverhältnisse im 19. Jahrhundert* (Göttingen, 1988); M. Poovey, *Uneven Developments: The Ideological Work of Gender in Mid-Victorian England* (Chicago, 1988); and L. Davidoff and C. Hall, *Family Fortunes* (Chicago, 1987).

7. D. Blackbourn and G. Eley, *The Peculiarities of German History: Bourgeois Society and Politics in Nineteenth-Century Germany* (Oxford and New York, 1984), p. 160; R.J. Evans, *The Feminist Movement in Germany, 1894–1933* (London, 1976).

society."[8] Perhaps, then, the German bourgeoisie's cultural success actually contributed to continuing gender inequality as much as its political failure did. Indeed, Blackbourn argues that "bourgeois dominance in Germany was most effective where it was most silent and anonymous, where its forms and institutions came to seem most natural."[9] In no other area of social existence was this "naturalization" more evident than in the area of gender relations. A radical minority sought to expose this naturalization while the moderate majority of liberals – together with conservatives – sought to justify it.

Louise Dittmar (1807–84) was the most articulate representative of the radical liberal position on gender in the Vormärz.[10] Questions about women's nature – and their potential equality with or persistent difference from men – constantly recurred in her writings. So too did questions about the relationship between individual consciousness and oppressive social conditions, the power of ideology, and the possibilities for historical change. Her writings exposed the ways in which prominent liberal philosophers had naturalized sexual difference, and promoted a radical strand of liberalism that recognized the equal right of every individual to seek his or her full potential. In her struggle with these issues, Dittmar extended the limits of two major theoretical frameworks available in her day: the philosophy of liberalism, with its organizing concepts of freedom, equality, happiness, reason, and progress, and the philosophy of religious dissent, with its critical analysis of the links between an authoritarian state and an authoritarian God, its challenging of the barriers between the human and the divine, and its language of moral urgency.

8. J. Kocka, "Vorwort," in Frevert, *Bürgerinnen*, p. 9.

9. Blackbourn and Eley, *Peculiarities*, p. 204.

10. Until recently no research had been done on Dittmar, but in the last few years she has become the subject of intensive study. Excerpts from Dittmar's writings were first reprinted in R. Möhrmann, ed., *Frauenemanzipation im deutschen Vormärz* (Stuttgart, 1978), pp. 55–58, 62–64, 92–103, 126–49, and 208–19. She was included in the women's history encyclopedia by D. Weiland, *Geschichte der Frauenemanzipation in Deutschland und Österreich* (Düsseldorf, 1983), pp. 71–72. A comprehensive overview of Dittmar's works and a literary analysis are provided by R.-E. Boetcher Joeres in "Spirit in Struggle: The Radical Vision of Louise Dittmar (1807–1884)," and a reconstruction of Dittmar's biography is provided by C. Klausmann in "Louise Dittmar (1807–1884) – Ergebnisse einer biographischen Spurensuche," both in R.-E. Boetcher Joeres and M. Burkhard, eds., *Out of Line/Ausgefallen: The Paradox of Marginality in the Writings of Nineteenth-Century German Women*, a special issue of *Amsterdamer Beiträge zur neueren*

Dittmar was born in Darmstadt into the family of a treasury official (*Oberfinanzrat*) and thus into the comfortable ranks of the German Protestant bourgeoisie. Although Dittmar's father worked at the court of the grand duke of Hesse-Darmstadt, the family did not have conservative leanings. Christina Klausmann has recovered biographical information showing that at least two of Dittmar's brothers had ties to leftist circles. One was a friend of Georg Büchner's, and one married the daughter of C.W. Leske – Karl Marx's Darmstadt publisher – in whose home many radicals gathered. These familial ties must have reinforced Dittmar's own political leanings.[11] As the one unmarried daughter, Dittmar was weighed down by many domestic duties and was unable to receive any formal education; nevertheless, she published nine books in the space of five years. The first two, *Bekannte Geheimnisse* (1845) and *Skizzen und Briefe* (1845) covered a wide range of political and social issues and addressed women's disenfranchisement in scathing terms. Four books on religious topics followed: *Der Mensch und sein Gott* (1846), *Lessing und Feuerbach* (1847), *Vier Zeitfragen* (1847), and *Charakterisierung der nordischen Mythologie* (1848). *Vier Zeitfragen* was the reprint of a lecture she delivered to the Mannheim Monday Club (*Montagsverein*), a small group of religious dissenters dedicated to cooperation between women and men, Jews and Christians. The applause and encouragement she received from this group gave her the courage to acknowledge authorship of her previous books. Two poetry collections followed: *Wühlerische Gedichte* (1848) and *Brutus-Michel* (1848), both celebrating leading revolutionaries and criticizing the Frankfurt Parliament. Klausmann has also found evidence that Dittmar delivered further lectures – to audiences in Mainz and Darmstadt – in the course of 1848.[12]

In January 1849 Dittmar founded a journal entitled *Soziale Reform*, in which she printed not only her own essays, but also articles by others, with a majority addressing women's issues. The journal folded after only four issues, but the essays in it were reprinted, along with some new ones, in a book entitled *Das Wesen der Ehe nebst einigen Aufsätzen über die soziale Reform der Frauen* (1849). The essays on marriage in this book, collectively

Germanistik 28 (1989): 279–301 and 17–39, respectively.

11. Klausmann, "Louise Dittmar," pp. 15–20.
12. Klausmann, "Louise Dittmar," pp. 28–29.

entitled *Das Wesen der Ehe* (The Essence of Marriage), were
republished separately in 1850, and this is the last book Dittmar
ever managed to publish. Despite the fact that her theological
writings had been favorably reviewed by numerous newspapers
from Hamburg to Halle,[13] and that her own newspaper had
attracted contributions from some of the leading democrats and
women's rights advocates of her day,[14] she was unable to find a
publisher in the postrevolutionary years.[15] During the years of
reaction, publishers probably found the causes Dittmar advocated simply too risky to take on.

Although Dittmar became more specific and concrete in her
suggestions for improving women's lot in her writing during the
revolution, the overwhelming consistency of themes in Dittmar's writings – many of which were written concurrently
despite their publication in sequence – permits them to be
discussed as a unit. It was not so much the revolution that
opened a space for Dittmar and women like her, but rather the
general atmosphere of prerevolutionary turmoil and especially
the atmosphere of religious turmoil. The 1840s were marked not

13. See the reviews of L. Dittmar, *Der Mensch und sein Gott in und außer dem
Christenthum* (Offenbach a.M., 1846) in *Kirchliche Reform: Monatsschrift für freie
Protestanten aller Stände* (Halle, September 1846), pp. 38–39, and in the *Mannheimer Abendzeitung*, 23 May 1846, p. 550. See also the review of L. Dittmar,
Lessing und Feuerbach (Offenbach a.M., 1847) in *Kirchliche Reform* (Halle, October
1847), pp. 38–39. The inside back cover of L. Dittmar, *Vier Zeitfragen beantwortet
in einer Versammlung des Mannheimer Montag-Vereins* (Offenbach am Main, 1847)
advertised *Mensch* and listed further newspapers that favorably reviewed it,
among them the *Hamburger Telegraph*, the *Hanauer Zeitung*, and the *Vaterland*
(Darmstadt).
14. Contributors included Louise Otto, Otto Wigand, Ludwig Bamberger,
Johanna Küstner, Karl Fröbel, and Claire von Glümer. Klausmann has identified
one of the anonymous pieces as belonging to Malwida von Meysenbug. See
Klausmann, "Louise Dittmar," p. 32. Gudrun Wittig has listed Fanny Lewald,
Ida von Düringsfeld, and Ida Frick as Dittmar's collaborators. See G. Wittig,
*"Nicht nur im stillen Kreis des Hauses": Frauenbewegung in Revolution und nachrevo-
lutionärer Zeit, 1848–1876* (Hamburg, 1986), p. 72.
15. Letters from Dittmar to the writer Lorenz Diefenbach give evidence of her
eagerness to keep writing and her difficulties in finding a publisher. See, for
example, Dittmar to Diefenbach, 2 October 1852, and 3 December 1852, Univer-
sitätsbibliothek Giessen, Nachlaß Diefenbach. It is also important to note that –
with the exception of Louise Otto's *Frauen-Zeitung*, which was not forced to shut
down until 1852 – none of the other women's newspapers outlasted the revolution. Mathilde Franziska Anneke's *Kölner Frauenzeitung*, founded in September
1848, had to be shut down after the authorities confiscated the third issue.
Louise Aston's *Freischärler für Kunst und soziales Leben* lasted for seven issues,
from November to December 1848. Louise Marezoll's *Frauen-Spiegel*, also begun
in 1848, disappeared as well. See Wittig, "Nicht nur im stillen Kreis," pp. 70–72.

only by the rise of neopietistic orthodoxy in Protestantism and a revival of pilgrimages and relic worship in Catholicism, but also by the rise of protest movements within each denomination. The Protestant Friends of Light (*Lichtfreunde*) promoted theological rationalism, and the German Catholics (*Deutschkatholiken*) promoted separation from Rome, congregational self-determination, freedom of belief for the individual, and an end to priestly celibacy and to the practice of the confessional. The German Catholics' name was misleading – they also attracted many dissatisfied Protestants, and the vast majority of radical liberals in the Vormärz had some connection to this movement.[16] Both the Friends of Light and the German Catholics were also renowned throughout Germany for their openness to women's participation in congregational life.[17] It is therefore no coincidence that Dittmar's first opportunity to speak publicly was given her by a German Catholic splinter group, the Monday Club.

That which distinguished Dittmar from her contemporaries in such an atmosphere was neither her political point of view – her political writings clearly placed her within the camp of "radical liberals" or "radical democrats" (to use the terms of the time), to which many 1848 revolutionaries also belonged – nor the fact that she advocated an expansion of women's rights, for a substantial number of women and men in her time did so as well.[18]

---

16. For background on the dissenting movements and on the general religious atmosphere, see: C.M. Holden, "A Decade of Dissent in Germany: An Historical Study of the Society of Protestant Friends and the German-Catholic Church, 1840–48" (Ph.D. diss., Yale, 1954); J. Brederlow, *"Lichtfreunde" und "Freie Gemeinden": Religiöser Protest und Freiheitsbewegung im Vormärz und in der Revolution von 1848/49* (Munich and Vienna, 1976); W. Graf, *Die Politisierung des religiösen Bewußtseins* (Stuttgart-Bad Cannstatt, 1978); C. Rehm, *Die katholische Kirche in der Erzdiözese Freiburg während der Revolution 1848/49* (Freiburg and Munich, 1987); J. Sperber, *Popular Catholicism in Nineteenth-Century Germany* (Princeton, 1984).

17. For documentation of women's status within dissenting congregations, see C.M. Prelinger, *Charity, Challenge, and Change: Religious Dimensions of the Mid-Nineteenth-Century Women's Movement in Germany* (New York, 1987); S. Paletschek, "Die Stellung der Frau im Deutschkatholizismus und in den freien Gemeinden im ausgehenden Vormärz und zu Beginn der Reaktionszeit" (M.A. Thesis, University of Hamburg, 1983); A. Lotz, "'Die Erlösung des weiblichen Geschlechts': Frauen in deutschkatholischen Gemeinden," in C. Lipp, ed., *Schimpfende Weiber und patriotische Jungfrauen: Frauen im Vormärz und in der Revolution 1848/49* (Moos and Baden-Baden, 1986).

18. For an overview of nineteenth-century German women writers' views on gender, see the superb study by K. Goodman, *Dis/Closures: Women's Autobiography*

Dagmar Herzog

What distinguished her was the theoretical and philosophical quality of her analysis of the female condition, and the incisiveness of her dissection of the reigning liberal conception of gender relations. Most other women's rights advocates were democrats, like Dittmar, and all advocated greater economic, educational, and political opportunities for women, but most – like Louise Otto, Fanny Lewald, and Kathinka Zitz-Halein – continually linked their demands for equality with a concern for maintaining women's femininity and difference from men. They distanced themselves from "those who have brought the phrase 'emancipation of women' into discredit by degrading the woman into a caricature of the man," as Otto put it in the opening issue of her *Frauen-Zeitung*.[19] Dittmar differed from Louise Aston as well, whose much mythologized advocacy of free love, atheism, and cigar-smoking obscured the fact that her writings, despite their critique of loveless marriages, rarely challenged prevailing gender conceptions.[20] Dittmar's writings, by contrast, revealed that she was both firmly within the liberal tradition and at the same time one of its most sophisticated critics.

in Germany between 1790 and 1914 (New York, 1986). For primary documents, see Möhrmann, *Frauenemanzipation;* G. Hummel-Haasis, ed., *Schwestern zerreißt eure Ketten: Zeugnisse zur Geschichte der Revolution von 1848/49* (Munich, 1982); and R.-E. Boetcher Joeres, ed., *Die Anfänge der deutschen Frauenbewegung. Louise Otto-Peters* (Frankfurt, 1983). Analyses of individual women's views are provided by S. Zucker, "Female Political Opposition in Pre-1848 Germany: The Role of Kathinka Zitz-Halein," in J.C. Fout, ed., *German Women in the Nineteenth Century* (New York, 1984); N. Kaiser, "Marriage and the Not-So-Simple Life in the 1840s," in J. Hermand and R. Grimm, eds., *From the Greeks to the Greens: Images of the Simple Life* (Madison, 1990); and H. Adler, "On a Feminist Controversy: Louise Otto vs. Louise Aston," in R.-E. Boetcher Joeres and M.J. Maynes, eds., *German Women in the 18th and 19th Centuries* (Bloomington, 1986). Overviews of women's activity in the Vormärz and the revolution are provided by L. Secci, "German Women Writers and the Revolution of 1848," in Fout, *German Women;* and Lipp, *Schimpfende Weiber.*

19. L. Otto, "Programm," *Frauen-Zeitung,* 21 April 1849, p. 1.
20. For example, see L. Aston, *Aus dem Leben einer Frau* (Hamburg, 1847). Dittmar's utter disinterest in a flamboyant lifestyle or masculine dress, however, unfortunately did not prevent other women's rights advocates from feeling threatened by the "masculinity" of her mind. She was perceived as less than appropriately feminine by both Kathinka Zitz-Halein and Johanna Küstner. See Klausmann, "Louise Dittmar," pp. 29 and 37, and Boetcher Joeres, "Spirit," p. 299. Indeed, Klausmann and Boetcher Joeres speculate that it was this lack of support from other women as well as the unfriendly political climate that ultimately led Dittmar to stop writing.

Dittmar had no difficulty articulating precisely what she thought the problem was. "Since my earliest youth," she wrote in 1849, "I found nothing more painful than the lack of respect for and devaluation of my sex. . . . All the conditions in which women find themselves seemed to me insulting and inadmissible."[21] The difficulty, as she pointed out, was in finding a solution, and so she tried to tackle the problem from many different angles: "I seize upon whatever can help me with this, thus I seized upon the social movement, thus the religious movement."[22] Here Dittmar clearly stated her method: to appropriate anything from the conceptual frameworks available in her day that could assist her in developing an explanation for women's condition. Two themes in Dittmar's writings particularly illuminate her critique of liberalism from a liberal perspective. The first is the tension between arguing for women's equality with men and arguing for women's special capacities and needs. The second is the tension between her attacks on Christianity's oppression of women and her reliance on biblical language. These two tensions recur throughout her entire oeuvre, with numerous experimental variations. By juxtaposing Dittmar's work with an article on gender relations by Carl Theodor Welcker, one of the most prominent liberals of her day, and by examining her arguments more closely, the logic of allowing the different strategies to remain in tension will become clear.

Equality and Difference in Liberal Thought on Gender

When early nineteenth-century German liberal philosophers and statesmen tried to reconcile their own demands for greater political freedom with a new justification for the exclusion of women from public life, they frequently invoked the laws of nature as a means to resolve this philosophical dilemma.[23] They

21. L. Dittmar, "Erwiderung," in *Das Wesen der Ehe nebst einigen Aufsätzen über die soziale Reform der Frauen* (Leipzig, 1849), p. 109. Hereafter, this text will be designated *Soziale Reform*, to distinguish it from the essays on marriage (*Das Wesen der Ehe*), which were reprinted in 1850.

22. Dittmar, *Vier Zeitfragen*, p. ii.

23. Although dualistic thinking about the sexes has a long history, it was not until the late eighteenth and early nineteenth centuries – with Rousseau and his popularizers – that sexuality was thought to exert a central influence on character

based their theory of society on the necessity for polar opposition between the sexes, arguing that this opposition was so crucial a cornerstone to the entire edifice of German society that any attempt to demand women's equality endangered that natural difference on which the social order depended.

This set of assumptions was articulated by a wide range of late eighteenth- and early nineteenth-century political philosophers, novelists, poets, authors of prescriptive tracts, and politicians.[24] It was exemplified by Carl Theodor Welcker's 1838 article on "Geschlechtsverhältnisse" (Relations between the Sexes) in the *Staats-Lexikon* that he edited with Carl von Rotteck.[25] The *Staats-Lexikon* represented the cumulative and synthetic statement of southwest German liberal self-understanding in the prerevolutionary years. As Leonard Krieger noted, it was "the most influential organ of political liberalism in pre-March Germany," and Karin Hausen and Carola Lipp have specifically demonstrated how representative Welcker's ideas on gender were.[26]

---

formation and therefore to have relevance for political life. For several decades older views of gender roles based in social status coexisted with the new biological views. For background on the relationship between biology and political discourse see I.V. Hull, "'Sexualität' und bürgerliche Gesellschaft," and U. Frevert, "Bürgerliche Meisterdenker und das Geschlechterverhältnis," both in Frevert, *Bürgerinnen*; T. Laqueur, "Orgasm, Generation, and the Politics of Reproductive Biology," in *Representations*, no. 14 (Spring 1986): 1–41; K. Hausen, "Family and Role Division: The Polarization of Sexual Stereotypes in the Nineteenth Century – An Aspect of the Dissociation of Work and Family Life," in R.J. Evans and W.R. Lee, eds., *The German Family* (London, 1981); M. Bloch and J.H. Bloch, "Women and the Dialectics of Nature in Eighteenth-Century French Thought," and L.J. Jordanova, "Natural Facts: A Historical Perspective on Science and Sexuality," both in C.P MacCormack and M. Strathern, eds., *Nature, Culture, and Gender* (Cambridge, 1980); and L.J. Jordanova, *Languages of Nature: Critical Essays on Science and Literature* (New Brunswick, 1986).

24. Many of these thinkers are discussed in V. Hoffmann, "Elisa und Robert oder das Weib und der Mann, wie sie sein sollten: Anmerkungen zur Geschlechtercharakteristik der Goethezeit," in K. Richter and J. Schönert, eds., *Klassik und Moderne: Die Weimarer Klassik als historisches Ereignis und Herausforderung im kulturgeschichtlichen Prozeß* (Stuttgart, 1983). Excellent discussions can also be found in Frevert, "Bürgerliche Meisterdenker," Hull, "'Sexualität,'" and K. Hausen, "'. . . eine Ulme für das schwanke Efeu': Ehepaare im Bildungsbürgertum, Ideale und Wirklichkeiten im späten 18. und 19. Jahrhundert," all in Frevert, *Bürgerinnen*. Further context is provided by E. Kennedy and S. Mendus, eds., *Women in Western Political Philosophy* (New York, 1987).

25. C. Welcker, "Geschlechtsverhältnisse," in C. von Rotteck and C. Welcker, eds., *Staats-Lexikon oder Encyclopädie der Staatswissenschaften*, 1st ed., vol. 6, (Altona, 1838), pp. 629–55.

26. Krieger, *The German Idea*, p. 31; K. Hausen, "Family and Role Division"; C. Lipp, "Frauen und Öffentlichkeit: Möglichkeiten und Grenzen politischer

Welcker's article also usefully demonstrates how the various elements of liberal thought on gender were intimately intertwined. Indeed, Dittmar herself singled out Welcker's article on gender relations in the *Staats-Lexikon* as particularly representative of the German liberal position on women.

In "Geschlechtsverhältnisse" Welcker articulated the centrality of gender for middle-class national, religious, and political identity. Welcker wrote: "And this Christian and German family life – the greatest and most hopeful progress in the whole history of humanity – . . . such a family life is underestimated by new theories and considered a matter of indifference for civilization and for freedom. . . . *As if the free dignified family and the free dignified life of the state did not mutually support each other, and as if they did not also in their decline pull each other down!*"[27] For Welcker, the life of the state and the life of the family were interdependent; one goal of his article was to define a model for family life that would ensure the continued health of the state.

Welcker's article began with a historical overview of gender relations in earlier societies; he pointed out the continuing progress in women's lot from the "despotism" and "harems" among Babylonians and Persians, through the moderate improvements of the Hebrews, Greeks, and Romans, up to the Germanic peoples, with their high regard for women. He argued that the Christian-German state of his day represented the peak of civilization and, at the same time, staunchly insisted that no further progress was necessary. He was as deeply opposed to those "ultra-democrats" who argued for women's legal and political equality with men (he singled out Harriet Martineau, Jeremy Bentham, Charles Fourier, and Claude-Henri de St. Simon for special censure) as he was to the supposed "Oriental despots." However, after chronicling dynamic

---

Partizipation im Vormärz und in der Revolution 1848," and C. Lipp, "Liebe, Krieg und Revolution: Geschlechterbeziehung und Nationalismus," both in Lipp, *Schimpfende*. See also U. Gerhard, "Die Rechtsstellung der Frau in der bürgerlichen Gesellschaft des 19. Jahrhunderts: Frankreich und Deutschland im Vergleich," in J. Kocka, ed., *Bürgertum im 19. Jahrhundert*, vol. 1 (Munich, 1988), pp. 464–68. The fact that Welcker's article was republished unchanged in 1847 in the second edition of the *Staats-Lexikon* and that a shortened version – which nevertheless contained all the same arguments – was published in 1862 in the third edition further indicates the "staying power" of his views.

27. Welcker, "Geschlechtsverhältnisse," pp. 648–49 (emphasis in the original).

historical change, Welcker had to find a logical reference point *outside* history if he wanted to argue against further change.

The historical overview was followed by a long philosophical section in which Welcker defended his adamant disapproval of women's equality by referring to the laws of nature and the difference between the sexes inscribed in those laws. He concluded this section by declaring triumphantly that all his arguments against women's equality in no way undermined the liberal ideal of a society based on contract or consensus. "Even if all our major arguments about immorality and depravity, injustice and unnecessariness of unconditional equality . . . do not apply to a few exceptions . . . nevertheless this unconditional equality and the overthrow of our prevailing social order must also be rejected in legal terms. This rejection, namely, absolutely does not impair the principle of social contract or consensus, but rather is appropriate to it."[28] Here Welcker summed up his justifications for female subordination and, in the same breath, assured his readers that this in no way undermined the liberal concept of society. Nothing could state more clearly the way liberal self-understanding and female subordination were linked.

Welcker's article also provides a particularly revealing example of how philosophers formulated their beliefs about gender relations in terms of the unchanging laws of nature, rather than mutable manmade laws. Welcker states:

> Our more perfect present-day natural-rights and Christian theory of state no longer subordinates humanity to the state or the human being to the citizen as the Greek and Roman [theories did]. Rather, it makes human rights the foundation of citizen rights, thereby founding the equality of the latter on the equality of the former. And yet such manifold inequality between man and woman, such a great difference in their life-tasks and in their strengths, and consequently also in their legal circumstances, is already determined by nature.[29]

Welcker here reconciled his pride in the equal rights his society extended to all males with the attempt to legislate women's exclusion from that political society. Significantly, he justified that exclusion by referring to nature and the "natural" relations between men and women.

28. Ibid., pp. 650–51.
29. Ibid., p. 630.

Welcker's philosophical starting-point for his reflections on the political rights of women was the sexual act. The roles he thought women and men played in procreation determined, in his view, their character traits, their appropriate behavior in the family, and their appropriate relation to the political realm. The fundamental precondition for procreation, as well as for all other activities, was that the sexes must remain in polar opposition. Welcker wrote: "[The two sexes] can, in accordance with the most universal law of nature, simultaneously maintain their own essential definition and maintain their fundamental attraction and harmonious union for their common life-purpose only when they are in polar opposition and connection."[30] Basically elaborating on a model of magnetic attraction, according to which connection is only possible through opposition, Welcker went on to define the precise content of that opposition by positing that the man takes the more "active" and "external" role in procreation, the woman the more "passive" and "internal." After intercourse, man is *"freer"* to take responsibility for "other *external* activity." But woman's "life-goal is love" and her responsibility is for the *"lasting maintenance of the species through inner development."*[31]

This model of sexual behavior and differentiation of character traits in turn had consequences for family life and political life: women's main focus should be the family, man's the public realm of business and politics. All transgressions of these spheres assigned by nature were disgusting to Welcker: "The only thing in the whole moral world as repugnant and perverted as the masculine woman [*Mannweib*] is the effeminate man [*weibischer Mann*]."[32] The ideal arrangement was a lifelong loving marriage in which the woman was the priestess at the cozy hearth while the man triumphantly rushed out each day to attend to business, and returned home to quiet happiness.[33]

In the pages that followed, Welcker elaborated his belief that women's femininity was the cornerstone of a healthy and stable society, because only a "truly feminine" mother could raise children appropriately, teaching them in the family how to control sensual drives. "Wherever women become degenerate,

---

30. Ibid., p. 636.
31. Ibid., p. 637 (emphasis in the original).
32. Ibid., p. 641.
33. Ibid., p. 644.

civic virtue and strength will disappear as well. Only if the strongest of all sensuous drives are subordinated to the domination of moral good sense first in the family – the foundation and plant nursery [*Pflanzschule*], the prototype of the state association – can the permanent victory of [moral good sense] be hoped for in the state as well."[34] This quote not only indicates that Welcker placed a heavier burden on the woman to remain feminine than on the man to remain masculine, but also reveals Welcker's contradictory application of "nature." While Welcker relied on nature to assign character traits and appropriate spheres of activity, nature and natural drives were also apparently dangerous enough to be placed under state control. This was particularly evident when Welcker discussed the social decline resulting from lax divorce and adultery laws[35] and when he discussed appropriate punishments for "crimes of the flesh."[36] On the one hand, nature determined that women must be "truly feminine." On the other hand, one apparently could not rely on nature to keep women (and passions) in their place without state control.

Thus, the differentiation of traits, tasks, and spheres between the sexes had to be enforced by law, and women could not be allowed to participate directly in shaping political policy. The health of the state, according to Welcker, required the maintenance of sexual difference, and *any* transgression of that difference through demands for legal equality could not be tolerated. When Welcker discussed how unnecessary a referendum on the question of women's rights would be, the way he phrased the choices – "whether for their womanliness or for manly rights dangerous to them" – once again revealed the opposition he perceived between womanliness and rights.[37] In an explicit attack on the St. Simonians, Welcker wrote that "those who by

34. Ibid., p. 647.
35. Ibid., pp. 646 and 660.
36. For example, Welcker argued that "the disorderly drives and passions that underlie these crimes are of such a nature and strength, and they cause such ruinous incitements, that if we do not oppose them with a mighty dam of law and of that morality that is protected and supported by the law, and through the public conscience and legal punishment and shame keep awake the slumbering consciousness of individuals, they will spread faster than all other criminal passions, find incitement and nourishment and soon shatter all the essential foundations of a dignified and healthy social life." See ibid., p. 659.
37. Ibid., p. 650.

unilaterally following an abstract rule of equality ignore the laws and barriers of nature and demand more rights for women than [women], according to those laws and barriers, can possibly want, destroy this holiest and most solid foundation of human and civic virtue and happiness [i.e., family life] yet again."[38] He thus reiterated the decisive opposition between equality and difference in liberal thought.

Dittmar's Struggle within the Liberal Framework

Dittmar's choices of rhetorical strategies for advocating women's rights were made with Welcker's argument in mind. On the one hand, Dittmar frequently insisted that women were logically included in the liberal ideals of freedom, equality, and human rights. On the other, she also frequently invoked the special qualities liberal philosophers ascribed to women to justify a widening of women's sphere. Finally, however, Dittmar challenged Welcker's opposition between equality and difference and proposed new definitions for these two terms. She also redefined the appropriate role of the state, urged reconsideration of what was natural and what was unnatural, and advocated dynamic historical change in contrast to Welcker's plea for social stasis.

Dittmar demanded equality for women in a variety of ways. In her newspaper, *Soziale Reform* – and particularly in the essay collection on marriage ("Das Wesen der Ehe") within it – she addressed those who "start with the premise that personal freedom is a right and a necessity" and specifically defended women's right to education, to a career and economic self-sufficiency, and to participation in making and administering the laws that affect women.[39] Writing in the midst of revolution, Dittmar also effectively employed the metaphor of political freedom for other marginal groups in order to expose the way freedom and equality were denied to women. "The political position of the man with respect to the woman is that of the patrician to the plebeian, the free [person] to the slave."[40]

---

38. Ibid., p. 650.
39. L. Dittmar, "Die männliche Bevormundung," in *Soziale Reform*, p. 15; L. Dittmar, "Der weibliche Antheil an sozialen Reformen," in *Soziale Reform*, p. 16; L. Dittmar, *Das Wesen der Ehe* (Leipzig, 1850), pp. 22, 40–41, and 72–73.
40. Dittmar, *Wesen*, p. 19.

Furthermore, she remarked, "it is surprising the way the political standpoint of a people is mirrored in all relationships. The protection of women under the law resembles the constitutional system like one drop of water [resembles] another; concessions, empty promises, palliatives."[41]

Dittmar was hopeful that "true democrats" would have a different perspective, "that all true democrats will carry the democratic principle, the full granting of rights and the full enjoyment of personal freedom, also into this area. . . . It is therefore a logical consequence that, as soon as the democratic principle has achieved victory, the essence of marriage will undergo a complete transformation."[42] Although Dittmar's faith in the democrats' commitment to women's rights was (in hindsight) somewhat naive,[43] the important point is the way she argued that equality among men should be accompanied by equality between men and women. She used similarly liberal language in "Vier Zeitfragen," the lecture delivered in Mannheim in 1847: "Let us say it loud and clear, we *demand* happiness; we consider it our *right*."[44]

Already in 1845, however, Dittmar had directly criticized those who did not extend the liberal ideal of freedom to all individuals, including women. In *Skizzen und Briefe* she pointed out that the language and concepts of liberalism, which claimed to be universal, were actually gender-bound in their application by philosophers. "In those who doubt the feasibility of [woman's]

41. Ibid., pp. 17–18.
42. Ibid., p. 18.
43. It is important not to underestimate the democrats' commitment to egalitarianism within marriage, which went far beyond anything that conservatives or moderate liberals recommended, and many democratic men – revolutionaries like Gustav Struve or Robert Blum, dissenting preachers like Johannes Ronge or Carl Scholl – advocated greater equality for women. As Lipp points out, the classic liberal theory of the state used a patriarchal model of the family in theorizing gender relations, whereas "the democratic natural rights theories that the left-liberals also championed, by contrast, emphasized far more the aspect of equality of the sexes." See Lipp, "Frauen und politische Öffentlichkeit," p. 295. At the same time, however, democrats still tended to assume that men and women had specifically masculine and feminine character traits. As Lipp notes, "Also in the thinking of the democratic movement, then, the polar definition of gender characteristics found an echo. Love and feeling were assigned to women as a specifically feminine quality, and at the same time [women], in their emotionality, were romantically elevated." See Lipp, "Liebe, Krieg und Revolution," p. 364.
44. Dittmar, *Vier Zeitfragen*, p. 2 (emphasis in the original).

freedom, I cannot help doubting their understanding of it as well as their comprehension of female nature. They search about in all of existence to find an unconditionally free situation for the human being [*Mensch*] but strictly speaking, they only understand this to mean the man [*sie begreifen im eigentlichsten Sinn nur den Mann darunter*]."[45] In this text, Dittmar also addressed the way male self-understanding depended on defining women as the antithesis to men. "I am suspicious of all characterizations of women that start from their antipodes, the men. . . . They [the men] are not fair enough to acknowledge that there could be a life that is more beautiful and more appropriate for women without fearing that their male nature has been violated."[46] In her explicit attack on Welcker's article, Dittmar echoed and expanded this theme. "The whole [Geschlechtsverhältnisse] article," she explained, "starts from the premise and the endeavor to subordinate the woman to the man and to justify all existing legal and moral conditions relating to the woman."[47] She further decried "these liberals of 1830, how they do not even concern themselves with finding the causes of social abuses, but rather only prove their historical necessity and development."[48]

What seemed natural to Welcker, Dittmar argued, was really the result of social conditioning. For example, she pointed out that to provide no educational opportunities for the woman, to educate her for nothing else but domesticity, "and then to say, 'that is her destiny,' does that not mean that she is being *pre*destined?"[49] In another essay Dittmar was even more explicit in her attack on the way "nature" was used to limit women's possibilities: "What is nature, what is destiny? Is nature not itself changeable? Is the destiny of humans not something arbitrary? Truly, to legislate here is to be very presumptuous or very narrow-minded. It is possible that women will occasionally fail against nature, but who will have to suffer for it? Against their destiny? Who is insolent enough to force one on them?"[50]

Dittmar argued that given the freedom to develop them-

45. L. Dittmar, *Skizzen und Briefe aus der Gegenwart* (Darmstadt, 1845), p. 88.
46. Dittmar, *Skizzen*, p. 94.
47. Dittmar, *Wesen*, p. 6.
48. Ibid., p. 7.
49. Ibid., pp. 55–56 (emphasis in the original).
50. L. Dittmar, "Aphorismen," in *Soziale Reform*, p. 119.

selves, women could develop all the same talents as men. She insisted that no sphere need be closed to women:

> There is almost no field of social life that could then not be cultivated by and for [the woman]. For example, the immense kingdom of natural science, chemistry, mechanics, and their multitude of practical applications; psychology, medicine, from doctoring the soul down to physical nursing; intellectual and physical education, from poetry, philosophy, and mathematics down to ABC and one times one; from the practicing of artistic postures down to athletics; the field of art . . . from the nurturing of creative genius down to mechanical copying.[51]

All that was needed, Dittmar reasoned, was an equal opportunity for women to acquire an education. Dittmar recommended the establishment of polytechnical institutes for women,[52] and a "grand interlocking set of institutions," financed by the state but run by women, that would prepare women for the careers of their choice.[53]

In the same texts in which Dittmar argued for women's potential equality with men and exposed the ways "nature" was used to veil the effects of social conditioning, she also frequently argued that women were indeed different from men, that women's higher nature had not been recognized, and that women's special ways of seeing the world had been undervalued. In *Skizzen und Briefe* Dittmar criticized the male ideal: "That which they like to declare to be masculine is really only the world-destroying, by no means the world-delighting, principle."[54] In *Vier Zeitfragen* she explained that her goal was "to rouse an idea in the woman that alone will be capable of tearing her out of the errors, scorn, and indignity into which she has fallen, simply because she has never been recognized in her higher nature and therefore has been overwhelmed with scorn and humiliation by society since time immemorial."[55] And in *Soziale Reform* she suggested that "every more far-reaching female activity must be carried out by women collectively. . . . In

---

51. Dittmar, "Der weibliche Antheil," p. 16.
52. Ibid., p. 16.
53. Dittmar, *Wesen*, p. 40.
54. Dittmar, *Skizzen*, p. 94.
55. Dittmar, *Vier Zeitfragen*, p. v.

collectivity everything can be made possible in a way appropriate to [woman's] peculiarity."[56]

The identification of women's higher nature and special difference was also the outstanding feature of the collection of essays Dittmar published under the title *Das Wesen der Ehe*. While this was the same work in which she made her most explicit recommendations for advancing women's equality, these essays were also replete with the language of the "natural attraction of opposites" used by Welcker. For example, she wrote that "for a completely human marriage we insist on spiritual love as a precondition. . . . [The] development of physical science, specifically chemistry, convinces us that the laws of relatedness of souls are founded on the same laws."[57] She concluded that "the whole universe is dominated by the principle of male and female; without this contrast there would be no dynamic motion."[58] In *Das Wesen der Ehe* Dittmar accepted the identification of women with emotion and men with reason so prevalent in her time, but turned this association to women's advantage by arguing that

> if we want to make life more human, and not only more manly, then the man seems to be just as unself-sufficient as the woman. . . . Just as the eye and the ear perceive in different ways, and one can measure and weigh the same things in different ways using either size or scales, and every narrowing or limiting, every subordination of these absolutely valid assessments must lead to wrongheadedness, mistake, deceit, and confusion; so also with the subordination and limitation of the female judgment and its influence on the shaping of life.[59]

In this text, Dittmar also placed particular emphasis on women's specific vulnerabilities as women. She argued that divorce should be made easier – she went so far as to suggest that the state should have no role in controlling divorce at all – that the state should take responsibility for childcare,[60] and that the state should protect women against men when necessary. Dittmar maintained with particular fervor that divorce trials

56. Dittmar, "Der weibliche Antheil," p. 16.
57. Dittmar, *Wesen*, p. 4.
58. Ibid., p. 70.
59. Ibid., p. 29.
60. Ibid., p. 72.

were far more injurious to women than to men. "The sensibilities of the man," she wrote, "are not directly damaged by the state intervention: he is the one who has the choice, he is the property owner, there are no moral restraints on him, he is the one who can bring about a separation in various ways, and finally, his feelings, even in the most repugnant divorce trial, are not put on public display like those of the woman."[61] Dittmar shocked her readers by rejecting any role for the state in either marriage or divorce.[62] Such a rejection of state involvement in private lives could be considered a classically liberal position. But Dittmar knew that other liberals would not agree. In a wry letter to an anonymous woman, published in *Soziale Reform*, Dittmar contended that to be an overt atheist in her society was easier than to challenge the institution of civil marriage.[63]

At the same time, Dittmar challenged other liberals to consider in what situations the state's involvement would be most useful – not in controlling marital fidelity, but rather, as she put it, in "protecting female honor," in protecting women from dependency and abuse. The state mistook its own role as self-appointed protector of women and thereby exposed its lack of true concern for women's needs. The state, Dittmar maintained,

> should be the representative of female rights, should protect the holiness, the inviolability of female nature, this is demanded by the individuality of the woman. It should understand the woman as woman, understand her not only in her right to be human but also in her right to be female, and not let the latter lead to an impairment of her personal freedom; it should guard this [personal freedom] doubly, against the encroachments of the external world and against the world of men, and thereby protect her against her husband as against every other man.[64]

When Dittmar spoke of the protection of female honor, she did

61. Ibid., pp. 22–23.
62. Boetcher Joeres and Klausmann have located an angry response to Dittmar's critique of civil marriage by her contemporary Johanna Küstner Fröbel in K. Fröbel and J. Fröbel, *Hochschulen für Mädchen und Kindergärten als Glieder einer vollständigen Bildungsanstalt* (Hamburg, 1849).
63. Dittmar, "Erwiderung," p. 110. Klausmann has suggested that this woman was the well-known writer Malwida von Meysenbug.
64. Dittmar, *Wesen*, p. 21.

not only mean guaranteeing women's "inviolability"; she also insisted that the state should protect female honor by freeing women from the compulsion to get married as a means for economic survival.[65] This was the basis for her demands for guaranteeing women's right to work and for state financing of women's education.

But by no means did Dittmar aim to transfer women's dependency from their husbands onto the state: "But so that the woman does not get into the same dependency-relationship and disproportionate relationship to the whole of society that she is in now in relation to the man, it is necessary that just like the man she be able to decide her own matters, manage them herself, and carry them out. And to this end she must . . . consult with other women about ends and means."[66] This call for collective female endeavor recurred in Dittmar's writings. It was evident not only in her defense of women's clubs[67] but also in her decision to launch the journal *Soziale Reform*, through which she sought to provide a forum for just such "collective consultation" between women over their own matters.[68]

Dittmar's Redefinition of Welcker's Terms

How, then, can we make sense of these two seemingly contradictory lines of argument in Dittmar's writings? One explanation lies in the way Dittmar redefined equality itself. For Welcker, equality implied sameness, and thus he could reject equality between the sexes on the basis of their biological differences. Dittmar redefined equality to mean not sameness, but rather the irrelevance of differences for certain purposes, for example, for the purpose of getting an education, being economically self-supporting in the career of one's choice, or having the right to participate in political decision making. A further explanation can be found in the way Dittmar redefined the state. As the passages from *Das Wesen der Ehe* indicate, Dittmar's vision of the ideal state was far removed from that of her contemporaries. Her model state was utopian, a state that guaranteed women's freedom and women's equality. This state

65. Ibid., p. 73.
66. Ibid., p. 39.
67. Ibid., p. 73.
68. L. Dittmar, "Ein Brief an die Herausgeberin," in *Soziale Reform*, p. 107.

would take women's specific needs as women into account, and would thereby make women *more* capable of achieving equality with men.

But the logic of letting the two strands of argument remain in tension becomes even clearer if we examine the ways that Dittmar redefined nature. In contrast to many of her contemporaries, Dittmar believed that nature, left to its own devices, was good. She therefore challenged Welcker's distrust of nature and implicitly exposed the liberals' effort to reinforce nature with legal constraints. Here she took liberal concepts to their logical conclusion, assuring her readers that social anarchy would not ensue if the state no longer intervened in marriage:

> The *freed* woman, who no longer needs to sell herself, the economically independent woman, will oppose the frivolity and instability of the man with a mighty dam. The man will then *constantly* have to strive for her love. . . . In this way we have a natural balance: in her natural faithfulness a counterpart to his natural unfaithfulness. But his tendency toward unfaithfulness also provides a constant challenge for her to awaken his love over and over again. . . . In this reciprocity lies the solution to the whole problem without any assistance from the state. Nature has everywhere created its own shores, that keep even the most turbulent sea in its bounds.[69]

For all her sentimental language, Dittmar was in essence contesting the *Staats-Lexikon*'s definition of nature and challenging Welcker and others to take their stated faith in the laws of nature seriously. Whereas Welcker said laws should provide a "mighty dam" against sexual drives,[70] Dittmar contended that women themselves could provide that "mighty dam." Furthermore, Dittmar removed nature from its position of opposition to abstraction and instead located it in opposition to state intervention and legal constraint. This displacement allowed her to label all that subordinated women as "unnatural."

What was unnatural, Dittmar argued, were the *conditions* under which women were forced to live. The expectations placed on women were unnatural, and especially the institution of marriage was unnatural. This formulation undermined the *Staats-Lexikon* link between "nature" and a particular model of

69. Dittmar, *Wesen*, pp. 15–16 (emphasis in the original).
70. Cf. fn. 36.

domesticity and family. In *Das Wesen der Ehe*, for example, Dittmar suggested that "without [spiritual love] marriage is immoral, unnatural."[71] Welcker could have agreed. But Dittmar went on to draw different conclusions: she argued that "not letting the woman freely develop her emotional or spiritual life . . . in combination with the [economic and legal] dependency of the woman, leads the woman unconditionally into the man's power and lets him abuse his power in the most unnatural and nature-defiling way."[72] At another point, she argued that the involvement of the state in marriage and divorce was an "unnatural intrusion of state power."[73]

Furthermore, it is significant that Dittmar chose not to argue the direct opposite of Welcker's claim that "woman's life-goal is love." Instead of countering that women were not interested in or motivated by love, Dittmar instead focused on the "unnatural" distortion of women's capacity for love in her society:

> Especially in the case of women this desire is suppressed, weakened and clouded through an unnatural upbringing, through moral thumbscrews, and through the most clever principle of deadening. We must therefore not . . . let ourselves be persuaded into the assumption that the love of women can be awakened by a command here, be held in check there, be bought with a position, a provision here, be banned with an external necessity there, in short, that it could be, according to inclination, allowed to develop a few degrees of warmth, [and then] soon be turned down to below the freezing point.[74]

In *Skizzen und Briefe* Dittmar made an argument that similarly placed the blame for whatever "unnaturalness" a woman might evince on the external conditions of her life. She claimed that if

71. Ibid., p. 4.
72. Ibid., pp. 29–30.
73. Ibid., p. 19.
74. Ibid., pp. 9–10. Even when Dittmar did not explicitly use the terms "natural" and "unnatural," the links she had established between "nature" and "love," on the one hand, and "civil marriage," and "unnaturalness," on the other, made her meaning abundantly clear: "And for love, which springs out of the most heated yearning for satisfaction, for this thirst of the soul, to which asylum does he [the stupid Philistine] direct it? To the prison of civil marriage, this economic and political asylum of unfreedom. Love is something he does not know, it is not listed in his *Staats-Lexikon*, he only knows 'gender relations,' legitimate and illegitimate." See ibid., p. 32. Here she again took a scornful stab at Welcker's claim that "woman's life-goal is love."

women overstepped the "proper" bounds of their sex in the past it was because social conditions were unnatural.[75] She also put it this way: "If life were in proper relation to both sexes, the woman would develop as much power, courage, energy, and greatness of soul, as much spirit and talent as the man in his sphere. One would nowhere see in her a flaw, an inferiority as in the past, where she required almost superhuman powers and often was really forced to step out of her female nature in order to express the fundamental idea of her soul."[76] This statement can be read as a response to the many epithets against "masculine women" (*Mannweiber*) circulating in the 1840s. But it also suggests a different resolution to the equality-difference tension: that every individual woman should be able to express "the fundamental idea of her soul."

Dittmar proposed yet another view of nature, one that emphasized the differences between *individual* natures, regardless of sex, and argued that what was natural was whatever was peculiar to a given individual. For example, in commenting on the recent plethora of prescriptive texts for women, she declared pointedly: "There are no more and no fewer women as they should be than there are men as they should be."[77] In the same vein, she argued that "only that which contradicts the nature of a being is unnatural; aside from that, everything that is, is natural. Whether it contradicts the external demands on it or not, in no way diminishes its inner legitimacy."[78] Significantly, Dittmar here associated nature with inner personal impulses and not with prescribed behavior differentiated according to gender.

Indeed, one of Dittmar's most effective resolutions of the equality-difference dilemma was to redefine Welcker's notion of difference. Instead of only focusing, as he did, on the differences between men and women, she continually emphasized the differences *among* women. This emphasis on individual peculiarity and diversity and the need to encourage individual self-development found its most urgent expression in the language of religious dissent.

75. Dittmar, *Skizzen*, pp. 101, 102.
76. Ibid., pp. 92–93.
77. Ibid., p. 110.
78. Ibid., p. 96.

Religious Dissent: A Way Out of the Liberal Dilemma

Welcker had identified his vision of ideal family life as not only German but also Christian. By implication, then, to propose an alternate model of gender relations was to open oneself to attack as an atheist, a subverter of the faith. Dittmar refused to accept such a dichotomy. Her vision for society drew strength from a submerged strand within Christianity. Not only did Dittmar recognize the deep resonance that religious language would have in an era of religious revival on both the right and the left, but she also tapped into a philosophy that was potentially far more radical than even the secular egalitarianism advanced by the Enlightenment. On the one hand, Christianity in her day was associated with the preservation of power in the king, ignorance and superstition in the masses, and pious submissiveness on the part of wives. On the other hand, however, the Christian tradition contained within it a strand that emphasized the equal dignity and worth of every individual, a tradition of prophetic denunciation of injustice, and faith in the possibility of a complete transformation and renewal of the world, the creation of justice on earth.

There is an unresolved tension in Dittmar's writing between scathing attacks on the hypocrisy and oppressiveness of the Christian churches and a reliance on a language and a conceptual framework that can only be described as deeply religious. For example, in *Skizzen und Briefe* Dittmar told the story of Beate, a woman burned at the stake for heresy and witchcraft in the seventeenth century. In her final words to the townspeople, Beate says, "I had no God and no faith, for I had your God, and I cursed Him because He could not unite the spirit and the bodily senses, because He directed the striving soul only towards heaven and filled it with scorn and loathing for earthly needs. . . . Abandon the God who does not comfort the penitent and take in the lost!"[79] Both anti-Christianity and deep religiosity are evident here. At another point in *Skizzen und Briefe*, Dittmar similarly argues: "They do not acknowledge that there is only One God, who is everywhere where He is recognized, not where He is sent burnt offerings."[80] Calling socialism "the

---

79. Ibid., p. 82.
80. Ibid., p. 24.

realization of the Christian principle,"[81] Dittmar proclaimed that "the new Lord is neither the God in the machine nor the God in the church but certainly the God in the heart and in the *deed*."[82]

Dittmar contended that Christianity in particular had inhibited women's capacity to develop their own independent convictions. "Who else still went to church," Dittmar asked, "but the unenlightened *Volk* and the female sex, that still believed itself forced to sacrifice its own convictions to the tyranny of convention?"[83] Dittmar constantly referred in her writings to the desperate need to awaken a feeling of self-worth in women. "I know," she wrote, "what a Sisyphus-work one burdens oneself with when one espouses the cause of the female sex. . . . Since [the woman] has no sense of self-esteem, or has rather a limitless self-contempt, she must necessarily assume that he who takes on her cause is her enemy."[84] Dittmar consistently asserted the rights of the individual to determine him- or herself, to follow an inner ideal:

> Without a sense of self-worth the human being has not even achieved the *lowest* level of humanity. I therefore lay claim to self-worth for *every* person, lay claim to it for each sex equally. The *individual peculiarity*, without which people themselves and all of life are *without charm*, without which there is no happiness, no progressive development, no self-revelation of the spirit, this individual peculiarity depends solely upon that sense of self-worth, and can never fully express itself without freedom.[85]

To emphasize the sanctity of each individual and the sacredness of the right to self-determination, Dittmar followed the example of Ludwig Feuerbach and argued that what was human *was* divine and that there was no higher perfection than potential human perfection.[86] To argue anything else would have

---

81. Ibid., p. 31.
82. Dittmar, *Mensch*, p. 83 (emphasis in the original).
83. Ibid., p. 67.
84. Dittmar, *Skizzen*, p. 111.
85. Dittmar, *Vier Zeitfragen*, p. 6 (emphasis in the original).
86. Ludwig Feuerbach (1804–72) was best known as the author of *The Essence of Christianity*, first published in 1841. Feuerbach argued that what people worshipped as a God was really only the projected image of their own potential perfection. In projecting perfection onto a fictive being, they denied their own worth: "Man in relation to God denies his own knowledge, his own thoughts, that he may place them in God. Man gives up his personality." See L. Feuer-

been to concede that humanity had limits and that oppression and evil were inevitable components of human life. Dittmar wrote in 1847: "When I candidly say I am not religious, all I am saying is I am not – indeed I hate – that which one usually takes it to mean; my nature consists in *resistance against injustice*, not in *pious tolerance* of the seemingly inescapable. And I believe that only the *misunderstanding* of the truly religious (*that* which was *the basis* of all reforming efforts) interprets spiritual independence as irreligiosity."[87]

This "spiritual independence" was Dittmar's highest goal, and she argued that it was irreconcilable with faith in God. In *Der Mensch und sein Gott* Dittmar wrote that "the evils of our time lie precisely in that lack of thinking-for-oneself that is a result of faith, for the faith in a power that takes care of us leads to faith in [a power] that does our thinking for us."[88] In *Lessing und Feuerbach* she again argued that "as long as we assume the existence of a 'higher' reason, we must naturally despise our own [reason]."[89] Dittmar extended her argument to include equality between Jews and Christians, with absolutely no reservation. "A community that only recognizes Christians," she declared in defending Jewish rights, "carries the seed of destruction within itself, because it proclaims loudly that the human being is worth nothing to it."[90] That statement could only come from someone who had redefined Christianity entirely in human and earthly terms. Dittmar's own "spiritual independence" demanded that all individuals be seen as ends in themselves: "Each individual will and must be considered and treated as an end in himself, as he is, and the purpose of the

---

bach, *The Essence of Christianity*, trans. George Eliot (New York, 1957), p. 27. This particular idea of Feuerbach's occurred in endless variations in Dittmar's work. Dittmar also credited Feuerbach with helping her to see the links between divine authority and all other authorities that oppressed women. "Feuerbach's *Essence of Christianity* gave me the courage," she wrote, "in battling the highest authority [i.e., God] to simultaneously battle against every *authority imposed from above*. . . . Without smashing the last hidden fetter, the most hidden little thread that so mysteriously creeps over, we cannot free ourselves from the aftereffects of a morality that entangles us from earliest adolescence on and that, particularly for the female sex, becomes a practically impenetrable web." See Dittmar, "Erwiderung," p. 110.

87. Dittmar, *Vier Zeitfragen*, p. iii (emphasis in the original).
88. Dittmar, *Mensch*, p. 68.
89. Dittmar, *Lessing*, p. 42.
90. Dittmar, *Mensch*, p. 79.

whole should lead to transforming unity into the greatest possible diversity."[91] Dittmar would reject any faith that excluded Jews or oppressed women.

Dittmar would go to extremes, if need be, in denying the existence of divinity outside of humanity, for in her time no one could know what perfection human beings were capable of once the authorities of state and church had been removed. In 1846 Dittmar wrote:

> The era no longer wants to honor a dead biblical literalism since what matters is to shape life newly out of itself. [The era] struggles for fulfillment of a dream that it has sought for millenia in heaven, it is searching for peace of mind. It wants to establish a new idea, . . . a bible that declares human beings as an association in the here and now, and that awakens the powers of the inexhaustible *human* spirit for *this* life. To create this living bible is the task of all thinking and truthful people; it is their divine calling to let the new *savior* be resurrected, to realize the miracles, to raise the dead, to heal the sick, to multiply loaves and make fire from water. . . . Our church is the world, our religion is reason, our Christianity is Humanity, our statement of faith is freedom, our worship service is the truth.[92]

Finally, however, as the above passage already indicates, no other language but religious language could express the urgency with which Dittmar felt a total transformation of individual souls and social structures to be necessary and legitimate. For example, to underscore the legitimacy of her demand for justice for women, Dittmar concluded an essay on women's rights in her newspaper *Soziale Reform* with a passage that, for readers schooled in the New Testament, created clear echoes between women and the early Christian disciples:

> Poor and without rights, oppressed legally and in principle, physically unsuited for battle, intellectually deprived, . . . limited in her means, scorned, ridiculed, repressed, and persecuted with the full weight of a life-ethic that is hostile to her – where should she gather strength, where should she plow and sow without land? . . . And yet she will plow and sow and reap a thousand times over, like no other worker in the vineyard of the Lord![93]

91. L. Dittmar, "Der Selbstzweck der Menschheit," in *Soziale Reform*, p. 6.
92. Dittmar, *Mensch*, pp. 81–82 (emphasis in the original).
93. Dittmar, "Die männliche Bevormundung," p. 15.

This passage reverberates with and reformulates at least two biblical passages: one from the Apostle Paul's Second Letter to the Corinthians and one from the Gospel of Matthew about God's just treatment of laborers in His vineyard.[94] Dittmar thus laid claim to an ancient language of justice and reinterpreted it to incorporate women.

To appreciate her work in this regard more fully, Dittmar must be placed in the context of an international phenomenon of utopianism, a hybrid blend of liberalism, radical Christianity, and various strands of early socialism. This strand of the European radical tradition was, it has been argued, frequently more attentive to women's rights than later "scientific" socialism was.[95] The 1840s in Germany were a utopian moment when a complete social transformation seemed possible, if only the old authorities of God and king, church and state, could be swept away. It was possible at that time to believe that nature, left to its own devices, would make all things good.

Dittmar identified the possibilities of the moment: "I view the whole content of history as the striving to bring humanity to consciousness of itself, to a feeling of its dignity, to an understanding of its destiny."[96] Her goal was to make sure that women were included in any project of social transformation. In 1849, she wrote in her newspaper:

> For [the female sex] the "self-purpose of the human being" must become the female gospel. With social reform the Reformation story of [women] begins. More than a female Huss and Luther will rise and press for the letter of the gospel, and hammer her articles against the indulgences. The truth, that the human being only exists for his own sake, is written too deeply into the human heart to fail to catch fire, as soon as life itself throws in the spark. And it did that.[97]

And she concluded: "The liberation of women will be the greatest revolution, not only of our time, but of all times, for it will break chains that are as old as the world."[98] But for various

94. Compare 2 Corinthians 6:4–5, 8b–10, and Matthew 20:1–17.
95. This position has been forcefully argued by B. Taylor in "Socialist Feminism: Utopian or Scientific?" in R. Samuel, ed., *People's History and Socialist Theory* (London, 1981).
96. Dittmar, *Mensch*, p. iv.
97. Dittmar, "Der weibliche Antheil," p. 16.
98. Dittmar, "Aphorismen," p. 119.

reasons peculiar to German history – having to do with the timing of industrialization, the timing of revolution, the strength of political conservatism and the nature of the established churches – utopianism of this sort did not gain ground in Germany the way it did in England and France.[99] Even though the initial success of the religious dissenting movements opened a space in which demands for women's rights could be put forward already before the revolution of 1848–49, the space that had been opened closed again all too soon. The small organized women's movement that emerged in the 1860s was dedicated to women's right to work and to the personal autonomy and political equality with men that would accompany that right to work. But by 1871, as Herrad Ulrike Bussemer has shown, the women's movement had once again turned to arguments about women's superior sensibility and morality in an (amazingly successful) effort to appear less threatening to male liberals – their potential political allies – and to broaden their social base.[100] Whether these women were aware of Dittmar's efforts is not known, but it is clear that her philosophical struggles anticipated the dilemmas that would confront later feminists.

Dittmar's writings are important both for the history of German feminism and for the history of German liberalism. Even though she may not have satisfactorily or completely resolved the tension between equality and difference, the philosophical issues with which she wrestled exposed a core of self-contradiction within liberalism and the limits of the liberal vision. In raising these issues, Dittmar posed a challenge that liberals to this day have not met. The debates between moderate and radical liberals that characterized the Vormärz extended far beyond the choice between constitutional monarchy and democracy into the fundamental realm of gender relations. Debates about gender raised questions central to the self-understanding of the rising bourgeoisie as it defined and redefined itself in relation to other classes. Reconstructing aspects of these debates in the 1840s, however, sheds light not only on the limits of liberalism but also on its early potential. The tragedy is that the

---

99. For a comparative perspective, see B. Taylor, *Eve and the New Jerusalem: Socialism and Feminism in the Nineteenth Century* (New York, 1983); and C. Goldberg Moses, *French Feminism in the Nineteenth Century* (Albany, 1984).

100. See H.U. Bussemer, "Bürgerliche Frauenbewegung und männliches Bildungsbürgertum, 1860–1880," in Frevert, *Bürgerinnen*.

most visionary German liberals – those who proposed that equality could and must be reconciled with individual and group diversity – were driven into exile or silenced in the wake of the revolution. This loss of vision has had profound consequences not just for the future of gender politics but also for that of class and religious politics as well.

3
Liberalism, Modernization, and the Social Question in the Kingdom of Saxony, 1830–90

Richard J. Bazillion

To study German liberalism in the nineteenth century, from either a regional or a national perspective, is to wrestle with an ambiguous conception of modernity. How, liberals asked themselves, ought Germany to be ruled in an age when French political theory, British capitalism, and industrialization had challenged the institutional structure of society? This proved to be a vexing question, both at the time and in retrospect; for the victory of liberal economics during the century's middle decades was not accompanied by change in the political realm. Modernization transformed the manufacturing economy and the organization of labor, but spared the monarchical state. Though Germany embraced imported technologies and economic doctrines, it showed less enthusiasm for constitutional experimentation. Even in the kingdom of Saxony, where new ideas readily won a hearing, liberals proposed relatively modest forms intended to reserve public affairs for men of property and education.[1]

Scholars of comparative modernization, such as Reinhard Bendix and Barrington Moore, Jr., have emphasized the interaction of economic development, the decline of social hierarchies,

1. The best recent discussions of liberalism in its German context are J.J. Sheehan, *German Liberalism in the Nineteenth Century* (Chicago, 1978); and D. Langewiesche, *Liberalismus in Deutschland* (Frankfurt a.M., 1988). Economic change in the German states is studied from a regional perspective in F.B. Tipton, Jr., *Regional Variations in the Economic Development of Germany in the Nineteenth Century* (Middletown, Conn., 1976); S. Pollard, *Peaceful Conquest: The Industrialization of Europe, 1760–1970* (Oxford, 1981); R. Fremdling and R.D. Tilly, eds., *Industrialisierung und Raum: Studien zur regionalen Differenzierung im Deutschland des 19. Jahrhunderts* (Stuttgart, 1979).

and broader access to political power.[2] Modernization within the Atlantic community eventuated in a democratic society by combining all three processes. Developments followed a similar, but by no means identical course in central Europe, where conditions produced a less dynamic interplay among economic, social, and political change. Nineteenth-century Germany, for example, retained a ruling oligarchy based, in Theodore Hamerow's words, on an "alliance of status and influence" that assured "the continuation of a concept of civic leadership derived from a preindustrial hierarchical society."[3] That compact rested, as James J. Sheehan has pointed out, on the willingness of government to promote economic growth and to admit "enlightened public opinion into the policy-making process."[4] Despite misgivings about the bureaucratic state, liberals had therefore sought early in the industrial age to ease the political tensions associated with rapid economic growth by means of limited government intervention.

Rather than confront legitimate authority, the liberal bourgeoisie initiated a process of reform that gradually brought government under the rule of law. The corporate privileges of church, nobility, and guild underwent intense scrutiny in the liberal press. Burghers and entrepreneurs demanded and received legal recognition of property rights. As educated commoners gained access to the public service, bourgeois interests claimed the attention of government. In the kingdom of Saxony and elsewhere, particularly after 1830, business and industry won political influence in the state. By mid century their success had enabled the middle class to "claim to represent the general interest of society."[5]

This "silent bourgeois revolution," which produced a modern capitalist economy but not a liberal parliamentary system, is clearly evident in Saxony, where the rate of economic develop-

2. See R. Bendix, "Modernisierung und Soziale Ungleichheit," in W. Fischer, ed., *Wirtschafts- und sozialgeschichtliche Probleme der frühen Industrialisierung* (Berlin, 1968); R. Bendix, *Kings or People: Power and the Mandate to Rule* (Berkeley, 1978); B. Moore, Jr., *Social Origins of Dictatorship and Democracy* (Boston, 1966).

3. T.S. Hamerow, *The Birth of a New Europe: State and Society in the Nineteenth Century* (Chapel Hill, 1983), p. 331.

4. Sheehan, *German Liberalism*, p. 44.

5. David Blackbourn calls this process a "silent bourgeois revolution" and emphasizes the contrast between liberalism's influence in economics and in politics in D. Blackbourn and G. Eley, *The Peculiarities of German History: Bourgeois Society and Politics in Nineteenth-Century Germany* (Oxford, 1984), p. 190.

ment after 1800 rivaled that of Rhenish Prussia. Traditional political and economic institutions represented by the bureaucratic state and the craft guilds found themselves under mounting pressure. "Modern" notions such as constitutional rule, organized political parties, economic deregulation, freedom of the press, religious liberty, and the public administration of justice gained favor among the Saxon bourgeoisie. A liberal movement emerged in the 1830s to press the claim of an educated and propertied middle class to share power with the traditional ruling elite.

Liberalism attracted those intellectuals, businessmen, and civil servants who believed that the state ought to encourage capitalist initiative by loosening economic regulation. During the middle decades of the century, when industrialization conquered the traditional economy, Saxon liberals dwelt on the implications of economic change: a party-based political system, fair representation of the interests of factory industry, cabinet ministers responsible to the legislative majority, municipal self-government, and national unification. Excluded from power except for a brief interval in 1848, liberalism nevertheless proclaimed the inevitability and indivisibility of progress long after the "March days" of 1848.

Synonymous with progress to most liberals, economic modernization in fact ruined many working-class Saxons, especially journeymen in the declining crafts. Weaving, typesetting, printing, and tailoring were the occupations most susceptible to mechanization.[6] Artisans who plied these trades suffered chronic unemployment, a fate shared by construction workers in the kingdom's largest cities, where boom-and-bust cycles in the building industry were common.[7] Endemic poverty and the ferment associated with it comprised the "social question" of the 1830s and 1840s. As capitalist industry surged ahead in the following decades, efforts to organize the new factory working class for political action created the nucleus of imperial Germany's social democratic movement.

---

6. H. Zwahr, "Zur Konstituierung des Proletariats als Klasse: Strukturuntersuchung über das Leipziger Proletariat während der industriellen Revolution," in H. Bartel and E. Engelberg, eds., *Die großpreußisch-militaristische Reichsgründung 1871*, 2 vols. (Berlin, 1971), vol. 1, pp. 526–27, 534.
7. F. Stolle, *Die sächsische Revolution, oder Dresden und Leipzig in den Jahren 1830 und 1831* (Leipzig, 1835), pp. 220–21.

Because of Saxony's accelerated pace of modernization in the nineteenth century, the region provides an inviting field for the study of the relationships among economic development, social unrest, and political reform. A small state surrounded by powerful neighbors, Saxony had to be innovative in order to survive. The Elbian kingdom occupied some 14,960 square kilometers in the heart of Germany, bordering on Prussia to the north and the Austrian empire to the south. With slightly fewer than two million people in 1849, two-thirds of them urban dwellers, Saxony had the second highest population density in Europe. Between 1750 and 1850 a demographic revolution increased the population by 82 percent. Burdened by relatively unproductive agriculture, Saxony became a net importer of food after 1815. Severe pressure on the country's balance of payments stimulated industrialized manufacturing for the export market. Economic development then attracted immigration, which helped to swell a population whose natural rate of increase was already high.[8]

Demographic growth and technological innovation proved to be mutually reinforcing. By 1831 62.5 percent of Saxony's spinning mills had been mechanized; factories in the industrial center of Chemnitz employed between fifty and three hundred hands. According to Rudolf Forberger, Saxony had completed the first phase of its industrial revolution by the early 1830s.[9] Thirty years later only 25 percent of the population earned its living on the land, compared with 56 percent engaged in industry, mainly in the manufacture of textiles. Small and middle-sized enterprises, each employing an average of eleven workers, predominated in the kingdom at large.[10]

8. K. Große, *Geschichte der Stadt Leipzig von der ältesten bis auf die neueste Zeit*, 2 vols. (Leipzig, 1842), vol. 2, p. 704; K. Blaschke, "Industrialisierung und Bevölkerung in Sachsen im Zeitraum von 1830 bis 1890," *Historische Raumforschung* 5 (1965): 69, 71; Blaschke, *Bevölkerungsgeschichte von Sachsen bis zur industriellen Revolution* (Weimar, 1967), pp. 99ff.; F. Burkhardt, "Die Entwicklung der sächsischen Bevölkerung in den letzten 100 Jahren," *Zeitschrift des sächsischen statistischen Landesamtes* 77 (1931): 2. Sources for these population data are: Pollard, *Peaceful Conquest*, p. 357, n. 27; H. Kiesewetter, "Bevölkerung, Erwerbstätige und Landwirtschaft im Königreich Sachsen, 1815–1871," in Pollard, ed., *Region und Industrialisierung*, pp. 91–93.

9. R. Forberger, *Die industrielle Revolution in Sachsen, 1830–1861* (Berlin, 1982), pp. 26, 35; Forberger, "Zur Auseinandersetzung über das Problem des Übergangs von der Manufaktur zur Fabrik," in *Beiträge zur deutschen Wirtschaftsgeschichte des 18. und 19. Jahrhunderts* (Berlin, 1962), p. 181.

10. R. Zeise, "Zur Rolle der sächsischen Bourgeoisie im Ringen um die

A long mercantile history and willingness to experiment with new technology helped Saxony to acquire the features of an industrial society by 1815. Textiles and metal-fabricating became the mainstays of the new economy, which in turn relied heavily on foreign trade to pay for the imported food required by a burgeoning population. Convinced of the need to safeguard business and industry, Saxony's rulers facilitated the transition from a traditional to an industrial economy. Bureaucratic reformers, notably Albert Christian Weinlig (1812–73)[11] in the ministry of the interior, cautiously deregulated the guild-dominated economy between 1849 and 1861. One reason for the relatively slow implementation of industrial freedom (*Gewerbefreiheit*) and occupational mobility (*Freizügigkeit*) was the government's concern for the fate of large numbers of workers forced to survive in a competitive marketplace once the guild organization of labor had broken down. Another, of course, was the fear of provoking social unrest on a scale similar to the revolutionary ferment of 1848–49. Recent history had taught Saxon bureaucrats to appreciate the destabilizing effects of modernization and to beware of the social consequences of economic change.

With the rise of an industrial society came the reorganization of labor. From 1830 on, handicraftsmen in a variety of trades faced intensifying competition from mechanized industry situated mainly in Chemnitz, Leipzig, Dresden, and the Zwickau district.[12] Friedrich Georg Wieck, a prominent factory-owner, proclaimed in 1845 that "any kind of opposition [to the factory] is fruitless, even dangerous; progress is indispensable, and to facilitate it no means may be spared and no measures

---

wirtschaftspolitische Vormachtstellung in Deutschland in den fünfziger und sechziger Jahren des 19. Jahrhunderts," in Bartel and Engelberg, eds., *Die großpreußisch-militaristische Reichsgründung 1871*, 1: 235.

11. Weinlig received a medical degree from the University of Leipzig, but habilitated there in mineralogy and technology. After teaching economics in Erlangen for a year, he joined Saxony's interior ministry in 1846 and served briefly as minister in 1849. He headed the trade, industry, and agriculture department until his death. The standard biography is P. Domsch, *Albert Christian Weinlig: Ein Lebensbild nach Familienpapieren und Akten* (Chemnitz, 1912). See also S. Moltke and W. Stieda, eds., *Albert Christian Weinlig in Briefen von ihm und an ihn* (Leipzig, 1931).

12. Between 1834 and 1852 the populations of Zwickau, Dresden, and Chemnitz increased by 112.3, 57.6, and 62.6 percent, respectively. "Die Städte des Königreichs Sachsen," *Zeitschrift des statistischen Bureaus des Königlichen Sächsischen Ministeriums des Innern*, vol. 1 (1 February 1855), p. 2.

rejected."[13] Entrepreneurial spirit, official encouragement, accessible raw materials and markets, and a virtually inexhaustible labor supply promoted industrial expansion and hastened the decline of artisan manufacture. Although one in every 13.4 Saxons was a handworker in the 1840s – compared with a 1:20.5 ratio in Prussia – most of these were handloom weavers who found themselves increasingly at the mercy of factory competition.[14] By the end of the 1840s, two-thirds of all Saxons lived in towns and villages, and 51.3 percent of the labor force worked either as handicraftsmen or factory hands.[15] Ten years later, the Saxon economy supported the largest industrial/artisanal working class in Germany.[16] By then the "social question" had become less an issue of endemic poverty than concern with the proliferation of artisan masters whose economic prospects were marginal at best. Reluctance to suppress the guilds slowed progress toward complete occupational mobility and encouraged the survival of antiquated manufacturing methods. Craftsmen, moreover, had ample time to organize political oppositon to the spread of factory industry and to *Gewerbefreiheit*.

Politics in Saxony reflected the tensions inherent in the revolutionary change in the organization of labor created by industrialization. Radicalism flourished in an environment of conflict between two large manufacturing sectors, one traditional and the other modern. From the 1840s on, democracy attracted the small producers and craftsmen who suffered economically from competition with the factories. Led by the charismatic writer, Robert Blum, the democrats dominated Saxon politics in 1848–49. The government crushed their organization after the Dresden uprising in May 1849 and jailed those convicted of insurrection. Many former democrats joined the social democratic movement, based in Leipzig, in the mid-1860s.[17]

13. F.G. Wieck, *Die Manufaktur- und Fabrikindustrie des Königreichs Sachsen* (Leipzig, 1845), p. 2.
14. R. Weber, *Die Revolution in Sachsen, 1848/49: Entwicklung und Analyse ihrer Triebkräfte* (Berlin, 1970), p. 4.
15. R. Zeise, "Zur sozialen Struktur und zur Lage der Volksmassen auf dem Lande am Vorabend der Revolution von 1848/49 in Sachsen," *Jahrbuch für Wirtschaftsgeschichte* 1 (1968): 240.
16. "Zur Statistik der Handwerke im Königreiche Sachsen, 1849 und 1861," *Zeitschrift des statistischen Bureaus des königlichen sächsischen Ministeriums des Innern*, 9/10 (September–October 1860): 107.
17. Democratic leaders, some of them old '48ers, disapproved. Emil Adolf Roßmässler, who headed the Leipzig Workers' Association (*Arbeiterverein*),

In Saxony, an overwhelmingly Lutheran country where the Protestant tradition of self-help colored attitudes toward poverty, the churches failed to mediate the class struggle. There was no constituency in Saxony for the Social-Catholic movement of the 1860s or for the Center Party after unification.[18] When Ferdinand Lassalle, Wilhelm Liebknecht, and August Bebel made a political issue of the social question, confrontation between Social Democracy and the bourgeois parties set the tone for Saxon political life. Saxony first gained notoriety as a hotbed of radicalism in 1849 as a result of the Dresden uprising. Leipzig became a socialist mecca after 1863, when Lassalle founded his General German Workingmen's Association there. By the early twentieth century Saxony had acquired the sobriquet "red kingdom."

Liberalism emerged as a coherent ideology after the country became a constitutional state in 1831. Liberal doctrine appealed mainly to businessmen, upper-level civil servants, merchants, factory owners, and academics. An informal party system that included democratic, moderate, and conservative groupings existed by decade's end. Saxon liberalism reflected the views of Leipzig's commercial bourgeoisie, supported intra-German free trade, and grasped the political implications of the customs union concluded with Prussia in 1834.[19] Bourgeois influence was particularly apparent, at the subministerial level, in the departments of foreign affairs and interior as well as in the lower house of the legislature. Reforms enacted by the government of Bernhard von Lindenau (1779–1854) permitted commoners, many of whom held liberal ideas, to hold public office. Although they entered the bureaucracy's upper reaches gradually over the

---

feared that labor's activism would destroy "the pleasant constellation of political parties in Germany" and that it "could drive the propertied classes into the arms of reaction once again." H.-P. Katlewski, "Sozialer Liberalismus und soziale Bewegung im 19. Jahrhundert," in K.J. Rivinius, ed., *Die soziale Bewegung in Deutschland des neunzehnten Jahrhunderts* (Munich, 1978), p. 91.

18. See W.O. Shanahan, *German Protestants Face the Social Question* (Notre Dame, Ind. 1954), pp. 192–94. D. Warren, Jr., *The Red Kingdom of Saxony: Lobbying Grounds for Gustav Stresemann, 1901–1909* (The Hague, 1964), p. 21. Saxony's 200,000 Catholics constituted less than 5 percent of the population.

19. Zeise, "Zur Rolle der sächsischen Bourgeoisie," p. 265. Biedermann, for example, was a lifelong resident of Leipzig and a municipal politician of note. His first work on the "German question" appeared early in his career: *Das deutsche Nationalleben in seinen gegenwärtigen Zuständen und in seiner fortschreitenden Entwicklung* (Leipzig, 1841).

next ten years, these liberal sympathizers made their presence felt. One official who accompanied his aristocratic minister to a diplomatic conference in 1833 wrote that his role was to be "an expert guardian of the Constitution" in order to insure that his superior did not do anything which "would get us in trouble with our assembly [*Stände*]."[20]

Lindenau encouraged his noble colleagues and their bourgeois subordinates to work harmoniously together to implement innovations like municipal self-government, the abolition of the peasantry's residual feudal obligations, the professionalization of government departments, judicial independence, and rationalization of the tax structure. A law enacted in 1840 permitted nonguild enterprises to function in the villages, where the free labor market encouraged industrial development. These were the first steps toward deregulation of the economy, a process that culminated in 1861 with the introduction of full occupational mobility. Reforms initiated by enlightened bureaucrats in the 1830s belonged to the modernization process that created a constitutional state, a class society, and the factory system.

Technological change and the application of steam power began to affect the organization of production early in the nineteenth century. By the 1840s the government was regularly granting concessions to entrepreneurs who wished to build factories in the countryside, outside the jurisdiction of the urban guilds.[21] These "closed establishments" (*geschlossene Établissements*), as contemporaries called them, were clustered in the Erzgebirge region around the city of Chemnitz, where underemployed handloom weavers provided a ready labor force for the new textile mills. One of Leipzig's leading printers, B.G. Teubner, installed a steam-driven press in 1826, and the famous F.A. Brockhaus publishing house soon followed suit. Completion of the Leipzig-to-Dresden rail line in 1839 inaugurated Saxony's transportation revolution.

20. H. Göpner, *Beiträge zur Entwicklungsgeschichte der Parteien in den sächsischen Kammern I. Der Landtag von 1830–40* (Leipzig, 1913), p. 108; G. Schmidt, *Die Staatsreform in Sachsen in der ersten Hälfte des neunzehnten Jahrhunderts* (Weimar, 1966), p. 132. Saxony acquired its first two bourgeois cabinet members in 1858. University-educated commoners had filled subministerial posts for many years previously and influenced policy-making from positions of considerable authority.

21. "Konzessionen zur Errichtung von Maschinenbauanstalten und Fabriken," Staatsarchiv Dresden, Ministerium des Innern [hereafter StAD, MdI] vols. 1–2 (1836–71), no. 1275a–1275b.

As mechanization and the factory system advanced, weavers, spinners, printers, and smiths protested their declining wages and lost jobs. Saxony's earliest outbreak of Luddism occurred in 1830, when printers in the Brockhaus firm tried to destroy one of the company's modern presses.[22] A year of unrest in 1830–31, provoked in large part by high unemployment in the building and manufacturing trades, convulsed the kingdom's two largest cities. Those who testified before a commission of inquiry into the disorders cited a variety of causes, including foreign competition with domestic producers, the high price of beer, and workingmen's fondness for cheap brandy. One witness asserted: "The people's opinion with respect to these matters is this: Join the Prussian tariff system in order to have latitude for trade and commerce."[23] Saxony followed this advice in 1834, but artisanship continued to suffer the ravages of technological unemployment. The Leipzig riot of 12 August 1845 stemmed from motives similar to those uncovered fifteen years before, plus a number of economic, political, and religious grievances now shared by the bourgeoisie.[24] Liberals now routinely applied the term "social question" to the constellation of unemployment, poverty, and the growth of radical ideas such as socialism.[25]

Middle-class businessmen and intellectuals discovered the social question in the 1830s and gave it considerable attention during the following decade.[26] Outbreaks of artisan unrest and political protest threatened to culminate in revolution if the problem remained unsolved. In the view of some bourgeois reformers, industrialization offered an answer. These reformers

---

22. H. Brockhaus, *Aus den Tagenbüchern Heinrich Brockhaus*, vol. 1 (Leipzig, 1884), p. 163; Stolle, *Sächsische Revolution*, pp. 16–17.

23. StAD, Kreishauptmannschaft Leipzig, no. 3849–3852.

24. Background on the social crisis in Saxony during the years of industrial expansion is provided in two articles by the author: "Social Conflict and Political Protest in Industrializing Saxony, 1840–1860," *Histoire sociale/Social History* 17, no. 33 (May 1984): 79–92; "Urban Violence and the Modernization Process in Pre-March Saxony, 1830–31 and 1845," *Historical Reflections* 12, no. 2 (Summer 1985): 279–303.

25. The best example, in a Saxon context, is Karl Biedermann, *Vorlesungen über Sozialismus und die soziale Frage* (Leipzig, 1847).

26. Germany's foremost interpreter of the social question was the Kiel University economist Lorenz von Stein. His major works were *Der Sozialismus und Communismus des heutigen Frankreichs: Ein Beitrag zur Zeitgeschichte* (Leipzig, 1842), and *Geschichte der sozialen Bewegung in Frankreich von 1789 bis auf unsre Tage*, 3 vols. (Leipzig, 1850–55).

believed that the new factory proletariat, although paid meager wages, enjoyed more stable employment prospects than did the handicraftsmen. "I at least know of no factory," declared one Saxon industrialist, "that, in the constant flux of business, takes on a throng of workers today in order to abandon them, with wife and child, to penury and communal welfare."[27]

Entrepreneurs and liberals who advocated industrialization agreed that the new factories offered a solution to the social question. Most of them opposed guild restrictions on the mobility of labor and demanded legal measures against attempts by workers to organize. Friedrich Georg Wieck, for example, one of the great modernizers of Saxony's textile industry, counted among his advantages the absence "in our Germany" of the "self-destructive mania of workers' associations for forcing up wages and regulating labor."[28] He preferred that pay scales be dictated by the marketplace and advised the government not to copy England's factory legislation. "Our low wages," asserted Wieck, "are a weapon against England's industry, which we ought not to lay down."[29] Technological innovation and clever management were the keys to prosperous industry and thus to improved living standards for workers.

Businessmen who petitioned the state to give them tariff protection – but to keep its regulatory hand off their affairs – nevertheless urged the government to address the social question. In a letter to the ministry of the interior written in 1839 a group of spinnery operators acknowledged their "moral obligation" to protect the welfare of their workers. They also made it clear that the government would have to step in when business downturns forced them to lower wages below the subsistence level.[30] Factory hands who relied on the solicitude of their employers could therefore expect to be left in the lurch when business conditions turned sour. The government itself was unlikely to be able to offer much help in such circumstances. During the late pre-March period, when the economy stumbled

---

27. Heinrich Bodemer, quoted in *Der Herold: Eine Wochenschrift für Politik, Literatur und öffentliches Gerichtsverfahren*, 9 July 1845.

28. F.G. Wieck, *Industrielle Zustände Sachsens: Das Gesammtgebiet des sächsischen Manufaktur- und Fabrikwesens, Handels und Verkehrs* (Chemnitz, 1840), p. 82.

29. Ibid., p. 83.

30. Ibid., p. 99.

and food prices rose dramatically, little could be done to ease the plight of hungry workers.

Liberals regarded the social question as a vital issue, because to leave it unresolved would invite turmoil among the lower classes. Karl Biedermann (1812–1901), a faculty member at the University of Leipzig and a prominent journalist, belonged to the group of liberal intellectuals and businessmen who sought an answer to the social question in collaboration with the state.[31] He delivered a series of public lectures in 1847 in which he warned that radical socialism might well seduce the masses if economic distress were allowed to fester. The idea of worker self-help appealed to him, as a man who himself had come from humble origins. "I am convinced," he declared, "that [the] principle of association . . . is capable of unlimited extension and perfection, and . . . can eliminate a very great number of social evils, if not eradicate them completely. This can be accomplished without attempting a radical reform of the whole social order."[32] Biedermann wholeheartedly endorsed the cooperative movement that his friend Hermann Schulze-Delitzsch (1808–83) founded in the 1860s.[33] While teaching courses for the Leipzig workingmen's educational association, he became in fact the mentor of a young woodworker named August Bebel.[34]

Bourgeois progressives, to be sure, sometimes overlooked the human consequences of mechanization and economic change: technological unemployment, dangerous working conditions, child and female labor, and overcrowded housing.[35] Liberals

31. During a long political career, Biedermann served on the Leipzig city council, the Frankfurt Parliament, the Gotha Assembly, the Saxon Landtag, and the first German Reichstag. A prodigious author, he wrote many works on contemporary German history, philosophy, and educational theory. See his autobiography, *Mein Leben und ein Stück Zeitgeschichte: Eine Ergänzung zu des Verfassers "Dreißig Jahre deutscher Geschichte"*, 2 vols. (Breslau, 1886).

32. Biedermann, *Vorlesungen über Sozialismus und die soziale Frage*, p. 99.

33. On Schulze-Delitzsch see F. Thorwart, *Hermann Schulze-Delitzsch: Leben und Wirken* (Berlin, 1913), and F. Thorwart, ed., *Hermann Schulze-Delitzschs Schriften und Reden*, 5 vols. (Berlin, 1909–13).

34. Biedermann, *Mein Leben*, 2: 212.

35. T.S. Hamerow made this point, which D.G. Rohr challenged. Writing some years later, J.J. Sheehan concluded that "a great many liberals" worried about industrialization's consequences for the *Mittelstand*. They preferred a healthy artisanal sector to unrestricted factory production. See T.S. Hamerow, *Restoration, Revolution, Reaction* (Princeton, 1958), p. 63; D.G. Rohr, *The Origins of Social Liberalism in Germany* (Chicago, 1963), pp. 9–10; Sheehan, *German Liberalism*, pp. 31–32.

consequently remained less popular in the kingdom at large than were their radical-democratic rivals, who wished to reform the guild system and not to destroy it as a social institution.[36] Liberals, for their part, saw no point in trying to revive the charitable role once played by the guilds. Yet one of the distinguishing features of Saxon liberalism was its social conscience, personified by the movement's leading figure, Karl Biedermann, and by the founder of the cooperative movement, Hermann Schulze-Delitzsch.

Although Saxon liberalism turned its attention to the problems of an industrializing society, in the end it failed to provide the modern proletariat with a political home. Until 1849–50, liberals placed economic development and constitutional reform on the same plane. Thereafter they concentrated their political vision on German unification, their economic policy on industrial expansion, and their social thought on the utility of self-help efforts among the working class. Guildsmen remained indifferent to the liberals' national program, and independent masters – though not necessarily their journeymen – vigorously opposed factory construction and unrestricted entry into trades. Only the liberal-sponsored workingmen's educational associations of the 1860s attracted a following, by appealing mainly to intelligent laborers bent on self-improvement. In general liberalism offered little comfort to workers whose livelihoods depended on such endangered crafts as blacksmithing, knifesmithing, nailsmithing, leatherworking, soapmaking, or wheelwrighting.

As proponents of modernization, dedicated for the most part to laissez-faire economics and political reform, the liberals inspired a mixed reaction in the state. On the one hand, the government shared their commitment to industrial development and their concern for the plight of handicraftsmen struggling in an increasingly competitive marketplace, and stood shoulder to shoulder with the liberals against republicanism and, later, against Social Democracy. On the other hand, Saxony's rulers utterly rejected the suggestion made in 1849 by Biedermann's moderate liberals that economic growth and free

36. Less privileged members of society also identified them with the bourgeois-liberal oligarchy that ruled the largest cities. See H. Zwahr, "Vom feudalen Stadtregiment zur bürgerlichen Kommunalpolitik," *Jahrbuch für Regionalgeschichte* 7 (1979): 7–34.

trade within the Prussian–German Customs Union (the *Zollverein*) implied closer political ties between the two neighboring states.[37] The repressive government of Friedrich Ferdinand von Beust (1809–86) excluded liberals from the political arena.[38] Midcentury liberalism thus found itself ostracized by a particularistic government, rejected by labor, and under suspicion by patriotic Saxons of all classes. Liberal ideas nevertheless exerted considerable influence behind the scenes, especially within the Ministry of the Interior, whose officials formulated the government's economic policy. It was they who somehow had to settle the everlasting disputes between the craft guilds and factory owners.

For years Saxony's artisans had petitioned the government to reform the organization of labor. They demanded an end to the fragmentation of guilds in the same trade, controls on the migration of rural artisans to the cities, journeymen's and masters' examinations that took better account of "the intelligence and scientific training" of artisans, and protection against unfair competition from mechanized industry. By no means did the guildsmen confuse a revised set of trade regulations with *Gewerbefreiheit*, which the independent masters greatly feared.[39] Liberal proponents of modernization, who promoted industrial development at the expense of the guilds' special interests, found a solution to over-regulation of the economy in industrial freedom and open access to the skilled trades.

In 1855 the Saxon Landtag conceded that the old, comfortable symbiosis between merchants and craftsmen could be preserved no longer. Decades of tinkering with the rules under which the guilds exercised their authority had resulted in administrative chaos. Factory industry and steam-powered transportation had

37. Richard von Friesen, who served for many years in the Saxon cabinet, accused those liberals who had supported the Prussian Union project of 1849 of desiring "an incorporation of Saxony in Prussia." Friesen, *Erinnerungen aus meinem Leben*, 2 vols. (Dresden, 1880), vol. 1, p. 265. Saxony's leading historian rebutted this claim in T. Flathe, "Die Memoiren des Herrn von Friesen," *Historische Zeitschrift* 46 (1881): 1–47.

38. Zeise, "Zur Rolle der sächsischen Bourgeoisie," pp. 237, 249. Beust believed the *Zollverein* to have been a political mistake – although incontrovertibly an economic success – because it implied eventual absorption of the middle states by Prussia.

39. Letters from the Innungsmeister-Verein, Leipzig, 7 December 1853, the Gewerbeverein, Waldheim, 23 January 1855, and the Gewerbeverein, Pirna, 14 April 1855, to the interior ministry, StAD, MdI, no. 1385a.

rendered the complicated system of traditional monopolies obsolete.[40] Weinlig proposed in 1857 to limit the guilds' authority to urban areas, but to preserve their right to oversee entry into trades. He also suggested that the examination system be reformed and that wages and working hours be regulated. At the same time, politically neutral economists in the Saxon Ministry of the Interior tried to define a "factory" so that these "closed establishments" could be exempted from guild regulations. By protecting guild labor against raids by factory owners, while at the same time giving industry free access to the nonguild labor pool, they hoped to allow artisanry and mechanized production to coexist.[41] Opposition from both guildsmen and factory owners quickly doomed this attempt to reach a compromise.

Although a liberal sympathizer, Weinlig doubted the wisdom of setting the labor market free from its long-standing constraints. According to his biographer, he "foresaw that chaos would follow the introduction of unrestricted *Gewerbefreiheit*," and he therefore wished to initiate "a process of development that [would] reinfuse the surviving hulks of the guilds with purpose and substance."[42] Yet he rejected pleas from established masters to resurrect the guilds' ancient privileges, for to do so would obviate the potential advantages of free enterprise and the new technology. As for the economy that lay outside guild regulation and in which poverty and sickness cried out for government action, Weinlig argued that "we must seek to be of assistance, not by reactivating and extending the old guild system through the extinction of large industry, which we cannot do without, but rather through the creation of a new corporative system, in which large industry can and shall take part."[43] Weinlig considered "very developed industry" to be essential to Saxony's economic health. The emergence of a factory proletariat placed on the government a heavy social responsibility, which, in Weinlig's view, it could not afford to shirk.

Saxony's rulers clearly did not wish to create two hostile

---

40. "Bericht der dritten Deputation der zweiten Kammer," 16 July 1855, p. 441, StAD, MdI, no. 1385.
41. Draft of the *Gewerbeordnung* of 1857, StAD, MdI, no. 1385c.
42. Domsch, *Weinlig*, p. 45.
43. "Einleitung und allgemeine Motive zu dem Entwurfe einer Gewerbeordnung für das Königreich Sachsen," p. 11, StAD, MdI, no. 1385c.

economies by reforming the guild system on the one hand, while sanctioning total industrial freedom on the other. As had been the case since 1848–49, the government hesitated to act until convinced that deregulation of the economy would not provoke social unrest.[44] The cabinet did not proclaim industrial freedom until 15 October 1861, the year after Austria had done so. In any event, journeymen frustrated by the difficulty of achieving master status under the old dispensation welcomed the introduction of *Gewerbefreiheit* as an opportunity for upward mobility. Only the established, highly conservative artisan groups persisted in their hostility toward an open economy. The government therefore felt secure in ignoring the guildsmen's jeremiads against economic reform.[45]

Liberals who appreciated Weinlig's strategy now turned their attention to skilled, intelligent workers, such as August Bebel, whom they hoped to enlist in the self-help movement. In addition to inculcating the middle-class values of diligence and thrift, the educational associations aimed to equip their members with enough knowledge to get ahead in a competitive economy. The associations indeed proved to be especially popular in the industrializing Leipzig district, where the urban labor force grew to 21,400 over the ensuing decade.[46]

Together with the former democratic leader, Emil Roßmäßler, prominent Leipzig liberals such as Biedermann and Hermann Schulze-Delitzsch proposed adult education and producer-consumer cooperatives as their answer to the social question.[47] In later years they expressed satisfaction with the results of their experiment. "If we can console ourselves with anything at all about the desolate wastes that made up German politics after 1850," wrote Biedermann at the end of the century,

44. "Das Gewerbegesetz betr. Gutachten des Staatsrathes über den Entwurf von 1857," StAD, MdI, no. 1385d.
45. These were, if anything, more vituperative than the petitions directed to the Frankfurt Parliament in 1848. See StAD, MdI, no. 1385g.
46. Egon Schumann, "Über die industrielle Revolution in Leipzig von 1830 bis 1871," *Sächsische Heimatblätter* 4 (1973): 168. H. Zwahr calculated the number of factory workers to be forty-seven thousand with 35 to 40 percent of them resident in the city proper in 1875. See his *Zur Konstituierung des Proletariats als Klasse* (Munich, 1981), p. 321.
47. Biedermann founded the manual-training movement in the early 1880s, in the belief that the schools "must concern themselves with practice as well as theory" and provide "training to work." See Biedermann, *Die Erziehung zur Arbeit, eine Forderung des Lebens an die Schule*, 2d ed. (Leipzig, 1883), p. 48.

"it is with the activity of our people . . . in economic and social concerns. The principle of self-help and association . . . fostered a sense of well-being and produced astonishing material as well as equally significant ethical results."[48] Although forty years had passed since Biedermann first addressed the social question, he remained committed to the principle of associationism in which he and his fellow reformers among the bourgeoisie believed so deeply.

Optimistic to the end, Biedermann failed to realize that the rise of an industrial society had rendered the liberals' ideal of class harmony obsolete. So quickly did factory industry expand after 1861 that the field for individual initiative among skilled craftsmen narrowed drastically. Liberalism, moreover, had nothing to offer the industrial proletariat that had only its labor to sell in a marketplace ruled by *Gewerbefreiheit*. Schulze-Delitzsch himself realized that labor was developing its own political agenda, to which liberals would have to respond if they were ever to constitute a mass party.[49] But there proved to be nothing in the program of bourgeois liberalism capable of winning over the new working class. The liberal National Association (Nationalverein), founded in 1859 to promote unification under the auspices of Prussia, illustrated the point. In an effort to discourage political activity among the lower classes, the Nationalverein would accept workers only as "honorary members."[50] Bebel rejected the nonpolitical role in which liberals had cast the working class. He consequently drew away from his liberal mentors, accusing them of "worrying about every kind of popular movement" and "constantly pinning their hopes on [their] rulers."[51]

Others in Leipzig shared Bebel's desire that labor acquire an independent political voice. First on the scene were Lassallean organizers, who founded the General German Workingmen's Association (Allgemeiner Deutscher Arbeiterverein) in 1863.

48. Biedermann, *Dreißig Jahre deutscher Geschichte*, 2 vols. (Breslau, 1896), pp. 179–80.

49. Gustav Mayer, "Die Trennung der proletarischen von der bürgerlichen Demokratie in Deutschland, 1863–1870," in H.-U. Wehler, ed., *Radikalismus, Sozialismus und bürgerliche Demokratie* (Frankfurt a.M., 1969), p. 112.

50. This is what Schulze-Delitzsch himself told a large gathering of workers in Leipzig in January, 1863. See A. Bebel, *Aus meinem Leben* (Berlin, 1930), pp. 69–70.

51. Ibid., p. 48.

Lassalle's party had two great liabilities, one of which was its founder's sympathy for a Prussian-led Germany. Lassalle's rivals in the workers' movement, particularly the Saxons, spurned *Kleindeutschland*, an idea so closely associated with the Frankfurt Constitution and indeed with the Customs Union. Memories of the role Prussian troops had played in crushing the Dresden uprising of May 1849 remained vivid in the 1860s, and Berlin insisted on excluding Austria from the *Zollverein*.[52] Second, Lassalle's notion of state-aided cooperatives promised limited economic benefits to the industrialized working class, which was coming to see both the social question and its own political rights in a rather different light.

Saxony became the center of an independent proletarian mass party soon after Wilhelm Liebknecht, a socialist agitator deported from Prussia, arrived in Leipzig in the summer of 1865. Bebel joined forces with the newcomer that winter, after severing ties with Biedermann's liberals. Within a year the two allies had combined their talents in agitation and organization to create the Saxon People's Party (Sächsische Volkspartei). Infused with the hatred of Prussia (*Preußenhaß*) characteristic of Saxon democracy, the socialist movement repudiated the liberal vision of German unification. Socialists also reached their own conclusions with respect to what they called the "labor question" posed by a capitalist economic system. Although the first party program, submitted to a convention held in Chemnitz on 19 August 1866, said nothing about class struggle or the defeat of capitalism, socialists clearly intended to solve the labor question by political means.[53] Two years later, the Nürnberg party congress resolved that "the political movement is the indispensable vehicle of the economic liberation of the working classes."[54] Socialists thus invaded the very arena from which the liberals had long sought to exclude workingmen.

Even before the amalgamation of the Lassallean and Bebel-

---

52. Although willing to sign bilateral trade agreements with Austria, as it did, for example, in 1853, Prussia refused to admit its rival to the *Zollverein*. Recalling Berlin's capitulation to Austria three years earlier, Rudolf von Delbrück warned that an "economic-political Olmütz" would result were Vienna to enter the Customs Union. Bernhard Schulze, "Wirtschaftspolitische Auffassungen bürgerlicher Demokraten im Jahrzehnt der Reichseinigung," in Bartel and Engelberg, eds., *Großpreußisch-militaristische Reichsgründung*, pp. 381–82.

53. Mayer, "Trennung," p. 133.

54. Ibid., p. 149.

Liebknecht organizations, which was consummated at Eisenach in 1869, the social question had become a political issue to the workers' party. This development presaged a complete break with bourgeois democracy, which, like moderate liberalism, could not abide a politically active working class. The democrats tried time and again to accommodate labor, but reluctantly conceded that the social question as defined by socialists meant conflict between the class that possessed and the class that labored. Moderate liberals found themselves equally at a loss. What Biedermann called his own "false pride" in his contribution to the welfare of labor prevented him from going "head to head" with the agitators, thus leaving them free to organize an autonomous workers' movement.[55]

Once the Social Democratic Workers' Party (Sozialdemokratische Arbeiterpartei) came into existence and established ties with Marx's International, reconciliation with the middle-class parties became impossible. Regardless of whether socialists in fact wished to carry through a revolution, liberals took their rhetoric at face value and assumed the worst. Bebel himself offered no reassurance during a polemical contest with the democrats in the course of 1870. "Freedom ceases," he announced, "at the point where it impinges on another's sphere of activity, that is to say, where it encroaches on equality."[56] Socialists bluntly dismissed the liberals' faith in individual initiative and self-help. Access to education, the right to organize, social insurance schemes, and a broader franchise would no longer suffice: Social Democracy wanted power in the state.

On 1 November 1870 Bebel wrote to the old democratic firebrand Johann Jacoby that "from this moment on, although blows may fall upon us like hail, the future belongs to us."[57] Emerging at last from beneath the wing of the bourgeoisie, the social democrats established themselves within the political system of imperial Germany. Their presence tended to drive everyone else to the right. Had Germany's political institutions allowed power to migrate gradually from the traditional elite to a new set of rulers that reflected the class composition of an industrial society, Bebel's optimism might have been justified.

55. Biedermann, *Mein Leben*, 2: 213.
56. Quoted in Mayer, "Trennung," p. 172.
57. Quoted in ibid., p. 176.

But liberals insisted that men of property must control the balance of political power. Instead of growing disenchanted with Bismarck's authoritarian system, liberals tended to view the state as the protector of "individual liberty, order, [and] material interests, indeed, of the supremacy of the bourgeoisie itself, and frankly against the masses."[58]

The economic downturn that began in the early 1870s made allies-in-adversity of liberals, industrialists, and the state. With the onset of the postunification recession, Prussia imposed protectionism on its new empire. Textile manufacturers in Saxony had never supported free trade under the *Zollverein,* nor had the country's mining, machine-building, and paper industries.[59] On the other hand, enterprises vulnerable to foreign competition, such as factories producing finished goods for export, welcomed higher tariffs. The demise of free trade forced National Liberals to reconsider basic principles and old alliances in light of new realities. Ignoring advice from friends in the merchant community, Saxon National Liberals in the Reichstag accepted the increased duties on imported agricultural products and textiles out of concern for the national economy.[60]

A sense of impending danger on the home front, as well as anxiety over German industry's ability to compete in world markets, also persuaded National Liberals to vote for the Anti-Socialist Law and for Bismarck's social insurance bills. They regarded both measures as interactive means of both depoliticizing the social question and banking the fires of class conflict that had been ignited by Social Democracy. Saxony's National Liberals appreciated the Chancellor's antisocialist strategy all the more because of their own general unpopularity. For patriotic Saxons had resented the liberal nationalists' support

58. This perfectly accurate observation came from Friedrich Julius Stahl, surely no friend of liberalism, in 1868. Quoted in S. Schmidt, "Liberale Parteibewegung und Volksmassen während der bürgerlichen Umwälzung in Deutschland, 1789–1871," *Zeitschrift für Geschichtswissenschaft* 26, no. 5 (1978): 407.

59. Seventy-five industry representatives signed a petition to the Landtag opposing the *Zollverein* treaty of 1862. They objected to specific tariff schedules, not to the agreement itself. Zeise, "Zur Rolle der sächsischen Bourgeoisie," p. 254.

60. W. Zorn, "Wirtschafts- und sozialgeschichtliche Zusammenhänge der deutschen Reichsgründungszeit (1850–1879)," in Helmut Böhme, ed., *Probleme der Reichsgründungszeit, 1848–1879* (Cologne, 1968), p. 305, as well as Sheehan, *German Liberalism,* pp. 186–88.

of Prussia in 1866, and the party was finding it difficult to recruit enough dedicated workers to manage its own affairs.[61] During the 1870s, in fact, National Liberals had to run under the banner of Reich Association for Saxony (Reichsverein für Sachsen) in order to identify themselves as members of a loyal antisocialist front that also included Conservatives and Progressives. The National Liberal Party did poorly under its own name in the 1880s, years in which the Conservatives usually elected more than twice as many deputies to the Landtag.[62]

In a state where political Catholicism had no following, middle-class voters gave the National Liberals and Conservatives together a majority in the lower house. The two "law-and-order" parties joined forces in 1896 to legislate the three-class voting system in an effort to stem the socialist tide. This right-wing partnership kept Social Democracy at bay for the next thirteen years. Although the socialists elected twenty-three Reichstag deputies in 1901 – under universal male suffrage – not one Social Democrat sat in the Landtag. By adopting the restrictive Prussian franchise of 1850, the National Liberals repudiated a central feature of the Frankfurt Constitution. Fear of the politically organized working class made them allies of an authoritarian state.[63]

The federal National Liberal party, in its 1898 convention, denounced "the abasement of all the ideals we hold dear" by Social Democracy.[64] Liberals refused to believe that Eduard Bernstein's conciliatory gestures meant anything more than simply a change in tactics. "None of us," warned their manifesto, "can observe the depths of Social Democratic revisionism's heart. Opposition to the 'Patriarchs' [i.e., Bebel and Liebknecht] may be a temporary expedient."[65] A vigilant state offered the best defense against the socialist menace. National Liberals appreciated that Bismarck, who understood the connection between social policy and national security, had created an executive with the power to act decisively against subversion.

61. Biedermann, *Mein Leben*, 2: 343.
62. Sheehan, *German Liberalism*, p. 227.
63. Ibid., p. 222; Warren, *Red Kingdom*, pp. 21–23; John L. Snell, *The Democratic Movement in Germany, 1789–1914* (Chapel Hill, 1976), p. 374.
64. Quoted in Herbert Schwab, "Nationalliberale Partei (NLP), 1867–1918," in D. Fricke, ed., *Die bürgerlichen Parteien in Deutschland, 1830–1945*, 2 vols. (Leipzig, 1970), vol. 2, p. 362.
65. Quoted in ibid., p. 363.

Karl Biedermann, retired for more than twenty years from the leadership of the Saxon National Liberal party, concurred both in his associates' evaluation of the political situation and in their general satisfaction with the results of Bismarckian *Sozialpolitik*. The chancellor, he had written in the 1880s, "has embarked on an immense undertaking in the area of social policy . . . that rests on firm foundations: autonomy and the principle of associationism."[66] In his last book on the social question, which was published in 1900, Biedermann declared himself content with the results of imperial Germany's social legislation. He approved of the factory regulations, insurance schemes, and land reform efforts that comprised the state's social welfare program. The process of reform, however, had gone as far as it could "without completely transforming the organization of labor."[67] From the collaboration between the state and private enterprise he drew exactly the conclusion Bismarck had intended, namely, that existing socioeconomic arrangements still had considerable vitality. The middle class should consequently mobilize to fight "a battle of life and death" with socialism in which "the prize of victory is of inestimable value . . . : social peace."[68] Biedermann clearly hoped that acceptance of Bismarck's reforms by the middle class would "tilt the balance in favor of parliament" but he had no desire to weaken the state's ability to protect itself.[69]

Intimidated by the sudden rise of Social Democracy, liberals demanded that the state guarantee political stability. They concluded that a government that was subject to the rule of law rather than to shifting legislative majorities offered the best protection to national interests. They preferred a forceful yet constitutional state to one that risked its long-sought unity for so dubious a principle as popular sovereignty. Thus, neither on the regional nor on the national level did liberals encourage genuine

66. Biedermann, *Mein Leben*, 2:351.
67. Biedermann, *Vorlesungen über Sozialismus und Sozialpolitik* (Breslau, 1900), p. 173.
68. Ibid., p. 205.
69. Langewiesche, *Liberalismus*, pp. 175–76. Germany's need to solve simultaneously the social and national questions forced liberals to ponder parliamentarization in light of socialism's apparent threat to national security. Their dilemma is analyzed in Ernst Schraepler, "Die politische Haltung des liberalen Bürgertums im Bismarckreich," *Geschichte in Wissenschaft und Unterricht* 5 (1954): 529–44.

parliamentary reform. Instead they supported a "universal but unequal ballot" within Saxony and Prussia as a means of ensuring that propertied interests would retain their control of the government.[70] As Dieter Langewiesche points out in his recently published history of German liberalism, liberals no longer pursued a parliamentary system after 1880. "Only a minority of National Liberals" regarded such a constitution as desirable in the years preceding World War I.[71] They feared its consequences for the monarchical tradition and glimpsed the specter of democratization behind institutions such as the universal franchise and ministerial responsibility. Furthermore, none of the liberal parties in Germany sought a mass base among the electorate. Refusing to present themselves as "representatives of bourgeois class interests," they forced the middle class to join a variety of nonpolitical economic interest groups in order to make its voice heard.[72]

This is not to say that German liberalism deserves to be judged a failure. On the contrary, it accomplished tasks of historical importance during the nineteenth century and thereafter. Social and economic modernization of the nation resulted from the work of numerous bureaucrats, intellectuals, entrepreneurs, and statesmen. But that is not the whole story. Although liberal reformers had amassed an impressive record by century's end, they had not completed their political agenda of the 1840s. Against their contributions to the renovation of German society must be set their inability, indeed their unwillingness, to build a parliamentary system.

Liberalism was, above all, a conception of how a modern society ought to be governed. Gains made by the liberal bourgeoisie as a class, as well as its services to German society, stand in contrast to this unfulfilled hope. How were basic principles of freedom and equality before the law to be incorporated into the political system?[73] From the movement's beginning in the 1830s, social justice, worker self-help, and constitutional rule were prominent liberal values. They found expression in measures such as legalization of workers' associations, social insurance,

70. Langewiesche, *Liberalismus*, p. 223.
71. Ibid., p. 217.
72. Warren, *Red Kingdom*, p. 74.
73. R. Koch, *Deutsche Geschichte, 1815–1848: Restauration oder Vormärz?* (Stuttgart, 1985), p. 96.

vocational education, the cooperative movement, and municipal self-government. Liberal-minded bureaucrats in both Saxony and the Reich reshaped the institutions of an industrializing society. They helped to alter the standards of political legitimacy by asserting the idea of a more open ruling elite, one capable of promoting economic growth and providing a reasonable level of social security. Having discerned the kernel of a German nation-state in the *Zollverein*, Karl Biedermann and his fellow liberals helped forge a national consciousness in the face of opposition from particularistic governments. Although suspicious of a politically conscious working class, liberals argued persuasively for a right of association that permitted labor to build its party structure legally. The sum of these efforts has legitimately been called a "silent bourgeois revolution."[74]

The liberal middle class, however, wielded its influence most effectively at the local level. The Saxon Landtag of 1869–70, for example, adopted liberal proposals that urban administrative units be enlarged to include the industrial suburbs and that industry be given political representation.[75] The state and national governments proved to be less open to the idea that political power ought to reflect the relative balance of interests in society. Liberals themselves downplayed ministerial responsibility because they feared that Social Democracy would benefit most from a parliamentary system similar to that of Britain. The modernization process that transformed imperial Germany's economy and opened its society to men of property consequently left the nation's political institutions untouched. Notwithstanding the "dynamic character and relative liberality" of Wilhelmian Germany,[76] the central government remained largely impervious to change. Only in municipal affairs did politics encourage new leaders to challenge the status quo.

74. Blackbourn declares that "the silent revolution was most impressive precisely where it was most silent." See Blackbourn and Eley, *Peculiarities*, p. 288. Bourgeois influence emanated, above all, from the permanent civil service, which was open to liberal ideas from the 1830s onward.
75. Urban development and administration in nineteenth-century Saxony is surveyed in K. Blaschke, "Entwicklungstendenzen im sächsischen Städtewesen während des 19. Jahrhunderts (1815–1914)," in H. Matzerath, ed., *Städtewachstum und innerstädtische Strukturveränderungen: Probleme des Urbanisierungsprozesses im 19. und 20. Jahrhundert* (Stuttgart, 1984), pp. 44–64.
76. J. Kocka, "German History before Hitler: The Debate about the German Sonderweg," *Journal of Contemporary History* 23 (1988): 10.

"Modernization," as Hans-Ulrich Wehler has said, "does not lead in every case to increased [political] participation, but rather can absorb energies and alienate [people] from politics."[77] The decline of liberal politics regionally and nationally in the 1880s and 1890s illustrates Wehler's point. A process that began in Saxony during the mid-1870s became visible in national affairs by 1900, as political reform slipped from view. Although liberals participated vigorously in many special interest and professional groups such as the Association for Social Policy (Verein für Sozialpolitik) and in municipal councils, they developed "a certain distaste for party organization and electoral agitation."[78] Formerly active "political professors" disengaged themselves from the fray, as did the bureaucrats once so prominent in liberal ranks. Educated and propertied Germans lost their interest in and respect for political activity. Generally satisfied with the results of Bismarck's statecraft, they forged an alliance with the state that lasted as long as the empire itself.

77. H.-U. Wehler, *Modernisierungstheorie und Geschichte* (Göttingen, 1975), p. 23.
78. Sheehan, *German Liberalism*, p. 233.

4

The Limits of Liberal Politics in Berlin, 1815–48

Jonathan Knudsen

In recent years our understanding of the "making" of early German liberalism has been extended by new methods of socio-historical analysis that in turn have revitalized the study of liberalism as a cultural process. We can now observe, by region and at key moments in the decades between 1815 and 1848, with what tenacity liberals resisted the repressive policies of the German Confederation, even as they managed to infiltrate key institutions and reshape fundamental aspects of German politics, culture, and economy.[1] How and why the liberal system of ideas proved to be persuasive and adaptable is less easily answered once we abandon the whiggish framework of liberalism itself. We understand increasingly that liberalism historically consisted of a loose family of ideas which could be creatively combined in a local and often idiosyncratic manner. This has been one reason for the continuing debate over "true liberalism": is the presence of certain subcomponents in the family of liberal ideas necessary for us to name an individual or

1. The research for this article was conducted in Berlin and Göttingen in 1988–89 under the auspices of a Fulbright Fellowship. I would like to express a special gratitude to Manfred Gailus and to my colleagues at the Max-Planck-Institut für Geschichte in Göttingen for their criticism, support, and encouragement.
   In the following two valuable essay collections: see W. Schieder, "Probleme einer Sozialgeschichte des frühen Liberalismus in Deutschland," in W. Schieder, ed., *Liberalismus in der Gesellschaft des deutschen Vormärz*, Geschichte und Gesellschaft, supp. 9 (Göttingen, 1983), pp. 12–14 and I. Cervelli, "Deutsche Liberale im Vormärz: Profil einer politischen Elite (1833–1847)," in Schieder, ed., *Liberalismus*, pp. 312–40; W. Kaschuba, "Zwischen deutscher Nation und deutscher Provinz: Politischer Horizonte und soziale Milieus im frühen Liberalismus," in D. Langewiesche, ed., *Liberalismus im 19. Jahrhundert*, Kritische Studien zur Geschichtswissenschaft, vol. 79 (Göttingen, 1988), pp. 83–108. Also the recent synthesis by D. Langewiesche, *Liberalismus in Deutschland* (Frankfurt a.M., 1988), pp. 34–38.

group liberal?[2] The direct answer would appear to be no, for in liberalism's evolution it is not easy to find any particular element common to all those who called themselves liberals. Religious toleration, freedom of speech and assembly, free trade, equality before the law, the right of equal access to education and occupation, the commitment to constitutional government – any of these could be found to be missing from the views of representative liberal thinkers.[3]

In the pre-1848 period, therefore, liberalism was a movement best understood in its difference: it was a set of stylistic variations emanating from a dynamic political and cultural configuration; these variations, in turn, were rooted in changing social, cultural, and occupational subuniverses.[4] As a consequence, liberalism only acquired meaning in its elaboration, for instance, by place as Rhenish or East Prussian liberalism; by group or occupation, as bureaucratic or aristocratic liberalism; and by commitment to some aspect of the belief system, especially in terms of the principle of equality, as *juste milieu*, free trade, or radical liberalism. Significantly, liberalism placed itself within a concrete political spectrum of right to left that differed by place: thus more than one contemporary noted that Rhenish liberalism constituted a different set of reflections, habits, and rhetorical gestures than liberalism in Königsberg or southwest Germany.

Berlin is a particularly complex example of the variations within the liberal movement. The presence of the court, the large numbers of military and state administrative personnel,

2. H. Rosenberg, *Politische Denkströmungen im deutschen Vormärz*, Kritische Studien zur Geschichtswissenschaft, vol 3 (Göttingen, 1972), pp. 13–14, 25–42; L. Gall, "Liberalismus und 'bürgerliche Gesellschaft': Zu Charakter und Entwicklung der liberalen Bewegung in Deutschland," in L. Gall, ed., *Liberalismus*, 3d ed. (Königstein/Ts., 1985), pp. 162–87; J.S. Shapiro, *Liberalism and the Challenge of Fascism: Social Forces in England and France (1815–1870)*, 2d ed. (New York, 1964). J.J. Sheehan, *German Liberalism in the Nineteenth Century* (Chicago, 1978), intro. to pt. 1.

3. Lothar Gall's search for a "true liberalism" within the diversity of the early movement is striking in its rich, detailed, and specific understanding of liberal ideas and figures in the pre-1848 decades. See especially Gall's "Liberalismus und bürgerliche Gesellschaft" cited above and his "Der deutsche Liberalismus zwischen Revolution und Reichsgründung," *Historische Zeitschrift* 228 (1979): 98–108. See Wolfgang Mommsen's well-taken reservations: "Der deutsche Liberalismus zwischen 'klassenloser Bürgergesellschaft' und 'organisiertem Kapitalismus': Zu einigen neueren Liberalismus-Interpretationen," *Geschichte und Gesellschaft* 4 (1978): 77–90.

4. Rosenberg, *Politische Denkströmungen*, esp. p. 29.

the hypervigilance of the censors, the arbitrary and blanket repression of political expression affected every sector of public affairs and severely inhibited the development of the liberal movement in the capital. Politically critical visitors – Heinrich Heine, Ludwig Börne, and Johann Jacoby, for instance – or an observer such as Henry Dwight, the son of the president of Yale University, constantly remarked on the more numerous restrictions on personal freedom in Berlin.[5] In a certain sense a public political life did not emerge until late in the period. When Johann Jacoby visited Berlin in the early 1830s he wrote that he would describe "the views about public life, not public life itself. Because we have none. Everything is *private* here; the *privy councillors* make sure of that."[6]

Consequently political life in the capital was highly provincial and directed simultaneously toward the monarch, the court, and the state's officials. Ernst Dronke wrote his history of Berlin in 1846 on this basis – as the history of the central government and not as the history of urban politics.[7] Friedrich Saß concluded in another contemporary history also published in 1846 that Berlin was condemned to royalist piety and political "indifferentism."

As the royal residence Berlin had become more accustomed than other cities to the theatricality and sparkle that the monarchical always attaches to itself, and this pleasure in monarchical pomp has contributed not a little to reinforcing in the population an acceptance of the status quo as the most natural, simple, and unavoidably necessary condition of things. Naturally the masses express this tie between the ruling principle and the city not as a spirit of party but

5. H. Heine, "Briefe aus Berlin," *Sämtliche Schriften*, ed. K. Briegleb, 12 vols. (Munich, 1981), vol. 3, pp. 51, 55–56; L. Börne, *Berliner Briefe, 1828*, ed. L. Geiger (Berlin, 1905), pp. xxxiii, 43; J. Jacoby, *Bilder und Zustände aus Berlin*, 2 vols. (Altenburg, 1833), vol. 1, p. 8; H.E. Dwight, *Travels in the North of Germany* (New York, 1829). Dwight wrote, p. 166: "Conscious as every Prussian is that the almost omniscient eye of the government, through the medium of its system of *espionage* is fixed upon him, and that a single word expressed with boldness, may furnish an occasion for transferring him to Koepnic or Spandau; he becomes of course, in every circle, suspicious of those around him, sustains a negative character in his conversation, advances those indefinite opinions which are harmless, and if he does not commend, he takes very good care never to censure the proceedings of government."
6. Jacoby, *Bilder und Zustände aus Berlin*, vol. 1, p. 51.
7. E. Dronke, *Berlin* (Berlin [East], 1987).

rather as an indifferentism with respect to all political groups who fall into a condition of decided protest with the present situation.[8]

The communal political bodies, through their majority in the council, contributed to the privatizing of politics, royalism, and indifference for they, together with the state and the magistracy, prevented detailed reporting of and public attendance at their meetings until just before the revolution.[9] Contemporaries were forced to read the papers from Leipzig, Augsburg, and Königsberg to learn about events in Berlin. Adolf Streckfuß (1823–95), the novelist and historian of Berlin, wrote of these years before 1840: "There were no political associations; the ever watchful police would not have allowed them to be founded. The most stringent control by the censor closed the press to every political activity. None of the newspapers dared to discuss daily affairs freely. Only papers outside Prussia could report events there, [and] these were not read in those days by the city's citizenry."[10]

The suppression of political life in the capital generated characteristic patterns of resentment and passive resistance in the pre-1848 period. Periodically the latent social and economic discontent in the pre-1848 years burst forth with political overtones, but open revolt came almost exclusively from the artisanate and working poor. Food riots broke out during the French occupation in 1808; there was also the "tailors' revolution" of 1830, the "fireworks revolution" of 1835, and the "potato revolution" of 1848.[11] The political liberals among Berlin's

8. F. Saß, *Berlin in seiner neuesten Zeit und Entwicklung, 1846*, new ed. with an afterword by Detlef Heikamp (Berlin, 1983), p. 93.

9. K. Kettig, "Gemeinsinn und Mitverantwortung: Beiträge zur Geschichte der Berliner Stadtverordnetenversammlung, zugleich eine Würdigung des Stadtverordnetenvertreters Heinrich Kochhann," *Der Bär von Berlin* 12 (1963): 13–14, 27; A. Streckfuß, *500 Jahre Berliner Geschichte: Von Fischerdorf zur Weltstadt*, 4th ed. (Berlin, 1886), vol. 2, pp. 905–8. For the general issue of public access to communal political life see J.J. Sheehan, *German Liberalism*, p. 10.

10. Streckfuß, *500 Jahre Berliner Geschichte*, vol. 2, p. 772; similar judgments appear on pp. 750 and 789.

11. H. Bock, *Die Illusion der Freiheit: Deutsche Klassenkämpfe zur Zeit der französischen Julirevolution 1830 bis 1831* (Berlin [East], 1980), pp. 169–82; Streckfuß, *500 Jahre Berliner Geschichte*, vol. 2, pp. 785–87; excerpts from contemporaries in R. Köhler and W. Richter, *Berliner Leben, 1806–1847* (Berlin, 1954), pp. 45–46, 245–48; D. Meyer, *Das öffentliche Leben in Berlin im Jahr vor der Märzrevolution* (Berlin, 1912), pp. 86–98; M. Gailus, "Pöbelexzesse und Volkstumulte im Berliner Vormärz," in M. Gailus, ed., *Pöbelexzesse und Volkstumulte in Berlin: Zur Sozialgeschichte der Straße (1830–1980)* (Berlin, 1984), pp. 1–43.

class of burghers (*Bürgertum*), however, were far more subdued in these years. Their "progressive" political attitudes were still predominantly shaped by an Enlightenment culture that had been molded by the long reign of Friedrich II and the generation of Lessing, Mendelssohn, Nicolai, and Teller. This Berlin Enlightenment had balanced a particular type of theological cosmopolitanism with a rather slavish monarchism and had sharply separated civil society from notions of burgher self-rule.[12] Such a tradition of etatism (*Etatismus*) and administrative paternalism (*Bevormundung*) seemed to contemporaries to have culminated in the Stein-Hardenberg reform effort for revolution from above.

The continuing presence in the capital of survivors from the reform period dictated that into the 1840s much of the visible political debate was still formulated in terms of the tradition of enlightened bureaucratic reform. These state officials, as a number of recent historians have argued, maintained a group cohesiveness in and out of power[13] through which they dominated the formulation of liberal political attitudes in the capital. For this reason local debate focused on the Stein-Hardenberg reforms, particularly the Municipal Law (Städteordnung) of 1808, as it came to be attacked by a variety of retrenching social and political interests; on the heritage of the Frederickian policy of religious toleration and theological rationalism as it came to be assaulted by the neo-pietist orthodoxy; and on maintaining free market relations against efforts to restore the guilds.

Yet the tone of this debate was no longer optimistic, for the bureaucratic reform movement had failed to sustain or broaden the political consensus that had burst forth in the wars against the French. The subsequent political witch-hunt initiated by the Carlsbad Decrees forced the following generation to reconstruct a progressive political tradition in the midst of doubts concern-

---

12. See the critical reference to "geschmeidige Anpassung" by W. Dreßen, "Berliner Freiheit," in J. Boberg et al., eds., *Exerzierfeld der Moderne: Industriekultur in Berlin im 19. Jahrhundert* (Munich, 1984), p. 32.

13. Schieder, "Probleme einer Sozialgeschichte des frühen Liberalismus in Deutschland," p. 15; H. Rosenberg, *Bureaucracy, Aristocracy, and Autocracy: The Prussian Experience, 1660–1815* (Cambridge, Mass., 1958), pp. 180–83, 204, 210–21; B. Vogel, *Allgemeine Gewerbefreiheit*, Kritische Studien zur Geschichtswisssenschaft, vol. 57 (Göttingen, 1983), pp. 48–67; R. Koselleck, *Preußen zwischen Reform und Revolution: Allgemeines Landrecht, Verwaltung und soziale Bewegung von 1791 bis 1848* (Stuttgart, 1967), pp. 337–43.

ing the Enlightenment inheritance. Enlightened attitudes were now filtered in an idiosyncratic manner, through various forms of idealism, the experience of war against the French in the nationalist "uprising," and the Christian-Germanic reaction. Natural rights theory, Kantianism, Hegelianism, utilitarianism, Smithianism, Germanic nationalism, and etatist thinking of various shadings all fed into the Berlin opposition. In its experience of disappointment and political terror, the postrevolutionary generation also went through a lengthy phase of resignation that caused it to engage in its own forms of retrenchment. In addition, the continuous task of mediating between the administrative carriers of the repressive state apparatus and the liberal survivors in the administration buttressed the widespread ideological tendency among the state's officials to redefine the bureaucracy itself as civil society and to constitute that bureaucracy as a separate estate. For these reasons, Berlin's liberal political life until the late 1830s was a conscious retreat from the opening produced by the French occupation and the Stein-Hardenberg reforms.

The precise shape of this retreat, the modes of accommodation to the police powers of the state, the forms of opposition and resistance are difficult to describe. What evidence we have survives in the muted record of a sharply restricted public debate in the form of pamphlets and treatises on constitutional life and in private letters, memoirs, and diaries that could not be easily confiscated.[14] If we seek to go beyond individual figures of the opposition and study the various institutions and social groups that fashioned political life in this period – the state officials and city administrators, the university professoriat, the publishers and free intellectuals, the resident nobility, the artisanate and entrepreneurs, we are faced with difficulties that prevent us from easily following the lead of Hartmut Zwahr and others.[15] With notable exceptions, such as the work on Berlin's

14. Kettig, "Gemeinsinn und Mitverantwortung," pp. 8–9; G. Kutzsch, "Der Staat und die Stadt Berlin," *Der Bär von Berlin* 17 (1968): 7–8. The publication of critical memoirs was subject to censorship until late in the century: the continuous effort to suppress the posthumous publication of Varnhagen von Ense's diaries and the sentencing of his niece Ludmilla Assing to prison terms in 1862 and 1864 is a case in point. H. Houben, *Verbotene Literatur von der klassischen Zeit bis zur Gegenwart*, 2 vols. (Berlin and Hanover, 1924–28), vol. 1, pp. 600–601.

15. H. Zwahr, "Zur Klassenkonstituierung der deutschen Bourgeoisie," *Jahrbuch für Geschichte* 18 (1978): 21–83. See also F. Simhart, *Bürgerliche Gesellschaft*

minorities and the young Hegelians, we lack basic studies of the city's social and political elites.[16] We know almost nothing of the magistracy or the city council as social groups.[17] We know more about the manner in which the free market system reshaped economic life on the eve of industrialization, but we still know relatively little about how new social groupings shaped the economy and how that economy in turn reconstituted the social forces.[18] Marriage patterns and family ties, wealth and education, the structure of clientage, the distribution of patronage – these matters which comprise the glue of politics in an age of notables are largely unexplored. Thus Berlin in these decades is an exemplary witness to Jürgen Kocka's account of our inadequate knowledge of the German *Bürgertum* in the nineteenth century.[19] At this stage, then, the study of liberals and the liberal movement in Berlin remains more a history of liberal ideas than one would like.

The remainder of this essay, which forms part of a larger

und Revolution: Eine ideologiekritische Untersuchung des politischen und sozialen Bewußtseins in der Mitte des 19. Jahrhunderts, dargestellt am Beispiel einer Gruppe des Münchner Bildungsbürgertums, Studien zur bayerischen Verfassungs- und Sozialgeschichte, vol. 9 (Munich, 1978).

16. See for instance S. Wenzel, *Jüdische Bürger und kommunale Selbstverwaltung in preußischen Städten*, Veröffentlichungen der Historischen Kommission zu Berlin, vol. 21 (Berlin, 1967), pp. 19–69; and the recent model study by Wolfgang Eßbach, *Die Junghegelianer: Soziologie einer Intellektuellengruppe*, Übergänge, vol. 16 (Munich, 1988).

17. Of the older studies most valuable remain P. Clauswitz, *Die Städteordnung von 1808 und die Stadt Berlin: Festschrift zur hundertjährigen Gedenkfeier der Einführung der Städteordnung* (Berlin, 1908); Meyer, *Das öffentliche Leben in Berlin*, pp. 26–39; and E. Kaeber, "Die Oberbürgermeister Berlins seit der Steinschen Städteordnung," *Jahrbuch des Vereins für die Geschichte Berlins* 2 (1952): 5–114. Of the more recent research see especially J. Kutzsch, "Berlins Bürgermeister, 1808 bis 1933," *Der Bär von Berlin* 25 (1976): 7–29; Kettig, "Gemeinsinn und Mitverantwortung," pp. 7–27; and J. Wetzel, "Oberbürgermeister Heinrich Wilhelm Krausnick und die Berliner Kommunalpolitik von 1834 bis 1862," "*. . . taub für die Stimme der Zeit,*" *Zwischen Königstreue und Bürgerinteressen: Berlins Oberbürgermeister H.W. Krausnick von 1834 bis 1862* (Berlin, 1986), pp. 9–83.

18. See for instance L. Baar, *Die Berliner Industrie in der industriellen Revolution* (Berlin [East], 1966), pp. 139–67; J. Bergmann, *Das Berliner Handwerk in den Frühphasen der Industrialisierung* (Berlin, 1973); I. Mieck, *Preußische Gewerbepolitik in Berlin, 1806–1844: Staatshilfe und Privatinitiative zwischen Merkantilismus und Liberalismus* (Berlin, 1965).

19. J. Kocka, "Bürgertum und bürgerliche Gesellschaft im 19. Jahrhundert: Europäische Entwicklungen und deutsche Eigenarten," in J. Kocka, ed., *Bürgertum im 19. Jahrhundert: Deutschland im europäischen Vergleich*, 3 vols. (Munich, 1988), vol. 1, pp. 14–15. See also the comments by Schieder, "Probleme einer Sozialgeschichte des frühen Liberalismus," p. 16.

project on liberal culture in Berlin during the first half of the nineteenth century, considers three related manifestations of liberal political life. It begins by looking at the institutional constraints to communal politics, then considers the views of two prominent liberal survivors of the Stein-Hardenberg reform era, and finally outlines the pattern of extrainstitutional political activity in the years before 1848.

The Communal Political System

Nineteenth-century liberalism in the cities grafted itself onto older traditions of self-rule.[20] Berlin and the cities of Brandenburg-Prussia, however, had fewer such traditions to which to adapt. Except for the churches – and their significance should not be underestimated – those institutions in Berlin open to a liberal politics were all relatively new: the municipal government created by the Municipal Law of 1808 and the newly founded university (1810) under the quasi-protection of Minister Altenstein.[21] Prior to the reform legislation, the monarchy had always intervened directly in the city's administrative, economic, and political affairs. Such intervention in the eighteenth century, for example, had given the Huguenot and Jewish minorities positions of economic privilege out of proportion to their actual numbers. It had also led to the elimination of the vestiges of self-rule. By the eighteenth century the royal administration, through its *Steuerräte* and police president, had assumed police powers and control over public assistance. The magistracy, as a consequence, had largely lost its independent political functions and economic independence, and we have little knowledge of its survival as a social caste.[22] As a political

20. For the later period see the suggestive essay by J. Sheehan, "Liberalism and the City in Nineteenth-Century Germany," *Past and Present*, no. 51 (1971): 116–37.

21. Outside the official institutions, of course, there were many informal associations and voluntary groups that had already begun to characterize cultural life prior to 1800 and continued during the Restoration – reading societies, lodges, salons such as that of Varnhagen von Ense, inns, coffeehouses, and smoking rooms. For the Restoration period D. Hertz rightfully stresses the break with prerevolutionary salon culture. See her *Jewish High Society in Old Regime Berlin* (New Haven 1988), pp. 269–85. Of the extensive literature, the best contemporary descriptions of Berlin's associational and public life remain those of Saß, *Berlin in seiner neuesten Zeit und Entwicklung*, 1846, and Dronke, *Berlin*.

22. Clauswitz, *Städteordnung von 1808*, pp. v–vi, 19–26, 30; K.-H. Börner,

body the citizenry was also divided because significant groups of the specially privileged or *Eximirten* had particular judicial and political arrangements with the state. The large numbers of nobles, royal officials, and members of the religious minorities (Huguenots and Czech Brethren; the Jews were a quite different and special case) also prevented the formation of a corporate political spirit. "We knew that we lived in a police state," wrote Heinrich Kochhann, master baker and liberal member of the city council from the late 1830s. "[We] subordinated ourselves for better or worse to the printed provisions of the law and recognized the particular police president as the authoritative and responsible representative of all burgher interests."[23]

Drafted in the brief period of legislative renewal, the Stein-Hardenberg Municipal Law of November 1808 sought a radical solution to a number of fiscal and institutional problems, while recognizing that they might only be solved by granting greater local autonomy.[24] In Berlin, as in the other cities affected, the Municipal Law sought to mobilize the urban classes within broad but clearly circumscribed boundaries and thus to generate a renewal that would not undermine the fundamental patterns of bureaucratic absolutism. The problems of reorganization were many, and in the end the reforms did not allow Berlin enough autonomy to set aside the traditional barriers between self-government and administration from above. The Municipal Law was not able to create a fiscal administration capable of

---

"Beginn der bürgerlichen Umwälzung in Berlin: Einführung der preußischen Städteordnung," *Jahrbuch für Geschichte* 35 (1987): 153–55.

23. H.E. Kochhann, *Tagebücher*, ed. A. Kochhann, 4 vols. (Berlin, 1905–7), vol. 2, pp. 22–23.

24. The best summaries remain H. Heffter, *Die deutsche Selbstverwaltung im 19. Jahrhundert*, 2d rev. ed. (Stuttgart, 1969), pp. 84–103, and E.R. Huber, *Deutsche Verfassungsgeschichte seit 1789*, vol. 1 (Stuttgart, 1960), pp. 172–78. The lengthy literature on the introduction of the Municipal Law in Berlin is basically dependent on Clauswitz, *Städteordnung von Berlin*, pp. 54–109. Of those who have reworked the archival material, see K. Schrader, "Die Verwaltung Berlins von der Residenzstadt des Kurfürsten Friedrich Wilhelm bis zur Reichshauptstadt unter besonderer Berücksichtigung der Stellung der Stadtverwaltung zu der oberen preußischen Staatsbehörden und mit einem Abriß der Behördengeschichte der Berliner Regierung" (Ph.D. diss, Berlin [East], 1963), pt. 2, pp. 16–25; and Börner, "Beginn der bürgerlichen Umwälzung," pp. 168–72. See also Berthold Schulze, "Die Einführung der Städteordnung in Berlin und der Mark," *Jahrbuch für brandenburgische Landesgeschichte* 10 (1959): 11–17; and G. Kautzsch, "Verwaltung und Selbstverwaltung in Berlin unter der ersten Städteordnung," *Jahrbuch für brandenburgische Landesgeschichte* 13 (1962): 22–40.

paying the debts and taxes owed the state along with the new burdens handed to the city. The reforms brought to Berlin a major increase in financial burdens, chiefly in the form of the debt from the French occupation and the poor relief system that had previously been a royal responsibility. But other burdens were transferred as well: the responsibility for garbage collection, lighting, paving, and funding the schools. For these reasons the Restoration brought with it gradual administrative adjustments that actually became part of a pattern of erosion and reversal of the self-rule that had been granted. After 1810 judicial and police matters were taken from the magistracy. The city's courts became royal institutions and the French colony lost its legal privileges. Similarly the state's high officials and the military remained under special legal jurisdictions. Furthermore, between 1815 and 1850, the Ministry of the Interior assumed control over the schools and religious life. The expansion of the city, the growth of the poor relief burden, the need to pave the streets and provide lighting brought with it a willingness by the magistracy to sacrifice political power in exchange for the state's assumption of control of the increased indebtedness. Thus, without consulting the council, the police president made individual contracts with companies to provide services – in this case the British for gas and lighting – that went against the future interests of the city. All of these examples reveal the pattern of administrative centralization that asserted itself once again in the 1820s.[25]

The continuous encroachment by the state reduced the political arena to a very small number of issues. This, in turn, seems to have prevented clear political distinctions and cleavages from developing. The arena of public expertise was equally small, reduced as it was to administration by district of the churches and the poor relief system.[26] It was in local administration that most of Berlin's political notables – those who were not royal administrators, pastors, or university teachers – received their

25. In addition to the above literature, especially Clausewitz and Schrader, see also I. Mieck, "Von der Reformzeit zur Revolution (1806–1847)," in Wolfgang Ribbe, ed., *Geschichte Berlins*, 2 vols (Munich, 1987), vol. 1, pp. 503–12.

26. See the discussion in J.F. Geist and K. Kürvers, *Das Berliner Mietshaus, 1740–1862* (Munich, 1980), pp. 124–50 and throughout; also valuable for its fiscalism is the report by the poor relief commission, *Die öffentliche Armenpflege in Berlin, mit besonderer Beziehung auf die vier Verwaltungs-Jahre 1822 bis 1825* (Berlin, 1828).

practical training in government.[27] Such training unfolded within a tradition of administrative preeminence that excluded the opportunity to discuss or alter policies. As state councillor Streckfuß stated (1841): "In those transactions involving duties toward the state or the individual, it is in the nature of the matter that those responsible cannot decide whether they want to fulfill their duty or not."[28] The training thus instilled patterns of frugality divorced from patterns of political principle and political responsibility.

We have few documents describing the work and relations of the "lord mayor" (*Oberbürgermeister*), "mayor" (*Bürgermeister*), city council, and the state in these first decades under the Municipal Law, but those that survive let us glimpse the efforts to channel, restrict, and discipline the city council. The Municipal Law created an electoral system in which a restricted electorate of citizens – those possessing a trade, property, or earning 150 talers yearly in smaller cities or 200 talers in larger cities – chose councillors by district; these in turn elected the magistrates and the mayoral officers. There are continuous comments regarding political apathy in Berlin until the early 1840s, and with Paul Clauswitz we may accept the argument that citizenship was often acquired simply in order to practice a craft or a trade.[29] The statistics of the city administration for the years 1828–48 reveal that on average 5 to 6 percent of the population was enfranchised; participation gradually increased from about 40 percent in the first years of the century to over 70 percent after 1840. In absolute terms the active electorate ranged from 8,200 in 1828, when the statistics begin, to 19,000 in the stormy elections of 1848.[30]

27. See the comments by Kochhann, *Tagebücher*, vol. 2, p. 22, vol. 3, pp. 35–37; C. Knoblauch in R. Knoblauch, "175 Jahre Knoblauchsches Haus: Aus Tagebüchern und Akten des Familienarchivs," *Zeitschrift des Vereins für die Geschichte Berlins*, no. 52 (1935): 63–64; and K.F. Klöden, *Jugenderinnerungen*, ed. K. Koetschau (Leipzig, 1911).
28. Karl Streckfuß, *Die beiden preußischen Städteordnungen verglichen* (Berlin, 1841), p. 44.
29. Clauswitz, *Städteordnung von 1808*, p. 197. See also Kettig, "Gemeinsinn und Mitverantwortung," pp. 11–12.
30. Städtische Behörde, ed., *Bericht über die Verwaltung der Stadt Berlin in den Jahren bis incl. 1840* (Berlin, 1842), p. iv; Magistrat, ed., *Bericht über die Verwaltung der Stadt Berlin in den Jahren 1841 bis incl. 1850* (Berlin, 1853), pp. 6–8. On this problem see Clauswitz, *Städteordnung von 1808*, pp. 196–97; Kettig, "Gemeinsinn und Mitverantwortung," p. 11; Wetzel, "Oberbürgermeister H.W. Krausnick," p. 18; Koselleck, *Preußen zwischen Reform und Revolution*, pp. 571–73.

Most of Berlin's population thus remained disenfranchised, but a sizable number of the *Kleinbürgertum*, small traders and artisans, acquired political rights for the first time. Since large numbers of the state administration, the nobility, and the officer corps were without citizenship or chose not to participate, the *Kleinbürgertum* came to dominate in the council to a greater degree than their social status would have warranted. This led to complaints from the city's notables about distance and alienation from the council. Carl Knoblauch (1793–1859) wrote to the Freiherr vom Stein that the council looked as if it had been "brought together by accident and had not been selected";[31] and the Freiherr vom Stein formulated matters even more crudely: "A substantial inadequacy in the present municipal constitution is [found in] the degrading of the citizenry by the intruding riffraff, the swinish multitude, as Mr. Burke says, the crass opposition existing between the city councillors and the magistrates."[32]

Those who voted, moreover – and we are actually talking about approximately 130 men as heads of households in each of the 102 districts of the city – appear to have exercised their franchise with less than the required sense of deference. They appear to have chosen councillors who, on the one hand, elected and reelected professional administrators as magistrates but, on the other, elected quasi-opposition figures as their *Oberbürgermeister* and *Bürgermeister*.[33] These highly qualified men had in some manner shown independence from the state, but such independence cannot necessarily be equated with political liberalism. Leopold von Gerlach (1757–1813), for example, had been chief inspector of the Berlin administration and had been shunted aside for his anti-French attitudes; he was a decided critic of the Stein-Hardenberg reforms and was still elected as the first *Oberbürgermeister*.[34] Friedrich von Baerensprung (1777–1841), a member of the Christian-German Table Society who was dismissed and imprisoned for dueling with Hardenberg's coworker Christian Scharnweber (1770–1822), also appears to have been chosen at first as *Bürgermeister* and

31. Knoblauch, "175 Jahre Knoblauchsches Haus," p. 64.
32. Freiherr vom Stein, *Briefe und amtliche Schriften*, ed. W. Hubatsch, 10 vols. (Stuttgart, 1957–74), vol. 6, p. 984.
33. Kaeber, "Die Oberbürgermeister Berlins," pp. 54–65, esp. p. 59.
34. Börner, "Beginn der bürgerlichen Umwälzung," pp. 184–85.

then as *Oberbürgermeister* because of a similar combination of intellectual independence and opposition to the French.[35] Such choices by the council suggest the form of unfocused resistance to authority that often characterized public life in Berlin throughout the nineteenth century and is captured in Adolf Glaßbrenner's literary figures.[36] But they also reveal the social boundaries between the various administrative competencies and the almost nonexistent room for maneuver in a system where the king ratified the selections. Those elected to the highest city offices possessed lengthy state administrative experience and were thus embedded in the state apparatus and the networks of political patronage outside the city. In this sense the elections reflected only a modest degree of political autonomy.

The Municipal Law thus created a communal political system that was relatively closed to liberal politics in the decades before 1840. Yet even this minimal opening constituted a permanent threat to the basic patterns of administrative control, for the Municipal Law tied certain aspects of local self-rule to the elections of the city councillors and the subsequent elections of the magistracy and the mayor. Therefore it kept the principle of representation alive and raised expectations for self-rule that contrasted with the failure of the monarchy to implement the promised constitution. The Berlin city council, furthermore, was one of those communal bodies that, political loyalty aside, constantly fought for its right of administrative oversight against encroachment by the *Oberbürgermeister, Bürgermeister*, and the state administration. In this sense the struggle over the principle of self-rule forged alliances over procedure and oversight at the local level; it transformed nascent liberal and conservative political allegiances into a vague oppositional attitude that substituted for more substantial political distinctions.

35. H. Sembdner, ed., *Heinrich von Kleists Lebensspuren*, vol. 1 (Frankfurt a.M., 1984), p. 372; G. Kutzsch, "Berlins Bürgermeister 1808 bis 1933," *Der Bär von Berlin* 25 (1976): 10.

36. H. Denkler, "Einleitung und Editionsbericht," in Adolf Glaßbrenner, *Unterrichtung der Nation*, ed. H. Denkler et al., vol. 1 (Cologne, 1981), pp. 31–34; I. Heinrich-Jost, *Literarische Publizistik Adolf Glaßbrenners (1810–1876): Die List beim Schreiben der Wahrheit*, Dortmunder Beiträge zur Zeitungsforschung, vol. 31 (Munich, 1980).

Liberal Revisionism

Before the 1840s, however, the state and its administrators most often sought to suppress the tiny gestures of independence and the right of access to the political system by small artisans and traders. Even administrators once committed to the idea of representative government gradually sought to transpose communal political matters into the realm of administration. This retreat from self-rule forms the background to the lengthy campaign to rewrite the Municipal Law which culminated in the revision of 1831. In part the struggle over revision was connected with instituting a uniform municipal code in the Prussian lands lost or not yet acquired in 1808, but in Berlin and the other cities where the original code had been introduced, it brought with it a sustained effort to restrict the franchise and restore greater powers to the magistrates and central administration. The debate signaled a willingness by the state to tolerate public discussions that concerned restricting rights already granted. It also signaled a willingness by the city's "liberal" state officials to separate themselves from their electoral base and thus to restrict their own political independence from the state.

The two chief protagonists in Berlin, the historian Friedrich von Raumer (1781–1873) and the state councillor Adolf Streckfuß (1779–1844), were both survivors of the Stein-Hardenberg reform era.[37] In the late twenties neither had as yet acquired his future power or popularity. Both were state officials outside the communal system; they were linked by common friendships; and they met each other through their memberships in associations such as Zelter's Singakademie.[38] I focus on their views briefly in order to indicate the basic pattern of their inegalitarian liberalism.

Raumer, nephew of Leopold von Gerlach and closely connected in the early years to the romantic circle in Berlin (Adam

---

37. For the chief texts, see F. von Raumer, *Über die preußische Städteordnung, nebst einem Vorworte über bürgerliche Freiheit nach französischen und deutschen Begriffen* (Leipzig, 1828), and his *Zur Rechtfertigung und Berichtigung meiner Schrift über die preußische Städteordnung* (Leipzig, 1828). Also K. Streckfuß, *Über die preußische Städteordnung: Beleuchtung der Schrift des Herrn Prof. von Raumer unter gleichem Titel* (Berlin, 1828), his *Katechismus für Stadtverordnete der preußischen Städte* (Berlin, 1832), and his *Die beiden preußischen Städteordnungen verglichen*.

38. Knoblauch, "175 Jahre Knoblauchsches Haus," *Zeitschrift des Vereins für die Geschichte Berlins*, no. 52 (1935): 67; and no. 53 (1936): 128.

Müller and Achim von Arnim), had been an intimate coworker in Hardenberg's finance commission. His values were drawn from that curious mixture of romantic medievalism, royalism, aristocratic arrogance, and liberal individualism that makes it so difficult to generalize about the historical movement of liberalism in the pre-1848 period. Within the finance commission he had been committed to economic liberalism and peasant emancipation, causing a break with the conservative friends of these years. Kleist had even challenged Raumer to a duel when the struggle over Hardenberg's reforms caused his *Berliner Abendblätter* to lose access to privileged information.[39] Raumer resigned from the government to pursue an academic career, becoming a professor of political science in 1819 in Berlin, where he was also named a member of the censorship commission (*Oberzensurkollegium*).[40] But he remained an outspoken advocate of freedom of speech and religious toleration. Blunt speeches before the king and the Academy of Sciences caused him in 1831 first to resign from the censorship commission and then in 1847 from the Academy of Sciences. Resigning from the Academy made him a popular figure in Berlin: he was elected to the city council in 1847 and later served in the foreign ministry of the Frankfurt Parliament.[41]

Streckfuß was a central figure within the state administration. Although he never acquired Raumer's popularity, he too was esteemed by the public, having been nominated by the council as *Oberbürgermeister* in the midst of the crisis over *Oberbürgermeister* Baerensprung's tenure in office. He was also honored shortly before his death as the twentieth honorary citizen of the city.[42] Born in poverty, a scholarship student, poet, tutor of Italian, and later translator of Tasso and Dante, he had been a member of the Saxon administration when the division of Saxony in 1815 brought him into Prussian service. Due to Streckfuß's close ties

39. Sembdner, *Kleists Lebensspuren*, pp. 354–81; K. Günzel, *Kleist: Ein Lebensbild in Briefen und zeitgenössische Berichten* (Stuttgart, 1985), pp. 334–42.

40. W. Friedrich, "Friedrich von Raumer als Historiker und Politiker" (Ph.D. diss., Leipzig, 1929), pp. 14–17 and throughout; Vogel, *Allgemeine Gewerbefreiheit*, pp. 86–90.

41. F. von Raumer, *Vermischte Schriften*, 3 vols. (Leipzig, 1852–54), vol. 1, pp. 1–24, 36–49, 77–87; and his *Litterarischer Nachlaß*, 2 vols. (Berlin, 1869), vol. 1, p. 1.

42. K. Streckfuß, *Adolf Karl Streckfuß*, Beiträge zur mittelalterlichen, neueren und allgemeinen Geschichte, 16 (Jena, 1941), esp. pp. 24–25, 37–39.

with the Körner family, he was recommended to then minister Wilhelm von Humboldt, who arranged for his entry into the central administration in Merseburg. He gradually was entrusted with all matters connected with the Municipal Law. His Italian translations served as the basis for intellectual contact with the crown prince, who came to act as his patron, eventually elevating him to the council of state (*Staatsrat*) once the prince became king.

There is no autobiographical indication why Raumer wrote his pamphlet, *Über die preußische Städteordnung*, but it clearly summarized the resentments against and efforts at restricting the franchise that had gathered force in the twenty years since the Municipal Law had been introduced. If there is no space to explore his narrow arrogance in detail, we note that his views undoubtedly emerged from that attitude of paternalistic liberalism historians have come to associate with Prussia and Berlin. In Raumer's thought, moreover, there were also aspects of the gentry liberalism observable among the nobility.[43]

Raumer was royalist and antirevolutionary; he was overtly Christian, attacking "the atheistic philosophy of the eighteenth century";[44] he was also decisively neo-corporatist and rejected popular sovereignty, which he referred to as "atomistic," "Rousseauist," and "populist." But in spite of his support of free trade capitalism, he also deplored the "rule of wealth" and sought to establish a new patriciate based on a clerisy of the educated.[45] Such views allowed him to answer his own question – "whether civic freedom grows or does not grow to the extent that more individuals take part in the government; whether it resides more in the constitution or in the administration" – in favor of retrenchment.[46] He stressed, for example, that the collegial Prussian administration was superior to a system of

---

43. Besides Koselleck, *Preußen zwischen Reform und Revolution*, pp. 398–415, 564–75, and Vogel, *Allgemeine Gewerbefreiheit*, 97–132, see Vogel's recent reflections, "Beamtenliberalismus in der Napoleonischen Ära," in Langewiesche, ed., *Liberalismus im 19. Jahrhundert*, pp. 45–54; and R. Vierhaus, "Liberalismus, Beamtenstand und konstitutionelles System," in Schieder, ed., *Liberalismus in der Gesellschaft des deutschen Vormärz*, pp. 39–54. H. Obenaus, "Gutsbesitzerliberalismus: Zur regionalen Sonderentwicklung der liberalen Partei in Ost- und Westpreußen während des Vormärz," *Geschichte und Gesellschaft* 14 (1988): 304–28.

44. Raumer, *Über die preußische Städteordnung*, p. 10.

45. Ibid., pp. 7 and 54 respectively.

46. Ibid., pp. 2–3.

unrestricted communal participation.[47] Raumer committed himself, as a result, to an overtly discriminatory political system, arguing that popular sovereignty was incommensurate with monarchy.[48] Consequently he sought to strengthen the powers of the magistracy with respect to the council; he recommended restricting the franchise by raising wealth requirements, establishing a two-tiered system of passive and active electors, and changing the pattern of voting by district to one of voting by corporation, so that the power of the educated could come to predominate. "We should persuade ourselves that officials, clergymen, professors, schoolteachers, etc., those who are at present completely cast aside or have isolated and ineffective positions, should be united in corporations and engaged in activities for the good of the whole."[49] These views were plainly in line with that form of administrative liberalism that had emerged in the Restoration. It is not without justification, moreover, that Raumer was accused of being linked to the French ultras.[50]

Karl Streckfuß defended the Municipal Law in the rationalist language of the administrative liberal, but in such a way that it could be accepted by a "strict royalist."[51] In his view royalism was not opposed to civic freedom. "No one can doubt," he wrote, "that the throne is safest and most secure when it rests on the contentment of its subjects. . . . The contentment of a people, however, only proceeds from civic freedom – from that freedom in which each can move in independence within his circle of activity, unencumbered by the barriers of the law and secure from the effects of arbitrary rule."[52] For these reasons he rejected Raumer's neo-corporatist arguments for elections by guilds and defended the fundamental right of the council to oversee the magistracy.[53] Still Streckfuß came to accept Raumer's basic demand to restrict the electorate by raising

47. Ibid., pp. 13–15.
48. Ibid., p. 57.
49. Ibid., p. 53.
50. W. Perschke, *Versuch einer Metakritik der Kritik der Herrn von Raumer, Streckfuß, Horn, Wehnert und Theil über die preußische Städteordnung als Commentar zu dem Gesetze* (Leipzig, 1829), p. 17.
51. Streckfuß, *Über die preußische Städteordnung*, p. 20.
52. Ibid., p. 21.
53. Ibid., pp. 63–65 and 75 and 95, respectively.

property requirements and dividing the citizenry into active and passive parts.[54]

The debate between the two Berliners produced numerous responses whose individual views fall outside the scope of this essay.[55] It is striking, however, that Freiherr vom Stein closely followed the debate, seeking to use his connections and influence to orchestrate the revisions of 1831 in his own restrictive manner. From the correspondence we know that Raumer, Streckfuß, and the councillor Carl Knoblauch wrote and visited him. `We also know that Raumer and Knoblauch shared his more conservative reform ideas. Furthermore, the responses from the Rhineland (Freiherr von Ulmenstein) and Silesia (Wilhelm Perschke) were far more progressive defenses of the Municipal Law. Freiherr von Ulmenstein, royal Prussian state councillor in Düsseldorf, directly rejected the "oligarchical" tendencies of the Berliners, stressing instead that citizenship should be expanded into state citizenship.[56] Last, we can see that the debate between Raumer and Streckfuß dealt with the problem of forming a new restricted elite. Raumer used the language of corporatism to constitute a new patriciate influenced by an educated meritocracy. Streckfuß, on the other hand, sought to establish a more open elite based on wealth and interest. In both cases, however, we witness their effort to exclude the lesser class of burghers (*Kleinbürgertum*) and resist the growing democratic pressures from below.

The Evolution of a Noninstitutional Liberal Opposition

If we pause to consider the significance of the political restraints on communal political life and liberal politics in Berlin, we can

---

54. Ibid., pp. 50 and 53–54.

55. Of the many responses from non-Berliners, the most significant are Perschke, *Versuch einer Metakritik*; and H.C. Freiherr von Ulmenstein, *Die preußische Städteordnung und die französische Communalordnung mit Rücksicht auf die Schriften des Herrn Professors von Raumer und des Herrn Geheimen-Ober-Regierungsraths Streckfuß* (Berlin, 1829). The debate can also be followed in the correspondence between the Freiherr vom Stein and the city councillor C. Knoblauch. On this entire problem see Clausewitz, *Städteordnung von 1808*, pp. 145–47; Knoblauch, "175 Jahre Knoblauchsches Haus," no. 52, pp. 67–70; Freiherr vom Stein, *Briefe und amtliche Schriften*, vol. 7, pp. 260–62, 538–45.

56. Freiherr von Ulmenstein, *Die preußische Städteordnung*, pp. 76–77, 95, and 133–42.

begin by questioning the extent to which liberal aspirations were different in Berlin than elsewhere. Liberal values developed in the first half of the nineteenth century as part of an alternative view of life and thus as part of a larger pattern of opposition and secular nonconformity. Liberals sought to establish a constitutional life, reshape the economy, and reformulate the cultural traditions in their own image. But under conditions as they existed in the capital, where political repression was particularly intense, the liberal movement unfolded without ready access to the political instruments and without the ability to develop into a mass movement. This situation was surely not unique to the Prussian capital, though the intensity of the political repression may have been. Political repression allowed the traditions of bureaucratic reform to dominate and largely prevented full articulation of the implicit cultural code. In this environment, then, liberals did not develop clear ideological divisions or overt political habits. Rhetorically simplified, we can say that Berlin produced social institutions requisite for a liberal culture, and it produced individual liberal spokesmen; but until the 1840s that city revealed only the most muted of liberal politics. This separation between a liberal culture and a liberal politics became characteristic of the form assumed by liberalism within the Prussian domains. It was based on accepting a division between the institutions of civil society and those of the state, with the consequent internalization by the population of traditions of paternalistic domination. This pattern led Fritz Stern and others to speak generally of German "illiberalism" and then to describe illiberalism as a particular cultural pathology. The term, however, does not allow us to explore the range of commitment to inegalitarian *v*alues within the liberal value system itself, nor does it permit us to discern the concrete institutional mechanisms and modes by which such values were internalized and reproduced.[57] In this sense we must reconsider Gabriel Motzkin's global claim that, in order to establish itself in nation-states with highly centralized bureaucracies, liberal or democratic society must produce a sharp polarization in worldviews.[58] Liberal

---

57. See F. Stern, *The Politics of Cultural Despair: A Study in the Rise of the Germanic Ideology* (Berkeley, 1974). See also K.H. Jarausch, "Illiberalism and Beyond: German History in Search of a Paradigm," *Journal of Modern History* 55 (1983): 268–84.

58. G. Motzkin, "Säkularisierung, Bürgertum und Intellektuelle in Frankreich

culture was layered and self-contradictory, as was the Enlightenment movement from which it largely emerged; it did establish itself in resistance and opposition, but not in every arena. In Berlin liberalism flourished especially in the city's associational, religious, and cultural life, but not in its political institutions. Yet the voluntary associations, unlike the parish church or an open parliamentary life, continued to appeal to specific groupings and encouraged social and cultural segmentation.

The restrictive nature of the communal political system meant that the extraparliamentary liberal culture developed only slowly and under great pressure from the state. We need to place before us the heritage of a flowering Enlightenment culture that gradually lost its intellectual élan and social coherence. The political persecution of opponents in the Restoration, the so-called *Demagogenverfolgung,* cut far deeper into civic life than we often assume, for not only did figures of the fraternity and gymnastics movement face dismissal and imprisonment but so too did administrators, doctors, teachers, publishers, and clergymen.[59] The newly formed university was especially affected until the mid-1820s, when a truce was finally declared.[60] Besides the dismissal of the professor of theology Wilhelm De Wette (1780–1849) and the continuing stress placed on Friedrich Schleiermacher (1768–1834), other, minor figures such as Leopold von Henning (1797–1866), Hegel's teaching assistant, were persecuted. Henning's was a typical case, since he was imprisoned for ten weeks without charges ever being filed or an apology given. As a result, only a few liberal voices were heard in the university within these years. In the 1830s, for instance, Eduard Gans (1797–1839) held public lectures on European history from 1789 that were attended by hundreds of listeners. Although Minister Altenstein protected Gans, he nevertheless forced Gans to end public lectures that defended Enlightenment reform traditions. Gans then turned to lecturing on the Prussian

---

und Deutschland während des 19. Jahrhunderts," in Kocka, ed., *Bürgertum im 19. Jahrhundert,* vol. 3, p. 142.

59. On this problem see the excellent recent essay by K. Kettig, "Demagogenverfolgung in Berlin im Jahre 1819," *Der Bär von Berlin* 37 (1988): 7–57.

60. M. Lenz, *Geschichte der Königlich Friedrich-Wilhelms-Universität zu Berlin,* vol. 2, pt. 1 (Halle, 1890), pp. 34–176, 184.

legal code in order to continue exploring links between politics and the law.[61]

Until very late in the pre-1848 period, therefore, we can observe various acts of accommodation and resistance in the extrainstitutional political life of Berlin, but we cannot describe a coherent political movement. The revolutions of 1830, while altering perceptions in Berlin, do not appear to have quickened the tempo of political life substantially, as they did elsewhere in Germany.[62] The death of Friedrich Wilhelm II, however, marked the more substantial break with the Restoration. Heinrich Kochhann noted in his diaries that the city council began to be filled with a new generation of liberal activists around 1840; a new "citizens' association" was founded, although it was soon forbidden to discuss political issues. The council meetings were eventually opened to public scrutiny.[63] Political gatherings like the one celebrating the visit of Professor Welcker in 1841 reveal a new capacity to organize protest within Berlin, but political organizing was carried out by a left Hegelian opposition that began to differentiate itself from the liberal movement.[64] Indeed, the visit of Professor Welcker was a turning point in the growing split between a left liberal democratic vision and the inegalitarian liberalism of the reform bureaucracy. For a brief moment in the early 1840s the young Hegelian intellectuals in Berlin began to form alliances with the working-class movement in the city and to lead political opinion outside Berlin.[65] Such views, as we know, were sharply attacked and met with the loss of academic positions and exile. If political life became somewhat more fluid in the 1840s, it was still the case that the pattern of repression prevailed in Berlin until revolution broke out in March 1848.

61. Ibid., pp. 495–97; H.G. Reissner, *Eduard Gans: Ein Leben im Vormärz,* Schriftenreihe wissenschaftlicher Abhandlungen des Leo Baeck Instituts, vol. 14 (Tübingen, 1965), pp. 131–38.

62. W. Schmidt, "1830: Zäsur in der deutschen Geschichte und Beginn einer neuen Etappe in der Entwicklung der revolutionären Demokratie," *Zeitschrift für Geschichtswissenschaft* 34 (1986): 992–1013.

63. Kochhann, *Tagebücher,* vol. 3, pp. 36–40; Kettig, "Gemeinsinn und Mitverantwortung," pp. 18–20.

64. Hirsch, "Die Berliner Welcker-Kundgebung: Zur Fruhgeschichte der Volksdemonstrationen," *Archiv für Sozialgeschichte* 1 (1961): 27–43.

65. G. Mayer, "Die Anfänge des politischen Radikalismus im vormärzlichen Preußen," *Zeitschrift für Politik* 6 (1913): 1–113; idem, "Die Junghegelianer und der preußische Staat," *Historische Zeitschrift* 121 (1920): 413–40; J. Toews, *Hegelianism: The Path toward Dialectical Humanism, 1805–1841* (New York, 1980), pp. 362–66; Eßbach, *Junghegelianer,* pp. 183–204, 206–8, 210–12.

5

Arms and the People

The Bürgerwehr *of Lower Franconia in 1848 and 1849*

James F. Harris

The following essay is informed by the profound changes that have occurred and are occurring in historical writing on Germany in the past generation. Many recent analysts of modern Germany have turned from political and institutional to social history, in the process adopting many of the techniques of the social sciences.[1] The results have been impressive, but the practitioners have themselves been subjected to criticism founded on two quite different points.[2] The first is that social historians have not fully uncovered the social base of society because of their overemphasis on elites, one predicated on the assumption that self-interest, while not unique to the upper and upper-middle classes, possessed more power at those levels to mold society and the state.[3] The second argues that the theoretical

---

1. Historians are currently bombarded by articles on German historiography. G. Iggers, *New Directions in European Historiography*, rev. ed. (Middletown, Conn., 1984), describes the turn to social history, but precedes recent stages of the debate. For the latter see R.J. Evans, "The New Nationalism and the Old History: Perspectives on the West German *Historikerstreit*," *Journal of Modern History* 59, no. 4 (December 1987): 760–97. Also see K.D. Barkin's "From Uniformity to Pluralism: German Historical Writing since World War I," *German Life and Letters* 34 (1980–81): 234–47, and the excellent analysis by K.H. Jarausch, "Removing the Nazi Stain? The Quarrel of the German Historians," *German Studies Review* 11, no. 2 (May 1988): 285–301.
2. First stated in D. Blackbourn and G. Eley, *The Peculiarities of German History: Bourgeois Society and Politics in Nineteenth-Century Germany* (Oxford and New York, 1984), an expanded version of their *Mythen deutscher Geschichtsschreibung: Die gescheiterte bürgerliche Revolution von 1848* (Frankfurt a.M., 1980), a far more suggestive title. Also see G. Eley, *From Unification to Nazism: Reinterpreting the German Past* (Boston, 1986) and D. Blackbourn, *Populists and Patricians: Essays in Modern German History* (Boston, 1987), for a closer examination of both authors' ideas.
3. The best example is J. Kocka, *Facing Total War: German Society, 1914–1918*

James F. Harris

assumptions about both political movements and social classes are too simplistic.[4] This latter charge hinges largely on the claim that current research has revealed that all classes, certainly the middle and lower, are far more complex and internally divided than previously thought.[5] An even more basic criticism of social history has been that it has ignored politics in concentrating on the specifics of the daily life of common people at home or in the work force.[6]

Analysis of the *Bürgerwehr* or civil militias of Lower Franconia provides the historian with more than merely an interesting story because it engages several major themes in German history: the relationship of the middle class to liberalism and the revolution of 1848, the "revolutionary" nature of that revolution, the related question of the apolitical nature of the German people, and the linkage of social structure with political action. In this regard, the specificity of the experience of the civil militias in northern Bavaria determines the extent to which all these themes may be illuminated. A major assumption in this latter approach is that such analysis must focus on the grass roots, in this case the rural communities (*Landgemeinden*) of Lower Franconia.

One of the most important issues in the history of nineteenth-century political development is the role of the middle class. It is now clear that the middle class was far more complex than historians originally thought. Members of the *Bürgerwehr* were drawn largely from the "old" middle class of craftsmen, small-shop owners and dealers, lower-level officials, and small landowners. The following essay will describe the political role of the civil militias of northern Bavaria during the 1848 revolution in terms of both their social composition and their political

(Cambridge, Mass., 1984), pp. 5–10 and 171–76, but esp. 164ff., where the author details the failure of his model. More generally see H.-U. Wehler, *The German Empire, 1871–1918* (Leamington Spa, 1985).

4. This is true both of the argument that German history should not be written only with an Anglo-French model in mind, as well as the more specific assertion that many historians have not got their facts straight – see M.L. Anderson and K.D. Barkin, "The Myth of the Puttkamer Purge and the Reality of the *Kulturkampf*," *Journal of Modern History* 54, no. 4 (December 1982): 647–86.

5. J. Kocka, ed., *Bürger und Bürgerlichkeit im 19. Jahrhundert* (Göttingen, 1987), esp. the editor's own "Bürgertum und Bürgerlichkeit als Probleme der deutschen Geschichte vom späten 18. zum frühen 20. Jahrhundert," pp. 21–63.

6. See G. Himmelfarb, *The New History and the Old* (Cambridge, Mass., 1987), pp. 13f.

goals and activities. It will show that this segment of the middle class, one that was very large and probably predominant in Bavaria, was anything but passive in *both* 1848 and 1849, but that it is difficult to use terms such as "liberal" to describe it. As will become apparent, the civil militias were important forms of political mobilization because of their obvious relation to military force in the midst of revolution.

The need for military weapons in a revolution would seem to be a given, but such was not the case in Germany in 1848. Revolutionary leaders succeeded in their demands for an end to censorship, the approval of freedoms of speech, assembly, and political organization, as well as an agreement by the governments involved to share power with popularly elected representative bodies, *before* any significant amount of force was used. The pressure actually employed to secure these concessions took the form of assemblies, demonstrations, and crowds. Moreover, responsibility for much of what little physical violence did occur was governmental, even if the monarchs quickly gave in to popular pressure and decided not to contest the issue with the crowds by force. In Thomas Nipperdey's pithy description: "It is astonishing how quickly and completely the old powers capitulated; they gave up without firm resistance; . . . None of the monarchs considered counterrevolution, although monarchy remained a potential counterrevolution."[7]

It was just as well that German revolutionaries did not need either weapons or an organized military force in order to produce a German "Glorious Revolution," as they possessed neither. In Unterfranken (Lower Franconia), one of seven Bavarian provinces east of the Rhine,[8] records show the virtual nonexistence of firearms in the general population. Early reports

---

7. Popular violence in southwest Germany had little effect on the revolution; in Berlin ca. 250 people died following a decision by the *military* to disperse a loud, but not violent, crowd. The best short description is in T. Nipperdey, *Deutsche Geschichte, 1800–1866: Bürgerwelt und starker Staat* (Munich, 1984), pp. 598–99, 602, and 604–5. P. Reichensperger, *Erlebnisse eines alten Parlamentariers im Revolutionsjahre 1848* (Berlin, 1882), pp. 57–58, saw the Berlin *Bürgerwehr*, with twenty-five thousand weapons distributed indiscriminately and with elected officers, as a danger to the republic. So also R. Gneist, *Berliner Zustände: Politische Skizzen aus der Zeit vom 18. März 1848 bis 18. März 1849* (Berlin, 1849), pp. 22–23.

8. Only the Pfalz lay west of the Rhine; although Bavarian, it was administered under a very different set of laws and had a politically more radical population. See M. Spindler, ed., *Handbuch der bayerischen Geschichte*, vol. 4: *Das neue Bayern* (Munich, 1975), pp. 62ff.

noted the absence of weaponry, as for example in the *Landgericht*[9] (district) of Hammelburg where 1,431 men in twenty-one *Gemeinden* (communities or municipalities) enrolled in militias, although none possessed so much as a single gun.[10] As late as September 1848, a report to Munich in the form of a table containing data on all known militias in Lower Franconia listed several whole districts without guns. Yet the government had already made 4,500 flint-lock muskets available to a portion of the 23,000 men who had enrolled in the various militias. Many of the reporting officials described the units in their districts as "unarmed" – or, more poignantly, armed with "agricultural implements" and with sticks and clubs. To the north in Neustadt am Saale the district director reported some guns in Neustadt itself, apparently obtained from the state, but added that the remaining twenty-two communities would "in the event of need be equipped with straightened scythes attached to shafts," the rural reversal in 1848 of "beating swords into ploughshares." These reports themselves are the best testimony to the lack of weapons in Bavaria; the communities and militias requested weapons because they had none.[11] In a revolution that is commonly described as failing because it lacked weapons and military structure,[12] this early and apparently easy acquisi-

---

9. The lowest level of the central state structure, headed by a *Landrichter* (district director).

10. "Abgabe von Waffen, Munition u. Bildung von Sicherheitswachen. Aemter Berichte. Jg. 1848," 17 May 1848, Regierungs-Abgabe 1943/45, Bayerisches Staatsarchiv, Würzburg (hereafter BStaAW), Faszikel 1781. Further citation will give document, date, archival designation, and Faszikel no.

11. See "Die im Jahre 1848 in Folge politischer stattgehabter Störung der öffentlichen Ruhe und Sicherheit und die desfalls ergriffenen Maßregeln für Abgabe von Waffen, Munition u. Bildung von Sicherheitswachen, etc., März bis August 1848," and "Übersicht sämmtlicher im Regierungsbezirk von *Unterfranken und Aschaffenburg* gebildeten Sicherheitswachen und freiwilligen Landwehrkorps," listing all communities possessing such corps, total enrollment, and number and type of weapons, both in BStaAW, 1777. The latter, although dated 4 September 1848 on the cover, includes a note on the last page reading "finished 20 July 1848," indicating an even earlier completion date.

12. This is implicit in classic treatments like T. Hamerow, *Restoration, Revolution, Reaction: Economics and Politics in Germany, 1815–1871* (Princeton, N.J., 1958), esp. pp. 116–18 and 192–93; what is universally noted is the failure or unwillingness of the "revolutionaries" to destroy existing governments. In his *Lebenserinnerungen, 1823–1899* (Stuttgart, 1931), p. 116, the Württemberg liberal Otto Elben wrote that in the homeland of Paul Pfizer, not much thought was given to the question of power, and the common hope was that the National Assembly would solve all problems.

tion of weapons must be understood before we can properly assess the role of the militias in the revolution.[13]

Lists of reforms emanating from popular assemblies in the first days of the March revolution in Bavaria usually included some form of militia or process for arming the people,[14] and the first concrete organization of militias dates from the second and third weeks of March.[15] Agreement by the government in Munich to many of these demands testified to its fear of the crowd. Of course King Ludwig I's position had already been seriously compromised by his dalliance with Lola Montez.[16] Under the dual pressure of intense personal criticism and snowballing political opposition, Ludwig formally abdicated on 20 March in favor of his son Maximilian, who had already agreed to take over on the sixth.[17] Among the freedoms apparently agreed to,

13. Little has been written about the military or quasi-military aspects of the 1848 revolution. P. Sauer's *Revolution und Volksbewaffnung: Die württembergischen Bürgerwehren im 19. Jahrhundert, vor allem während der Revolution von 1848/49* (Ulm, 1976) is an interesting narrative lacking social analysis; so, too, is W. Steinhilber's *Die Heilbronner Bürgerwehren 1848 und 1849 und ihre Beteiligung an der badischen Mai-Revolution des Jahres 1849* (Heilbronn, 1959); but K. Obermann, "Die soziale Zusammensetzung der Bürgerwehr in Köln 1848/49," *Jahrbuch für Wirtschaftsgeschichte* 4 (1970): 141–58, provides data for Cologne. E. Schwalm's *Volksbewaffnung, 1848–1850, in Schleswig-holsteinische Erhebung* (Neumünster, 1961) is limited in social analysis to only a few members' lists. F. Voss, *Bürgerwehr in Neuwied von 1648 bis 1856* (Leipzig, 1969), is thin and disappointing for 1848. C. Nobiling, *Die Berliner Bürgerwehr in den Tagen vom 19ten März bis 7ten April 1849: Ein unfreiwilliger Beitrag zur Geschichte der Märzereignisse* (Berlin, 1852), and O. Rimpler, *Die Berliner Bürgerwehr im Jahre 1848 von ihrer Organisation am 19. März bis zu ihrer Auflösung am 11. November: Aus den hinterlassenen Papieren des Commandeurs der Berliner Bürgerwehr* (Brandenburg a.H., 1883), are still useful for Berlin, but lack a social dimension. The anonymous *Das Volk in Waffen im Sinne der Demokratie: Ein Bild aus den Märztagen* (Berlin, 1887) likewise gives more flavor than substance.

14. *Allgemeine Zeitung* (Augsburg) (hereafter *AZ*), no. 63, 3 March 1848, p. 998, dated Ulm, excerpted from the *Karlsruher Zeitung*. For a more complete statement of these hopes and demands, see F. Welfauh, *was erwartet das Volk, was erwartet Deutschland von Bayerns Ständen?* (Munich, 1848), a printed list of goals, clearly from spring 1848.

15. *AZ*, no. 69, 9 March, dated 7 March 1848, noting formation of student companies; and Munich, dated 8 March 1848, stating that sixteen companies had drilled.

16. See the still useful description in M. Doeberl, *Entwicklungsgeschichte Bayerns*, 3 vols. (Munich, 1931), vol. 3, edited by M. Spindler, pp. 135–42.

17. Ibid., pp. 144–45. D. Langewiesche, "Die politische Vereinsbewegung in Würzburg und in Unterfranken in den Revolutionsjahren 1848/49," *Jahrbuch für fränkische Landesforschung* 37 (1977): 200, who writes that Ludwig's decisions on the 6th made a liberal or even moderate-democratic revolution in Bavaria "superfluous."

however reluctantly, by the retiring monarch was the right to form security defense forces. In fact the students at the University of Munich seem to have been the first to ask permission to establish such an organization. The same occurred at the University of Würzburg, in the capital of Lower Franconia, sometime before 15 March. Thus the provincial governor of Lower Franconia reported the formation of a security force (*Sicherheitswehr*)[18] by the students "as has occurred in other university cities," warning that this preempted the formation of a more trustworthy and reliable citizen security force and requesting release of arms by the war ministry in order to prevent the growth of bad feeling.[19]

Soon students and citizens formed self-defense units under a wide variety of names throughout Bavaria and then promptly asked the state for arms. On 19 March the governor of Lower Franconia reacted by informing all lower offices that while "very many" requests had been received, the government in Würzburg had no weapons available. If danger threatened, he urged the organizations to arm themselves as best they could, perhaps by arranging directly with established *Landwehr*[20] units for the use of their surplus weapons.[21] The central government also exhibited caution, making nonmilitary offices responsible for all weapons distributed by arsenals unless given prior approval by the regular military commanders. Military offices were to supply guns directly to approved volunteer *Landwehr* units only in pressing cases where a clear and present danger existed.[22]

The first decree related to the *Bürgerwehr* under King Maximi-

18. Names varied, but the most common were: *Freiwillige Landwehr, Sicherheitswache (wehr), Stadtwehr, Volkswehr,* and *Bürgerwehr.* All are translated as "militia." *Regierungs-Präsident* is best translated as "governor."

19. Governor (gov.) of Lower Franconia (LF) to the Ministry of the Interior (MInn) in Munich, Würzburg, 19 March 1848, BStAW, 1777.

20. The *Landwehr* was an older structure within the jurisdiction of the War Ministry; it was under its own commander and by 1848 acted as a peace-keeping force. P.E. Rattelmüller, *Das bayerische Bürgermilitär* (Munich, 1969), is really a description of the *Landwehr*; pp. 31–35 provide a list of the several hundred *Landwehr* units as of 1809! Maximilian became commanding general of the *Landwehr* on 19 March 1848, the day before he became king. Also see W. Kopp, *Würzburger Wehr: Eine Chronik zur Wehrgeschichte Würzburgs* in *Mainfränkische Studien* 22 (1979), on the local *Landwehr* and the elements of the regular army in Würzburg.

21. 19 March 1848, BStAW, 1777.

22. 20 March 1848, ibid.

lian II's signature – and perhaps the most important in the history of the Bavarian civil militias in 1848 – came on 7 April.[23] This decree granted sons of citizens who had reached their legal majority and other inhabitants of a reliable character the right to join volunteer *Landwehr* units under elected officers if such units were approved by the local provincial governor and the regular *Landwehr* commander in accordance with the exclusionary clause of the *Landwehr* statutes. Delivery of weapons, at least infantry flintlock muskets, sabers, and cartridge pouches, would be made by state arsenals to approved militias against guarantee of the quick and undamaged return of the equipment. Most of the restrictive clauses of the earlier directives of 19 and 20 March were thereby nullified, and, as the governor immediately published the full text of Maximilian's more permissive decree in the local governmental *Intelligenz Blätter*, all of Lower Franconia soon realized that they were now permitted to form militias. Moreover, since this information appeared in an official publication, self-defense seemed to be encouraged by the state.[24]

In line with this policy change, the Ministry of the Interior for Church and Educational Affairs[25] notified the senate of the University of Würzburg that students could now have a volunteer *Landwehr* for the purpose of maintaining order and, provided they subordinated their unit to the regular *Landwehr*, would shortly receive weapons.[26] Reluctantly, the *Landwehr* commander of Lower Franconia notified the governor of the decree of 7 April, making sure he understood that the regular *Landwehr* would always share control of the new units.[27] In little more than a month from the first glimmerings of protest, weapons had been acquired from a reluctant government.

The demand for weapons was so great and so immediate that the state acted to keep track of a process that was getting out of hand by requiring, on 15 April and 4 May, all local offices to

23. MInn to the gov. of LF, Munich, 7 April 1848, ibid.
24. Gov.'s draft letter conveying this information to the *Intelligenz Blätter*, Würz., 15 April 1848, ibid.
25. Bavaria had two ministries of the interior, one of which dealt specifically with "Church and Education"; unless otherwise stated, reference here is to the unmodified Ministry of the Interior.
26. MInn for Church and Education to gov. of LF, Munich, 12 April 1848, BStAW, 1777.
27. Würzburg, 13 April, ibid.

report on the establishment of militias and, most important, to provide data on their strength both in manpower and weaponry.[28] By 3 May the state knew that at least 22,025 guns had already been distributed. Consequently the War Ministry decided to limit to 6,000 the number of weapons available to each of the provinces, except for Oberbayern and Schwaben-Neuburg, which were allotted 8,000 each. State planners appear to have assumed that demand would continue and exceed these limits. To cushion the expected negative response to this move, the provinces were told that they could borrow the unused portion of another province's quota; moreover, exceptions to these limits could be made if needed.[29]

Governmental motivation behind this disbursement is still not entirely clear, but certainly the state responded to outside pressure and neither took the initiative nor *deliberately* encouraged the spread of militias. There is no compelling evidence that the state ever trusted or relied on the militias. At all times the government tried to control them, most notably by putting them under the jurisdiction of the *Landwehr* and regular army or, more subtly, by requiring local communities to guarantee the return of the weapons under pain of financial cost of replacement. With the sole exception of student groups, the state dealt only with communities and not with individuals or political groups. As the arsenals were scattered throughout the state and distributed weapons at the behest of regional or local authorities, the state did not know who had those weapons or even how many had been disbursed.

But the goals of the militias were also not entirely clear. One of few sources for the study of their intentions is their statutes.[30]

---

28. MInn to all provinces, Munich, 15 April and 4 May, ibid. Such information gathering was a hallmark of Maximilian's reign. See L. Lenk, "Revolutionär-Kommunistische Umtriebe im Königreich Bayern: Ein Beitrag zur Entwicklung von Staat und Gesellschaft, 1848–1864," *Zeitschrift für bayerische Landesgeschichte* 28 (1965): 555–622.

29. MInn to Gov. of LF, Munich, 13 May 1848, BStAW, 1777. The guns distributed by 3 May were provided as follows, by province: Oberbayern (2,492), Niederbayern (no report), Pfalz (6,491), Oberpfalz and Regensburg (409), Oberfranken (400), Mittelfranken (3,236), Unterfranken and Aschaffenburg (1,452), and Schwaben-Neuburg (7,545). As guns were undoubtedly distributed in Niederbayern as well, the total should probably be much higher.

30. Unfortunately, fewer of these have survived in the records. Some, e.g., Würzburg, printed their statutes, which were then copied or adapted by other communities.

With little variation all militias prescribed the type of uniform to be worn, defined eligibility so as to exclude the unreliable, provided for the election of officers, and laid down rules for drilling with weapons and for the calling of the troops to action. A few examples give a sharper picture of these organizational rules. All units defined the forces as locally defensive in nature, even while proclaiming their loyalty to the fatherland.[31] But in Neustadt am Saale the members wished to be called on only in serious cases where the regular force was insufficient; the district director commented that, understandably, members did not wish to be used as special police in beer riots.[32] Schönau's statutes specifically stated that the troop was to be used chiefly within the municipality.[33] The men of Hilders went a bit further, telling the government that all signatories had agreed "at any time to devote themselves to the service of the fatherland, should an enemy troop approach our border."[34] In rural Seilert the mayor produced a notice accompanying the brief statutes and headed Neighbors![35] It read: "It is well known to all of you that all of Europe, all of Germany, is shaken, aroused. Danger threatens from all sides – disorder and bad thinking is to be found in all directions. It is, therefore, above all necessary that we stick together – ; that *everyone* thereby strive to suppress any disorder, so as to obtain the goal that is only achievable through quiet and order!"[36]

Communities treated eligibility in varying ways. In Seilert the statutes did not mention restrictions, while others, as in Neustadt am Main, echoed the directive of 7 April nearly verbatim. In Schönau all men and boys over eighteen with no criminal record were acceptable. But the membership lists rarely show the appearance of members of bad character, as for example in Neustadt am Main where two men were described as immoral for having caused pregnancies out of wedlock and for breaking

---

31. The symbols of fatherland, e.g., in Schweinfurt, were mixed: black-red-gold was combined with blue-white.
32. District Director Welsch to gov. of LF, Neustadt am Saale, 23 July 1848, BStAW, 1778 (same Faszikel title as 1777).
33. N.d., probably April 1848, BStAW, 1781.
34. Hilders, early on 28 April 1848, ibid., 1777.
35. "Neighbor" here probably meant "local citizen"; see K.-S. Kramer, *Die Nachbarschaft als bäuerliche Gemeinschaft: Ein Beitrag zur rechtlichen Volkskunde mit besonderer Berücksichtigung Bayerns* (Munich-Pasing, 1954), esp pp. 12–17.
36. Seilert, 21 April 1848, BStAW, 1778.

windows in the school.[37] Some lists had a column for good character, *Leumund*, but as the result of prior screening it was nearly always marked "good." For organizations trying to pry guns out of hesitant state armories, it made little sense to submit lists that contained ne'er-do-wells.

Uniforms also varied greatly, a few units dictating complex directions in this regard. Cost of the uniforms was sometimes born by the communities, sometimes by the individual members, but only one community asked its members to pay for their arms, which were much costlier. In this sense, the militias do not seem to have constituted an exclusive class structure in rural Bavaria, at least not at the rank-and-file level. In addition, jurisdiction was seldom a problem from the communal standpoint, as nearly all were quite willing to act under *Landwehr* orders. Most statutes required drill with weapons on pain of a fine, but such exercises were to be held "within the community" and on Sundays or holidays or "when it would not interfere with work."

Descriptions of the organization, dress, and social activities of the *Bürgerwehr* tend, unfortunately, to trivialize the phenomenon and to distract from the more important fact of the pervasiveness of these institutions. According to governmental records, 23,047 men in Lower Franconia alone had joined self-defense forces by late summer of 1848, even if fewer than one in four possessed a firearm.[38] In a province with a total population of 583,076 representing 130,256 families in 1846,[39] this was a large number and a radical change from the Vormärz. Two hundred ninety-nine separate local militia organizations existed in all but eight of the forty-nine governmental districts in Lower Franconia. The various militias were therefore the single most prevalent product of the revolution, outnumbering all political organizations put together and appearing at an earlier date.[40]

---

37. For Seilert, above, n. 36; Neustadt am Main, 21 April 1848, BStAW, 1778, and 5 May 1848, BStAW, 1781; for Schönau, above, n. 33.

38. "Übersicht," see n. 11 above.

39. "Bevölkerung des Civil-Standes der sämmtlichen Polizeidistrikte in Unterfranken und Aschaffenburg: Nach der Unions-Volkszählung des Monats Dezember 1846", BStAW, Regierung von Unterfranken, Faszikel 1670, aggregated here only at the district level.

40. Langewiesche, "Vereinsbewegung", pp. 195–233 and 213, n. 87, found no membership lists for the 283 political associations, p. 233, reported in the *Politische Wochenschrift* for 8 April and 17 June 1849. The eight districts not

Assuming that all units elected officers, as stated in the 7 April directive and as the statutes unanimously indicate, and that the eligibility requirements were probably more open than in the elections to parliament, it was the *Bürgerwehr* that first introduced political activity to most of Bavaria in 1848. By any standards, these organizations were democratic structurally, if not ideologically, and they were progressive by comparison with the most common form of communal structure in which only heads of families or householders could vote.

Emphasis on the *total* militia enrollment in Lower Franconia obscures what was fundamentally a communal, grass-roots experience. This is what accounts for the enormous variety, not always trivial, in statutes, dress, and eligibility. The *Bürgerwehr* were an expression of local pride and of local rights vis-à-vis the central state. This explains in part the insistence by one community after another that they deserved weapons because they had done all those things that the decree of 7 April listed. Now the state should carry out its side of the implied agreement and deliver the weapons. There is no reason to see these requests, sometimes demands, for weapons as an attack on the state in the sense of rebellion. Rather, this was the locality taking advantage of the situation to assert itself, even at some financial cost! Nor was this an act of counterrevolution. For while nearly all of the communities spoke about threats to "peace and order," there were no reports of any specific acts, uprisings, or even potential upheavals in any of the correspondence relating to requests for arms in early 1848. The documents do not indicate that the communities ever contemplated use of the weapons against their own citizens.

As proof of their right to weapons as well as their need for them, a large number of communities wrote to the provincial government in Würzburg announcing the formation of security organizations and emphasizing their support for "peace and order." Without being asked, nineteen included lists of their enrolled members, seventeen of which provided information on each member's occupation and often on his residence, age, and marital status as well. They did this voluntarily, probably in order to enhance their chances of getting the weapons. Keeping

---

reporting a militia may have possessed one or more and either not reported it or not reported its formation by 20 July (see above, n. 11).

143

Table 1. Distribution of All Reported *Bürgerwehr* Members in Lower Franconia by Occupation (In Numbers and Percentages)

Occupation	No.	Percentage (N = 1,140)
Crafts:		
(Master)	(141)	(12.4)
(Generic)	(324)	(28.4)
(Journeymen)	(79)	(6.9)
(Apprentices)	(4)	(0.4)
Total for crafts	548	48.1
Peasantry	224	19.7
Merchants	58	5.1
Business	23	2.0
Clerks	46	4.0
Higher officials	73	6.4
Lower officials	45	4.0
Workers	108	9.5
Professionals	15	1.3
Total	1,140	100.1[1]
No data & illegible	118	
Unmarried only	116	
Total	1,374	

1. Exceeds 100 percent due to rounding.
Source: All data is from Regierungs-Abgabe 1943/45, 1777, 1778, 1781, BStAW.

in mind that the nearly 1,400 listed members are not a statistically significant sample and were self-selected, it is still worth noting the occupational distribution of those membership lists for Lower Franconia for which there is data. Table 1 provides the numerical and percentage distribution of enrolled members.

Table 2 attempts to compress a great deal of data about the militias in the individual communities into a more easily recognizable format. Column 1 portrays each community's *Bürgerwehr* in terms of the preponderance of a specific occupational category or a mixture of two or more categories expressed in numbers and as a percentage of total militia members (column 4). Column 2 provides data on the unmarried members (again in numbers and as a percentage of column 4), and column 3 presents the average age of each group where data was available. Column 4 gives the total in each defense force and its

Table 2. *Bürgerwehr* Membership: Occupational Predominance,
Marital Status, and Age by Community

Community	Predominant occupations	No. & percentage unmarried	Average age	No. in Militia	No. of Families
Arnstein	Crafts (62%)	10 (36%)	—	28 (9%)	314
Damm	Peas (29%)/Cr (26%) & Workers (35%)	30 (33%)	37.3	92 (21%)	444
Dettelbach	Cr (49%)/Peas (19%)	50 (34%)	—	148 (33%)	450
Dettingen	Peas (75%)	—	37.3	46 (35%)	130
Ebern	Cr (77%)	—	—	137 (59%)	234
Hafenlohr	Cr (86%)	—	29.4	14 (7%)	207
Hilders	Cr (77%)	—	—	50 (25%)	200
Hofheim	Cr (69%)	—	—	102 (50%)	205
Kleinostheim	—	—	—	70 (26%)	270
Mainaschaff.	Peas (32%)/Cr (32%) & Workers (24%)	22 (50%)	30.9	44 (20%)	218
Memmelsdorf	Cr (53%)	—	—	70 (46%)	154
Miltenberg	Cr (44%)/Com (35%)	45 (79%)	30.5	57 (9%)	628
Neustadt a.M.	Workers (70%)	8 (80%)	29.1	10 (5%)	198
Oberbessenbach	Peas (63%)	—	—	48 (30%)	162
Orb	Cr (48%)/Ofc (21%)	104 (43%)	—	244 (34%)	718
Schweinfurt	Com (37%)/Ofc (28%) & Cr (25%)	—	—	183 (11%)	1,695
Seilert	Peas (71%)	29 (36%)	33.5	80 (35%)	229
Wiesentheid	Cr (46%)/Ofc (25%)	18 (28%)	—	65 (30%)	216

1. Data for Arnstein, Dettelbach, Ebern, Hilders, Hofheim, Miltenberg, Orb, Schweinfurt, and Wiesentheid are from the 1852 census; all other data in this column are from the
1858 census, see n. 45 above.

Source: All data are from the lists in Faszikeln nos. 1777, 1778, 1781 in BStAW. Abbrevi-
ations are: Peas = peasant, Cr = crafts, Com = commercial (including here both
Merchant and Business categories), and Ofc = officials (including here both upper
and lower categories). Kleinostheim is included only for total numbers of militia
members.

percentage of column 5, which gives the number of families in
each community as of either 1852 or 1858.

The first and most obvious fact that emerges from this data is
that distribution of militia members' occupations was not uniform in the seventeen reporting communities. Six were predominantly craft-oriented,[41] three were agricultural,[42] one was

41. Apprentices were miniscule in number; journeymen ("Gesellen") were
also relatively few, but nearly 60 percent of the remainder were listed only as
"bakers" or "shoemakers," i.e., not specifically as masters. In the small, rural
towns of Bavaria, a simple generic entry of this sort probably indicated lack of a

145

largely worker,[43] and seven were mixed, but with crafts present in every town. This occupational structure generally mirrored Lower Franconia itself: the province combined numerous small agricultural communities with fewer, but also numerous, craft-dominated towns and villages, the whole spiced only now and again with a small number of trade and commercial[44] centers. In 1852 three-quarters of the people of Lower Franconia were engaged in agriculture as compared to about 19 percent in trade, commerce, and crafts. But this exaggerates the agricultural element and must be modified because 27 percent of the "agricultural" population consisted of rural day laborers, most possessing a house or land, and another 20 percent worked both in agriculture and at a trade or craft.[45]

Nine communities identified men as unmarried in addition to their occupational entry or, in some cases, in place of one. In Dettelbach, for example, all single men were entered on a separate list without any occupational designation at all. In Orb all unmarried militia members (104!) appeared on a separate list, but several were identified either as possessing a trade or as

---

guild structure, and presumably such men possessed a small shop with few or no journeymen or apprentices. See S. Volkov, *The Rise of Popular Antimodernism in Germany: The Urban Master Artisans, 1873–1896* (Princeton, N.J., 1978), pp. 16ff. and 100ff.; Mack Walker, *German Home Towns: Community, State, and General Estate, 1648–1871* (Ithaca and London, 1971), pp. 73–107; and Spindler, ed., *Handbuch* 4, no. 2:799f.

42. Peasants usually appeared as "Bauer" in these lists, but "Häcker" (grape growers) are included. As a group peasants were underrepresented here by comparison to their percentage of the population in 1852.

43. Largely in agriculture, not factory work; Damm was an exception (see above, n. 53).

44. There were fewer merchants and more dealers, e.g., in hops, wine, and cattle.

45. "Bevölkerung des Königreichs Bayern nach Alter und Geschlecht, Familienverhältnissen, Religionsbekenntnissen, Erwerbsarten und Ständen, dann Zahl und Bestimmung der Gebäude, auf Grund der Aufnahme vom Monate Dezember 1852," bound with *Beiträge zur Statistik des Königreichs Bayern* (Munich, 1850). Only the 1858–61 censuses provided data at the communal level. See "Tabelle über die Familien- und Seelenzahl der Civil- und Militärstandsbevölkerung von Unterfranken und Aschaffenburg nach dem Ergebnisse der Unions-Volkszählung vom Monate Dezember 1858," BStAW, Regierung von Unterfranken, Faszikel, 1670, in some cases updated in pencil to 1861. For 1861, see Königliches Statistisches Bureau, ed., *Verzeichnis der Gemeinden des Königreichs Bayern mit ihrer Bevölkerung im Dezember 1861, geordnet nach Kreisen, Verwaltungs-Districten und Gerichtssprengeln, unter Beifügung der einschlägigen Rentämter, Forstämter und Baubehörden* (Munich, 1863). Unfortunately both 1858 and 1861 provide only numbers of families and people without occupational data.

sons of citizens who did. Only a very few actual citizens, whether peasant, craft, commercial, or worker were identified as unmarried, but more than half of all men in Lower Franconia over age fourteen were unmarried.[46] The average age of the unmarried men in the militias for whom there was data was nearly twenty-seven, whereas all men together averaged nearly thirty-four. If militia membership were expressed as a percentage of married couples rather than families it would be much higher.[47] In these militias, older, married men predominated.

The fact that a defense force, even one that met little action, was dominated numerically within the ranks by older, married heads of families is surely significant. As it seems natural to believe that more rather than fewer younger men would volunteer, many young men must have been excluded, probably because they were perceived as less responsible. In this milieu the possibility that they might have been rebels is very small. Exclusion of younger, unmarried men was normal in rural Bavaria before 1848. Many communities limited municipal citizenship to married men. Even the common political practice of signing petitions sent to the king or parliament conformed to this same exclusionary rule. In addition to marriage, possession of an established trade, craft, land, or permanent employment could also be necessary to the acquisition of citizenship status in these traditional municipalities.[48] The high proportion of unmarried men on a few lists explains the government's decree permitting, where needed, the enrollment of citizens' sons and reliable visitors. Had these not been included, eligibility might have been so exclusionary as to encourage disobedience. The point is that such exclusion was normal in this communal society in a way that was not true of cities like Munich, Würzburg, or even Aschaffenburg, and it is unreasonable to

---

46. According to the 1852 census, n. 45 above, 52 percent. Some of those without designation may have been unmarried.

47. In 1852 there were 84,369 married couples compared to 117,301 families; see above, n. 45 . W.R. Lee, *Population Growth, Economic Development, and Social Change in Bavaria, 1750–1850* (New York, 1977), p. 18, shows a population decline in the late eighteenth century and a growth rate slower than much of Germany after 1800.

48. See Walker, *German Home Towns*, pp. 73–77. D. Langewiesche, *Liberalismus und Demokratie in Württemberg zwischen Revolution und Reichsgründung* (Düsseldorf, 1974), p. 173, states that journeymen, factory workers, day laborers, and servants were excluded from the *Bürgerwehr* in more radical Württemberg.

expect that this practice would change overnight because of events in distant Munich, Berlin, or Vienna.

What is impressive in these lists of *Bürgerwehr* members is not the expected predominance of established, older, married citizens from recognized and traditional occupations, but rather the appearance of men from a variety of occupations with lower status, including factory workers, day laborers, and servants. Unlike parts of Saxony, where workers seem to have been deliberately excluded from militias,[49] there is no record of exclusion of any workers as such in Lower Franconia. Of course, neither day laborers nor factory workers became officers, even noncommissioned officers, so far as the records indicate, but there is nothing unusual in that in a still very status-conscious society. Additionally, the large number of Bavarian day laborers owning homes or land (80 percent!) may account for their acceptance as compared to Saxony.[50]

Complete lists of officers exist for five of the communities (Ebern, Hofheim, Memmelsdorf, Schweinfurt, and Würzburg)[51] and provide a limited profile of the elected leadership group. Craftsmen, nearly all of them masters, were important here too, holding a plurality of positions in two organizations (Hofheim, 5 of 13 officers, and Memmelsdorf, 3 of 8) and dominance in Ebern (14 of 18). But in the larger cities of Schweinfurt and Würzburg officials dominated, holding 9 of 13 and 14 of 21 of the leadership posts, respectively. Indeed, there were no craftsmen elected to any officer positions in Würzburg! Peasants were even less successful, holding only two positions in one organization, Memmelsdorf. Commercial and retired military men outnumbered the peasantry in the officer lists, just the opposite of what one might expect from the weight of their numbers among the rank and file. Based on limited data, the leaders of traditional

49. R. Weber, *Die Revolution in Sachsen, 1848/49: Entwicklung und Analyse ihrer Triebkräfte* (Berlin, 1970), p. 126; citing, e.g., the *Vogtländische Anzeiger* for 12 April 1848 that arming was understandable, but only for the "genuine, true people, not a raw class in whose hands the weapons would become murder tools." Obermann, "Soziale Zusammensetzung," esp. pp. 157–58, makes essentially the same point based on more circumstantial evidence in the large city of Cologne.

50. In 1852 (see above, n. 45) 94,392 of 118,592 day laborers owned a house or land.

51. Only the officer lists survive for Würzburg; but, according to the "Übersicht" (see above, n. 11), the total enrollment was quite large, perhaps as many as 1,800, 400 of them students.

society – and they were heavily officials – led the *Bürgerwehr* in Lower Franconia.

But none of this is surprising. In general it reflects what happened at the elections to both the Frankfurt and Bavarian parliaments, where the *Honoratioren* – literally, men with position and reputation – won election.[52] Precisely the same thing happened in the *Bürgerwehr*, varying with the size and type of community. The composition of both the rank-and-file membership as well as the officership of the defense organizations in Lower Franconia roughly reflect the social structure of society and its dominant values. Change may be seen in the appearance of a large group of factory workers in Damm, where they constituted some 25 percent of the membership with identifiable occupations, as well as in the number of clerks (*Kommis*) who accounted for 11 and 21 percent of enrollments in Miltenberg and Schweinfurt, respectively. Nevertheless, society as a whole was nonindustrial and not very modern.[53]

The size of the *Bürgerwehr*, especially when expressed as a percentage of the number of families in 1858, is probably very accurate – if anything it is a bit conservative, as the number of families in 1846 was much lower. This is significant because it was the male heads of family who predominated in the *Bürgerwehr*. Indeed, as a percentage of the heads of family in the age range of twenty to forty years, which was most heavily represented in the militia membership, the actual proportion of militiamen must unquestionably have been higher. It must be noted here that if the militia enrollment figures from September 1848 for the 299 communities with militias are totaled, they constituted about 11 percent of the adult male population and perhaps as much as 27 percent of married citizens. This was a society acting in unison.

Following this description and analysis of the social composition of the *Bürgerwehr*, we must turn our attention to the purpose and use of a quasi-military force of over 23,000 scattered in small units over an area roughly the size of Yellowstone National Park, about 3,200 square miles. By all accounts they were

52. J. Sheehan, *German Liberalism in the Nineteenth Century* (Chicago, 1978), pp. 60ff.; D. Blackbourn, *Class, Religion, and Local Politics in Wilhelmine Germany: The Centre Party in Württemberg before 1914* (New Haven, 1980), pp. 14–15.

53. Spindler, ed., *Handbuch* 4, no. 2:782ff. Damm was very near the larger city of Aschaffenburg and was annexed to it later in the century.

poorly armed (despite the 4,500 government weapons), poorly trained (if at all), and seldom mobilized. The lack of action unquestionably suited most of the members who desired their beloved "peace and order" even, or especially, in the middle of a revolution. It seems clear, although not provable using these documents, that they feared foreign invasion or bloody rebellion by faceless urban masses more than anything else and were quite happy when neither occurred. They wanted to do their duty to the community and even to the fatherland, but they wanted to do it at home. Yet there was little to do there, as they did not perceive public assemblies and the formulation of petitions for or against issues like a bill of rights, the Frankfurt Constitution, or Jewish emancipation as disturbances of "peace and order." Violence to persons or property was what rural Bavarians perceived as a disturbance, and that, for the most part, did not occur.

It is difficult to label these organizations as revolutionary or counterrevolutionary. The militias were willing to suppress threats to "peace and order," but always in the form of concrete attacks on their community. They did not attack revolutionary ideas any more than they promoted them. If we accept the proposition that the *Bürgerwehren* generally reflected their communal environment, then the militias in Lower Franconia did just that – and no more. Elsewhere, in Berlin, Saxony, Schleswig-Holstein, Baden, and Württemberg, where there was at least some revolutionary activity, the *Bürgerwehr* was also proportionately more revolutionary; yet typically the great majority opted for the status quo, whereas only a small minority favored revolutionary change and violence.[54]

To put all of this more directly, there was no revolution in Lower Franconia in 1848 or 1849. There was a series of reforms, most of them requested long before 1848. That these reforms became law or practice nearly overnight in consequence of a great deal of popular pressure and an overly fearful pair of monarchs does not make these changes "revolutionary" in any sense other than that of the rapidity of the change. To the extent

---

54. For instance, L. Radler, *Die Stadt Schweidnitz und die Revolution von 1848* (Hamburg, 1933), pp. 73ff., describing the bloody clash there between *Bürgerwehr* and army that left eleven dead and many wounded. My thanks to Richard Breitman for allowing me to see his manuscript paper on the Berlin *Bürgerwehr*, describing the experience there as less than truly radical.

that they followed all that was happening in the outside world of Munich, Berlin, Vienna, and Frankfurt am Main, the militiamen of Lower Franconia, along with most of their fellows elsewhere, found it relatively easy to accept the reforms. Some reforms helped them and some did not, but only a few were seen as serious threats, and the means used to counter even those were neither military nor paramilitary – they were democratic and employed the political tools of assembly and petition. Although this is not the purpose of this essay, it is possible to trace the expressions of sentiment on major issues within these communities through study of the petition process, an approach that will aid our understanding of political change at the grassroots level of society.[55]

The German revolution of 1848 did fail, but it is not easy to pinpoint the day of the "failure." The military defeat at Rastatt must be seen as only the final blow delivered against those intent on defending the *already* defunct Frankfurt Parliament. Vienna in October 1848, Berlin in November 1848, the refusal of the king of Prussia to accept a crown in spring 1849, and the opposition of states like Prussia and Bavaria to the Frankfurt Constitution in spring 1849 were all serious setbacks to the revolution. Study of the "failure" of 1848 is also made difficult by the lack of agreement on *what* constituted the revolution. In theory the only "revolutionary" regime was that of the archduke John in Frankfurt, but in reality even this regime was hardly revolutionary. Ministries changed in the major capitals, but they were never more than moderately liberal and soon reverted to a conservative coloration. On the other hand, the reformist legislation passed by the various states essentially survived, and even the attempts to modify it in a conservative sense took years. Viewed from this perspective the failure of the revolution was a very gradual and never complete process that lasted well into the 1850s. It may be easier as well as more accurate, at least in describing Lower Franconia, to argue that the revolution was never successful in gaining power and hence never really lost it.

---

55. Thus the irony of the "democratic" opposition to Jewish emancipation in December–January 1849–50. See my article "Public Opinion and the Proposed Emancipation of the Jews in Bavaria in 1848–1850," *Leo Baeck Institute Yearbook* 34 (1989): 67–79. The most common reaction to the *Grundrechte* and the Frankfurt Constitution was also the petition.

So too with the *Bürgerwehr*. In retrospect it is apparent that the government began to respond more negatively to requests from the various corps in the summer of 1848, perhaps influenced by the fear inspired in Germany by the June Days in France. In July 1848 the Bavarian government instructed its officials to forbid the use of special flags for local militia units and noted that there was no need for "complete" arming and equipping of militias, adding that the entire *Landwehr* system was about to be changed in any case and the cost of such outfitting might soon be superfluous – a financial note with appeal to frugal communities.[56] In early 1849 Bavaria began to alter its position on the supply of arms to the militias. This came after a tumultuous autumn in Frankfurt where two conservative delegates were murdered by scythe-wielding mobs, in Vienna where the revolutionaries were crushed by the military, and in Berlin where, in a tense atmosphere, the king moved the parliament to Brandenburg and began the process of modifying the proposed constitution in a conservative direction. In response to an unusually persistent request for arms from two communities, the government in Munich decided that, because of the "increase in the [size] of the army required by conditions," in order to restrict new deliveries of guns as much as possible and "simultaneously to win as much time as possible" the provincial governors in Bavaria were to make it known that the War Ministry was not in a position to promise further delivery of arms.[57] This stopped short of a decree against further distribution of arms, but it was clearly a major step toward such a policy.

In March 1849 the government continued its movement away from support for the *Bürgerwehr*. This occurred just after serious and bitter debate about acceptance of the bill of rights proposed by the National Assembly in Frankfurt am Main, and just before a major crisis over nonacceptance of the Frankfurt Constitution. The government in Munich notified the provincial governors that they should be ready to undertake the task of securing the return of unneeded weapons as units diminished or dissolved.[58]

56. MInn to the Kammer des Innern (branch of MInn in the province) and to the Landwehr Kreis Kommando in LF, Munich, 19 July 1848, BStAW, 1778.
57. MInn, Munich, 25 January 1849, ibid.
58. MInn, Munich, 5 March 1849, and gov. to the lower offices, MInn, 26 March 1849, both in ibid.

In his directive to lower officials the governor referred to "somewhat changed conditions," by which he meant the rapidly growing disquiet among democrats as they realized that the Frankfurt Constitution would not be accepted by the major states. In Bavaria and much of Germany the greatest test of the revolutionary will of both leaders and followers, of both parliamentarians and their electors, occurred in spring 1849 over the nonrecognition of the national constitution. Ultimately this led to a valiant but doomed effort by a complex mixture of participants in Baden to support a rump Frankfurt parliament by military means against the far more powerful and better-trained Prussian troops. The revolutionaries in the states of Baden and Württemberg proved that they could mobilize enough people there to cow the monarchs in about the same fashion as they had in spring 1848. But nationally two major differences existed between the two popular struggles: on the one hand, public opinion in 1849 seems weaker perhaps because it was now divided into two relatively equal and opposed groups; on the other, in 1849 a military arm existed in the form of volunteer corps, some of them *Bürgerwehr* units or parts of those units, which possessed arms. At first no one, revolutionaries included, had any good idea how many people or militias would support the Frankfurt Constitution.

In the final analysis, most of Bavaria proved to be far less radical than Baden, Württemberg, or Saxony. The Bavarian Palatinate on the left bank of the Rhine was the exception and contributed strongly to support for the Frankfurt Constitution and the struggle in Baden. In the remaining seven-eighths of Bavaria east of the Rhine, conditions varied between relative quiet in the older provinces of Upper and Lower Bavaria and serious upset in Franconia and parts of Swabia. In Upper, Middle, and Lower Franconia state officials exhibited great concern and were under no illusions about the popular irritation with the king's decision.[59]

News of Maximilian II's rejection of the Frankfurt Constitution broke on 28 April 1849. The first reaction in Franconia appeared

59. Gov. to the MInn, Munich, Bamberg, 4 May 1849, Bayerisches Hauptstaatsarchiv, Munich [hereafter, BHStA], MInn, Faszikel 45536, "Oberfranken: Unruhen wegen der deutsche Verfassungsfrage," 018–023. Sheets in this file are numbered from 001 on and those numbers are provided following the Faszikel number, as here, 45536, 018–023.

in Bamberg on 29 April in the form of an appeal "To the People of Franconia!"[60] The broadsheet called on all fellow citizens to support the Frankfurt Constitution and "force" the government to recognize it. It argued that no power could resist the spontaneous will of a people and urged people to speak out in assemblies, to choose committees and to empower them to lead the "great movement." A similar piece directed to Middle Franconia, although also printed in Bamberg on the 29 April, addressed itself to "Our Fellow Citizens in the Army" arguing that their loyalty should be to the Frankfurt Constitution and that supporting it would not be a violation of their oath.[61] In Würzburg on 14 May, an elected committee of the *regular Landwehr* publicly addressed their commander, Count von Recliteren-Limpurg, arguing that the *Landwehr* was part of the German people and owed loyalty to the Frankfurt Constitution.[62] From the beginning of the protest against the rejection of the constitution, democrats in Franconia were conscious of the role to be played by the military and quasi-military forces. They were not unique.

The Bavarian government officials in Franconia appear to have never trusted the militias and to have lost whatever faith they had originally had in the *Landwehr*. In Bamberg the state viewed the broadsheet "To the People of Franconia" as "capable of generating treason" and promptly confiscated it.[63] The governor was convinced that the "revolutionary party" in Germany was currently concentrating its efforts on provoking an uprising in Bavaria.[64] Civil as well as military authorities agreed on the probability of an uprising, on the unreliability of the militia and *Landwehr*, and on the need for reinforcement by the regular army.[65] They assumed, as stated in their report of 1 May, "that in any case the democratic party intends to be master of the *Volkswehr* [militias] and thereby to become an armed force." All government officials were concerned with a change in recruitment by the militias tending now toward

60. Ibid., 004.

61. By the Congreß von fränkischen demokratischen Vereinen, ibid., 45538, "Mittelfranken: Unruhen wegen der deutschen Verfassungsfrage," 014.

62. Würzburg, 14 May 1849, ibid., 46038, "Unterfranken und Aschaffenburg: Unruhen wegen der deutschen Verfassungsfrage." Sheets in this file are not numbered.

63. Report of the city commissioner to the gov. of Upper Franconia, 30 April 1849, ibid., 45536, 005–008.

64. Gov. von Stenglein to MInn, Munich, 4 May 1849, ibid., 018–023.

65. Meeting of 1 May 1849, 9 A.M., ibid., 024–026.

the "fringe elements" that had resulted in a corps that had to be seen as "hostile." The petition supporting the Frankfurt Constitution by the *Landwehr* showed, they stated, on which side it would stand in case of a conflict. There had even been talk in the newspapers of uniting the militias and *Landwehr* under a common command.[66] Consequently, the governor began to take steps to have surplus weapons from the militias returned to the arsenals.[67]

Comparing the situation in spring 1849 to the previous year, the governor of Upper Franconia reported that there were now so many democrats in the *Landwehr* "that [one could] not count on the performance of the *Landwehr* as in the prior year's events and that also the *Volkswehr* in its most recent composition and tendency is more for than against the democratic party."[68] In Wunsiedel the district director reported trouble and described the *Landwehr* as one-third solid republican and the militia as providing parades and cheers for the radicals Hecker and Struve.[69] Melchior von Stenglein, the governor, later explained the unreliability of the *Landwehr* in more prosaic terms: most members were agriculturalists, vineyard owners, or field workers and depended for the entire year on the work of the moment – they had no time for other pursuits.[70] Presumably, Stenglein implies, those men would have been more conservative. But, with almost no exceptions, the militias were not nearly so radical in 1849 as they appeared in the fears of state officials.

In both Upper and Lower Franconia the regular military was a vital part of the equation pitting state against people. In Bamberg the authorities uniformly dismissed the militias and *Landwehr* as sources of support even when they did not see them as sources of outright opposition. All discussions of measures for maintaining order concentrated on the availability of regular troops: in the early days they asked for reinforcements, later

66. Meeting of 8 May 1849, 3 P.M. in Bamberg, ibid., 068–073. I have found no evidence to support the state's claim about a change in membership, but it merits study.

67. Meeting of 7 May 1849, 3 P.M., ibid., 074–075.

68. Gov. v. Stenglein to MInn, Bamberg, 22 May 1849, ibid., 118–121. Stenglein did not feel that the situation in Franconia as a whole was as dangerous as thought a month earlier. Also, see report of the city commissioner (Ihl) and the *Bürgermeister* (Glaser), same date to Stenglein, ibid. The reference to the role of the *Landwehr* in the previous year is intriguing, but lacks corroborating evidence.

69. District Director Fürst to v. Stenglein, Wunsiedel, 14 May 1849, ibid., 154.

70. V. Stenglein to MInn, Bamberg, 5 June 1849, ibid., 208–10.

they begged the military to extend their stay.[71] In Upper Franconia the authorities felt it necessary for the troops to be visible throughout the province and not merely in Bamberg. There the requests were partially successful, and, in addition, the governor was able to transfer six hundred men from Bayreuth. It is not clear, and may never be, whether the presence of troops in and around Bamberg was the reason why the province remained calm or whether there really was no serious tendency in that direction regardless of the eagerness of democratic leaders and the fears of state officials.

All of the conditions described in Upper Franconia existed in magnified form in Lower Franconia. Sentiment was more strongly for the Frankfurt Constitution and against the government. As a result, the state officials were more cautious and fearful, and the need of regular troops was perceived to be much greater. In part this stemmed from Lower Franconia's geographic location; not only were events in radical Saxony to be feared as in Upper Franconia, but so too was the radical influence from neighboring Hessen, Württemberg, Baden, and Frankfurt itself.[72] The populace there was more active, as evidenced by incidents in which students seized arms from the university, townspeople clashed with regular army troops, soldiers gave arms to the people, and the regular *Landwehr* challenged its commander over the issue of recognition of the Frankfurt Constitution.[73] Even if none of these

71. Meeting of the five civil and military leaders, v. Stenglein absent, of 30 April 1849, ibid., 005–008, and the meeting of 2 May 1849 at 3 P.M. with v. Stenglein, both in ibid., 027–030 and 005–008. The upsets in Saxony occasioned renewed requests for troops for the Hof area on the Saxon border. See Stenglein to MInn, Bamberg, 5 May 1849, the city commissioner's and *Bürgermeister's* reports, Bamberg, 22 May 1849, requesting troops to stay, 143–46, and Stenglein to MInn, Bamberg, 5 June 1849, 208–10, all in ibid.

72. See, e.g., reports on Aschaffenburg from the gov. of LF (probably Leopold Graf Fugger von Glött) to MInn, Würzburg, 29 April 1849; on Hessen, Saxony, and the Odenwald, 11 May 1849; and on Orb on 28 May 1849, all in ibid., 46038. According to W. Schärl, *Die Zusammensetzung der bayerischen Beamtenschaft von 1806 bis 1918* (Kallmünz, Bavaria, 1955), pp. 197–98, Glott retired in 1849.

73. Ringelmann (MInn) and Forster (MInn, Church and Education), to gov. of LF, 15 May 1849, and the gov. of LF to MInn, Würzburg, 21 May 1849, on the student crisis; commander of the *Landwehr* of LF to the Kammer des Innern in Würzburg, 16 May 1849; gov. of LF to MInn on the problem of soldiers and arms in the Royal II Army Corps, Würzburg, 17 May 1849; and gov. of LF to MInn on the bad feelings and incidents between soldiers and civilians, Würzburg, 20 May 1849, all in BHStA, 46038.

incidents was revolutionary, they appeared as more symptomatic of a movement tending in that direction than in Upper Franconia.

By the testimony of the governor, the man most directly concerned with the maintenance of peace, Lower Franconia differed most because it had been abandoned by the government. From the beginning, the authorities in Lower Franconia saw little use in either the militia or the *Landwehr*[74] and attempted, evidently unsuccessfully, to disarm them in early May.[75] The better-thinking citizens, reported the governor, Count Fugger von Glött, supported recognition of the Frankfurt Constitution as the only way to avoid worse problems; only an "imposing military reinforcement" in the form of regular troops could reverse the situation.[76] On 21 May he stated flatly that the situation looked bleak and that the worst scenario would be a general arming of the people.[77] In Würzburg, both a full battalion of the city watch and the regular *Landwehr* were needed to keep order.[78]

The government in Munich seems to have believed the reports emanating from Würzburg, for it sent instructions on how to prepare for a state of siege there – but no troops.[79] The governor described his position as "embarrassing" because he could not enforce the laws – for example, the confiscation of treasonous publications.[80] As the military was restricted to the citadel, the help needed in Orb and Miltenberg could not be sent. That, in turn, allowed local militias and individuals to exercise with guns and to form *Freischaren*, or guerrilla units. It was, he wrote, the "highest time" for taking energetic measures for the actual disarming of the militias and the dissolution of the *Märzvereine* – a widespread liberal-democratic political association – both of which, to his great concern, had not occurred.[81] Later that same day he took the extraordinary step of writing the following: in the face of great danger to the fatherland, "we see ourselves obligated to lay before your royal majesty again

74. Gov. of LF to MInn, Würzburg, 29 April 1849, ibid.
75. Gov. of LF to all district directors, 10 May 1849, ibid.
76. Gov. of LF to MInn, 11 and 17 May 1849, ibid.
77. Gov. of LF to MInn, 21 May 1849, ibid.
78. Gov. of LF to MInn, 22 May 1849, ibid.
79. MInn (Church and Education) Forster, covering letter to the gov. of LF with these plans, Munich, 26 May, 1849, ibid.
80. Gov. of LF to MInn, Würzburg, 26 May 1849, ibid.
81. Gov. of LF to MInn, Würzburg, 28 May 1849, ibid.

unconditionally the pressing plea from our heart for the final and *rapid* decision about the German constitutional question." Recognizing that it was not his place so to advise the government, he justified his action on the basis of the danger resulting from the scarcity of troops outside of Würzburg at such a key point in time.[82] His pleas for more troops continued on 1 June, but without success.[83] In the end the situation in Lower Franconia remained peaceful because counterrevolutionary action elsewhere succeeded – radical activity could not flourish in a single isolated area for long.

Lack of an uprising in Lower Franconia owed little to the presence of regular army troops, for there were few in the province. But except for a few scattered incidents, there seems to have been no significant sentiment favoring revolution.[84] Petitions that voiced criticism of the government were widespread, but they were merely an expression of opinion in a state where sentiment was nearly evenly divided on the issue. Nevertheless, the government saw all of this as damning the militias. As noted already, the interior ministry officials on the scene did not trust the militias, but neither did the army, as witnessed by the report of an army observation corps sent to Lower Franconia in early June, probably as the result of the reports from the provincial governors of the three Franconian provinces. Luder, the commander, wrote to Theodor von Zwehl, minister of the interior, on 17 June stating that the royal government should never entrust arms to any citizens not in support of the government and certainly not to any opposed to it. Any weapons in the custody of such people should be removed by force.[85] This, it seems clear, was the beginning of the end for both the *Bürgerwehr* and the regular *Landwehr*.

In late June 1849, while resistance in Baden was fizzling out, the Bavarian state ordered the return of those weapons no longer needed for the maintenance of security. In response to questions about which units might continue to possess state arms, the ministry stated that it would "hold the principle in mind that only those [units] that guaranteed full surety that the

82. Same date, separate letter, no time given, ibid.
83. Gov. of LF to MInn, Würzburg, 1 June 1849, ibid.
84. Langewiesche, "Vereinsbewegung," pp. 226–28, demonstrates this point for Lower Franconia conclusively.
85. Luder to v. Zwehl, Munich, 17 June 1849, BHStA, 45536.

weapons would be used to uphold legal order" would be permitted "temporary" possession of them. More ominously, those
who "[thought] they could use force to secure their political
outlook against the will of the state" would be required to return
the weapons. The ministry concluded its instructions to the
governors with the assurance that there would be no difficulty
in carrying out these instructions, as the regular army would
support the officials with any necessary armed might.[86] The
governor in Lower Franconia issued an almost exact copy of this
order to his subordinates, only softening the wording about
enforcement a bit.[87] On 9 January 1850 the *Bürgerwehr* were
finally informed that, because of a "new organization of the
Landwehr," all weapons must be collected. Hence all militias
were to be temporarily suspended. It reassured those who had
supported legal order and who had protected the endangered
legal structure that the government would hasten to their aid if
danger threatened in the future.[88] The message was clear – the
state was again strong, and it, not the locality, would deal with
insurrection. The state asked *all* of the organizations to return
weapons, although it is hard to see more than a few as actively
antigovernmental except in the political sense of opposition
through petition. No community resisted.

Thus the *Bürgerwehr* in Bavaria came to an end by state decree
in the winter of 1850. The role of the militias in Lower Franconia
– and probably in Bavaria and Germany – in 1848 and 1849 does
not comfortably fit our view of "revolution." Citizen militias
were neither revolutionary nor counterrevolutionary. Yet they
were clearly political and even democratic in structure. Moreover, they were not trusted by the state, which was, after all, a
centralized state long at odds with decentralized power structures. Reflecting a very large part of Bavarian society – arguably the
majority outside of a few big cities – the *Bürgerwehr* were an
expression of rural community life. As such, they and their history
belong only tangentially to the history of the revolution of which
they were never an integral part. To be understandable,

86. MInn to provincial governors, Munich, 22 June 1849, BStAW, 1778.

87. Same order as in n. 78 above, "In the Name of the King," Würzburg, 28
June 1849, ibid.

88. Geo. Gus. Hohe, Regierungs-Direktor, Kammer des Innern, to all offices,
9 January 1850, ibid.; later that year Hohe was appointed governor of the Pfalz,
see Schärl, *Zusammensetzung*, p. 201.

their experience should be seen in the context of a communal society that changed only a little in 1848 and whose continued development would be increasingly important much later in the century as "politics" spread downward within the "centralized" state.[89] If we are to understand the local politics of the later period, as David Blackbourn has cogently argued we should,[90] it would be well to begin with its development in this earlier period.

Several conclusions seem warranted. The experience in Lower Franconia calls into question the degree to which the 1848 revolution was genuinely "revolutionary" – either in the more superficial aspect of the use of force or in the more profound sense of substantive change. Many liberals who have been seen as revolutionary probably should be described as much more moderate, in roughly the same way as the *Bürgerwehr* appears – that is, not as the state saw them, as radical, democratic, revolutionary, and undependable, but as they really were – desirous of "peace and order."[91] It must be emphasized that the militias appear to be definitely dominated numerically by peasants and rural craftsmen and were generally considered conservative and politically apathetic; yet they were active without being either revolutionary or liberal in any normal use of those terms. Middle-class and liberal were not synonymous. The rural folk of Lower Franconia were not apolitical in 1848 or 1849 but rather the opposite.[92] What they wanted and how they were willing to act to obtain these goals is another matter, one that merits closer study if we are to understand the emergence of political life in Germany.

89. As G. Eley has persuasively argued vis-à-vis 1848 for Germany as a whole in *The Peculiarities of German History*, pp. 51–59.

90. Blackbourn, *Class, Religion, and Local Politics*, pp. 10–18. One can also profitably turn to recent studies of the sixteenth century for stimulation: see esp. P. Blickle, *The Revolution of 1525: The German Peasants' War from a New Perspective*, translated by T.A. Brady, Jr., and H.C.E. Midelfort (Baltimore and London, 1981).

91. See Nipperdey, *Geschichte*, pp. 605–6, who argues that the liberal strategy, following the initial success of "revolution," turned immediately to "reform" – "die Revolution hat gesiegt, es lebe die Reform – das war die liberale Strategie." See C. Kleßmann, "Zur Sozialgeschichte der Reichsverfassungskampagne von 1849," *Historische Zeitschrift* 218 (1974): 282–337, esp. pp. 297 and 313ff., for a different view of this period.

92. For a discussion of the apolitical German, see S. Suval, *Electoral Politics in Wilhelmine Germany* (Chapel Hill, N.C., 1985), pp. 3–9 and 257.

6

Associational Life and the Development of Liberalism in Hanover, 1848–66

Michael John

The growth of voluntary associational life in nineteenth-century Germany has received considerable attention from historians in recent years. Associations based on voluntary membership and at least notional indifference to the social status of participants have been contrasted with the involuntary, status-bound, corporate organization of the society of estates and are commonly seen as central features of the modernization of German society. Associations were, it is argued, both cause and effect of the dissolution of the old order. At the same time, such associations often developed more distinctly political functions. Several historians have pointed to the "crypto-politicization" of ostensibly unpolitical organizations during the period before 1848. Nor was this phenomenon restricted to the Vormärz period, but rather extended through the second half of the nineteenth century and beyond. Voluntary associations possessed a variety of functions with regard to the development of German politics, including the creation of a training ground for politicians, the provision of a local organizational base for political parties, and the reflection of the unity and power of the bourgeoisie and other social groups in Germany. This last aspect has received particular emphasis in some very recent studies, in which it has been argued that associations "were a major vehicle for bourgeois aspirations to social leadership."[1]

1. D. Blackbourn and G. Eley, *The Peculiarities of German History: Bourgeois Society and Politics in Nineteenth-Century Germany* (Oxford, 1984), p. 197; cf. R. Koshar, *Social Life, Local Politics, and Nazism: Marburg, 1880–1935* (Chapel Hill/London, 1986). See in general T. Nipperdey, "Verein als soziale Struktur im späten 18. und frühen 19. Jahrhundert," in T. Nipperdey, *Gesellschaft, Kultur, Theorie: Gesammelte Aufsätze zur neueren Geschichte* (Göttingen, 1976), pp. 174–205;

Associational life had other important features as well. In the first place, a general connection existed between the vitality of local associational life and the ebb and flow of the liberal/ nationalist cause in the first two-thirds of the nineteenth century. Indeed, it is clear that the development of German nationalism before 1848 was very much conditioned by its being organized into the new forms of associational life.[2] The Wars of Liberation and their immediate aftermath saw the development of a powerful trend toward the formation of organizations such as gymnastics clubs, which had strong links with the nationalist cause. The suppression of most of these clubs by the states followed in the reaction of the 1820s, but many were refounded during the nationalist revival that began in the late 1830s. Thomas Nipperdey has pointed to the development of a "passion for associations" around 1840,[3] which reached a peak in 1848–49 and involved enormous growth in both the number and range of German associations. The reaction after 1849 involved the return of legal restrictions on political associations and the development of a system of political policing of suspect organizations by the states. Finally, the revival of nationalist politics in the late 1850s and early 1860s was accompanied by a considerable increase in the level of organizational activity.

A second important aspect of the development of associational life in Germany was its connection with the state and local authorities. Associational life may have acted as a force for the emancipation of citizens from the constraints of the old order and in many cases served as a focus of opposition to the established political authorities. Nevertheless, there was always an element of ambiguity in the relationship between the associations and the government bureaucracies. In their pursuit of solutions to the problems of government in the nineteenth century, bureaucrats came to recognize the value of certain types of organization, such as chambers of commerce and the

---

D. Langewiesche, "Die Anfänge der deutschen Partei – Partei, Fraktion und Verein in der Revolution von 1848/49," *Geschichte und Gesellschaft* 4, no. 3 (1978): 324–26; K. Tenfelde, "Die Entfaltung des Vereinswesens während der Industriellen Revolution in Deutschland (1850–1873)," in O. Dann, ed., *Vereinswesen und bürgerliche Gesellschaft in Deutschland* (Munich, 1984), pp. 55–114.

2. D. Düding, *Organisierter gesellschaftlicher Nationalismus in Deutschland (1808–1847): Bedeutung und Funktion der Türner- und Sängervereine für die deutsche Nationalbewegung* (Munich, 1984), passim.

3. Nipperdey, "Verein als soziale Struktur," p. 175.

official agricultural associations, which sprang up in most German states during the first half of the nineteenth century. At a local level, urban authorities frequently founded associations to mobilize support for certain specific goals, particularly in the realm of social and educational policy. In some places this patronage by the authorities went so far as to embrace groups such as gymnastics and shooting clubs, which were seen as politically suspect elsewhere.[4] In general, the authorities' ambivalence towards associational life may be said to have paralleled that felt by many liberals toward the power of the state. In each case a feeling of optimism about the possibilities inherent in the new practices and organizational forms of the nineteenth century was tempered by feelings of vulnerability. Liberals feared the bureaucracy's propensity to abuse the state's power; civil servants were often afraid that the development of associational life would outgrow their ability to control it. This is exactly what happened in the early months of 1848, when – to cite a contemporary conservative – "associations shot up everywhere like mushrooms out of the ground."[5] A similar situation developed in the very different context of the early 1860s and provided an indispensable basis for the liberals' strength in the first decade after 1866.

The kingdom of Hanover followed many of these patterns fairly closely. Eighteen hundred forty-eight saw the creation of political associations in almost all of the towns. In towns such as Hanover, Göttingen, Hildesheim, and Celle there was a brief

---

4. See for example G. Stüve, *Johann Carl Bertram Stüve nach Briefen und persönlichen Erinnerungen*, 2 vols. (Hanover/Leipzig, 1900), vol. 1, p. 331, and vol. 2, pp. 189–90; G. Kratzsch, "Vereine mit idealen Zwecken im 19. Jahrhundert: Ein Beitrag zur Vereinsgeschichte der Provinz Westfalen," in H. Döllinger et al., eds., *Weltpolitik, Europagedanke, Regionalismus: Festschrift für Heinz Gollwitzer zum 65. Geburtstag am 30. Januar 1982* (Münster, 1982), pp. 198, 201, and 206–7; I. Tornow, *Das Münchner Vereinswesen in der ersten Hälfte des 19. Jahrhunderts, mit einem Ausblick auf die zweite Jahrhunderthälfte* (Munich, 1977), p. 92; Nipperdey, "Verein als soziale Struktur," pp. 197–99.

5. H. Bodemeyer, *Die hannoverschen Verfassungskämpfe seit 1848* (Hanover, 1861), vol. 1, p. 53. On the states' ambivalence toward the growth of associations, see Tornow, *Münchner Vereinswesen*, pp. 246–48, and the rather abstract comments in G. Wurzbacher, "Die öffentliche freie Vereinigung als Faktor soziokulturellen, insbesondere emanzipatorischen Wandels im 19. Jahrhundert," in W. Ruegg and O. Neuloh, eds., *Zur soziologischen Theorie und Praxis des 19. Jahrhunderts* (Göttingen, 1971), p. 107; for the liberals' ambivalence toward the state, see J.J. Sheehan, *German Liberalism in the Nineteenth Century* (Chicago and London, 1978), chap. 3.

flowering of democratic radicalism led in the main by groups such as practicing lawyers, who managed to mobilize a broadly lower middle-class and working-class following. By late 1848 there were over one hundred political associations in the kingdom, but the overwhelming majority seems to have been relatively weak and primarily concerned with local issues. Certainly, the local political context prevented the construction of a broad popular coalition for the achievement of liberal goals, whether in alliance with or against the government. The Hanoverian government after March 1848 pursued domestic policies, which fulfilled many moderate liberal demands and enjoyed considerable popular support. At the same time, it resolutely opposed the attempts by the Frankfurt Parliament to create a national constitution, which would, it was feared, abrogate the sovereignty of the Hanoverian state. This combination of liberal domestic and conservative foreign policies effectively produced a stalemate in Hanoverian politics that could not be overcome before the revolution collapsed.[6]

The 1850s saw the dissolution of most of the active political groups founded in 1848–49, police action against radical leaders, and the close supervision of associational life by the authorities. In consequence, the kingdom of Hanover experienced much of the renunciation of overt political activity and the "retreat into sociability," which has been observed in other German states. These developments led to a relocation of liberal activity into forms of organization that refused to practice overt politics. In Celle, the artisanal association survived the 1850s as a result of its ostensibly unpolitical stance and was thought by the police to have dominated the elections in the town. In Hildesheim liberal opponents of the government were able to win every election for the Landtag held during the 1850s.[7] In these towns and

---

6. M. Botzenhart, *Deutscher Parlamentarismus in der Revolutionszeit, 1848–1850* (Düsseldorf, 1977), pp. 381ff. and 595–606; K. Kurmeier, *Die Entstehung der nationalliberalen Partei Hannovers* (inaug. diss., Göttingen, 1923), pp. 22–26; N. Matern, *Politische Wahlen in Hildesheim 1848 bis 1867* (phil. diss., Bonn, 1959), chaps. 2–3.

7. Tenfelde, "Entfaltung des Vereinswesens," pp. 69–70; for events in Württemberg, see D. Langewiesche, *Liberalismus und Demokratie in Württemberg zwischen Revolution und Reichsgründung* (Düsseldorf, 1974), pp. 262–64. On Celle, see *Hannoversche Nachrichten*, 21 January 1857, the police report of 10 February 1855 in Niedersächsisches Hauptstaatsarchiv Hanover (hereafter NHStA) Han., 80 Lüneburg I, no. 750, and T. Offermann, *Arbeiterbewegung und liberales Bürgertum*

elsewhere, the 1850s saw the survival (and sometimes the flourishing) of certain forms of associational life – for example, workers' educational associations that enjoyed the support of local liberals and democrats.[8] This concentration on local, seemingly unpolitical (or apolitical) forms of activity probably did much to ensure the survival of liberalism in the period of reaction.

The case of workers' educational associations deserves closer attention in that it highlights the difficulties facing the state's attempts to create a climate unfavorable to liberal politics in the years after 1848. The first such association had been founded in the town of Hanover in August 1845 and became one of the most important bases for democratic radicalism in the town in 1848–49. Under growing police pressure in the following years, this and other, similar associations (most of which had been founded in the autumn of 1848) renounced political goals in order to survive. By 1853 no workers' educational association in the kingdom retained any direct political commitment, and some associations (for example, that of the town of Hanover) actually increased their membership in the three years after that date – that is, in the very period in which the Hanoverian reaction reached its height. In December 1857 the government ordered increased surveillance of workers' associations, but the results were very limited. By 1865 there were twenty-two workers' associations in the kingdom with 2,900 members, and most had some connection with local liberal groups.[9]

The practice of renouncing direct political activity was by no means restricted to workers' associations. After 1848 the police were generally empowered to dissolve political associations and an association's renunciation of political commitments was a sine qua non of survival in most areas of Germany during the

---

in Deutschland, 1850–1863 (Bonn, 1979), p. 301, n. 195; for Hildesheim, see Matern *Politische Wahlen*, chaps. 4–7.

8. K. Birker, *Die deutschen Arbeiterbildungsvereine, 1840–1870* (Berlin, 1973), pp. 106–13; G. Scheel, "Die Anfänge der Arbeiterbewegung im Königreich Hannover: Zwischen Integration und Emanzipation," *Niedersächsisches Jahrbuch für Landesgeschichte* (hereafter *NJfL*) 48 (1976): 59–62; for a view that underplays the involvement of urban elites in workers' educational associations, see Offermann, *Arbeiterbewegung und liberales Bürgertum*, pp. 300–302.

9. Scheel, "Anfänge der Arbeiterbewegung," pp. 21–33 and 38–53. For a different view, see E. Pitz, "Deutschland und Hannover im Jahre 1866," *NJfL* 38 (1966): 110–11.

1850s. Recent studies of other states have stressed, however, that the "retreat into sociability" implied in the categorical exclusion of political discussion from associational life was by no means solely a tactical response to these changes in policing practices. The exclusion of politics corresponded to the basic wishes of many members of the associations, for whom the divisive experiences of 1848–49 had been traumatic. In many associations it appears that the very notion of "sociability" involved the avoidance of partisan divisions. This helps to explain why the urban history of nineteenth-century Germany was littered with examples of sociable organizations, whose names (*Harmonie, Eintracht, Concordia,* and so on) expressed their members' desire for a type of unity that would transcend the divisions of party politics. Most studies also concur that periods of high political excitement such as 1848–49 had a negative effect on sociable associations, with lower membership figures and levels of organizational activity being noted for many areas. Indeed, as in the case of the workers' educational associations, it seems that the period of most extensive "depoliticization" after 1853 saw the revival in the fortunes of many "unpolitical" clubs, the gymnastics association in the town of Lüneburg being a case in point. The history of organized gymnastics in the kingdom of Hanover suggests that those who wished to keep politics out could almost always defeat those who wished to use the associations principally as a vehicle for political agitation. Moreover, the German League of Gymnasts (Deutscher Turnerbund), which had been founded in 1848, survived only in northwestern Germany after 1850, with its center in Hanover. It did so solely because its members rejected the political radicalism of gymnastics associations elsewhere.[10]

This aversion to political activity on the part of many voluntary associations posed difficulties for those who wished to mobilize such associations in support of liberal political goals. It did not by any means condemn such attempts to automatic

10. H. Schulze, *Die Bedeutung der nordwestdeutschen Turnvereine für die Einheitsbewegung und die Entwicklung der Turnkunst, 1816–1866* (phil. diss. Marburg, 1935), pp. 13–15; Offermann, *Arbeiterbewegung und liberales Bürgertum,* p. 110; for comparisons, see W. Meyer, *Das Vereinswesen der Stadt Nürnberg im 19. Jahrhundert* (Nuremberg, 1970), pp. 65–66; Tornow, *Münchner Vereinswesen,* pp. 237–39; T. Braatz, *Das Kleinbürgertum in München und seine Öffentlichkeit von 1830–1870: Ein Beitrag zur Mentalitätsforschung* (Munich, 1977), pp. 23–35; Kratzsch, "Vereine mit idealen Zwecken," p. 196.

failure. The period between the revolution of 1848 and the annexation of Hanover by Prussia in 1866 saw many examples of the tense and often contradictory relationship between liberalism and associational life in the kingdom. Liberal spokesmen consistently defended the right to form associations, condemned the hostile police practices connected with the Hanoverian state,[11] and participated in attempts to establish new associations. One liberal newspaper compared the relationship between associational life and freedom to that between oxygen and fire.[12] Yet the translation of such principles into an active form of politics was never simple, and the success of the liberals in taking over much of the associational life of the kingdom of Hanover by 1866 requires explanation. As will be seen, that success was far more the product of the ineptitude of opposing forces than of an easy conquest of associational life arising out of some natural affinity between that form of social action and the precepts of liberal politics.

A major aspect of the history of associational life in the two decades after 1848 was the limited effect of the clubs' avoidance of politics. The Hanover gymnastics club, for example, sought to avoid involvement in politics but nevertheless harbored a desire for national unification, for which physical exercise was seen as a suitable preparation. In reaction to the upsurge of nationalist enthusiasm in the wake of the Italian war of 1859, the Lüneburg gymnastics club supported the view of its counterpart in Hamburg that individual members might behave patriotically, but that no association should seek to influence government policy.[13] Recent research has emphasized that social and political engagement were related activities and that the retreat into sociability should not be equated with any meaningful level of depoliticization. Certainly, the fact that social clubs often extended access to reading matter produced by the opposition should be taken seriously as an aspect of the liberals' mobilization of public opinion. So too should the evidence that local elites often belonged to a range of organizations, which often transcended the

---

11. For a statement of the belief that, while the Hanoverian law of associations was not a particular problem, the powers of the police were, see, F.A. Lange, "Die deutschen Turnvereine und die Vereinsgesetze," *Deutsche Turn-Zeitung* 10 (1865): 405.
12. *Zeitung für Norddeutschland*, 18 January 1859.
13. Schulze, *Die Bedeutung der nordwestdeutschen Turnvereine*, pp. 14, 35.

divide between politics and sociability.[14]

These considerations help to explain the attention paid by the police to the type of reading material provided by associations and to the personnel of the association's committees. The police rightly recognized that the crucial point was not the particular direction of a given association's activities, but its place in the overall network of social and political life in a given area. Thus, a report of January 1858 on associational life in the governing district (*Landdrostei*) of Lüneburg expressed concern about a number of local associations on the basis of the presumed political sympathies of their members, and recommended that the artisans' association in Celle should be watched. A similar report on associational life in the town of Hanover showed an equal sensitivity to the political dangers inherent in social organizations and recommended close attention to the capital's gymnastics, singing, and lawyers' associations because of their leading roles in the events of 1848.[15] In 1857 the police chief of Celle reported that the opposition's successes in the local elections were the result of its ability to influence opinion through the local artisans' credit association, despite that body's lack of overt political activity. However, the law forbade the police to do much more than express suspicions based on the assumed sympathies of the leadership groups in associations as long as explicit political activity was avoided.[16] This fact and the seeming impotence of the police in dealing with the burgeoning nationalist movement in the early 1860s suggests that the rule of law had made serious inroads into public life, even in the Hanover of King George V – a state that was a byword for reaction in pre-1866 Germany.

Most studies concur in seeing 1859 as a turning point in the history of the liberal/nationalist movement. The combination of

14. See in general Nipperdey, "Verein als soziale Struktur," pp. 192–94; Tornow, *Münchner Vereinswesen*, pp. 237–46; Birker, *Arbeiterbildungsvereine*, pp. 107, 112.

15. See the *Verzeichnis* on associational life in the *Landdrostei* Lüneburg of January 1858, NHStA Han., 80 Lüneburg I, no. 755; *Polizei-Direktion* Hanover report, 9 January 1858, NHStA Han., 80 Hanover I A, no. 717.

16. *Polizei-Direktion* Celle, report of 31 January 1857, NHStA Han., 80 Lüneburg I, no. 756. Cf. M. John, "Liberalism and Society in Germany, 1850–1880: the case of Hanover," *English Historical Review* 102 (1987): 587–88 for more details. On the legal constraints placed on the Hanoverian authorities with regard to the suppression of associations, see Offermann, *Arbeiterbewegung und liberales Bürgertum*, pp. 69–70, 95–97.

the onset of the New Era in Prussia and the Italian war led to a heightening of public interest in the nationalist cause and triggered the foundation of the National Association (Nationalverein). A major aim of the National Association lay in the conquest and mobilization of public opinion through the creation of an interlocking series of associations at a local and regional level, linked together wherever possible by national organizations. This meant both attempts to use existing associations as political bases for the *kleindeutsch* cause and a program of establishing new associations for the same purpose. Activities such as organized shooting, singing, and gymnastics experienced a considerable revival in the early 1860s, and national leagues of shooters and singers were established with strongly nationalist overtones.[17]

An important, although as yet imperfectly understood, aspect of this associational activity concerned the derivation of political benefit from the many anniversary celebrations of the years between 1859 and 1866. In many ways, the centenary celebrations of the birth of Schiller in November 1859 provided the model here. Coming at a time when educated public opinion had already been aroused in a nationalist direction by the events of the previous months, the *Schillerfeier* that took place in most German towns provided great opportunities for nationalist agitation. The celebrations, which characteristically took the form of performances of Schiller's plays, processions, ceremonial speeches, and dinners, tended to be organized by specially convened committees, whose composition was of great interest to political activists. In Stuttgart, a *Schillerverein* came into existence at the end of 1858 that was dominated by the local singing club (*Liederkranz*), which had strong attachments to the liberal/ nationalist cause. In Kiel, the preparations for the celebrations were led by supporters of the National Association and this pattern was repeated in many German towns. In Hildesheim, the mayor and municipal council, where support for the National Association was strong, succeeded in converting the

17. T.S. Hamerow, *The Social Foundations of German Unification, 1858–1871: Ideas and Institutions* (Princeton, 1969), pp. 331–58; D. Düding, "The Nineteenth-Century German Nationalist Movement as a Movement of Societies," in H. Schulze ed., *Nation-Building in Central Europe* (Leamington Spa, 1987), pp. 44–49; Sheehan, *German Liberalism*, pp. 95–97; Offermann, *Arbeiterbewegung und liberales Bürgertum*, pp. 165–86.

Schiller celebrations into a nationalist demonstration. There is little doubt that this marked a new stage in the nationalist movement, and historians have rightly drawn attention to the "national pathos" of the Schiller celebrations. In a similar vein, the novelist Wilhelm Raabe saw them in 1872 as the birth of the unity of the German people.[18]

In the years after 1859, this type of activity was to grow in significance. The centenary celebrations of Fichte's birth in May 1862 and the fiftieth anniversaries of the battles of Leipzig (1863) and Waterloo (1865) provided ample opportunities for nationalist agitation. The first of these gave the Berlin section of the National Association the chance to attract an audience of around 3,500 people and led to the association's acquiring 502 new members. In Kiel, the Fichte anniversary committee was once more dominated by the National Association and culminated in an illegal toast to the association. Once again, developments in the kingdom of Hanover paralleled those elsewhere. In Göttingen, the police alleged that the Fichte celebrations were used to conceal a National Association dinner attended by Rudolf Bennigsen, Johannes Miquel, and Gottlieb Planck, the three leading Hanoverians in the association. Almost all of the 116 people present were, it was alleged, liberal sympathizers. Similar events occurred in various parts of the kingdom of Hanover in connection with the celebrations of the battles of Leipzig and Waterloo.[19]

Despite the National Association's evident concern that these

18. See in general A. Ludwig, *Schiller und die deutsche Nachwelt* (Berlin, 1909), pp. 400–419 (for Raabe, p. 401); W. Real, "Pfingstversammlung und Abgeordnetentag (1862): Eine Studie zur Geschichte der politischen Willensbildung in der Ära der Reichsgründung," in K. Stephenson and A. Scharff, eds., *Darstellungen und Quellen der deutschen Einheitsbewegung im neunzehnten und zwanzigsten Jahrhundert*, vol. 8 (Heidelberg, 1970), pp. 164–66; for Stuttgart, see O. Elben, *Das Schillerfest in Schillers Heimath Stuttgart, Ludwigsburg und Marbach, den 9. 10. und 11. November 1859* (Stuttgart, 1859); cf. Langewiesche, *Liberalismus und Demokratie*, pp. 289–90; for Kiel, see J. Wetzel, *Theodor Lehmann und die nationale Bewegung in Schleswig-Holstein* (Neumünster, 1971), pp. 146–47; for Hildesheim, see Matern, *Politische Wahlen*, p. 108.

19. *Die Fichte-Feier der Berliner Mitglieder des National-Vereins, 19. Mai 1862: Ein Erinnerungsblatt* (Berlin, 1862), pp. 3–4; Wetzel, *Theodor Lehmann*, pp. 150–51; *Polizei-Direktion* Göttingen, report of 20 May 1862, with list of participants, NHStA Han., 80 Hildesheim I E, no. 477, fos. 286–92. Schulze, *Die Bedeutung der nordwestdeutschen Turnvereine*, pp. 45–46.; R. Lembcke, *Johannes Miquel und die Stadt Osnabrück unter besonderer Berücksichtigung der Jahre 1865–1869* (Osnabrück, 1962), pp. 228–29.

celebrations be used as a means of agitation, however, it would be wise to consider certain qualifications with regard to their effectiveness. In the first place, there was the question of the regional distribution of support for the association. It has long been recognized that one of the major, perhaps *the* major, determinant of support for the liberal/nationalist cause was the length of time a given region had been part of Hanover. The territorial settlement of 1815 had considerably enlarged the kingdom, adding East Friesland and the areas around Osnabrück and Hildesheim to the dynastic possessions of the Guelph monarchy. Each of these areas saw the development of hostility to the Guelph monarchy, with the native populations convinced that the government was determined to neglect their interests and, in the cases of the towns, to interfere in their rights of self-administration. Such feelings did a great deal to prepare the ground for the expansion of support for the National Association, which found the bulk of its support in the recently acquired regions. In East Friesland, which had been part of the Prussian monarchy in the late eighteenth century, the nationalist cause derived particular strength from the widespread preference for Prussian as opposed to Hanoverian rule. Elsewhere, as in Hildesheim, liberals were quick to seize on the opportunities provided by the citizens' belief that the Hanoverian royal house was prejudiced against their local interests, especially with regard to the construction of railways. In Hildesheim, Osnabrück, and the towns of East Friesland, there was considerable (if at times reluctant) support for annexation by Prussia in 1866. The kingdom of Hanover thus provides ample evidence for the connection between political regionalism and nationalist enthusiasm. The two came together in a hostility to the political status quo of the German Confederation.[20]

20. See the general comments in H. Berding, "Staatliche Identität, nationale Integration und politischer Regionalismus," *Blätter für deutsche Landesgeschichte* 121 (1985): 373–78; Kurmeier, *Entstehung*, pp. 90–106; B. Ehrenfeuchter, "Politische Willensbildung in Niedersachsen zur Zeit des Kaiserreiches: Ein Versuch auf Grund der Reichstagswahlen von 1867 bis 1912, insbesondere seit 1890" (phil. diss. Göttingen, 1951), pp. 40–41, 54–56, 265; Lembcke, *Miquel und die Stadt Osnabrück*, pp. 8–10; E. Pitz, "Deutschland und Hannover im Jahre 1866," pp. 130–31; H. Borkenhagen, *Ostfriesland unter der hannoverschen Herrschaft, 1815–1866* (Aurich, 1924), traces the development of opposition in East Friesland. For Hildesheim, see H.-M. Tiebel, *Hildesheim und die königlich hannoversche Regierung: Ein Beitrag zur Städtegeschichte Niedersachsens im 19. Jahrhundert*

The evidence suggests that this regional factor was of the greatest importance in the success of liberal associational activity, and it might be argued that, without an existing background of hostility to the Hanoverian monarchy, liberal calls for the development of sympathetic associations tended to be relatively unsuccessful. In the towns of East Friesland, there can be no doubt about the central role played by supporters of the National Association in the foundation of new gymnastics clubs in the early 1860s. These clubs subsequently took on directing functions in the committees for the celebration of the anniversary of the battle of Leipzig and, later, in the Schleswig-Holstein committees. In Osnabrück the new gymnastics club was closely associated with the National Association, as a result of which it apparently had little appeal for the predominantly Roman Catholic population of the surrounding countryside and villages. In Hildesheim, on the other hand, there was a different outcome. Here the strong support for the National Association in the municipal council was countered by a numerically rather stronger *großdeutsch* group and a sizeable Roman Catholic population. An attempt by a *kleindeutsch* nationalist, August Gottsleben, to set up a pro-National Association gymnastics club led to a split and the creation of an opposing club with the significant title of *Eintracht*.[21] This provides an important indication that the National Association could not expect to have everything its own way with regard to the activities of ancillary organizations.

This impression is certainly confirmed by the uneven response to the activities of National Association activists elsewhere. In Münden, the local authorities reported in early 1861 that a printer named Scriba who was in constant contact with Miquel in Göttingen used the gymnastics club to disseminate National Association propaganda. However, an attempt to use the *Bürgerverein* of Münden to collect signatures for a National Association petition failed, and the instigator resigned as a result. When Scriba went to Hameln for the same purpose, however, he discovered to his surprise that two gymnastics

---

(Hildesheim, 1956), p. 3 and passim; cf. Matern, *Politische Wahlen*, pp. 20–25, 146–48.

21. Schulze, *Die Bedeutung der nordwestdeutschen Turnvereine*, pp. 43–52. For the relative strengths of the *kleindeutsch* and *großdeutsch* groups in Hildesheim in 1863, see Matern, *Politische Wahlen*, p. 118.

clubs existed in the town and apparently departed when he was firmly told that gymnastics clubs did not have "secondary goals" (*Nebenzwecke*).[22] Much the same might be said of Celle, a town where radical elements had a considerable organizational base. The police reported in September 1860 that it had no difficulty in influencing the contents of the gymnastic club's statutes and that there were plenty of conservative members. When local "democrats" attempted to exploit the founding ceremony of the club in October 1861, they were repulsed by the club's committee, an event that led to the refusal of the town's council to take part.[23] The same sorts of difficulties were experienced when attempts were made to take over shooting clubs for the *kleindeutsch* cause. In the case of Münden, the sources once again reveal the strength of conservatism among the town's population, and conservatives seem to have dominated the shooting society of Hildesheim, at least until 1861. According to the local police, this dominance explained the National Association's tactics of attempting to insert its supporters into the society's committee. Even a desire to participate in the German Shooting Festival in Frankfurt in 1862 – an event that the police associated with the National Association – was, it seems, not necessarily an indication of sympathies with the political aims of the Association.[24]

There was thus nothing particularly inevitable about the contribution of voluntary associations to the *kleindeutsch* cause. The 1860s saw many attempts to create anti-National-Association groups, at both local and national levels, as was shown by the foundation of such organizations as the *Großdeutscher Verein* in Hildesheim and the nationwide *Deutscher Reformverein* in 1861–62. The latter organization tended to feed off the hostility to Prussia, which was prevalent in many areas of southern Germany. The *Reformverein*'s most recent student, Willy Real, has emphasised the fact that Hanover was alone among the states in northern

22. Sattler to *District-Commando* Göttingen, 2 and 6 February 1861, Homeyer to *Landdrostei* Hildesheim, 10 February 1861, NHStA Han., 80 Hildesheim I E, no. 477, fos. 252–53, 262–63, 268–69.

23. *Polizei-Direktion* Celle to *Landdrostei* Lüneburg, 29 September 1860 and 7 October 1861, NHStA Han., 80 Lüneburg I, no. 757.

24. *Magistrat* Münden to *Landdrostei* Hildesheim, 6 June 1862; Meyer to *Landdrostei* Hildesheim, 24 May 1862; and *Polizei-Direktion* Hildesheim to *Landdrostei* Hildesheim, 4 June 1862, NHStA Han. 80 Hildesheim I E no. 576, fos. 3–4, 8–10, 49–52.

Germany in offering the organization significant possibilities of success. These possibilities were a direct consequence of the successes of the National Association between 1859 and 1862 and mobilized support around the doubts felt by many Hanoverians (some of a moderately liberal persuasion) about the dangers of Prussian expansionism. Branches were established in a number of towns that were otherwise strongholds of liberal nationalism – Harburg, Celle, Hildesheim, Göttingen – and by February 1863 the organization had 1,500 members in the kingdom of Hanover. This made it considerably stronger in terms of the size of its membership than the National Association. In many cases, it appears, local citizens were prompted to join the *Reformverein* by their disapproval of the pro-National-Association policies promoted by their municipal councils.[25]

It seems therefore that the liberal nationalists faced considerable problems in turning the upsurge of associational life in the early 1860s to their advantage. Even in those towns where they could benefit from preexisting local hostility to rule by the Guelph dynasty, their limited appeal became clear as opposing forces began to use the liberals' own techniques against them. Only in East Friesland was the National Association's evident pro-Prussianism an advantage; elsewhere, many urban property owners were at best lukewarm about this salient aspect of the National Association's program. Yet, beneath this uncertainty about Germany's future among Hanover's property owners lay a deeper coherence, whose precise contours require analysis. The creation of the *Reformverein* in the kingdom illustrated the divergence of opinions about the best way toward a German nation-state and about the form that that state should take. In Hanover, the *Reformverein* represented a combination of political elements, ranging from conservative reactionaries to moderate liberal federalists. The very name of the organization was an implicit admission that the political status quo was unsustainable and that no policy of out-and-out reaction had any possibility of success in the long term. Moreover, the leadership of the *Reformverein* considered the political future within the con-

---

25. W. Real, *Der Deutsche Reformverein: Großdeutsche Kräfte zwischen Villafranca und Königgrätz* (Lübeck and Hamburg, 1966), pp. 90–93; cf. Matern, *Politische Wahlen*, p. 111. On the background to the foundation of the Hanoverian branch of the *Reformverein*, see F. Köster, *Hannover und die Grundlegung der preußischen Suprematie in Deutschland, 1862–1864* (Hanover, 1978), pp. 63–65.

text of *national* reform, involving the further development of the German Confederation towards a form of statehood that would allow for the survival of the princely dynasties within a federal state based on agreements between those dynasties. That sort of program was a far cry from the position adopted by reactionary politicians such as Count Wilhelm Friedrich von Borries, who discouraged the initial attempts to set up a counter-organization to the National Association in August 1861.[26]

The Hanoverian government tolerated the *Reformverein* but did not welcome its activities. The implicit rift between the bureaucracy and the *Reformverein* became increasingly explicit in 1863–64 as a result of mounting agitation over Schleswig-Holstein. In contrast to the position of most of the middle states, the kingdom of Hanover failed to support the claims of the Augustenburg dynasty, a policy that aroused powerful opposition. This was to have extremely important consequences in that it provided a framework within which the political differences between the National Association and the *Reformverein* could be submerged in common "patriotic" activity. Both organizations agreed in opposing the policy adopted by the German "Great Powers" (i.e., Prussia and Austria) and in pressing the Augustenburg dynasty's claims. Fueled by powerful memories of the battle of Leipzig, a sizable number of organizations were formed in late 1863 to collect money for Schleswig-Holstein and to agitate for "a national act" on the part of the government. On 21 November 1863, a meeting held in the town of Hanover saw a prominent member of the National Association calling for the burial of political differences in patriotic activity. Seven days later a similar meeting was called in Hildesheim on the joint initiative of the National Association and the *Reformverein*, and a Schleswig-Holstein committee was formed. This pattern was repeated in Harburg, Lüneburg, and other towns in the kingdom in November and December 1863. By March 1864 there were at least eighty-eight Schleswig-Holstein associations and committees in the kingdom of Hanover, in which the National

---

26. Real, *Reformverein*, pp. 28–29. On Borries, who led the Hanoverian reaction from 1855–62 as minister of the interior, see R. Wöltge, *Die Reaktion im Königreich Hannover, 1850–1857: Die Rückbildung des Verfassungsgesetzes und die Reformversuche an den Provinziallandschaften* (phil. diss. Tübingen, 1932); M.L. Anderson, *Windthorst: A Political Biography* (Oxford, 1981), pp. 76–82.

Association and the *Reformverein* found a certain degree of common ground.[27]

The Schleswig-Holstein movement was a critical development in the internal politics of Hanover in the early 1860s. It provided the essential framework within which the collapse of a meaningful reform conservatism and the extension of the liberals' hold over public opinion took place. Despite the liberal election victory of June 1863, there are grounds for thinking that the fortunes of the National Association were beginning to wane as a result of hostility to the domestic policies of Bismarck in Prussia, the activities of the *Reformverein*, and the appointment of the moderate Windthorst-Hammerstein ministry in succession to that of the hated reactionary Borries in December 1862.[28] The Schleswig-Holstein question provided unprecedented opportunities for political agitation precisely because it was an unequivocally *national* issue that did not require clarity of thinking about the issue which divided the Hanoverian middle classes most – i.e., the form of a future German nation-state. The fact that *großdeutsch* and *kleindeutsch* views could find common ground on the question of Schleswig-Holstein gave added force to the growing consensus in Hanoverian public opinion regarding domestic political reforms.[29] Moreover, the Schleswig-Holstein issue provided the impetus to a hitherto unprecedented level of political activity in Hanover largely because it was perceived to be a "national" rather than narrowly party-political question. A meeting in the town of Hanover on 20 or 22 November 1863 attracted an audience of around 10,000, and meetings in Harburg and Hildesheim at the end of the month were attended by 2,000 people. By July 1864, the Hanoverian Schleswig-Holstein committees had collected nearly 65,000 guilders for a cause that at no point showed any sign of success in terms of its principal goals.[30] This constituted an intensity of political activity far greater than anything the kingdom had experienced since 1848.

27. J. Daebel, *Die Schleswig-Holstein-Bewegung in Deutschland, 1863/64* (phil. diss. Cologne, 1969), pp. 71–77, 228; Matern, *Politische Wahlen*, pp. 132–36.

28. Kurmeier, *Entstehung*, pp. 67–68; cf. Köster, *Hannover und die Grundlegung der preußischen Suprematie*, pp. 115–17.

29. Matern, *Politische Wahlen*, p. 123.

30. Daebel, *Schleswig-Holstein-Bewegung*, pp. 60, n. 3, 282; Matern, *Politische Wahlen*, pp. 135–36; *Polizei-Direktion* Harburg, report of 26 November 1863, NHStA Han., 80 Lüneburg I, no. 776.

Recent scholarship has convincingly shown that the resolution of the Schleswig-Holstein question in 1864 delivered a mortal blow to the *Reformverein*. Bismarck's success in forcing Austria into a subordinate position effectively destroyed the *großdeutsch* position as a practical possibility. Although the Hanoverian branch of the *Reformverein* outlasted all other local branches, it was riven by internal disagreements that led in August 1864 to the secession of some eighty members on the grounds that it was too liberal. The destruction of the possibility of a coherent *großdeutsch* politics was accompanied by the effective takeover by the National Association of the local Schleswig-Holstein committees.[31] This is not to say that the National Association supported Bismarck's policy concerning Schleswig-Holstein. Indeed, 1864 was a year of considerable difficulties for the association in that Bismarck's failure to pursue a "German" (i.e. pro-Augustenburg) policy in Schleswig-Holstein, coupled with the failure of the Prussian government to solve the constitutional conflict in a liberal way, presented a depressing picture from the *kleindeutsch* point of view. In Hanover, the association's activities seem to have been overcome by lethargy, which declined only with the fall of the Windthorst-Hammerstein ministry in October 1865 and the reversion to an unmistakably reactionary course by the king.[32] Yet if the *kleindeutsch* position in 1864 was unenviable, that of the *großdeutsch* camp was more or less impossible, for it presumed an evidently unrealistic leadership role in the German question on the part of Austria. To that extent, the Schleswig-Holstein question changed the relative fortunes of the National Association and the *Reformverein* decisively to the advantage of the former.

A further feature of the agitation concerning Schleswig-Holstein was the leading role played by gymnastics clubs. Here, it seemed, was an issue on which the clubs could demonstrate their nationalist credentials without breaking their self-imposed injunction to avoid political activity. At this point it must be remembered how narrow the common conception of what constituted "political" activity really was. As was noted above, the avoidance of politics by no means precluded a generalized

---

31. Real, *Reformverein*, pp. 183–84, 204–5; Daebel, *Schleswig-Holstein-Bewegung*, pp. 75, 213.
32. Kurmeier, *Entstehung*, pp. 69–71.

commitment to the patriotic cause. A commonly expressed view in the gymnastics movement of the 1860s was that the clubs were "patriotically German . . . but they were not political on the grounds that (unlike the National Association) they did not regard the realization of a particular political form of unity as a fundamental goal."[33] This distinction between a broad patriotic commitment and politics was, to be sure, an ideology in Karl Mannheim's sense of a fiction cloaking reality.[34] In view of the situation in the early 1860s, a commitment to national unity clearly involved powerful beliefs of a political nature. Yet there are good reasons for thinking that broad sections of the German middle classes sincerely believed in the compatibility of support for nationalism and avoidance of political activity. For that reason alone, the strength of German nationalism in public opinion cannot be adequately gauged in terms of the modest size of organizations such as the National Association.[35]

The Schiller festivals of 1859, the celebrations of the battles of Leipzig and Waterloo, and the Schleswig-Holstein movement all testified to the extent to which the nationalist mood had permeated Hanoverian public opinion before Bismarck's "revolution from above." As time went on, the National Association came to realize that the generalized commitment to nationalism offered political possibilities that were denied to more narrow, partisan organizations, which sought to promote the association's goals. On 30 August 1863, a major gymnastics festival was held in Göttingen at the instigation of Miquel, who had organized the event so that it coincided with a sharpshooting festival. Among the 400 to 600 people present were Bennigsen and Planck, the other major Hanoverian leaders of the National Association. Yet, despite this clear link with the National Association, Miquel was careful to argue that the gymnasts' avoidance of direct party politics was correct. He particularly warned against "turning the gymnasts' associations into either political clubs or gymnastics schools and thereby losing sight of the political and social importance of the gymnastics movement."

33. A. Baur, "Das Vereinsturnen in Deutschland," *Deutsche Turn-Zeitung* 8 (1863): 179.

34. K. Mannheim, *Ideology and Utopia: An Introduction to the Sociology of Knowledge* (London, 1936).

35. See L. O'Boyle, "The German *Nationalverein*," *Journal of Central European Affairs* 16 (1957): 333–52.

Shortly afterwards, the National Association's weekly magazine confirmed that gymnastics associations should be dissuaded from pursuing party-political goals. In the opinion of the historian of gymnastics in northwestern Germany, this approach helped the gymnastics clubs when the fortunes of the National Association stagnated in 1864.[36]

There are thus grounds for thinking that the strength of the *kleindeutsch* cause depended on its ability to make itself into the sole effective representative of a nationalism that was widely perceived to be apolitical. The National Association gained a significant advantage from its stand on the Schleswig-Holstein issue, because it involved the assertion of an essentially federalist policy toward national unification. Outside East Friesland, the *kleindeutsch* nationalists in Hanover had little to gain and a lot to lose from the seeming connection between their cause and that of Prussian expansionism. The kingdom's population, like that of the other states north of the Main, was far more likely to accept Prussian leadership in the national cause if it did not entail the creation of a centralized Greater Prussia.

As we have seen, the Schleswig-Holstein issue provided the occasion for a convergence over domestic policy issues between the National Association and the *Reformverein*. An important part of that convergence was the shared belief in the desirability of a German nation-state in which local and regional variations were maintained through adoption of a federal form of government and the feared "unitary state" (*Einheitsstaat*) was avoided.[37] There is every reason to think that people like Bennigsen and Miquel were sincere in their belief in the compatibility of Prussian-led national unification and the survival of respected local institutions. Despite differences in emphasis with respect to the possibilities inherent in rule by Prussia, it seems probable that the leaders of the National Association in Hanover accepted an essentially North German conception of liberal politics, which helped them to build bridges with other shades of opinion in the kingdom. This approach, associated with the work of people such as Friedrich Dahlmann and Johann Carl Bertram von Stüve, emphasized among other things respect for

36. *Deutsche Turn-Zeitung* 8 (1863): 278 and 286; Schulze, *Die Bedeutung der nordwestdeutschen Turnvereine*, pp. 50–52, 67, and 75.
37. See. S. Na'aman, *Der Deutsche Nationalverein: Die politische Konstituierung des deutschen Bürgertums, 1859–1867* (Düsseldorf, 1987), pp. 14 and 22–23.

the historical basis of the state and its local institutions and the importance of local self-administration. Outside East Friesland, support for annexation by Prussia before the war of 1866 was extremely rare in the *kleindeutsch* camp. After the war, which solved this problem through military force, the Hanoverian leaders of the new National Liberal Party showed themselves determined to maintain the integrity of Hanover's institutions against the centralizing impulses of Prussia's bureaucrats. An address of 1 October 1866, which called for unified legislation on economic and military affairs coupled with "protection for the peculiarities of the new provinces and especially of our land, which have grown up out of history, morals, and legislation" found the support of the leaders of the National Association but also of many members of the *großdeutsch* movement. There was, it seems, little difference between the parties on programmatic questions in late 1866, and the way was clear for a relatively unified approach to the question of the form of the new state. It was no surprise, then, that the leaders of the National Liberal Party in Hanover found it possible to stand together with their *großdeutsch* opponents in defense of Hanoverian traditions in the discussions held in Berlin in July and August 1867, thereby winning important concessions from Prussia.[38]

The basic consensus about political issues, which involved support for national unification but hostility to centralization, had its roots in the same political and cultural milieu that spawned a distinction between nationalist commitment and party politics. In a sense, it may be argued that the policies pursued by King George V's governments, especially that of Count von Borries, made possible a liberal/conservative coalition that was ultimately responsible for the ascendancy of the National Association. Borries's great achievement was to destroy the bases of a coherent reform conservatism. His attempt

---

38. From an enormous literature, see above all H. Barmeyer, "Die hannoverschen Nationalliberalen, 1859–1885," *NJfL* (1983): 65–85; H. Barmeyer, *Hannovers Eingliederung in den preußischen Staat: Annexion und administrative Integration, 1866–1868* (Hildesheim, 1983), pp. 81–123 and passim; W. Frauendienst, "Zur Assimilierung Hannovers durch Preußen nach 1866," *NJfL* 14 (1937): 310–44; Kurmeier, *Entstehung*, pp. 119–24 (on the address of 1 October 1866), 140–42, 147–48, and 166–68; H.A. Schmitt, "From Sovereign States to Prussian Provinces: Hanover and Hesse-Nassau, 1866–1871," *Journal of Modern History* 57 (1985): 24–56; in general, see H. Heffter, *Die deutsche Selbstverwaltung im 19. Jahrhundert: Geschichte der Ideen und Institutionen* (Stuttgart, 1950), pp. 470–92.

to rule from the center, which involved constant and unconstitutional encroachments on the much-prized rights of self-administration enjoyed by the towns and rural communes, created an opposition within the very groups in society that had the most to lose from the end of the monarchy – i.e., the nobility. Above all, the regime's vigorous but unsuccessful intrusions into associational life (however innocuous the activities of the association in question) reflected a complete inability to recognize the ways in which the rules of the political game had changed since the 1840s. Thus, the provincial agricultural associations of Hildesheim and Osnabrück (both of which were led by opponents of the National Association) were deliberately starved of funds because of the regime's fear of any independent political activity.[39] As we have seen, reactionary bureaucrats like Borries were always suspicious of attempts to create political organizations, even those like the *Reformverein* that offered the possibility of an effective counterweight to the National Association. This explains the bitter complaint of Oskar Meding, a leading figure in Hanoverian *großdeutsch* politics, that "the Hanoverian bureaucracy had no conception of a public party politics that did not allow itself to be commanded by the green table [of the ministry]." Instead, the Hanoverian government used repression and vain attempts to stimulate a cult of the Guelph monarchy in order to bolster its position. Given the political realities of the 1860s, such policies had little chance of success without being underpinned by a workable political organization.[40]

The effect of the Borries ministry was undoubtedly to push public opinion in the direction of the National Association, or at least in the direction of the generalized nationalist commitment that played so large a part in the Hanoverian politics of the 1860s. As Stüve wrote in May 1861, "at present, opposition to a bad system [of government] and the National Association are identical in the country."[41] Yet of all the aspects of the Borries regime that undermined the monarchy's support, it is probable that the frequent bureaucratic incursions into the sphere of

39. [A. Lammers], "Hannovers Reactionsjahre," *Preußische Jahrbücher* 3 (1859): p. 537; Stüve, *Johann Carl Bertram Stüve*, 2: 292–94.

40. O. Meding, *Memoiren zur Zeitgeschichte*, vol. 1 (Leipzig, 1881), p. 148; on the cult of the Guelph monarchy, see Anderson, *Windthorst*, p. 79.

41. Stüve, *Johann Carl Bertram Stüve*, 2: 300, Stüve to Braun, 18 May 1861.

municipal self-government were the most important. By the 1860s, liberal nationalists had gained control over most of the urban councils with the exception of the town of Hanover. This control was greatly facilitated by the frequent clashes with the central bureaucracy in the late 1850s and early 1860s. By seeking to avoid clashes between the towns' governments and their elected assemblies, local leaders of a liberal persuasion sought to present themselves as the defenders of the town's historic privileges against an overweening, despotic government. Conversely, the Borries ministry in particular tended to encourage disputes between the town governments and their assemblies as a pretext for interventions in local affairs. Urban leaders such as Miquel rightly saw the importance of a form of politics in which the town councils were seen as the united representatives of local interests against the central government. After 1870, a similar policy was pursued for the same reasons by the National Liberal mayor of the town of Göttingen, Georg Merkl.[42]

There is very little doubt that control over municipal councils was vital to the liberals' political strength in the kingdom of Hanover and elsewhere. A major consequence was that it fostered tendencies towards an apolitical approach to politics that was, as we have seen, so characteristic of the internal life of many of Germany's voluntary associations. Hostility to the pretensions of bureaucratic rule from the center could be presented as a defense of the interests of the whole town, rather than as partisan politics. Nor did the connections stop there. In many Hanoverian towns, the leaders of local government were at the center of attempts to expand the range of nationalist associational activity. The police reports concerning nationalist activities in the town of Harburg consistently stressed the leadership given to the local nationalist movement by the mayor, August Grumbrecht. The Schleswig-Holstein movement in Harburg, Lüneburg, and elsewhere was dominated by members of the local council.[43] By 1863–64, there were clear signs that liberal nationalists in the municipal councils were finding it possible to

42. On the government's policy with regard to the town of Osnabrück, see Stüve, *Johann Carl Bertram Stüve*, 2:283–84; Lembcke, *Miquel und die Stadt Osnabrück*, pp. 206–7; G.J. Merkl, *Erinnerungen an meine fünfundzwanzigjährige Thätigkeit als Bürgermeister von Göttingen* (Göttingen, 1897), pp. 15–16.
43. See the many reports on Harburg politics in NHStA Han., 80 Lüneburg I, no. 771; and *Landdrost* of Lüneburg, report of 14 December 1863, NHStA Han., 80 Lüneburg I, no. 753.

weld together the defense of local autonomies, the dominant political issues of the kingdom of Hanover, and a broad commitment to the promotion of the nationalist cause.[44]

The role of associational life in promoting a commitment to an apolitical nationalism among the citizens of Hanover was certainly very great. The fact that it was the National Association that derived the greatest benefit from this was mainly the result of external political factors and the ineptitude of the Hanoverian government, particularly with regard to its relationship with local government and the integration of its more recently acquired territories. Associational life was by no means *necessarily* liberal, but the interplay of foreign and domestic political developments in the late 1850s and early 1860s gave the *kleindeutsch* activists the upper hand as the representatives of the broader nationalist cause. The sterility of the politics practiced by the Guelph monarchy effectively left the field to the National Association. This failure to develop an alternative nationalist politics is vital in any explanation of the long-term strength of National Liberalism in Hanover after 1866.

The events of the 1850s and 1860s were also vital in defining the approach of Hanoverian liberals to politics after 1866. The major characteristic of Hanoverian liberal nationalism was its association of nationalism with local rights of self-administration. The studiously nonpartisan, but generally liberal *Osnabrücker Zeitung* captured this blend of nationalism and localism perfectly when it claimed that "our German fatherland can achieve political unity without succumbing to the evil of centralization. Indeed our national duty lies essentially in a sensible linking of the idea of national unity and local independence."[45] The power of such sentiments emerged clearly in May 1866, when Grumbrecht called for the towns to be "a barrier against the continually growing power of the state."[46] A report subsequently written on the basis of the reactions of

44. See *Polizei-Direktion* Harburg, report of 24 April 1864 on a meeting the previous day which had called for the restitution of Stüve's Municipal Government Ordinance of 1851 as part of a package of reform proposals, in NHStA Han., 80 Lüneburg I, no. 772.

45. *Osnabrücker Zeitung*, 18 May 1864, quoted in C. Henke, *Die Osnabrücker Presse von der Märzrevolution 1848 bis zur Gegenwart* (inaug. diss., Münster, 1927), p. 44.

46. Quoted in R. Nürnberger, "Städtische Selbstverwaltung und sozialer Wandel im Königreich und in der Provinz Hannover während des 19. Jahrhunderts," *NJfL* 48 (1976): 11.

senior figures in municipal government to the annexation of the kingdom concluded that "the German duties of the Prussian state urgently require the decisive promotion of the rights of communal and provincial self-administration."[47] The central point was not that Prussia was popular (always excepting the special case of East Friesland). Grumbrecht himself expressed opposition to the annexation in 1866, and very few members of the National Association positively welcomed it.[48] Rather, it was that the widespread unpopularity of the Guelph monarchy had strengthened the conviction that the solution of Hanover's domestic problems and German national unification were inextricably linked. Bennigsen had come to this conclusion in the mid-1850s;[49] by the mid-1860s many Hanoverians who were otherwise suspicious of the National Association had come to similar conclusions. There is every reason to think that the bureaucracy's repeated interference into local government and associational life played a central role in this alienation of support among Hanover's property-owning classes.

The relationship between associational life and local government was in many ways symbiotic. The police rightly suspected that influence over associations was crucial to the liberal opposition's ability to win local elections. On the other hand, urban governments tended to found new associations in order to bolster their position or, as in the case of the Schleswig-Holstein movement, to create a framework through which political agitation might find expression. Moreover, the ostensible apoliticism of the associations found its counterpart in the emphasis of liberal leaders in the municipal councils on the representation of their community, if necessary against the central bureaucracy. Here, we see the liberals' success in blending the old and the new – the defense of the "home town" with the assertion of the national cause. This blend helped to legitimate and give substance to one of the key features of German liberalism – the belief that the liberal movement represented a unitary *Volk*, in which partisan divisions at best played a secondary role and at

47. Quoted in ibid., 12.
48. [A. Grumbrecht], *Politische Betrachtungen für die Gegenwart und die nächste Zukunft von einem alten (nicht Alt-) Liberalen* (Bremen, 1866), p. 3; cf. Kurmeier, *Entstehung*, pp. 95–98.
49. H. Oncken, *Rudolf von Bennigsen: Ein deutscher liberaler Politiker*, vol. 1 (Stuttgart and Leipzig, 1910), pp. 280–88.

worst were to be treated with disdain.[50] As a recent study of local politics in the town of Konstanz has suggested, liberalism was strongest when it managed to translate the social contacts built up in the associations into effective local political control.[51] The bureaucracy and police repeatedly complained that local governments were exceeding their proper sphere of authority (i.e., local affairs) and were engaging in partisan propaganda, but were in practice able to do very little to curb such practices.[52] With the collapse of the *Reformverein*, the liberals came close to achieving a monopoly of public opinion formation in many of Hanover's towns.

These features of Hanoverian politics were of the greatest importance in the years after 1866. The National Liberals remained substantially stronger there than in the Reich as a whole largely because they remained the only real expression of the nationalist cause. The prevalence of Guelph particularism among the province's nobles removed any real possibility that an alternative, pro-Prussian conservatism would emerge. The survival of the Guelph movement into the Weimar Republic reflected the curious fact that the Hanoverian royal house could arouse considerable political support only after its eviction from the throne. The government badly needed that sort of organized support in the years before 1866, but its manner of governing removed any possibility of such support developing. As a result, Hanoverian National Liberalism could thus remain the principal representative of an apolitically nationalist, liberal-conservative, progovernmental coalition for far longer than was possible in most areas of the Reich.[53]

50. On the "home town" tradition, see above all M. Walker, *German Home Towns: Community, State and General Estate, 1648–1871* (Ithaca and London, 1971), chap. 12, which draws out well the link between the ideology of the home town and "the ubiquitous yearning for organic wholeness" (p. 426). On the self-image of German liberalism as the representative of a united *Volk*, see Sheehan, *German Liberalism*, chap. 7 and L. Gall, "Liberalismus und 'bürgerliche Gesell-schaft': Zur Charakter und Entwicklung der liberalen Bewegung in Deutschland," *Historische Zeitschrift* 220 (1975): 324–56.

51. D. Bellmann, "Der Liberalismus im Seekreis (1860–1870): Durchsetzungs-versuch und Scheitern eines regional eigenständigen Entwicklungskonzeptes," in G. Zang, ed., *Provinzialisierung einer Region: Zur Entstehung der bürgerlichen Gesellschaft in der Provinz* (Frankfurt, 1978), pp. 213–14.

52. See for example the correspondence on Miquel's alleged attempt to do this in Göttingen in February–March 1858, NHStA Han., 80 Hildesheim I E, no. 474.

53. See John, "Liberalism and Society," pp. 591–98, for a more extended treatment of this subject.

7

Notable Politics, the Crisis of German Liberalism, and the Electoral Transition of the 1890s

Geoff Eley

Tradition, Change, and German Political Culture

One influential approach to German political history before 1914 has stressed the structural embeddedness of popular political allegiances. This in its turn is linked to certain general assumptions about the longer-term formation of German political culture. At one level, such assumptions reflect a conception of German differences from "the West," which was axiomatic for both the liberal and Marxist traditions of the late nineteenth and early twentieth century and became central to explanations of the origins of Nazism after 1945. Thus for Karl Dietrich Bracher, the doyen of postwar West German political history in this sense, the "ultimate cause" of Nazism went right "back to the beginning of the nineteenth century," and derived from "the deep schism between German and Western political thought."[1] As is well known, this view is also attached to a particular reading of the 1848 Revolution, when the German bourgeoisie is thought to have failed in its liberalizing mission. Consequently, a set of inherited cultural dispositions combined with

1. Cited by G. Barraclough, in "Mandarins and Nazis," *New York Review of Books*, 19 October 1972, p. 42. An earlier version of this essay is scheduled to appear in *Quaderni Storici*. It is an adaptation and further development of arguments presented in my *Reshaping the German Right: Radical Nationalism and Political Change after Bismarck* (New Haven and London, 1980), and is complementary to another essay, "Anti-Semitism, Agrarian Mobilization, and the Crisis in the Conservative Party: Radicalism and Containment in the Foundation of the *Bund der Landwirte*, 1892–1893," written during 1982 and set to appear in the long overdue volume edited by J.C. Fout, *Politics, Parties, and the Authoritarian State: Imperial Germany, 1871–1918* (New York, forthcoming). It forms part of a continuing study of German liberalism between the 1860s and 1920s.

the debacle of 1848 and the subsequent failure of the 1860s (when the German bourgeoisie allowed itself to be coopted into Bismarck's nonliberal solution of the German question) to deprive Germany of the social force necessary for a healthy and vigorous liberalism. The configuration that accompanied German unification, therefore, which is usually presented as a dynamic economy developing within an unreformed political framework, in which preindustrial elites maintained their dominance against the rising forces of a modern society, is thought to have defined the parameters of German development in the next fifty years. This particular combination of economic modernity and political backwardness – involving the "unusually protracted retardation of democratization as against industrialization" – produced the strains and stresses that led ultimately to the catastrophe of 1933.[2]

This argumentation has been at the heart of the so-called *Sonderweg* thesis, the idea that German history followed a special or peculiar path of political development between 1848–71 and 1945.[3] This view of German exceptionalism has usually been based on a combination of political and intellectual or cultural history grounded in a social analysis of the primacy of preindustrial elites, namely, the Junkers and their equivalents in the bureaucracy and the military. At the same time, there is a deeper sociological dimension to the argument that harks back to the notion of deep-rooted cultural traits and derives in part from two flimsy but influential essays by Talcott Parsons in the 1940s, on "Democracy and Social Structure in Pre-Nazi Germany" and "Some Sociological Aspects of Fascist Movements."[4]

2. The quoted phrase comes from M.R. Lepsius, "Parteiensystem und Sozialstruktur: Zum Problem der Demokratisierung der deutschen Gesellschaft," in G.A. Ritter, ed., *Die deutschen Parteien vor 1918* (Cologne, 1973), p. 56.

3. Current debates about the *Sonderweg* thesis were initiated to a great extent by D. Blackbourn and G. Eley, *The Peculiarities of German History: Bourgeois Society and Politics in Nineteenth-Century Germany* (Oxford, 1984), and its earlier and shorter German version, *Mythen deutscher Geschichtsschreibung* (Frankfurt, 1980). The historiographical literature relevant to this discussion is now extremely large and still growing. Among the more recent and helpful are H. Grebing, *Der "deutsche Sonderweg" in Europa, 1806–1945: Eine Kritik* (Stuttgart, 1986); and J. Kocka, "German History before Hitler: The Debate about the German *Sonderweg*," *Journal of Contemporary History* 23 (1988): 3–16. However, Grebing neglects much of the English-language discussion, and Kocka presents an extremely partial view of its contribution to this literature.

4. See his *Essays in Sociological Theory* (Glencoe, 1964), pp. 104–41.

The strongest more recent formulation can be found in Dahrendorf's classic *Society and Democracy in Germany*, where the political deficit of German backwardness is traced back to a deeper-lying social structure: "The social basis of German authoritarianism, thus of the resistance of German society to modernity and liberalism, consisted in a structural syndrome that held people to the social ties in which they had found themselves without their doing and that prevented them from full participation."[5] Taken in plenitude, this has been an enormously attractive line of interpretation, promising as it does the integration of political, cultural, and sociological forms of explanation. With respect to political culture, moreover, there has been a particularly influential version of the argument, contained in the essays of M. Rainer Lepsius, and it is worth considering this in more detail.

Lepsius begins with the persistence of crucial "elements of a preindustrial social order," and locates this in an argument about the inadequate integration of competing and mutually exclusive political subcultures in the life of the state. In his view, the German party system was to stay tightly fettered in a field of conflict already defined before the foundation of the Reich, which remained highly resistant to "modern" political concerns like the "achievement of democratic institutions" or the "realization of claims on social equality." Political loyalties remained "fixed" on regional, local, confessional, and other particularist interests, rather than developing with the times and contributing to the integration of the emergent citizenry inside a participant political culture comparable to those of the West. The result was the abnormal persistence of a mutually reinforcing structure of self-sealing, culturally autonomous "social-moral milieus," each with its characteristic party representation. Lepsius distinguishes four major examples of this kind: a conservative one that was "Protestant, agrarian, regionally closed, and wedded to traditional paternalistic precepts"; that of the Catholic Center; that of the *Mittelstand*; and that of the Socialists.[6] Together, he argues, their existence lent an imposing stability and continuity to the entire period between 1871 and 1933. Increasingly, each became entrenched behind a wall of defensive preoccupations,

---

5. R. Dahrendorf, *Society and Democracy in Germany* (London, 1968), p. 404.
6. Lepsius, "Parteiensystem und Sozialstruktur," pp. 64ff.

concerned with its own particularistic interests and integrity as opposed to a more pluralist conception of the interest of the whole, and cemented by carefully nurtured subcultural identity. Even the rise of Social Democracy, with its 4.2 million voters by 1912, failed to alter this situation. The labor movement itself formed a higly organized defensive subculture, and its growing strength merely deepened the others' attachment to "preindustrial conceptions of value." This created and entrenched "a moral frontier between the bourgeois-confessional communities of sentiment and the labor movement," which militated against the "structural conditions of industrial society" and prevented Germany's gradual democratization.[7]

Over the last quarter century, this has proven a compelling analysis. It has recently been given a new twist by Stanley Suval's general study of Wilhelmine electoral politics.[8] Drawing on the work of the cultural school of U.S. electoral history (most notably that of Paul Kleppner), he argues that "religion, ethnicity, nationality, and race," combined with the impact of a politically interventionist state, were more salient to the lines of political cleavage in Wilhelmine Germany than was class in some exclusive or primary sense. On this basis, he distinguishes between four "social groupings" that broadly coincide with Lepsius's "social-moral milieus," together with two additional smaller ones based on the Jewish and Polish minorities; the Conservatives/East-Elbian rurals, the Center Party/German Catholics; the Social-Democrats (SPD)/working class; and a fourth with a more fragmented party-political representation, based on the Protestant *Bürgertum* and *Mittelstand*. He then argues that Wilhelmine elections had the effect of asserting and confirming the differences between these stable camps.[9]

At the same time, Suval departs from Lepsius in two ways. On the one hand, he presents the electoral system in a far more positive light. He builds a persuasive case for seeing the Wilhelmine polity as increasingly organized around a stable political

7. Ibid., p. 73. See also M.R. Lepsius, "Demokratie in Deutschland als historisch-soziologisches Problem," in T. Adorno, ed., *Spätkapitalismus oder Industriegesellschaft* (Stuttgart, 1968), pp. 197–213. Both essays have acquired classic status and enormous influence over the last two decades.

8. See S. Suval, *Electoral Politics in Wilhelmine Germany* (Chapel Hill, N.C., 1985).

9. Ibid., pp. 55–119.

culture articulated through the process of voting, which served to affirm people's basic allegiance and commitments in an integrative and thoroughly modern way. In fact, far from being a source of fragmentation and instability as Lepsius maintained, the lines of cleavage and affiliation were delivering the bases of cohesion. As Suval shows, the electoral process was not really susceptible to the authoritarian direction and plebiscitary manipulation many historians have claimed to detect, and adult males exercised their votes remarkably unencumbered by corruption, paternalism, deference, and intimidation. On the contrary, the Wilhelmine period was marked by a continuous and constructive politicization of the electorate: "Turnout increased; dropoff decreased; local councils became politicized; the number of voters engaged in more intensive campaign activity rose enormously. This is the Wilhelmine system."[10] This was leading to the growth of a stable political culture, which was at least comparable to contemporary electoral systems: "Wilhelmines were voting for past, present, and future as embodied in continuing and durable social groupings. The Wilhelmine inheritance then was a series of stable commitments by a politicized electorate exercising its citizenship roles."[11] As Suval argues in his conclusion, this has major implications for the question of continuity and our understanding of Weimar and its instabilities: rather than crippling Weimar democracy, the Wilhelmine legacy may have been one of its positive foundations.

On the other hand, he also discovers considerable flux and indeterminacy in one of Lepsius's four "social-moral milieus" (that of the Protestant *Bürgertum* and/or *Mittelstand*) that undermine the force of structural continuity Lepsius finds descending from the 1860s and 1870s. Here Suval points to the attempt to form a new "social grouping" in the three decades before 1914 that could replace the liberal ascendancy of the unification decades – an anti-Socialist and patriotic bloc based on the Protestant bourgeoisie and petty bourgeoisie, coordinated by the government for antidemocratic ends. The space for such a strategy was opened by the break-up of liberal hegemonies in Protestant Germany in the face of the politicization of the 1890s, which created the possibility of transforming the old liberal

10. Ibid., p. 36.
11. Ibid., p. 257.

constituency into a new one loyal to the government. Although this remained fairly amorphous in organization terms before 1914, the aspiration lent much unity to the politics of the government and dominant classes, and corresponded to the never-quite-realized *Sammlungspolitik* that occupies such a central place in the historiography of the Wilhelmine years. In particular, Suval also points to a "radical populist" version of this effort, taking various forms but ultimately moved by a fierce brand of nationalist ideology that threatened to outflank the government from the right.[12]

Suval's reevaluation of the Wilhelmine polity is salutary. By freeing the years before 1914 from their usual place in the teleology of German exceptionalism, by considering the Wilhelmine era in "its own terms," and by simultaneously defining a more realistic basis for cross-national comparison, he casts Wilhelmine electoral behavior in an illuminating light. The issue of comparison is explicitly enjoined, and this "normalizing" of pre-1914 politics is the very opposite of the untheoretical neohistoricism with which such analysis is frequently tagged.[13] Moreover, by standing Lepsius on his head – that is, by seeing the various subcultures as training grounds of active citizenship and as the building blocks of an integrated political culture rather than an entrenched obstruction – Suval supplies an alternative to the most patently misleading aspects of Lepsius's argument, namely, the idea that there was no significant realignment of political forces or popular allegiances between the founding period of unification and the outbreak of the First World War, let alone in the collapse of the Weimar Republic in 1930–33. In fact, as I and others have argued, the 1890s constituted a major moment of flux, bringing a basic shift in political alignments and a striking upsurge of popular mobilization.[14] In this sense the

12. Ibid., pp. 149–60.
13. For a discussion of this point, see Blackbourn and Eley, *Peculiarities*, pp. 29ff.
14. See especially G. Eley, *Reshaping the German Right: Radical Nationalism and Political Change after Bismarck* (New Haven and London, 1980); and D. Blackbourn, *Class, Religion, and Local Politics in Wilhelmine Germany: The Centre Party in Württemberg before 1914* (New Haven and London, 1980). See also W. Mock, "'Manipulation von oben' oder Selbstorganisation an der Basis? Einige neuere Ansätze in der englischen Historiographie zur Geschichte des deutschen Kaiserreichs," *Historische Zeitschrift* 232 (1981): 358–75; R.G. Moeller, "The Kaiserreich Recast? Continuity and Change in Modern German Historiography," *Journal of Social History* 17 (1984): 655–83.

decade was a vital moment of transition between two distinct electoral "systems," the Bismarckian and the Wilhelmine in Suval's terms. One configuration of dominant-class politics, in which the leading force was liberal, was replaced by another, in which a more complex and fragmented array of forces took shape. The purpose of this paper is to explore some of the terms of this difficult and unresolved transition.

Liberalism, Popular Politics, and the Flux of the 1890s

The key change of the 1890s was this: between the early 1860s and the end of the 1880s the dominant fraction of the Bismarckian power bloc had been *liberal* – and even after 1879 national politics had still been structured by the parliamentary strength of the various liberal groupings – but by the start of the next decade this liberal predominance was already starting to decompose, and by 1900 it was in fragments. The 1887 elections were the last in which the National Liberals recovered something like their former strength of the 1870s before sinking in subsequent elections to a fairly even plateau of some forty-five to fifty-five seats.[15] In its heyday the party had a continuous belt of seats stretching from Baden in the southwest through the Palatinate, Prussian and Grand Ducal Hesse, Prussian Saxony, and Hanover, flanked by Thuringia and Saxony, and culminating in Schleswig-Holstein in the north. But by 1898 that predominance had fallen apart, with the permanent loss of some forty seats. This was accompanied by a similar crisis in these regions. As Dan White concludes, "After 1896, when the Hessian National Liberals lost their broad margin in the second chamber, no regional liberal party in South Germany exclusively controlled its state legislature."[16]

Moreover, electorally this National Liberal predominance was

15. In the first elections under the empire the National Liberals won 125 of the 382 seats, rising in 1874 to 155 out of 397, or 39 percent of the total. Under the pressure of the antisocialist and protectionist agitation of the late 1870s, this representation declined to 128 in 1877 and 99 in 1878, and by 1884 the rather confused alignments among the liberal groupings as a whole left the party with only 51 seats. The National Liberal share of the popular vote fell from its peak of 29.7 percent in 1874 to 12.9 percent in 1884. After 1887 (99 seats, 22.3 percent of the vote), the party averaged 48 seats and 13.7 percent of the popular vote.

16. D.S. White, *The Splintered Party: National Liberalism in Hessen and the Reich, 1867–1918* (Cambridge, Mass., 1976), p. 151.

rural as much as it was *urban*. The party had come to power at the end of the 1860s as the voice of popular regional coalitions against aristocracy and reaction. This applied to Prussian Hesse and Hanover no less than to the more obvious cases of Bavaria, Württemberg, and – preeminently – Baden. In the Grand Duchy of Hesse, for instance, they were the patent beneficiaries of unification, which swept the liberals to office with forty-one out of fifty seats in the first elections of 1872. There resulted a close symbiosis (which was typical of the regions just mentioned) of liberal notables (*Honoratioren*) and state officials, in which the social primacy of the former acquired extra shape and visibility from the dispatch of administrative functions in the local and regional context: provincial commissions, district committees, school boards, chambers of commerce, agricultural associations, and so on. A discriminatory property franchise, both for the Prussian Landtag and for the provincial and district assemblies, then backed the "natural" leadership of such liberal notables with some extra legal security. Ideologically – and culturally – the broader basis of this coalition was cemented by the *Kulturkampf*, which was vital to its popular legitimacy in the 1870s.[17] In the towns this went together with a definite social milieu (which is conceptually consistent with Lepsius's "social-moral milieu," but at the same time much more sociologically specific), where intermarriage, kin, business networks, associations from school and university, religious observance, philanthropy, cultural events, and the social arena of the club all worked to keep the mechanisms of identity and influence well oiled.[18] Although present in the countryside, these associations

17. The popular-cultural aspects of the *Kulturkampf*, and the sometimes near-utopian aspirations invested in it by liberal activists, are a neglected dimension in the literature. But see the following: G. Schmidt, "Die Nationalliberalen – eine regierungsfähige Partei? Zur Problematik der inneren Reichsgründung, 1870–1878', in Ritter, ed., *Deutsche Parteien*, p. 120; L. Gall, "Die partei- und sozialgeschichtliche Problematik des badischen Kulturkampfes," *Zeitschrift für die Geschichte des Oberrheins* 113 (1965): 151–96; U. Tal, *Christians and Jews in Germany: Religion, Politics and Ideology in the Second Reich, 1870–1914* (Ithaca and London, 1975), pp. 81–120; G. Zang, ed., *Provinzialisierung einer Region: Zur Entstehung der bürgerlichen Gesellschaft in der Provinz* (Frankfurt, 1978), esp. the essays by D. Bellmann, W. Trapp, and Zang himself.

18. Detailed social-historical studies of local associational life in late nineteenth century Germany are still badly needed. For general suggestions, see T. Nipperdey, "Verein als soziale Struktur in Deutschland im späten 18. und frühen 19. Jahrhundert," in *Gesellschaft, Kultur, Theorie: Aufsätze zur neueren*

were less finely developed, and liberal predominance rested necessarily far more on the initiative and standing of a few leading personalities.

But in destroying the dominance of the National Liberals in German politics, the collapse of their support in the countryside was quantitatively much more important than the Social Democratic Party's (Sozialdemokratische Partei Deutschlands or SPD) gains in the towns. In this sense the major solvent of existing political alignments in the 1890s was an unprecedented agrarian radicalism, one that could already be detected in 1890, but that is normally associated with the launching of the Agrarian League (Bund der Landwirte or BdL) in 1893. In fact, this agrarian mobilization was initiated not so much by the grievances of the Junkers – hostility to Caprivi's commercial treaties and the threat of lowered tariffs – as by the distinctive long-term problems of the smaller farmer, above all by indebtedness and its sources, rural depopulation, the erosion of ancillary enterprise like brewing and rural crafts, the apparent pro-urban biases of government, and so on. A series of conjunctural factors exacerbated this small-farmer resentment, including the disastrous foot-and-mouth epidemic of 1891–92, the severe drought of the following year, and the higher taxes attached to the Army Bill of 1892–93. Furthermore, the institutional consolidation of the rural class structure, particularly via the emerging mechanisms of interest representation, inevitably militated against the satisfaction of peasant demands. Smaller producers had small hope of sharing in the benefits of a growing economy without positive intervention from the state in the form of tax relief, cheap credit, or the construction of railway branch-lines, and there was little sign that the government was prepared to move in that direction.

Not surprisingly, therefore, peasant protest took the form of an antiplutocratic populism, through which a variety of enemies – the nobleman, the priest, the big city, the educated gentleman,

---

Geschichte (Göttingen, 1976), pp. 176–205; and O. Dann, "Die Anfänge politischer Vereinsbildung in Deutschland," in U. Engelhardt, V. Sellin, and H. Stuke, eds., *Soziale Bewegung und politische Verfassung* (Stuttgart, 1976), pp. 197–232. The pioneering monograph, which has set new standards in this regard, is R. Koshar, *Social Life, Local Politics, and Nazism: Marburg, 1880–1935* (Chapel Hill and London, 1986). See also H. Freudenthal, *Vereine in Hamburg: Ein Beitrag zur Geschichte und Volkskunde der Geselligkeit* (Hamburg, 1968).

an unfeeling distant government, and, of course, the middle-man and the Jew – could be easily conflated into a single image of oppression. The scenario of rural unrest thus produced was common to most parts of central and southern Germany, with further traces in the rest of the country depending on the character of the social structure. The political forms varied, from political anti-Semitism in Hesse to independent peasant radical-ism in parts of Bavaria, and a redeployed Catholic radicalism in Baden. In Württemberg the launching of an independent state Center Party coincided with the climax of traditional radical democracy in the People's Party, and both took much of their impetus from rural discontents and aspirations. Now, in each of these cases it was *National Liberalism* and its regional equivalents that became the butt of rural complaints, although in Bavaria the Center also came in for its share. In general, this amounted to a new spontaneous activation of rural voters *beyond* the existing frontier of party control and representation, in ways that threatened the hold of existing parties on their traditional sup-port.

Here I want to draw attention not only to the social and ideological bases of this challenge, but also to the popular mode of its organization. A new *style* of politics was being launched. At one level this can be measured simply by the expansion of the electorate, in all the ways stressed by Suval and earlier by Blackbourn and myself, including the rising rates of participa-tion, the intensity of electioneering, the increase in the numbers of run-off ballots, the rising costs of campaigning, and so on. But the very fact of electoral competition itself was changing the nature of the rural political process. The hustings were a new experience for large numbers of constituencies. Georg von Hert-ling contrasted sharply his uneventful return for a Rhineland seat in the 1880s with the intensive village campaigning needed in his new Bavarian seat by 1896, and this may be taken as emblematic of the general experience of the decade.[19] Politics had previously been conducted by small groups of notables, connected more by social prestige than by any organized party associations, who generally met perfunctorily a few weeks be-fore the polling day to select a candidate, and who rarely

19. G.V. Hertling, *Erinnerungen aus meinem Leben*, 2 vols. (Munich, 1919–20), vol. 2, p. 176.

indulged in serious electioneering. This informality – that is, the absence of an *organized* context for local political life, in effect the absence of a local public sphere – was the counterpart to the National Liberals' postunification hegemony. But such olympian detachment from the vulgarities of grass-roots campaigning was becoming unrealistic in the new conditions of the 1890s, when winning a seat began to require "working" a constituency well in advance.[20]

Otto Böckel's victory in Marburg on an independent anti-Semitic and rural populist platform in 1887 is now well established as the classic manifestation of the new politics against the old. Here a small clique of leading personalities had customarily managed the election without a major rally, and Böckel's opponent proceeded as before, arriving three weeks before the poll to meet with a few merchants, teachers, and *Bildungsbürger* (i.e., the local National Liberal establishment in Marburg) behind closed doors. In the meantime, however, Böckel was stumping the villages, achieving maximum visibility among the peasantry, and building the popular momentum for his unexpected triumph. For our purposes, the striking thing about this movement was to be its longer-term durability, organized around a collective identity and sense of élan that at the time was quite unusual outside the SPD. For example, this involved a conscious playing on popular traditions (among other things, by reappropriating the iconography and legacies of 1848), and by presenting himself as a colorful "man of the people" in contrast to the effete and distant elite, Böckel was gambling not only on the local peasantry's democratic populism, but also on its recently violated Hessian patriotism, for the Prussian annexation of 1867 had added a further dimension to the complexities of the peasantry's cultural discontents. The organized infrastructure of the movement was provided by the freshly created Central German Peasants' Union (Mitteldeutscher Bauernverein) and its auxiliaries, but Böckel's tireless agitational drive was the real key to his success. In addition to quantity – in the first four months of 1890 he held over sixty rallies – style was crucial. His progress was accompanied by marching bands or "torchlight processions

---

20. Aside from the evidence assembled in Suval, *Electoral Politics*, see also D. Blackbourn, "The Politics of Demagogy in Imperial Germany," *Past and Present* 113 (November 1986): 152–84.

that marched from village to village singing Lutheran hymns and patriotic songs. Mounted peasant youths guarded his wagon while hosts of followers, all wearing the blue cornflower as an identifying party badge, trailed along behind."[21] Politics here were popular and celebratory and have to be seen in their specific local context.[22]

Nor can these politics be regarded as "manipulative" in origin.[23] The popular *origins* of this rural radicalism become clearer if we note that the SPD was also making gains in the countryside at this time. By 1898 the SPD took 26.5 percent of its popular vote from small communities of less than two thousand people, or some 15 percent of the votes cast in such places. Many of these were in industrial Thuringia and Saxony, or in the hinterlands of the great urban strongholds of Hamburg, Berlin, Nuremberg, Königsberg, and so on. But this should not obscure the party's progress in rural areas proper. By 1898 the SPD was "not only the strongest party of the town, but also the third strongest party in the village."[24] This was true of two areas with little developed industry in particular: in Mecklenburg and the province of East Prussia, where big-estate agriculture dominated, and in Protestant small-farming areas like Hesse, central Württemberg, and the northern Palatinate. This should not be exaggerated, of course. The SPD hardly conquered the German countryside, and its failure to develop a creative national policy for the peasantry remained one of its biggest deficits after the abortive discussions of 1894–95.[25] But *symptomatically* the

21. R.S. Levy, *The Downfall of the Anti-Semitic Political Parties in Imperial Germany* (New Haven and London, 1975), p. 56.

22. The best and most intensive treatment of the Böckel movement is now D. Peal's unpublished dissertation, "Anti-Semitism and Rural Transformation in Kurhessen: The Rise and Fall of the Böckel Movement" (diss., Columbia University, 1985), currently being revised for publication.

23. The manipulative view of agrarian mobilization has been most closely associated with the work of H.-J. Puhle. See esp. *Agrarische Interessenpolitik und preußischer Konservatismus im Wilhelminischen Reich, 1893–1914*, 2nd ed. (Bonn-Bad Godesberg, 1975); and "Conservatism in Modern German History," *Journal of Contemporary History* 13 (1978): 701–7. I have discussed Puhle's work critically in "Anti-Semitism, Agrarian Mobilization, and the Crisis in the Conservative Party: Radicalism and Containment in the Foundation of the *Bund der Landwirte*, 1892–1893," in J.C. Fout, ed., *Politics, Parties, and the Authoritarian State: Imperial Germany, 1871–1918* (New York, forthcoming).

24. H. Hesselbarth, *Revolutionäre Sozialdemokraten, Opportunisten und die Bauern am Vorabend des Imperialismus* (East Berlin, 1968), pp. 247f.

25. The whole question of the SPD and the countryside remains an area of terrible neglect. Aside from Hesselbarth, *Revolutionäre Sozialdemokraten*, see H.G.

party's new presence in the countryside reflected a general element of turmoil in the accustomed pattern of allegiance. For the rural electorate, voting for the SPD became one among a repertoire of radical affiliations in the volatile circumstances of the 1890s.

The entry of the new politics into the villages could be dramatic in its disruption of old solidarities. Thus, in 1888, in the Oberhessian village of Lindheim, a left-wing candidate contested the reelection of the local mayor, who had normally been presented as a matter of course by the prosperous National Liberal farmer Richard Westernacher and other local notables; the unexpected success of the left candidate split the village down the middle, producing breakaways in the choir and the savings bank, two camps in the church, and general feuding.[26] With experiences like these, National Liberals might be forgiven for conflating the problem of the SPD with that of the anti-Semites, because they were both associated with overturning the comfortable certainties of local politics. By 1898 the SPD had made the second ballot in three of the six Hessian rural constituencies, and these were also precisely the centers of anti-Semitic advance: in Giessen the SPD vote rose from 19 to 33 percent; in Friedberg-Büdingen from 17 to 34 percent; and in Bensheim-Erbach from 11 to 27 percent. In 1887 the National Liberals had won all three of those seats on the first ballot, yet were now reduced to 30, 35, and 44 percent, respectively. In Hesse as a whole the National Liberal share of the poll fell from 42 to 31 percent between 1893 and 1898, while the SPD's climbed from 22 to 35 percent.[27]

During the 1890s, therefore, the adaptability of the old anti-socialist parties was being challenged in a big way. On the one hand, the lifting of the Anti-Socialist Law in 1890 had liberalized

Lehmann, *Die Agrarfrage in der Theorie und Praxis der deutschen und internationalen Sozialdemokratie* (Tübingen, 1970). The best general discussion is in A. Hussain and K. Tribe, *Marxism and the Agrarian Question*, vol. 1: *German Social Democracy and the Peasantry, 1890–1907* (London, 1981).

26. K.E. Demandt, "Leopold von Sacher-Masoch und sein oberhessischer Volksbildungsverein zwischen Schwarzen, Roten und Antisemiten," *Hessisches Jahrbuch für Landesgeschichte* 18 (1968): 182.

27. For a detailed breakdown of the SPD's performance in rural constituencies, see Hesselbarth, *Revolutionäre Sozialdemokraten*, pp. 241–50. See also K. Saul, "Der Kampf um das Landproletariat: Sozialistische Landagitation, Grossgrundbesitz und preußische Staatsverwaltung, 1890 bis 1903," *Archiv für Sozialgeschichte* 15 (1975): 167–77.

the conduct of political life to the advantage of the SPD, which, aside from its conquest of the towns, had, in October 1890, immediately issued the slogan "Out into the Countryside!"; on the other hand, the political temperature was also being raised, as we saw, by a variegated process of independent rural politicization. The formation of the BdL in early 1893 by a group of Conservative landowning politicians, partly to immunize the East Elbian countryside against any further progress of the anti-Semites and partly to begin seizing command of the rising agrarian mobilization by channeling it into an opposition to the Caprivi government's commercial treaties, was one response to this situation; and, measured in the most immediate terms – the sealing of East Elbian society against the agitation of the SPD – the initiative can be counted a success, because in 1898 the meager SPD vote in the backwaters of West Prussia, Posen, and Pomerania dwindled even further. But in areas like these, where a combination of big-estate agriculture and transmuted seigneurial authority kept the rural population in a state of well-entrenched deferential subordination, the challenge of popular politics was least urgent. In Catholic agricultural regions, by contrast, where the SPD vote also slumped in 1898 from its already modest totals, the anti-Socialist counterattack was much more of a creative achievement. For in Rhineland-Westphalia, Baden, Württemberg, and Bavaria, the Center Party was faced not with a subordinated class of landless laborers, but with a freshly mobilizing independent peasantry.

When it began expanding its organization in the early 1890s, the Center was partly responding to the new volatility in the southern countryside, where agrarian self-interest conjoined with older traditions of parish-pump radicalism to produce a more complex political formation than in the Prussian east. But there was also a larger political dimension to this expansion of the party's activity. The development of a modernized Catholic subculture of party, trade union, self-help, and cultural agencies was also partly the conscious initiative of the leadership. The Center managed more rapidly than any other established party to reconstitute itself for full-scale competition with the SPD after 1890. The old guard certainly hankered for the former certainties of the now-defunct Anti-Socialist Law. But the coming generation around Ernst Lieber appreciated the need to fight the SPD on the new ground. The construction of the People's Association for Catholic Germany (Volksverein für das Katholische Deutschland) in autumn 1890 on broad ideological foundations instead of the narrower confessional ones that some older voices had wished; the parliamentary opposition to fresh exceptional laws; and the gradual move toward Christian trade unionism were all signs of this trend. As the Hessian Center leader Philipp Wasserburg, a self-styled "clerico-democrat," put it when opposing the government's abortive Revolution Bill in 1895: "Police and Church for once are irreconcilable opposites."[28]

By comparison, the National Liberals were far less adaptable. They failed to emulate the Conservatives and Center by going on the offensive as a national and regional party in the 1890s. Where the latter busied themselves with building an organization for moderating the independence of the new agrarian movements, the National Liberal Party failed to produce a comparable response. Both the Conservatives and the Center managed to reconstitute themselves in a new representative relationship with old rural constituencies; ideologically, this involved far-reaching processes of innovation, through which diverse movements of rural discontent were rationalized into a single "agrarian interest" and the *Mittelstand* was simultaneously constructed as a "natural" support for right-wing politics. But not only did the National Liberals fail to create new popular organizations for recouping the lost ground; they also formed a dangerous alliance with the newly founded BdL, which certainly gave them short-term advantages in the 1893 elections, but simultaneously gave a hostage to fortune. When the BdL sank roots in Hesse and Hanover in the spring of 1893, for example, it turned naturally to National Liberal farmers for its support. Almost without exception, the leaders were to be prominent National Liberal notables, and the League's local structures meshed neatly with those of the existing liberal-dominated Agricultural Associations.[29]

---

28. H. Gottwald, "Zentrum und Imperialismus" (diss., Jena, 1966), pp. 96f.

29. See White, *Splintered Party*, pp. 143f.; J.C. Hunt, "The 'Egalitarianism' of the Right: The Agrarian League in South-West Germany, 1893–1914," *Journal of Contemporary History* 10 (1975): 515ff. In 1893 seven of the nine National Liberal candidates for the Reichstag elections in Hesse were endorsed by the BdL, and the other two were broadly sympathetic. For the more complex situation in Hanover, see G. Vascik "Rural Politics and Sugar in Germany: A Comparative Study of the National Liberal Party in Hanover and Prussian Saxony, 1871–1914" (diss., University of Michigan, 1988).

The contrast with the Center is revealing. The problems facing the National Liberals in Hanover, Hesse, and the Palatinate were much the same as those of the Center in Bavaria and the southwest. Both were faced with a new kind of popular activity in rural areas that outgrew the conventional framework of *Honoratiorenpolitik* and demanded innovation. Both were also anxious, in their different ways, to defend their existing character as parties of disinterested principle, "reconciling and harmonizing the opposing economic aspirations in our midst," as one leading National Liberal put it.[30] But whereas the Center managed to keep its own integrity as a party, the National Liberals in effect subcontracted the task of maintaining their rural presence to a potentially hostile independent partner – the BdL – which possessed its own national apparatus and a special relationship to another party, the Conservatives east of the Elbe. This was an absolutely crucial turning point: rather than adapting and renovating their own organization, the National Liberals abandoned vital political space to an agrarian movement that would eventually strike out on its own in decidedly *nonliberal* directions. In this sense, the BdL's ability to insert itself politically between the National Liberal Party and its historical rural constituency in certain regions was the key development of the 1890s. Indeed, the impact of the new league was much greater here, in the central belt from Hanover down to Württemberg, than in the areas east of the Elbe. In the east it merely serviced an existing system of neo-seigneurial domination; in these other regions it delivered new allies into the Conservative camp and fractured the National Liberals' political confidence.

To illustrate the National Liberal predicament, it is worth returning to the earlier example of the Hessian village of Lindheim. In small communities such as this one, with only a few hundred inhabitants, liberal prestige needed little organization beyond the usual savings club for the smaller farmers. Something more elaborate was normally produced by special circumstances. One of the latter might be the arbitrary presence of a particularly vigorous philanthropist such as Leopold Sacher-Masoch, who came to Lindheim in 1887 – just as Böckel was beginning his career in nearby Marburg across the border in

---

30. A. Hobrecht in June 1897, quoted in L.F. Seyffardt, *Erinnerungen* (Leipzig, 1900), p. 595.

Prussian Hesse – and launched his short-lived Oberhessian League for Popular Education (Oberhessischer Volksbildungs-verein) in January 1893.[31] But this kind of initiative died almost as soon as it began. More commonly, the liberal notables were stirred into action by the intrusion of an unwelcome competitor, whether anti-Semite, Socialist, or some other type of radical. Thus the bitter village election for the Lindheim mayor in 1888 was followed the next year by the establishment of a farming school for girls under the auspices of the Upper Hessian Agricultural Association (Oberhessischer Landwirtschaftlicher Verein) and directly inspired by the local National Liberal notable, Richard Westernacher. By 1890 such liberals were facing a still more politicized environment. Otto Böckel's movement had now reached into the Grand Duchy of Hesse, where it found the local leadership of the ex-National Liberal farmer Philipp Köhler, who helped launch the Central German Peasants' Association, which by mid-1892 claimed fifteen thousand members in some four hundred branches. Thus, when the BdL was launched in Upper Hesse in 1893 it was no surprise to find Westernacher on its committee together with other leading National Liberal farmers. In these circumstances National Liberal activity had a natural agrarian direction once it was challenged for its traditional village support. Badly needing a local apparatus to fight the anti-Semites and the SPD, it was hardly surprising that the National Liberals welcomed the sudden appearance of the BdL.[32]

To put this example into a somewhat stronger context, it is worth contrasting the Grand Duchy of Hesse with another liberal stronghold, namely, Schleswig-Holstein. This counterexample shows quite well how the problems of the National Liberal notability in Hesse derived from a particular rural social regime. Schleswig-Holstein shows the agricultures of independent peasants and big estates existing as separate economies in virtually contiguous proximity. In many ways the province was a microcosm of German agriculture's main features at the turn of the century: a highly productive rich and middle peasantry in the fertile marshlands of the west, conducting a commercial,

---

31. Demandt, "Leopold von Sacher-Masoch," pp. 177f., 182, and 192ff.
32. Ibid., p. 185f.; Levy, *Downfall*, pp. 55–60; White, *Splintered Party*, pp. 136ff. For a more detailed discussion of these general points, see Eley, "Anti-Semitism, Agrarian Mobilization, and the Crisis in the Conservative Party."

mechanized agriculture that had rapidly converted to livestock, and with vigorous traditions of political freedom; big noble estates in the hilly east, more persistent in grain cultivation and slower to respond to the changed conditions of the world market; and, sandwiched between them, the poor freeholding peasants of the sandy Geest, generating only small surpluses that had to be supplemented from wage labor for other farmers and industry. The provincial agricultural associations had long been dominated by the eastern estate-owners, whose influence was further entrenched by the legal incorporation of the new Chamber of Agriculture in 1895 on a restricted franchise. However, in the meantime some progressive agronomists had launched a Cooperative Federation in 1883 for smaller farmers not accommodated by the associations, and by 1900 this numbered some two hundred affiliates. Moreover, the economic division corresponded to a political one, because the conservatives could maintain a serious presence only in the eastern districts. The two conservative parties had never won more than two of the province's ten Reichstag seats before 1893, and by 1903 they had been eliminated altogether. By contrast, the liberals kept and even extended their hold on the peasantry between the 1890s and 1914, taking seven of the ten seats in 1912. In *this* kind of setting there was little scope (or even need) for an organization like the BdL. Its possible field of activity was circumscribed by the peasantry's historical liberalism, and it managed little progress among the prosperous farming districts of the west.[33]

In Schleswig-Holstein, in other words, the contradiction between peasant and estate agriculture was articulated inside an existing division of political allegiance, in which the confident liberalism of prosperous independent farmers drew fresh strength from direct comparisons with the big estates. Here the juxtaposition *validated* liberalism as an ideology of rural politics and enabled the old populist coalition of the 1860s and 1870s, which defined itself against the Prussian aristocracy, to persist much longer than elsewhere. But in the second of our examples,

33. The classic ecological analysis of agrarian politics in Schleswig-Holstein is R. Herberle, *From Democracy to Nazism: A Regional Case Study on Political Parties in Germany* (New York, 1970), pp. 23ff. See also G. Freifrau v. Schrötter, "Agrarorganisation und sozialer Wandel (dargestellt am Beispiel Schleswig-Holsteins)," in W. Rüegg and O. Neuloh, eds., *Zur soziologischen Theorie und Analyse des 19. Jahrhunderts* (Göttingen, 1971), pp. 123–44.

that of Hesse, liberalism was itself the political vehicle of the landowning oligarchy, and could be adapted to peasant dissatisfactions with far greater difficulty. Of the three Hessian provinces, only in Rhenisch Hesse "where the influence of the relatively weak territorial aristocracy had been crushed under the French occupation of 1793–1815" and where the "better-off peasants and townsmen" had been the main economic beneficiaries was something like the buoyant farming society of western Schleswig-Holstein reproduced.[34] Significantly, perhaps, the National Liberals had an easier time surviving politically in the two Rhenish Hessian constituencies of Bingen-Alzey and Worms-Heppenheim than elsewhere in the Grand Duchy.

In the two other provinces of Starkenberg and Upper Hesse the social contrasts were much stronger: the former with an industrial belt in the north from Darmstadt to Offenbach, a fertile farming zone in the southwest along the Rhine and the Bergstrasse, and the much poorer Odenwald in the southeast; the latter more uniformly agricultural, but divided by the Vogelsberg into a more prosperous west and a backward east. It was in Upper Hesse, the most northerly of the Hessian provinces, where the disparities were greatest and the bigger farmers controlled the best land and facilities, that the existing political alignments – that is, the National-Liberal-dominated structures of *Honoratiorenpolitik* – were most vulnerable. For here the poor smallholding peasantry confronted the combined liberal predominance of local nobility and improving farmers (the Richard Westernachers of the region) without the benefit of an existing peasant radicalism to provide a strong counter-hegemonic alternative. Of course, Hessian National Liberals had originally built their political success on a broad popular coalition against the traditional aristocratic order: as late as 1881 liberals in the adjoining Prussian Reichstag constituency of Hanau-Gelnhausen-Bockelheim had entered the elections with the slogan "Junkers and priests together/Put townsmen and peasants in tether."[35] But by the end of the 1880s this popular leadership had ossified into a fresh set of oppressive paternalistic relations, which could only be fractured by a new and independent peasant politics. In

---

34. White, *Splintered Party*, p. 20f.
35. "Junker und Pfaffen im Bund/Richten Bürger und Bauer zu Grund!," cited in ibid., p. 100.

fact, Upper Hesse formed the southern rim of a region stretching westwards to Siegen, northwards to Göttingen, and eastwards into Thuringia, which was to return a fairly stable bloc of anti-Semitic and radical agrarian deputies from 1893 to the First World War, and such a breakthrough could be achieved in the Hessian context only through a frontal collision with the landed liberal establishment.[36]

The failure of the Hessian National Liberal Party to accommodate the needs of smaller farmers in the changed conjuncture of the late 1880s and 1890s, either by adapting the existing Agricultural Associations for a drastically expanded service activity, or by some organized innovation by the party itself, had far-reaching implications. Basically, they vacated a political space whose noisy invasion by new political forces eventually brought their very survival as a serious political force in the countryside into question. Thus, significantly, Otto Böckel's movement won most of its support in the poorer agricultural areas in the north of the Grand Duchy, where chronic indebtedness, bad soil, inadequate transportation, and backward technology combined to depress the smallholding peasants. In the western areas across the Rhine (much as in the marshlands of Schleswig-Holstein), on the other hand, a prosperous class of richer peasants with strong traditions of political independence predominated, and Böckel's anti-Semitic radicalism made few inroads into the established and more deeply rooted liberal support.[37] While we remain remarkably ignorant about the social basis of German liberalism between the 1860s and the turn of the century, it may well be that such contrasts were paradigmatic for liberal survival before the First World War. In that case, National Liberal *Honoratiorenpolitik* – the informal structure of politics that entered a crisis in the 1890s, that presumed popular allegiances rather than organizing them – may be related to one kind of sociopolitical regime in the countryside as opposed to another, in which landholding systems, the forms and bases of peasant emancipation, and degrees of peasant

36. Although the specific inflection is my own, this account is condensed from the following sources: White, *Splintered Party*, esp. pp. 123ff.; R. Mack, "Otto Boeckel und die antisemitische Bauernbewegung in Hessen, 1887–1914," *Wetterauer Geschichtsblätter* 16 (1967): 113–47; Demandt, "Leopold von Sacher-Masoch," pp. 180–84; and Peal, "Anti-Semitism and Rural Transformation."
37. White, *Splintered Party*, pp. 20f. and 137–40.

political independence provide the important variables. Where liberals remained a vital force in the countryside before 1914 – for example, in Oldenburg, parts of Hanover, and parts of Pomerania, as well as Schleswig-Holstein and Rheinhessen – it is to the existence of a broadly based, early-emancipated, and commercially successful peasant agriculture that we may have to look.

Stabilization on a Reduced and Fragmented Basis

What, then, was the outcome of these processes in the 1890s? By using the BdL's resources, National Liberals in Hesse and Hanover (in the latter with far more difficulty) managed to arrest their party's electoral decline. Between 1898 and 1903 the total liberal vote rose from 31.9 to 35.5 percent in Hesse and from 27.3 to 29.2 percent in Hanover. In the towns, on the other hand, where the threat came from the SPD, the National Liberals' needs were rather different, and there was no urban equivalent of the BdL to do the party's organizational work. In Darmstadt the National Liberal vote plummeted disastrously from 49.3 percent in 1893 to only 32.7 percent in 1898, while the SPD's rose from 31 to 45.4 percent. By 1898, each of the three big urban constituencies in Baden – Pforzheim, Mannheim, and Karlsruhe – had fallen to the SPD. Furthermore, National Liberal problems were compounded in southwest Germany by a notable invigoration of local Center parties, responding to the incipient independence of their own agricultural voters. In Hesse the Center polled 10.4 percent in 1893, but 13.1 percent in 1898 and 17.1 percent in 1903, whereas for Baden the figures were 29.9, 35.5, and 40.7 percent, respectively. In the Palatinate, finally, where the National Liberals held all six of the Reichstag seats in 1893, each of these factors converged to produce a crisis of dramatic proportions. For one thing, in contrast to the deal struck in Hesse, the National Liberal adjustment to the BdL's new organizational presence proved extremely stormy. Massive pressure was exerted by the BdL on National Liberal committees for the adoption of sympathetic agrarian candidates for the elections of 1898, and where this proved impossible, as in Kaiserslautern, an independent BdL candidate was put up. This produced a traumatic upheaval in the region's National Liberal Party, and the atmosphere became "so embittered and disordered by the invasion of unscrupulous agrarian rabble-rousers" that all six sitting deputies declined renomination. Moreover, while the National Liberals were dividing on the agrarian issue when confronted with the aggressive intervention of the BdL, they had to cope simultaneously with a much stronger challenge from the SPD and a firmed-up bloc of Center votes. In the event they managed to hold on to four of their six seats, but at the cost of disastrous inner-party tensions and a reluctantly "agrarian-ized" public profile. Their total vote also slumped from 47.7 to 34.5 percent.[38]

Elsewhere, the political mobilizations of the 1890s left the National Liberals increasingly dependent on alliances with other parties, especially in industrial regions like the Ruhr, the Kingdom and the Prussian province of Saxony, and Thuringia. Here the commonest alignments were regional continuations of the Cartel with the Conservatives and Free Conservatives – the three-party electoral coalition struck by Bismarck against the Center in 1887 – in which the three parties aimed for an agreed slate of candidates. In the two Saxonies this enabled the National Liberal vote to hold up quite well after 1887, although it tended to be distributed across different constituencies from election to election depending on the varying terms of the electoral pact.[39] But in the neighboring Thuringian states matters were complicated by the strong left-liberal presence dating from the National Liberal secession of 1881. Consequently, the National Liberal vote there always pulled two ways, either before the poll itself, when the parties tried to agree on a common nomination, or actually during the voting. Thus in the 1893 Coburg election a left liberal defeated the National Liberal in a three-way contest, largely by attracting the votes of the defeated Socialist. But by 1898 the National Liberals had

38. See the detailed report in *Heidelberger Zeitung*, 14 May 1898.

39. In 1893 the Conservatives fielded candidates in Mittweida, Chemnitz, Zwickau, and Reichenbach, but deferred to the National Liberals there in 1898 and 1903, while in rural Leipzig and Glauchau the arrangement worked the other way around. In 1893 a clash of Conservatives and National Liberals occurred in only three of the Kingdom of Saxony's twenty-three constituencies, and in only two of the twenty in the Prussian province of the same name; in 1898 the figures were three in each; and in 1903 one in the former, five in the latter. See T. Klein, "Reichstagswahlen und -abgeordnete der Provinz Sachsen und Anhalt, 1867–1918," in W. Schlesinger, ed., *Zur Geschichte und Volkskunde Mittel-deutschlands: Festschrift für Friedrich von Zahn* (Cologne and Graz, 1968), vol. 1, pp. 65–141.

dropped out, to be replaced by a BdL candidate and an anti-Semite, who seem to have divided the former National Liberal votes between them with a smaller third share probably going to the left liberal; this time the latter defeated the Socialist in the runoff. In 1903 the National Liberals reappeared and won the seat. This pattern was repeated in nearby Gotha, where in 1898 the former supporters of an absent National Liberal gravitated towards a Conservative and a left liberal in a ratio of two to one. In 1903 in Schwarzburg-Sondershausen the intrusion of an anti-Semite attracted so much National Liberal support that the left liberals abandoned their own candidacy and united with the National Liberal rump. In Schwarzburg-Rudolstadt there were two left liberals facing the Socialist in 1893, and a left liberal and a National Liberal in 1898, but in 1903 the intervention of the BdL cut the National Liberal share of the vote by over 65 percent.

In this sort of area, where industry had penetrated deep into the countryside, and agriculture, handicrafts, and industrial production coexisted in jumbled proximity, the dangers of the new agrarian mobilization for the National Liberals' mixed sociology of rural and urban *Honoratioren* were especially sharp. In an area like Hesse, the loss of National Liberal support in town and country could be confronted separately, and to some extent the party's development in the two sets of environments could assume different trajectories, although again ultimately at the cost of the party's coherence. But in Thuringia the two processes intersected *inside* individual Reichstag constituencies, and local National Liberals were finding it much harder to maneuver independently between a strong left liberal tradition and a new agrarian presence. This completed a national picture of some complexity, in which National Liberal relations with the BdL covered everything from outright hostility (as in Schleswig-Holstein and Baden) and embittered accommodation (as in Hanover and the Palatinate) to harmonious cooperation (as in Hesse) and kaleidoscopic confusion (as in Saxony and Thuringia). Most commonly, this diversity introduced a powerful element of internal conflict into the party's counsels, leading to frequent local splits, acrimony, and loss of direction.

Geoff Eley

The Reordering of the Public Sphere:
Liberalism in Transition

Where does this leave us in relation to the starting point of this essay? Most obviously, it confirms the importance of the 1890s as a decade of flux, in which one structure of politics was replaced by another. This occurred partly at the level of government with Bismarck's departure from office in 1890 and the opening of a period of divided and uncertain national administration that lasted until the major ministerial reconstruction of summer 1897. But the reorientation of national policy under Caprivi's chancellorship (1890–94), particularly in the areas of economic and social policy, also undermined the stability of the old Bismarckian governing coalition, at the heart of which had been a National Liberal Party joined increasingly since 1878–79 to a Conservative alliance based on an ideology of industrial-agrarian cooperation. During the 1890s – which in global terms were marked by processes of accelerated capitalist industrialization, the end of the depression, and the transition to imperialism – the conflicts of interest and outlook between industry and agriculture became harder to contain within the Bismarckian framework of propertied solidarity and "Schutz der nationalen Arbeit." Simultaneously, the forms of public life underwent some dramatic transformations, with an expanding electorate, new technologies of propaganda and communication, and new levels of active organization. In the 1890s, the masses dramatically entered politics, which were now placed on a transformed popular basis. This brought a major enlargement of the public sphere and a vital redefinition of the political nation. As new popular forces in town and country began to mobilize, the bases of political life itself began to change. *Honoratiorenpolitik*, as the highly exclusive and informally structured system of notable politics that characterized the restrictive public sphere of the unification decades, was the casualty of this compound process. As David Blackbourn says, "Politics itself underwent a change as it acquired the imprint of popular aspirations."[40]

The strong conception of conservative structural continuity associated with Lepsius – that there was little scope for political movement within the postunification political system, that the

---

40. Blackbourn, *Class, Religion, and Local Politics*, p. 18.

parties were incapable of outgrowing "the traditional framework of order," and that "from the 1860s until 1929" they "remained bound to their original communities of sentiment and their inaugural conflicts," as Wehler puts it – makes no sense in the light of this fundamental shift.[41] As we saw, the absence of bourgeois revolution between 1840 and 1870 is supposed to have frozen German political life in a "preindustrial" and authoritarian mold, shaped by a set of exclusive and self-perpetuating "social-moral milieus." Yet, far from revealing a static and inward-looking continuity in this way, the history of the parties between the 1860s and 1929 contains a far-reaching process of decomposition and regrouping, with an initial phase centering on the 1890s and a later, more protracted one beginning after 1909. In each of these two phases, the nonsocialist parties were reconstituted in a radically different relationship with a vital popular constituency, first with the peasantry and then, in a process that lies beyond the scope of this essay, with the petty bourgeoisie.

At the level of the polity as a whole, therefore, the 1890s brought a reordering of the public domain – a fundamental change in the scale and intensity of political life, in the levels of popular participation, and in the terms on which public discourse was conducted. Such changes were articulated in and around the electoral process, and they marked the transition, as Suval has described it, from the Bismarckian to the Wilhelmine electoral system. The mobilizations of the 1890s had the effect of thoroughly shaking up existing political allegiances, whose volatility unlocked the party-political configuration bequeathed by the 1870s and 1880s. As I have argued, for the National Liberals in particular this was a traumatic encounter. The given practices and assumptions of *Honoratiorenpolitik* were most completely embodied in the local and regional hegemony of National Liberal groupings. After Bismarck's famous turn to the right in 1878–79 had dislodged the National Liberal Party from its previous role as principal governing party, National Liberal influence in national politics continued to subsist on the same structure of informally constituted sociopolitical leadership. By the end of the 1890s, that older structure of politics had largely

41. H.-U. Wehler, *Das Deutsche Kaiserreich, 1871–1918*, 6th ed. (Göttingen, 1988), p. 80.

fallen apart, to be replaced by an emerging mass-political frame-work. By 1898–1903, as I suggested, the crisis of National Liberal electoral fortunes had been brought under control, although the party's national parliamentary strength had to stabilize at a much lower level than before. Moreover, in some ways the new political climate after 1897 returned the National Liberals to their former role as the governing party par excellence, although in a far less secure form and now in an effective partnership with a freshly "governmentalized" Center Party. Basically, the government's retreat from the anticonstitutional brinkmanship of the mid-1890s – a time when the Kaiser's circle regularly flirted with antisocialist exceptional legislation, and even an antiparliamentary coup d'état – combined with the extremism of agrarian demands to reemphasize the National Liberals' governmental value.

To this extent the National Liberals could feel that they had successfully ridden the storm. Despite their declining electoral base, and the turmoil of the local political process, they had upheld the value and procedures of moderate constitutionalism on which the empire had been founded – for example, by blocking the government's various illiberal initiatives, including the Revolution Bill of 1894–95, the Prussian Law of Association or "little Anti-Socialist Law" of 1896–97, and the *Zuchthausvorlage* of 1899 (a legislative initiative to restrict picketing), all of which were defeated by firm National Liberal/Center opposition – and could regard themselves again as the natural party of government. By and large, the key legislative achievements of the turn of the century – from the completion and passage of the Code of Civil Law, to the Navy Laws of 1898 and 1900, and the painfully wrought agrarianism of the tariff settlement of 1902 – could be regarded as characteristically *National Liberal* measures. But, more realistically, this was the Indian summer of National Liberalism, in its classical 1870s form, and over the longer term the existing liberal tradition was shown to have been irretrievably undermined by the upheavals of the 1890s. Once the social foundations of *Honoratiorenpolitik* had disappeared, the old notability could not maintain itself indefinitely at the level of parliamentary governance without reconstituting a viable mass-political base. To close, therefore, it is worth saying a few words more about the National Liberals' situation in 1900, as they faced the challenge of the coming decade.

First, the party made little effort at organizational renovation. Although new constitutions were adopted in 1892 and again in 1905, the National Liberal leadership remained a self-constituted oligarchy of notables: neither local agents nor occasional delegate meetings were integrated into decision making, and the striking feature of the organizational consolidation was the degree to which ordinary activists remained largely uninvolved. In a way, the old *Honoratiorenpolitik* was simply reproduced at a new level of constitutional formality. On this evidence, the adjustment to a new style of mass politics was by no means a natural stage in the history of parties, in which they brought their practice into line with the demands of a new age and its technologies. When the National Liberals encountered demands for a stronger local rootedness of political life, in fact, they responded very slowly and with extreme reluctance. By comparison, both the Center and the Conservatives managed a far quicker response – the former via the political elasticity of the Catholic Church and its social relations, the latter by a remarkable improvisation (the BdL) in a crisis of its moral authority in the countryside. The larger context of these innovations, deriving from the concurrent radicalizations of the peasantry and labor, failed to elicit a comparable response from the National Liberals, whether in organization or ideology.

Second, at an ideological level the National Liberals' main response to the 1890s was a conservative one, namely, the recourse to old and trusted verities. Faced with new processes of popular mobilization, and with the dissolution of the party's historic constituency into hostile sectionalisms pulling in opposite directions, the party's leaders retreated into a celebration of the National Liberal heritage. At the party's key preelection delegate meeting in May 1898, all three keynote speeches by Rudolf von Bennigsen (1824–1902), Friedrich Hammacher (1824–1904), and the younger Ernst Bassermann (1854–1917) took this line: the party had originated in the 1860s as the champion of liberalism, national unity, and sociopolitical compromise; and now – as Germany's historic *Mittelpartei* – its role was once again to mediate among the different economic interests, both for the sake of the nation as a whole and for its own party-political survival.[42] At its most grandiloquent, this meant

42. *Allgemeiner Delegiertentag der Nationalliberalen Partei* (Berlin, 1898), pp. 9f., 13, and 15–26.

invoking the party's character as a historical community of sentiment, what Arthur Hobrecht (1824–1912), another National Liberal leader, called "the cement of history, the cement that a long period of common effort in great tasks and of common struggles over great questions necessarily produced."[43] More prosaically, it meant a stronger emphasis on "national questions," including everything from *Weltpolitik* and the navy, to the strengthening of the state fabric and the defense of the "idealist heritage of the German people," as Professor Wilhelm Kahl (1849–1932), another leading National Liberal, put it.[44] One form of this was the reassertion of the maxims of the *Kulturkampf*, and in the Rhineland the most enthusiastic celebrants of the National Liberal past in the late 1890s tended to cling most stubbornly to the tried "anti-ultramontane" slogans. But it also produced a stronger stress on foreign policy, naval armaments and colonies, the subjection of the national minorities, and the aggressive "defense of German *Kultur.*"

Third, when considered with the organizational deficit mentioned above (which amounted to a failure to take the problem of population mobilization sufficiently seriously), this recourse to a traditional conception of the nation left the National Liberal establishment extremely vulnerable to a new criticism from *within* its own milieu. A further dimension of the ferment of the 1890s, not as salient in electoral terms as the agitation of the countryside but over the longer term no less important, was the emergence of a new category of nationalist pressure groups, whose active elements came invariably from a strong National Liberal background. This was especially true of the Pan-Germans and the Navy League, but applied more generally as well to an emerging cohort of professional and semi-professional functionaries and propagandists, who devoted themselves mainly to this sphere of activity. The absorption of such people into that which elsewhere I have called a distinctive "radical-nationalist milieu" was not incompatible with a continuing National Liberal affiliation. But such activists increasingly came to regard the popular political inactivity of the National Liberal establishment as a symptom of a more fundamental ideological malaise. Invariably, the histories of the

---

43. Seyffardt, *Erinnerungen,* p. 595.
44. *Allgemeiner Delegiertentag,* p. 72.

nationalist pressure groups revolved around serious tension between a National Liberal and more broadly conservative notability and a new generation of activists who accused them of being insufficiently responsive to the political needs of the day. In fact, much of the motive force for the radical nationalism produced in such organizations came from a growing impatience with an existing style of establishmentarian politics – that is, with *Honoratiorenpolitik* in the sense discussed above. In effect, radical nationalists took the National Liberal stress on the national interest, radicalized it, and connected its primacy to the new realities of popular mobilization imposed by the 1890s. The electoral crisis of National Liberalism in the 1890s, and the peculiar deficits of the party's response to the challenge of the new politics, thus spawned what eventually became a further extra-parliamentary challenge to its faltering popular credibility. On the one hand, the inflexibility of National Liberal *Honoratiorenpolitik* – its inability to create a new apparatus for the recruitment and continuing involvement of what should have been the party's natural and most active supporters – allowed the creation of an independent space for radical-nationalist activity in the nationalist pressure groups, which was originally compatible, or at least nonantagonistic, with National Liberal allegiance, but which soon ran increasingly into conflict with it. On the other hand, the party's continuing neglect of popular politics and the attendant frustrations of the radical nationalists then delivered the materials for a full-scale critique from this new quarter.[45]

In this sense, the emergence of radical nationalism was a symptom of the broader changes this essay has been discussing – a sign that the older structure of notable politics was passing into a period of ideological as well as sociopolitical crisis: that is, its assumptions were being brought into question by a new kind of activist middle-class challenge. If there was an innovative impulse from within the National Liberal milieu itself, therefore, it came from a new activist grouping, which saw the need for popular mobilization and argued that it should be conducted on

---

45. I have developed this argument in detail in *Reshaping the German Right*. For a summary, see also G. Eley, "Some Thoughts on the Nationalist Pressure Groups in Imperial Germany," in P. Kennedy and A. Nicholls, eds., *Nationalist and Racialist Movements in Britain and Germany before 1914* (London, 1981), pp. 40–67.

a populist-nationalist footing. This is the fourth and final point I wish to make. To the extent that the National Liberal Party managed to regenerate itself before 1914, it did so ultimately by seeking to assimilate the energies released by the nationalist pressure groups. Gustav Stresemann, who himself entered politics via the new popular agitations of the late 1890s and was active in support of the radical-nationalist leadership of the Navy League in 1903–8, was a principal architect of this strategy. There were certainly other impulses for liberal regeneration, among them the process of left-liberal concentration between 1905–6 and 1910, which itself had also originated in the complex dynamics of the 1890s. But in the National Liberal Party as such, the openness of the Stresemann-Bassermann leadership that succeeded the postunification generation of Bennigsen and Hammacher to this broader process of liberal coalescence was accompanied by this wager on the radical-nationalist temper of the new middle class – that is, the white-collar, managerial, administrative, and professional strata, who seemed to be the most enthusiastic supporters of the nationalist pressure groups. Here the motivating ideology was populist, but also heavily antisocialist and antidemocratic, and this too was a consequence of the 1890s.

8

German Liberalism in the Second Empire, 1871–1914

Dieter Langewiesche

The development of German liberalism from the founding of the Second Empire to the outbreak of the First World War is usually depicted as one of continuous decline. This is understandable since the liberal parties lost political influence to the same extent that the conservative and Catholic parties, as well as the Social Democrats, gained in electoral strength. In the first Reichstag elections of 1871 the liberal parties held 52.9 percent – an absolute majority – of the seats between them, whereas in the last elections of 1912 they received only 21.9 percent. Thus, the decline of the German liberal parties is beyond doubt. It would, however, be misleading to reduce the history of liberalism between 1871 and 1914 to one of decline. Liberal ideas pervaded German society and strongly influenced the prevailing political culture. Liberal parties helped establish the legal, social, and economic foundations of the national state at the same time that they established a modern infrastructure necessary for urban life in the cities. Thus liberalism had an impact on the general character of German political life that cannot be measured by election results alone.[1]

The Decline of the Liberal Parties as a Process of Political Normalization

In the 1860s and 1870s the liberal parties were not simply "normal" parties that could be placed on the same level with

1. The author would like to express his appreciation to Larry Jones, Friedrich Lenger, and Patricia O'Brien for their assistance in translating this essay. The most important works on German liberalism in imperial Germany are quoted by J.J. Sheehan, *German Liberalism in the Nineteenth Century* (Chicago and London, 1978), and D. Langewiesche, *Liberalismus in Deutschland* (Frankfurt, 1988).

other parties. On the contrary, they were the opinion-leaders and standardbearers of the German national movement. Liberal organizations spearheaded this movement, one that reached far beyond the spectrum of political liberalism. Those who longed for a German national state without Austria felt a sense of affinity for the national movement that the liberals had set in motion, even if they might not have accepted the political, social, and economic specifics of the liberal program.

This admittedly exceptional situation could not be maintained for long. The normalization of political life in the German national state meant that the liberals would lose their exceptional position, that they would be transformed from the embodiment of the whole national movement to simply one party among others. This process of normalization was completed by the late 1870s, when the conservatives made their peace with the new national state and political Catholicism was able to overcome at least a measure of its national isolation with the initial dismantling of the *Kulturkampf*.

In the 1878 Reichstag elections the various liberal parties together received 33.6 percent of the total popular vote, while in 1912 they still held 25.9 percent. Over the same period of time the conservatives lost even more, falling from 26.6 percent in 1878 to 12.2 percent in 1912, while the German Center Party (Deutsche Zentrumspartei), considered by many historians to be Germany's most stable political party, declined from 23.1 percent in 1878 to 16.4 percent in 1912. If one considers the absolute number of votes, the liberal parties were far more successful, with a gain of 63 percent between 1878 and 1912, than either the conservatives, with a loss of 3 percent, or the Center, with a gain of 50 percent.[2] Thus the liberals were quite successful in terms of absolute numbers despite the fact that they were losing in relative terms. This apparent paradox is not difficult to explain. While the gains of the liberal parties and the Center could keep pace with a population growth of approximately 50 percent between 1878 and 1912, they could not match a dramatic rise in voter turnout that amounted to 112 percent.[3] The politicization

2. On liberal election results in the Second Empire, see Langewiesche, *Liberalismus in Deutschland*, pp. 133–64, 308–9 (Table 4), as well as G.A. Ritter and M. Niehuss, *Wahlgeschichtliches Arbeitsbuch: Materialien zur Statistik des Kaiserreichs, 1871–1918* (Munich, 1980), and S. Suval, *Electoral Politics in Wilhelmine Germany* (Chapel Hill, N.C., 1985).
3. In 1878 there were 5.78 million and in 1912 12.26 million electors.

of German society that manifested itself in the rapidly rising voter turnout benefited the Social Democrats above all. Liberals were especially vulnerable to Social Democratic competition, as both groups recruited the bulk of their support from the Protestant and secularized electorate and were not particularly successful among Catholic voters.

The groups to which liberalism could appeal were thus rather limited in number. Not only was the Catholic third of the population excluded from the potential liberal electorate, but there were other limitations as well. Liberalism lost Protestant workers to the Social Democratic Party, which from 1890 on received more votes than any other German party. Among Protestant urban middle classes and Protestant peasants liberalism had to compete with the conservative parties, which were also thoroughly Protestant. Within these structural limitations – limitations indeed unparalleled in the rest of Europe[4] – German liberalism proved surprisingly successful at the polls. This success is easily overlooked if one simply compares subsequent election results with the exceptional situation of the 1870s when the Social Democrats were still a splinter group, the conservatives stood in opposition to the newly founded national state, and the Center was widely regarded as the party of the empire's Catholic enemies. Whoever supported the national state could therefore only vote for one of the liberal parties. The political polarization that was inherent in this situation, however, had to be overcome if the national state, originally created through military force, was ever to legitimize itself on the basis of broad popular support. Thus the declining support for the liberal parties during the first decade of the German Empire must also be seen as a measure of the inner consolidation of the national state that had emerged from three successive wars in the 1860s. This process of inner consolidation and political normalization would not have been possible if the liberals had retained the exceptional position they enjoyed in the 1860s and 1870s. It may be one of the great ironies of German history that the liberal

---

4. In this respect, see D. Langewiesche, "Liberalismus und Bürgertum in Europa," in J. Kocka, ed., *Bürgertum im 19. Jahrhundert: Deutschland im europäischen Vergleich* (Munich, 1988), vol. 14, pp. 1–34; as well as the essays in D. Langewiesche, ed., *Liberalismus im 19. Jahrhundert: Deutschland im europäischen Vergleich*, Kritische Studien zur Geschichtswissenschaft, vol. 79 (Göttingen, 1988).

parties had to pay for the surprisingly rapid consolidation of the national state with the loss of their own political hegemony. Their success as a national movement was reflected in their weakness as political parties.

The Liberal Era to the "Second Reichsgründung"

The constitutions of the North German Confederation of 1867 and the German Empire of 1871 were only provisional in nature. The decision as to whether the center of political power would rest with the monarch or with parliament was deferred until some point in the future. Yet while the Reichstag was essential for the conduct of national politics, the liberals were not able to establish a government responsible to parliament. Above all, the liberals failed to subject the military, the strongest base of the Prussian-German monarchy, to the annual budgetary prerogatives of the Reichstag. The central problem of the Prussian constitutional conflict over rule by king or rule by parliament was thus carried over into the imperial state. Whether or not the makeshift constitution could be developed into an effective parliamentary system of government was a question that only the future could answer.

The liberals were optimistic. Although they had split over the issue of compromise in the constitutional conflict of 1862–66, both the National Liberal Party (Nationalliberale Partei) and the left-liberal German Progressive Party (Deutsche Fortschrittspartei) were convinced that the national state had the potential to develop along liberal lines. Their willingness to compromise did not mean that they were ready to renounce power. The emergence of the German national state as the result of three victorious wars had left them no choice but to compromise if they did not want to jeopardize their long-standing goals. For the liberals to try to deprive the monarch of his exclusive powers over the military at the very moment when the new nation-state had emerged victorious over Denmark, Austria, and France would have invited almost certain defeat. As the first Reichstag elections in 1871 indicated, such a move would not have received the support of the German population. Even at the height of national euphoria in 1871, the liberal representatives of the national movement had received only 46.6 percent of the total popular vote and 52.9 percent of the seats. The voters rewarded those National Liberals who had been ready to compromise with 30.1 percent of the votes and 32.7 percent of the seats in the Reichstag, whereas the left liberals received only 9.3 percent of the vote and 12.3 percent of the seats.

Liberal hopes of being able to liberalize and parliamentarize the national state on a step-by-step basis cannot be dismissed as a mere illusion. The historian must be careful not to judge the aspirations of 1871 from the perspective of 1918. In spite of all the defeats that the liberals suffered in the constitutional arena, they also experienced a remarkable string of successes. Thus Eduard Lasker was right when he counted the period between 1866 and the late 1870s among "the most magnificent phenomena in the history of reform in Prussia and Germany, if not the history of reform of all civilized nations. . . . In all areas of legislation with the exception of taxes and finances a compromise was reached even on proposals by the government and demands by parliament where an agreement seemed at first to be completely out of reach or at least out of reach for the foreseeable future."[5] Lasker went on to present a proud record of reform. The constitutions of the North German Confederation and the German Empire, the penal code and other judicial laws, the reform of the monetary system and the founding of the national bank, the imperial commercial code and the law on joint-stock companies, the imperial court and the creation of national offices, the national press law, and even the various military laws were all seen as the prelude to still further improvements. No less important were various reforms in Prussia, such as the county ordinance and the laws for self-determination and administrative courts.[6]

It was not only the National Liberals who were proud of this record of reform. Despite all their criticism, the Progressives also celebrated these successes that seemed to be liberalizing the national state in the very first decade of its existence. Even Max Weber, who had always sharply criticized the Wilhelmine

5. *Aus Eduard Laskers Nachlaß,* edited by W. Cahn (Berlin, 1902), pp. 9 and 52f. See also J.F. Harris, *A Study in the Theory and Practice of German Liberalism: Eduard Lasker, 1829–1884* (Lanham, Md., 1984); as well as Langewiesche, *Liberalismus in Deutschland,* pp. 165–80.

6. See H. Heffter, *Die deutsche Selbstverwaltung im 19. Jahrhundert: Geschichte der Ideen und Institutionen,* 2d ed. (Stuttgart, 1969), pp. 453–653; and E.R. Huber, *Deutsche Verfassungsgeschichte seit 1785,* 2d ed. (Stuttgart, 1970), vol. 3, pp. 833–1028, and vol. 4, pp. 361–64.

middle class for lacking the will to power, looked on the 1870s as the "heyday of the Reichstag" to which "the vast majority of those imperial institutions that still possessed any value whatsoever had to be attributed."[7] Even if the liberals had fought more determinedly with the founder of the Second Empire over formal parliamentary rights, they could not have achieved more – and they almost certainly would have endangered what they had in fact achieved.[8] Sharing Weber's conviction, most liberals in the 1860s and 1870s already looked forward to the time after Bismarck, whose reckless policies they had come to deplore more and more ever since the 1870s.

Rudolf Haym, an unflappable admirer of Bismarck, lamented in 1881 that the imperial chancellor had undermined the hopes of liberalizing the German government. But without Bismarck, or even less in opposition to him, nothing could be achieved.[9] Julius Hölder, the undisputed head of the Württemberg National Liberals, spoke of Bismarck's "violent character" and called him "a modern majordomo" and "Ivan the Terrible!" "A nation," Hölder concluded, "does not have great men at its top for nothing."[10] The founding of the empire had elevated Bismarck to the status of a national hero, and any open struggle against him for more political power for parliament did not seem feasible.

Weber reported that it had been the liberals' fondest hope, one they often expressed amongst themselves, to "steer through the regency of this grand personality." Their aim was to preserve imperial institutions for the day when "politicians of ordinary dimensions" would lead the nation-state.[11] The liberals could not foresee that Bismarck and his imperial master, with-

---

7. M. Weber, "Parlament und Regierung im neugeordneten Deutschland (1918)," in M. Weber, *Gesamtausgabe*, vol. 15, *Zur Politik im Weltkrieg: Schriften und Reden, 1914–1918*, edited by W.J. Mommsen and G. Hübinger (Tübingen, 1984), pp. 441, 443. See also W.J. Mommsen, *Max Weber und die deutsche Politik, 1890–1920*, 2d ed. (Tübingen, 1974).

8. Weber, "Parlament und Regierung," p. 442.

9. *Ausgewählter Briefwechsel Rudolf Hayms*, ed. H. Rosenberg (repr. Osnabrück, 1967), p. 325. See also L. Gall, *Bismarck: Der weiße Revolutionär* (Frankfurt, 1980), pp. 459–591.

10. *Das Tagebuch Julius Hölders, 1877–1880: Zum Zerfall des politischen Liberalismus in Württemberg und im Deutschen Reich*, ed. D. Langewiesche, Veröffentlichungen der Kommission für geschichtliche Landeskunde in Baden-Württemberg, vol. A 26 (Stuttgart, 1977), pp. 242 and 248.

11. Weber, "Parlament und Regierung," p. 442.

out whose support the chancellor's Bonapartist rule would not have been possible, would direct imperial politics for two decades. Neither could they foresee that the "first *Reichsgründung*" of 1871 would be followed by a second in 1878–79, one of a completely different nature. For while the first had created the framework of the modern nation-state, the second, at the end of the 1870s, concluded the liberal phase of that state's development. In 1871 liberals looked with optimism to a future that seemed to be theirs; after 1878 they felt as if they were standing on the ruins of their own hopes.

Wilhelm Oncken, the biographer of the National Liberal leader Rudolf von Bennigsen, has described what happened at the end of the 1870s as the "greatest inner upheaval of modern German history."[12] The leader of the Center, Ludwig Windthorst, on the other hand, spoke of "the bankruptcy of liberalism,"[13] and the liberals as well were aware that a new epoch had begun. What occurred at the end of the 1870s to change this feeling of enthusiasm into one of disillusionment?[14]

The fact that the founding of the German Empire took place during a period of economic well-being did much to increase the political appeal of the national movement and greatly facilitated the reconciliation of the interest antagonisms that existed within the movement. Moreover, a German nation-state seemed to promise economic progress, and the liberals were its principal advocates and beneficiaries. It was only in the 1860s that liberalism and laissez-faire had become synonymous. The liberals, in turn, were able to profit politically from this as long as the economic boom continued. But when there was a marked slowdown in economic growth after 1873 and increasingly large segments of the population were hit by the crisis, liberalism became the great political loser. Liberal economic beliefs were

12. H. Oncken, *Rudolf von Bennigsen: Ein deutscher liberaler Politiker nach seinen Briefen und hinterlassenen Papieren* (Stuttgart-Leipzig, 1910), vol. 2, p. 302.

13. Quoted in H.-E. Matthes, *Die Spaltung der Nationalliberalen Partei und die Entwicklung des Linksliberalismus bis zur Auflösung der Deutsch-Freisinnigen Partei, 1878–1893* (diss., Kiel, 1953), p. 122.

14. See H. Rosenberg, *Große Depression und Bismarckzeit: Wirtschaftsablauf, Gesellschaft und Politik in Mitteleuropa* (Berlin, 1967), as well as H.A. Winkler, "Vom linken zum rechten Nationalismus: Der deutsche Liberalismus in der Krise von 1878/79," *Geschichte und Gesellschaft* 4 (1978): 5–28, and Gall, *Bismarck*, pp. 526–91; Sheehan, *Liberalism*, pp. 181–88; Langewiesche, *Liberalismus in Deutschland*, pp. 164–80.

discredited, and with them the liberal parties. Eduard Lasker described the hostile attitude which the liberals had to face in the following way: with the end of economic well-being "discontent spread over all the regions of the empire, throughout all classes of the population, and created an atmosphere in which every man inhaled the scent of unhappiness with every breath. It was not difficult for rabble-rousers to exploit this discontent, nor was it difficult for them to charge the ruling groups with [responsibility for] it."[15]

The economic crisis did not automatically force the National Liberals from their position as an unofficial government party. A number of developments over which the liberals had no control converged to produce what has been called the "great turn-around of 1878."[16] The disillusionment with economic liberalism was only one of these developments. That Bismarck could use this to free himself from parliamentary dependence on the liberals, however, stemmed from a number of important factors. Among the most significant was the reorientation of Prussian conservatism in the 1870s.[17] In making their peace with the German national state, the Prussian conservatives had given Bismarck new possibilities for parliamentary coalitions. The repeal of some of the measures associated with the *Kulturkampf* of the late 1870s had had a similar effect. Bismarck was quite ruthless in exploiting the political maneuvering space this afforded him, and he forced through decisions that placed a heavy burden on liberalism and drove the liberal parties into repeated splits in the period that followed 1879.

First, Bismarck used the pressure of an electorate mobilized by propaganda to pressure the National Liberals into supporting the antisocialist laws. In this way they helped to undermine the constitutional state that was rightly seen as the quintessence of liberalism. At the same time, this decision intensified the gulf separating the liberal parties. Together they had pushed through the development of the constitutional state; now they fought each other over a central liberal issue. The National Liberals did indeed secure their position as an unofficial mem-

15. *Aus Laskers Nachlaß*, p. 95.
16. Weber, "Parlament und Regierung," p. 442.
17. The most recent work is J.N. Retallack's *Notables of the Right: The Conservative Party and Political Mobilization in Germany, 1876–1918* (Boston, 1988).

ber of the government by supporting these antisocialist laws; they lost this position, however, in 1879, in the controversy over the reform of imperial finances. Bismarck received the necessary majority only with the help of the conservatives and the Catholic Center. The liberal forces that had played such a prominent role in the founding of the German Empire now joined the Social Democrats in opposing the government on a critical issue. During that same year, a group of fifteen liberal representatives abandoned the National Liberals' parliamentary delegation and accepted the new tariffs that had ended the era of German free trade.

Free trade had never been one of the central tenets of German liberalism. Only during the economic boom of the 1860s and 1870s had German liberals become staunch defenders of free trade principles. The demoralization felt by liberals over Bismarck's change of course on trade policy, however, did not derive solely from the fact that they had become advocates of free trade out of principle. More important, the controversy over the tariffs showed that the economic interests had gained more and more influence over the political decision-making process during the 1870s. This development hit the liberals in their most vulnerable spot. The idea of the national state as a guarantee of political, economic, social, and cultural progress stood at the center of their program. This all-encompassing idea of the nation had given liberalism an integrative potential that had extended far beyond the liberal bourgeoisie. This potential, however, was inevitably weakened by the rise and spread of interest politics. Political liberalism was no longer perceived as a necessary ingredient of economic progress, and consequently the conflict of economic interests within the middle classes became increasingly apparent. The primacy of politics over economics was thus obscured.

The rise of interest politics hit the liberals particularly hard, as their preeminence as a national movement had depended on the validity of their claim that they represented not the interests of specific groups but those of the entire nation. Now the liberals were in danger of being pulverized between the various interest groups. Eugen Richter, who became the leading left-liberal spokesman in the 1870s, resolutely condemned the new state protectionism. It would carry "class interest" into politics "from above," claimed Richter. "That is far more dangerous than socialist agitation from the other side."[18] At the same time, the National Liberal Heinrich Rickert bemoaned the "inferno of predatory interests" that would throw everybody into "confusion" – "agrarians, protectionists, supporters of guilds, tax reformers of opposing camps, ultramontanists, Bismarckians, socialists, liberal trade-unionists, bigots, free-traders who wanted no tariffs at all but did not want to pay direct taxes either, blatant militarists and their polar opposites."[19] His political friend Franz von Stauffenberg considered the entire future of liberalism to be in danger: "*Only* personal interest still has weight with the people. Our part seems to be over and done with, and I am becoming less and less able to do anything against the increasingly powerful feeling that that for which I have worked for half of my life amounts to nothing. . . . The very thought of party politics disgusts me beyond belief."[20]

Thus it was a profoundly different liberalism that emerged in 1880 from the National Liberal split.[21] On the surface this split was brought on by the military law of 1880 that fixed the military budget for another seven-year period and the laws that ended the *Kulturkampf*. More basic causes, however, lay in the differing perspectives that had emerged within the liberal camp on which direction the party should take in the future. Those who remained with Rudolf von Bennigsen in the National Liberal Party bowed to the imperial chancellor. "As long as a man of this historical stature and authority is in office," argued Bennigsen, one must compromise with him.[22] Only now the National Liberals were deferring their hopes for the parliamentarization of the German Empire until some point in the distant future. This was a turning point in the history of German liberalism. It also deepened the political gulf that existed within the liberal camp, as the left liberals remained resolutely opposed to Bismarck's

18. Quoted in I.S. Lorenz, *Eugen Richter: Der entschiedene Liberalismus in Wilhelminischer Zeit, 1871–1906* (Husum, 1981), p. 93.
19. Quoted in *Im Neuen Reich, 1871–1890: Politische Briefe aus dem Nachlaß liberaler Parteiführer*, ed. P. Wentzcke (Bonn-Leipzig, 1925, repr., 1967), p. 210.
20. Ibid., pp. 290–91.
21. See Sheehan, *Liberalism*, pp. 189–218; Matthes, *Spaltung*, passim; Langewiesche, *Liberalismus in Deutschland*, pp. 177–80 and 211–27; D.S. White, *The Splintered Party: National Liberalism in Hessen and the Reich, 1867–1918* (Cambridge, Mass., 1976).
22. *Rudolf von Bennigsens Reden*, ed. W. Schultze and F. Thimme (Halle a.d.S., 1922), vol. 2, p. 84.

policies. The reversal on tariff policies, the end of the *Kultur-kampf*, coalitions with the Conservatives and the Center, the beginning of governmental social policy – all this seemed to be part and parcel of what the left liberals disparaged as a policy of "favoring all against all."[23] Ludwig Bamberger, who penned these words in his famous tract "Die Sezession," called upon the German middle classes to show whether or not they would "measure up to their vocation" and secure "the peaceful development of human culture." He saw this culture threatened by a "state socialism" in conservative disguise that united antiquated with utopian ideas, or, as he himself put it, "reaction with socialism!"[24]

The changing character of political life described by Bamberger could already be seen in the second *Reichsgründung*, and it went on to complete triumph in the Wilhelmine era after 1890. The politicization of society was now qualitatively different. Around 1880 it had been still unclear whether the liberal parties would adjust to these changes. Neither the left liberals nor the National Liberals possessed a recipe that could be followed quickly; both were preparing for a time after Bismarck. While the National Liberals sought to influence imperial politics through acquiescence, the left liberals prepared themselves for opposition.

"World Politics" and Inner Reform: Liberalism in the Wilhelmine Era

The era after Bismarck failed to fulfill liberal expectations. Politics now meant something completely new: almost all spheres of life became more and more organized, many were politicized, and even in spheres as far removed from politics as sports and popular education, organizations with different worldviews competed against each other. A convinced Social Democrat did not attend a class offered by Catholic organizations and vice versa. They read different papers, borrowed their books from

23. For the most recent treatment of this problem, see H.-J. von Berlepsch, *"Neuer Kurs" im Kaiserreich? Die Arbeiterpolitik des Freiherrn von Berlepsch 1890 bis 1896* (Bonn, 1987).

24. L. Bamberger, "Die Sezession" (1881), in *Gesammelte Werke*, vol. 5 (Berlin, 1897), pp. 129, 131, and 134. See also S. Zucker, *Ludwig Bamberger* (Pittsburgh, 1975).

different libraries, and belonged to different trade unions – and their children attended different kindergartens, even when they lived in the same part of town. Their wives probably shopped in different cooperatives, and they would never go to the same festivities. As long as they felt ostracized from the politically and culturally dominant society, Social Democrats and Catholics would organize within relatively closed subcultures.[25] For the liberals, however, such a close identification with a particular milieu was inconceivable in light of their claims to represent the nation as a whole. It was therefore impossible for liberals to withdraw into a self-contained milieu to build up organizational support for their politics. At the heart of liberal claims for the universality of their political program lay the determination to speak for the entire nation rather than for any specific group of the population.

By the second *Reichsgründung* at the end of the 1870s German liberals had succeeded to a considerable degree in making good this claim. In the Wilhelmine era, however, this was no longer the case. This was not because the national principle had lost its integrative potential. On the contrary, even those parties that had originally been labeled the enemies of the empire, such as the Center and the Social Democrats, now claimed to represent the political interests of the "true" nation. Moreover, a number of national mass organizations such as the Pan-German League (Alldeutscher Verband) and the German Naval League (Deutscher Flottenverein) had also emerged on the political scene.[26] Their appeal to all sectors of the population demonstrated that the integrative potential of nationalism remained powerful. In fact, it had actually increased, as there was no other ideology in the age of imperialism that could compete with the mass appeal of demands for a German "world politics," for a German "place in the sun." Yet, whereas the liberals had been the principal

25. See V.L. Lidtke, *The Alternative Culture: Socialist Labor in Imperial Germany* (Oxford, 1985). For two, more recent contributions see D. Kramer, *Theorien zur historischen Arbeiterkultur* (Marburg, 1987); and D. Langewiesche, "The Impact of the German Labor Movement on Workers' Culture," *The Journal of Modern History* 59, no. 3 (1987): 506–23.

26. For further details, see R. Chickering, *We Men Who Feel Most German: A Cultural Study of the Pan-German League, 1886–1914* (London, 1984); G. Eley, *Reshaping the German Right: Radical Nationalism and Political Change after Bismarck* (New Haven, 1980); and J. Dülffer and Karl Holl, eds., *Bereit zum Krieg: Kriegsmentalität im Wilhelminischen Deutschland, 1890–1914* (Göttingen, 1986).

representatives of the nation until the second *Reichsgründung*, now they were of only secondary importance in articulating the idea of German nationhood. A nationalism that had transformed itself into imperialism had no place within a liberal politics of integration.

To be sure, the liberal parties shared the imperial aspirations of the German nation and tried to benefit from them.[27] This was all the more understandable as the connection between "world politics" and the requirements of a rapidly modernizing industrial society corresponded to the political and social models that liberals had developed for the nation-state. To retreat from national "world politics" would have resulted in the defection of middle-class supporters from liberal parties. Even then, however, most liberals did not advocate an aggressive imperialism. For although the National Liberals were the "colonial party par excellence"[28] and hoped to reap benefits from "each high tide of national emotion" and each "fight for national needs,"[29] they propagated a rather moderate form of social imperialism, according to which the German nation would give "cultural blessings" and would receive in return "countries seemingly without masters."[30] They hoped that enhanced power abroad would translate into social harmony at home as well as in the colonies.

The hope of using "world politics" as a means of liberalizing the German Empire was even more pronounced in the political calculations of left-liberal imperialists. Their demand for a German "world politics" was accompanied by an opening in social and political life that gave left liberalism new opportunities for growth and development. The coalition of National Liberals, left liberals, and conservatives that made up the Bülow bloc lasted only a few years, from 1907 to 1909, whereas the grand bloc (*Großblock*) "from Bassermann to Bebel" functioned only briefly,

27. See W.J. Mommsen, "Wandlungen der liberalen Idee im Zeitalter des Imperialismus," in K. Holl and G. List, eds., *Liberalismus und imperialistischer Staat: Der Imperialismus als Problem liberaler Parteien in Deutschland, 1890–1914* (Göttingen, 1975), pp. 109–47; as well as P. Theiner, *Sozialer Liberalismus und deutsche Weltpolitik: Friedrich Naumann im Wilhelminischen Deutschland* (Baden-Baden, 1983).

28. H. Gründer, *Geschichte der deutschen Kolonien* (Paderborn, 1985), p. 65.

29. *Politisches Handbuch der Nationalliberalen Partei* (Berlin, 1908), pp. 772 and 775.

30. Ibid., pp. 585 and 587.

from 1909 to 1913, in Baden.[31] But the rigid political barriers had nevertheless been broken. Left liberals and Social Democrats had moved closer together and had even worked together for periods of time in the Reichstag. Even the Center was an occasional participant in these coalitions. Thus "the Weimar coalition" was already emerging in the last years before the outbreak of World War I, although only in embryonic form and as an uncertain possibility. There is no way of knowing, however, whether a functioning permanent coalition could have emerged on its own, or whether the parliamentarization and democratization of the Second Empire could have been achieved without defeat in World War I and the ensuing revolution.

Social Liberalism in the Cities and in the Empire

Social liberalism developed in the German Empire at both imperial and local levels. The origins of governmental social policy in the 1880s have often been analyzed[32]; the same cannot be said, however, of the social and welfare measures taken by the various German municipalities.[33] The reason for this may very well be that historians have tended to look for the origins of German social liberalism in imperial politics. The fruits of such a search have been meager and disappointing.[34] To conclude from this, however, that German liberalism did not have a social component would be misleading, for the German variant of social liberalism was born in the cities. Inasmuch as this is a largely neglected field of investigation, it would be impossible to provide more than a rough outline of the problem here.[35]

31. B. Heckart, *From Bassermann to Bebel: The Grand Bloc's Quest for Reform in the Kaiserreich, 1900–1914* (New Haven, 1974); J. Thiel, *Die Großblockpolitik der Nationalliberalen Partei Badens, 1905–1914* (Stuttgart, 1976); T. Eschenburg, *Das Kaiserreich am Scheideweg: Bassermann, Bülow und der Block* (Berlin, 1929). See also the titles quoted in Langewiesche, *Liberalismus in Deutschland*, pp. 221–27.

32. See G.A. Ritter, *Sozialversicherung in Deutschland und England: Entstehung und Grundzüge im Vergleich* (Munich, 1983); and Berlepsch, *"Neuer Kurs" im Kaiserreich?* pp. 15–63.

33. For further details, consult J. Reulecke, *Geschichte der Urbanisierung in Deutschland* (Frankfurt, 1985), pp. 56–67; and W.R. Krabbe, *Kommunalpolitik und Industrialisierung: Die Entfaltung der städtischen Leistungsverwaltung im 19. und 20. Jahrhundert* (Stuttgart, 1985).

34. See the recent essays in K. Holl, G. Trautmann, and H. Vorländer, eds., *Sozialer Liberalismus* (Göttingen, 1986).

35. A more explicit treatment can be found in Langewiesche, *Liberalismus in*

In the second half of the nineteenth century urban social policy meant above all else the expansion and improvement of the urban infrastructure. Without improvements in sanitation in the areas of water supply and waste disposal, rapid urbanization would have had more catastrophic results, as in the case of Hamburg, where in 1892 the last great German cholera epidemic claimed the lives of more than eight thousand people.[36] The larger cities developed services that included gas and electricity as well as municipal slaughterhouses and tramways. Schools were built, along with public baths and parks, and theaters and museums were either erected or placed under municipal ownership. In city after city German liberals played a key role in establishing an ever-increasing number of municipal services. It may seem paradoxical that those cities that were Social Democratic strongholds at the time of Reichstag elections voted liberal in local elections. This, however, stemmed from an undemocratic suffrage designed to secure middle-class hegemony in the cities. At the turn of the century, only 50 to 60 percent of those in Prussia who were eligible to vote for the Reichstag could vote in city council elections. In Hamburg and Rostock, this percentage was as low as 23 and 8 percent, respectively.

Together with the Center and conservatives, therefore, the liberals defended the dominance of the bourgeoisie in the cities. But theirs was not a bourgeois special-interest politics. On the contrary, they used their political strength in the cities to expand the urban infrastructure and to introduce social reforms that would benefit all social strata. Political illiberalism and the will for social reform thus merged together in municipal social liberalism. Perhaps one can even go so far as to suggest that political illiberalism was a major prerequisite for the commitment to social reform that characterized municipal liberalism in Wilhelmine Germany. Because they could sustain themselves politically against Social Democracy, liberals found the strength to pursue a policy of reform that did not conform to the accepted picture of bourgeois liberalism. There was, however, a far more important reason behind this policy. Even the left liberals had

---

Deutschland, pp. 187–211. See also J.J. Sheehan, "Liberalismus and the City in Nineteenth-Century Germany," *Past and Present* 51 (1971): 116–37.

36. R.J. Evans, *Death in Hamburg: Society and Politics in the Cholera Years, 1830–1910* (Oxford, 1987).

initially opposed governmental social policy because they feared that an authoritarian state that had become a shield against the social risks of life could no longer be liberalized. Ludwig Bamberger thus saw bourgeois society becoming entangled in a "life or death" struggle if a governmental system of social insurance were to be adopted. This would create a "social tower of Babel" in which liberality would become extinct under state supervision.[37] The National Liberals had indeed allowed the anti-socialist laws to pass; they nevertheless refused to turn the workers into state pensioners, as Bismarck wanted to do.

Right-wing liberalism supported governmental social insurance; left liberalism rejected it. Within the liberal camp, therefore, there was no clear right-left division that encompassed all spheres of politics. Whoever like the National Liberals enjoyed close ties to the state and its conservative elite supported the beginnings of a state social insurance program. Whoever like the left liberals demanded political reforms rejected the idea of giving the state responsibility for one's social existence. At the imperial level, both political *and* social progressivism seemed utterly incompatible with German liberalism. This, in turn, was a direct consequence of the conservative second *Reichsgründung* of the late 1870s. Those who opposed the German state as it developed from 1880 on could not accept its social policy. Only under the radically changed circumstances that existed at the turn of the century did left liberals abandon their opposition to the government's social insurance system. Only then could political and social liberalism come together. In municipal politics, however, such a line of confrontation had never existed. The cities had managed to preserve a large degree of administrative autonomy against state governments throughout Germany and could therefore serve as a testing ground for a brand of liberal politics that proved far more reform-oriented than at the level of either the individual states or the empire itself.

In the cities the liberals possessed a degree of political influence they never enjoyed at the imperial level. After the turn of the century the power of the Reichstag increased but true parliamentarization could not be achieved. The situation in the cities was different, for here success at the polls automatically translated into governmental responsibility. Liberalism took

---

37. Bamberger, *Sezession*, pp. 131–33.

advantage of this opportunity and transformed itself into a more socially conscious form of liberalism. As far as the public was concerned, however, this transformation was of secondary importance, for the fate of individual liberal parties was determined far more by what happened at the imperial than at the municipal level. Still, until sufficient work has been done, one may assume that the municipal social liberalism of the Wilhelmine Empire helped to lay the foundation for the cooperation among liberalism, Social Democracy, and the Center that would emerge in the Weimar Republic.

Liberalism and the Crisis of the Bildungsbürgertum

The central values and goals of the German liberal movement have always been supplied by the educated bourgeoisie (*Bildungsbürgertum*). Not even the more economically influential elements of the German bourgeoisie have been able to challenge its preeminence in the articulation of liberal principles.[38] From the beginning of the nineteenth century to the "liberal era" of the newly founded national state, this particular form of liberalism proved immensely successful because it offered a comprehensive vision of progress. From a political point of view, the liberals of the German national movement espoused a program that let them embrace the future in essentially optimistic terms. As the goal of a powerful nation-state – by its very definition a politically egalitarian *Rechtsstaat* as well – seemed after 1867 to be rapidly nearing its realization, liberalism reached the zenith of its popularity. This was no less true in the economic sphere, where liberals proudly proclaimed a golden future and praised industrialization as the way to a better life for all. The necessary complement to material progress was the nation-state, which, according to the liberals, would also be a *Kulturstaat*. The nation and the national state were thus the guiding stars of the optimistic view of the world with which the educated bourgeoisie had transformed liberalism into a persuasive doctrine of progress.

At the end of the nineteenth century all of this suddenly changed. To be sure, the idea of the great nation still fascinated

38. In this respect, see D. Langewiesche, "Bildungsbürgertum und Liberalismus im 19. Jahrhundert," in Jürgen Kocka, ed., *Bildungsbürgertum*, 4:95–121. See also U. Engelhardt, *"Bildungsbürgertum": Begriffs- und Dogmengeschichte eines Etiketts* (Stuttgart, 1986).

the masses, but the liberals were no longer masters of this idea. The populist mass organizations that promised the Germans of the Wilhelmine era a "place in the sun" had usurped the heritage of liberalism as a force of national integration. The liberals tried to fight this loss of influence but were unsuccessful. The old ideas with which they had established themselves as the political vanguard of progress had outlived themselves and were no longer capable of competing with the new views of the future that Social Democracy and conservative populists had to offer. The liberal *Bildungsbürgertum*, which up to this point had always shaped liberalism programmatically and led it organizationally, was no longer equal to this task. Other social groups that might have taken its place simply did not exist. The reasons why the *Bildungsbürgertum* could no longer exercise its traditional leadership role within the German liberal camp have gone essentially unresearched. A few pointed suggestions must therefore suffice.

After the turn of the century a number of cultural diagnoses appeared revealing a deep sense of uncertainty and apprehension. In one work from 1913 the following passage can be found: "The times in which we live are indeed the most stirring and exciting of all times. . . . Eternal values give way to the sensations of the day, and the epochal degenerates into the ephemeral!"[39] Nothing appeared to have any permanence. The old foundations first of physics, then of painting, were shattered. One had, as the historian Adalbert Wahl lamented, "destroyed an old view of the world and had not yet found anything new to put in its place." Like many of his contemporaries, Wahl was hoping for a "great constructive spirit" that would create "from the ruins of an old worldview a new structure [that would be] clearly recognizable for the laity as well."[40]

It is not a question of whether these diagnoses of the times were accurate or not. Most important here is that large portions of Germany's educated bourgeoisie felt as if they were standing on thin ice. The cultured bourgeoisie had always justified its claim to social preeminence – a claim that in Germany had been widely accepted – with its cultural status. "Culture," however,

39. D. Sarason, ed., *Das Jahr 1913: Ein Gesamtbild der Kulturentwicklung* (Leipzig and Berlin, 1913), p. v.
40. A. Wahl, *Deutsche Geschichte von der Reichsgründung bis zum Ausbruch des Weltkriegs* (Stuttgart, 1932), vol. 3, p. 27.

no longer seemed sufficient to distinguish this self-conscious social elite from "the masses." The fact that the latest discoveries in the natural sciences were no longer comprehensible and that artists were constantly exchanging one avant-garde style for another improved the opportunities of the masses to become more directly involved in the process of cultural production at the same time that it undermined the cultural monopoly of the educated elites. The producers of culture seemed to devalue the capital of the cultured bourgeoisie by continually casting new commodities into the cultural market. Many of the cultured bourgeoisie regarded this development as a kind of cultural expropriation. For "culture" was their most important form of capital, the ground on which their social status rested. And now this capital had been reduced to nothing.

Seen from the perspective of the Weimar Republic, it is possible to establish three separate stages in the expropriation of the German *Bildungsbürgertum*. The postwar inflation and the manner in which it had been ended had resulted in the material expropriation of significant portions of Germany's *Bildungsbürgertum*. By the same token, they looked upon the revolutionary transition from Second Empire to Republic as an act of political expropriation by which the supposedly uncultured masses, in the form of the socialists and the Catholics, had come to power. The sense of cultural expropriation that the German *Bildungsbürgertum* had experienced since the last decade of the nineteenth century contributed in no small way to the political paralysis of German liberalism. German liberalism had always recruited its ideas and political spokesmen from the ranks of the Protestant bourgeoisie. But as the social source of its creative energy atrophied, political liberalism lost its dynamism. The liberal era in Germany had reached its end.

9

German Liberals and the Genesis of the Association Law of 1908

Eleanor L. Turk

Throughout most of the nineteenth century, German political organization was inhibited by a plethora of restrictive state laws. Unification and empire did little to change this situation. Although Article 4 Section 16 of the Imperial Constitution of 1871 gave the national government the right to regulate associations, until 1899 state laws prevailed. Only in 1908 was the right of association defined on a national basis. Within this maze of monarchical control and particularism, German liberals had to develop both the ideology and the techniques of political action. In the Bismarckian period from 1871 to 1890, this took place under the shadow of exceptional laws designed especially to suppress the rise of mass political factions, the Catholic Center Party and the Marxist Social Democratic Party. Once the exceptional law strategy was abandoned, more "normal" political interaction could begin. But in the 1890s the traditional parties were confronted not only with the mass ideological parties, but also with the rise of numerous special-interest pressure groups. German politics, therefore, never developed the trend toward consensus parties that alternate between being in power and being the "loyal opposition." Squeezed between a paternalistic conservative state and increasingly effective ideological and special-interest groups, German liberals struggled to achieve goals that included civil liberty and a responsible parliamentary government.

In evaluating the role of liberalism in the German Empire between 1871 and 1918, it is necessary to observe that the transition from absolute monarchy to constitutional monarchy was accomplished by "revolution from above" rather than by constituent assemblies. Of the twenty-five states that combined to form the empire in 1871, only five had constitutions written after the formation of political parties in the 1860s. As a result, in all but the three free cities, the "founding fathers" in Germany were hereditary monarchs and their hierarchical aristocratic bureaucracies.[1] They preempted the important political negotiations and compromises among influential middle-class sectors of society that characterized constitution building in the west European republics.

The earliest state constitutions were promulgated to uphold the conservative monarchies of the German Confederation, which was established by the Congress of Vienna in 1815 and which endured until 1866. Although some of the states had deliberative bodies, these Diets of Estates tended to consist of hereditary aristocrats and appointed representatives of corporate bodies such as cities or professions. Where elected bodies did exist, the voting laws, like the oligarchical three-class franchise in Prussia, were designed to protect aristocratic privilege. The oldest constitution, enacted in Saxe-Meiningen in 1829, permitted only a minimal right of association closely controlled by the government:

> Art. 28. Subjects shall not be forbidden to form societies for purposes that are not *per se* unlawful; but the right . . . shall be obtained by them only with the consent of the State.[2]

After the failure of the bourgeois revolutions of 1848, political activism of any sort was regarded as dangerous by the monarchist governments. Cannily, they used the constitution against political groups. The Prussian Constitution, introduced on 31 January 1850, reflected the prevailing conservative apprehension:

> Art. 29. All Prussians shall be entitled to meet in closed rooms, peacefully and unarmed, without previous permission from the authorities.

1. States with constitutions written before 1850 included Baden, Bavaria, Braunschweig, Hesse-Darmstadt, Lippe, Saxony, Saxe-Altenburg, Saxe-Meiningen, and Württemberg. In the 1850s constitutions were developed in Anhalt, Oldenburg, Prussia, Reuß jüngere Linie, Saxe-Coburg-Gotha, Saxe-Weimar-Eisenach, Schwarzburg-Rudolstadt, Schwarzburg-Sondershausen, and Waldeck. Mecklenburg-Schwerin and Mecklenburg-Strelitz had no constitution. Those written after 1867 were for Bremen (1894), Hamburg (1879), Lübeck (1907), Reuß ältere Linie (1867), and Schaumburg-Lippe (1868). E.H. Zeydel, ed., *Constitutions of the German Empire and German States* (U.S. Government Printing Office, Washington, D.C., 1919.)
2. Zeydel, *Constitutions*, p. 370 (emphasis in the original).

But this provision does not apply to open-air meetings, which shall be subject to whatever restrictions the law may prescribe, even requiring previous permission from the authorities.

Art. 30. All Prussians shall have the right to form associations for such purposes as do not contravene the penal laws.

The law shall regulate, with special regard to ensuring the public security, the exercise of the right guaranteed by this and the preceding article [29].[3]

This was augmented on 11 March 1850 with the Association Law, which stipulated registration of associations together with their bylaws and membership lists, mandatory surveillance of their activities by police authorities, and the exclusion of minors, women, and students from associations that "discuss political matters in their meetings." Any communication among political organizations was prohibited. Violations could result in forced closure of the meeting or organization and fines or imprisonment for participants.[4] Following the Prussian example, on 13 July 1854 the Confederation Diet also moved, to suppress popular nationalism and liberalism by requiring the states to ban potentially subversive organizations and disband existing groups espousing socialist or communist goals. The Diet denied women, minors, and apprentices the right of association. It, too, prohibited any collaboration or communication between political associations. Any remaining group activity was to be subject to observation by agents of the local police.[5]

Every German state but tiny Waldeck passed laws either to define or to restrain political associations and assemblies. These varied from state to state, but their cumulative effect was the same: they contained the growth and development of political movements. Typical provisions required political associations to submit lists of their officers and members and their bylaws to local police, to provide police with the agenda of their meetings, and to permit police agents to attend them. These agents could shut down those meetings if they deviated from the scheduled

---

3. Ibid., p. 227.

4. "Die landesrechtlichen Vorschriften, betreffend das Vereins- und Versammlungsrecht," *Drucksachen zu den Verhandlungen des Bundesrats des Deutschen Reichs* (hereafter *Drucksachen*), no. 159, Appendix 1, vol. 12 (Berlin, 1907), pp. 1–3.

5. *Drucksachen*, no. 159, Appendix 2, vol. 12, pp. 12–13.

agenda or if they threatened public order. Women, minors, apprentices, and students were barred from political associations by many states. Similarly, public political meetings had to obtain police permission twenty-four to forty-eight hours in advance and submit to police surveillance. Permission could be refused if the authorities believed that the meetings would disrupt order or encourage discussion of illegal matters, such as criminal or revolutionary acts. Women and minors were prohibited from attending. In Mecklenburg-Strelitz no open-air political meetings were allowed.[6] In particular, provisions like Article 8 of the Prussian Association Law of 1850 and Article 4.b of the Confederation Association Law of 1854 imposed a significant and long-lasting impediment. Known as the *Verbindungsverbot*, this prohibition against cooperation, collaboration, or correspondence among political organizations deprived political associations and pressure groups of effective vertical organization from local committee through to national party executive. It also prevented them from working with their counterparts in other states. Thirteen states adopted this restriction.

German liberalism focused first on the problems of unification and economic development, goals attainable only through collaboration with nationalist elements. The monarchies were accepted as necessary participants in this process. But the unification of Germany left the old constitutions and association laws intact. The imperial constitution, implemented 1 July 1871, was a treaty among monarchs, not the product of a national constituent assembly. The political parties thus conformed to state restrictions, especially that of the *Verbindungsverbot*, even after unification. This particularly affected the local committees, which were required by state laws to remain separate from each other. District and state committees also developed, but they could not consist of designated representatives of the local committees, nor could they communicate with those bodies. Where state committees existed, these bans could be circumvented by annual party conventions, when adherents could assemble as individuals and elect a separate central committee to function until the next convention. Of course, these were prohibited from collaborating with similar organizations in other states.[7]

6. Ibid., no. 159, Appendix 3, vol. 12, pp. 1–96.
7. E.R. Huber, *Deutsche Verfassungsgeschichte seit 1789*, vol. 4, *Struktur und Krisen des Kaiserreichs* (Stuttgart, 1969), pp. 7ff.

Bismarck's experiments with exceptional laws against the Catholics and the Social Democrats were totally counterproductive; by 1890 reaction to them had developed the two largest political constituencies in the empire. Thus, when debate began in 1894 over the right of association in Germany, the liberals had already entered a period of decline. In the national elections of 1893 they had attracted only 32.7 percent of the voters, having lost ground significantly in such former strongholds as Prussia, Saxony, and Württemberg.[8] They welcomed this controversy on principle and used it eagerly as a way to reverse their decline in success at the polls. There are three discernible stages in their campaign for the law. When the government introduced measures mainly to curtail political rights, such as the Anti-Revolution Bill of 1894 and the Prussian Association Law of 1897, the liberals were in the forefront of the opposition. Indeed, they countered with persistent demands for national legislation to end the *Verbindungsverbot*. When the focus next turned to economic issues, however, the efforts of management to restrain workers' organizations split the liberals. The final stage found liberals conceding to conservative and Prussian demands to restrict the association and assembly rights of ethnic minorities in exchange for association rights for women. Yet without liberal persistence the state laws of the 1850s might have prevailed.

The controversy began in June 1894, when an Italian anarchist assassinated the president of France. Kaiser Wilhelm reacted by demanding a stringent law to curtail oppositional political activity. His chancellor, General Leo von Caprivi, was as reluctant to propose inroads on the state prerogatives as he was to make the Reichstag the forum for radical propaganda on the issue. Wilhelm was impatient with Caprivi's unwillingness to act. By 1 September 1894 he was even ready to replace Caprivi in order to get his own way, not only against the left, but also against agrarian conservatives who opposed Germany's new free trade treaties.[9] On 6 September at a gala banquet in Königsberg with the Prussian provincial Landtag, Wilhelm personally removed five of the most intransigent conservatives from the guest list

---

8. G.A. Ritter and M. Niehuss, *Wahlgeschichtliches Arbeitsbuch: Materialien zur Statistik des Kaiserreichs, 1871–1918* (Munich, 1980), pp. 83–96.
9. J.C.G. Röhl, *Germany Without Bismarck* (London, 1967), p. 114.

and admonished the nobility in his speech for "misunderstanding" and "combating" him, even opposing him: "But gentlemen, opposition by the Prussian nobility to their King is an absurdity! . . . I direct to you my call: 'On to the battle for religion, for decency and order against the parties of revolution. . . . Forward with God, and dishonor to him who deserts his King!'"[10]

Yet Caprivi still resisted. Meeting with the emperor on 6 October he again objected to presenting to the Reichstag a measure that was sure to spell defeat for the government.[11] In the Prussian cabinet on 12 and 19 October he battled conservative ministers over the basic rights of organizations. He wanted only to outlaw associations proven dangerous to public order. They demanded measures to prevent suspicious groups from organizing at all or from holding meetings. Outvoted, Caprivi was forced to accept the proposal "that associations that threaten the public peace or security are to be forbidden." Minors and women would be banned from political associations and their meetings, although working women could attend meetings related to discussions of their work. Caprivi also had to agree to present the measure to the Reichstag.[12]

Angry and discouraged, Caprivi submitted his resignation on 23 October. The emperor immediately rejected it and drove to the Chancery to assure Caprivi of his continuing confidence and support.[13] That provoked the Prussian minister-president's resignation, which the emperor also rejected. Two days later Caprivi informed the emperor that he had surveyed all but three of the non-Prussian states and that they were against submitting national legislation on an association law at this time. They felt

10. *Kreuzzeitung*, 7 September 1894, no. 419.
11. P. Eulenburg to Bülow, 6 October 1894. Bundesarchiv Koblenz, Nachlaß Bernhard Fürst von Bülow (hereafter BA: NL Bülow), no. 75, pp. 103–6.
12. The minutes of the 12 October meeting are printed in E. Zechlin, *Staatsstreichpläne Bismarcks und Wilhelms II: 1890, 1894* (Stuttgart and Berlin, 1929), pp. 193ff. [Prussian Cabinet] Protocol, October 19, 1894. "Geheime Akten betreffend der Staatsministerial und Kronrats Protokolle," Auswärtiges Amt, Abteilung A, American Committee for the Study of the War, German Foreign Ministry Archives, 1867–1920, Reel ACP 202 (hereafter ACP 202), pp. 21–35.
13. Caprivi, letter to his brother, 23 October 1894; Berlin Hauptarchiv, Nachlaß Caprivi, rep. 92, no. 5. The text of Caprivi's resignation is in Zechlin, *Staatsstreichpläne*, pp. 204–7, and a partial translation is in J.A. Nichols, *Germany After Bismarck: The Caprivi Era, 1890–1894* (New York, 1958), p. 350.

that the timing was wrong and that prospects of passage were poor. But, fundamentally, they did not wish to cede their local control for the uncertainties of a national law.[14] Bavaria would have to admit women to association meetings, and Württemberg, Baden, and Hesse would have to impose the preventive ban where none existed. These states much preferred their own laws to the changes demanded by the Prussians. Caprivi's evidence appeared irrefutable. But that very day the emperor was handed a clipping from the *Kölnische Zeitung* that contained, to his outrage, a complete and accurate account of his private meeting with Caprivi on the problem two days before.[15] Embarrassed and furious, Wilhelm bitterly accepted the resignations of both men. He summoned to Berlin the elderly Prince Chlodwig zu Hohenlohe-Schillingsfürst, then serving as governor-general of Alsace-Lorraine, and appointed him Prussian minister-president and federal chancellor.

The papers were filled with excited discussion and speculation over the scandal, but Hohenlohe went about his business calmly. Acceding realistically to the wishes of the states, he persuaded his Prussian colleagues on 31 October to delete the section on the association law. The revised bill was submitted to on 16 November to the Bundesrat. It was approved there and passed on to the Reichstag in early December.[16] Entitled "The Bill to Amend and Extend the Penal Code, Military Penal Code, and the Press Laws," the measure was popularly dubbed the "Umsturzvorlage," the Anti-Revolution Bill.

The first of the three required readings of the bill began in January 1895 and lasted through five days of partisan positioning. An alignment emerged between the Center Party, whose ninety-six members found the call to protect religion promising, and the seventy-two Conservatives. As the two largest factions

---

14. Caprivi to Wilhelm, 25 October 1894, Bundesarchiv Koblenz, Nachlaß Chlodwig Hohenlohe [hereafter BA: NL Hohenlohe], no. 1596.

15. Eulenburg and his conservative colleagues had been hoping to oust Caprivi, and there is therefore considerable controversy among historians about the "leak" of this private conversation to the liberal press. See Nichols, *Germany After Bismarck*, pp. 351–54; Röhl, *Germany Without Bismarck*, pp. 116–17; J. Haller, *Aus dem Leben des Fürsten Philipp zu Eulenburg-Hertefeld* (Berlin and Leipzig, 1926), pp. 162–66.

16. [Prussian] Cabinet minutes October 31, 1894, ACP 202; "Entwurf eines Gesetzes . . ." (undated) NL Hohenlohe, no. 1596; Bundesrat no. 103, November 16, 1894.

in a legislature of 397, they led the movement to submit the bill to committee. Through committee hearings that lasted into April they converted the bill into a measure that protected religion instead of affording the state protection against revolutionaries. With the liberals leading the opposition, this version of the bill was summarily rejected by the plenum on 11 May 1895.[17]

Although the liberals were quick to reject the reactionary Anti-Revolution Bill, they immediately rejected a socialist initiative to grant unrestricted rights of association and assembly to all German citizens, regardless of sex, and to abrogate existing laws to prevent collective action for the improvement of wages or working conditions. Several liberal speakers and a member of the Polish faction, however, initiated a call for the government to present a unified national association law, although they declined to specify desirable provisions.[18]

Undaunted by his defeats in both the Bundesrat and the Reichstag, Wilhelm next pressed for stricter legislation in Prussia. Accordingly, the Prussian minister of the interior, Ernst von Köller, went rapidly to work. On 15 September he forwarded to Hohenlohe proposals for four alternatives: a wholly new association law containing "the desired provisions"; a revision of the existing association law; other possible amendments to the existing law; and a short new antisocialist law. Although he preferred the last, he felt the second would be easier to pass.[19] He coupled this with a vigorous campaign against the socialist press and in November 1895 sent the Prussian police to raid the homes of over seventy Berlin socialists presumed to be violating the Prussian *Verbindungsverbot*. The police indicted forty-five men and two women and closed eleven socialist organizations, including six Reichstag election committees and the party executive committee.

This aggressive action infuriated Hohenlohe, and Köller was

17. *Stenographische Berichte über die Verhandlungen des Reichstages* (hereafter *Verhandlungen des Reichstages*), vol. 141, pp. 224–32; vol. 142, pp. 1155–1209 and 2242–44. The committee members included 9 Conservatives, 8 from the Center, 7 liberals, 3 socialists and a Pole. Ibid., vol. 138, p. 339.

18. Ibid., vol. 140, pp. 1997–2024 and 2083–2107.

19. Köller to Hohenlohe, September 1895, with Appendix, BA: NL Hohenlohe, No. 1600.

forced out of the ministry.[20] In the Reichstag, the left-liberal Radicals began an immediate counteroffensive by proposing the text of a national association law: "All Germans are entitled to form associations without any prior official permission, and are entitled to hold meetings, unarmed, whether in private rooms or in the open air. Further, any association is entitled to enter organized activities with other associations to pursue common goals."[21]

The socialists resubmitted the measure that had failed so dismally in May. In the Reichstag session of 29 January 1896 they deemphasized the workers' rights issue, which had been the focus of their earlier initiative. Instead, they pointed to similarities between socialist organizations and the bylaws of the Conservative Party, the Landlords' League, and other prominent industrial, professional, religious, and cultural organizations, asserting that the ban was a sword of Damocles hanging over them all.[22]

On 8 February 1896 the Reichstag began debate on the Radicals' association bill. The Center Party spokesman complained that if Köller's actions against the socialist organizations were upheld in court, all party organizations would be in danger. He proposed a resolution urging the government to submit, as soon as possible, a "unified codification of the public rights of association and assembly."[23] The National Liberals concurred. But when the government failed to respond, the house voted on 18 February to submit the Radicals' bill to a committee for further review.

On 26 February a second legislative group took up the issue. After twenty years of preparation, a unified imperial Civil Code was under review by the Reichstag. In committee, debate began over the legal definition of an association and the nature of its rights under the new legal code. The majority voted that all organizations, except those with specifically economic goals, could obtain legal status simply by registering with local authorities.

---

20. See E-T.P.W. Wilke, *Political Decadence in Imperial Germany: Personnel-Political Aspects of the German Government Crisis, 1894–97* (Urbana, Ill., 1976), pp. 131–55.
21. *Verhandlungen des Reichstages*, vol. 143, pp. 617–26; vol. 151, pp. 126–37.
22. Ibid., vol. 143, pp. 617–26.
23. Ibid., vol. 144, pp. 831–47.

The government spokesmen argued that the Bundesrat would never accept this.[24] The committee persisted, however, voting on 18 March to exclude minors from political organizations and meetings, to end the *Verbindungsverbot*, and to require only a forty-eight-hour notice of meetings to facilitate traffic arrangements.[25]

In May the Prussian case against the Social Democrats finally came to court. The *Verbindungsverbot* was on trial as well, and, to the government's disappointment, thirty-two of the defendants were acquitted and six of the eleven associations reinstated. The state was required to pay court costs for all those acquitted. The party executive committee and four election committees were dissolved as a result of the court rulings, however.[26] Under the impact of this verdict the Reichstag began the second reading of the Radicals' association law. The new committee version endorsed not only the Radicals' call for an unhampered association right, but also the socialists' demand that legitimate labor organizations be exempt from the laws for political associations.[27] But there was a serious split among the committee's liberal members. Ernst Bassermann, a National Liberal leader, had been elected as spokesman for the committee, but had refused to present its report. The task was left to Heinrich Rickert, a Radical. Rickert introduced the report by revealing that the two conservative factions and the government representatives had neither attended nor voted in the discussions. Rickert was understandably uncertain about final approval for the bill. He challenged the government to state whether it was willing to accept an interim measure just to end the *Verbindungsverbot*. Karl von Boetticher, the imperial secretary for internal affairs, hedged his answer: the Bundesrat had not discussed the right of association since the states had objected to including it in the 1894 Revolution Bill, and the Bundesrat was not required to discuss any Reichstag matter until it had passed the second reading. Unsatisfied, the bill's supporters paraded to the ros-

24. Reported in the *Kreuzzeitung*, 27 February 1896, no. 97.
25. *Kölnische Zeitung*, 19 March 1896, no. 257.
26. E.L. Turk, "The Berlin Socialist Trials of 1896: An Examination of Civil Liberty in Wilhelmian Germany," *Central European History* 19 (1986): 323–42.
27. A Prussian court decision in 1886 classified unions as political organizations because they aimed to "influence public affairs." This subjected them to police surveillance and regulation. See K. Saul, "Der Staat und die 'Mächte des Umsturzes,'" *Archiv für Sozialgeschichte* 22 (1972): 302–5.

trum. Although most urged acceptance of the committee's report, they also said that they would be willing to accept an interim measure ending the *Verbindungsverbot*. The Center Party decided to cast its vote in favor of the committee report in order to force a discussion in the Bundesrat, and on that cue the bill successfully passed its second reading in the Reichstag.[28]

On 7 June the Civil Code committee of the Reichstag resumed its discussion of the right of association. The government had rejected its proposal for simple registration of associations. The Center proposed exceptional status for political, religious, and educational organizations, but urged the government to submit an acceptable association law, especially one defining the rights of workers' organizations.[29] It was clear that the government would have to make some sort of statement on the issue, especially if it wanted to protect the smooth passage of the Civil Code.

Eberhard von der Recke, Prussian minister of internal affairs, consulted with envoys from the other German states. On 13 June he reported to the Prussian cabinet that they were unanimously against the Reichstag's bill but divided over an interim measure to end the *Verbindungsverbot*. He also informed the cabinet that a Reichstag committee, led by National Liberal Ernst Bassermann and including representatives of all but the Conservative Party, had formed to submit an interim measure to end the *Verbindungsverbot*: "Domestic associations of any nature may enter into organizational relationships. Existing state laws to the contrary are abrogated." The cabinet rejected that proposal. Now even Prussia preferred to leave control of the association laws to the individual states.[30]

Bassermann had formed the "Independent Committee for the Passage of an Interim Law to Regulate the Right of Association" on 11 June 1896. He had written the proposal, which Recke had read to the Prussian cabinet, as a substitute for the committee draft at the Reichstag's third reading of the association law bill on 16 June. A petition endorsed by 260 of the Reichstag's 397 members supported the proposal, and Bassermann spoke

---

28. *Verhandlungen des Reichstages*, vol. 146, pp. 2387–2404.

29. *Kreuzzeitung*, 7 June 1896, no. 263.

30. Cabinet minutes, 13 June 1896, Geheimes Staatsarchiv der Stiftung Preußischer Kulturbesitz, Berlin-Dahlem (hereafter: GSA), rep. 90, no. 394, STM 2972.

vigorously on behalf of this majority. Rickert again demanded clarification from the government, and Boetticher replied that the state governments would reject action at the national level. Nevertheless, the majority voted to amend the proposed association law with the Bassermann version. In that form it passed its third and final reading.[31] Thus the Reichstag abandoned its efforts to formulate a national association law and put the issue to the states. The Bundesrat simply ignored the action.

Fearing that the Center Party's strategy and the momentum behind the Bassermann proposal might endanger the Civil Code, Hohenlohe decided it was time to intercede. On 27 June he went to the rostrum of the Reichstag and urged patience while Boetticher discussed the *Verbindungsverbot* with the states. He assured the members that this amelioration would take place in the various state legislatures before the Civil Code came into effect on 1 January 1900. That satisfied the Center. Bassermann concurred, but added the proviso that if the governments did not take action within the year, the Reichstag should reserve its right to act on the matter.[32] The Civil Code gained easy approval during the summer.

True to his word, Hohenlohe announced in his first speech to the new Prussian Landtag session on 18 November 1896 that a bill on the association law was forthcoming. On 27 November Recke, the Prussian minister for internal affairs, submitted the draft to the cabinet. It proposed ending the elaborate registration procedures and the ban on women at political meetings as well as abrogating the *Verbindungsverbot*. But it also included controversial innovations. The police were given authority to *prohibit* meetings that they decided might be subversive; they could dissolve associations or meetings that they found to be *immoral* or dangerous. And, although it would require amending the Prussian Constitution, minors were henceforth to be

---

31. *Verhandlungen des Reichstages*, vol. 146, pp. 2667–76; vol. 153, p. 2198. The socialists tried to reintroduce the matter into the Civil Code, proposing: "The state laws that forbid organizational relationships among political associations are abrogated. Organizations of employers designed to discuss more favorable wages and working conditions are not subject to state [association law] regulations." The progressives also tried to insert the Bassermann version. However, both measures were rejected in committee, and a Conservative-Center majority rejected them as amendments in the plenary session. Ibid., vol. 146, pp. 2735–49; vol. 153, pp. 2250–56.

32. *Verhandlungen des Reichstages*, vol. 146, pp. 3016–3123.

barred from organized groups. Recke argued that these measures were necessary "compensations" for the other changes.[33]

The cabinet waited until early April 1897 before tackling these issues. Disagreement over the preventive ban emerged. Recke discussed it with party leaders. He reported that the National Liberals both in Prussia and in the Reichstag were adamantly opposed to the proposal, arguing that Hohelohe had said nothing about "compensations." As the government relied on a conservative-liberal majority in the Prussian lower house, and as neither the Prussian upper house nor the king would countenance the simple elimination of the *Verbindungsverbot*, Recke advised postponement.[34] Hohenlohe was able to persuade Wilhelm to accept elimination of the preventive ban on meetings, although the king insisted on retaining the restrictions on minors.[35] Despite the misgivings of the cabinet, Hohenlohe sent the draft forward in that form in order to redeem his pledge to the Reichstag.

For the first time in over a decade, the National Liberals found themselves with real political influence in both the Prussian Landtag and the Reichstag. In the Prussian Landtag, where the deputies were elected through a plutocratic three-class ballot, the Conservatives and Free Conservatives controlled 203 of the 433 seats, only 14 short of an absolute majority. The Center had 97 seats, the National Liberals 79, and the divergent left-liberal Radicals 20.

The National Liberals were the only Landtag faction with a larger national than Prussian constituency.[36] They had to walk a narrow line between preserving their place in the Prussian

33. Minister of the Interior, 27 November 1896, Appendix 1, GSA, 3. Hpt. Abt. AA., No. 1176, 2 16020.

34. Cabinet minutes, 2 April 1897, ibid., STM 1526. See also cabinet minutes, 9 April 1897, GSA, 3. Hpt. Abt. AA., no. 1177, STM 1640, as well as Fürst Chlodwig zu Hohenlohe-Schillingsfürst, *Denkwürdigkeiten der Reichskanzlerzeit*, ed. Karl Alexander von Müller (Stuttgart and Berlin, 1931), pp. 328–29.

35. Recke and Marschall to Hohenlohe, 10 April 1897, BA: NL Hohenlohe, no. 1606.

36. Only 25 (47.2%) of the 53 National Liberals in the Reichstag came from Prussia. By contrast, 82% of the Conservatives, 71% of the Free Conservatives, and 54% of the Center Party delegates in the Reichstag were from Prussia. Even the Social Democrats, whom the three-class franchise kept out of the Prussian Landtag, elected 21 (47.7%) of their 44 Reichstag delegates in 1893 from Prussia. Prussian districts elected 236 of the 397 Reichstag deputies. This analysis compiled from M. Schwarz, *MdR: Biographisches Handbuch der Reichstage* (Hanover, 1965).

coalition and retaining their non-Prussian voters. Their tactics were extraordinarily bold. In the Reichstag Bassermann reintroduced and secured passage of his bill to end the *Verbindungsverbot*. Then, to the shock and outcry of the liberal press and southern constituents, the Prussian contingent of the party voted with the conservatives for the Prussian Association Law, even with the ban on minors. They approved it through three readings in the lower house and also approved the constitutional amendment necessary to deprive minors of their right to participate in political groups. Predictably, however, when the bill went to the Prussian upper house, the aristocratic conservatives quickly converted it into an exceptional law against the Social Democrats and the anarchists. A Radical delegate marveled that the left was now depending on on the reactionary Prussian upper house to help defeat the bill.[37] Indeed, in this version it even embarrassed Hohenlohe, and he advised his colleagues to take a neutral stance. Confident, however, that they had liberal support, the ministers agreed to "recommend" this reversion to the lower house.[38]

When the revised bill was presented to the lower house on 24 July the deputies waited through five tense hours of heated debate, wondering how the National Liberals would vote. Finally the issue was put to the test. An absolute majority of members present was 208. In a vote by roll call, the reactionary bill garnered only 206 votes, the only government bill to be defeated in the entire session of the Landtag. The National Liberals had held; the intransigent Conservatives were blamed for the bill's defeat.[39] Yet for all their magnificent party discipline, the National Liberals had accomplished little. The Bundesrat ignored the passage of the Bassermann bill in the Reichstag, and the *Verbindungsverbot* remained untouched in Prussia. Only tiny Reuß jüngere Linie, one of the smallest states of the empire, took the necessary action to eliminate it.

On 18 June 1897, at the height of the debate over the Prussian Association Law, Emperor Wilhelm II placed the right of association in an entirely different context. Speaking before a group of

37. *Kölnische Zeitung*, 23 June 1897, no. 579.
38. Cabinet minutes, 29 June 1897, BSA, 3. Hpt. Abt. AA., no. 1177, STM 2955.
39. E.L. Turk, "Holding the Line: The National Liberals and the Prussian Association Law of 1897," *German Studies Review* 2 (1979): 297–316.

textile workers in Bielefeld, he claimed that he wanted protection for the German workers and the "ruthless suppression of any revolutionary impulses and the stiffest penalties for those who would try to prevent any person who wishes to work from doing so."[40] Then, during the summer, he shuffled the government to remove ministers sympathetic to social concerns and replace them with men he felt would work to control social and economic agitation in order to build industry and help Germany become a prestigious international power.[41] Finally, on 6 September 1898 the emperor announced at a military review in Oeynhausen that he would fulfill his Bielefeld pledge with a law that would "stipulate that any and all persons, whoever they may be, who try to prevent a willing worker from working, or who try to persuade him to join a strike, will be punished by a term in prison at hard labor. . . . Law and order must be maintained."[42]

Wilhelm had neglected to warn his ministers about the speech. They were shocked and dismayed at his statements,[43] knowing that the outcry following the Oeynhausen speech had essentially killed any chance for such a measure. They stalled as long as they could, but finally, at the emperor's demand, submitted "The Bill to Protect Willing Workers" to the Reichstag on 1 June 1899. It specified penalties for coercion or boycott on behalf of a strike or "agitation for a lockout or strike" in any industry essential to national security.[44] This bill had been thoroughly anticipated by the partisan press and widely discussed for two years. They had dubbed it the "Prison Bill" and taken predictably partisan positions, the Center and left against the conservatives. Yet the National Liberals were divided, as liberal principles were confronted by patriotic nationalism and concern for the industrial economy. Initially voting in caucus to

40. *Kreuzzeitung*, 19 June 1897, no. 282.

41. Analysis of the impact of these personnel changes on social policies and politics is provided in M. Schmidt, *Graf Posadowsky: Staatssekretär des Reichsschatzamtes und des Reichsamtes des Innern* (Halle, 1935), pp. 40–88. For the more traditional political narrative, see Röhl, *Germany Without Bismarck*, pp. 229–51; and Wilke, *Political Decadence*, pp. 262–78.

42. *Schultheß Europäischer Geschichtskalender* 39 (1898): 158–59.

43. Hohenlohe, *Denkwürdigkeiten*, pp. 451–53. See also K.E. Born, *Staat und Sozialpolitik seit Bismarcks Sturz* (Weisbaden, 1957), pp. 147–48.

44. *Verhandlungen des Reichstages*, vol. 179, pp. 2238–98.

support the bill,[45] they belatedly reversed their position during the first reading on 22 June and voted not to send it to committee for further review. This augured yet another defeat for the government, which recessed the Reichstag until November.

Throughout the summer the National Liberals debated the bill among themselves. When the legislature reconvened, a group of twenty-four National Liberals, a bare majority of their faction of forty-seven, submitted a three-section compromise proposal. The first section called, again, for the end of the *Verbindungsverbot*. The second supported peaceful collective bargaining and picketing in legally announced strikes; but coercion of workers or employers to join job actions could be punished by jail sentences or fines. The third section canceled all the items of the government's bill.[46] The socialist newspaper *Vorwärts* waggishly dubbed this the "Half-Prison Bill." In a loud and unruly session on 19 November the house rejected this compromise measure and the government's original bill.

Following this resounding defeat, the emperor abandoned his efforts to curtail civil liberty. The liberals, however, moved resolutely to reintroduce the bill to end the *Verbindungsverbot*. In the end, Hohenlohe's sense of honor made the difference. He was determined to redeem his pledge to the Reichstag that the states would eliminate the ban. By threatening to resign, he secured Wilhelm's assent.[47] When Bassermann, for the third year in a row, proposed his bill to end the *Verbindungsverbot* on 6 December 1899, Hohenlohe announced that the Bundesrat would approve. The Reichstag vote on the "Lex Hohenlohe" came quickly, and the ban passed quietly out of existence on 7 December, a major victory for liberal principles and persistence.[48]

The liberals turned next to a social aspect of the association law, in the final phase of their reform efforts. In April 1902 Bassermann led a group of Reichstag members in the call for the abrogation of state laws preventing women from participating in associations and assemblies dealing with issues of social policy. Working women vigorously complained at their arbitrary exclu-

---

45. *National-Zeitung*, 16 June 1899, no. 372.
46. *Verhandlungen des Reichstages*, vol. 175, p. 252.
47. Hohenlohe, *Denkwürdigkeiten*, pp. 447–48.
48. *Verhandlungen des Reichstages*, vol. 168, pp. 3245–55.

sion from discussions of their own wages and working conditions. Numerous petitions to the Reichstag supported their demands. Indeed, the Social Democrats made this a major issue in the national elections of 1903 and increased their Reichstag mandate by twenty-five seats. The National Liberals also gained five seats in 1903, the only one of the "state supporting" parties to show an increase. The Prussian-based Polish Party, campaigning as an oppressed and aggrieved minority, was the only other party to increase its mandate in the election. Its primary demand was the unrestricted use of the Polish language in church, education, and public meetings.[49]

By December 1903 the Polish question had begun to concern the Prussian minister of the interior. In a memo to the cabinet Freiherr Hans von Hammerstein pointed to a recent court decision that permitted the Polish language in public meetings; he felt this increased their opportunity for separatist and anti-Prussia agitation. He continued by suggesting that in view of the numerous petitions to grant association rights to women, it was an opportune time to amend the Prussian Association Law's restraints on women in exchange for greater control of the Polish minority. The draft list of amendments that he attached omitted the restrictions on women and minors, as well as the requirement that associations register their membership with the police. But in the compensations he proposed, Hammerstein made the German language a requirement for all meetings in which "public affairs" were discussed. He also significantly raised the catalogue of penalties, in some instances from a fine of 150 marks to one of 600 marks.[50] The other ministers preferred to postpone discussion until the next session,[51] and Hammerstein died in 1905 without action having been taken.

At the national level, the secretary of the interior, Count Arthur von Posadowsky-Wehner, tried another approach. He

---

49. In the 1903 elections the Conservatives, Free Conservatives, and Center each lost 2 seats; the various minorities – Hanoverians, Alsatians, Anti-Semites, and others – lost a combined total of 13. The Danes returned one member in each of the 1898, 1903, and 1907 elections. The Polish party also grew in 1903 from 14 to 16 representatives. Ritter and Niehuss, *Wahlgeschichtliches Arbeitsbuch*, p. 40.

50. Hammerstein to Bülow, 4 December 1903, BA: R43F Reichskanzlei 2603 (microfilm of Deutsches Zentralarchiv 2240), STM 4697.

51. Votum, Kultusminister [v. Studt], 25 April 1904, BA: R43F Reichskanzlei 2603 (microfilm of Deutsches Zentralarchiv 2240).

agreed that it was time to admit women to vocational and social organizations.[52] Reichstag delegates from the Radical and Center parties had been proposing such a bill since 1890. A law to that effect could strengthen the nonsocialist workers' organizations and meet the demands for women's rights without having to sacrifice state controls over political organizations. He announced his intentions to the Reichstag in January 1904 and began negotiations with Bundesrat representatives to gain the support of the states. The task took him until October 1906, due to state concerns about the impact of the bill on their own labor codes.[53]

The bill on vocational associations went to the Reichstag in November 1906. The draft opened trade unions to women and minors, but excluded farm workers, domestics, and civil servants. Across the board the party spokesmen criticized the measure for what it did and did not do, but voted on 27 November to send the bill to committee for discussion and amendment. When the government suddenly dissolved the Reichstag on 13 December and called for new elections, Posadowsky's bill died in committee.[54]

The Bülow government had dismissed the Reichstag because the Center-led majority had refused to grant the military credits needed to subdue an uprising in one of Germany's African colonies. The election of 1907 was, therefore, somewhat of a vendetta, as the call went out to the "state-supporting" Conservatives, Free Conservatives, National Liberals, and Radicals to build a bloc against the "national enemies" – the Catholic Center, the Social Democrats, and the increasingly vocal minority Polish party that voted with them. This campaign, fought over the concept of patriotic imperialism, revealed how ending the *Verbindungsverbot* had changed the nature of German politics. The day after the Reichstag was dissolved Radical and National Liberal leaders met in Berlin to plan a cooperative election campaign. Following that, leaders of the four bloc parties met regularly in the offices of the Prussian Conservatives to coordinate their activities. They were backed by funds that

52. Votum, Posadowsky, 17 June 1904, ibid.
53. P. Rassow and K.E. Born, *Akten zur staatlichen Sozialpolitik in Deutschland, 1890–1914* (Wiesbaden, 1959), pp. 150–51.
54. *Verhandlungen des Reichstages*, vol. 218, pp. 3860–79, 3881–3906, 3907–28, 3937–55; vol. 226, pp. 4998–5030.

the Central Association of German Industrialists had funneled through the Free Conservative Party and distributed among the parties and pro-bloc associations. Of the estimated 600,000 marks distributed in this manner, the Navy League received approximately 30,000 to publish and deliver election publicity. One of the most active electioneers was the Imperial Union for Combating Social Democracy, founded after the socialist gains in 1903 "to encourage cooperation between the various non-socialist parties" and to assist in their campaign efforts. Working through a network of 287 local groups, 340 affiliated organizations, and 22 labor unions, it sought energetically to defeat the socialists.[55] Before 1900 this kind of cooperation would have been blocked by the *Verbindungsverbot*. This extraordinary party collaboration and the involvement of the special-interest associations with the political parties made the election of 1907 one of the most bitterly fought in the history of the Second Empire.

The bloc parties' strategy forged a stunning victory, even though they polled only 43 percent of the votes on the first ballot. By cooperating to back a single candidate in the run-off elections, bloc parties were able to increase their Reichstag majority from 177 to 216. The opposition parties elected only 168 delegates. The Social Democrats suffered the greatest defeat – their representation declined from 81 to 43 members. The Center Party actually gained 5 seats and retained its plurality, but because the bloc did not need Center support to build a majority, the party actually lost political leverage. The Poles gained 4 seats, but the other minorities (Alsatians, Danes, and Guelphs) shared a loss of 6 seats.[56]

Bülow convened the new Reichstag on 19 February 1907. Six days later he paid the debt he had incurred for the liberals' support by announcing that the government would submit the long-awaited draft of a national association law to the Reichstag. Over the summer the Prussian Cabinet developed a bill that was close to Hammerstein's proposals, and on 11 October 1907 they presented it to the Bundesrat. It granted the rights of association and assembly to all citizens of the empire, regardless

55. G.D. Crothers, *The German Elections of 1907* (New York, 1968), pp. 114 and 161–63.
56. Ibid., pp. 174–75.

of sex and age. New associations had one week to give local authorities a register of officers, bylaws, and the number of members in the German language. All organizations had to give authorities twenty-four-hour notice of public meetings to discuss "public affairs" and twelve-hour notice of any election meeting. A significant innovation was a paragraph stipulating that all public meetings were to use the German language unless given official exemption by state authorities. Police surveillance would continue at public meetings, but the convener, not the police, would be responsible for dismissing the assembly for use of a foreign language or exhortations to violence or disorder. Penalties were assessed at the six-hundred-mark level. State laws affecting religious organizations, as well as the right of farmworkers and domestics to organize, were unaffected by the Prussian proposal.[57]

In the Bundesrat on 12 November 1907 the states' resistance to this interference was made clear by the variety of amendments they offered: Baden and Hamburg wanted power to prevent some associations and assemblies; Saxony insisted that all outdoor meetings discussed "public affairs" and needed police surveillance; and Bavaria, Saxony, Baden, and Mecklenburg wanted to retain their ban on minors.[58] They were outraged to learn that Bülow had first consulted the parties rather than the states,[59] and that the bloc was inalterably opposed to the ban on minors.[60] But the Prussians held firm, and the Bundesrat reluctantly approved the bill with its major provisions intact. It was forwarded to the Reichstag on 22 November 1907.

The first reading of the association law in the Reichstag began on 9 December. It was impassioned but predictable. Bethmann-Hollweg explained that the law would eliminate unnecessary police interference in associations and assemblies without sacrificing the controls necessary to maintain public order; the law also would respect the desirable aspects of existing state association laws.[61] A Conservative spokesman followed him to the podium. Expressing concern about the impact of the language paragraph on the "loyal" Lettish, Masurian, and

57. *Drucksachen*, no. 159, vol. 12.
58. Rassow and Born, *Akten*, pp. 293–96.
59. Ibid., p. 298.
60. Ibid., p. 301.
61. *Verhandlungen des Reichstages*, vol. 229, pp. 2091–93.

Wendish minorities, he objected to the new freedom for women and minors in associations. Despite these reservations, he pronounced this a timely and workable compromise and recommended that it be forwarded to a committee to prepare the second reading.[62] The Center spoke next. Acknowledging the benefit to women and minors, it rejected the language paragraph, the high penalties, and the exclusion of legal protection for religious associations and orders, farmworkers, and civil servants.[63] The spokesman for the National Liberal Party welcomed the bill liberals had demanded for thirty-seven years and spoke of it as a significant improvement to the laws of Prussia and the major states. He urged the house to consider the real benefits of a uniform national law and be willing to compromise. His major concern was that a concrete definition of the term "public affairs" was needed in order to assess the application of the law to the many economic, social, and political associatons that it would affect. He felt it was natural that a meeting in Germany should be conducted in the German language, but also expressed concern for the "loyal" minorities.[64] The Social Democrats condemned the continuing emphasis on the rights of the police rather than the citizens, and especially attacked the language paragraph as an effort to curtail the efforts of labor unions to organize the many minority and foreign workers flocking to industrial jobs. Indeed, the socialists preferred the old Prussian law to this dangerous innovation.[65]

In the subsequent two days of debates, these themes and objections were echoed by representatives of the minority parties. More vociferous, however, were the radical spokesmen, who likened the language paragraph to a new exceptional law. If the purpose of the clause was to facilitate police surveillance, then the police in those districts should learn the local languages![66] Nevertheless, all agreed to submit it to committee and work to develop an acceptable bill.

The committee locked horns over the bill from December through the following March, and reported out a bill full of

62. Ibid., pp. 2095–98.
63. Ibid., pp. 2098–2105.
64. Ibid., pp. 2105–11.
65. Ibid., pp. 2111–23.
66. Ibid., p. 2134.

astonishing compromises.[67] The Conservatives had forced through the exclusion of minors from associations and assemblies.[68] The Radicals, however, had succeeded in changing the term "public affairs" to "political affairs"[69] and in limiting application of the bill to "political" associations and meetings. This exempted trade union activities from police surveillance, as their efforts to obtain better wages and working conditions were specifically protected under the Industrial Code.[70] The penalties were reduced to the 150-mark level. In addition, the National Liberals succeeded in pushing through a compromise on the highly controversial language paragraph stipulating that in regions where the non-German population totaled 60 percent or more, meetings could be conducted in both languages for the next twenty years, after which all residents were expected to be sufficiently prepared to hold their meetings in the German language.[71] Moreover, the bloc parties maintained sufficient solidarity to defeat efforts by the Center and Social Democrats to end police surveillance entirely, and to extend civil liberty to workers still denied the right to organize: farm workers, domestics, and civil servants. The government representatives had warned that they would withdraw the bill rather than submit to those concessions.[72] Although a number of revisions were proposed during the second reading by the Center and left, they were rejected. One by one the paragraphs of the revised bill were put to the vote, often by roll call. Even the hotly contested language paragraph passed, by a vote of 196 to 177.[73] The compromise worked; the bloc held firm through the third reading on 8 April. The government, eager to have the matter

67. Ibid., vol. 246, pp. 4823–4924. These exhibits contain the full committee report and the amendments proposed by the factions. This material is discussed in reports of the Bundesrat representatives in Rassow and Born, *Akten*, pp. 307–42.

68. Rassow and Born, *Akten*, p. 325.

69. Ibid., p. 319.

70. Ibid., pp. 308 and 315.

71. This compromise was initiated by a government proposal that stipulated a minimum 75 percent ethnic population in the district and would have permitted the use of the foreign language for only ten years. "Entwurf eines Gesetzes," BA, R43F Reichskanzlei 2604 (microfilm of Deutsches Zentralarchiv 2241), p. 155. See also B. Heckart, *From Bassermann to Bebel: The Grand Bloc's Quest for Reform in the Kaiserreich* (New Haven, 1974), pp. 61–63.

72. Rassow and Born, *Akten*, p. 314.

73. *Verhandlungen des Reichstages*, vol. 232, pp. 4694–96.

completed before the upcoming Prussian elections, agreed that it would go into effect on 1 May 1908.[74]

Shaped more by politics than principle, the Association Law of 1908 was the crowning achievement of the liberals' participation in the Bülow bloc. It was a logical capstone to their efforts, starting with the action against the *Verbindungsverbot*, to regain political leverage and promote reform in Prussia and in the empire. But this success was too costly. In their rush to join Bülow's bloc the National Liberals had antagonized their non-Prussian constituencies. Although they had gained 6 seats in Saxony, they had lost a total of 10 seats from Bavaria, Baden, Hesse, and Thuringia. The left liberals had similarly gained 13 seats in 1907, mainly in Prussia and Saxony where government support gave them credibility among the antisocialist middle class. But the compromises that the liberals so assiduously shepherded through the committee alienated both the right and left. In the elections of 1912, which were dominated by the mass parties of the Social Democrats and Center, National Liberal seats dropped from 54 to 45, a smaller mandate than their delegation of 51 in 1903. The left liberals, who combined in 1910 to form the Progressive Peoples' Party (Fortschrittliche Volkspartei) were only slightly more successful, losing only 7 seats for a total of 42 delegates.[75]

The German liberals had achieved their major goal in 1871 with German unification. During the 1880s they had struggled and splintered, unable to coalesce around another issue.[76] The debate over the right of association that began in 1894 reinvigorated the liberals at a time when the new mass parties of the Center and left were seizing the political initiative. The liberals provided the crucial swing votes to prevent the passage of restrictive laws in Prussia and the Empire. Their dogged persistance forged the first step toward a national association law with the elimination of the *Verbindungsverbot*. The results of that change were clearly demonstrated during the election in 1907 of the Bülow bloc, a stunning victory for collaborating parties and special interest organizations. And, under liberal aegis, the Association Law of 1908 was the one real legislative

74. Rassow and Born, *Akten*, p. 392.
75. Ritter and Niehuss, *Wahlgeschichtliches Arbeitsbuch*, pp. 83–96.
76. D. Langewiesche, *Liberalismus in Deutschland* (Frankfurt a.M. 1988), pp. 134–36.

accomplishment of the bloc, indeed, one of the rare bills to be passed over the objections of the Bundesrat. Their success on these issues, out of all proportion to the size of their legislative factions and constituencies, affirmed the vigor of liberal leadership and the importance of liberalism in moderating the many strident political voices of the empire.

10

The Decline of Liberal Professionalism
Reflections on the Social Erosion of German Liberalism, 1867–1933

Konrad H. Jarausch

During the triumph of political liberalism, academics reshaped their callings into liberal professions. In the heady 1870s, university graduates were no longer content to be servants of the state but wanted to become independent practitioners, pursuing their livelihood unfettered by government control. In line with the internal liberalization of the Second Reich, doctors and lawyers transformed their quasi-bureaucratic vocations into free professions.[1] Only sixty years later, liberal professionalism was vanishing and political liberalism lay prostrate. The failure of liberal remedies to resolve their existential crisis led professionals to embrace neoconservative or racist alternatives, while the collapse of the bourgeois parties hastened the demise of the Weimar Republic.[2] This astounding parallel reversal occurred in two separate, yet linked arenas. Preoccupied with pursuing professionalism, expert groups played a leading role in the general alliance created by bourgeois reformers. Searching for a firmer social basis for mass participation, liberal parties sought to cultivate the professions as one of a handful of constituent groups. The gradual breakdown of their mutually beneficial relationship holds the answer to a crucial question: How did the decline of liberal professionalism contribute to the social erosion of German liberalism?

1. J.J. Sheehan, *German Liberalism in the Nineteenth Century* (Chicago, 1978), pp. 123ff.; C. Huerkamp, *Der Aufstieg der Ärzte im 19. Jahrhundert* (Göttingen, 1985), pp. 254ff.; and H. Siegrist, ed., *Bürgerliche Berufe* (Göttingen, 1988), pp. 11ff.
2. L.E. Jones, *German Liberalism and the Dissolution of the Weimar Party System, 1918–1933* (Chapel Hill, 1988), p. 476; M.H. Kater, *Doctors under Hitler* (Chapel Hill, 1989); and K.H. Jarausch, *The Unfree Professions: German Lawyers, Teachers, and Engineers, 1900–1950* (New York, 1990).

Konrad H. Jarausch

Although often invoked, the societal reasons for the failure of liberal politics have rarely been explored in detail. Due to insistent objections to the *Sonderweg* thesis, Hans-Ulrich Wehler has narrowed his emphasis on the modified persistence of premodern patterns into a specific "deficit in liberal civic political culture."[3] Pointing to "a silent bourgeois revolution," his Anglo-American critics have argued more effectively for a shifting of perspective than they have researched the occupational underpinnings of "middle-class hegemony."[4] The concomitant assertion of the "illiberal" character of German society and culture has hardly proven any more convincing, since "illiberalism," defined only by what it rejected, turned out to be an exceedingly slippery concept.[5] More specifically focused on the travails of the educated was the search for the elusive *Bildungsbürgertum*.[6] Although suggesting commonalities in "cultivation," knowledge-based work, and cultural style, this debate has been unable to agree on the timing and causes of this social formation's dissolution.[7] Political historians have generally been aware of the importance of professionals as leaders of liberal parties, but rarely have they bothered to investigate lawyers or other university graduates.[8] In contrast, scholars interested in

3. Cf. H.-U. Wehler's *Das Deutsche Kaiserreich, 1871–1918* (Göttingen, 1980), 4th ed. (now translated into English), versus his essay "Wie bürgerlich war das Kaiserreich?" in J. Kocka, ed., *Bürger und Bürgerlichkeit im 19. Jahrhundert* (Göttingen, 1987).

4. D. Blackbourn and G. Eley, *Mythen deutscher Geschichtsschreibung: Die gescheiterte bürgerliche Revolution von 1848* (Frankfurt, 1980), now in expanded English edition; D. Blackbourn, "The Discreet Charm of the German Bourgeoisie," in *Populists and Patricians* (London, 1987), pp. 67ff.; and G. Eley, *From Unification to Nazism* (Boston, 1986), pp. 11ff.

5. R. Dahrendorf, *Society and Democracy in Germany* (Garden City, 1967); and F. Stern, *The Failure of Illiberalism* (New York, 1972); versus K.H. Jarausch, "Illiberalism and Beyond: German History in Search of a Paradigm," *Journal of Modern History* 55 (1983): 268f.

6. K. Vondung, ed., *Das Wilhelminische Bildungsbürgertum* (Göttingen, 1976); W. Conze and J. Kocka, eds., *Bildungsbürgertum im 19. Jahrhundert* (Stuttgart, 1985), vol. 1; and U. Engelhardt, *"Bildungsbürgertum": Begriffs- und Dogmengeschichte eines Etiketts* (Stuttgart, 1986).

7. J. Kocka, "Bildungsbürgertum – Gesellschaftliche Formation oder Historikerkonstrukt?" in idem, ed., *Das Bildungsbürgertum in Gesellschaft und Politik* (Stuttgart, 1989); K.H. Jarausch, "Die Krise des deutschen Bildungsbürgertums im ersten Drittel des 20. Jahrhunderts," in Kocka, *Bildungsbürgertum*; and H.-U. Wehler, "Deutsches Bildungsbürgertum in vergleichender Perspektive – Elemente eines 'Sonderwegs,'" in Kocka, *Bildungsbürgertum*.

8. Sheehan, *German Liberalism*, pp. 19ff.; Jones, *German Liberalism*, pp. 5f.; and the other essays in this volume.

the professions have focused more on the occupational "professionalization project" than on the experts' broader political involvement.[9] Despite much sophisticated debate, the interrelationships between liberalism and the rise of the professions, as well as the professionals and the fall of liberal politics, have yet to be examined.

Such an inquiry requires a rethinking of the relationship between professions, the state, and politics. Instead of representing objective expertise, professionalism needs to be understood as a deeply political practice, involving struggles within the occupation, with clients, bureaucrats, and professors. Similarly, professionalization should be seen as a process of change in the structure of academically trained occupations, a process that evolved through various stages, each contingent upon general societal conditions.[10] Moreover, the state should not be treated as an abstraction but must be concretized as people, interests, and policies, all grounded in social conflicts. Different levels of "stateness," i.e., varying degrees of bureaucratic control, tend to lead to distinctive professional responses, which change drastically over time even within the same country. The linkage between the professions and the state can be found in the convergence of political efforts by experts to advance professionalization and government policies in the realms of law, health, and education, among others. In mediating between practitioner organizations and bureaucratic decisions, political parties play a crucial role. Beyond cultural expectations, expert allegiances depend on the articulation of their interests, the politicians' effectiveness in advancing their cause, and the government's responsiveness to their wishes.[11] As spokesmen for individual or collective rights, lawyers tend to come closest to the political process, doctors intervene in social issues, and teachers often participate in public debate. Other professionals

9. Siegrist, *Bürgerliche Berufe*, passim, and the essays in G. Cocks and K.H. Jarausch, eds., *German Professions, 1800–1950* (New York, 1990).
10. M. Burrage, K.H. Jarausch, and H. Siegrist, "An Actor-based Framework for the Study of the Professions," forthcoming in M. Burrage and R. Torstendahl, eds., *The Professions in Theory and History* (London, 1990). Cf. also H. Siegrist, "Bürgerliche Berufe: Die Professionen und das Bürgertum," in his volume on *Bürgerliche Berufe*, pp. 11ff.
11. A.J. Heidenheimer, "Comparing Status Professions: The Evolution of State-Profession Relationships of Lawyers and Physicians in Britain, Germany, and the US," forthcoming in his volume on the state and the professions.

such as engineers remain for the most part mute. As it was not somehow foreordained, the deliberalization of the *Bildungsbürgertum* should therefore be investigated as a result of complex interactions among aspiring professions, evolving governments, and changing policies.[12]

The Rise of Liberal Professionalism

In nineteenth-century Central Europe, academic occupations "professionalized from above," as the middle classes were weak and political participation infrequent. Founded during the Middle Ages, learned occupations such as that of jurist originally flourished in corporate bodies within a system of patronage politics. During the era of enlightened absolutism, cameralist governments transformed these callings into quasi-official positions so as to increase public welfare in their "police state."[13] As prerequisites for more efficient public service, successive regulations demanded academic training and established two-tiered state examinations that created a uniform body of qualified practitioners. Achieved by lawyers between 1723 and 1808, this occupational homogenization took doctors from 1725 until the suppression of surgeons in 1852, and secondary teachers struggled for unity from 1810 until the school compromise in 1901.[14] As a corrective to arbitrary charges, fixed fee schedules, loyalty oaths, and official titles such as the Prussian "Justizkommissar" gave the emerging professions a quasi-bureaucratic aura. Tight regulation of practice and government supervision of discipline left little room for autonomy, while the overwhelming prestige of public service made bureaucrats the role models for the educated middle class. Before the emergence of organized public life, associations tended to be local, and were devoted to scientific progress and sociability rather than to

12. K.H. Jarausch, "The German Professions in History and Theory," in Cocks and Jarausch, eds., *German Professions*, pp. 9–26. Cf. C. McClelland, *The Rise of the German Professions* (Cambridge, 1990).

13. M. Raeff, *The Well-Ordered Police State: Social and Institutional Change through Law in the Germanies and Russia, 1600–1800* (New Haven, 1983); and R.S. Turner, "The *Bildungsbürgertum* and the Learned Professions in Prussia, 1770–1830," *Histoire sociale* 13 (1980): 105ff.

14. H. Titze, "Bildungsauslese und akademischer Berufszugang," especially "Grundzüge der historischen Professionalisierung mit besonderer Berücksichtigung der Zugangsnormierung" (Ms., Göttingen, 1987).

vocational aims. In the professional arena, the government dominated practice, universities controlled education, and practitioner income and prestige governed socioeconomic well-being. As long as the public was denied participation, change could only come from bureaucratic reform.[15]

In response to such outside domination, the struggle for professional emancipation and representative government combined into a single liberal crusade during the first half of the nineteenth century. In law, the reform discourse of the *Bildungsbürgertum* focused on individual rights, thereby making the lawyer a natural leader in the campaign for popular participation in government. In medicine, wide-ranging demands for the improvement of public health supported the claims of scientifically trained doctors to superiority over nonacademic healers and midwives. In education, broadly based hopes for liberating citizens through cultivation aided the emergence of academic teachers of neohumanist *Bildung* in the classical gymnasiums.[16] By the 1840s this impetus spilled out of the university lecture halls into pages of uncensored journals and prompted attempts to found scholarly and occupational associations. In spite of vocal participation by academics in national conferences and the Frankfurt assembly during 1848 – over one-third of the deputies were professionals – the political failure of the revolution dashed all hopes for an improvement of the professional life.[17] With the restoration governments intent on stamping out bureaucratic liberalism, progressive practitioners were forced into the emerging opposition parties. In various state houses, lawyers, teachers, and doctors comprised between one-seventh and one-fifth of all liberal deputies in the 1860s.[18] Bureaucratic reluctance to improve legal services, health-care delivery, or public education pushed professionals into a critical stance, ready to

15. H.-U. Wehler, *Deutsche Gesellschaftsgeschichte, 1815–1848/9* (Munich, 1987), 2:221ff.; and J. Caplan "Profession as Vocation: The German Civil Service," in Cocks and Jarausch, *German Professions*.
16. H. Siegrist, "Public Office or Free Profession? The German Attorney in the Nineteenth and Early Twentieth Centuries," in Cocks and Jarausch, *German Professions*; C. Huerkamp, "The Making of the Modern Medical Profession, 1800–1914," ibid.; and A.J. La Vopa, "Specialists against Specialization: Hellenism as Professional Ideology of German Classical Studies," ibid.
17. Sheehan, *German Liberalism*, p. 57. See A. La Vopa, *Prussian Schoolteachers, 1763–1848: Profession and Office* (Chapel Hill, 1980) and K.H. Jarausch, *Deutsche Studenten, 1800–1970* (Frankfurt, 1984), pp. 47ff.
18. Sheehan, *German Liberalism*, pp. 82, 161–65.

embrace free advocacy, an open medical market, or autonomous schools.

Despite some bureaucratic remnants, the recasting of the professions during the liberal era was surprisingly far-reaching. Doctors had long chafed under the official requirements of loyalty oaths, licenses, mandatory assistance, bureaucratic discipline, and quarterly reporting. In 1869 the reform movement managed to have medical practice included in the new trade regulations of the North German Confederation, freeing competition among all healers and only protecting those who bore the title of "doctor." In order to achieve full *Kurierfreiheit*, the majority of physicians was even willing to forego legal prohibition of charlatanism.[19] Lawyers similarly objected to bureaucratic admission controls, titles, fee schedules, or disciplinary supervision as long as economic risks remained privatized as remuneration by individual clients rather than public pay. After long parliamentary struggles, the new Imperial Lawyers' Code (Rechtsanwaltsordnung or RAO) of 1878 established uniform regulations for the entire Reich, created a unified attorney profession (*Rechtsanwalt*), freed admission to practice, and initiated self-discipline through a series of chambers (*Anwaltskammern*). But the embattled compromise still contained etatist elements in training (identical with judges), localization (admission to one place), official fee schedules (restricting unfair charges), and continuing court monopoly (*Anwaltszwang*). Led by the newly founded German Lawyers' League (Deutscher Anwaltverein of 1871), most attorneys were willing to run the risks of open competition in their desire to escape government tutelage and establish a truly *freie Advokatur*.[20] Buoyed by the increasing demand for qualified services, the reforms of the liberal decade freed qualified professionals in private practice.

The emergence of liberal professionalism had profound political implications. Practitioners were divided on the economic merits of opening up competition, as some feared to leave the shelter of bureaucratic protection. But many expected the free-

19. C. Marx, *Die Entwickelung des ärztlichen Standes seit den ersten Dezennien des 19. Jahrhunderts* (Berlin, 1907), pp. 32ff.; Huerkamp, *Aufstieg der Ärzte*, pp. 254ff.
20. A. Weißler, *Geschichte der Rechtsanwaltschaft* (Leipzig, 1905), pp. 562ff.; and K.F. Ledford, "A Social and Institutional History of the German Bar in Private Practice, 1878–1930" (diss., Johns Hopkins University, Baltimore, 1988), pp. 39ff.

ing of the market to improve services by increasing the number of practitioners and sharpening their skills. Following British and French examples, liberal leaders such as Rudolf von Gneist and Rudolf von Virchow advocated a more active conception of citizenship.[21] Making practice free from official censure seemed an essential precondition for full participation in public life. While removing some hated restrictions, the thrust of the reform was also altruistic and political. The drastic restructuring of medical and legal practice was only possible due to the ideological agreement and practical cooperation of professional spokesmen, reformist bureaucrats, and liberal party leaders. Not surprisingly, the professions (with public officials excluded) provided over one-fifth of the membership of the National Liberal fraction and over one-third of the deputies of the Progressive Reichstag delegation in the Second Empire. Almost half of these parliamentarians were lawyers, and slightly fewer were teachers and professors, while doctors and other practitioners remained fairly rare. In party conventions and regional assemblies, professionals were similarly active and influential.[22] Originating in the classic free professions, this liberal spirit also infused other academic careers such as teaching and eventually permeated the entire *Bildungsbürgertum*. A surprising break with its bureaucratic origins, liberal professionalism combined practice and politics into one emancipatory thrust.

During the last decades of the nineteenth century, the market gamble of the professions produced severe academic overcrowding. From the early 1860s to 1890 university and technical enrollment more than doubled, from 14,631 to 32,020, then stagnated until 1893–94 before expanding to 71,676 by 1914. These growth waves increased the number of law students from 2,420 in 1860 to 5,321 in 1881, paused, then resumed to create 11,976 by 1906, and finally receded to 9,896 in 1914. Moving somewhat in the opposite direction from law, medicine started with 2,108, surged to 10,149 by 1890, fell back to 7,483 in 1903–4, and then advanced again, to 18,189 by 1914. Similarly, the

---

21. R. von Gneist, *Freie Advokatur: Die erste Forderung aller Justizreform in Preußen* (Berlin, 1867); and R. von Virchow, *Gesammelte Abhandlungen auf dem Gebiete der öffentlichen Medicin und der Seuchenlehre* (Berlin, 1879).

22. Calculated from Sheehan, *German Liberalism*, pp. 160, 162, 193, 206, and 240ff. Cf. D. White, *The Splintered Party: National Liberalism in Hessen and the Reich, 1867–1918* (Cambridge, 1976), pp. 225ff.

number of teaching candidates rose to 7,802 in 1882, declined to 4,854 in 1891–92, and then increased to 23,288 in 1912.[23] Propelled by the foundation of new gymnasiums, the recognition of modern secondary training and the eventual admission of women, the increase in propertied and lower middle-class students created ever more graduates clamoring for entry into professional careers. While growing prosperity and public hiring absorbed much of the expansion, the Göttingen economist Wilhelm Lexis argued in 1891 that from 1880 on there had been 1,023 future lawyers too many, that after 1890 there had been an excess of 1,987 physicians, and that since 1880 there had been over 3,000 more teachers than necessary.[24] With entry into legal and medical practice free, the number of attorneys trebled, from 4,091 to 12,297, that of doctors rose from 13,728 in 1876 to 30,558 in 1909, and Prussian teachers in male secondary schools quintupled, from 2,702 in 1860 to 13,624 in 1915. No wonder that intensified competition and longer waiting times for state appointment led to public hysteria about the dangers of an "academic proletariat." The fear of overcrowding, constantly reiterated, spawned a new kind of educational protectionism.[25]

Another unintended consequence of liberal professionalism was the rise of academic anti-Semitism. Due to the opening of careers, Jewish enrollment in Prussian universities increased to over 9 percent of all students in the late 1880s. This 7.5-fold overrepresentation particularly affected the free professions, with "Mosaic" students amounting to 17.3 percent in medicine and to 9.8 percent in law, whereas government reluctance to appoint Jewish teachers depressed the proportion in the philosophical faculty to below-average levels, about 6.5 percent between 1886–87 and 1911–12.[26] Hence, the Berlin anti-Semitism contro-

23. H. Titze, ed., *Das Hochschulstudium in Preußen und in Deutschland, 1820–1944* (Göttingen, 1987), pp. 28f., 86ff.; and Jarausch, *Students, Society, and Politics in Imperial Germany: The Rise of Academic Illiberalism* (Princeton, 1982), pp. 23ff.

24. W. Lexis, *Denkschrift über die dem Bedarf Preußens entsprechende Normalzahl der Studierenden der verschiedenen Fakultäten* (Berlin, 1891); and H. Titze, "Die zyklische Überproduktion von Akademikern im 19. und 20. Jahrhundert," *Geschichte und Gesellschaft* 10 (1984): 92ff.

25. Figures from Jarausch, *Unfree Professions*, Appendix Table A.5a; Huerkamp, *Aufstieg der Ärzte*, p. 151; and R. Bölling, *Sozialgeschichte der deutschen Lehrer* (Göttingen, 1983), p. 17.

26. N. Kampe, "Jews and Antisemites at Universities in Imperial Germany," *Leo Baeck Yearbook* 30 (1985): 357ff. and 32 (1987): 43ff.

versy in the early 1880s, initiated by Heinrich von Treitschke's polemical call "the Jews are our misfortune," evoked a strong echo among nationalist and Protestant students. Anti-Semitic activists founded Associations of German Students (Vereine Deutscher Studenten or VDSt) that barred Jewish members and made social exclusion the central issue in campus politics. Due to novel agitational methods and clever election alliances, these Vereine Deutscher Studenten gradually spread their racial hatred into traditional corporations such as the *Burschenschaft*. Although some smaller dissident student groups such as the Freie Wissenschaftliche Vereinigung and the Freistudentenschaft resisted, Jewish youths largely withdrew into their own newly founded associations.[27] Part of the *Bildungsbürgertum*'s general turn towards illiberalism, the youthful embrace of anti-Semitism introduced a dangerous racial cleavage into the professions. Steeped in liberal values, the majority of adult practitioners continued to reject prejudice, but many of their younger successors, frustrated by the prospect of unemployment, were all too quick to blame their talented and industrious Jewish competitors.[28]

The liberalization of practice increased tensions within the professions. Faced with a great influx of newcomers, many attorneys clamored that entry into judicial studies or into the legal career should be barred. Although the lawyers' conventions in 1894, 1905, and 1911 rejected a *numerus clausus*, a growing minority of discontented practitioners discarded economic liberalism.[29] Sharpening competition also forced more beginners to settle at the lower district courts without being allowed to practice at the superior courts, increasing their share among attorneys from 4 percent in 1880 to 23 percent in 1915. The emergence of second-class lawyers unleashed a fierce struggle for simultaneous admission in the *Anwaltstage* (lawyers' conventions) of 1905, 1907, and 1913, without resolving the

27. Jarausch, *Students, Society, and Politics*, pp. 266ff.; and N. Kampe, *Studenten und "Judenfrage" im Deutschen Kaiserreich: Die Entstehung einer akademischen Trägerschicht des Antisemitismus* (Göttingen, 1988).

28. K.H. Jarausch, "Akademischer Antisemitismus: Eine verdrängte Studententradition," forthcoming in *Internationales Archiv für Sozialgeschichte der deutschen Literatur* (1990).

29. F. Ostler, *Die deutschen Rechtsanwälte, 1871–1971* (Essen, 1982, rev. ed.), pp. 63ff.; and Ledford, "History of the German Bar," pp. 285ff.

dispute.[30] The advance of medical science and the proliferation of private physicians similarly increased the number of specialists to about one-quarter of all Prussian doctors in 1909. As specialization brought more money and higher prestige, generalists and rural physicians fiercely resented the rise of a "superior" group of doctors.[31] While physicians failed in banning quackery, medical associations slowly succeeded in creating self-governing chambers (Prussia in 1887) and limiting competition through self-disciplinary honor courts (Prussia in 1899).[32] Among secondary teachers, rapid expansion triggered a "school war" between partisans of classical and modern training. Only after the granting of quasi-equality to nonhumanist institutions could the profession come together in a unified association, the Philologenverband.[33] The professions responded to these internal strains by opting for a form of neocorporatism that sought some collective safeguards without jettisoning the liberal legacy.

During neocorporate professionalism the politics of experts grew more divisive and less liberal. Problems of overcrowding, created by the freeing of access, growing cleavages within careers, desire for self-government, and selection of philosophical priorities could not be resolved by practitioners themselves, but required government action. Having just escaped bureaucratic tutelage, the professions turned back to the state for help during the last years of the nineteenth century. Intimately involved in the creation of the German Civil Code (Bürgerliches Gesetzbuch or BGB) in 1896, lawyers settled for legal uniformity rather than insisting on a full adoption of their liberal agenda.[34] Although initially welcoming the establishment of health insurance as a way to increase demand for their services, doctors vigorously

30. Ostler, *Deutsche Rechtsanwälte*, pp. 80ff.; and Ledford, "History of the German Bar," pp. 325ff.

31. Huerkamp, *Aufstieg der Ärzte*, pp. 167ff.

32. Ibid., pp. 261ff, Cf. R. Spree, *Soziale Ungleichheit vor Krankheit und Tod* (Göttingen, 1982), pp. 138f.

33. J.C. Albisetti, *Secondary School Reform in Imperial Germany* (Princeton, 1983); and S.F. Müller, "Verbandsinteressen der Lehrer an höheren Schulen am Ende des 19. Jahrhunderts," in M. Heinemann, ed., *Der Lehrer und seine Organisation* (Stuttgart, 1977), pp. 235ff.

34. M.F. John, "The Politics of Legal Unity in Germany, 1870–1896," *Historical Journal* 28 (1985): 341ff.; and idem, "The Peculiarities of the German State: Bourgeois Law and Society in the Imperial Era," *Past and Present* 119 (1988): 105ff.

polemicized against their domination by bureaucratic and sometimes socialist insurance boards. The Hartmannbund, founded
as a special-interest organization in 1900, even resorted to
strikes in order to push through its neoliberal demand for "free
physician choice" against the public *Krankenkassen* (health insurance funds).[35] As officials, secondary-school teachers similarly organized in an independent way to formulate their
demands, but then pressured the government for pay equality
with judges and for uniform academic titles.[36] In order to be
effective, professional associations established direct channels
to the bureaucracy and sought to broaden their political base in
the Reichstag. While three-quarters of the lawyer deputies still
clung to the liberal parties, one-tenth belonged to the Center
Party and a few were Socialists or Conservatives. Although over
half of the secondary teacher parliamentarians remained liberal,
one-quarter preferred Catholic affiliations and one-eighth Conservative ties.[37]

Based on competence and connections, the power of liberal
professionals rested on the cities and local communities
throughout the greater part of the empire. In the 1850s and
1860s progressive practitioners promoted the founding of a web
of prepolitical associations in order to advance the national
constitutional cause. As effective speakers and organizers,
Bildungsbürger typically led singing societies, gymnastic groups,
and especially the Schiller celebrations of 1859. While these
organizations provided the essential infrastructure for liberal
politics, the working class eventually rejected bourgeois leadership claims and created a dense associational network of its
own.[38] Due to graduated suffrage systems, liberal parties controlled many city councils; for instance, in 1911 they dominated
60 percent of the councils of Rhenish and Westfalian towns.
Bolstered by their business ties and legal expertise, private and
public lawyers played a leading role within urban self-

35. Huerkamp, *Aufstieg der Ärzte*, pp. 224ff., 279ff.
36. Jarausch, *Unfree Professions*, chap. 1.
37. Langewiesche, *Liberalismus in Deutschland*, pp. 312f.; and Jarausch, *Unfree Professions*, chap. 3.
38. J. Link, "Harmony, Unity, and Loyalty: The *großdeutsch* Patriotism of the *Männergesangvereine* in the 1840s" (MA thesis, Chapel Hill, 1984); M. John, "Associational Life and the Development of Liberalism in Hanover, 1848–1866," in this volume; Langewiesche, *Liberalismus in Deutschland*, pp. 114ff.; and V. Lidtke, *The Alternative Culture* (New York, 1985), pp. 21ff.

government, such as the Frankfurt or Munich councils and the Hamburg Senate, until the extension of the vote gradually undercut the influence of cultivated *Honoratioren*. This local power base made for strong expert representation in liberal and progressive parties in regional parliaments and state organizations, in contrast to the more conservative higher officials.[39] Within the cities, professional influence rested on the superior problem-solving capacity of communal experts in urban problems such as mass schooling, power and light, transportation, sanitation, etc. But in the parties, experts tended to serve as individuals rather than as group representatives, and politicians hesitated to push professionalization, uncertain as to whether professionals were numerous enough to organize as a mass base.[40]

During the Second Reich, the professionals' commitment to liberalism evolved in surprising twists. Given the tradition of state control of academic callings, the liberal restructuring of the professions during the 1860s and 1870s was remarkably complete. Against lingering bureaucratic allegiances, medicine and law transformed themselves into free professions, practitioners like Eduard Lasker played a leading role in the liberal parties, and general liberal attitudes reigned supreme in educated circles.[41] Similarly unexpected was the illiberal onslaught of the 1880s and 1890s due to free market overcrowding, Bismarck's rejection of political liberalism, and the rise of anti-Semitic *völkisch* ideologies. Unable to break the liberal bonding of most professionals, these countercurrents created considerable strain within academic occupations, pushing them towards a neocorporate compromise between competition and security.[42] Around 1900 the relationship between the professions and liberalism began to fracture, with an impatient, progressive minority ready

39. R. Evans, "Liberalism and Local Politics in the German City, 1860–1914" (manuscript, Norwich, 1988); and Langewiesche, *Liberalismus in Deutschland*, p. 200.

40. See. J. Reulecke, *Geschichte der Urbanisierung in Deutschland* (Frankfurt, 1985); and Dan Mattern's dissertation on Greater Berlin around the turn of the century (in preparation).

41. J.F. Harris, *A Study in the Theory and Practice of German Liberalism: Eduard Lasker, 1829–1884* (Lanham, 1984).

42. D.K. Müller, *Sozialstruktur und Schulsystem: Aspekte zum Strukturwandel des Schulwesens im 19. Jahrhundert* (Göttingen, 1977); L. Gall, *Bismarck: Der Weiße Revolutionär* (Frankfurt, 1980); and H. Schulte, *The Tragedy of German Inwardness*, forthcoming (Hamilton, 1990).

to embrace socialism. At the other end of the spectrum, those custodians of culture who were frightened by the pace of change embraced the imperial dreams of the Pan-German League (Alldeutscher Verband or ADV) and other patriotic pressure groups: "Nearly the majority of the League's local leadership consisted in fact of teachers, civil servants, doctors, and lawyers." With Friedrich Naumann combining elements from both extremes, centrist professionals sought to refurbish their legacy in a neoliberal, often socially responsible, and imperialist way.[43] While the rhetoric of academic freedom and of free professional practice implied in the concepts *freie Advokatur, freie Arztwahl* continued to dominate, the erosion of liberalism's professional and ideological underpinnings had begun.

The Crisis of Liberal Professionalism

"Initially the *Bürgertum* was quite stunned by the outbreak of the revolution." Deploring their horror at the collapse of the Second Reich, democratic lawyer Erich Eyck urged a distraught middle class to turn defeat into liberation.[44] In the turbulent December of 1918 the newly formed German Democratic Party (Deutsche Demokratische Partei or DDP) appealed to bourgeois unity in support of a "great party" of liberals, ready to endorse the fledgling Weimar Republic. As a bulwark against Socialist radicalism, the DDP promised democratic reform balanced by orderly government. Election flyers supported employee aspirations for collective bargaining and protection of patent rights, which might please embattled engineers. Officials and teachers were promised "recognition of their well-earned rights," improved pay, more liberal bureaucratic rules, and acceptance of their organizations. According to the signatures on announcements, the DDP mobilized numerous lawyers and educators, but this program failed to address free professionals such as

43. Jarausch, *Students, Society, and Politics*, pp. 356ff.; quote from R. Chickering, *We Men Who Feel Most German: A Cultural Study of the Pan-German League, 1886–1914* (Boston, 1984), pp. 103ff., 316ff.; and R. vom Bruch, "Gelehrtenpolitik und politische Kultur im späten Kaiserreich," in G. Schmidt, ed., *Gelehrtenpolitik und politische Kultur in Deutschland, 1830–1930* (Bochum, 1986), pp. 77ff.

44. E. Eyck, *Des deutschen Bürgertums Schicksalsstunde* (Leipzig, 1919), p. 20. According to G. Hollenberg, "Bürgerliche Sammlung oder sozialliberale Koalition?" *Vierteljahrshefte für Zeitgeschichte* 27 (1979): 392ff., the role of the middle class in the revolution is still largely unresearched.

attorneys or doctors, some of its core constituency.[45] When traditionalist members of the middle class, who still longed for "authority, monarchy, and the bureaucratic state," founded a German People's Party (Deutsche Volkspartei or DVP), a right-liberal alternative to democratic politics reemerged. More attuned to the needs of the "intellectual middle class," the DVP tried to harmonize the interests of all officials or teachers, but was willing to recognize the superiority of advanced academic training.[46] Confronted with Bolshevik revolutionary promises, democratic egalitarian appeals, liberal meritocratic rhetoric, and conservative monarchist exhortations, where would professionals turn?

At first it seemed as if the revolution might strengthen the professionals' commitment to liberal politics. Left-wing experts created councils of intellectual workers to promote "cultural political radicalism," and in some larger cities separate *Lehrerräte* (teacher soviets) sprang up among teachers, asking for a greater voice in school decisions. Victims of previous discrimination, such as probationary teachers (*Studienassessoren*), marginal practitioners (lower-court attorneys), and women demanded the internal democratization of professional structures and practices. When existing elites were slow to change, radical pressure groups emerged, such as the "free association for law and socialism," the League of Decided School Reformers (Bund entschiedener Schulreformer or BeS) or the Reichsbund Deutscher Technik (National League of German Technology).[47] With former leaders cowed and the majority of practitioners hesitating, progressive professionals managed to push through a number of impressive reforms, such as the admission of women to

45. "Wahlaufruf!" and appeals to National Liberals, Young Liberals, "Angestellte und Arbeiter," as well as "An alle Beamten im Reichs-, Staats-, und Gemeindedienst!" in *Allgemeine Werbeflugschriften der DDP* (Berlin, 1918). More specific pamphlets in the series *Deutschlands Wiederaufbau* by B. Marwitz, C. Köhler, and Prof. Rönneburger were addressed to lawyers, white-collar employees, and secondary teachers, respectively.

46. B. Marwitz, *Deutsche Demokratie und nationaler Liberalismus* (Berlin, 1919), p. 65; "Reichsausschuß der DVP in Hamburg," *Nationalliberale Correspondenz* 48 (1921), no 132; and "Beamtentagung der DVP," ibid., nos. 183 and 185.

47. Kritische Justiz, ed., *Streitbare Juristen: Eine andere Tradition* (Baden-Baden, 1988), pp. 129ff.; W. Böhm, "Lehrer zwischen Kulturkritik und Gemeinschaftsutopie: Der Bund entschiedener Schulreformer," in M. Heinemann, ed., *Der Lehrer und seine Organisation* (Stuttgart, 1977), pp. 191ff. Cf. Jarausch, *Unfree Professions*, chap. 2.

legal practice in 1922 and the appointment of a greater number of female principals. Leftist experts, in control of ministerial bureaucracy, tried to make justice more accessible to laymen through arbitration, to democratize the internal structure of the school through parent or pupil councils, and to popularize technology by removing it from bureaucratic or capitalist control. The discrediting of imperial hierarchies and customs allowed a sizable discontented minority of experts to attack the problems of neocorporate professionalism by democratic and social reforms. At the same time, the victory of parliamentarianism over bureaucratic authority increased the power of political parties, prompting practitioners to become more openly involved in liberal organizations so as to create a working relationship with the republic.[48]

Weimar's economic and political chaos, however, inhibited the bonding of professionals to the democratic state. While the privations of the war were considered transitory, the tribulations of the ensuing peace, such as the reintegration of veterans, had a lasting negative effect. For former soldiers, the academic overcrowding and glut on the job market seemed like a betrayal, since insurance funds limited the admission of physicians to medical practice and only a minority of trainees qualified for the appointment list.[49] More devastating still was the impact of hyperinflation. Despite periodic legislative adjustment, legal case loads declined and lawyers' fees lagged behind the spiraling deterioration of buying power, which was wiping out the savings and pensions of many free professionals. Similarly, teachers' salaries eroded dramatically and intermittent parliamentary raises failed to keep up with runaway prices.[50] Instead of solving the professional crisis, rigorous stabilization

48. Ostler, *Deutsche Rechtsanwälte*, pp. 143ff.; F. Hamburger, "Lehrer zwischen Kaiser und Führer: Der deutsche Philologenverband in der Weimarer Republik" (diss., Heidelberg, 1974); and R. Viefhaus, "Ingenieure in der Weimarer Republik," in R. Rürup, ed., *Technik, Ingenieure, und Gesellschaft* (Düsseldorf, 1981), pp. 292ff.

49. M. Beatus, "Academic Proletariat: The Problem of Overcrowding in the Learned Professions and Universities during the Weimar Republic, 1918–1933" (diss., Madison, 1975); and K.H. Jarausch, "Die Not der geistigen Arbeiter: Akademiker in der Berufskrise, 1918–1933," in W. Abelshauser, ed., *Die Weimarer Republik als Wohlfahrtsstaat* (Stuttgart, 1987), pp. 280ff.

50. F. Eulenburg, "Die sozialen Wirkungen der Währungsverhältnisse," *Jahrbücher für Nationalökonomie und Statistik*, 3. Folge 67 (1924): 748ff.; and Jarausch, *Unfree Professions*, chap. 2.

measures in 1924 added insult to injury. In the name of general deflation (*Preisabbau*), attorneys' fees were drastically slashed, thereby complicating economic recovery. As part of the 16.3 percent reduction of Reich bureaucratic personnel (*Beamtenabbau*), about 10 percent of Prussian secondary teachers were simply dismissed. Even engineers who had largely escaped the ravages of inflation through full employment were now fired due to rationalization measures.[51] The troubled course of general politics, from the shame of Versailles and the quasi-civil war with Communist insurgents and right-wing Free Corps to the traumatic Ruhr struggle, did little to endear the Republic to the educated middle class. As Weimar cabinets were slow to respond to their needs, professionals often felt abandoned by liberal politics.

To succeed in the sharp organizational struggles of the Republic, professional associations transformed themselves from loose collections of notables into tight interest groups. In the German Lawyers' League (Deutscher Anwaltverein or DAV), a confederation of local chapters turned into a national mass membership organization with elaborate representational structures. In the Secondary School Teachers' Organization (Philologenverband or PhVb), the central executive grew from an amateur board to a full-time office staffed by paid functionaries. In the Association of German Engineers (Verband Deutscher Ingenieure or VDI), a complex committee system evolved to reflect various interests and constituencies, complemented by a profitable publishing enterprise.[52] Intent on gaining more public influence, professional associations mounted vigorous press campaigns to enhance their image. Time and again, functionaries tried to place colleagues into national or state ministries so as to help shape administrative decisions as well as legislative proposals from their inception. To make up for small numbers, professionals also resorted to coalition building with powerful allies, such as creating a front of the "free professions," joining

51. For the resentment against stabilization cf. DVP, ed., *Beamtenpolitik* (Berlin, 1924), p. 12f.; M.L. Hughes, *Paying for the German Inflation* (Chapel Hill, 1988); and Jarausch, *Unfree Professions*, chap. 3.

52. Ostler, *Deutsche Rechtsanwälte*, pp. 221ff.; H.C. Laubach, "Die Politik des Philologenverbandes im Reich und in Preußen während der Weimarer Republik," in Heinemann, ed., *Lehrer*, pp. 249ff.; and R. Stahlschmidt, "Der Ausbau der technisch-wissenschaftlichen Gemeinschaftsarbeit 1918 bis 1933," *Technik*, pp. 348ff.

broader organizations of public officials (National League of Higher Officials – Reichsbund höherer Beamter or RhB) or founding associations for the promotion of technology. In hope of a stronger legislative voice, professional associations encouraged their members to enter political parties. Secondary school teachers created "parliamentary councils" to communicate their needs to friendly politicians while the parties organized committees for officials. As the neocorporate chamber movement failed to make progress during Weimar, experts developed a new style of interest group professionalism so as to advance their cause.[53]

Gradually the attachment of professionals to the liberal parties weakened, as experts became more and more disappointed in the practical returns of democratic policies. In the DDP leadership lawyers played a leading role (around one-third), while teachers were especially strong in the Prussian Landtag fraction, and there was even an occasional engineer. In the DVP party core, higher officials (and especially secondary teachers) were the strongest group (at one-fifth of the membership) after the one-half industrial-commercial interests, while free professionals amounted only to one-thirteenth.[54] If Reichstag members are any indication, during the republic the allegiance of professionals to the liberal parties weakened as more experts embraced socialist or communist causes, while larger numbers also joined the Catholic Center or the conservative DNVP. Intent on immediate reform, the more radical innovators turned further to the left, while traditionalists with religious ties went further to the right, for the Center and DNVP were more active in promoting the simultaneous admission of attorneys and in defending the superiority of the secondary schools.[55] Although generally sympathetic to their complaints, the DDP did not do enough: it only opposed the imposition of the *Gewerbesteuer* on free professionals, supported moderate school reform, and demanded greater independence for technical employees. Due to its ties

53. Jarausch, *Unfree Professions*, chaps. 2 and 3.

54. L. Albertin, ed., *Linksliberalismus in der Weimarer Republik: Die Führungsgremien der DDP und der DStP, 1918–1933* (Düsseldorf, 1980), p. xvi; and L. Döhn, *Politik und Interesse: Die Interessenstruktur der DVP* (Meisenheim, 1970), pp. 79ff.

55. W.L. Patch, "Class Prejudice and the Failure of the Weimar Republic," *German Studies Review* 12 (1989): 35ff.; and Jarausch, *Unfree Professions*, chap. 3.

with the RhB, the DVP voted with bourgeois initiatives for the salary increase for higher officials in 1927, and despite its business dependence it supported lawyer and engineering fee revision.[56] Instead of renewing their emotional attachment to liberalism, professionals espoused a more pragmatic republicanism of self-interest.

The devastating impact of the Great Depression on training, jobs, and pay shattered this interest group professionalism. Due to the business downturn, the number of students shot up to record heights. By summer 1931 enrollment peaked at 138,000, increasing legal studies enrollments to 20,839, bloating the philosophical faculty to 44,492, and raising technical numbers to 23,749.[57] Academic overcrowding produced a renewed oversupply of professionals. By 1933, 10,065 Prussian law trainees were clamoring for admission to the bar, bringing the number of attorneys to 19,440, more than double what it had been in 1921. Between 1919 and 1932 the number of doctors rose by 58 percent to 52,518. While 4,065 Prussian probationary teachers waited for a government job, financial exigency reduced annual public hiring to four new appointments and actually cut positions back to 15,299 in 1933. With technical colleges turning out over 13,000 graduates per year, the number of engineers doubled to 215,957 between 1925 and 1933, outstripping demand.[58] As the depression reduced the number of available jobs, alarmist publications argued with inflated figures, claiming that about 50,000 graduates were unemployed. Particularly hard hit were engineers and technicians: a full one-third of these professions was out on the street by 1933![59] Professional troubles were com-

56. Deputy H. Beythien on "Freie Berufe" in A. Kempkes, ed., *Deutscher Aufbau* (Berlin, 1927), pp. 260f. Cf. Albertin, *Linksliberalismus*, pp. 54, 292, and 494; and Döhn, *Politik und Interesse*, pp. 245ff.

57. Figures from Titze, *Das Hochschulstudium in Preußen und Deutschland*, pp. 29ff.

58. Ostler, *Deutsche Rechtsanwälte*, pp. 202ff; M.H. Kater, "Physicians in Crisis at the End of the Weimar Republic," in P. Stachura, ed., *Unemployment and the Great Depression in Weimar Germany* (London, 1986), pp. 49ff.; A. Nath, *Die Studienratskarriere im Dritten Reich* (Frankfurt, 1988), pp. 35ff.; and K.-H. Ludwig, *Technik und Ingenieure im Dritten Reich* (Düsseldorf, 1974), pp. 44ff.

59. W. Hartnacke, *Bildungswahn – Volkstod!* (Munich, 1932); and B. Gleitze, "Die Berufszählung der technischen Berufe," *Zeitschrift des Vereins deutscher Ingenieure* 79 (1935): 1342f. Cf. Beatus, "Academic Proletariat," pp. 220f.; and Jarausch, "The Crisis of the German Professions, 1918–1933," *Journal of Contemporary History* 20 (1985): 379ff.

pounded by impoverishment. Due to a precipitous decline of business, lawyers' average income dropped by 50 percent to 5,520 Mk between 1928 and 1933, raising the proportion of poor attorneys (under 3,000 Mk) to over one-third while the number of "proletarianized doctors" similarly increased. Imposed by emergency decrees, the deflationary Brüning salary cuts reduced secondary teacher earnings by a cumulative 30 to 40 percent! At the same time, working conditions in law firms, high schools, and factories deteriorated dramatically.[60]

The ensuing "crisis of professional consciousness" eroded the ideological underpinnings of liberal professionalism. Lawyers began to move away from legal individualism towards some kind of left- or right-wing collectivism. Most doctors continued to fight "socialized medicine" in the *Krankenkassen*. Annoyed by excessive experimentation, teachers sought to reassert discipline and pedagogical authority in the classroom. Threatened by unemployment, engineers propagated various kinds of technocracy through a vague formula of "working for the community" (*Gemeinschaftsarbeit*).[61] Some progressive professionals developed more radical socialist ideas, such as legal insurance or free legal aid, ambulatory clinics, job-sharing among all teachers, and socialization of industry. But the majority pulled back from the evident risks of liberalism and clamored for the restoration of authoritarian security. Traditionalist attorneys tried to dam the flood of newcomers and insisted on tightening ethical standards against unfair competition and corruption. Physicians tried to gain control of the sickness funds. Academic teachers tried to displace less trained competitors and women from their institutions. Trained engineers agitated for title protection against unlicensed technicians.[62] A more insecure minority

60. Dr. Thalheim, "Über die Einkommenslage der deutschen Rechtsanwälte," *Juristische Wochenschrift* 62 (November 1932); A. Bohlen, *Die Lebenshaltung der höheren Beamten* (Leipzig, 1932); and O. Holbach, "Die Lage der Ingenieure," in *Die Lage der akademischen Berufe* (Berlin, 1932). Cf. Jarausch, *Unfree Professions*, chap. 4.

61. S. Feuchtwanger, "Idee und Wirklichkeit in der deutschen Anwaltspolitik," *Juristische Wochenschrift* 61 (1932): 1091ff.; N. von Hammerstein, ed., *Deutsche Bildung? Briefwechsel zweier Schulmänner, 1930–1944* (Frankfurt, 1988), pp. 15–54; and J. Herf, *Reactionary Modernism: Technology, Culture, and Politics in Weimar and the Third Reich* (Cambridge, 1984), pp. 154ff.

62. S. Feuchtwanger, *Der Staat und die freien Berufe: Staatsamt oder Sozialamt?* (Königsberg, 1929); Nath, *Studienratskarriere*, pp. 171ff.; and material in Jarausch, *Unfree Professions*, chap. 4.

began to follow the rantings of the *völkisch* fringe about the "rebirth of German law," the restoration of racial health, the abolition of "excess democracy" in the school, or the restoration of a technical corporate elite.[63] Even if they were hit no worse than other strata, professionals tended to project their particular problems into a generalized notion of "cultural crisis." As liberalism seemed to be responsible for the economic difficulties and the *Kulturkrise*, they began to grope for a more compelling ideology.

The failure of liberal solutions to the crisis hastened the professionals' desertion of liberalism. After three decades of debate, desperate lawyers abandoned the *freie Advokatur* and limited access to the bar. Teachers in Bavaria, Baden, Württemberg, Saxony, and Hesse similarly demanded a *numerus clausus*, while Prussian educators championed the creation of work for unemployed colleagues. Engineers started a private work service (*Ingenieurdienst*) that allowed beginners some trial job experience.[64] Hampered by complicated interest-group pressures, governmental responses to these professional demands were too little and came too late. The ponderous bureaucracy preferred to research the causes of overcrowding; it initiated lengthy interministerial negotiations that resulted in a catalogue of ineffective countermeasures. Attorneys experienced no relief of these conditions. Doctors did eliminate their economic dependence on the fund bureaucracy through new *Kassenärztliche Vereinigungen*. But teachers were counseled to employ sharper meritocratic selection of students and trainees – cold comfort for those who were to be weeded out. Similarly, engineers were left at the mercy of the free market.[65] Since professionals were relatively few (between three and four hundred thousand) and disunited, liberal politicians rarely paid attention to them in spite of their *Mittelstand* rhetoric. The protectionist demands of experts ran counter to basic tenets of laissez-faire. The strategy of reliance on voluntary cooperation could not alleviate the

63. R. Finger, *Die Sendung des Rechtsanwalts* (Munich, 1930); W. Hartnacke, *Die Überfüllung der akademischen Berufe* (Dresden, 1932); and Ludwig, *Technik*, pp. 44ff.

64. DAV, ed., *Stenographischer Bericht über die 29. AV* (Berlin, 1932); F. Behrend, "Erinnerungen an die Tätigkeit des Ph-Vb," *Höhere Schule* 7 (1954): 165ff.; and Viefhaus, "Ingenieure," pp. 336f.

65. R. Schairer, *Die akademische Berufsnot: Tatsachen und Auswege* (Jena, 1932); Kater, "Physicians in Crisis," pp. 67ff.; and Jarausch, *Unfree Professions*, chap. 4.

magnitude of suffering; an increase in competition appealed only to the strong and the predicted decrease of enrollment, although eventually realized, took too long to bring about any relief. No wonder that many professionals felt abandoned by liberal leaders and politicians.[66]

Nazi professionals were quick to exploit this weakness with propaganda. The National Socialist journal *Deutsches Recht* accused liberalism of bringing about "a decline in the popular sense of justice" and of spreading "distrust in the judiciary." Grounded in "the swamp of the West and Asiatic-Marxist subhuman instincts," a Jewish "jurisprudence of decadence" alienated Germans from their own law.[67] While racist physicians polemicized against the biological deterioration of the *Volk*, rightist teachers ranted that the "democratic-liberal-Marxist system" was ruining not only education but also the country as a whole. Due to the "liberal-democratic" bias of educational associations, "the present system will unscrupulously throttle the teaching profession."[68] Leading *völkisch* engineers as well engaged in the crass "industrial and money-based thinking" of capitalism that was responsible for depression unemployment.[69] Nazi activists astutely linked general criticism of Weimar problems to specific complaints by professionals. Not burdened by governmental responsibility, they promised a racial purge of lawyers, suggested a complete stop of teachers' admissions and jobs for trainees, and hinted at a technocratic reordering of industry. A minority of practitioners was so distraught over the crisis that it abandoned its liberal heritage and joined the Nazi bandwagon. To focus its appeals, the NSDAP founded professional affiliates for lawyers in 1928 (Nazi Jurists' League – Bund Nationalsozialistischer Deutscher Juristen or BNSDJ), teachers and doctors in 1929 (Nazi Teachers' League – Nationalsozialistischer Lehrer-

66. Beythien, "Die DVP, der kaufmännische und gewerbliche Mittelstand und die freien Berufe," pp. 2561ff.; and H. Reif, *Mittelstandspolitik* (Berlin, 1928), vol. 9 of the *Schriftenreihe für politische Werbung* of the DDP.

67. W.M. Reiter, "Zur Einführung," *Deutsches Recht* 1 (1931): 1f.; H. Frank, "Erwachen des deutschen Rechts," *Deutsches Recht* 1 (1931): 3ff.

68. "Pädagogische Zeitenwende," *Nationalsozialistische Lehrerzeitung* 10 (November/December 1931): 1ff.; "Das klassische Fundamentalwerk über Erziehung und Bildung im NS Staat," *Nationalsozialistische Lehrerzeitung* 2 (February 1932): 2ff.; "Ein Kennzeichen des Systems: Das 'Assessoren-Elend,'" *Nationalsozialistische Lehrerzeitung* 3 (1932): 13f.

69. G. Feder, "Geleitwort," *Deutsche Technik* 1 (1933): 1; and F. Lawaczeck, "Kapitalistische Wirtschaft – Volkswirtschaft,' *Deutsche Technik* 1 (1933): 2ff.

bund or NSLB; and Nazi Doctors' League – Nationalsozialistischer Ärztebund or NSÄB), and engineers in 1931 (League of
German Architects and Engineers – Kampfbund Deutscher Ar-
chitekten und Ingenieure or KDAI), which had attracted between 3 percent and 10 percent of their colleagues by January
1933.[70] Although limited, these inroads reveal that the societal
basis of liberalism was crumbling: "The last supports of the
liberal systems are shaking. 'German teacher,' your time has
come."[71]

The Social Erosion of Liberalism

The social erosion of liberalism was precipitated in part by the
problems inherent in liberal professionalism. The restructuring
of the free professions during the foundation of the German
Empire was a tenuous compromise between lingering state
control and novel market freedom. Whereas considerable super-
visory rights remained with the government, all the risks of
practice were privatized. Already during the Second Reich,
liberal professionalism was encountering difficulties with
academic overcrowding, racial prejudice, elite hierarchy, mis-
ogynist attitudes, and practitioner dominance. The initial Weimar reforms sought to democratize the neocorporate professions of the late empire by empowering disenfranchised
minorities, granting women legal equality, and partially laiciz-
ing practices. Supported by a progressive minority, these piece-
meal changes aroused considerable resentment in the
traditionalist majority, which recalled the Second Reich as a
golden age. When renewed overcrowding, hyperinflation,
stabilization dismissals, and depression unemployment impov-
erished many experts and threatened the survival of some
marginal practitioners, liberal leaders and policies were made
into a scapegoat. A progressive minority sought to develop

70. K. Willig, "The Theory and Administration of Justice in the Third Reich"
(diss., University of Pennsylvania, Philadelphia, 1975), pp. 334ff.; W. Feiten,
Der Nationalsozialistische Lehrerbund (Weinheim, 1981), pp. 40ff.; F. Kudlien, *Ärzte
im Nationalsozialismus* (Cologne, 1985), pp. 18ff.; J.C. Guse, "The Spirit of the
Plassenburg: Technology and Ideology in the Third Reich" (diss., Lincoln,
1981), pp. 36ff.
71. "Die letzten Stützen des liberalistischen Systems wanken: Deine Zeit
'Deutscher Lehrer,' bricht an," *Nationalsozialistische Lehrerzeitung* 12 (December
1932), pp. 1ff. Cf. also Jarausch, *Unfree Professions*, chap. 4.

liberalism further, in a socialist direction, and proposed collectivist solutions. But the majority of professionals opted for self-protection through the restoration of authoritarian patterns, while a more radical fringe sought even more drastic *völkisch* and racist remedies. Liberal professionalism lost its hold when it proved unable to cope with the crisis of the professions during the 1920s and failed to develop convincing forward-looking alternatives.[72]

The professions' alienation from liberalism also stemmed from the ineffectiveness of liberal politicians in mobilizing support. Although they were overrepresented in the leadership of liberal parties, professionals only rarely used their influence to advance their own occupational cause. As spokesmen for the interests of others, attorneys had great difficulty in formulating their own demands. Teachers tended to be preoccupied with general cultural issues and considered engagement in material questions to be undignified. In comparison with other middle-or lower-class groups in the electorate, the professional constituency seemed small, and support for its special requests often risked triggering a mass backlash. Calls for practitioner protection also clashed with free trade principles, rendering liberal politicians ideologically deaf to professional needs. When democratic parties attempted to organize the professional constituency in their own affiliates, the results were disappointing. While the Republikanische Richterbund did exert pressure on jurist circles, its total membership was a mere eight hundred jurists – hardly an impressive electoral base. When the founding of teacher organizations failed, politicians preferred working through the leaders of established professional associations. But their official neutrality in partisan struggles muffled liberal voices even if the general ideological direction of groups like the German Teachers' League (DLV) was decidedly progressive (DDP).[73] The contradictions within fragmented middle-class interests made it difficult for liberalism to address the special needs of the professionals. As the wishes of professionals had a

72. K.H. Jarausch, "Die unfreien Professionen: Überlegungen zu den Wandlungsprozessen im deutschen Bildungsbürgertum, 1900–1950," in J. Kocka, ed., *Bürgertum im 19. Jahrhundert: Deutschland im europäischen Vergleich* (Munich, 1988), pp. 124ff.

73. B. Schulz, *Der Republikanische Richterbund, 1921–1933* (Frankfurt, 1982), pp. 40ff.; R. Bölling, *Volksschullehrer und Politik: Der Deutsche Lehrerverein, 1918–1933* (Göttingen, 1978), pp. 114ff.

low priority on the legislative agenda, the liberal parties obtained few concrete improvements for their academic adherents.

In the final analysis, a series of unforeseen disappointments broke the bond between the professions and liberalism. A mere decade after the consolidation of liberal professionalism, the emergence of organized capitalism undercut the economic basis of "free field" competition among practitioners. Just when a state of law and culture (*Rechts- und Kulturstaat*) seemed firmly established in government, the general intellectual climate shifted toward inwardness, irrationalism, and pessimism. At the moment of triumph of the rule of notables (*Honoratioren*), the rise of mass politics began to transfer power towards interest groups.[74] In a neocorporate compromise, the professions maintained their liberal ethos in this hostile environment by clinging to the *freie Advokatur*, the *freie Arztwahl*, or academic freedom in the classroom. The initial Weimar years offered a surprising chance to resume the liberal advance – that is, until economic and political chaos as well as traditionalist backlash transformed the broad reform impetus into interest group professionalism.[75] Eventually the cumulative crises of hyperinflation, stabilization, and depression initiated a multidimensional desertion of the republic: in their own realm, many professionals abandoned liberal practices and clamored for authoritarian solutions; in the general cultural arena, the majority of the educated middle class drifted toward neoconservative ideas and flirted with *völkisch* promises; and, in a political sense, the social basis for liberal parties crumbled, allowing the Communist and Nazi extremes to deadlock parliamentary government.[76] Half a century after its proud and hopeful inception, the alliance between the professions and liberalism dissolved, unable to overcome adverse structural changes and crisis challenges.

The deliberalization of the professions illuminates the problems of the survival of liberalism within an illiberal society. Contrary to popular belief, the decline of liberal professionalism

---

74. M. Ramsey, "The Politics of Professional Monopoly in 19th Century Medicine," in G. Geison, ed., *Professions and the French State* (Baltimore, 1985), pp. 225ff. Cf. H.A. Winkler, ed., *Organisierter Kapitalismus* (Göttingen, 1974); H. Schulte, ed., *The Tragedy of German Inwardness?* (Hamilton, 1990); and T. Nipperdey, *Die Organisation der deutschen Parteien vor 1918* (Düsseldorf, 1961).

75. K. Jarausch, "Die Krise des Bildungsbürgertums in dem ersten Drittel des zwanzigsten Jahrhunderts," in J. Kocka, ed., *Bildungsbürgertum*, vol. 4.

76. L.E. Jones, *German Liberalism*, pp. 476ff.

was due neither to the persistence of preindustrial habits nor to the prevalence of bourgeois hegemony.[77] Instead it was the very success of liberal advances in law, culture, economy, and polity that brought on the illiberal and anti-Semitic backlash of the 1880s. Similarly, the neoliberal impetus manifest in the founding of the Weimar Republic was stopped only by the unprecedented economic and political crises of the 1920s. Paradoxically, liberalism was strong enough to mount a credible threat to competing clerical and conservative ideas; but at the same time liberal currents were not so powerful as to prevent consummate statesmen or unforeseen chaos from shaking their hold on the *Bürgertum*. Once its mission of unification and constitutional government had largely been achieved, liberalism sank back to the status of one political movement among others. Amidst the many reasons for its failure to democratize the empire or to maintain the republic, the effective destruction of "the social fabric of German liberalism" looms large.[78] The experience of the professions suggests that the explanation may be found less in long-range structural obstacles than in the contingent historical disappointments of liberal constituent groups. Offering an attractive liberating vision in early industrial society, liberalism had no compelling answers and seemed to be intellectually bankrupt during the crises of mature capitalism. No wonder that disappointed supporters turned away and embraced seemingly more vigorous authoritarian and *völkisch* alternatives.

The voices of two secondary teachers illustrate the eclipse of liberalism among professionals during the last Weimar years. Typical Protestant *Bildungsbürger*, the Latinist Otto Schumann and the Germanist Martin Havenstein taught at gymnasiums in Berlin and Frankfurt. Dedicated to scholarship, involved in pedagogical questions, and concerned about professional advancement, their candid correspondence reveals a growing disaffection with liberal principles and the Weimar Republic after 1930. Both philologues criticized the democratic school-reform

---

77. Phrase from Sheehan, *German Liberalism*, pp. 1ff. Cf. H.-U. Wehler, *The German Empire, 1871–1918* (Leamington Spa, 1985) versus D. Blackbourn and G. Eley, *The Peculiarities of German History: Bourgeois Society and Politics in Nineteenth-Century Germany* (Oxford, 1984); and the refinements of the argument in "Wie bürgerlich war das Kaiserreich," *Bürger und Bürgerlichkeit im 19. Jahrhundert* (Göttingen, 1987).

78. Langewiesche, *Deutscher Liberalismus*, pp. 133ff., 280ff.; Jones, *German Liberalism*, p. 481.

plans as "monkey business" (*Affentheater*), expressing their dislike of experimentation and progressive youth psychology. Scholarly frustration fed a general cultural pessimism about the future: "On one side an intellectualist hyperculture with ridiculous blindness and arrogance, and on the other side a frightening brutality and lack of decency." Fed up with "the confusion with which we are governed," they increasingly complained about "the party mismanagement from which we suffer." Both were worried about the rise of middle-class extremism: "What shall become of the once so broad bourgeois middle that carried our culture for centuries?" While finding "much unsympathetic about the [Nazi] movement" such as its *Radau-Antisemitismus*, they saw its leveling of social distinction as "something good and great" that "*might* perhaps lead us to salvation." As "many professionals already sympathize with his movement," Schumann wished that Hitler would draw more of the cultivated into his party in order to safeguard German culture: "This is our *only* hope."[79] In a desperate attempt to salvage some aspects of the liberal legacy, confused professionals welcomed a cure that was to turn out worse than the disease.

79. Hammerstein, *Deutsche Bildung?* pp. 15–54.

11
German Liberalism and the Alienation of the Younger Generation in the Weimar Republic

Larry Eugene Jones

The dramatic decline of the German liberal parties in the Weimar Republic stemmed from a variety of factors so closely intertwined that it becomes difficult, if not impossible, to disentangle one from another. The legacy of schism within the German liberal movement, the destabilizing effect of what was popularly known as the "national question," the general course of social and economic development in the 1920s and early 1930s, the increasingly prominent role of organized economic interests in German political life, the failure of liberal efforts to create a united bourgeois party, and the increasing disaffection of Germany's industrial elite all combined to sap the vitality of political liberalism in the Weimar Republic and to condemn the German liberal parties to a slow, if not irreversible, decline.[1] No less significant as both a symptom and a cause of liberalism's declining political fortunes between 1918 and 1933 was the alienation of the so-called younger generation from the two liberal parties that occupied the center of Weimar's political

1. For a comprehensive treatment of the failure of the German liberal parties during the Weimar Republic, see L.E. Jones, *German Liberalism and the Dissolution of the Weimar Party System, 1918–1933* (Chapel Hill, 1988). The completion of this essay was made possible by grants from the American Council of Learned Societies, the National Endowment for the Humanities, the National Humanities Center, and the Canisius College Faculty Fellowship Program. Professor Hans Mommsen was kind enough to provide the author with access to the papers of his father, Wilhelm Mommsen, while Erich Lüth graciously granted permission to use the papers he had deposited in the Forschungsstelle für die Geschichte des Nationalsozialismus in Hamburg. The minutes of the editorial board of the *Kölnische Zeitung* (referred to in the notes as the "Büchner-Protokolle") were made available by Kurt Weinhold. The author would like to take this opportunity to thank not only these, but all those whose cooperation made the completion of this essay possible.

Larry Eugene Jones

stage for the better part of a decade, the German Democratic Party (Deutsche Demokratische Partei or DDP) and the German People's Party (Deutsche Volkspartei or DVP). To be sure, the alienation of the younger generation was hardly confined to the two liberal parties. Both the German Center Party (Deutsche Zentrumspartei) and the right-wing German National People's Party (Deutschnationale Volkspartei or DNVP) as well as the Social Democrats (Sozialdemokratische Partei Deutschlands or SPD) experienced considerable difficulties of their own in attempting to integrate the younger generation into their organizational structure. In no case, however, were the consequences of this failure more apparent or more profound than in the case of the two liberal parties.

The literature on generational conflict and the role it played in the rise of National Socialism is indeed extensive.[2] For the most part, the principal thrust of this literature has been to examine the extent to which a direct line of continuity can be traced from the rebellion of the German youth movement in the Wilhelmine period to the alienation of the younger generation and the rise of National Socialism in the Weimar Republic.[3] Yet for all the interest that the problem of generational conflict in the Weimar Republic has attracted, little attention has been devoted to the efforts of the more established bourgeois parties to overcome the alienation of the younger generation and – at least in the case of the DDP and Center – to win it over to the support of the Weimar Republic. After all, these parties were acutely aware of

2. For a survey of this literature, see P. Stachura, "Deutsche Jugendbewegung und Nationalsozialismus," *Jahrbuch des Archivs der Deutschen Jugendbewegung* 12 (1980): 35–52. Of the more recent contributions to this discussion, see above all else M. Kater, "Generationskonflikt als Entwicklungsfaktor in der NS-Bewegung vor 1933," *Geschichte und Gesellschaft* 11 (1985): 217–43; H. Mommsen, "Generationskonflikt und Jugendrevolte in der Weimarer Republik," in T. Koebner, R.-P. Janz, and F. Trommler, eds., *"Mit uns zieht die neue Zeit": Der Mythos Jugend* (Frankfurt a.M., 1985), pp. 50–67; and E. Domansky, "Politische Dimensionen von Jugendprotest und Generationenkonflikt in der Zwischenkriegszeit in Deutschland," in D. Dowe, ed., *Jugendprotest und Generationenkonflikt in Europa im 20. Jahrhundert: Deutschland, England, Frankreich und Italien im Vergleich* (Brunswick and Bonn, 1986), pp. 113–37.
3. For example, see M. Kater, "Bürgerliche Jugendbewegung und Hitlerjugend in Deutschland 1925 bis 1939," *Archiv für Sozialgeschichte* 17 (1977): 127–74, and I. Götz von Olenhusen, "Die Krise der jungen Generation und Aufstieg des Nationalsozialismus: Eine Analyse der Jugendorganisationen der Weimarer Zeit," *Jahrbuch des Archivs der Deutschen Jugendbewegung* 12 (1980): 53–82.

288

the problem that the alienation of the younger generation posed to their political effectiveness, and they fully realized that their own survival, as well as that of the political order with which they were so closely identified, depended on the success of their efforts to win the support of those young men and women who had grown to political maturity since the last years of the Second Empire. The purpose of this essay, therefore, will be to examine the efforts of the German liberal parties to attract the support of the younger generation and to explain why by the beginning of the 1930s these efforts had ended in failure. Particular attention will be devoted to the outcome of the 1928 Reichstag elections, both as an index of the younger generation's alienation from the established liberal parties and as the catalyst for a renewed attempt on the part of the two liberal parties to recapture the support of the younger generation. This, in turn, coincided with a revival of political activity on the part of Germany's liberal youth that manifested itself not only in the emergence of young liberal clubs throughout much of the country, but also in a concerted campaign for a reform and realignment of the German party system that culminated in the ill-fated founding of the German State Party (Deutsche Staatspartei or DStP) in summer 1930 as the last grand attempt to rebaptize the Weimar party system in the spirit of the younger generation. The State Party's failure to overcome the cleavages that had become so deeply embedded in the structure of Weimar party politics, however, only intensified the estrangement that had developed between the younger generation and the established liberal parties. As liberal efforts to create a new political home for the younger generation continued to falter, its political isolation and its vulnerability to seduction by the facile idealism and relentless dynamism of the Nazi movement became increasingly apparent.

In Weimar political parlance, the term younger generation was characteristically vague and embraced at least two distinct cohort groups. On the one hand, the term referred to those who had grown to political maturity in the last years of the Wilhelmine Empire and whose social and political values had been shaped in no small measure by their experiences in the German youth movement. Not only had this segment of the younger generation received its baptism of fire in the trenches of World War I, but it had returned to civilian life in 1918 only to find the Reich it had gone off to defend in a state of complete chaos. At the same time, the term younger generation also included those who had reached adulthood since the end of World War I and whose formative experiences were of the deprivation of the war and immediate postwar years.[4] Within these two cohort groups, the liberal parties concentrated their efforts on two specific subgroups. The first of these was youth broadly defined, without reference to the specific social character of those to whom the two liberal parties directed their appeal. In this regard, both the DDP and DVP sought to establish a foothold within what still remained of the prewar German youth movement in all of its sociological heterogeneity.[5] This was then augmented by a more direct appeal to young academics and university students, a group that continued to recruit itself almost exclusively from the ranks of Germany's bourgeois elite.[6] Other groups – and most conspicuously working-class and rural youth – received little in the way of overt attention except as part of the more general appeal that the two liberal parties directed toward all of those who had once belonged to the German youth movement.

The political alienation of German youth in the Weimar Republic represented the culmination of a process that had begun

---

4. On the validity and technique of cohort analysis, see P. Loewenberg, "The Psychological Origins of the Nazi Youth Cohort," *American Historical Review* 76 (1971): 1457–1502. Unfortunately for the purposes of this investigation, Loewenberg has confined his analysis to those for whom the deprivations of war and the immediate postwar period constituted the formative experience and therefore has little to say about how his analysis might be applied to the so-called front generation. A far more serious defect of Loewenberg's argument, however, is his failure to incorporate a social or class dimension into his analysis. It is naive to assume, for example, that middle-class and working-class youth experienced the deprivations of the war and the postwar period in the same ways. On the so-called front generation, see the extremely perceptive contemporary essay by E. Jung, "Die Tragik der Kriegsgeneration," *Süddeutsche Monatshefte* 27, no. 5 (May 1930): 511–34.

5. On the history of the German youth movement in the Weimar Republic, see W. Laqueur, *Young Germany: A History of the German Youth Movement* (New York, 1962), pp. 99–187, and P. Stachura, *The German Youth Movement, 1900–1945: An Interpretative and Documentary History* (New York, 1981), pp. 38–117.

6. On the politics of the German student movement during the Weimar Republic, see W. Zorn, "Die politische Entwicklung des deutschen Studententums, 1918–1931," in K. Stephenson, A. Scharff, and W. Klötzer, eds., *Darstellungen und Quellen zur Geschichte der deutschen Einheitsbewegungen im neunzehnten und zwanzigsten Jahrhundert* (Heidelberg, 1965), 5: 223–307. On the early years of the Weimar Republic, see the detailed study by J. Schwarz, *Studenten in der Weimarer Republik: Die deutsche Studentenschaft in der Zeit von 1918 bis 1923 und ihre Stellung zur Politik* (Berlin, 1971).

during the last decades of the Second Empire. One of the more interesting features of Wilhelmine political culture was the existence of a youth movement that rejected the social and moral conventions of Wilhelmine Germany in hopes of investing life with a deeper meaning through fellowship and communion with nature. Though avowedly apolitical in its initial manifestations such as the Wandervögel, the German youth movement was profoundly alienated from the way in which Germany had developed since the founding of the Second Empire and espoused a disdain for modern political life that drew much of its inspiration from the *völkisch* ideas of Paul de Lagarde and Julius Langbehn. Although the movement became increasingly politicized with the approach of war, efforts to unite the older members of the youth movement under the aegis of the Free German Youth (Freideutsche Jugend) in a common crusade for the reformation of German public life lacked clear ideological direction and foundered on the antipathy that the rank and file of the German youth movement felt toward the very idea of partisan political activity. At the same time, however, the German youth movement remained fervently nationalistic and went off to the front in 1914 with an enthusiasm that was naive, if not suicidal.[7]

Following the end of World War I and the collapse of the Second Empire, the founders of the DDP moved quickly to mobilize the idealism of the German youth movement on behalf of Germany's new republican order. Animated by the hope that youth's longing for political change might translate itself into active support for the fledgling German republic, the Democrats made a concerted bid for the support of younger generation in the campaign for the January 1919 elections to the National Assembly.[8] Their efforts were aided in no small measure by the fact that at the height of the November revolution the National Association of National Liberal Youth (Reichsverband der nationalliberalen Jugend), the youth cadre of the prewar National Liberal Party (Nationalliberale Partei or NLP), had defected to

7. For example, see K. Jarausch, "German Students in the First World War," *Central European History* 17 (1984): 310–29.

8. For example, see E. Staedel, *Die Pflicht der Jugend: Ansprache gehalten im Auftrag der Demokratischen Partei am 5. Januar 1919 in Darmstadt* (Darmstadt, [1919]). See also Gesamtverband des Jungliberalen Reichsverbandes, "An unsere jungliberalen Freunde!" in *Allgemeine Werbeflugschriften der Deutschen demokratischen Partei* (Berlin-Wilmersdorf, 1918), pp. 8–9.

the DDP and actively supported its efforts to establish a foothold in the younger generation.[9] Following the elections, the leaders of the DDP moved to consolidate their party's position in the younger generation by founding the National League of German Democratic Youth Clubs (Reichsbund Deutscher Demokratischer Jugendvereine) under the leadership of Max Weißner.[10] This organization, which held its first national congress in April 1919 before meeting for a second time in conjunction with the DDP's Berlin party congress later that summer,[11] called upon German youth to defend the Weimar Constitution, to struggle for a revision of the Versailles Treaty, to work for the creation of economic democracy at home, and to reject "racial hatred and the whipping up [*Aufpeitschung*] of all lower instincts."[12] A sister organization known as the National League of German Democratic Students (Reichsbund Deutscher Demokratischer Studenten) was subsequently founded under the chairmanship of Wilhelm Mommsen for university matriculants throughout the country in an attempt to stem the sharp swing to the right that had begun to manifest itself at German universities.[13] This organization augmented its appeals for the creation of a "national and social democracy" in which the divisions of class and

9. B. Marwitz, *Deutsche Demokratie und nationaler Liberalismus*, Deutsche Demokratische Ziele, no. 6 (Berlin, 1919).

10. For an early statement of the movement's goals, see M. Weißner, "Die Jugend in der Deutschen demokratischen Partei," in H. Kugelmann, ed., *Die deutschdemokratische Jugendbewegung: Ihre Ziele und Bestrebungen* (Berlin-Zehlendorf, n.d. [1919]), pp. 7–10. On the history of the Young Democratic movement, see E. Schein, "Die demokratische Jugendbewegung," in R. Thurnwald, ed., *Die neue Jugend*, Forschungen zur Völkerpsychologie und Soziologie, vol. 4 (Leipzig, 1927), pp. 239–51, and H.-O. Rommel, "Die Weimarer Jungdemokraten," *Liberal* 13 (1971): 915–24. The latter is based without attribution on Schein's essay.

11. "Tagung des Reichsbundes Deutscher Demokratischer Jugendvereine im Festsaal des Herrenhauses zu Berlin am 18. und 19. Juli 1919," in Reichsgeschäftsstelle der Deutschen Demokratischen Partei, ed., *Bericht über die Verhandlungen des 1. Parteitags der Deutschen Demokratischen Partei abgehalten in Berlin vom 19. bis 22. Juli 1919* (Berlin, 1919), pp. 347–63.

12. Deutscher demokratischer Jugendverein Groß-Berlin, "Jugend heraus!" *Mitteilungen für die Mitglieder der Deutschen Demokratischen Partei* 2, no. 5 (May 1920): 180–81.

13. In this connection, see W. Mommsen, "Studentenschaft und Demokratie," *Die demokratische Jugend* 1, no. 1 (10 October 1919): 11–15. See also W. Mommsen, "Studentenschaft und demokratischer Staat," *Die Hilfe* 26, no. 25 (17 June 1920): 376–78, and W. Mommsen, "Demokratische Arbeit an den Hochschulen: Zum Jenaer Studententag am 6. und 7. Oktober," *Der Demokrat* 2, no. 40 (6 October 1921): 769–71.

confession would be submerged with a series of specific proposals for educational reform aimed at improving the legal
status of students and their place in the administrative life of the
universities.[14]

Their commitment to the creation of a genuine German democracy notwithstanding, the Young Democrats remained deeply
divided between those like Heinrich Landahl who had come out
of the Free German youth movement and who supported the
general goals of the party, but were disinclined to become more
actively involved in its internal affairs and political activists like
Ernst Lemmer who were strongly committed to pursuing their
goals within the framework of the DDP. At the DDP's Nuremberg Youth Day (Reichsjugendtag) in April 1920 the Young
Democrats relaxed their organizational ties to the DDP and
elected Landahl as their national chairman in what was generally regarded as a formal triumph for the Free German wing.[15]
By the same token, the National League of German Democratic
Students tried to put some distance between itself and the DDP
in hopes of establishing a foothold among those young academics
who had become disaffected from the existing party system and all
it supposedly stood for.[16] The drift away from the party reached
a climax in the summer of 1922 when the Young Democrats
celebrated their "spiritual independence" from the DDP with a
demonstration in Kassel that commemorated the struggle for
national and democratic independence of the early nineteenth
century and that claimed for themselves the legacy of those who
had marched to the Dörnberg and Hambach castles some ninety
years earlier. The highpoint of the demonstration came on the
final day of the congress when more than 1,200 Young Democrats donned the frock of the Wandervögel and marched to
the Dörnberg, where Lemmer, Landahl, and Mommsen
exhorted them to become more actively involved in the struggle
to realize the goals of their spiritual ancestors from the

---

14. Reichsbund deutscher demokratischer Studenten, "An die deutsche
Studentenschaft," *Die demokratische Jugend* 2, nos. 9/10 (10 May 1920): 128–29.

15. Schein, "Die jungdemokratische Bewegung," p. 241.

16. In this respect, see the manuscript of the unpublished memoirs that
Mommsen wrote after the end of World War II, pp. 19–20, in the private
possession of his son, Professor H. Mommsen of the Ruhr-Universität Bochum.
For an insight into the thinking behind this strategy, see W. Mommsen, "Jugend
und Politik," *Die Hilfe* 27, no. 29 (15 October 1921): 458–60.

1830s.[17] Yet, impressive as this demonstration was, it did little to heal the deep-seated divisions that had developed within the ranks of the Young Democratic movement.[18] This became all too blatantly apparent in the spring of 1923 when, under the impact of the Franco-Belgian occupation of the Ruhr and the continuing collapse of the mark, the activist wing under Lemmer managed to regain control of the Young Democrats' national organization through a coup d'état that left the Free Germans around Landahl with no alternative but to secede from the movement.[19]

If the Democrats moved quickly to establish a foothold within German youth and student movements, the leaders of the German People's Party found themselves severely hampered in their overtures to the younger generation both by the general confusion that surrounded their party's founding in December 1918 and by the defection of the National Liberal youth cadre to the rival DDP. Initially the leaders of the DVP had hoped to compensate for their lack of a youth organization by working within the German National Youth League (Deutschnationaler Jugendbund or DNJ), an ostensibly nonpartisan organization in which all those committed to the reconstruction of the fatherland on the basis of German-Christian culture could unite.[20] This arrangement, however, became increasingly untenable as the right-wing DNVP tried to politicize the DNJ for its own partisan purposes. By the fall of 1919 the situation within the DNJ had deteriorated to the point where a break was no longer avoidable, and in September Gustav Stresemann, the founder and dynamic young chairman of the DVP, resigned from the organization's executive committee in protest against the way in which the DNVP had violated the DNJ's political neutrality.[21] In the meantime, the DVP's state and local chapters had already

17. See *Junge Demokratie 1832 und 1922: Auf dem Dörnberg und dem Hambacher Schloß* (Frankfurt a.M., [1922]).

18. For example, see H. Preuß, "Von Cassel bis Frankfurt," in *Der Herold* 4, no. 38 (May 1923): 57.

19. Schein, "Die demokratische Jugendbewegung," pp. 242–44. See also the report of the Young Democratic conference in Jena, 17–18 November 1923, in *Der Demokrat* 4, no. 17 (20 November 1923): 198–200.

20. On the founding and program of the DNJ, see W. Foellmer, *Der deutschnationale Jugendbund: Vorschläge und Anregungen* (Berlin, 1919).

21. *Deutsche Jugend – Deutsche Volkspartei*, Jugend-Schriften der Deutschen Volkspartei, no. 5 (Berlin, 1924), pp. 10–15. See also W. Reichardt, "Ein Rückblick auf die Geschichte der Jugendbewegung," *Schaffende Jugend* 3, no. 15 (1 August 1926): 231–35.

begun to establish youth organizations of their own in Bochum, Dortmund, and a number of other cities in the Rhine-Ruhr basin.[22] In October 1919 the party's national leadership decided to coordinate this activity and to encourage its spread into other parts of Germany by creating the Youth Cadre of the German People's Party (Jugendgruppen der Deutschen Volkspartei) under the honorary chairmanship of Protestant pastor Hans Luther.[23] As in the case of the DDP, the leaders of the DVP also created a sister organization for university matriculants known as the National Student Committee (Reichsstudentenausschuß) of the DVP from its founding in 1922 until the beginning of 1925, when it reconstituted itself as the National Committee of University Groups of the German People's Party (Reichsausschuß der Hochschulgruppen der Deutschen Volkspartei) with chapters at more than thirty German universities.[24] At the heart of the ideological appeal with which the leaders of the DVP sought to galvanize these elements in support of their party lay a unequivocal commitment to the two cardinal tenets of the National Liberal legacy to which the DVP had laid claim: a belief in the value of the individual personality and an equally powerful faith in the historical mission of the German nation.[25] In bidding for the support of these groups, however, the leaders of the DVP did not allow their party's youth and student organizations the autonomy that they enjoyed within the DDP, but took special pains to ensure that they were subordinated to the

22. For example, see H. Fretlöh, ed., *Deutschlands älteste deutschvolksparteiliche Jugendgruppe* (Bochum, 1922), pp. 5–10, and *Festschrift zum zehnjährigen Bestehen des Deutschen Jugendbundes, Jugendgruppe der D.V.P., Dortmund am 20. Mai 1929* (Dortmund, [1929]), pp. 3–6, both in Hauptstaatsarchiv Düsseldorf (hereafter HStA Düsseldorf), NL Klingspor, vol. 4–II/37–46 and 4–III/152–64.

23. In this respect, see the report by H. Garnich in Deutsche Volkspartei, Reichsgeschäftsstelle, ed., *Bericht über den Zweiten Parteitag der Deutschen Volkspartei am 18., 19. und 20. Oktober 1919 im Kristallpalast in Leipzig* (Berlin, 1920), p. 60. See also *Wie wird die Arbeit in einer Jugendgruppe der Deutschen Volkspartei am zweckmäßigsten geleitet?* Jugendschriften der Deutschen Volkspartei, nos. 1–2 (Berlin, 1921).

24. K. Göbel, "Reichsausschuß der Hochschulgruppen der Deutschen Volkspartei," in Michael Doeberl et al., eds., *Das akademische Deutschland*, 4 vols. (Berlin, 1931), 2: 603–4. See also K. Göpel, *Von Art und Arbeit der Hochschulgruppen: Rede auf der Reichstagung der Hochschulgruppen der Deutschen Volkspartei zu Köln am 4. Dezember 1925*, Hochschulschriften der Deutschen Volkspartei, no. 1 (Berlin, 1925).

25. O. Brües, *Die deutsche Jugend und der liberale und nationale Gedanke* (Berlin, 1919).

overall goals of the DVP's national organization by staffing key leadership positions with party functionaries.[26]

Despite vigorous efforts on the part of both the DDP and DVP to integrate the younger generation into their own organizational structure, the vast majority of the younger generation remained outside of the orbit of the established bourgeois parties.[27] In large part this phenomenon stemmed from the fact that by the beginning of the 1920s the younger generation had begun to develop its own specific form of organization in what was commonly known as the Bund.[28] Many of the Bünde that surfaced in the immediate postwar period possessed close ties to the prewar German youth movement and consciously sought to perpetuate its values and idealism in the wake of defeat and revolution. Of these, the most significant was the Young German League (Jungdeutscher Bund), which Frank Glatzel, Wilhelm Stapel, and a small group of conservative intellectuals had founded on Burg Lauenstein in August 1919 in an attempt to unite those who had been left homeless by the demise of the Free German youth movement on a *völkisch*-national basis.[29] Others, like Artur Mahraun's Young German Order (Jungdeutscher Orden), were essentially veterans' organizations that sought to transform German political life in the spirit of the

26. A. Kempkes, "Die Organisation der Deutschen Volkspartei," in A. Kempkes, ed., *Deutscher Aufbau: Nationalliberale Arbeit der Deutschen Volkspartei* (Berlin, 1927), pp. 21–22. See also "Satzungen des Wahlkreisjugendausschusses der Deutschen Volkspartei Westfalen-Süd," 9 July 1921, HStA Düsseldorf, NL Klingspor, 4–II/273–77.

27. Although membership statistics for the various political youth organizations that existed during the Weimar Republic are virtually nonexistent, contemporary estimates placed the strength of the National League of German Democratic Youth Clubs at approximately 20,000. On the other hand, Adolf Kempkes's claim at the DVP's Stuttgart party congress in December 1921 that the party's youth organization had attracted 40,000 members seems to have been greatly inflated. For Kempkes's report, see *Nationalliberale Correspondenz*, 2 December 1921, no. 251. Of the various political youth organizations that existed in Germany after the end of World War I, only those that were affiliated with the German Center Party enjoyed any real success in attracting and retaining the support of the younger generation. See N. Körber, *Die deutsche Jugendbewegung: Versuch eines systematischen Abrisses* (Berlin, 1920), pp. 5–9.

28. For a more thorough examination of this phenomenon, see F. Raabe, *Die bündische Jugend: Ein Beitrag zur Geschichte der Weimarer Republik* (Stuttgart, 1961).

29. F. Glatzel, "Der Jungdeutsche Bund," in Bundesamt des Jungdeutschen Bundes, ed., *Jungdeutsches Wollen: Vorträge gehalten auf der Gründungstagung des Jungdeutschen Bundes auf Burg Lauenstein vom 9.–12. August 1919* (Hamburg, 1920), pp. 11–32. See also Glatzel, "Die Jungdeutschen," in R. Thurnwald, ed., *Die neue Jugend*, pp. 191–77.

"front experience."[30] In neither case, however, did those Bünde that became politically active during the Weimar Republic profess much in the way of sympathy for the symbols and institutions of Germany's new republican order. On the contrary, the leaders of the *bündisch* movement held parliamentary democracy responsible for having exacerbated the social, confessional, and regional antagonisms that divided the German people and dismissed political parties as a concrete manifestation of the national divisiveness that had accompanied the introduction of parliamentary government. This, in turn, was complemented by a vague commitment to the creation of a new social order based upon the principle of the *Volksgemeinschaft* as an alternative to the fragmented and atomized character of modern mass society. In a similar vein, the Bünde also lamented the triumph of economic egoism and longed for a return to some sort of precapitalist order based upon the "front experience" and the "socialism of the trenches."[31]

The emergence of the Bünde as an increasingly prominent feature of Germany's political culture, however, was only one aspect of a more general legitimacy crisis that began to affect the German party system in the second half of the 1920s. Not only had the stabilization of the mark in the winter of 1923–24 inflicted severe and in some cases unexpected economic hardship on different segments of Germany's beleaguered middle classes, but the fact that the Reichstag and the parties that constituted it had been excluded from any sort of meaningful role in the stabilization process severely compromised the legitimacy of the German party system in the eyes of Germany's middle-class electorate. This, in turn, impinged most heavily upon the DDP and DVP, which, of all the nonsocialist parties that dotted the German political landscape in the middle of the 1920s, were most closely identified with the pluralistic multiparty system that had developed in Germany since the end of

---

30. On the emergence and early development of patriotic associations in the Weimar Republic, see J. Diehl, *Paramilitary Politics in Weimar Germany* (Bloomington, 1977).

31. Raabe, *Jugend*, pp. 115–30. See also G. Schroeder, "Der Sozialismus der nationalen Jugend," *Der Arbeitgeber: Zeitschrift der Vereinigung der Deutschen Arbeitgeberverbände* 20, no. 8 (15 April 1930): 218–20, and J. Winschuh, "Bündische Bewegung und Sozialpolitik," *Soziale Praxis: Zentralblatt für Sozialpolitik und Wohlfahrtspflege* 39, no. 24 (12 June 1930): 561–55.

the previous century.[32] The deepening legitimacy crisis that descended on the German party system in the second half of the 1920s was characterized not only by the continued decline of the German liberal parties, but also by the rise of special-interest parties like the Business Party of the German Middle Class (Wirtschaftspartei des deutschen Mittelstandes) or the Christian-National Peasants' and Farmers' Party (Christlich-nationale Bauern- und Landvolkspartei), the increasingly prominent role of organized economic interests in the German political process, and increasingly frequent appeals for a reform and reorganization of the German party system.[33] The net effect of these developments was to intensify the political alienation of the younger generation at the same time that they heightened its desire to become more actively involved in shaping Germany's national destiny.

Even though many of the Bünde remained self-consciously elitist and never sought to attract a mass or popular following, their presence on the Weimar political scene severely complicated the task facing the German liberal parties in their efforts to attract the support of the younger generation. There was, as more than one liberal politician was quick to point out, a fundamental incompatibility between Bund and party that stood in the way of all efforts to integrate the younger generation more fully into the institutional fabric of German political life.[34] Throughout all of this, the youth and student organizations affiliated with the two liberal parties found themselves pushed more and more to the periphery of German liberal politics. This was particularly true of the Young Democrats, where hopes that Lemmer's election to the Reichstag in December 1924 heralded the beginning of a new era in the history of the DDP and its relationship to the younger generation remained unfulfilled. Above all else, the Young Democrats were disturbed by the support that the idea of a united liberal party as propagated by the newly founded Liberal Association (Liberale Vereinigung)

32. In this respect, see L.E. Jones, "In the Shadow of Stabilization: German Liberalism and the Legitimacy Crisis of the Weimar Party System, 1924–30," in G. Feldman, ed., *Die Nachwirkungen der Inflation auf die deutsche Geschichte* (Munich, 1986), pp. 21–41.

33. For further details, see Jones, *Liberalism*, pp. 225–305.

34. T. Heuß, "Parteien und Bünde," *Wille und Weg: Eine politische Halbmonatsschrift* 4, no. 2 (15 April 1928): 40–46.

seemed to enjoy on the DDP's right wing. In the course of their attacks against the Liberal Association and the concept of liberal unity, the leaders of the Young Democrats categorically rejected the ideological premise upon which a united liberal party was to be founded and insisted that liberalism and democracy were fundamentally incompatible political creeds. In the Young Democratic lexicon liberalism was synonymous with the political representation of organized economic interests, and, as good Democrats who placed the welfare of the nation as a whole before that of any of its constituent interests, they would have nothing to do with it.[35] At the same time, however, the Young Democrats took special pains to reaffirm their loyalty to the DDP and pledged to work for its internal regeneration so that it might fulfill its historic mission as a party of national and social reconciliation.[36] Yet for all of the enthusiasm that Lemmer and his associates were able to bring to task of regenerating the DDP, membership in the National League of German Democratic Youth Clubs declined from an estimated 20,000 at the beginning of the Weimar Republic to less than 2,300 by the end of 1926. By the same token, the National League of German Democratic Students had been decimated by the social, economic, and political crises of the early 1920s and had only recently begun to rebuild its national organization.[37]

Nor was the situation in the German People's Party any more encouraging. For although the DVP's youth and student organizations had managed to survive the runaway inflation of the early 1920s and the traumatic national crisis of 1923 in substantially better shape than their counterparts in the DDP, the party continued to experience considerable difficulty in attracting the support of the younger generation. While party leaders attributed much of this to the general antipathy of the German youth movement toward the existing political system, they also cited their own reliance on liberal slogans and liberal ideas as a major reason for their inability to secure a breakthrough into the

35. For example, see H.-W. Gyßling, "Demokratie, Liberalismus und das deutsche Staatsproblem: Vortrag beim Reichsführertag der Deutschen Demokratischen Jugend in Bamberg am 3. Oktober 1926," *Der Herold* 7, no. 71 (November 1926): 208–12.
36. E. Lemmer, "Hinein in die Politik," *Berliner Tageblatt*, 22 October 1926, no. 499.
37. W. Stephan, *Die Deutsche Demokratische Partei im Berichtsjahr 1926: Jahresbericht der Reichsparteileitung* (n.p., [1927]), pp. 24–26.

ranks of the younger generation. Yet rather than reject liberal-ism altogether as the Young Democrats had done, the leaders of the DVP's youth organization tried to rectify this situation by appropriating the style and form of the German youth move-ment at the same time that they tried to clarify their party's ideological goals.[38] Here they enlisted the cooperation of none other than German foreign minister and DVP party chairman Gustav Stresemann. Speaking before the Union of German Students (Verein Deutscher Studenten) at the University of Berlin in July 1926, Stresemann reminded his audience of the role that the German liberal movement had played in the founding of the Second Empire and exhorted the current gener-ation of university students to become more actively involved in the efforts to remold the existing German state in the spirit of those national and liberal values that had served the Reich so admirably in the struggle for German unification. It was not in negation and opposition but in support of the state, Stresemann admonished his listeners, that the true vocation of German youth lay.[39] By reaffirming their commitment to liberalism and by infusing that commitment with a strong dose of German nationalism, Stresemann and his associates hoped that it would be possible to win the support of at least a majority of those three to four million voters who would be going to the polls for the first time in the national elections scheduled to take place in 1928.[40]

If Stresemann and the leaders of the DVP were hopeful that the 1928 Reichstag elections would bring about a reversal in the electoral behavior of the younger generation, the outcome of the elections could not have come as a greater disappointment. At no point in the history of the Weimar Republic was the failure of the German liberal parties to attract and retain the support of the

38. W. Husen, "Zur Lage in unserer Jugendbewegung," May 1926, in HStA Düsseldorf, NL Klingspor, 4–II/94–95. See also W. Reichardt, "Wir und die deutsche Jugendbewegung," *Schaffende Jugend* 3, no. 16 (15 August 1926), pp. 243–49.

39. G. Stresemann, "Student und Staat," in G. Stresemann, *Reden und Schrif-ten: Politik – Geschichte – Literatur, 1897–1926*, edited by R. v. Rheinbaben, 2 vols. (Berlin, 1926), 2: 262–302. In a similar vein, see F. Kruspi, *Student, Staat und Volk*, Hochschulschriften der Deutschen Volkspartei, no. 4 (Berlin, 1926).

40. W. Husen, "Millionen von Jungwählern," in "Zur Jugendarbeit der Deutschen Volkspartei im Wahljahr 1928," n.d., HStA Düsseldorf, NL Kling-spor, 4–III/234.

younger generation or the effects of that failure upon the electoral fortunes of the two liberal parties more apparent than in the May 1928 Reichstag elections. After the last national elections in December 1924, the DDP and DVP had seen their share of the national electorate decline from 16.2 to 13.5 percent.[41] While much of this could be attributed to the success of middle-class splinter parties like the Business Party and the Christian-National Peasants' and Farmers' Party, the leaders of the German liberal parties also saw a direct correlation between their own parties' poor performance at the polls and the alienation of the younger generation. Voter abstention reached a record high in the 1928 Reichstag elections as more than ten million eligible voters failed to vote. And this, as liberal analysts were quick to point out, stemmed in no small measure from the apathy of the younger generation.[42]

The outcome of the 1928 Reichstag elections marked a watershed in the efforts of the two liberal parties to win the support and cooperation of the younger generation. Over the course of the next two years both the DDP and DVP launched determined efforts to overcome the political alienation of the younger generation and to reintegrate it into the organizational fabric of German liberal politics. In November 1928 Stresemann initiated a reform of the DVP national organization that made improving the party's image and effectiveness among the younger generation one of its major goals.[43] In a similar vein, the Democrats tried to rejuvenate their party organization by electing Lemmer to the cochairmanship of the DDP managing committee and by creating a number of openings in the party leadership for other representatives from the Young Democratic movement.[44] These efforts coincided with a revival of political

41. Jones, *Liberalism*, pp. 302–4.
42. For an example of the contemporary literature on the "generation gap" from a liberal perspective, see Ziegler, "Die übersprungene Generation," *Deutsche Stimmen* 40, no. 12 (20 June 1928): 357–62, and W. Stephan, "Die 'Führerkrise' oder der Generationswechsel in der Politik," *Wille und Weg* 4, no. 16 (15 November 1928): 378–81, as well as R. Wolff, *Ideenkrisis – Parteienwirrwarr: Eine historisch-politische Betrachtung* (Berlin, 1931), pp. 66–78, and A. Dix, *Die deutschen Reichstagswahlen, 1871–1930 und die Wandlungen der Volksgliederung* (Tübingen, 1930), pp. 32–37.
43. In this respect, see the minutes of the DVP managing committee, 5 December 1928, AA: NL Stresemann, 3164/103/174572–77, and of the first meeting of the DVP organizational committee, 20 December 1928, ibid., 174587–88.
44. Minutes of the DDP executive committee, 23 March 1929, in L. Albertin,

interest on the part of Germany's liberal youth and the emergence of young liberal clubs throughout the country. The first of these was the February Club (Februar-Klub), which a group of young intellectuals with close ties to the local DVP founded in Cologne in February 1928 in an attempt to forge a closer bond between their generation and the political system from which it had been all but excluded.[45] This was followed in December 1928 by the founding of the Quirites in Berlin and in the spring of 1929 by the establishment of young liberal clubs in Stuttgart, Freiburg, and Heidelberg.[46] By far the most important of the young liberal groups to surface in the aftermath of the 1928 Reichstag elections, however, was the "Front 1929," which was founded in March 1929 by Stresemann's personal friend and biographer Rochus von Rheinbaben. Recruiting its membership almost exclusively from the ranks of Berlin's bourgeois intelligentsia, the Front 1929 sought to establish itself as the crystallization point around which all those genuinely interested in a reform of German public life could unite, and it actively solicited the cooperation of national political figures from all of Germany's major bourgeois parties.[47] The true spirit behind the founding of the Front 1929, moreover, was Gustav Stresemann. Outraged over the way in which he had been treated by his own party's right wing, Stresemann had become disenchanted with the way in which the German party system had developed since the founding of the Weimar Republic and privately encouraged

---

ed., *Linksliberalismus in der Weimarer Republik: Die Führungsgremien der Deutschen Demokratischen Partei und der Deutschen Staatspartei, 1918–1933* (Düsseldorf, 1980), pp. 486–87.

45. On the founding and goals of the February Club, see Winschuh's remarks at its first meeting in Cologne on 10 February 1928, BA: NL Sieling (Kleine Erwerbung, 484), 1. For a statement of its objectives, see E. Regh, "Der Februar-Klub," *Frankfurter Nachrichten*, 31 March 1929, no. 90.

46. For further details, see Jones, *Liberalism*, pp. 326–29. For the best contemporary sources on these developments, see K. Göpel, "Entwicklung und Stand der politischen Reformbestrebungen der jungen Generation," *Hochschulblätter der Deutschen Volkspartei* 4, no. 30 (May 1929): 1–4 (BA: R 45 2/6/11–14), and Reichsgemeinschaft junger Volkspartei, *Aufmarsch und Ziel* (Lobau, [1929]), pp. 17–24, as well as the report by Mansfeld at an editorial conference of the *Kölnische Zeitung*, 22 March 1929, in "Büchner-Protokolle: Redaktionssitzungen der Kölnischen Zeitung 22. März 1929 bis 2. Dezember 1935."

47. R. v. Rheinbaben, "'Front 1929' und ihr Gedankenkreis," *Frankfurter Nachrichten*, 31 March 1929, no. 90. See also "Richtlinien der Front 1929," n.d., BA: NL Koch-Weser, 101/103.

Rheinbaben in his efforts to bring about its reform and realignment.[48]

By no means were the various young liberal groups that surfaced in the aftermath of the 1928 Reichstag elections in total agreement on the shape and form of the liberalism they espoused. Some, like the February Club and the League for the Regeneration of Political Life (Bund zur Erneuerung des politischen Lebens) in Freiburg, espoused a commitment to the traditional values of political and economic liberalism,[49] while others, most notably the Heidelberg Coalition for Young German Politics (Heidelberger Arbeitsgemeinschaft für jungdeutsche Politik), stood on the extreme left wing of the German liberal movement and made no effort to conceal its disenchantment with the liberal ideas and slogans of the past.[50] The Front 1929, on the other hand, espoused a general disdain for all ideological distinctions and sought to unite all of those elements in German political life that earnestly desired a reform of Germany's parliamentary system in a united front stretching from the right wing of the DDP through the Center and DVP to the left wing of the DNVP.[51] The common denominator uniting all of these groups was a deep and abiding distrust of the role that organized economic interests had come to play in German political life since the end of World War I. If for these groups the regeneration of German liberalism was synonymous with a reform of the German party system as it had evolved since the founding of the Weimar Republic, this, in turn, was synonymous with an end to the "tyranny of economic self-interest" that had become such a prominent feature of German political life in the second half of the 1920s.

In their crusade for a reform and regeneration of the German

---

48. On Stresemann's relationship to the Front 1929, see Mansfeld's report, 22 March 1929, "Büchner-Protokolle," as well as the memorandum of Stresemann's remarks during a conversation with Rheinbaben and Stein, 26 April 1929, AA: NL Stresemann, 3164/105/174987–88. See also G. Stresemann, "An die Jugend," *Nationalliberale Correspondenz*, 29 December 1928, no. 235.

49. For example, see J. Winschuh, "Liberale Erneuerung," *Deutsche Führerbriefe*, 27 October 1928, in BA: NL Sieling (Kleine Erwerbung 484), 1.

50. For further information on the Heidelberg Coalition for Young German Politics, see Kind's report at a meeting of the action committee of the February Club, 28 April 1930, BA: NL Sieling (Kleine Erwerbung 484), 2.

51. Rheinbaben to Stresemann, 23 March 1929, AA: NL Stresemann, 3176/78/169430–35.

party system, the leaders of the young liberal movement were soon to be joined by another organization that promised to provide them with the mass popular base they sorely needed, Artur Mahraun's Young German Order. The publication of Mahraun's *Das jungdeutsche Manifest* in December 1927 marked the beginning of a critical new period in the history of Mahraun's organization. For not only did *Das jungdeutsche Manifest* assail the "partyism" of German public life as the source and symbol of Germany's national fragmentation, but it also outlined a program for the peaceful evolution of the Weimar Republic into a higher and more perfect form of democracy inspired by the "front experience" and based upon the concept of the *Volksgemeinschaft*.[52] To be sure, Mahraun's political program lay outside the orbit of traditional German liberalism and actually had more in common with the antisystem romanticism of the German youth movement than it did with basic values of the German liberal tradition as it had evolved in the nineteenth and twentieth centuries. In point of fact, Mahraun's concept of the *Volksgemeinschaft* was explicitly antiliberal in that it both subordinated the individual to the welfare of the nation as a whole and espoused a hierarchical political order based upon one's innate leadership ability.[53] At the same time, however, Mahraun's willingness to pursue his goals within the framework of the existing system, his categorical rejection of schemes for the forcible overthrow of the Weimar Republic, and his vigorous defense of Stresemann's foreign policy clearly set the Young German Order apart from the other patriotic associations that dotted Germany's political landscape in the second half of the 1920s. By the same token, no one was more vehement in his denunciation of organized economic interests and the role they

52. A. Mahraun, *Das jungdeutsche Manifest* (Berlin, 1927), esp. pp. 7–10, 61–93, and 197–203. On the early history and development of the Young German Order, see Mahraun's own account in A. Mahraun, *Gegen getarnte Gewalten: Weg und Kampf einer Volksbewegung* (Berlin, 1928), pp. 153–78. For further details, see Diehl, *Paramilitary Politics*, pp. 222–27, as well as the monographs by K. Hornung, *Der jungdeutsche Orden* (Düsseldorf, 1958), pp. 51–86, and A. Kessler, *Der jungdeutsche Orden in den Jahren der Entscheidung I (1928–1930)* (Munich, 1975), pp. 7–29.

53. The antiliberal character of the Young German program is most apparent in R. Höhn, *Der bürgerliche Rechtsstaat und die neue Front* (Berlin, 1929). For the most comprehensive statement of the Young German ideology, see A. Mahraun, *Parole 1929* (Berlin, 1929), pp. 3–34.

had come to play in German political life than Mahraun himself.[54]

Galvanized into action by the election of right-wing extremist Alfred Hugenberg to the DNVP party chairmanship in October 1928, Mahraun and the leaders of the Young German Order began to cultivate closer ties with representatives of the young liberal movement through the spring and summer of 1929.[55] But the Order's agitation for a reform and consolidation of the German party system posed a perplexing problem for the leaders of the German liberal parties, who feared that the movement might very well slip out from under their own control. The response of the two liberal parties to this dilemma was characteristically different. For whereas the leaders of the DDP evinced genuine sympathy for the aspirations of the younger generation and were anxious to cultivate closer relations not only with the young liberal front but also with Mahraun and the Young German Order,[56] the leaders of the DVP, with the notable exception of Stresemann and Economics Minister Julius Curtius, remained deeply suspicious of the campaign for a reform of the German party system and feared that this campaign foreshadowed the founding of still another political party.[57] It was to counter this danger that a group of young DVP activists under the leadership of Frank Glatzel and Josef Hardt founded the Reich Association of Young Populists (Reichsgemeinschaft junger Volksparteiler or RjV) as a special organization distinct from the DVP youth cadre for young party members between the ages of twenty-five and forty. The aim of this organization, as Glatzel explained in his keynote address at the RjV's founding ceremonies in Weimar in May 1929, was to infuse the DVP with the spirit of the younger generation and to free it from the domination of outside economic interests so that it would be in a position to attract the support of those who, regardless of their

54. For example see A. Mahraun, *Das jungdeutsche Manifest*, pp. 61–80.
55. For example, see the exchange of letters between Mahraun and Rheinbaben in *Der Jungdeutsche*, 7 March 1929, no. 50. For Mahraun's antipathy towards Hugenberg and the Pan-German circles behind him, see A. Mahraun, *Die neue Front: Hindenburgs Sendung* (Berlin, 1929), pp. 7–70, 87–104.
56. Entry in Koch-Weser's diary, 27 February 1929, BA: NL Koch-Weser, 39/11–13.
57. For example, see Scholz to Stresemann, 26 March 1929, AA: NL Stresemann, 3164/104/174786–89, and Moldenhauer to Stresemann, 4 April 1929, ibid., 3164/105/174933–66.

current party affiliation, had become disenchanted with the existing party system. Only then would the DVP be in a position to fulfill its historic mission as the crystallization point around which "the great state party of the national middle" could form.[58]

Fears that the younger generation's campaign for a rejuvenation of the German party system might culminate in the founding of a new political party mounted in the wake of the Young German Order's decision in March 1929 to initiate a "People's National Action" as the first step toward a renewal of German public life.[59] This action, which drew to a climax with three mass demonstrations in Dortmund, Danzig, and Dresden in the summer and early fall of 1929,[60] clearly raised the specter of a new political party. With the initiation of Hugenberg's campaign against the Young Plan in the summer of 1929 and Stresemann's untimely death the following October, Mahraun and his associates felt that they could ill afford to wait any longer, and at a confidential meeting of the High Chapter of the Young German Order on 12–13 October they decided to proceed with the founding of a new middle party.[61] Meanwhile Erich Koch-Weser had already begun to explore the possibility of a new political party with Josef Winschuh of the Cologne February Club and other spokesmen for the young liberal front,[62] and at its Mannheim party congress in the first week of October the DDP party leadership opened up fifteen positions on its execu-

---

58. On the founding of the RjV, see A. Meier, "Das Ergebnis von Weimar," *Deutsche Stimmen* 41, no. 11 (5 June 1929): 321–29, and RjV, *Aufmarsch und Ziel*, pp. 24–37. For the text of Glatzel's speech, see "Zusammenschluß junger Volksparteiler," n.d., BA: R 45 2/6/19–31. For Glatzel's goals, see his letter to Winschuh, 25 March 1929, BA: R 45 2/69/417–19, as well as his speech, "Die Deutsche Volkspartei als Partei der Volksgemeinschaft," in Hindenburgbund-Jugendgruppen der Deutschen Volkspartei, *Staatsbürgerliche Jugend: Unsere Reichsschulungswoche in Braunlage/Harz vom 22. bis 27. April 1930* (Berlin, [1930]), pp. 3–5. On relations between the RjV and the DVP youth cadre, see Glatzel's remarks at a meeting of the DVP National Youth Committee (*Reichsjugendaus-schuß*), 23 March 1930, HStA Düsseldorf, NL Klingspor, 4–III/83–86.

59. Protocol of the Nineteenth High Chapter of the Young German Order, 26–27 January 1929, BA: R 161/12. See also A. Mahraun, "Volksnationale Aktion," *Der Meister* 4, no. 6 (March 1929): 243–54.

60. Kessler, *Der jungdeutsche Orden*, pp. 46–61.

61. Protocol of the Twenty-Third High Chapter of the Young German Order, 12–13 October 1929, BA: R 161/12.

62. For example, see Koch-Weser's notes for a conversation he had with Winschuh on 18 October 1929, BA: NL Koch-Weser, 101/91–101.

tive committee for representatives from the younger generation.[63] But as the Democrats took what appeared to be the first steps towards the creation of a united liberal party, the Young Democrats were torn by a bitter leadership crisis that had profound implications for their relationship to the party as a whole. For whereas Lemmer, as national chairman of the Young Democratic League, was fully prepared to cooperate with a paramilitary organization like the Young German Order in the crusade for a reform of the existing party system,[64] the more pacifist elements of the Young Democratic movement around Hamburg's Erich Lüth remained adamantly opposed to any concessions on the question of armaments and military policy that might make an accommodation with the DDP more palatable to Mahraun and his associates.[65] By the same token, the Young Democrats opposed the DDP's abrupt turn to the right in the aftermath of the 1928 Reichstag elections and were especially critical of the strong commitment to the defense of middle-class economic interests that the party had made with the promulgation of its new economic program at the Mannheim party congress in October 1929.[66] In the meantime, relations between Lüth and Lemmer continued to deteriorate until the former was officially expelled from the Young Democrats in February 1930 as punishment for his breach of discipline in publicly attacking Lemmer's leadership of the movement.[67] Although Lüth was successful in appealing his expulsion and was allowed to rejoin the movement in an act of public reconciliation,[68] the episode

63. Report by Mansfeld, 8 October 1929, "Büchner-Protokolle."

64. E. Lemmer, "Hinein in die Politik," *Vossische Zeitung*, 22 June 1929, no. 148.

65. On the leadership crisis within the Young Democratic movement, see Lemmer to Lüth, 27 June 1929, Forschungsstelle für die Geschichte des Nationalsozialismus in Hamburg (hereafter cited as FGNS Hamburg), 751–9/1, as well as the report in the *Dortmunder General-Anzeiger*, 16 October 1929, ibid.

66. H. Muhle, "Zum jungdemokratischen Wirtschaftsprogramm: Diskussionsrede auf dem Mannheimer Parteitag," *Der Herold der deutschen Jungdemokratie* 10, no. 10 (October 1929): 146–47. See also the report by Mansfeld, 8 October 1929, "Büchner-Protokolle." For the details of the DDP's new economic program, see Jones, *Liberalism*, pp. 342–44.

67. Lemmer to Lüth, 7 February 1930, FGNS Hamburg, 751–9/2. See also E. Lüth, "Die Säuberungskrise bei den Jungdemokraten," *Dortmunder General-Anzeiger*, 30 January 1930, FGNS Hamburg, 751–9/2.

68. In this respect, see Lemmer to Lüth, 12 March 1930, as well as the protocol of a meeting of the Young Democratic leadership from the Reich, Berlin-Brandenburg and Hamburg, 16 March 1930, both in FGNS Hamburg, 751–9/2.

nevertheless revealed deep-seated cleavages within the Young Democrats that placed their loyalty to the DDP in serious doubt.

In the course of the negotiations that Koch-Weser conducted in the aftermath of Stresemann's death, it became increasingly apparent that the new leadership of the DVP was by no means as interested in the creation of a united liberal party as Stresemann had been. At the same time that Koch-Weser and the leaders of the DDP were courting the favor of Mahraun and the leaders of the young liberal movement,[69] the election of Ernst Scholz as Stresemann's successor to the DVP party chairmanship encountered strong opposition from the young activists on his party's left wing.[70] Although Scholz was able to placate his critics with an appeal for the consolidation of all "state-supporting bourgeois forces" at the DVP's Mannheim party congress in March 1930,[71] this was denounced with great fanfare by Mahraun and his associates as an attempt to shore up the position of those "anonymous plutocratic forces" that had dominated German political life ever since the founding of the Weimar Republic.[72] Relations between the DVP and the young liberal elements on its left wing became increasingly strained when in the spring of 1930 the "People's National Action" reconstituted itself as the People's National Reich Association (Volksnationale Reichsvereinigung or VNR) in preparation for the Saxon state elections that had been set for 22 June.[73] Frus-

69. For example, see the minutes of the DDP managing committee, 23 January 1930, in Albertin, ed., *Linksliberalismus*, pp. 521, as well as the memoirs by the DDP secretary general from 1922 to 1929, W. Stephan, *Acht Jahrzehnte erlebtes Deutschland: Ein Liberaler in vier Epochen* (Düsseldorf, 1983), pp. 175–78.

70. For example, see Glatzel to the members of the DVP central executive committee, 11 December 1929, BA: NL Jarres, 40.

71. See the speech by E. Scholz in Deutsche Volkspartei, Reichsgeschäftsstelle, ed., *8. Reichsparteitag der Deutschen Volkspartei in Mannheim vom 21. bis 23. März 1930* (Berlin, [1930]), pp. 3–6. For the young liberal response to Scholz's appeal, see the speeches by Glatzel and Rodens, in ibid., pp. 6–7. For the background of this appeal, see Jones, *Liberalism*, pp. 355–57.

72. For example, see K. Pastenaci, "Sammlungsparole," *Der Jungdeutsche*, 23 April 1930, no. 94.

73. For the VNR's ideological orientation, see A. Mahraun, *Der Aufbruch: Sinn und Zweck der Volksnationalen Reichsvereinigung* (Berlin, 1929), pp. 53–77, as well as Mahraun's speech in Volksnationale Reichsvereinigung, *Der erste Reichsvertretertag am 5. und 6. April 1930* (Berlin, 1930), pp. 14–59. On the VNR's decision to enter the Saxon elections, see Mahraun to the VNR's local chapters, 21 May 1930, BA: NS 26/875.

trated by Scholz's passivity in the matter of bourgeois unity, the leaders of the young liberal front chastised the DVP party chairman for his insensitivity to the aspirations of the younger generation in a move that contained the implicit threat of a general secession on the part of the young liberal elements around Winschuh and Rheinbaben.[74] The Reich Association of Young Populists, on the other hand, continued to reaffirm its loyalty to the DVP and worked desperately to reform the party from within so that a break between it and the young liberal front could be averted.[75]

It was against the background of these developments that the Reichstag was dissolved on 18 July 1930. Immediately after the dissolution of the Reichstag the leaders of the young liberal front met in Berlin to draft a letter exhorting the leaders of the various nonsocialist and nonconfessional parties that stood to the left of the DNVP to set aside their differences for the sake of a united effort in the forthcoming Reichstag elections.[76] In response to this letter, the leaders of the young liberal front met with representatives from all of the parties from the DDP to the newly founded Conservative People's Party (Konservative Volkspartei) on the afternoon of 25 July but were frustrated by the lack of agreement they found among the various participants about the ultimate shape the proposed initiative on the behalf of bourgeois unity should take.[77] In the meantime, however, Mahraun and the leaders of the Young German Order had been meeting secretly with Koch-Weser and representatives from the Democratic party leadership for the past several days to discuss what quickly developed into plans for founding a new political party.[78] When Koch-Weser and Mahraun informed the leaders of the young liberal front of their plans at a second meeting later

74. Croon, Rodens, and Sieling to Scholz, 22 May 1930, BA: NL Sieling (Kleine Erwerbung 484), 2.

75. See Glatzel to Jarres, 23 June 1930, with "Vorschlag eines Aktionsprogramms der Reichsgemeinschaft junger Volksparteiler," n.d., BA: NL Jarres, 41.

76. *Kölner Tageblatt*, 5 August 1930, no. 391. For the general outlines of this proposal, see R. v. Rheinbaben, "Der erste Schritt: Ein praktischer Vorschlag zur Parteireform," *Berliner Börsen-Courier*, 24 July 1930, no. 339.

77. A protocol of this meeting, apparently written by a participant from the RjV, has been preserved among the records of the Brunswick DVP district organization, Stadtarchiv Braunschweig (hereafter cited as StA Braunschweig), GX6/612.

78. On the DStP, see Jones, *Liberalism*, pp. 369–72. From the Young German perspective, see Kessler, *Orden*, pp. 102–33.

that evening and announced that they were actively seeking the cooperation of the younger generation in launching the new party, the unity of the young liberal front quickly evaporated. For whereas Glatzel and the spokesmen for the RjV refused to commit themselves to the founding of a new political party and tried to dissuade Koch-Weser and Mahraun from going ahead with their plans, not only Rochus von Rheinbaben from Front 1929 but also Josef Winschuh from the February Club movement and Theodor Eschenburg from the Quirites agreed to throw their support behind the new party.[79] When the founding of the German State Party was officially announced on the morning of 28 July, all three signed the appeal heralding its arrival and the rebirth of the German party system that this was supposed to mean.[80]

The founding of the German State Party on 28 July 1930 represented a concerted attempt on the part of the Democratic party leadership to secure a breakthrough into the ranks of the younger generation and to overcome that cleavage between *Bund* and party that had become such a prominent feature of Weimar's political culture. Not only were the Democrats hopeful that the Young German Order and its allies in the VNR would provide the German bourgeoisie with the spiritual cement it so sorely needed,[81] but the "Manifesto of the German State Party," which the founders of the new party issued on 22 August,[82] was essentially a reformulation of traditional Democratic objectives in the vocabulary of the German youth movement. But if the founding of the DStP was conceived as an attempt to overcome the political alienation of the younger generation and to pave the way for its reconciliation with the

79. Protocol of the meeting between representatives from the young liberal front and the various bourgeois parties, 25 July 1930, StA Braunschweig, GX6/612. For the RjV's position, see Glatzel's remarks before the DVP national committee, 31 July 1930, BA: R 45 II/32/295–307, as well as his article, "Die jungen Volksparteiler und die Staatspartei," *Berliner Börsen-Courier*, 1 August 1930, no. 354. See also J. Winschuh, "Junge Generation vor die Front!" *Kasseler Tageblatt*, 3 August 1930, no. 212; and T. Eschenburg, "Die Deutsche Staatspartei," *Berliner Börsen-Courier*, 29 July 1930, no. 347.

80. Press release from the founders of the DStP, 28 July 1930, BA: NL Koch-Weser, 105/47.

81. Remarks by Bäumer before the DDP executive committee, 25 July 1930, in Albertin, ed., *Linksliberalismus*, p. 561.

82. A. Mahraun, *Die Deutsche Staatspartei: Eine Selbsthilfeorganisation deutschen Staatsbürgertums* (Berlin, 1930), pp. 41–48.

existing political system, then this effort was undercut by two ominous developments. First of all, the left wing of the Young Democratic movement regarded the DDP's alliance with the paramilitary Young German Order as a betrayal of the pacifist principles for which it had always stood and refused to support the new party. At a special convention in Nuremberg on 3 August 1930 they proceeded to reconstitute themselves as the Union of Independent Democrats (Vereinigung Unabhängiger Demokraten) in a move that received strong support from the leaders of the Young Democratic movement in Berlin-Brandenburg, Hamburg, and Nuremberg.[83] This came as a direct affront to Lemmer, Hans Muhle, and the leaders of the Young Democrats' national organization, all of whom were attracted to the Young German Order's political idealism and who enthusiastically endorsed the new party as a frontal assault against the role that organized economic interests had come to play in German public life.[84] An even more ominous development, however, was the refusal of Glatzel and the Reich Association of Young Populists to support the new party. For not only had Glatzel reached a private agreement with Scholz whereby his election to the Reichstag on the DVP national ticket had been assured,[85] but those members of the RjV who either belonged to the Young German Order or had joined the DStP were summarily expelled from the organization before it met in Kassel on 3 August to discuss its relationship to the new party. As a result, Glatzel was able to keep the RjV's representatives from Frankfurt, Lübeck, and Berlin from introducing a resolution at Kassel in support of a reconciliation between the DVP and DStP and

83. In this respect, see E. Lüth, "Vortrupp der neuen Linken," *Das Tagebuch* 11, no. 32 (16 August 1930): 1295–97, and O. Stündt, "Die alte Fahne treu! Von Gründung, Zweck und Ziel der Vereinigung unabhängiger Demokraten," *Das Echo der jungen Demokratie* 12, nos. 8/9 (August–September 1930): 111–17. For further details on organized pacifism within the DDP, see Karl Holl, "Pazifismus oder liberaler Neo-Imperialismus? Zur Rolle der Pazifisten in der Deutschen Demokratischen Partei," in Joachim Radkau and Imanuel Geiss, eds., *Imperialismus im 20. Jahrhundert: Gedenkschrift für George W. Hallgarten* (Munich, 1976), pp. 171–95.

84. See the remarks by Muhle and Körber before the DDP party council, 30 July 1930, in Albertin, ed., *Linksliberalismus*, pp. 569–72, as well as the appeal by Lemmer and Mahraun, "An die deutsche Jugend!" *Der Herold* 11, nos. 7/8 (July–August 1930): 43.

85. In this respect, see Kruspi to the RjV local chairman, 8 August 1930, BA: R 45 II/6/221–23, and Glatzel to Scholz, 12 August 1930, BA: R 45 II/5/41–49.

succeeded in securing the passage of a resolution that denounced the founding of the State Party as a "one-sided distortion of the ideal of bourgeois unity" as originally articulated by the DVP.[86]

Whatever momentum Koch-Weser and the founders of the DStP had hoped to generate for their efforts to galvanize the German bourgeoisie into a dynamic political force was soon exhausted in the wake of the bitter counterattack that Scholz and the leaders of the DVP directed against the new party through the remainder of the campaign. In this respect, Scholz was particularly angered by the way in which Koch-Weser had gone behind his back in search of support from the leaders of his party's left wing. What emerged from the campaign, therefore, was not the picture of bourgeois solidarity that the leaders of the DStP had hoped to project, but rather a picture of a badly divided and factious party system that only confirmed everything the leaders of the younger generation had been saying about it for the past two years. As a result, the State Party's hopes of establishing itself as a bridge between the younger generation and the existing party system turned to bitter ashes as it went down to a demoralizing defeat in the September 1930 Reichstag elections. Whatever the reasons might have been, the DStP lost approximately one-fifth of the votes the DDP had received in the 1928 Reichstag elections as well as five of the twenty-five seats the DDP had held in the previous national parliament. At the same time, the DVP lost more than one million of the 2.7 million votes it had received in 1928 and saw its parliamentary strength fall from forty-five to thirty mandates. Between them the two liberal parties had seen their share of the popular vote slip from 23 and 22.2 percent in the 1919 and 1920 national elections respectively to 13.5 percent in May 1928 and 8.4 percent in September 1930. In the case of both the DDP and DVP, a major cause for their stunning defeat was their inability to mobilize the estimated five million new voters who went to the polls in a national election for the first time in 1930. And the

86. For further details, see the reports in the *Kölnische Zeitung*, 4 August 1930, no. 421, and the *Berliner Börsen-Courier*, 5 August 1930, no. 359, as well as the open letter from Heide to Scholz, *Berliner Börsen-Courier*, 5 August 1930, no. 360, and the appeal from Bente to the DVP youth organizations, *Berliner Börsen-Courier*, 12 August 1930, no. 372.

principal beneficiary of this failure was the National Socialist German Workers' Party.[87]

The outcome of the 1930 Reichstag elections bore vivid testimony to the persistent alienation of the younger generation from the existing political system and from the two liberal parties that, for better or worse, had courted it so assiduously for the past two years. The electoral verdict was particularly distressing to the founders of the German State Party, whose efforts to rebaptize the German party system in the spirit of the younger generation had been seriously compromised throughout the campaign by a series of disputes between the Young Germans and old-line Democrats like Hermann Höpker-Aschoff, Oskar Meyer, and Gustav Stolper over everything ranging from the party's ideological profile to the selection of candidates for the upcoming Reichstag elections.[88] With the DStP's demoralizing defeat at the polls in the September elections, the tenuous alliance on which the party had been founded began to unravel. Under these circumstances, the old-line Democrats around Höpker-Aschoff moved quickly to regain control of the party, first by blocking Koch-Weser's election as chairman of the DStP Reichstag delegation at its first caucus on 17 September[89] and then by setting conditions for the party's future development that the Young Germans found impossible to accept.[90] For their own part, Mahraun and the leaders of the Young German Order found their freedom of movement severely limited by a virtual

87. For the most recent discussion of this problem, see J. Falter, "The National-Socialist Mobilization of New Voters: 1928–1933," in T. Childers, ed., *The Formation of the Nazi Constituency, 1919–1933* (London, 1986), pp. 202–31. On the electoral fortunes of the two liberal parties, see Jones, *Liberalism*, pp. 386–88.

88. For an indication of Young German dissatisfaction with the situation within the DStP, see the bulletin from the Young German leadership to the leaders of the VNR, 16 August 1930, BA: NS 26/875. See also E. Eggeling, *Partei oder Bewegung? Der jungdeutsche Kampf und die Staatspartei* (Berlin, 1930), pp. 12–33. The most detailed source on the Young German secession is the lengthy memorandum prepared by W. Jänicke for the period from 17 September to 9 October 1930, BA: NL Jänicke, 56. For further details, see Jones, *Liberalism*, pp. 388–91.

89. See the postscript to Stolper's letter to Landahl, 16 September 1930, BA: NL Stolper, 44.

90. Eggeling, *Partei oder Bewegung?*, pp. 24–26. For further details, see Mahraun to Koch-Weser, 3 October 1930, BA: NL Koch-Weser, 107/49–50, as well as Mahraun's circular to the leaders of the VNR and Young German Order, 3 October 1930, and his remarks before the VNR executive committee, 17 October 1930, both in BA: NS 26/875.

rebellion that had erupted within the Order against the alliance with the DDP.[91] The impending crisis drew to a climax in the first week of October 1930 when the Young Germans announced their secession from the State Party with a bitter attack against Höpker-Aschoff and his associates for having betrayed the spirit in which the DStP had been founded.[92] With this turn of events, the attempt of Germany's liberal leadership to bridge the gap between party and Bund all but ended in failure. What had begun as a bold experiment on the part of Koch-Weser and the DDP party leadership to infuse new life into the German liberal movement and to fuse the "state-supporting" elements of the German bourgeoisie into a united phalanx capable of keeping it from falling under the seductive sway of National Socialism had degenerated into a bitter embarrassment for both them and the Young Germans.

The Young German secession from the German State Party in the fall of 1930 represented a critical episode in the failure of liberal efforts to attract the support of the younger generation for several reasons. In the first place, the leaders of the Young German Order had been severely chastened by the way in which their venture into the realm of German party politics had turned out, and they gradually retreated back into the murky world of antisystem politics from which the Order had originally emerged. At the same time, those Democrats like Koch-Weser and Lemmer who had thrown the full weight of their political reputations behind the alliance with the Young Germans found themselves targets of a vicious counterattack that in Koch-Weser's case resulted in the resignation of his Reichstag mandate and in the end of his political career.[93] Third, the young liberals who had supported the State Party so enthusiastically at the time of its founding in summer 1930 were embittered by the collapse of negotiations between the Democrats and Young Germans and were on the verge of bolting from the party themselves before the leaders of the DStP regained their confi-

91. For an indication of this, see "Kurzer Entwurf eines Vortrages, der nach Bedarf in jeder Weise erweitert werden kann," n.d., BA: R 161/17, as well as the protocol of the Twenty-Seventh High Chapter of the Young German Order, 12 December 1930, BA: R 161/12.

92. Eggeling, *Partei oder Bewegung?*, pp. 26–27.

93. Lemmer to Kluthe, 15 October 1930, BA: NL Kluthe, 12/46–47. On the circumstances of Koch-Weser's resignation, see his letter to Schmiedmantel, 11 October 1930, BA: NL Schücking, 50.

dence by offering Winschuh the parliamentary seat that Koch-Weser's resignation had left vacant.[94] By the same token, the unity of the Young Democratic movement had been severely damaged by the role that Lemmer and the organization's national leadership had played in the founding of the DStP. Not only did Lüth and the movement's supporters in Hamburg, Nuremberg, and Berlin-Brandenburg join disgruntled spokesmen for the DDP's left wing in founding the Radical Democratic Party (Radikaldemokratische Partei or RDP) in November 1930,[95] but the DStP's efforts to organize what still remained of the Young Democratic movement in the National League of State Party Youth (Reichsbund staatsparteilicher Jugend) met with strong reservations from erstwhile Young Democrats who harbored an abiding distrust of the new party.[96] By the summer of 1932 Young Democratic disenchantment with the DStP had become so widespread that many of the movement's most prominent leaders refused to support it in the Reichstag elections that had been set for 31 July.[97]

If anything, the feud over the State Party only exacerbated the divisions that already existed within the ranks of Germany's liberal youth and lent new credence to the arguments of those within the German youth movement who insisted that the existing party system was incapable of regeneration. The situation was only slightly better in the German People's Party, where relations between the RjV and the DVP youth cadre – renamed the Hindenburg League-Youth Cadre of the German People's Party (Hindenburgbund-Jugendgruppen der Deutschen Volkspartei) in the summer of 1929[98] – had been severely strained by the RjV's agitation for a realignment of the German

94. In this respect, see Winschuh's statement before the Cologne February Club, 25 October 1930, BA: NL Sieling (Kleine Erwerbung 484), 2, as well as his letter to Dingeldey, October 1930, BA: NL Dingeldey, 39/1.

95. For an indication of Young Democratic support for the RDP, see O. Stündt, "Die neue Linke greift an! Zum Gründungsparteitag der Radikaldemokratischen Partei in Kassel," *Das Echo der jungen Demokratie* 12, nos. 11/12 (November–December 1930): 161–64. For a brief history of the RDP, see B. Gutleben, "Radikaldemokratische Partei – Aufrechte Liberale ohne Erfolg," *Liberal* 28 (1986): 65–75.

96. For example, see Kluthe to Jaeger, 4 December 1930, BA: NL Kluthe, 11/14. See also Kluthe, "Was erwartet die Jungdemokratie von Hannover," [November 1930], BA: NL Kluthe, 44/132–34.

97. Kluthe to Lemmer, 22 June 1932, BA: NL Kluthe, 12/50.

98. *Berliner Stimmen: Zeitschrift für Politik* 6, no. 25 (22 June 1929): 2–3.

party system and the defection of the left wing of the young liberal movement to the DStP.[99] This, however, was only one aspect of the bitter internal crisis that erupted within the DVP following its defeat in the 1930 Reichstag elections and that was temporarily resolved with the election of a new party chairman, Eduard Dingeldey, in December 1930. The new party chairman had long supported the efforts to create a more meaningful role for the younger generation in the affairs of the party,[100] and his election as party leader was greeted enthusiastically by Glatzel and the leaders of the RjV.[101] But the hopes with which Glatzel and his associates had greeted Dingeldey's election to the party chairmanship failed to materialize. For in the final analysis Dingeldey was never able to establish his independence from the business interests that dominated the right wing of the party and soon embarked on a political course that drove a deep wedge between it and the RjV. Glatzel was an outspoken critic of Dingeldey's decision to break with the Brüning cabinet in October 1931,[102] and in February 1932 only ill health kept him from a breach of party discipline that almost certainly would have resulted in his expulsion from the DVP.[103]

The DVP's sharp swing to the right in the second half of 1931 and the conflict that this produced within the party leadership was accompanied by the emergence of a sharp split within DVP's youth and student organizations. For the most part, the leaders of the Hindenburg League stood on the right wing of the DVP and not only supported Dingeldey's decision to break with the Brüning government in the fall of 1931 but also hoped that

99. In this respect, see Hintzmann to Klingspor, 23 October 1930, HStA Düsseldorf, NL Klingspor, 4–III/34–36, as well as the report by Hintzmann in Führer-Brief no. 4, 26 January 1931, BA: NL Dingeldey, 54/9.

100. E. Dingeldey, "Jugend und Partei," *Frankfurter Nachrichten*, 31 March 1929, no. 90.

101. For example, see Glatzel to Dingeldey, 12 December 1930, BA: NL Dingeldey, 53/46–47, and 23 April 1931, BA: NL Dingeldey, 53/71–72, as well as F. Glatzel, "Um die Zukunft der Partei," *Die Reichsgemeinschaft: Blätter der "Reichsgemeinschaft junger Volksparteiler"* 1, nos. 5/6 (December 1930): 1–3. See also Glatzel's remarks at a meeting of the national leadership of the Hindenburg League, 19 April 1931, HStA Düsseldorf, NL Klingspor, 5/232–33.

102. For further details, see RjV Rundschreiben no. 10, 14 October 1931, StA Braunschweig, GX6/612, as well as F. Glatzel, "Selbstbehauptung oder Selbstpreisgabe?" *Die Reichsgemeinschaft* 2, nos. 17/18 (November 1931): 1–4.

103. *Kölnische Zeitung*, 27 February 1932, no. 114. See also Glatzel to Dingeldey, 3 March 1932, BA: NL Dingeldey, 53/169–70. For further details, see Jones, *Liberalism*, p. 441.

this would prepare the way for the establishment of closer ties with the forces of the so-called national opposition.[104] When Glatzel and five other DVP deputies broke with Dingeldey and the rest of the Reichstag delegation in supporting the chancellor in his showdown with the radical Right in October 1931, Ernst Hintzmann and the leaders of the Hindenburg League demanded that the DVP party chairman take disciplinary action against the renegade deputies and worked vigorously behind the scenes to undercut Glatzel's position as leader of the RjV.[105] Although Glatzel was absent from the Reichstag when this scenario repeated itself the following February, he continued to lend moral support in *Die Reichsgemeinschaft*, the RjV's official organ, to those DVP Reichstag deputies who had voted with the government even after they had been expelled from the party.[106] By this time, however, Dingeldey's supporters within the RjV had become so exasperated by Glatzel's repeated breaches of party discipline that at a meeting of the RjV leadership in Hanover on 20 March 1932 they tried to gain control of the organization. When this failed, the RjV delegates from Hesse-Darmstadt, Saxony, North-Westphalia, and Württemberg announced that they and their supporters were seceding from the organization.[107] Similar developments were afoot in the DVP's student organization, where efforts by the party's national leadership to suppress dissension and criticism of Dingeldey's political course led Friedrich Kruspi to resign as chairman of the DVP's National Committee of University Groups at the beginning of April 1932.[108] This in turn set the scene for the final break that came the following July when Glatzel, along with several other prominent DVP parliamentarians, seceded from the DVP

104. In this respect, see Klingspor to Hembeck, 22 July 1931, HStA Düsseldorf, NL Klingspor, 5, and Klingspor to Dingeldey, 12 October 1931, HStA Düsseldorf, NL Klingspor, 6–I, as well as the exchange of letters between Klingspor and Hintzmann, 5–7 October 1931, HStA Düsseldorf, NL Klingspor, 6–I/179–81.

105. Klingspor to Dingeldey, 20 November 1931, HStA Düsseldorf, NL Klingspor, 6–I/173–74.

106. F. Glatzel, "Der Sieg der staatspolitischen Front," *Die Reichsgemeinschaft* 3, nos. 3/4 (15 March 1932): 1–2.

107. For further details, see the protocol of the RjV delegate conference in Hanover, 20 March 1932, StA Braunschweig, GX6/613, as well as Wellmann to Dingeldey, 24 March 1932, BA: NL Dingeldey, 94.

108. For further details, see the correspondence between Kruspi and Dingeldey, 29 March–11 April 1932, BA: NL Dingeldey, 77/9–16.

in protest against the alliance that Dingeldey had concluded with the DNVP's Alfred Hugenberg for the upcoming Reichstag elections.[109]

Glatzel's resignation from the DVP in the summer of 1932 came as the last in a series of resignations that had completely decimated the left wing of the party. Yet as devastating as these developments were to the DVP's hopes of securing a break-through into the ranks of the more progressive and reform-minded elements of Germany's younger generation, they were almost immediately eclipsed by an even more sensational, if not scandalous, turn of events on the DVP's right wing. Ever since Dingeldey's break with the Brüning government in the fall of 1931, the leaders of the party's right wing had been pressuring the DVP party chairman into the establishment of closer political and organizational ties with the right-wing DNVP. This campaign, which received strong support from the Westphalian Stahlhelm, reached a dramatic climax in late February 1932 when the entire DVP district organization in South-Westphalia seceded from the DVP and defected to the DNVP. Among those who figured prominently in the secession was Hermann Kling-spor, the South-Westphalian district chairman of the Hindenburg Youth League who announced his resignation from the party on 11 March.[110] The furor over this scandal, which came just as the DVP was preparing for the state and local elections that had been scheduled to take place throughout much of the country on 24 April, had hardly died down when Ernst Hintzmann, the national chairman of the Hindenburg Youth League, announced his resignation from the DVP and all party offices just three days before the election.[111] Like Klingspor before him, Hintzmann also joined the DNVP, where the two former DVP youth leaders founded the German Youth League (Deutscher Jugendbund) in an effort to integrate those elements of the younger generation that had formerly belonged to the now defunct middle parties into the front of national regeneration that was beginning to

---

109. Glatzel to Dingeldey, 6 July 1932, BA: NL Dingeldey, 53/199–201.
110. For Klingspor's role in these developments, see his letters to Dingeldey, 8 and 27 February 1932, BA: NL Dingeldey, 46/64–66, 84–85, as well as the correspondence between Klingspor and Hintzmann, 3–17 March 1932, HStA Düsseldorf, NL Klingspor, 6–I/51–52, 125–26, and 132–33.
111. Hintzmann to Dingeldey, 21 April 1932, BA: NL Dingeldey, 122/39–43.

take shape on the German Right.[112]

By the summer of 1932 neither the German State Party nor the German People's Party could claim the loyalty of more than an infinitesimal fraction of those who belonged to the younger generation. To the growing dismay of Germany's liberal leadership, however, the alienation of the younger generation from the symbols and institutions of Weimar democracy no longer manifested itself in an aloofness from the very notion of partisan political activity but in active and in some cases enthusiastic support for the goals and ideals of National Socialism. Indeed, the enthusiasm with which the younger generation began to embrace the struggle against the Weimar system was reminiscent of the way in which the younger generation had responded to the call to arms in August 1914 and elicited surprise, if not astonishment, from the leaders of the German youth movement itself.[113] How, then, was the NSDAP was so successful in mobilizing the support of the younger generation whereas all of Germany's more moderate parties, including the two liberal parties, had failed? The answer to this question lies not merely in the profound change that had taken place in the material situation of the younger generation as a result of the Great Depression[114] or in the effectiveness of the student and youth organizations that the NSDAP had created as a way of attracting support from these sectors of the German population.[115] These factors would not have been decisive in and of themselves had it not also been for the fact that in the eyes of the younger generation all of Germany's more established political parties had become so thoroughly compromised by their identification with special economic interests that none of them offered any

112. Deutscher Jugendbund Westfalen-Süd, circular no. 1, 23 March 1932, HStA Düsseldorf, NL Klingspor, 6–I/48. For the organization's objectives, see H. Klingspor, "Sinn und Ziel nationalpolitischer Jugendarbeit," in Rundbrief des Deutschen Jugendbundes Westfalen-Süd, no. 3, April 1932, HStA Düsseldorf, NL Klingspor, 6–I/18–20.

113. For example, see W. Flirner, "Die Jugend im Kampf um Deutschland," *Das junge Deutschland: Amtliches Organ des Reichsausschusses der deutschen Jugendverbände* 27, no. 1 (January 1933): 1–11.

114. Götz von Olenhusen, "Krise und Aufstieg," pp. 61–65.

115. For further details, see P. Stachura, *Nazi Youth in the Weimar Republic* (Santa Barbara and Oxford, 1975), pp. 21–42, as well as M. Steinberg, *Sabers and Brown Shirts: The German Students' Path to National Socialism, 1918–1935* (Chicago, 1973), pp. 72–130, and G. Giles, *Students and National Socialism in Germany* (Cambridge, 1985), pp. 44–100.

hope for a solution to the crisis in which Germany found itself mired. When the younger generation began to lend its voice to the cacaphony of protest against the way in which the existing political system had consistently frustrated the formation of a genuine national consensus, this represented a dramatic intensification of the legitimacy crisis that had plagued the Weimar party system since the middle of the 1920s. For just as the legitimacy of the Weimar party system had been severely compromised by the ascendancy of organized economic interests and the emergence of middle-class splinter parties that placed special economic interests before the welfare of the nation as a whole, so was the younger generation now challenging the legitimacy of a system whose increasing fragmentation along lines of economic self-interest severely undermined its ability to define and articulate Germany's national interest.

While the revolt of the younger generation represented a crucial episode in the social and political dissolution of the German bourgeoisie that had been taking place ever since the last years of the Second Empire,[116] it would be misleading to suggest that the fate of German liberalism in the Weimar Republic was simply a consequence of patterns of political behavior that were already well established in the prewar period. This argument is fallacious for two reasons. Not only does it assign too great a significance to the role of continuity in explaining the failure of Weimar liberalism, but it also tends to overlook the extent to which the alienation of the younger generation – and particularly the intensity of that alienation – was directly related to the general course of social, political, and economic development during the Weimar Republic. In this respect the younger generation found itself caught at the juncture of two closely related impulses. In the first place, the series of national humiliations that Germany had suffered with the ratification of the Versailles Peace Treaty, the imposition of the London Ultimatum, the allied partition of Upper Silesia, and the Franco-Belgian occupation of the Ruhr had done much both to intensify the degree of national feeling that already existed within the ranks of the younger generation and to create a sense of national urgency that was to persist well after Germany had begun to

---

116. In this respect, see H. Mommsen, "Die Auflösung des Bürgertums seit dem späten 19. Jahrhundert," in J. Kocka, ed., *Bürger und Bürgerlichkeit im 19. Jahrhundert* (Göttingen, 1987), pp. 288–315.

recover from the ravages of the great inflation. At the same time, the increasing fragmentation of the Weimar party system and the increasingly prominent role that organized economic interests had come to play in German public life seemed to vindicate the skepticism of those who had always maintained that the existing political system was inimical to Germany's national welfare. The Young German Order's crusade against "partyism," the young liberal movement's agitation for a reform and rejuvenation of the German party system, and the Young Democratic campaign against the idea of a united bourgeois party were all facets of a concerted effort on the part of the younger generation to free the German party system from the tyranny of outside economic interests and to rebaptize it in the spirit of the younger generation. Not only were liberal politicians like Stresemann, Koch-Weser, and the DStP's Hermann Dietrich sympathetic to this sort of sentiment, but they also hoped that it could be harnessed to the banner of political liberalism. But as the ignominious fate of the German State Party and the outcome of the September 1930 Reichstag elections so clearly revealed, it was not German liberalism but the NSDAP that ultimately succeeded in galvanizing the antisystem sentiment of the younger generation into a national crusade against the very system of which the German liberal parties were such a conspicuous part.

12
Languages of Liberalism
Liberal Political Discourse in the Weimar Republic

Thomas Childers

The product of a lost war and a curious, stunted revolution, the Weimar Republic was born with a severe crisis of legitimacy from which it never really recovered. From the very outset of its brief, troubled existence in November 1918 to its demise with Hitler's appointment as chancellor in January 1933, the republic was besieged by opponents from the traditional conservative right, the radical left, and the fascist fringe. It knew no period of normalcy, not even in the so-called golden years of 1924–28, but staggered through a series of intense economic and political crises that would steadily erode its tenuous legitimacy and render its very existence increasingly problematic. The republic found no formula for consensus, even on the basic rules of political conflict, and its history is a story of unremitting ideological struggle that found expression in a clash of competing symbols, rituals, and languages.[1]

Among the enormous challenges confronting the new republic, not the least was the pressing need to fashion a new democratic political culture. This obviously entailed more than drafting and promulgating a constitution. The new democratic regime had to invent its own traditions, develop its own rituals, find its own political and social vocabulary. So, too, did its opponents, and, as a consequence, the political culture of the Weimar Republic quickly became a battleground of competing political symbols and languages. The two liberal parties of the

1. Studies of the Weimar Republic abound, but two strikingly creative and important recent additions to the literature deserve particular attention: D.J.K. Peukert, *Die Weimarer Republik: Krisenjahre der klassischen Moderne* (Frankfurt, 1987); and H. Mommsen, *Die verspielte Freiheit: Der Weg der Republik von Weimar in den Untergang, 1918–1933* (Munich, 1989).

period, the German Democratic Party (Deutsche Demokratische Partei or DDP) and the German People's Party (Deutsche Volkspartei or DVP), played central and highly revealing roles in that struggle.

Thanks to the research of recent years, we now know a great deal about the internal organization, tactics, policies, constituencies, and leading personalities of all the major Weimar parties.[2] Yet, despite this imposing research, we know surprisingly little about how those parties, including the liberal ones, actually constructed their public identities, targeted their constituencies, or formulated their appeals. What did they seek to convey to the German public, and how did they represent it, with what language and with what imagery? These are crucial issues in the analysis of political mobilization, and yet historians of the Weimar period, in contrast, for example, to historians of the French Revolution, have been surprisingly slow in turning their attention to them.[3]

All parties – in the Weimar Republic and in other contexts – formulate their positions on issues in a series of self-defining linguistic stances that distinguish them from their competitors. They use that language to evoke a distinct set of associations, to lay claim to certain historical lineages or to break with them, and to establish their ideological identity within a political landscape. Parties construct not only a set of issue-oriented policies but a rhetorical framework, a linguistic context in which they present and interpret the social and political environment. That semiotic structure, the political vocabulary, imagery, and allusions, is inextricably intertwined with their substantive policy positions and in some instances may acquire even great salience and significance. Political language may not always reflect "objective" social or political reality, but it does play a major role in shaping social and political perceptions. Thus, if we are to understand the formation of political consciousness and the

2. Of particular relevance to this discussion is L.E. Jones, *German Liberalism and the Dissolution of the Weimar Party System, 1918–1933* (Chapel Hill, 1988), which should serve as a model of how political history informed by social and economic analysis can be written.

3. See, for example, F. Furet, *Penser la Révolution française* (Paris, 1978); L. Hunt, *Politics, Culture, and Class in the French Revolution* (Berkeley, 1984); M. Ozouf, *Festivals and the French Revolution* (Cambridge, Mass.,1988); H.U. Gumbrecht, *Funktionen parlamentarischer Rhetorik in der Französischen Revolution* (Munich, 1987).

internal mechanisms of political mobilization, political language – or, more to the point, language*s* – must be systematically examined.

This essay, then, seeks to provide a point of departure for the examination of political language in the Weimar Republic. It is not intended to be an exhaustive analysis but rather to offer a set of introductory observations on the languages of liberalism and to suggest the considerable possibilities to be derived from a more systematic examination of the language of all the Weimar parties. Making liberalism the focal point of such an exercise recommends itself not only because both the DDP and DVP played important roles in the politics of the period but also because the tension between the two provides a particularly revealing glimpse into the problematics of generating a democratic political culture in the Weimar context. The history of the two liberal parties, their early successes and their gradual though relentless slide after 1920, is by now a familiar story in the scholarship and can be recounted here only in very condensed form.

Both liberal parties were founded in the midst of the revolution of 1918 as heirs to the liberal parties of imperial Germany. The DVP was essentially a successor organization to the old National Liberal Party, which had enthusiastically supported the imperial government's annexationist war aims, while the DDP was drawn primarily from circles close to the old Progressive Party. The latter had joined with the Social Democrats and German Center Party (Deutsche Zentrumspartei) to sponsor the ill-fated Reichstag Peace Resolution of 1917, and that coalition would reemerge in 1919 to form the so-called Weimar Coalition that would dominate the National Assembly and draft the constitution of the new republic. Despite efforts to form a united liberal party, a plan that would be revived at several points during the ensuing fourteen years, no merger was forthcoming, and in 1918 the two liberal parties entered the brave new world of republican Germany as bitter foes.[4]

Their similarities were many. Both the DVP and DDP endorsed a traditional liberal agenda on many issues, including

---

4. See Jones, *German Liberalism*, pp. 15–29 and 309–91; and L. Albertin, *Liberalismus und Demokratie am Anfang der Weimarer Republik: Eine vergleichende Analyse der Deutschen Demokratischen Partei und der Deutschen Volkspartei* (Düsseldorf, 1972).

the establishment of basic civil rights, the separation of church and state, the preservation of private property and the free enterprise system, careers open to talent (*freie Bahn dem Tüchtigen*), freedom of conscience, equality before the law, and the civil emancipation of women. In addition, each claimed to be a "people's party" capable of speaking for the nation, while at the same time pledging to protect the middle classes from the perils of socialism.[5] Yet major differences separated the two liberal parties, and those differences were reflected not only in the specifics of conflicting policy positions but in their fundamentally different approaches to the crucial problem of shaping a democratic political culture for the embattled Weimar Republic.

Among the bourgeois parties of the republic, only the DDP sought to construct a new language of democratic participation, a distinct political terminology for the new republic. Unlike the DVP, which condemned the revolution, lamented the loss of the monarchy, rejected the Weimar Constitution, and remained ambivalent about the new democratic order, the DDP rightly claimed to be "the first bourgeois party to place itself on the ground of the new realities created by the revolution." The conservative German National People's Party (Deutschnationale Volkspartei or DNVP) was, of course, overtly hostile to the new government, while the middle-class regional and special interest parties were at best ambivalent.[6] The Catholic Center, a charter member of the Weimar Coalition, certainly defended the new republican order in 1919 and thereafter, but its language, the political imagery of its rhetoric, was not focused on the republic as a new political entity but on the rule of law. "Monarchy and republic," the Center characteristically explained in 1920, using a rhetoric typical of its statements "are only forms, for which one can have greater or lesser preference. Above both, however, stands the law." While the party urged the acceptance of democracy, "whether the individual loves it or not," it made little effort to cultivate a new image of the citizen (*Staatsbürger*) of this

5. The founding programs of the DDP and DVP are found in E. Heilfron, ed. *Die deutsche Nationalversammlung im Jahre 1919* (Berlin, 1947), pp. 132–34 and 140–42. For the 1920 platforms see also W. Hartenstein, *Die Anfänge der Deutschen Volkspartei, 1918–1920* (Düsseldorf, 1962), pp. 210–11.

6. See W. Liebe, *Die Deutschnationale Volkspartei, 1918–1924* (Düsseldorf, 1956), and M. Schumacher, *Mittelstandsfront und Republik: Die Wirtschaftspartei – Reichspartei des deutschen Mittelstandes, 1919–1933* (Düsseldorf, 1972).

new democratic order. The Center's determination to defend Catholic interests meant pursuit of a politics of moderation and a defense of the rule of law against extremists of both the left and the right, but it did not translate into a language of democracy.[7]

In contrast to their bourgeois competitors, the DDP's commitment to the new democratic order was strikingly unequivocal. Rather than mourn the passing of the empire, the DDP forthrightly stated its recognition that "the revolution has created new conditions in Germany, that it means a break with the past, the old system. The old is gone beyond recall." During the campaign for the national constitutional assembly in January 1919, the DDP therefore proudly staked its claim to be "the first and as yet only bourgeois party openly and unconditionally to declare itself for the republican form of state."[8] With the passing of the old regime, the founders of the new party declared, "the path to the free people's state [*freier Volksstaat*] is open." In this new critical situation the Democratic Party hoped to mobilize "all those who, standing on the foundation of the republic, . . . do not want to deliver the fate of Germany to the reaction or to Social Democracy alone."[9] The time had come to rally to the "banner of Democracy," the party contended in an appeal to liberal voters. Given the threats to the republic from both left and right, the ambivalence of the DVP was counterproductive, even dangerous, the party asserted. "If the new freedom of the German Republic is to be defended, only a true and genuine democracy can help. Half measures will no longer do." Some former National Liberals had already "recognized the German Republic and declared themselves ready to help defend and develop it on the basis of a democratic weltanschauung,"[10] and the party appealed to others to join the cause as well.

7. The quotations are from "Zentrum und Demokratie," *Germania*, 30 May 1920. The goal of the Center, it was at pains to emphasize, was the creation of a genuine "Christian people's state [*christlicher Volksstaat*]." See, for example, "Anhänger und Freunde der Zentrumspartei," *Germania*, 3 May 1920. See also R. Morsey, *Die Deutsche Zentrumspartei, 1917–1923* (Düsseldorf, 1966).

8. L. Bergsträßer, *Die Deutsche Demokratische Partei und ihr Programm* (Greiswald, [1918]).

9. "Wahlaufruf," in *Allgemeine Werbeflugschriften der Deutschen Demokratischen Partei* (Berlin, 1918).

10. J. Rathje, *Deutsche Volkspartei oder Deutsche Demokratische Partei* (Berlin, 1919), pp. 2–3.

This resolute commitment to the new republican state and the DDP's close association with the Social Democrats quickly came under ferocious attack from the DVP and the parties of the right, all of whom sought to portray the Democrats as traitors to their class. The DDP's response to the attacks of their bourgeois rivals was to reject the inflammatory language of class conflict and to emphasize instead the forging of a new democratic political culture. For the Democrats, one campaign memo stated, the best response to the hostile slogans of their opponents was "the great idea that encompasses our program: 'Through the democratic state [we will achieve] equal rights for every citizen [*Staatsbürger*] and [equal] responsibility in rebuilding of our nation.' We cannot allow the campaign to pass without the attempt to hammer into every head, especially into the minds of the educated, the conviction that the establishment of the authority of the state, demanded by the right, will remain merely empty rhetoric if it is not based on the trust of the great mass of the citizens in their state." The old *Obrigkeitsstaat* of the empire had ultimately collapsed because it had lost the confidence and trust of wider and wider segments of the public. "Establishing the trust of the people . . . in the present state simply cannot be attained," the party warned, "if the democratic content of the present constitution is attacked."[11]

Although the democratic constitution had been drafted as an expression of the will of the majority, Theodor Heuß warned that "the spiritual acceptance and essential recognition of the democratically created republic in Germany is utterly deficient."[12] To fortify public identification with the constitution and the new state, the DDP was anxious to invent republican traditions. Thus, the party proposed the establishment of a "constitution day" to mark the anniversary of that document's promulgation. As a 1920 DDP leaflet put it, "The . . . constitution is the symbol of a people's freedom, its self-reliance, and its freely chosen responsibility of citizenship. . . . All truly free peoples of the earth view the day their constitution went into effect as the highest holiday on which all citizens, regardless of political or religious affiliations, join together in a common

---

11. "Wahlparolen," in *Das Demokratische Deutschland* 2, nos. 15/16 (25 April 1920): 257–61.
12. T. Heúß, *Der demokratische Staat und die Volksgemeinschaft* (Berlin, 1922).

commemoration. The anniversary of the German constitution must be such a day."[13]

A new spirit of democratic participation had to be fostered in Germany, the DDP contended, and from the beginning it struggled to shape a new sense of republican citizenship. Sensitive to charges from the right that it was insufficiently "national" in its orientation and that parliamentary democracy merely weakened the German state, the party labored to link its vision of democratic citizenship with a new national consciousness, a new *Staatsbewußtsein*. Far from weakening the country, the DDP argued, democracy was essential for Germany's future. Indeed, it was "the tragic fate of the German people that democratization and parliamentarization were not introduced . . . before the war." The catastrophes of the old regime might have been avoided, the party suggested, "if Germany had turned to democracy in time." In the country's grim postwar situation, the Democrats acknowledged, "we need a . . . strong national sentiment and a firm sense of state," but "both . . .," the DDP was confident, "will be strengthened by democracy. When the people . . . have influence over the course of their fate, when the individual citizen recognizes himself as a part of the state and as responsible for the state, his national feeling and his identification with the state will be strengthened."[14]

Democracy was not simply a form of government. "When we speak of democracy most people think only of a particular form of state . . . ," Anton Erkelenz explained, "a parliamentary regime with free suffrage and a few related things. For many the content of democracy is exhausted with this." As a consequence, its critics spoke of "formal democracy," which they maintained had "no deeper content." This was in part a linguistic problem, Erkelenz believed, since the German language, "otherwise so rich in words and concepts, is unfortunately rather poor in regard to politics." The language had "only one and the same word for the form of state and for the greater all-embracing social concept (*Gesellschaftsauffassung*) that stands behind it, namely 'democracy.'" Yet democracy, Erkelenz and the DDP maintained, was not simply a *Staatsform* but "a belief,

---

13. "Zum Jahrestag der Deutschen Reichsverfassung," DDP leaflet, 1920, in NSDAP Hauptarchiv (hereafter HA), reel 38, folder 756.

14. L. Haas, "Demokratie und Parteiwesen," Leitartikel für die Demokratische Werbewoche 26. März bis 2. April 1922, in HA/38/753.

an all-encompassing conception of society, a weltanschauung." It reflected the historic struggle to transcend classical elitist liberalism and "embrace the entire people, all citizens." That struggle had produced a form of state, the republic, that was no longer based on class domination but on "a free citizenry [*Freibürgerschaft*]" that shares "all influence and power" as well as "responsibility and duty." Under democracy, the party was at pains to emphasize, "the state no longer stands above the people and against the people but the people are the state."[15]

The German public, however, had to be taught to look beyond the terms, beyond the forms, to the essence of democracy. This would require great determination and commitment, Erkelenz felt, since "we have all grown up, have been educated, schooled, in a state that was still half feudal." The average citizen still did not fully comprehend that "his relationship to the democratic state is different from his relationship to the superficiality of Wilhelmine constitutionalism. Millions still do not understand that when they attack democracy, they are merely attacking themselves. The form of the democratic state is there, but we must still grow into it, must learn to absorb its content, its spirit, must learn to imbibe it like mother's milk." This was to be the great historic task of the DDP.[16]

To anxious members of the *Bürgertum*, worried by the powerful position of the SPD in the new Weimar state, the DDP endeavored to explain that creating a democratic people's state (*Volksstaat*) from the revolution of 1918 required cooperation with the German Social Democratic Party (Sozialdemokratische Partei Deutschlands or SPD). "In revolutionary times," the party explained, "one must take a clear, unequivocal stand. Whether for authoritarianism or majority rule, whether for monarchy or republic, whether *Beamtenstaat* [bureaucratic state] or *Volksstaat* [– all these] were and are questions that can only be answered with a yes or no." Only after one had taken a firm stand for one principle or the other, could one then make accommodations and compromises on specific issues. With the revolution and the abdication of the Kaiser and the other German monarchs, it had become an absolute necessity to work with the SPD. "Only in

15. A. Erkelenz, "Ideale der Demokratie," Leitartikel für die Demokratische Werbewoche 26. März bis 2. April 1922, in HA/38/753.
16. Ibid.

this way was it possible to educate the revolutionary elements [of that party] to practical work for the good of whole," the DDP explained, "only in this way could the great cleavage between Social Democracy and bourgeois elements that for decades has been a source of misfortune for the fatherland be bridged."[17]

The middle class, on the other hand, had to be convinced that Social Democracy was not its implacable enemy. It had to distinguish between the SPD's radical rhetoric of class struggle and its revisionist, pragmatic policies. "To cure the *Bürgertum* of this foolish worry" had been the great historic challenge to the old liberal parties, and they had failed miserably. The DVP, not to mention the other bourgeois parties, had learned nothing, the Democrats suggested,[18] but the DDP, despite the pernicious attacks of their bourgeois rivals, would continue to strive for productive cooperation with representatives of the working class so as to maintain domestic unity and broaden the definition of true democracy.[19]

From the very outset of its existence, the German People's Party had refused to join the DDP in efforts to construct a democratic political culture for the new republic. While its rhetoric was less inflammatory than that of the conservative DNVP, the People's Party initially condemned the new regime in both form and content. In its official platform of 1919 the party acknowledged the people's right to choose but made clear its strong preference for monarchy as the "form of state most consistent with the history and mentality of the German people." If the *Kaiserreich* could not be salvaged – and the DVP realistically knew that it could not – the party continued to cling to whatever symbolic vestiges of the old empire it could. The party, therefore, joined the DNVP in demanding "the restoration of the glorious red, black, and white colors of the Reich" and denounced the most prominent symbol of the new regime, the black, red, and gold flag of the republic.[20]

17. B. Marwitz, *Deutsche Demokratie und nationaler Liberalismus*, Schriftenfolge: Deutsch-demokratische Ziele, Heft 6 (Berlin, 1919).

18. Ibid.

19. E. David, "Koalition und Wahlkampf," in *Warum brauchen wir eine Regierung der Mitte?* (Berlin, 1920), pp. 3–6.

20. Reichsgeschäftsstelle der Deutschen Volkspartei, ed., *Grundsätze der Deutschen Volkspartei: Beschlossen auf dem Parteitag in Leipzig am 19. Oktober 1919* (Berlin, 1931).

The DVP viewed the collapse of the monarchy and the revolution as tragedies of colossal proportions, and the party's interpretation of both occupied a very prominent position in the early self-definition of DVP. Responding to a May Day poster depicting a common man freeing himself from chains and stepping across "broken crowns and swords into the sunlight of freedom," a prominent DVP politican commented in typical language that "the day on which the crowns and the sword were broken was not a day of joy for us but a day that marked the beginning of deepest degradation for our people, a day of disgrace and shame." The parties of the so-called Weimar Coalition – the Social Democrats, the Center, and the DDP – were held responsible for "the collapse of domestic solidarity" during the war and hence Germany's defeat. [21] The colors of the new republic were their colors, and, despite their appearance in the wars of liberation against Napoleon and in the revolution of 1848, the DVP condemned them as symbolic of internationalist forces "that already in Bismarck's day opposed the Reich." The new colors represented "the international efforts of the Zentrum [Black], which placed the world domination of the papacy above the Reich, international Social Democracy [Red], and international *Großkapital* [Gold], whose interests were represented by circles of the *Berliner Tageblatt*," a thinly veiled anti-Semitic reference to the newspaper's Jewish ownership. "The black, white, and red flag," on the other hand, was "the symbol of the German character [*deutsches Wesen*]," the DVP asserted, and "we therefore want to hold onto it."[22]

Despite these sentiments, the DVP was prepared to recognize "prevailing circumstances" and had neither the desire nor the ability to "hold back the wheel of history."[23] In early 1919 Stresemann denied that the DVP wished to be "the standard-bearer of a monarchist countermovement" but justified the party's acceptance of the new republic on pragmatic grounds alone. "The way to greater Germany (*Großdeutschland*)," a refer-

---

21. General Secretary Koester, *Gegen den schwarz-rot-goldenen Block: Vorträge für politische Ausbildungskurse der Deutschen Volkspartei: Ein Nachschlagebuch für den Wahlkampf* (Dortmund, 1920).

22. P.G. Reinhardt, *Die Deutsche Volkspartei und ihre Ziele: Vortrag gehalten am 27. Mai 1919 in der Aula des Nikolaigymnasiums in Leipzig vor den Oberklassen der höheren Schulen* (Leipzig, 1919), p. 12.

23. Ibid.

ence to the hoped-for union (*Anschluß*) with Austria, he explained, "and the way to domestic peace can only come on the basis of a republican form of government."[24] The DVP's lack of commitment to the new republic, however, was vividly reflected less than a year later when its leaders quickly accepted the conservative Kapp *Putsch* and in the subsequent Reichstag campaign vigorously condemned the DDP for its support of the general strike that had frustrated the hopes of the coup.[25]

After the elections in 1920, however, the party, under Stresemann's leadership, moved toward constructive participation in the new government. Later that year the DVP entered the cabinet, and in 1923 Stresemann briefly presided over a great coalition government as chancellor. Yet, despite this accommodation with the new system, the party's ambivalence about the republic remained a very prominent feature of its public discourse and its public image. Even in 1924, having already served quite prominently in several cabinets and eagerly seeking to play a role in the formation of a new government coalition, the DVP simply could not bring itself to offer an endorsement of the republic as such. The party's position was one of what Stresemann referred to as "national *Realpolitik*,"[26] and although the term was coined to describe the party's approach to Germany's foreign relations, it applied as well to the DVP's relationship to the republic.

The party's growing involvement in the government was, therefore, by no means portrayed as a commitment to the new democratic order but rather as a defense of that traditional liberal ideal, the *Rechtsstaat*. Although in subsequent years there would be variations on this theme, it would remain the standard rhetorical stratagem employed by the DVP to define the party's relationship to Weimar democracy. This device allowed the DVP to recognize the constitution as the binding basis of law and even participate in the government without, however, offering

---

24. G. Stresemann, "Kaiserreich, Revolution, Wiederaufbau: Rede auf dem Parteitag in Jena, 13.4.1919," in G. Stresemann, *Reden und Schriften: Politik – Geschichte – Literatur, 1897–1926*, edited by R. v. Rheinbaben, 2 vols. (Dresden, 1926), vol. 1, pp. 263–64.

25. See Jones, *German Liberalism*, pp. 62–66.

26. G. Stresemann, *Nationale Realpolitik: Rede auf dem 6. Parteitag der Deutschen Volkspartei in Dortmund am 14. November 1924*, Flugschriften der Deutschen Volkspartei, no. 54 (Berlin, 1924).

any philosophical support or legitimacy to the republican form of state. It was, therefore, quite characteristic of the DVP's self-presentation that it could condemn the revolution that had created the republic while acknowledging that the national assembly that followed had at least provided "a firm legal basis" for a new German state. After all, as one prominent DVP spokesman explained, "liberalism has always been the champion of the modern *Rechtsstaat*, . . . the champion of the constitutional state [*Verfassungsstaat*]."[27] Respect for the law, the party implied, meant respect for the existing constitution and "respect for the constitution," the party stressed, "must be linked to a respect for the state as such."[28]

Support for the *Rechtsstaat*, the constitution, "the state as such," were ideologically consistent constructions of considerable utility for the DVP. Defense of the German state, to which the party was increasingly committed after 1920, could be presented in the party's public pronouncements in such terms without actually endorsing the republic as such. In a "Manifesto of the German People's Party" issued in 1927 to commemorate the sixtieth anniversary of the founding of the National Liberal Party, the DVP typically explained that in deciding to participate in the government "the party had consciously put itself in the service of Germany." It had made its decision "without giving up its basic commitment to the great ideals of the past" – presumably the monarchic form of government – but had come, in what was for the DVP a typical formulation, to place "the welfare of the state above the form of the state [*Staatswohl über die Staatsform*]." The party's "liberal task" was to work with others to save what could be "useful for the salvation and reconstruction of the fatherland."[29]

When the DDP chided Stresemann's party about such ambivalence by warning that the threats from the radical left and right to the new democratic order demanded strong, unequivocal support for the republic, the DVP was not moved to take that step.

27. O. Most, "Der liberale Gedanke in der Deutschen Volkspartei," in Reichsgeschäftsstelle der Deutschen Volkspartei, ed., *Deutscher Liberalismus: Reden der Reichstagsabgeordneten Oberbürgermeister Dr. Most, Geheimrat Prof. D. Dr. Kahl, Reichsminister Dr. Stresemann* (Berlin, 1925), p. 14.

28. See the remarks of W. Kahl, in ibid., pp. 26–27.

29. "Das Manifest der Deutschen Volkspartei," in Reichsgeschäftsstelle der Deutschen Volkspartei, ed., *60 Jahr-Feier der Nationalliberalen Partei am 19. und 20. März 1927 in Hannover* (Berlin, 1927), p. 8.

If the republic was in danger, Stresemann suggested, it was "threatened psychologically the most by those who always have it on their lips and seek to make it a matter of partisan politics."[30] Similarly, efforts by the DDP to drum up support for the republic by generating democratic symbols, rituals, and rhetoric were dismissed contemptuously by the DVP as trivial and self-serving. "A republicanism worn for show is no guarantee of ability and character," the DVP's electoral platform declared during the fall campaign of 1924. "Parades with flags waving divert from the essential and lead to charges of arrogance and incitement. What is needed is not slogans, forms, and decorations. Only work and deeds, an awareness of responsibility and a sense of sacrifice lead to freedom." Far from offering the kind of endorsement of the republic demanded by the DDP, the DVP's platform stated that the party had entered the campaigns "in a battle for the constitutional state and a healthy economy" and concluded with the slogan, "Under the symbol of the old Reich colors, Black, Red, and White, we want to create a new, happy Germany."[31]

Defense of the Weimar state, no matter how philosophically distasteful, was therefore represented as a patriotic obligation for the DVP, and the party's service to Germany, the fatherland, and the nation rather than to the republic remained the central way of explaining the DVP's relationship with the new state. In Germany, the DVP explained, too many people had come to view the state not as *their* state but as one that served the special interests of others. Conditions in the new republic had merely exacerbated that prevalent attitude, and the great challenge confronting liberalism was therefore to restore the faith of the German people in the ideal of a state that would serve the interests of all. While the other Weimar parties represented specific class, religious, or regional interests, only a genuine people's party (*Volkspartei*) capable of speaking for the nation as a whole could restore confidence in the German state.[32]

The DVP sought to convince the public that it was just such a party. Its speakers and publications relentlessly asserted that

---

30. Stresemann , *National Realpolitik*, p. 23.
31. "Wahlaufruf der Deutschen Volkspartei," *Reichstagshandbuch 1924 III. Wahlperiode* (Berlin, 1925), pp. 139–41.
32. Most, "Der liberale Gedanke," p. 20.

the DVP represented exactly what its name implied, "a party of the entire German people, regardless of occupation [*Beruf*] or estate [*Stand*]."[33] For the DVP, the long-standing cleavages of German political culture could be overcome by only one thing, a commitment to the nation, a commitment embodied in the national liberal traditions of the DVP. It was "love of fatherland" that was missing in the new Germany, "a love of fatherland that sees in one's *Volksgenosse* [people's comrade] above all a brother; a love of fatherland that recognizes as its primary goal the creation of domestic solidarity and not the fomentation of discord that redounds to the advantage and pleasure of those beyond Germany's frontiers."[34] The DVP was uniquely qualified to revive that sense of nation, one of its spokesmen characteristically asserted, for in the construction of the "German People's Party, the emphasis lies on the word 'German.'"[35]

This emphasis on "love of fatherland," on "the national idea" served as the DVP's central conceptual and rhetorical device to transcend class, occupation, religion, and region, and it occupied a prominent position in the political discourse of the party. It was defined in two revealing ways. As a campaign reference booklet for the party's political operatives in 1920 noted, the DVP's "leading idea" was simply "the nation," followed by an espousal of "free activity and development of the individual personality, basically unfettered by state or clerical tutelage or direction."[36] This linkage of the nation to the individual was typical and reveals the key to the party's claim to transcend the basic social cleavages of German political culture. The DVP's "Basic Principles of 1919" phrased the relationship between nation, society, and individual in the following way:

> Since time immemorial the German character [*deutsches Wesen*] consists in striving for the free development of the individual and his

---

33. Reinhardt, *Die Deutsche Volkspartei und ihre Ziele*, p. 10.
34. Most, "Der liberale Gedanke," p. 6.
35. Reinhardt, *Die Deutsche Volkspartei und ihre Ziele*, p. 20.
36. Koester, *Gegen den schwarz-rot-goldenen Block*, p. 40. The DVP's definition of "freedom" was explained in numerous publications and speeches. "Liberalism desires freedom – freedom for the individual personality. Freedom is, for [liberalism], primarily individual freedom. Liberalism seeks, in other words, to create personalities. The value of the individual personality is the highest [principle]. It is the principle of progress." R. von Campe, "Liberalismus – Demokratie – Sozialismus," in *Deutsche Stimmen* 32, no. 22 (30 May 1920): 354.

uniqueness within the framework of a whole people. Cultivating this German character and creating recognition and respect for it in the world are the goals of the German People's Party. The DVP therefore represents the deepening and reconciliation of the liberal and social ideas on the basis of a commitment to the national state. It calls on all spiritual and ethical powers of the German people to cooperate in the inner renewal of *Volksleben* and the state on the basis of equality, earnest fulfillment of duty, and genuine love of fatherland.[37]

The DVP's claim to the status of a people's party thus rested rhetorically on its espousal of the liberal principle of individualism, which it equated with *deutsches Wesen* and hence with the nation. Yet it also operated with another definition of the nation that was very much in evidence in its efforts to mobilize a popular following. While the DDP sought to develop a new democratic definition of German citizenship for the republic, building bridges over the well-established social chasms of German political culture, the DVP from its very inception not only chose the language of classical liberalism, linking the "free personality," the free market, and German nationalism, but also adopted a confrontational language of class that would characterize its public campaigning throughout the Weimar era. Although the DVP tirelessly denied that it represented "the interests of a particular *Stand* [estate]" or that it was, as was often charged, "only a party of so-called heavy industry," it made crystal clear its operative social definition of "the nation." "We believe," the party asserted, "that a strong German *Mittelstand* [middle estate], a free, strong *Bürgertum*, and a robust *Bauernstand* [peasant estate] are the best pillars of the state,"[38] and it organized its campaigns around efforts to mobilize an almost exclusively middle-class electorate. Thus, while claiming to speak for the nation, the DVP eschewed the language of social reconciliation adopted by its liberal rival and sought to define itself on the Weimar political landscape as the stalwart defender of middle-class interests against the radicalism of the left and the class betrayal of the DDP.

The party had presented itself to the electorate in 1919 and 1920 as "the party of the German *Mittelstand*" and as a vociferous

---

37. Koester, *Gegen den schwarz-rot-goldenen Block*, p. 41.
38. Reinhardt, *Die Deutsche Volkspartei und ihre Ziele* p. 20.

opponent of the left.[39] Stresemann himself had set the tone for the party's first Reichstag campaign when he dramatically claimed that the whole of bourgeois culture was at stake. The election was nothing less than "a decision between European culture and Asiatic bolshevism," he asserted, and for that reason he regretted all the more "that the bourgeois left cannot bring itself to fortify the [bourgeois] unity front." Only a few months after the democratic regime was assaulted from the monarchist right in the Kapp *Putsch*, the DVP chose to enter the campaign under the slogan, "The enemy is on the left."[40]

Similarly, in 1924 the DVP campaigned as the champion of bourgeois unity against both the Social Democratic and liberal left. In that year the DVP proclaimed its support for the creation of a *Bürgerblock* coalition that would exclude not only the Social Democrats but also the DDP. The economic recovery of Germany and the slowly returning vitality of *Mittelstand* would be destroyed, the DVP repeatedly warned, "if radicalism and socialism rise to power."[41] The middle-class special interest parties, which had begun to multiply in 1923–24, were also condemned for bringing "confusion into bourgeois camp" and would, the DVP argued, merely "strengthen Social Democracy and weaken the national cause." German domestic recovery and the defense of German interests in international affairs, the DVP contended, could be achieved "only by a true victory of the bourgeois parties, with the exclusion of the Democrats, whose recent behavior can no longer be considered '*bürgerlich*.'"[42] Although the strategic position of the party would change from election to election thereafter, and the DVP would even serve again in a coalition government with the SPD between 1928 and 1930, the campaigns of the DVP were not designed to bridge existing social divisions within German political culture but to extract maximum electoral value from them.

Like its liberal rival, the DDP also claimed to be a genuine people's party and hence to speak for the nation, but its

---

39. See, for example, the 1919 DVP placard, "Die Deutsche Volkspartei: Die Partei des Mittelstandes," as well as the "Aufruf der Deutschen Volkspartei," reproduced in Heilfron, ed., *Die Deutsche Nationalversammlung*, pp. 132–34.

40. Stresemann's speech before the Reichsklub of the DVP, 29 May 1920, is reported in *Tägliche Rundschau*, 30 May 1920.

41. *Berliner Stimmen*, no. 13, 18 November 1924.

42. "Wählt für das Reich," *Berliner Stimmen*, no. 13, 18 November 1924.

language and political focus stood in sharp contrast to the those of the DVP. The founding program of the party had typically proclaimed that "the German Democratic Party is and will remain a true people's party because it does not represent any one-sided class interests."[43] Although such claims were frequently heard in 1919–20, when virtually all the new or reconstituted political parties claimed to be genuine people's parties, the DDP was exceptional in the extent to which the necessity of social reconciliation between the classes served as the focal point of its appeal. "We want to be composed of all strata [*Interessenschichten*] . . ., of all occupations, and therefore we do not represent the special interests of a *Stand* but, as a matter of principle, the reconciliation of the interests of the different *Stände*."[44]

Despite devastating electoral losses in 1920 and 1924,[45] the Democrats nonetheless continued to resist the divisive rhetoric of class conflict that characterized the other major bourgeois parties. "The raison d'être of our party," the DDP insisted in 1924, "is to prevent the disintegration of our people into two great groups. We feel that it is our responsibility to build bridges between segments of the people that otherwise threaten to split apart." In Germany's difficult situation, one prominent Democrat argued, the nation needed neither narrow interest parties nor confrontational class-based parties but "parties . . . that strive to mediate between natural social conflicts." In what was to be a typical DDP formulation, voters in 1924 were therefore urged to think "neither 'socialist' nor '*bürgerlich*' but democratic."[46]

While the other bourgeois parties, from the NSDAP to the DVP, invoked the imagery of "the *Volksgemeinschaft*" or "the nation" in developing a sociopolitical vocabulary that would allow them to transcend class, religion, and region, the DDP labored mightily to forge a new language of democratic citizenship. It

43. *Bergsträßer, Die DDP und ihr Programm.*
44. K. Petersen, *Zum Wahlkampf! Rede gehalten am 24. April 1920 in Görlitz* (Berlin, 1920).
45. See T. Childers, *The Nazi Voter: The Social Foundations of Fascism in Germany, 1919–1933* (Chapel Hill, 1983), pp. 34–64; and Jones, *German Liberalism,* pp. 67–80, 208–22, and 233–37.
46. "Nicht 'bürgerlich' oder 'sozialistisch' sondern demokratisch," *Berliner Tageblatt,* 14 November 1924.

was not the "nation" or the *"Volk"* or the "fatherland" but the citizen, the *"Staatsbürger,"* that formed the leitmotiv in the discourse of the DDP. The DDP had certainly experimented with the language of the *Volksgemeinschaft*, endeavoring after its first great electoral defeat in 1920 to demonstrate that the democratic terminology of the citizen (the *Staatsbürger*) was not inconsistent with that of the "people's comrade" (the *Volksgenosse*). "Whoever respects all German people's comrades equally" and whoever values "the *Volksganze* more than any special interest is in his innermost being a German democrat," one DDP appeal of 1922 explained. "The will to the *Volksgemeinschaft* is the catchword of German democracy."[47]

This terminology never vanished entirely from democratic discourse and, indeed, would acquire new prominence with the transformation of the DDP into the Staatspartei in 1930, but the party was clearly more comfortable speaking the language of citizenship. There was only "one effective remedy against the debilitating effects of the class conflict and political fragmentation," the party maintained in 1928, and that was to be found in genuine democratic citizenship. "There is one task that is more important than all others: we must create a spirit of German citizenship," the DDP asserted. "In the age of universal suffrage for men and women every German is a citizen," it explained. "'Citizen' is the most venerated title of democracy, of the republic. To be a citizen is the highest order. To feel oneself a citizen is the remedy . . . against fragmentation and narrow-mindedness." The DDP was uniquely qualified to lead in crafting that transcendent sense of democratic citizenship – the party relentlessly claimed – as it was "not a class party, not a *Standespartei*, not a caste party, but rather a party of all citizens [*Staatsbürger*]."[48]

Despite the linguistic exertions of both DVP and DDP to represent themselves as genuine people's parties, both sought to mobilize what were in effect almost exclusively middle-class constituencies and were therefore at pains to portray themselves as stalwart defenders of bourgeois interests against the Social

47. "Für Volk und Vaterland!" *Der Deutsch-Demokratische Landesbote*, 26 March 1922. See also "Demokratie, Republik und Volksgemeinschaft," DDP leaflet, 1922, HA/38/75.
48. *Der Demokrat: Mitteilungen aus der Deutschen Demokratischen Partei*, 9, no. 6 (18 March 1928).

Democrats. Although the DVP certainly assumed a more confrontational rhetorical posture in dealing with the left, the DDP was no less determined to condemn Marxism and claim credit for frustrating socialist efforts to expropriate the middle class. Moreover, in the rough and tumble of Weimar electoral politics, neither made more than cursory efforts to address working-class Germans, choosing instead to focuse their attention on the different elements of the *Mittelstand*. These appeals to the middle-class electorate were above all intended to locate the liberal parties along the major line of social cleavage in German politics by establishing their anti-Marxist credentials. The specifics of any issue under debate in the Reichstag was of secondary importance to this essential stratagem.[49]

Establishing their image as the staunch defenders of the beleaguered *Bürgertum* or *Mittelstand* against the Marxist left was, however, merely the first step for the liberal parties in defining themselves for the electorate. The German middle class to which such appeals were routinely made was by no means a social monolith, and the parties of the Weimar era were convinced that the most effective way of identifying and then mobilizing elements of the socially diverse middle-class electorate was to disaggregate the *Bürgertum* on the basis of occupation (*Beruf*). As a consequence, the bourgeois parties directed their appeals not only to the *Mittelstand* or *Bürgertum* as a whole but to highly defined occupational groupings – to shopkeepers, artisans, farmers, civil servants, white-collar employees, all well-organized vocational groups that seemed to convey middle-class status. Despite glaring differences in ideological orientation, all the bourgeois parties, from the NSDAP to the DDP, operated on the same assumption about the centrality of occupation in the formation of social identity in German political culture. Indeed, appeals to such *Berufsgruppen* represented the basic operational approach of all the bourgeois parties to German society throughout the Weimar period.[50]

Although the content of such appeals varied, all the bourgeois parties – and to a surprising extent the Marxist parties as well –

49. For liberal appeals to the various elements of the middle-class electorate see Childers, *The Nazi Voter*, pp. 38–40 and 50–102.

50. The following is developed at greater length in T. Childers, "The Social Language of Politics in Germany: The Sociology of Political Discourse in the Weimar Republic," *American Historical Review* (April 1990).

employed the same categories to disaggregate and target elements of the middle-class electorate. All began, of course, with the omnibus terms *Bürgertum* and *Mittelstand* when addressing the entire middle-class population. Although the two terms were often used interchangeably, the latter was frequently used to refer more specifically to the self-employed, especially to proprietors in handicrafts and retail trade (*Handwerker* and *Gewerbetreibende*) or, in the countryside, to family farmers and peasants (*Landwirte* or *Bauern*). These self-employed proprietors made up what contemporary German sociologists and others referred to as the "old middle class" (*alter Mittelstand*). White-collar employees (*Angestellte*) and civil servants (*Beamte*), two occupational groups that constituted the "new middle class" (*neuer Mittelstand*), were also targeted for recruitment by the bourgeois parties. These occupationally formulated appeals were supplemented by recruitment literature and events aimed at all the major religious and demographic components of German society – Protestants, Catholics, women, youth, and the elderly – but, nevertheless the social language of political mobilization in the Weimar Republic was noticeably dominated by the rhetoric of *Beruf*.[51]

Reflecting the centrality of *Beruf* in the sociology of Weimar politics, all the major parties maintained specialists in their organizations to cultivate support in the major occupational groups. All devoted numerous pamphlets to specific *Berufsgruppen*, held special recruitment campaigns or events for them, and produced a virtual torrent of leaflets elaborating their party's position on various economic and political concerns. The liberal parties were hardly exceptions. The inaugural platforms of the DVP and DDP in 1919 and 1920 contained sections devoted explicitly to peasants, artisans, and merchants, as well as to the white-collar employees and civil servants of the new middle class.[52] Typically, in 1924 the DVP's pamphlet series intended as a tool for use in recruitment activities devoted special issues to the civil service, white-collar employees, farmers, and the commercial *Mittelstand*. Not surprisingly, the DDP's Materialien zur demokratischen Politik issued an almost identical set of pam-

---

51. Ibid.
52. See Reichsgeschäftsstelle der Deutschen Volkspartei, ed., *Grundsätze der DVP*, and Bergsträßer, *Die DDP und ihr Programm*.

phlets in the same year.[53]

Great care was taken by the parties to determine the occupational identity of voters so that occupation-specific appeals could be delivered directly to their doors. A DDP memorandum dealing with tactics for the 1928 Reichstag elections, for example, stressed the importance of "mailing special leaflets . . . aimed at specific occupational strata [*Berufsschichten*] whose addresses" were to be determined "from address books and electoral lists." After dividing the population into categories such as "entrepreneurs, civil servants, *Mittelständler* of all sorts, teachers, etc.," leaflets and other materials dealing with their specific interests and concerns could be sent to them directly. This tactic was of obvious importance, the author of the memorandum concluded, since "the average German . . . is less interested in great political ideas than in the details, trifles, and narrower interests of his own special sphere."[54]

In making this observation, the DDP was merely acknowledging what for the major bourgeois parties was an increasingly problematic reality of Weimar political culture. Between the elections to the national assembly in 1919 and the final predepression Reichstag election in 1928, the DDP, DVP, and DNVP had witnessed a portentious fragmentation of middle-class electoral loyalties that would seriously undermine the stability of the Weimar party system well before the rise of Hitler's NSDAP. That instability was not reflected in a radicalization of the middle-class electorate – the Nazis in 1928 would receive less than 3 percent of the national vote – but in the emergence and proliferation of special-interest, single-issue, and regional parties. Parties such as the Business Party of the German Middle Class (Wirtschaftspartei des Deutschen Mittelstandes or WP), the

53. For the DVP, see *Angestelltenfragen im Reichstag*, Flugschriften der Deutschen Volkspartei, no. 51 (Berlin, 1924); *Mittelstandspolitik der Deutschen Volkspartei*, Flugschriften der Deutschen Volkspartei, no. 55 (Berlin, 1924); *Landwirtschaft und Parteipolitik*, Flugschriften der Deutschen Volkspartei, no. 57 (Berlin, 1924); and *Beamtenpolitik der Deutschen Volkspartei*, Flugschriften der Deutschen Volkspartei, no.58 (Berlin, 1924). For the DDP, see *D.D.P. und Landwirtschaft*, Materialien zur demokratischen Politik, no. 84 (Berlin, 1924); *D.D.P. und gewerblicher Mittelstand*, Materialien zur demokratischen Politik, no. 88 (Berlin, 1924); and *Beamtenfragen*, Materialien zur demokratischen Politik. no. 93 (Berlin, 1924).

54. A. Erkelenz, "Wie gewinnen wir die Reichstagswahlen?" in *Wie retten wir die Deutsche Republik* ([Berlin-Zehlendorf], [1928]), pp. 1–7.

Christian-National Peasants' and Rural People's Party (Christlich-
nationale Bauern- und Landvolkspartei), the German Peasants'
Party (Deutsche Bauernpartei), the Bavarian Peasant and
Middle-Class League (Bayerisher Bauern- und Mittelstands-
bund), the Christian-Social People's Service (Christlich-sozialer
Volksdienst), the Revalorization and Reconstruction Party
(Aufwertungs- und Wiederaufbaupartei), the Tenants' Party
(Mieterpartei), and a host of others sprouted like weeds along
the fringes of middle-class political culture in this period.
Moreover, each viciously attacked the mainstream liberal and
conservative "people's" parties for failing to represent their
specific sectarian interests, and each sought to mobilize different
elements of the middle-class electorate. Although all were ra-
bidly anti-Marxist, most were also vehemently opposed to
"supercapitalism" and espoused some vague notion of a corporatist economic and political order as a solution. Weimar's parliamentary democracy, most felt, was merely a sham, a system
that guaranteed the dominance of both big business and big
labor operating through the major parties.[55]

In 1919 such parties had accounted for a paltry 1.5 percent of
the vote, and they won only 3.7 percent in the first Reichstag
elections a year later. In 1924, however, after a year of almost
surreal hyperinflation and in the midst of a harsh stabilization
crisis, these middle-class alternative parties claimed 8.3 percent
of the national electorate, a figure that surpassed the percentage
won by the fading DDP and almost equalled the DVP's totals.
Equally distressing for the major liberal and conservative parties, the appeal of these *Interessenparteien* did not dissolve during
the period of relative economic and political stability that followed. In the regional elections of the woefully mislabeled
"Golden Twenties" the larger socially complex and ideologically
oriented parties of the bourgeois center and right saw their
constituencies continue to fragment, eroded by a plethora of
Lilliputian parties that rejected their socially integrative aspirations and championed the interests of specific occupational,
economic, and regional groups. In 1928, a year generally viewed
as the apex of Weimar's transient stability, approximately thirty

55. See T. Childers, "Interest and Ideology: Anti-System Politics in the Era of
Stabilization, 1924–1928," in Gerald D. Feldman, ed., *Die Nachwirkungen der
Inflation auf die deutsche Geschichte, 1924–1933* (Munich, 1985), pp. 1–20.

different political parties, the vast majority appealing to one element or another of the fractious *Bürgertum*, participated in the Reichstag elections, and the results vividly reflected the ongoing fragmentation of the middle-class electorate. In this last predepression campaign, the *Interessen-* and *Landesparteien* almost doubled their vote, claiming over 14 percent of the electorate. That total exceeded the combined vote of the DDP and DVP and almost equalled that of the DNVP. On the eve of the Great Depression almost a third of the middle-class electorate had already deserted their traditional political choices for special-interest or radical alternatives.[56]

Confronted with this unmistakable trend, the liberal parties were faced with a strategic dilemma of considerable proportions. Appealing to specific occupational or economic groups was axiomatic, indeed, it was an operational necessity in the political culture of the Weimar Republic, and the liberals had certainly organized much of their political mobilization efforts accordingly. Yet appealing to the narrow sectarian interests of shopkeepers, artisans, peasants, or white-collar employees greatly complicated the efforts of parties such as the DVP and DDP that endeavored to mobilize support across the different occupational and regional interests of the socially heterogeneous middle class. Given the differential impact of the postwar economic traumas of inflation, hyperinflation, and harsh stabilization on the different elements of the *Mittelstand*, finding common ground proved to be a considerable challenge for any party seeking to be a vehicle for middle-class integration.[57] Moreover, the radical system of proportional representation embodied in the Weimar Constitution virtually guaranteed the existence of numerous small parties which, although individually insignificant, were together capable of winning narrow sectarian support and hence weakening the major parties of bourgeois integration.[58] Thus, by 1928 the liberal parties were

56. T. Childers, "Inflation, Stabilization, and Political Realignment in Germany, 1924–1928," in G.D. Feldman, C.L. Holtfrerich, G.A. Ritter, P.C. Witt, eds., *Die deutsche Inflation: Eine Zwischenbilanz* (Berlin, 1982), pp. 409–31.

57. For the impact of the inflation on important elements of the *Mittelstand*, see R.G. Moeller, *German Peasants and Agrarian Politics, 1914–1924: The Rhineland and Westphalia* (Chapel Hill, 1986); A. Kunz, *Civil Servants and the Politics of Inflation in Germany, 1914–1924* (Berlin, 1986); and M.J. Hughes, *Paying for the German Inflation* (Chapel Hill), 1987.

58. Weimar's suffrage law entitled one mandate in the Reichstag for every

finding it increasingly difficult to formulate a credible political language that would allow them to address both sectarian interest and social integration.

Already in 1928 the DDP complained that Weimar was suffering from what it diagnosed as "the German malady." The symptoms of this uniquely Teutonic illness were "the absence of civic spirit [*Bürgergeist*], the absence of the will to power, and fragmentation into small groups and factions." These symptoms were compounded by "class spirit, caste spirit, racial hatred, envy, greed, and self-absorption [*Eigenblöderei*]." The German, the DDP complained, "never sees the complete whole, but only his own little troubles or his own special group." Only in Germany, the party believed, were "all developments in the nation and state judged from the worm's-eye view of the *Stammtisch* instead of according to great national exigencies." The results of this "German malady" were vividly reflected in the Weimar party system, with its wild proliferation of parties. "Everywhere," the DDP noted with bitter irony, "new parties are being founded: business parties, peasants' parties, reformation parties, house and property owners' parties (divided according to those houses with central heating and those without), tenants' parties, disabled veterans' parties, artisans' parties, etc." Soon "every German will have his own party, will be able to produce his own weltanschauung, hold his own meetings, and then finally vote for himself."[59]

The DVP agreed with the diagnosis. Between 1924 and 1930 the DVP tirelessly condemned the middle-class special interest parties and predicted dire consequences if the fragmentation within the bourgeois camp were not halted. It warned middle-class voters that support for bourgeois *Interessenparteien* would only ruin the *Mittelstand* by alienating "the other *Stände*." What was needed, it insisted, was a party that represented not narrow sectarian interests but "all *Stände*."[60] Attacking the Business

---

sixty thousand votes a party received in any one of the country's thirty-five electoral districts and allowed all surplus votes from districts where a party's candidates had been elected to be counted in a national pool. For further details see A. Milatz, *Wähler und Wahlen in der Weimarer Republik* (Bonn, 1965), pp. 41–51.

59. "Zum 18. März 1928," *Der Demokrat* 9, no. 6 (18 March 1928): 157–60, published also in "Die deutsche Krankheit," DDP pamphlet, 1928, HA/38/753.

60. "Der deutsche Mittelstand führt erbitterte Klage," DVP Leaflet, 1928,

Party, the largest of the special interest parties, the DVP scornfully dismissed the "narrowminded promises of this *berufsständische Interessenklique*," and called on middle-class voters to reject fragmentation and think in larger national terms. "It is the larger perspective in both domestic and foreign policy that determine Germany's future," it argued. "Neither the fatherland nor the *Mittelstand* will be served if now, following the lead of the Business Party, [everyone] mobilizes: a tenants' party, a revaluation party, the beggars, the Housing League, the Association for a Free Economy, and finally, if things continue in this vein, the Party of Black-Bread or White-Bread Eaters." Such sectarian obsessions would not, the DVP concluded firmly, save the *Mittelstand*.[61]

Inextricably linked to the problem of bourgeois fragmentation was a serious, if rarely articulated, dilemma for the liberals, a dilemma posed by the very language of middle-class political mobilization itself. In the discourse of all the bourgeois parties the occupational terms that stood at the center of their varied appeals tended to be linked with the corporatist imagery of *Stand*. References to the *Bauernstand*, the *Beamtenstand* (civil service estate), or even the *Angestelltenstand* (white-collar estate) pulse through the appeals of the bourgeois parties, especially – though certainly not exclusively – those on the right. By the late nineteenth century, however, this *ständisch* terminology was already a living anachronism, having clearly survived the passage of the social and economic conditions it had evolved to describe. The *ständisch* society evoked by the terms certainly did not exist during either the Wilhelmine or Weimar eras, and yet this language of estate continued to provide a remarkably powerful idiom for middle-class political culture. The terms thus remained, but their content had undergone considerable change since the genuinely preindustrial age. During the Weimar era, in fact, such language increasingly degenerated into a set of largely negative associations expressed most vividly in an implacable hostility not only to Marxism but to Weimar capitalism and parliamentarianism as well.[62]

Bundesarchiv Koblenz (hereafter BA), Zeitgeschichtliche Sammlung (hereafter ZSg.) 1/42/8(1).

61. "Ein Volltreffer war unser Flugblatt gegen die Zersplitterung," DVP leaflet, 1930, BA, ZSg. 1/42/8(2).

62. See Childers, "The Social Language of Politics."

Though employed by all the bourgeois parties, the language, the social vocabulary of middle-class political discourse itself, was not ideologically neutral. For the conservatives, special interest parties, and ultimately the National Socialists, this *ständisch* terminology was at least roughly consistent with the content of their appeals. Virtually all of the middle-class special interest parties, for example, called for the elimination of Weimar's liberal parliamentary system and capitalist economic order and demanded the creation of some form of *Ständestaat* in which the economic interests of the various *Gewerbestände* would find "representation based on occupational estate [*berufsständische Vertretung*]."[63] The DNVP, too, was at least superficially comfortable with this corporatist imagery and consistently couched its attacks on the Weimar system and the liberal/Social Democratic parties associated with it in the language of estate. For the National Socialists, of course, this *ständisch* vocabulary was used to develop the concept of the *Volksgemeinschaft* and constituted an essential element of their political language.[64]

Although both the DDP and DVP routinely spoke the lingua franca of *Berufsstand*, such language proved highly problematic for them. Neither of the liberal parties could encourage the corporatist economic and political solutions to Weimar's problems proposed by the special-interest, conservative, or fascist right, and their emphasis on the "free, individual personality," parliamentary democracy, or "economic freedom" was quite patently inconsistent with the both the imagery and substance of the *Ständestaat*. Yet no alternative language was available to them, and the efforts of the liberals to formulate one – the DDP's *Staatsbürgertum*, for example – were dismal failures. As the DDP put it in 1930, "We are in danger of seeing the idea of the people [*Volksgedanke*] being overwhelmed by the idea of occupation [*Berufsgedanke*] and the idea of the state being stifled by the idea of the party." Germany in 1930, the party complained, was "unsurpassed in the organization of . . . the occupational estate or economic stratum [*berufsständische oder wirtschaftliche Schicht*] but pathetic in the manifestation of the idea of state, in fitting

63. The implicit ideological content and the *ständisch* terminology of the single issue, special-interest, and regional parties are treated in Childers, "Interest and Ideology."

64. Childers, "The Social Language of Politics."

the self into a conception of the general welfare."[65]

These structural, representational problems were, of course, vastly exacerbated by the onset of the Great Depression and the growing radicalization of German political life. Both liberal parties suffered distressing losses again in 1928, and confronted by their own dwindling appeal and the first signs of a dramatic Nazi surge in a number of regional elections, the DVP and DDP began a perceptible drift to the right. For the DDP, the Mannheim party congress in 1929 signaled a significant shift in its orientation. Indicative of the new winds blowing through the party, one prominent speaker condemned "the radical metropolitan and cosmopolitan spirit of Berlin," and Erich Koch-Weser, the party chairman, "assailed Weimar's rampant "partyism" and "political horsetrading." In addition, the DDP adopted a new economic program that implicitly repudiated the party's commitment to "economic democracy," with its emphasis on fostering cooperation between management and *Arbeitnehmer*, and focused far greater attention on the plight of the economically strapped *Mittelstand*. A few months later, the DDP announced its intention of joining the rightist Young German Order (Jungdeutscher Orden) in the formation of a new political party that it hoped would become the basis for the long-sought party of bourgeois concentration.[66]

The new German State Party (Deutsche Staatspartei or DStP) remained formally committed to the republican state, but a significant shift in linguistic emphasis, signaled most obviously by the party's new name, was unmistakable. The DStP certainly declared its determination to continue "the struggle for the assertion and further constitutional development of the republic,"[67] but such formulations took a backseat to a new

65. W. Külz, *An alle, die starken und reinen Willens sind*, Materialien zur demokratischen Politik, no. 153 (Berlin, 1930). Külz's essay was intended to serve as a model for DDP speakers in the campaign. The DVP echoed these sentiments: "Either there are groups composed of occupations and occupational interests or there are parties, to whom the general welfare, the welfare of the state, stands higher than their momentary, usually changeable . . . occupational interests." See the remarks of F. Heller-Halberg, reported in *Der Elbwart: Blätter der DVP/Landesverband Hamburg*, 16 August 1930.

66. See A. Chanady, "The Dissolution of the German Democratic Party in 1930," *American Historical Review* 73 (1968): 1433, and Jones, *German Liberalism*, pp. 370–72.

67. "Kämpft für Reich und Volk," in *Der Demokrat* 11, no. 20 (20 October 1930): 457–58.

rhetorical turn. Stung by its own shrinking popularity and the mounting disaffection of many middle-class Germans with the regime, the DStP strained to disassociate itself from the very republican language that the DDP had struggled for years to create. In fact, the word "republic" appears only once in the party's founding manifesto. Even when pledging allegiance to the Weimar Constitution and the republic's controversial colors, its choice of words indicated this new distance: "The German State Party stands on the foundation of the Reich constitution and honors the state symbols."[68] Similarly, when offering constructive proposals for electoral and Reich reform, the language of the new party was far more critical of and distant from the republic than that of its predecessor. While proposing a new system of proportional representation, for example, the DStP condemned what it referred to as "the politically bankrupt party system" of Weimar and called for the transformation of the increasingly discredited and ineffectual republic into "a strong national German *Volksstaat*."[69]

Moreover, from its founding manifesto onward, the discourse of the DStP was focused far more sharply on preservation of the "state" than of the "republic." In the gathering economic and political crisis, the DDP/DStP characteristically insisted, Germany needed "a centrist bloc" that would "preserve the state from the radicals of the right and left."[70] The Nazis and the Communists were driving the country toward "civil war and revolution," the DStP warned, but significantly, the party chose to represent the polarization of German political life as a threat not to the republic but to "the security of the state."[71] In order to survive the crisis, the DStP asserted, "the Reich needs citizens and state-preserving parties that will place the interest of the state and the struggle for the state in the forefront [of their activities]."[72] "We must rediscover the idea of the state, which

68. "Der Aufruf zur Bildung der Deutschen Staatspartei," in Artur Mahrun, *Die Deutsche Staatspartei* (Berlin, 1930).

69. "Was ist die Deutsche Staatspartei," DStP leaflet, 1930, BA, ZSg. 1/27/20(2).

70. Ibid.

71. "Sammlung in der Deutschen Staatspartei," DStP leaflet, 1930, BA, ZSg. 1/27/20(2).

72. H. Dietrich, *Ziele und Aufgaben der Deutschen Staatspartei: Rede gehalten auf dem Gründungsparteitag der Deutschen Staatspartei, Hannover, den 9.11.1930* (Berlin, 1930).

we have lost," Hermann Dietrich declared, "and mobilize the groups close to us so that they see the struggle for this state . . . as their primary political objective."[73]

Symptomatically, the DDP's earlier emphasis on creating a new sense of democratic citizenship for the republic was also transformed in the discourse of the DStP. Whereas in 1928 the DDP had proudly stood before the electorate "on the basis of the republic," its successor, the new State Party, proclaimed that it was created "on the basis of the *Volksgemeinschaft*."[74] The DStP explained that "the social spirit of the . . . people's state demands [that we] transcend caste and class prejudices. A free citizenry must give itself social forms that outwardly document a mutual respect for all *Volksgenossen*. The citizens of a people's state should not judge one another by background or possessions but according to the value of the individual for the existence and future of the state and *Volk*."[75]

For the DVP no such rhetorical shifts were necessary. The party had never structured its discourse around a commitment to or defense of the Weimar Republic, even while serving in the cabinet, and thus its quite pronounced shift to the right after Stresemann's death in 1929 was less dramatic.[76] Yet the growing polarization of German political life, and especially the rise of the NSDAP in 1929–30, produced tremendous strains on the DVP's representation of its position in the party system. Having served in the Reich government since 1925, the DVP had undeniably become what the National Socialists referred to contemptuously as "a system party." As a consequence, the DVP found it increasingly difficult to articulate a rhetorical stance that would on the one hand permit the party to be sufficiently critical of the undoubtedly unpopular Weimar regime and at the same time allow it to defend "the state" against the radicals of both left and right.

Its solution, after serving for two years in the Great Coalition with the SPD, was to go on the offensive against the left,

73. H. Dietrich, "Die Staatspartei kämpft für Deutschlands Zukunft," in *Der Demokrat* 11, no. 16 (20 August 1930): 361–64.

74. "Das Manifest der Deutschen Staatspartei," in *Der Demokrat* 11, no. 17 (5 September 1930): 381–85.

75. Ibid.

76. For the DVP's shift to the right after Stresemann's death, see Jones, *German Liberalism*, pp. 352–60 and 395–434.

representing its mission as "a struggle to save the German state and the German economy." It renewed its summons to the German middle class to halt its "suicidal fragmentation" and rally in a "strong *staatsbürgerlicher Block* to counter the strong socialist bloc."[77] It would be a catastrophe, the party stressed, if "the German *Staatsbürgertum*" continued its internecine squabbles and in the process overlooked the fact "that the enemy stands on a blindly radical right and [on the left] with Social Democracy and Communism."[78] The terminology here is instructive. While the DDP/DStP routinely used the term *Staatsbürger* to convey a transclass conception of citizenship, for the DVP, which increasingly employed the term after 1930, it held a far more restrictive social meaning. In the vocabulary of the DVP, *Staatsbürger* or *Staatsbürgertum* essentially served as a transparent synonym for middle class or bourgeois.[79]

Although the DVP's new leader, Ernst Scholz, declared the party's willingness to deal with the SPD's more responsible elements and warned against the siren song of the National Socialists, the enemy for the DVP in 1930 remained on the left. "History always repeats itself," Scholz stated in a burst of characteristic rhetoric at the party's Mannheim party congress in March, "but people have not learned from it that what propelled the inundation of central Europe by the Huns or the violent expedition of Genghis Khan from central Asia into western Europe is being repeated today in the struggle of bolshevism against western culture." To "build a dam against this imminently threatening danger" was the task of the DVP.[80]

In this context it is perhaps not surprising that the DVP sought to deal with the rising National Socialist challenge by depicting the NSDAP as a party of the radical left, a tactic also

77. "Warum wieder Volkspartei?" in *Der Elbewart: Blätter der DVP/Landesverband Hamburg*, 23 August 1930.

78. "Der Sinn des Wahlkampfes," in *Nachrichtendienst Nr. 17 des Landesverbandes Schleswig-Holstein der DVP*, 12 August 1930.

79. The DStP's use of the term was also in transition in 1930, and it was certainly employed on some occasions to *imply* a more distinctly middle-class identity. See, for example, " Weil Sie das Staatsvolk und nicht den Interessenhaufen wollen!" DStP leaflet, 1930, Landesarchiv Berlin (LAB), Rep. 240, Acc. 2088, no. 88.

80. Scholz's remarks are found in Reichsgeschäftsstelle der Deutschen Volkspartei, ed., *8. Reichsparteitag der Deutschen Volkspartei in Mannheim vom 21. bis 23.3.1930* (Berlin, 1930).

employed by the DStP. Both repeatedly warned the *Mittelstand* about Nazi "socialism," hoping to exploit the leftist resonances found in much of Nazi rhetoric. "Whether national or international," the DStP typically decalared, "it is still socialism and, indeed, . . . of the most radical type." The *Bürgertum* should not be "fooled because the Nazis sit on the right in parliament or because they place the word 'national' before their socialist ideology," the DStP warned.[81] "They have nothing in common with the bourgeois parties that stand on the foundation of the capitalist weltanschauung," the DVP insisted. For a glimpse of what economic policy would be like in the Third Reich, the *Mittelstand* should look at the Soviet Union, where "interest slavery" had, indeed, been broken. "With their socialistic program, the Nazis are not one penny better than the other socialists," the DVP cautioned, and shopkeepers, artisans, peasants, and others in the German middle class were sternly warned "to beware of wolves in sheep's clothing."[82]

These warnings, coupled with the pronounced rightward shift of the DDP/DStP and DVP in 1929, failed to halt the decline of the liberal parties or to slow the breathtaking momentum of the National Socialists. Both liberal parties suffered a massive hemorrhage of electoral support to the radical right in the fall elections of 1930 and would never recover. Between 1930 and 1932 both parties were prominently associated with Brüning and his highly unpopular rule by emergency decree, and both suffered a string of humiliating losses in the regional and local elections. By 1932, a year of almost constant campaigning, their position had become largely untenable. Neither party was able to attract even 2 percent of the vote in the important Prussian Landtag elections in April and therefore entered the summer Reichstag campaign as little more than bourgeois splinter parties.[83]

In an effort to halt this disastrous slide, the DStP entered that campaign as an outspoken critic of the new reactionary government of Franz von Papen. Returning to the opposition, the DStP aggressively attacked Papen's "cabinet of barons" in language

---

81. "Hitlers Kern: Sowjetstern," DStP leaflet, 1930, BA, ZSg. 1/27/20(2).
82. "Herunter der Maske!" and "Rettet Deutschland!" DVP leaflets, 1930 BA, ZSg. 1/42/8(2).
83. See Jones, *German Liberalism*, pp. 435–75.

reminiscent of the DDP's earlier strongly republican rhetoric. The leitmotiv of the DStP's campaign was "the preservation of the republic and democracy," and it urged middle-class voters to "fight hard for the republic and against the cabinet of Junkers."[84] It also called on the *Bürgertum* to "awaken" to the ominous threat to individual freedom posed by the NSDAP.[85] The party continued to condemn the NSDAP as a manifestation of the radical left, emphasizing that "the socialism of Hitlerism is no less dangerous for the bourgeoisie than any other form of socialism."[86] Above all the NSDAP was portrayed as a threat to economic and political freedom. The party's spokesmen acknowledged that liberalism and all it stood for were under siege. Even "the word 'liberal' has been proscribed in Germany for the past few years," Carl Petersen lamented. "It has been ridiculed and mocked because its basic nature has not been recognized." The liberalism of 1932 was not Manchesterism, as Hitler suggested, and the DStP had no desire to revive the liberalism of a previous epoch. Liberalism stood for freedom, Petersen concluded, and freedom of every sort was in grave peril in Germany.[87]

In stark contrast to the DStP, the DVP entered the summer Reichstag campaign as a staunch supporter of the Papen government and in an electoral alliance with Alfred Hugenberg's DNVP. The DVP resolutely condemned the radicalism, hatred, and mass hysteria created by the National Socialists and demanded the formation of a "great national front," a "bloc of reason" to reform the discredited Weimar state.[88] In an effort to legitimize the unpopular Papen government, the party invariably portrayed its members as "the deputies of Reich President Hindenburg" and fervently urged the public to "give it a chance to work. Don't destroy the last hopes for peace and order by [encouraging] the thirst for power of those parties who can

84. See "Volk gegen Junker!" DStP leaflet, 1932, BA, ZSg. 1/27/20.

85. "Bürgertum erwache!" ibid.

86. Quoted from Schreiber at a meeting of the DStP executive committee, 5 April 1932, by E. Matthias and R. Morsey, "Die Deutsche Staatspartei," E. Matthias and R. Morsey, eds., *Das Ende der Parteien, 1933* (Düsseldorf, 1960), p. 54.

87. C. Petersen, "Durch nationale Demokratie zur deutschen Einheit," in H. Dietrich, C. Petesen, and R. Maier, *Der Weg der nationalen Demokratie: Reden auf der Kundgebung der Deutschen Staatspartei in Mannheim am 2. Oktober 1932* (Mannheim, n.d. [1932]).

88. "Was wir wollen, was wir fordern!" DVP leaflet, 1932, BA, ZSg. 1/42/8(3).

only destroy but can never work together." "Who do you want to follow," it characteristically asked voters, "the prophets of the masses or Hindenburg?"[89]

Yet, while the DVP warned against the "mass radicalism" of the Nazis, it also sharply intensified its antirepublican rhetoric, demanding an end to "the domination of party democracy" and "mass rule." "Our battle is against the Weimar party state," a DVP campaign circular to party operatives stated forthrightly.[90] In a construction that contained all the essential elements of the party's rhetorical appeal in 1932, the DVP issued the following call: "Down with the party state, whether black, red, or brown! Away with the wretched horse trading of the utterly mad mass parties! Bring on the clean German state that provides space and protection for Christian-national culture. Free our youth from the fog of mass slogans and offer a model of a healthy, private economic leadership based on individual responsibility."[91]

The DVP had "rejected the Weimar Constitution because it saw the current calamity coming," the party claimed, and now a far-reaching reform of the constitution was absolutely imperative in order to strengthen the authority of the state.[92] The DVP envisioned "a new Germany" that would not be "burdened by the shackles of a misconceived democracy and the onesided domination of political parties."[93] The DDP/DStP, with its lingering commitment to the Weimar state, had failed to understand the imperatives of the period and was therefore doomed. "The Democrats in Germany have become a sect," the DVP argued revealingly, "because they pray to a god who is long dead. Today democracy and the republic are no longer the issues of debate," the DVP contented, "The battle is for nothing less than the preservation of German culture, which is threatened everywhere by radicalism and dissolution, and for the existence of the German *Bürgertum*." For this reason, party

89. "Deutsche Wähler, Deutsche Wählerinnen!" and "Die DVP hat früh genug gewarnt!" DVP leaflets, 1932, BA, ZSg. 1/42/8(3).

90. *Nachrichtendienst Nr. 5 der rheinisch-westfälischen Arbeitsgemeinschaft der Deutschen Volkspartei: Reichstagswahl 1932*, BA, ZSg. 1/42/8(3).

91. "Wissen die Parteien, was sie wollen?" DVP leaflet, 1932, BA, ZSg. 1/42/8(3).

92. *Nachrichtendienst Nr. 5 der rheinisch-westfälischen Arbeitsgemeinschaft der DVP*, and "Die DVP hat früh genug gewarnt!" DVP leaflet, 1932, both in BA, ZSg. 1/42/8(3).

93. E. Dingeldey, quoted in the *Deutsche Allgemeine Zeitung*, 30 July 1932.

chairman Eduard Dingeldey explained, the DVP "had recognized the signs of the times and entered into an alliance with the [conservative] right."[94]

In 1932 both the liberal parties and the Weimar Republic suffered devastating political blows, and in the following year their long anticipated demise at last became a reality. The failure of the republic and Weimar liberalism, as the scholarship of the past decade has compellingly insisted, cannot be adequately explained as the product of long-term structural faults in German political and social development or within the liberal movement itself. Although long-term structural trends must be taken into account, understanding the failure of democracy in Germany after 1918 must begin with the political culture of the Weimar Republic itself. In any such analysis, the dynamics and mechanisms of political mobilization, the images, symbols, and languages employed in the political discourse of the period, should occupy a central position.

The language, or more accurately languages, of liberalism are particularly useful in analyzing the political culture of the Weimar Republic. For the liberal parties two important and revealing dilemmas structured their discourse throughout the period. All the major parties of the Weimar Republic were torn between the desire to speak for the nation – all claimed to be *Volksparteien* – and the very pressing need to cultivate specific social constituencies. The competing demands of social integration and sectarian interest plagued the major parties throughout the era, and the republic's radical system of proportional representation gravely exacerbated the problem.

The liberal parties struggled mightily with this dilemma but in the final analysis found it impossible to speak both the language of special interest and national (or even class) integration. This was in large part due to the fact that both the DVP and DDP had served prominently in the Weimar government during periods of severe economic hardship and as a result were held responsible for policies that had serious consequences for their socially diverse middle-class constituents. Under the circumstances, neither could formulate an appeal or find a credible language to transcend the divisions of middle-class politics. Neither the

94. "Die Demokraten in Deutschland," *Deutsche Allgemeine Zeitung*, 27 July 1932.

DVP's appeals to "the nation" or the DDP's invocation of "the German citizen" struck a responsive chord in the highly combative atmosphere of postwar Germany. Only the National Socialists, who were not burdened by government responsibility and hence not associated with either specific policies or specific interests, proved able to speak the language of both transcendent class solidarity and sectarian special interest.

For the liberal parties this dilemma had another important dimension. The lingering presence, indeed, prevalence of a powerful *ständisch* idiom in middle-class political discourse long after such preindustrial social formations had disappeared from German economic and social life created a serious, if dimly perceived problem for the liberals. Liberal policy, whether articulated by either the DVP or the DDP/DStP, represented the philosophical and historical antithesis of both the social values and political vision implied by such *ständisch* terminology and espoused in one form or another by the Nazis, conservatives, and special-interest parties. Yet the liberals could find no alternative language with which to address their middle-class constituents, and their inability to construct a credible alternative ultimately compelled them to operate on a linguistic terrain that was far more congenial to conservative or even fascist politics than their own. Moreover, by adopting the forms without the substance implied by such corporatist vocabulary, the DDP and DVP merely helped to confine the terms of bourgeois political discourse within a political language that was at its core inimical to their own liberal principles.

Finally, both liberal parties struggled throughout the Weimar era to define their relationship to the republic itself. For the DDP this meant from the outset a strong and unequivocal commitment to the new regime and a determination to shape a distinctly democratic political culture. The party was therefore closely identified both with the new state and with Social Democracy. Throughout its brief history the DDP strained to explain and justify both relationships, and much of its discourse reflects not only a defense of the republic but also a call for social reconciliation as a crucial step in creating a democratic civic culture. Only in 1930, after a demoralizing string of electoral catastrophes, did the party attempt to redefine those relationships by establishing the German State Party. Yet, in spite of that revealing change of name, the DDP/DStP remained inextricably linked in public discourse with Weimar – and with good reason. For unlike the SPD, with its relatively stable working-class constituency, or the Center, with its solid foundation in the Catholic community, the DDP more than any other party had forged its identity and staked its political fortunes on the Weimar Republic. One symptom not only of the DDP/DStP's growing isolation within the Weimar party system but also of the impending demise of Germany's republican experiment was the fact that by 1932 its increasingly desperate calls to defend the embattled republic found no echo among the bourgeois parties and little resonance in the middle-class electorate.

The DVP had, of course, adopted a different posture. Ambivalent from the beginning, the party never overcame its initial reservations about democracy Weimar-style, and this ambivalence was not in the least altered by repeated stints in the cabinet. Ten years after the party rejected the Weimar Constitution in the National Assembly, the DVP had quite clearly become a "system party," and yet, while pursuing a policy of government participation, the DVP consistently maintained a linguistic stance that sought to disassociate the party from the republic. Even under Stresemann's leadership, the DVP refused to join its liberal rival in efforts to create a democratic political culture for the new republic, choosing instead to defend its participation as a "patriotic duty" to the German fatherland or to the liberal principle of the *Rechtsstaat* but not, significantly, to the republic itself.

This rhetorical position paid modest political dividends for the DVP in the early Weimar years, allowing the party to enter the government while maintaining a critical distance from the republic, but it proved disastrous for both the party and Weimar democracy in the radicalized circumstances of the Great Depression. Having never committed itself to the republic, having never endeavored to buttress the republic's always tenuous legitimacy by offering an endorsement of the very republican order it served, the party found itself without a compelling defense of its own position or the regime's. Its continued verbal blasts at the left and its escalating attacks on Weimar's "misconceived democracy" were no match for the radical antisystem rhetoric of the NSDAP. Even with the Nazi peril looming ever nearer, the DVP could not bring itself to issue a clarion call to defend the beleaguered republic. Outflanked by the Nazis and trapped by their own history of rhetorical ambivalence, the leaders of the DVP could only issue tepid pleas for "moderation" or a "defense of the center," with the result that in the course of 1932 their party found itself without a constituency. For the DVP, policy and political language, practice and rhetoric had been out of sync since the early years of the republic, and too late, the party discovered that the latter might be as powerful as the former.

13

Symbols of Continuity and Change in Postwar German Liberalism
Wolfgang Haußmann and Hildegard Hamm-Brücher

Rebecca Boehling

The search for a liberal Germany would be incomplete without an exploration of the fate of liberalism after World War II. This essay will examine the Free Democratic Party (Freie Demokratische Partei or FDP), the organizational form of post-1945 German liberalism, first by summarizing the history of the party and its major traits, then by focusing in greater detail on two pivotal FDP leaders, Wolfgang Haußmann and Hildegard Hamm-Brücher. An approach that combines party history with biography should enable us to comprehend the idealized formulas and practical realities of postwar liberalism in the context of the coalition parliamentary system of the Federal Republic of Germany. It should also clarify the FDP's historical continuities and discontinuities with pre-1933 German liberalism.

The Free Democratic Party was founded in December 1948 at Heppenheim in Hesse as a united postwar German liberal party. The delegates there represented several liberal parties of various names that, following the collapse of the Third Reich, had been organized first at the local and then at the state and zonal level in the western parts of Germany. This local and state-level development restricted the national party's cohesion until the late 1950s. The extreme diversity and independence of the state party organizations (*Landesverbände*) meant that the national party long remained a "cartel of self-confident state-parties." It was not until the 1970s that the state organizations finally subordinated themselves programmatically and behaviorally to the *Bundespartei*.[1] The state organizations were, however, successful in

1. H. Vorländer, "Hat sich der Liberalismus totgesiegt?" in H. Vorländer,

achieving representation in all the state parliaments – except Schleswig-Holstein – prior to the founding of the Federal Republic, although they were dramatically outnumbered by their Christian Democratic and Social Democratic rivals.[2]

The fundamental nature of the postwar Free Democratic Party has been shaped by three major factors. First of all, although it was a new postwar party, the FDP had to deal with German liberalism's historical legacy. Second, because there was a great deal of liberal ideology that was coopted by the other major postwar West German parties, the FDP's existence has been dependent on finding both elements of traditional liberalism such as laissez-faire capitalism and new emphases on *Rechtsstaat* and individual freedom issues that have not been incorporated into the platforms of the other parties. Third, the limited appeal and thus small size of the FDP has made it dependent on the other major parties as potential coalition partners in order to be in power, while at the same time it has been able to exert more power than its size would normally merit precisely because it has provided the crucial number of seats to form the necessary majority to allow either the Social Democratic Party (Sozialdemokratische Partei Deutschlands or SPD) or the Christian Democratic Union (Christlich-Demokratische Union or CDU) to form a coalition government. Because of the legacy of German liberalism's historical schism, the FDP's limited ideological uniqueness and the party's role as a coalition builder, the FDP has had both a heterogeneous identity and membership.

One aspect of the heterogeneity within the FDP is the fact that institutional German liberalism's traditional division into right and left wings did not disappear after 1945. Until the late 1950s the FDP's main ideological and personnel differences were directly related to the old German Democratic Party (Deutsche Demokratische Partei or DDP) – German People's Party (Deutsche Volkspartei or DVP) divisions, which stemmed back even further to the old liberal split following the 1848 revolution. In the early postwar years former DVP policies and politicians were too closely associated with the rise of National Socialism to

---

ed., *Verfall oder Renaissancce des Liberalismus?* (Munich, 1987), p. 28.

2. C. Søe, "The Free Democratic Party," in H.G.P. Wallach and G.K. Romoser, eds, *West German Politics in the Mid-Eighties: Crisis and Continuity* (New York, 1985), pp. 123–24.

be able to exert much influence within the FDP,[3] although the early FDP did attract voters with these former affiliations and/or allegiances. Most of the early liberal leaders were former DDP members. This was especially true of southwest German liberals like Reinhold Maier, Theodor Heuß, and Wolfgang Haußmann[4] and Bavarian liberals like Thomas Dehler,[5] the dominant national party leaders both in terms of personnel and influence in the early years of the Federal Republic. Over time, however, and in certain regions more than in others, the more conservative wing came to vie for leadership positions within the FDP. It represented nationalistic and big business interests, sometimes to the point of exemplifying continuity not only with the former DVP but also with the old German National People's Party (Deutschenationale Volkspartei or DNVP).

Although the FDP has remained a unified liberal party, the tendency to revert back to upper middle-class recruitment, as in the case of the DVP, or to stress the lower middle class and the *Mittelstand*, as in the case of the DDP,[6] has recurred over and over again. In this particular respect, namely in the solicitation of voters and the intentional representation of special socioeconomic interests, many elements of continuity with pre-1933 German liberalism can be seen.[7] The result has been an attrition, rather than a break-up, of the party. In this respect the Germans have learned their lessons about the dangers of splinter parties; the minimal five-percent clauses in the state constitutions and the Basic Law discourage *Parteisplinterei* and add an incentive for small parties to do what is necessary to keep as many members within the fold as possible.

---

3. D. Hein, *Zwischen liberaler Milieupartei und nationaler Sammlungsbewegung: Gründung, Entwicklung, und Struktur der Freien Demokratischen Partei, 1945–1949* (Düsseldorf, 1985), pp. 55 and 193–95.

4. See U.D. Adam, "Politischer Liberalismus im deutschen Sudwesten von 1945–1978," in P. Rothmund and E.R. Wiehn, eds., *Die F.D.P./DVP in Baden-Württemberg und ihre Geschichte*, Schriften zur politischen Landeskunde Baden-Württembergs, vol. 4 (Stuttgart, 1979), pp. 220–54.

5. See B. Mauch, *Die bayerische FDP: Portrait einer Landespartei, 1945–1949*, Der politische Liberalismus in Bayern, Studienreihe des Thomas-Dehler Instituts, vol. 1 (Munich, 1981), pp. 15–27.

6. J.C. Hess, "Die Desintegration des Liberalismus in der Weimarer Republik," in Vorländer, ed., *Verfall oder Renaissance*, p. 105.

7. The rapprochement with Social Democracy which the social liberals have made could be compared with the DDP's role in the Weimar Coalition.

The virtual disappearance of both the German Democratic Party and its ill-starred successor, the German State Party, in the latter years of the Weimar Republic and the notoriety of the German People's Party as a result of its association with the rise of Nazism limited the potential numerical strength and influence of any postwar liberal movement. This was especially true when compared to the Social Democrats, who were able to continue to exist in exile and underground during the Third Reich. Their anti-Nazi credentials and their working-class base assured them of a sizable following in the postwar period. On the other hand, the Center Party and Bavarian People's Party broadened their appeal by forming the new Christian Democratic Union and the Christian Social Union (Christlich-Soziale Union or CSU) which were to include all nonsocialist Christian elements. The CDU/CSU predictably made inroads into potential liberal constituencies, such as the nonextremist Protestant antisocialists, who historically had often supported one of the liberal parties because the Center Party had been closed to them. Based on their historical legacy of structural weakness and a steadily decreasing following during the Weimar Republic, postwar German liberals could expect at best a restricted clientele. Compounding the liberals' postwar difficulties was the fact that after the shared experience of Nazi repression, all non-Nazi political parties recognized the necessity of stressing the principles of a *Rechtsstaat* and civil liberties traditionally associated with liberalism. Thus the only part of the liberal tradition that would not be coopted in some way by the other mainstream postwar parties was a commitment to the special socioeconomic interests of the German middle class and a call for a return to economic liberalism in the form of free trade and a free market economy.

Economic liberalism, however, was clearly on the defensive, at least with most Germans. Both the Christian Democratic Union and the Social Democratic Party worked out programs in the early postwar years based more or less on planned economies. This was to be expected of the Social Democrats. In the new CDU/CSU many local groups were convinced by the left wing of the old Center Party of the need for an adequate social net for all the returning POWs and Displaced Persons as well as for expellees and urban evacuees. Unlike the welfare system that originated during the Bismarckian era, this social net established a minimum standard of living as a fundamental civic right. The Free Democrats, on the other hand, felt that the Third Reich's emphasis on the collective *Volk* had convinced the Germans of the necessity of returning to individual political and economic freedom and of retreating from state intervention in the economy. They rejected the early postwar policies of social reform resulting from CDU/SPD cooperation such as pension guarantees and codetermination (*Mitbestimmung*) and clung to the Manchester school principles of liberalism.[8] While this may have limited the FDP's programmatic platform and thus restricted its membership and voter appeal, it also had its advantages, especially during the Allied occupation. As clear-cut proponents of old-style laissez-faire capitalism and a free market economy, the Free Democrats often found favor with the British and especially the American military government authorities. For example, in the British-American Bizonal Economic Council a small number of liberals were able to exercise a disproportionately large influence that would foreshadow the FDP's unique role in postwar West German politics.[9]

Economic liberalism was to find its most powerful West German advocate in Ludwig Erhard, whom the liberals successfully promoted for the important post of director of economic administration in the Bizonal Economic Council and who subsequently served as minister of economics under Chancellor Konrad Adenauer. Often dubbed the author of the "Economic Miracle," because his social market economy is generally given credit for the 1950s economic revival, Erhard initially was not aligned to any party. Although he eventually joined the CDU in the conviction that his neoliberal ideas were more needed there than in the FDP, where neoliberal economics already had solid support, most Free Democrats considered him one of their own.[10]

Despite its inability to attract a sufficient number of members or voters to surpass its small third-party status, the FDP has been able to shape various judicial, civil rights, and economic policies throughout the entire history of the Federal Republic. This is due to the fact that since 1949 the Free Democratic Party

8. Vorländer, "Hat sich der Liberalismus totgesiegt?" p. 26.
9. Søe, "The Free Democratic Party," p. 124.
10. Ibid., p. 133.

has been a junior member of all but two Bonn cabinets (from 1956 to 1961 and from 1966 to 1969). As the party that has tipped the scale to give the senior member of the coalition the necessary majority, it has received political posts and special concessions to a degree totally out of proportion to its small share of seats in the Bundestag.[11]

This special coalition role has affected the direction of the FDP's policies. Its policy orientation has been determined to a significant degree by the party, CDU or SPD, it was courting or being courted by, or with which it was trying to maintain a coalition. Thus the FDP's policies have been conditioned not only by their members' views of what constitutes modern-day liberalism, but also by what is programmatically feasible in a three-party – and now, with the recent successes of the Greens, a four-party – political system. Unable to achieve an absolute majority, both major parties have generally needed the FDP's support to form a coalition government. In order to exert a pivotal influence in coalition building, the FDP has had to draw sufficient voter support to surpass the minimum five-percent clause for parliamentary representation. Its acknowledgment of these prerequisites for achieving any significant influence in the political life of the Federal Republic has exposed it to charges of opportunism. To be sure, a kind of structural opportunism is inseparable from its role of majority creator. But this structural opportunism does not preclude an advocacy of liberal principles, nor does it imply that all FDP politicians are equally pragmatic. The liberals' emphasis on individualism has undoubtedly survived, not just in a Lockean sense, but also in terms of intraparty nonconformity. Compared to the other major parties, the FDP exercises the least collective party discipline; given its small size, it surprisingly often encompasses the most heterogeneous viewpoints, as illustrated in the two figures under examination in this study, Wolfgang Haußmann, the more pragmatic, party-politics oriented Free Democrat, and Hildegard Hamm-Brücher, the more independent, individualistic liberal activist.

It is difficult to classify and define the FDP because its identity varies according to whether one is examining it as a coalition party, and thus where it stands vis-à-vis the other

11. Ibid., p. 115.

parties, or as a voter and/or member party.[12] Some contemporary West German historians such as Dieter Hein have identified two political groups among the early postwar liberals: advocates of a liberal milieu party versus proponents of a national catchall movement (*Sammlungsbewegung*)[13] intended to gather together all those Germans who did not sympathize with the social and economic programs of the SPD or the cultural policies of the CDU.[14] Although this classification is based on whom the party was trying to attract rather than on its ideology, the former group indeed had ideological connections with the so-called left liberals of the old DDP and specifically of the Friedrich Naumann tradition, whereas the latter group had stronger ties with the DVP and the DNVP. Those advocates of the FDP as a liberal milieu party emphasize the desired membership whereas the supporters of it as a catchall movement are more concerned with the voter potential.[15] The history of the FDP demonstrates that without sufficient voters the membership milieu is rendered powerless. The structural problems that beset the FDP as a coalition, voter, and member party are thus all integrally related.[16]

Although the political behavior of the FDP has been influenced by the historical traditions of German liberalism, the survival of the party has been determined by the political imperative of finding a platform that will attract a minimum of five percent of the voters in order to receive representation in the state and national parliaments.[17] Often the FDP has drawn support from voters who wished to moderate either the left wing of the SPD or the right wing of the CDU/CSU by forcing the necessity of a coalition. Thus, their vote was not so much a vote for the liberals as an exercise of control over or a corrective for the other two major parties.[18] As a result some political

12. Ibid., p. 120.
13. Hein, *Zwischen liberaler Milieupartei*, pp. 11–16.
14. J.M. Gutscher, *Die Entwicklung der FDP von ihren Anfängen bis 1961* (Meisenheim, 1984), p. 40.
15. Both Haußmann and Hamm-Brücher would have to be considered liberal milieu advocates.
16. Gutscher, "Entwicklung der FDP," p. 40.
17. C. Søe and H. Vorländer, "Der Kampf um Überleben und Einfluß: Rolle und Funktion der FDP in der westdeutschen Politik," in Vorländer, ed., *Verfall oder Renaissance*, p. 174.
18. Ibid., p. 188.

analysts have viewed the FDP primarily as a "safety valve" for fluctuating voters who have become temporarily disillusioned with one of the major parties without being prepared to support the other. Polls have indicated that many more West Germans support the continued existence and viability of the FDP than those who consider themselves FDP supporters or "liberals" or who actually have voted for the FDP.[19] Although the FDP often projects itself as the "alternative of 'the center' in West German politics," it does not always occupy the middle position between Christian and Social Democrats. Especially in the early years of the Federal Republic, when Wolfgang Haußmann stood in the forefront of the FDP, it often stood to the right of the former on economic issues and in more recent years, when Hildegard Hamm-Brücher was instrumental in shaping the party, to the left of the latter on civil rights issues.[20]

Wolfgang Haußmann and Hildegard Hamm-Brücher: Symbols of Continuity and Change

Wolfgang Haußmann and Hildegard Hamm-Brücher represent two trends within West German liberalism: one toward uniformity and one toward differentiation. As municipal politicians during the occupation period they played similar roles; yet they display sufficiently different characteristics in the FDP and in the political life of the Federal Republic to offer comparison and contrast. Both are mainstream liberals who have taken independent stands and who at times have helped shape the party in their own images. At the same time they have also remained loyal members of the FDP, a fact that is especially significant in a party with the highest turnover rate both of members and voters of any of the political parties in the Federal Republic.

The choice of these two individuals is deliberate. Unlike the more internationally known Free Democrats like Hans-Dietrich Genscher or Otto Graf Lambsdorff, Hamm-Brücher and Haußmann both started out as local-level and then state-level liberal politicians who within a decade of each other played major roles in the national party. This working one's way up through the party at its various levels of jurisdiction was characteristic of the

19. C. Søe, "Free Democratic Party," p. 113.
20. Ibid., p. 115; See also p. 124.

development of the FDP in the 1940s and 1950s, when the state party was a mere amalgamation of the leaders of the local chapters and the national party a facade for a cartel of state parties. Whereas Wolfgang Haußmann, as well as other leading Free Democrats of his generation like Theodor Heuß, Thomas Dehler, and Reinhold Maier, considered themselves promoters of their state parties first and foremost,[21] Hamm-Brücher transcended regional ties with Bavaria to serve in a Hessian state ministry and in the Bonn cabinet. Both Haußmann and Hamm-Brücher played a role in FDP politics already during the earliest postwar years, the occupation period, and although they have now retired from the public limelight, both continued to play instrumental roles behind the scenes in the FDP; thus, both deserve credit for shaping the entire era of postwar German liberalism.

In terms of symbolizing the diversity within the party, their eighteen-year age difference makes it possible to look upon them as the representatives of two different generations of postwar liberals. This generational cleavage is further underscored by the fact that Haußmann was inclined to identify upward with his father's and uncle's generation and his family's longstanding liberal traditions while Hamm-Brücher tended to identify downward with both the generation born during and the one born after the Third Reich, as reflected in her efforts in school and university reform in the 1950s and 1960s. The gender contrast seems even more obvious, although their political concerns cannot be categorized along stereotypical gender lines of traditionally male economic and foreign policy interests and traditionally female social and cultural concerns.

Wolfgang Haußmann was the appointed deputy lord mayor of Stuttgart from 1945 until 1946. During this first postwar year Haußmann joined with Theodor Heuß and Reinhold Maier in forming the Democratic People's Party (Demokratische Volkspartei) in Haußmann's home in Stuttgart as an attempt to unite the former DDP and DVP in southwest Germany. Hildegard Hamm-Brücher was one of the first two liberal representatives in the postwar Munich city council. When the FDP, known at the time as the Liberal Democratic Party (Liberal-Demokratische Partei or LDP), entered the Munich city council for the first time

---

21. Vorländer, "Hat sich der Liberalismus totgesiegt?" p. 28.

in 1948, the twenty-seven-year-old Dr. Hildegard Brücher was postwar Germany's youngest city councillor. Both of these liberals went on to play leadership roles in the FDP on both the state and national levels. Most obviously, Haußmann represents continuity with Weimar liberalism both as a former member of the DDP's steering committee for Württemberg from 1931 to 1933, as the son of Conrad Haußmann, the state secretary and DDP Landtag and Reichstag representative, and as the grandson of Julius Haußmann, one of the founders of Württemberg's People's Party (Volkspartei) and its successor, the German Progressive Party (Deutsche Fortschrittspartei). Hamm-Brücher, on the other hand, represents change not only in terms of her youth, gender, and lack of political ancestors but also, as will be shown, in her activist pursuit of democratic liberalism and her rapprochement with Social Democracy.

Wolfgang Haußmann was born in 1903 in Stuttgart into a Lutheran Swabian family whose liberal party ties stretched back to the Revolution of 1848. His grandfather, Julius Haußmann, was known as a brilliant organizer who had sacrificed a parliamentary career in order to build up support for and strengthen the roots of the Württemberg People's Party, which was founded in 1849, and later the Progressive Party, which was founded in 1863.[22] Wolfgang's father, Conrad Haußmann, had been one of the founders of the Progressive People's Party (Fortschrittliche Volkspartei), along with Friedrich Naumann. As vice president of the Weimar National Assembly in 1919, he had prepared the Weimar Constitution in cooperation with the other DDP members, Hugo Preuß and Friedrich Naumann.[23] Earlier, in November 1918 when Wolfgang was fifteen, his father had invited a number of liberal representatives over to their house to form a unified liberal party, the German Democratic Party, which, however, was not to remain unified.[24] Twenty-seven years later in the same house, Wolfgang would host the founding meeting of the Democratic People's Party (Demokratische Volkspartei), which became the most important

---

22. H.-O. Rommel, "Aufbau und Zusammenbruch der Demokratie in Württemberg," in P. Rothmund and E.R. Wiehn, eds., *Die F.D.P./DVP*, p. 144.
23. P. Rothmund, "Liberalismus am Ende? – Weimarer Zwischenspiel," in Rothmund and Wiehn, *Die F.D.P./DVP*, p. 171.
24. Ibid., p. 137.

regional party within the postwar Free Democratic Party.[25]

At age seventeen, in keeping with his family tradition, Wolfgang Haußmann joined the DDP's youth group, the Democratic Youth (Demokratische Jugend), and later became its Württemberg state chairman. Nine years later he was a member of the DDP executive committee, a post he held for two years before being forced out of politics by the Nazis.[26] After studying law at the Universities of Munich, Tübingen, and Heidelberg, Haußmann wrote his dissertation, "Die Durchsetzung des parlamentarischen Systems im Deutschen Kaiserreich."[27] Although his own active participation in a parliamentary system was interrupted by the Third Reich, Haußmann continued to practice law in Stuttgart after the Nazis came to power. In April 1945, as French troops were approaching Stuttgart, a group of non-Nazi men calling themselves the "Rettet Stuttgart" group met in Wolfgang Haußmann's home to plan how to circumvent *Reichsstaathalter* Murr's orders to destroy Stuttgart. Haußmann; Karl Weber, a police official; and another lawyer, Arnulf Klett, were able to convince Dr. Karl Strölin, the lord mayor at that time, not to carry out Murr's "scorched earth" orders. In turn Strölin recommended Klett as his successor to the arriving French troops who occupied Stuttgart. Haußmann was appointed Klett's deputy mayor.[28]

In the presence of the U.S. local military government commander, Lt. Col. Charles L. Jackson, Reinhold Maier, Theodor Heuß, and Wolfgang Haußmann founded the Democratic People's Party in Haußmann's home in Stuttgart on 16 September 1945.[29] According to Haußmann, it was called the Democratic People's Party[30] in order to draw on the tradition of the Württemberg People's Party. North Württemberg was the only place where the German liberals were organized earlier than the

---

25. Personal interview with W. Haußmann, Stuttgart, 30 November 1982.

26. *Stuttgarter Zeitung*, 3 July 1963.

27. "Wolfgang Haußmann," in *Wer ist Wer?* (Frankfurt a.M., 1975), p. 379.

28. W. Haußmann, unpublished manuscript, 17 March 1982, protocol of Süddeutsche Rundfunk lecture for "Dreizig Jahre Jubiläum des Landes Baden-Württtemberg," Stadtarchiv Stuttgart, p. 2. Also, personal interview with W. Haußmann, Stuttgart, 30 November 1982.

29. Ibid.

30. In the 1950s FDP was added after the acronym for the Democratic People's party, DVP. Eventually even the Baden-Württemberg party changed its name completely to FDP.

local Christian Democrats.[31] Both Maier and Heuß had hopes that the Democratic People's Party might become a catchall party for Christian middle-class forces, but Haußmann, like most tradition-oriented Stuttgart liberals, felt that a liberal party needed to be independent of social Christian forces.[32]

When the first postwar municipal elections were held in 1946, Wolfgang Haußmann received the highest number of votes of all councillors. His popularity led to the suggestion that he become lord mayor; even the SPD city council faction tried to recruit him as lord mayor. But Haußmann had a newborn daughter, and his leg injury from the last days of the war had not yet healed; with these personal reasons for hesitating, he threw his support to Klett instead. Apparently wary of Haußmann's popularity, Klett saw to it that Haußmann did not continue as his deputy.[33] While this did not mark the end of Haußmann's political career, it did set him on a similar course to that of his grandfather, who had been more involved in intra-party politics than in the public limelight. Haußmann headed the liberal Democratic People's Party (Württemberg FDP) delegation to the Stuttgart city council from 1946 to 1953. He also was elected as its representative to the 1946 state constitutional assembly, where he again chaired the liberal faction. Haußmann was to retain his seat in the Landtag from its postwar reconstitution until 1972. From 1946 until 1964 he served as the chairman of the state FDP executive committee. During this time he held overlapping posts within the party organization and in the state cabinets. From 1953 until 1966 he served as Baden-Württemberg's minister of justice. In this capacity his initiative led to the 1958 founding of the Central Office for the Investigation of National Socialist Crimes (Zentrale Stelle zur Aufklärung Nationalsozialistischer Gewaltverbrechen). From 1953 until the 1970s he was a member of the national party executive committee, and in 1955 he was selected to hold the post of national vice chairman of the FDP.[34] His commitment to German liberalism is clearly reflected in the many – often thank-

31. P. Rothmund und R. Wiehn, "Demokratie im Stammland," in Rothmund und Wiehn, *Die F.D.P./DVP*, p. 215.

32. Ibid., pp. 212–13. Cf. Hein, *Zwischen liberaler Milieupartei*, pp. 11–15.

33. Personal interview with W. Haußmann, Stuttgart, 30 November 1982.

34. *Stuttgarter Zeitung*, 3 July 1963. Cf. "Haußmann," in *Wer ist Wer?*, 1975, p. 379.

less – party posts that he accepted and in which he served selflessly.

If Haußmann's biography was marked by family liberal influences as a youth and more service in administrative posts within the FDP than in elected ones as an adult, this was not the case for his younger female colleague in Bavaria, Hildegard Hamm-Brücher. Hildegard Brücher was born on 11 May 1921 in Essen to a Jewish mother and Lutheran father. Family traditions, whether religious or political, had only a limited impact upon her because by the time she was eleven both of her parents had died.[35] Her attendance at schools in Berlin, Dresden, and Constance indicates that she probably developed no particular regional ties while growing up. From 1939 to 1945 she studied chemistry at the University of Munich, ultimately receiving her doctorate there.[36] Her first political engagement seems to have been during the war when she was involved with the White Rose student resistance group led by Sophie and Hans Scholl. Unlike most of her comrades, Hildegard Brücher was able to avoid detection and capture because of a timely hospitalization with pneumonia.[37]

After the end of the war the twenty-four-year-old Brücher first supported herself with temporary employment as a science writer with the *Neue Zeitung* in Munich, a newspaper sponsored by the U.S. military government. By late 1946 she was already a full-time employee of the education section, and in 1949 she became a member of the newspaper's editorial board.[38] In 1948 she interviewed Baden-Württemberg's minister of culture, Theodor Heuß, for the *Neue Zeitung* and in the midst of her probing questions made such an impression upon Heuß that he told her: "Mädle, Sie müsse in die Politik."[39] And enter politics

35. Personal interview with H. Hamm-Brücher, Munich, 1 July 1983.
36. "Hildegard Hamm-Brücher," in *Wer ist Wer?* (Frankfurt a.M. 1975), p. 358.
37. N. Pataky, "Versuch einer Einleitung zur Person," in H. Hamm-Brücher, *Vorkämpfer für Demokratie und Gerechtigkeit in Bayern und Bonn* (Bonn, 1974), p. 7. How Brücher avoided deportation, and what category of the Nuremberg Laws she fell under is unclear. Perhaps because of her parents' deaths prior to the Third Reich and her apparent adoption by relatives, she was able to conceal her mother's Jewish heritage.
38. Personal interview with H. Hamm-Brücher, Munich, 1 July 1983. Cf. *Wer ist Wer?*, p. 358.
39. "Miss, you must go into politics." Pataky, "Versuch einer Einleitung," p. 7.

she did. The Liberal Democratic Party, which had been formed in Munich in late November 1945, had received less than two percent of the vote in the first municipal elections in May 1946 and thus had no representatives in the fifty-member city council. But in 1948 it was able to elect two representatives to the city council with almost five percent of the popular vote. One of the representatives was Dr. Hildegard Brücher, who only after her election as a liberal candidate actually joined the Liberal Democratic Party. Unlike Württemberg, liberalism had never been very strong in Bavaria, especially outside of predominantly Protestant Franconia.[40] But, as in Württemberg, in Bavaria's new postwar liberal party the former DDP members far outweighed former DVP members, although the majority of elected politicians, like Brücher, had not belonged to any of the Weimar parties.[41]

In late 1949 Brücher received one of the first Fulbright grants to study at Harvard University for a year. On her return from the United States she married the municipal department head, Erwin Hamm, then and thereafter an ardent CSU administrator, whom she had met while serving as a city councillor. She continued to serve as Munich city councillor until 1954, and in 1950 she was elected to the Bavarian Landtag as well. She held a Landtag seat until 1966, when the FDP failed to reach the five-percent minimum, and then again from 1970 to 1976. In 1963 she became a member of the national executive committee of the FDP and in 1972 its vice chairperson.[42] When she was unable to take her seat in the Bavarian Landtag in 1966, the Ministry of Culture in the SPD-ruled state of Hesse called on her to serve as state secretary. The fact that a party other than the FDP and one outside her home state of Bavaria had asked her to serve reflects the extent of her local and national reputation, especially in educational reform.[43] In 1969 the new national FDP–SPD coalition government recruited Hamm-Brücher from Wiesbaden to Bonn to serve as state secretary in the Ministry for Education and Science.[44] In the last two Schmidt governments from 1976 to 1982 she served as minister of state in the Foreign

40. Mauch, *Die bayerische FDP*, pp. 13–23.
41. Ibid., p. 38.
42. Pataky, "Versuch einer Einleitung," p. 8. See also *Wer ist Wer?*, p. 358.
43. Ibid., pp. 38–41.
44. Ibid., p. 57.

Office and as a member of the Bundestag.[45] More recently, in the midst of the 1982 coalition deliberations in the Bundestag, Hamm-Brücher made national headlines with her moving speech against her party's decision to change coalition partners.[46]

A consideration of even these bare biographical facts provides a basis for comparison and contrast. In various ways both Haußmann and Hamm-Brücher typify traditional German liberals. They are both professionals, one a lawyer, the other a journalist; both possess academic degrees, one in law and one in science; both are Protestant. These sociological characteristics, typical of postwar FDP members, apply equally well to the majority of liberal representatives in the 1848/49 Frankfurt Parliament and thus display marked leadership continuity within German liberalism.

Haußmann was of course predisposed to join the German Democratic Party and later the FDP because of the liberal traditions within his family that dated back generations and because of his strong regional ties to Stuttgart and Württemberg, historically and even now a stronghold of political liberalism. Theodor Heuß once commented on the fact that both he and Wolfgang Haußmann had had the fortune of being raised in a political family tradition that understood both the enthusiasm and the resignation associated with the year 1848 in German history.[47] In some ways a script for a role within organized German liberalism had already been written for Haußmann.

Hamm-Brücher, on the other hand, had few family or regional roots that predisposed her to liberal affiliations. Weimar liberal parties had an unusually high number of Jewish members and voters because they advocated religious freedom and individual civil rights in a German society that was otherwise laden with anti-Semitism. Since Hamm-Brücher herself was not raised in the Jewish tradition, any connection would probably be indirect, as in a keener awareness of intolerance and of the difficulties confronted by minorities. Hamm-Brücher experienced what it was like to be a minority in terms of her gender in the FDP and in politics in general, although the FDP has had a

45. H. Schuchardt and G. Verheugen, eds., *Das liberale Gewissen* (Berlin, 1982), p. 187.

46. For a copy of her 1 October 1982 speech, see Schuchardt and Verheugen, eds., *Das liberale Gewissen*, pp. 30–33.

47. Rothmund and Wiehn, "Demokratie im Stammland," p. 213.

higher percentage of women members than either the SPD or CDU/CSU.[48] She was also in the minority as a Liberal, a Protestant and a non-Bavarian in Bavaria. This contrasts starkly with Haußmann's status in Württemberg as a native and Protestant in a predominantly Protestant state with strong liberal traditions. This difference may explain Hamm-Brücher's strong sense of individualism and her activist reputation. Without these traits, she would have scarcely survived in political life. She did not hesitate to take strong positions within the party as she was used to being in uncomfortable, minority positions. This did not go unnoticed, and comments like "Warum muß die Brücherin immer so offen reden?" from those chairing FDP meetings where Hamm-Brücher spoke were not infrequent.[49]

Both had been politically active as young adults, but because of the eighteen-year difference in their ages, Haußmann had entered politics through the more traditional route of the DDP party structure during the Weimar Republic, whereas Brücher entered through an underground resistance movement. This clearly shaped their future political behavior patterns as well. Brücher's liberalism was one of personal conviction and not of party allegiances or abstract tradition; it grew out of protest against Nazism and broadened to include protest against clericalism, religious and cultural intolerance, political and social inequality, and an elitist educational system. Haußmann, too, was involved in a resistance movement of sorts. But its motive was to stop the unnecessary destruction of Stuttgart at the end of the war and to prevent the scorched-earth policy from being followed through to its destructive conclusion. Haußmann was definitely an anti-Nazi, but relative to Hamm-Brücher his resistance was of a more pragmatic, practical nature than the ideologically motivated resistance of the White Rose students.

In terms of their formal roles within the party, their move up the hierarchy was not concurrent because of their age and experience level at the end of the war. Haußmann's pivotal accomplishment was the shaping and building up of the party in

48. D. Brighton and E. Kirchner, "Germany: The FDP in Transition – Again?" *Parliamentary Affairs* 37, no. 2 (Spring 1984): 188. In 1980, 23 percent of the FDP members were women. Of course, the percentage of FDP women in parliament was lower.

49. "Why must that Brücher woman always speak so openly?" Pataky, "Versuch einer Einleitung," p. 8.

Baden-Württemberg from the cofounding of the Stuttgart DVP in September 1945 up into the 1960s.[50] The role he played in the municipal and state DVP/FDP transcended regional boundaries. As chairman of the Württemberg DVP/FDP from 1946 until 1964, Haußmann headed the liberal core group that was to play such a disproportionately large role in the broader organization of the U.S. zone of occupation. Informally organized in the fall of 1946, this zonal organization became the nucleus of the national FDP, which was formed in December of 1948 under the chairmanship of another Württemberg liberal, Theodor Heuß. The organizational and ideological predominance of the Stuttgart liberals continued in the national party, where, according to a proud Haußmann: "The DVP became the germ cell of a general renewal movement of political liberalism."[51] Of all the state party chapters, the Baden-Württemberg FDP has been the most successful in both state and federal elections.

Unique to Württemberg's brand of DVP liberalism was its openness to early cooperation with the SPD in cultural and educational legislation. The crucial factor here was the display of moderation and the downplaying of class conflict by the regional SPD, as fostered by its leader, Carlo Schmid.[52] Nevertheless, when Reinhold Maier in 1950 formed an SPD/DVP (FDP) coalition in Baden-Württemberg in contrast with the composition of other state and national governments, his decision met with disapproval from more conservative state FDP organizations, like the one in Hesse, as well as from the national central committee.[53] But, to the benefit of individuals like Haußmann, the traditional structure of German liberalism prevailed, namely, as a party of regional notables whose independent, venerable personalities were needed to attract a following.[54] Thus the Stuttgart "notables" were able to hold their own against their more conservative colleagues, although ultimately the predominance of the Stuttgart and North Württemberg group may have restricted the development of other southwestern

50. Rothmund und Wiehn, "Demokratie im Stammland," p. 215.
51. Ibid., pp. 217–18. In the original: "Die DVP wurde zur Keimzelle einer allgemeinen Erneuerungsbewegung des politischen Liberalismus."
52. Adam, "Politischer Liberalismus," pp. 225–26.
53. Ibid., pp. 226–29.
54. Ibid., p. 221. S. Neumann coined the term "Honoratiorenstruktur" to describe the role of these notables within the party.

377

FDP chapters and thus the growth of the party in general. Although neither were social liberals nor particularly interested in social reform, both Maier and Haußmann – in tune with the old Württemberg DDP tradition – successfully resisted their fellow liberals' pressure to end this state coalition with the SPD.[55]

Haußmann's Democratic People's Party/FDP tried to avoid a left-right categorization, but in actuality it seemed to be to the left of the state chapters in Hesse and North Rhine-Westphalia with their nationalist programs and to the right of the Hamburg chapter with its social-reform-oriented Liberal Manifesto. In the autumn of 1953 Maier's government fell when he opposed Chancellor Konrad Adenauer over the latter's support of religiously segregated schools rather than *Simultanschulen*, schools that would provide both Catholic and Protestant religious instruction. The FDP remained in the Baden-Württemberg government, but in a grand coalition alongside the SPD and the CDU.[56] Besides conflicts with coalition partners, from late 1953 on Maier and Haußmann also had to contend with direct internal opposition from the new, more conservative leader of the FDP Landtag contingent, Eduard Leuze.[57]

Haußmann served as minister of justice in this grand coalition state government during its seven-year tenure. While in this post he successfully developed an independent judiciary, changed press laws to guarantee more journalistic freedom, and established the Central Office for the Investigation of National Socialist Crimes in Ludwigsburg.[58] Within the party, however, his leadership of the Baden-Württemberg party came under fire in 1957 when Maier left regional party politics to become the FDP national chairperson. In 1960, for the first time since his chairmanship began fourteen years earlier, he was challenged for the post at the state party congress. His rival, Eduard Leuze, was defeated by only nine votes.[59]

The 1960 state elections in Baden-Württemberg broke up the grand coalition. The SPD gained a considerable number of votes

---

55. Ibid., p. 231.
56. Ibid., p. 229–32.
57. Ibid., p. 234.
58. Wilhelm Hofmann, "Die Zeit der Regierungsbeteiligung," in Rothmund and Wiehn, eds., *Die F.D.P./DVP*, p. 271.
59. Ibid., pp. 234–35.

as a result of the 1959 Godesberg Program, which moved it more towards the center and modified its working-class identification. Nevertheless, the two losers, the CDU and FDP, were able to form a new government excluding their former partner. Haußmann stayed on as minister of justice. But, as FDP leader, he was implicitly held responsible for the electoral decline. When in the 1964 Landtag elections the party suffered further losses – and Haußmann himself lost his seat – he became vulnerable to his opponents on the left and the right wings of his party. The social-reform-oriented Young Democrats urged Haußmann to step down from either his post as minister of justice or his party chair. When he hesitated, the Young Democrats, who supported a coalition with the SPD, joined forces with Leuze's more conservative Baden group, which had never forgiven Haußmann for the 1950 coalition with the SPD, to force Haußmann to resign as party chair. His successor was Leuze.[60]

The ideological split in the FDP reduced its once disproportional influence as coalition builder in Baden-Württemberg. After the December 1966 elections CDU Interior Minister Filbinger was elected minister-president. Haußmann, with Chairman Leuze's support,[61] headed an official FDP commission designated to continue the coalition with the CDU. In the meantime the SPD was secretly negotiating with an unofficial left-wing FDP delegation. When Filbinger learned of the FDP's duplicity, he brusquely bypassed the liberals altogether. In a quick compromise the CDU and SPD reached an agreement on the one issue that had hitherto separated them, one that had historically been championed by the liberals: providing other alternatives to religiously segregated schools. Mirroring the new national government, Filbinger formed a CDU/SPD grand coalition.[62]

Once in opposition, the Baden-Württemberg FDP became even more divided, and the older Stuttgart Liberals like Haußmann served increasingly in a purely advisory function. In 1968 the Constance sociology professor, Ralf Dahrendorf, joined the state executive committee and brought new ideas and leadership to the state and national FDP. His entry into this position really marks a generational changing of the guard within the

60. Ibid., pp. 235–37.
61. Ibid., p. 277.
62. Ibid., pp. 239–40.

party leadership. This new generation of liberal politicians had a sharper sense of socioeconomic conflicts and the need for social reform as well as for a new approach to German-German relations and *Ostpolitik*. The 1969 state party congress revealed the structural and ideological transformation that had taken place within the party. There was no right-wing representation in the new executive committee, and even centrist old-timers like Haußmann and Maier were given no opportunity to speak. The election of the favorite of the Young Democrats, Martin Bangemann, to the executive committee was symptomatic of this early swing to the left.[63] Four years later Bangemann, the "enfant terrible of the *Altliberalen*," was elected state chairperson. But the party had continued its leftward trend in the interim so that Bangemann was now considered a moderate among the 1973 leadership.[64]

In the first two postwar decades, Haußmann was representative of a slightly left-of-center orientation within postwar liberalism, an orientation that played down nationalism and the conservatism associated with the old German People's Party. This was typical of that generation of liberals who had lived through the Third Reich as political opponents of the Nazis and who identified themselves with the traditions of the Weimar liberals Friedrich Naumann and Gustav Stresemann. However, already by the 1950s large numbers of party leaders and rank-and-file members had not been liberal opponents to Nazism and had had no connection with the pre-1933 liberalism, nor did they define themselves by reference to the traditions of one of the Bismarckian, Wilhelmine, or Weimar parties. In contrast to many of these liberals, Haußmann aligned himself with the left-wing of the party in the 1950s debates over admitting and even recruiting right-wing extremists, including neo-Nazis, into the liberal fold and over restoring pre-1945 German borders.[65] But Haußmann refused to be captured by ideological restraints. The abandonment of the CDU/CSU coalition out of protest against the *Spiegel* affair and the eventual switch from the CDU/CSU to the SPD in the 1960s led to a realignment of the left

63. Ibid., pp. 240–41.
64. Ibid., p. 245.
65. Hein, *Zwischen liberaler Milieupartei*, pp. 211–12. See also J.M. Gutscher, *Die Entwicklung der FDP von ihren Anfängen bis 1961* (Meisenheim, 1984), pp. 186–87 and 101–2.

and right based on the so-called German question and *Ostpolitik*. After a number of FDP members left the party over this realignment of the FDP leadership to the left,[66] Haußmann, with his more traditional liberal concerns about constitutionalism, legal rights, and laissez-faire capitalism, found himself marginalized to the right of the new generation of FDP liberals. This generational change marked the end of Haußmann's formidable influence within the southwestern and national FDP. Until his death, however, he remained professionally active, worked in state and national campaigns, and advised the party leadership.[67]

Within the FDP, Hamm-Brücher took over where Haußmann left off. In the 1960s she began to earn a name for herself outside the confines of Bavaria. Whereas Haußmann had been preoccupied with setting up and establishing the Baden-Württemberg and national FDP on firm ground, Hamm-Brücher was able to concentrate on issues of liberalism via a firmly established party. Her primary concern was equal rights and equal opportunity, particularly in the field of education, which she saw as a stepping stone to social, vocational, and personal advancement. Given the chronology of the student movement in the Federal Republic, across Europe, and in the United States, her agitation for educational reform in the 1960s was timely. Her promotion of the *Simultanschule* over totally religiously segregated schools and the *Gesamtschule*, a comprehensive, nontracked school, reflected both liberalism's traditional anticlericalism and her own individual commitment to the further democratization of West German society through educational reform.[68] She also spoke out for increasing the number of students and facilities at the universities so that more students of diverse socioeconomic backgrounds could attend. She saw the 1960s student activism, on the one hand, as a turbulent but final departure from the uncritical acceptance of nineteenth-century values as to the role of the state, church, and family in society, and, on the other hand, as a rash entry into a twenty-first century where all lifestyles and working conditions would be revolutionized. This

---

66. C. Søe and H. Vorländer, "Der Kampf um Überleben und Einfluß: Rolle und Funktion der FDP in der westdeutschen Politik," in Vorländer, ed., *Verfall oder Renaissance*, pp. 175–76.

67. Personal interview with W. Haußmann, Stuttgart, 30 November 1982.

68. See H. Hamm-Brücher, *Gegen Unfreiheit in der demokratischen Gesellschaft* (Munich, 1968), pp. 100–253.

1960s generation was, according to Hamm-Brücher, experimenting with the different forms and manifestations of democracy. Realizing that the primary influence for her own and older generations had been authoritarianism, she worked to encourage tolerance and understanding from and for both generations, whom she saw as caught in the midst of transition.[69]

Her views on educational reform were interrelated with her advocacy of women's rights. Schools were not only frequently segregated according to religion, but also according to the sex of the children, especially in Bavaria, where Hamm-Brücher began her political career. This resulted in situations where secondary schools for girls were not always available. Because girls were not admitted to the boys' schools, some were being denied the opportunity of pursuing careers and/or higher education that required this special schooling. Graduates of boys' schools were given priority over girls' schools for university admission as well as for civil service positions later in life; the assumption was that the man had to support a family whereas the woman was working for spending money. Hamm-Brücher fought against these practices from the time she was in the Munich city council through her career in the Bavarian *Landtag* and in her posts in the Wiesbaden and Bonn ministries.[70]

Hamm-Brücher's sense of feminism stemmed from her liberal emphasis on individual rights. In her stress on the necessity of education and training for women's emancipation,[71] she resembled Helene Lange, a woman prominent in the conservative wing of the Berlin feminist movement in the 1890s.[72] However, Hamm-Brücher did not want to direct women's education toward just the domestic or "female sphere," as Lange had done. Hamm-Brücher also resembled Gertrud Bäumer, an early twentieth-century liberal feminist, at least according to some definitions. Often described as the Friedrich Naumann of the women's movement,[73] Bäumer believed that the women's movement had to devote itself to reducing social tension and

---

69. See Hamm-Brücher, *Vorkämpfer für Demokratie*, pp. 21–22 and 42–53.
70. Hamm-Brücher, *Gegen Unfreiheit*, pp. 18–19. See also her *Vorkämpfer für Demokratie*, p. 16.
71. Hamm-Brücher, *Gegen Unfreiheit*, pp. 17–19.
72. R. Evans, *The Feminist Movement in Germany, 1894–1933* (Sage, London, 1976), pp. 27–28.
73. Ibid., p. 154.

class conflict through social reform and organized welfare work.[74] Although Bäumer felt that liberalism and women's emancipation shared a common intellectual and historical basis,[75] she was hostile to liberal individualism.[76]

Although Hamm-Brücher tended to identify less with the women's movement because of *its* emphasis on collectivism and *her* own marked individualism, she did stress the goal of social reform and was willing to work with other women to accomplish it. While in the Munich city council, for example, she participated with the women representatives of the SPD, KPD, and CSU – to the dismay of male colleagues – in cross-party female motions concerning social issues such as day care and youth criminality.[77] Like Lange and Bäumer, however, Hamm-Brücher had certain "bourgeois feminist" ideas about women's appropriate behavior. In a 1951 newspaper article on the role of a female city councillor, she wrote: "and finally *mit Haut und Haar* she must remain a woman – because there are certainly enough men already in the city council."[78] Given the sexist barriers that she had to overcome in order to be respected by all parties – a real feat in traditionally conservative Bavaria – she should be given credit for easing the entry of other women into state and national politics.

Although more well-known for her advocacy of educational and social reform, Hamm-Brücher did not shy away from more traditional domestic and foreign policy issues. She made a name for herself as an active opponent of any resurgence or continuing influence of Nazism in the young Federal Republic. For example, she fought for many years against the appointment of Theodor Maunz, the former Nazi constitutional expert, as Bavarian minister of culture. Her media campaign against Maunz

74. Ibid.

75. G. Bäumer, *Die Frau in Volkswirtschaft und Staatsleben der Gegenwart* (Stuttgart, 1914), p. 309.

76. Evans, *The Feminist Movement*, pp. 155–57.

77. In the Munich city council that was elected in 1948, 25 percent of the members were women. This was the highest percentage of female members compared both to pre-1948 politics and to politics between 1948 and 1982. For examples of these motions, see the following protocols in the Stadtarchiv München, Ratssitzungsprotokolle (RP) 722/9, Personalausschußsitzung of 7 April 1949, RP 722/1, Stadtratssitzung of 29 March 1949, and RP 722/2, Stadtratssitzung of 12 April 1949.

78. *Neue Zeitung*, 14 February 1951. As cited in Hamm-Brücher, *Gegen Unfreiheit*, p. 14.

and her personal letters to Minister-President Alfons Goppel finally succeeded in forcing his resignation in 1964, seven years after his first appointment.[79]

Hamm-Brücher took an independent stand on liberal foreign policy when she opposed the FPD presidium at the 1967 annual party congress by strongly supporting the recognition of the Oder-Neisse line as a permanent German border. Her intention was to promote an *Ostpolitik* that would improve relations with the German Democratic Republic, Poland, and Eastern Europe in general.[80] At the Foreign Office she worked for international understanding through increased cultural awareness of other countries, specializing in United States–West German relations.

Because of her strong sense of justice, her special emphasis on equal opportunity as a prerequisite for democracy, and her *Ostpolitik*, one might assume that Hildegard Hamm-Brücher was a left liberal. But she did not identify herself in that way. Only weeks after the 1982 coalition realignment she wrote, in a volume intended as a protest against the transformation of the FDP "to a conservative right-liberal economic party,"[81] that she did not belong to the left-wing of the FDP and that she firmly rejected any explicitly anticapitalist policies.[82] Like Haußmann, she rejected dogmatic left-right positions and stressed instead the breadth of liberal identity. She stated that none of the great Liberals of the twentieth century, such as Naumann, Stresemann, Rathenau, Heuß, or Dehler, could be labelled right or left liberals; instead they were always just "liberals" who embodied elements of both the right and the left.[83]

Although she did not want to be identified as a left liberal, Hamm-Brücher did support the 1971 social-liberal Freiburg Theses, which called for a "democratization of society" and a "reform of capitalism,"[84] and which led to a split between social liberals, who seemed to be moving more and more toward a redefinition of German liberalism beyond the nineteenth-century political liberalism of a John Stuart Mill or even the early

79. Hamm-Brücher, *Vorkämpfer für Demokratie*, pp. 23ff.
80. Ibid., p. 35.
81. Schuchardt and Verheugen, *Das liberale Gewissen*, Vorwort.
82. H. Hamm-Brücher, "Keine Neuauflage des 'Genscherismus,'" in Schuchardt and Verheugen, *Das liberale Gewissen*, p. 27.
83. Ibid., p. 25.
84. Søe and Vorländer, "Kampf um Überleben," pp. 175–76. See also Søe, "Free Democratic Party," p. 132.

twentieth-century social liberalism of Friedrich Naumann to a rapprochement with social democratic principles, and the more old-style Manchesterite liberals, who wanted to continue Ludwig Erhard–type policies. She saw the Freiburg Theses as a political bridge between conservative – including liberal – bourgeois policies and socialist policies that could facilitate exchange and compromise in both directions.[85] Hamm-Brücher also took a strong position on civil rights, especially during the height of RAF (Rote Armee Fraktion) terrorist actions and the so-called Hot Autumn of 1977. As a *Rechtsstaat* civil rights activist, Hamm-Brücher found herself on the left of the interparty divide with social-liberals like Günter Verheugen and Ingrid Matthäus-Maier against more old-style national liberals and traditional economic liberals like Otto Graf Lambsdorff on the right.[86] On 1 October 1982 during what has gone down in contemporary West German political history as the *Wende*, when the FDP left the coalition with the SPD in 1982 and brought the Helmut Schmidt chancellorship to a close,[87] Hamm-Brücher gave a strong speech in the Bundestag against her party's decision to facilitate the coalition realignment.[88] But she also appealed to liberals to pull together and seek ways to resolve the conflict. She considered the FDP's withdrawal from the coalition with the SPD a betrayal of the coalition agreement and an undemocratic action, because no new elections had been held to determine popular opinion.[89] It was ultimately the undemocratic method behind the *Wende* that upset her more than any ideology associated with the switch of coalition partners. Unlike most of her social-liberal colleagues who also strongly opposed the realignment and left the FDP in protest, Hamm-Brücher remained loyal to the party. Her tolerance for diversity within liberalism and her own self-identification as a liberal and a Free Democrat compelled her to stay in the FDP and to continue to influence it from within.

---

85. H. Hamm-Brücher, "Keine Neuauflage des 'Genscherismus,'" p. 27.
86. Søe and Vorländer, "Kampf um Überleben," p. 177.
87. Søe, "Free Democratic Party," p. 121.
88. Reproduced in Schuchardt and Verheugen, *Das liberale Gewissen*, pp. 30–33.
89. Hamm-Brücher, "Keine Neuauflage des 'Genscherismus,'" p. 27.

Conclusion

After this brief examination of continuity and change in postwar German liberalism, one would have to conclude that although some change occurred, it was generally neither drastic nor totally unrelated to previous trends in pre-1933 German liberalism. The most significant change was not within liberal ideology per se, but in the practice of liberalism in the more or less stable three-party system in the Federal Republic, where the FDP functioned as maker or breaker of coalitions. The postwar liberals, unlike their Bismarckian, Wilhelmine, or Weimar predecessors, did maintain a unified party. The left and right bifurcation did continue into the postwar period, although a significant number of Free Democrats, like Haußmann and Hamm-Brücher, refused to be labeled as right or left. When the party changed coalitions first in 1969 by joining the Social Democrats in Bonn and then again in 1982, when it switched over to the CDU/CSU, the FDP lost some right-wing national liberals in the first instance and some left-wing social liberals in the second. But these renegades did not form rival liberal parties.

This factionalism, however, is what has ultimately determined the party's survival. Without this internal division the party would not have been able to switch coalitions as easily as it did and thus would not have been able to attract as many swing voters. No matter what the FDP offered or gave up in its party platform to acquire the minimum five-percent electoral support, there were always Germans who voted for the FDP in order to moderate one or the other of the two sectarian parties. There is no reason to doubt that this tendency will continue in the future.

Historically, three fundamental issues have tormented Liberals: laissez-faire capitalism, the guarantee of individual privacy and freedom, and constitutionalism. Because these issues will continue to appear in various forms, there will always be a potential for membership in a liberal party, at least as long as the sectarian parties do not coopt them totally. Whether the FDP will be accepted as the liberal conscience of the nation is another matter. The prospects of the party will be determined by whether issues that coincide with these liberal concerns arise. Future Haußmanns and Hamm-Brüchers will emerge in their own ways over pressing issues, whether these be judicial, educational, or other kinds of reforms. The ambition for a liberal party continues to exist, and with current West German concerns about the protection of personal information and privacy rights, private television and private universities, treatment of "guest workers" (*Gastarbeiter*), the use of census information, the granting of political asylum, and the right of civil disobedience, there will continue to be liberal supporters in the Federal Republic. These types of issues will continue to attract liberals like Hamm-Brücher, while party men and women like Haußmann will be needed to keep the party infrastructure intact. How forcefully the FDP deals with issues like these within the constraints of its varying coalitions will depend on its members' engagement and will ultimately determine the success or failure of this liberal party within the West German political system.

14

Ludwig Erhard and German Liberalism – An Ambivalent Relationship?

A.J. Nicholls

Ludwig Erhard's (1897–1977) position in the history of German liberalism after 1945 is somewhat paradoxical. On the one hand, he is the person most clearly identified with economic policies that not only were highly successful, but also deserve to be regarded as "liberal." The restoration of the free price mechanism, the liberation of market forces, and the support for healthy competition against enemies on the right and the left – all these were liberal characteristics of Erhard's long period at the helm of the West German economy from 1948 to 1966.

On the other hand, Erhard played little part in the reestablishment of liberalism as a political force in Germany after the war. For years unburdened by party membership, he ran in election campaigns as a candidate of the Christian Democratic Union (Christlich-Demokratische Union or CDU), and indeed on more than one occasion could claim to be the electoral locomotive that hauled the rather ramshackle Christian Democratic train to victory over its rivals. The policy for which Erhard stood was not one of laissez-faire capitalism, but one of the "social market economy." "Social" was not a word that carried much conviction as a liberal slogan in Germany. German liberals had not been wholehearted in their efforts to improve the lot of the less fortunate members of society, even if they had enthusiastically adopted the term *Volksgemeinschaft* in the 1920s. Erhard's policy seemed more appropriate to a party with Christian principles and an influential trade union element in its ranks than to one associated with narrow middle-class interests.

This view of Erhard as the architect of Christian Democratic popularity in the Federal Republic has a great deal to commend it. Erhard himself propagated it with vigor, much to the annoyance of Konrad Adenauer.[1] It should not be assumed, however, that Erhard's relationship to German liberalism was unimportant. In terms of his career development and his ideology he was both affected by and had an important effect on the history of modern German liberalism.

Erhard himself came from a class and provincial background that might be described as quintessentially liberal. The city in which he was born, Fürth, was a commercial and industrial city in the province of Middle Franconia. The majority of its inhabitants were Protestants but, since they were incorporated into the mainly Roman Catholic kingdom of Bavaria, it was not surprising that liberal sentiments had developed strongly in the province during the nineteenth century. Fürth itself boasted a proud tradition of religious tolerance that extended even to the substantial Jewish population.[2] The political parties that did well there were the left-liberal Progressive People's Party (Fortschrittliche Volkspartei or FVP) and the Social Democrats (SPD). Although the Progressives had dropped behind the SPD by 1912, they still made a very respectable showing.[3]

Erhard was the child of a mixed marriage; he was brought up by his Protestant mother in her faith, with the approval of his Roman Catholic father. According to one account, priests of both denominations attended family celebrations, and Erhard was later to stress the atmosphere of religious tolerance he enjoyed as a child.[4] His father was an independent retailer and ran a haberdasher's shop. The son of peasant farmers, he was an archetypal "small man" who had left the countryside to take up a trade. Although he is supposed to have respected Bismarck, his politics seem to have been those of the Progressives. He admired Eugen Richter, who embodied a purist, almost

---

1. In the summer of 1949 an opinion poll showed Erhard clearly ahead of Adenauer in public popularity. Only Schumacher had an equal amount of support. K. Hohmann, "Ludwig Erhard, 1897–1977," in *Fränkische Lebensbilder* (Neustadt and Aisch, 1984), vol. 11, p. 224; see also D. Koerfer, *Kampf ums Kanzleramt Erhard und Adenauer* (Stuttgart, 1987), pp. 58–59 and 159.

2. K. Hohmann, "Aus dem Leben Ludwig Erhards: Die Jahre bis 1945," *Orientierungen zur Wirtschafts- und Gesellschaftspolitik* 11 (April 1982): 50–52.

3. *Statistisches Jahrbuch für das Königreich Bayern, 1913* (Munich, 1913), pp. 457–63. The term Progressive will be used to denote left-liberal in this period, although the party names changed over time.

4. Hohmann, "Aus dem Leben," p. 53, citing a recorded interview between Erhard and Hans Otto Wesemann. See also J. Lukomski, *Ludwig Erhard: Der Mensch und der Politiker* (Düsseldorf and Vienna, 1965), pp. 9–24.

Gladstonian liberalism that was hostile to government interference, public spending, and obstacles to market freedom.
Erhard later claimed that his father would defend this form of
progressive politics against colleagues of a conservative – or
more probably National Liberal – frame of mind.[5] Apparently
neither Social Democracy nor the Catholic Center Party made
much impact on the Erhard family.

It has to be remembered, of course, that by the outbreak of the
First World War German liberalism had changed a good deal
since the foundation of the German Empire in 1871. Belief in the
self-operating mechanism of the market, the benefits of free
trade, and the virtues of strict economy in public expenditure
were crumbling. Their place was being taken by national self-
assertiveness and the fear of rising social forces ostensibly hostile to liberalism. This fear related particularly to the growing
strength of Marxist social democracy, but in Bavaria the democratization of the franchise in 1906 also helped the (Roman)
Catholic Center Party, which was regarded by many German
liberals as a defender of obscurantism and a threat to the
national consciousness of the *Reich*.

As far as one can tell, these pressures had little direct effect on
the Erhard family, whose lower-middle-class character may well
have shielded young Ludwig from exposure to aggressive
nationalism in such bodies as the student corporations. He
himself did not study at a university but rather completed an
apprenticeship in textile retailing. He had no opportunity to
practice his trade, however, for by the time his apprenticeship
had ended in 1916 the Great War was in progress. He went
straight to the colors in an operational artillery unit despite the
fact that as a child he had been afflicted with infantile paralysis,
which had left him with a deformation of his right foot. Apparently he fought through the war showing courage and experi-
encing no little misfortune, contracting typhus in Rumania and
then being severely wounded by shell splinters on the Western
Front in the autumn of 1918. He ended the war in the hospital
and was discharged only in June the following year. During the
1920s he was regarded by the authorities as 25 to 30 percent
disabled. His body was clumsy, and he limped.[6]

5. For further details of Erhard's early life see Hohmann, "Ludwig Erhard,
1897–1977," pp. 211–18.
6. Hohmann, "Aus dem Leben," p. 52.; also V. Laitenberger, *Ludwig Erhard:*

It is interesting in this context to compare his personality with that of another handicapped politician, Kurt Schumacher. Schumacher lost an arm while fighting in World War I and later was to endure even more privation in Dachau concentration camp. His heroism is not in doubt. Nevertheless, as leader of the Social Democrats after 1945 his crippled condition created an embittered image, behind which lay a valiant but essentially gloomy disposition.[7] Erhard, however, always presented himself as an optimist. His somewhat misshapen figure became the symbol of a prosperous and even slightly hedonistic lifestyle, a symbol capped by the characteristic cigar in its holder. It was this sense of optimism that Erhard communicated to his political supporters in the Federal Republic, and it rubbed off on liberals as well as on Christian Democrats. For the former, it was an unusual sensation. Despair, or at least angst, could be seen as their most characteristic cultural trait.

Erhard's optimism was all the more remarkable in that his family circumstances seemed scarcely to justify it. In addition to his own poor health, the future of his father's business was bleak. The Weimar era was not a happy one for the small retailer. The inflation damaged middle-class savings; the subsequent retrenchment brought high interest rates, contraction of trade, and fierce competition from more efficient large-scale firms. When Erhard had to turn his attention to the condition of the family concern, it was too late; by 1928 it was clear to him that he would need a new source of income.[8] Yet, unlike some others, he did not seek an explanation for the family misfortune in the seductive anti-Semitic conspiracy theories peddled in nearby Nuremberg by Julius Streicher. For one thing, such rancor was foreign to his nature. For another, he was by this time thoroughly schooled in the theories of classical liberal political economy.

The story of Erhard's intellectual development is well known, but it deserves rehearsing at this point to illustrate the extent to which his attitudes deviated from the "orthodox liberalism" of

Der Nationalökonom als Politiker (Göttingen and Zurich 1986), pp. 11–13; and Lukomski, *Ludwig Erhard*, p. 12.

7. Cf. the sympathetic but by no means uncritical biography of Schumacher by L. Edinger, *Kurt Schumacher: A Study in Personality and Political Behaviour* (Stanford and London, 1965), in particular pp. 15–17.

8. Laitenberger, *Erhard: Der Nationalökonom*, p. 18.

the Weimar period. Owing to his frail health he was unable to enter into the family business when he was demobilized, but registered instead for a diploma course at a newly founded college of commerce (*Handelshochschule*) in Nuremberg. His mentor there was Wilhelm Rieger, who believed in the strict application of market principles to microeconomic problems. Hence he firmly rejected the concept of a "just price" so popular among small businessmen and insisted that prices be fixed according to the laws of supply and demand. He was also firmly attached to the need for the state to ensure sound money, a principle that had been overridden in the First World War and was apparently disappearing altogether in the early 1920s.[9]

Since Erhard proved a gifted pupil at the *Handelshochschule*, he decided to go on with academic studies and read for his doctorate at Frankfurt University under the guidance of Franz Oppenheimer, a political economist who had developed a somewhat idiosyncratic theory of what he termed "liberal socialism." This involved a rejection of both laissez-faire capitalism and Marxism. Instead, there should be a just social order with an economy based on free market competition protected by the state. Social justice could be achieved by ensuring that everyone had a fair access to the market. But for this to happen, there first had to be a redistribution of landed property, since the inequalities of land ownership were seen by Oppenheimer as the major obstacle to a just and successful economic system.[10]

Erhard certainly did not accept Oppenheimer's theories literally, and he later recalled that "social liberalism" – rather than liberal socialism – would be a description he preferred for his own views.[11] Nevertheless, he continued to have a high personal

9. C. Heusgen, *Ludwig Erhards Lehre von der sozialen Marktwirtschaft: Ursprünge, Kerngehalt, Wandlungen* (Bern and Stuttgart, 1981), p. 66.
10. H.F. Wünsche, *Ludwig Erhards Gesellschafts- und Wirtschaftskonzeption: Soziale Marktwirtschaft als politische Ökonomie* (Stuttgart, 1986), pp. 74–81.
11. See Erhard's introduction to F. Oppenheimer, *Erlebtes, Erstrebtes, Erreichtes: Lebenserinnerungen* (Düsseldorf, 1964), p. 5. Erhard wrote, "If you are in political life as I am, you will be relentlessly crossexamined [*auf Herz und Nieren geprüft*]. Are you just preaching for effect or do you really believe in a liberal socialism? Well, I reversed the adjective and the noun – incidentally, my friend Wilhelm Röpke did the same – and claimed that although "social liberalism" certainly shifted the emphasis somewhat, it nevertheless remained true to the principle at stake. It is in the same spirit." Whether Oppenheimer would have agreed with this is doubtful, but it is not without interest for the light it sheds on Erhard's own thought.

regard for Oppenheimer. He took from him a commitment to social responsibility and a belief that a market economy would function best when property was as widely distributed as possible. Oppenheimer's view that free competition needed state protection also left a lasting impression on Erhard.

Lastly, Erhard's employment from 1928 until 1942 in the Market Research Institute in Nuremberg, headed by Wilhelm Vershofen, strengthened his inclination to put the consumer at the center of his view of the economy. Consumer goods industries were the main clients of Vershofen's Institute, which was one of the first in Germany to import American market research techniques and apply them to microeconomic problems.[12] In Germany the views of heavy industry tended to carry much weight in public policy-making. Those views were favorable to cartels and price-fixing. Erhard's practical experience, as well as his inclinations, caused him to favor those branches of production that met the needs of consumers.

So far, one may not regard Erhard's training as particularly unusual. Certainly in the United States or Britain it would have been unremarkable, except perhaps for the stress on social responsibility drawn from Oppenheimer. In Germany, however, economists had adopted a nationalistic stance that placed production before consumption in their scale of values. Commitment to a rigorously competitive market and free trade came to be regarded as unnecessary, if not positively undesirable. Such classical economic theories smacked of doctrinaire "Manchesterism,"[13] an epithet that continued to have negative implications until well into the twentieth century when it was supplanted by "liberalistic" as a term of abuse.

One area in which this development could be noticed was in the attitude toward competition and restraints on trade. By the 1920s the power of cartels in Germany was already something of a legend, the legality of cartel agreements having been recognized by a decision of the supreme court of the Reich in February

---

12. Erhard was anything but a comfortably placed academic at the institute; he spent his early years on a part-time and poorly paid basis. See E. Schäfer, "Die Institutionszeit in Nürnberg," in G. Schröder et al., eds., *Ludwig Erhard: Beiträge zu seiner politischen Biographie, Festschrift zum fünfundsiebzigsten Geburtstag* (Frankfurt/Vienna, 1971), p. 604.

13. L. Albertin, *Liberalismus und Demokratie am Anfang der Weimarer Republik: Eine vergleichende Analyse der Deutschen Demokratischen Partei und der Deutschen Volkspartei* (Düsseldorf, 1972), pp. 258–59. See esp. fn. 305.

1897. Although some German liberals were willing to control monopoly enterprises, relatively few of them seemed particularly worried about cartels, which were widely accepted as "a fact of economic life."[14] Many on the left wing of the German liberal movement were impressed by the inevitability of the shift away from Adam Smith's vision of open markets towards a form of organized capitalism.

In the Weimar Republic even the newly founded German Democratic Party (Deutsche Demokratische Partei or DDP) that performed so well in the elections to the National Assembly in January 1919 did not espouse a clearly consumer-oriented liberal economic policy. The influence of industrial pressure groups within the party structure was too great for that,[15] as was the overriding influence of nationalism. The DDP was incensed at the harsh treatment of Germany by its former enemies, and free trade principles became a casualty of nationalist resentment. As Germany was temporarily forbidden to protect its markets under the Versailles Treaty, the restoration of tariffs became a symbol of national sovereignty.

From the outset, the ambivalence of the Democratic Party's economic program confused its supporters. Adopted in December 1919, it certainly rejected socialism by claiming that "general nationalization [*Verstaatlichung*] would mean a deadly bureaucratization of the economy and a fateful reduction in its output."[16] It supported private property and praised the initiative of the entrepreneur but made no mention of competition, the free market mechanism, or free trade. Quite apart from the fact that liberals at this time preferred to stress Germany's nationalist aspirations and blamed economic problems on war or the Treaty of Versailles, the constituency that they perceived themselves to have was such that no consensus could be achieved except on the basis of negative preferences.

The left wing of the DDP wished to combine social with political democracy, even though they denied espousing socialism. They seemed to favor some sort of controlled economy, and they certainly favored codetermination in industry and state

14. James J. Sheehan, *German Liberalism in the Nineteenth Century* (Chicago and London, 1978), p. 257.
15. Albertin, *Liberalismus und Demokratie*, pp. 167–81.
16. W. Treue, *Deutsche Parteiprogramme, 1861–1954* (Göttingen, Frankfurt, and Berlin, 1954), p. 125.

arbitration in labor disputes. On the other hand, more conventional liberals pressed for a return to market forces and were unsympathetic to trade unions. Early in 1919 the main threat had apparently come from socialism; later in the 1920s the power of industrial capital seemed more of a menace to employee interests.

In 1927 one of the DDP's leading economic spokesmen, Hermann Fischer of the Hansabund, advised that the party should avoid trying to work out a clearer program because it would simply create difficulties and not achieve anything practical.[17] When Gustav Stolper delivered a ringing encomium for the benefits of capitalism and the sovereignty of the consumer two years later, delegates at the Democratic Party Congress cheered enthusiastically, but his proposals for the economy ran afoul of objections from white-collar trade unions and the Democratic youth organization.[18] They also cut across plans to move closer to the nationalist Young German Order (Jungdeutscher Orden), a body imbued with romantic notions of comradeship inimical to market economics.

For most of its career, therefore, the DDP was struggling to face both ways, warding off enemies on the left and right. It had to steer between Scylla and Charybdis in economic matters, and this crippled its ability to offer clear-cut, intellectually satisfying alternatives to its Marxist or nationalist rivals.[19] Small wonder, then, that in 1930 the party was in such dire straits that many of its leaders decided to merge the party with the Young German Order to form the new State Party (Staatspartei), the main aim of which was a stronger and more centralized state. On economic matters it claimed to stand for a type of "social capitalism," which was supposed to encourage small businessmen and at the same time not obstruct the national state (*Volksstaat*). Cartels

17. W. Schneider, *Die Deutsche Demokratische Partei in der Weimarer Republik, 1924–1930* (Munich, 1978), pp. 163–64. See also Fischer's speech to the 1924 DDP Congress, in which he claimed that the Weimar Constitution had created a *Volksgemeinschaft* in Germany: Hermann Fischer, *Volk, Staat und Wirtschaft: Vortrag auf dem Parteitag der Deutschen Demokratischen Partei, 5 April 1924* (Berlin, n.d.).

18. Schneider, *Deutsche Demokratische Partei*, pp. 171–74.

19. E. Portner, *Die Verfassungspolitik der Liberalen, 1919: Ein Beitrag zur Deutung der Weimarer Verfassung* (Bonn, 1973), pp. 188–89; see also C. Maier, *Recasting Bourgeois Europe: Stabilization in France, Germany, and Italy in the Decade after World War I* (Princeton, 1975), pp. 444 and 457.

and trusts should be subject to controls, which would prevent them from suppressing independent initiative or imposing un-economic prices on others. But there was no clear commitment to competition, let alone free trade.

As far as the more conservative liberals in Stresemann's German People's Party (Deutsche Volkspartei or DVP) were concerned, their leader had always made clear his support for individual enterprise. He sympathized with small business in its struggles with mightier market competitors. In the early years of Weimar his party called for a rapid end to wartime controls on commercial activity. He seemed to have a real commitment to liberal economics. Nevertheless, Stresemann became so preoccupied with Germany's diplomatic weakness that he preferred to concentrate his supporters' minds on national questions rather than on economic policy. The almost mystical belief in an organic national community, the *Volksgemeinschaft*, was stressed at the expense of competitive individualism. Like the DDP, the DVP depended on support from industrial interests for which cartels were a necessary fact of life. The party's economic program was bland rather than challenging. It rested on the defense of private property and a commitment to aid various special interests such as the shipping industry or the free professions. There was a marked lack of any clear-cut economic strategy.[20]

Liberal parties in the Weimar Republic, then, were certainly united in their rejection of socialism. But they were unclear about the preferred alternative. No agreement was reached on a theoretically consistent economic system – what the Germans would call a *Wirtschaftsordnung* – as the concept of free competition ran counter to too many vested interests. Free trade was already regarded as quaintly old-fashioned. When, on 15 March 1929, the DDP minister of agriculture, Hermann Dietrich, told the Reichstag that there was not a single free-trader in the Democratic delegation (*Fraktion*), his comment was greeted with approval by his own supporters.[21] Cartels and price-fixing were

20. For the party program see Treue, *Parteiprogramme*, pp. 118–22 (DVP); pp. 150–52 (DStP). On Stresemann's views see L.E. Jones, "Gustav Stresemann and the Crisis of German Liberalism," in *European Studies Review* 4, no. 2 (April 1974): 145–51.

21. *Verhandlungen des Reichstages, IV. Wahlperiode, 1928, Stenographische Berichte*, vol. 424 (Berlin, 1929), p. 1494, also cited in Schneider, *Deutsche Demokratische Partei*, p. 198.

either accepted as practical necessities which should not be touched by "unworldly" academics, or else they were perceived as inevitable if regrettable characteristics of "late capitalism," ones that should indeed be registered with the authorities to ensure they were not damaging the public interest, but that should nevertheless be protected by the law. Robust free market ideologies were not prominent among German liberal political groups in the 1920s, as it was accepted that classical liberalism had in some mysterious fashion gone intellectually bankrupt.

The German economics profession was itself a house divided insofar as its prescriptions for the German economy were concerned. Writing in March 1929, the liberal economist Walter Eucken described how difficult it was to obtain clear formulations from his colleagues in the Association for [Economic and] Social Policy (Verein für Sozialpolitik) when dealing with "fact-grubbers and vulgar economists" on the one hand and a priori theorists detached from reality on the other.[22] He deplored the lack of a coherent theoretical foundation that could enable German economists to answer the questions put to them by politicians and the general public. In the 1930s he tried to remedy this defect by explaining the implications of economic laws for the everyday lives of Germany's citizens. He severely criticized German economists for relativizing economic laws and thereby losing confidence in themselves insofar as general theories were concerned. Instead, they had devoted their attention to specific areas of the economic process at particular moments in time. "In this way," he argued, "there spread among German economists a pedantic attention to detailed facts," which was really a betrayal of the scientific method, even if it would not in the end be able to smother the truth.[23]

Eucken and other economists of the younger generation such as Wilhelm Röpke and Alexander Rüstow certainly wished to revive the classical teachings associated with Adam Smith, to maximize competition in the Germany economy, and to preach the importance of working with market forces rather than

22. W. Eucken to A. Rüstow, 27 March 1929, Bundesarchiv Koblenz Nachlaß (hereafter BA: NL) Rüstow, vol. 2.
23. W. Eucken, "Die Überwindung des Historismus," in *Schmollers Jahrbuch* 62 (March 1938): 69. His more general explanatory work was *Nationalökonomie wozu?* (Leipzig 1938). See also Eucken, *Kapitaltheoretische Untersuchungen*, 2d ed. (Tübingen and Zurich, 1954), chap. 1.

against them. They were mostly associated with the remnants of left-liberalism in the early 1930s, but the political climate made it impossible for them to achieve much progress.[24] However, this was only symptomatic of the confusion within liberal ranks that existed on a wide range of issues. For just as many liberal voters were tempted to support National Socialism in 1932 and 1933, so some economists of liberal inclinations thought they might be able to educate the Nazis in economic reality. Their aim was to use the strong state that they assumed Hitler would create to overcome the pressures from interest groups, which seemed to be turning the German economy into a milk cow for subsidies and special privileges. In a famous speech to the Association for Social Policy in 28 September 1932, Rüstow himself had passionately urged the need for a strong state, not to direct the economy but to protect the free market against distortions and overly powerful economic subjects.[25]

Rüstow's own opposition to National Socialism was unequivocal, and he, along with Röpke, was soon forced into exile. Those who stayed behind no longer had the freedom to express their views with frankness; nevertheless, some of them seem to have hoped that Nazi bombast about "corporatism" might be turned to good use in that it might establish rules of procedure that would apply to all within a market framework. Franz Böhm, later to be a major architect of anti-cartel legislation, lost his job in the Third Reich for lack of subservience to Nazi doctrine. Yet in 1933 he had expressed the hope that the new possibilities could be used to create a legal framework within which competition would be protected.[26] Even Erhard himself discussed the possibilities of corporatism and a system of state-supervised cartels, although it can be inferred from his writings that he saw these as a lesser evil, and that he considered the free

---

24. Cf. A.J. Nicholls, "The Other Germany – the Neo-liberals," in R.J. Bullen, H. Pogge von Strandmann, and A. Polonsky, eds., *Ideas into Politics: Aspects of European History, 1880–1950* (London and Sydney, 1984), pp. 164–70.
25. See A. Rüstow, "Die staatspolitischen Voraussetzungen des wirtschaftspolitischen Liberalismus," in W. Koch, ed., *Alexander Rüstow: Rede und Antwort, 21 Reden und viele Diskussionsbeiträge aus den Jahren 1932–62* (Ludwigsberg, 1962), pp. 249–58.
26. F. Böhm, *Wettbewerb und Monopolkampf: Eine Untersuchung zur Frage des wirtschaftlichen Kampfrechts und zur Frage der rechtlichen Struktur der geltenden Wirtschaftsordnung* (Berlin, 1933; facsimile reproduction, 1964), pp. vi–xiv.

market to be the optimal solution.[27]

During the 1930s, German neoliberal economists worked to build up counterarguments to combat collectivism, corporatism, and nationalist attitudes toward trade. Characteristics of the neoliberal position were a commitment to free competition supported by the state and above all by the law. The latter should give no protection to cartels or contracts which restricted economic freedom. Prices and wages should be fixed by the laws of supply and demand. Consumers and not governments or special-interest groups should be sovereign in the marketplace. Support should be given to small businesses and small farmers, not by affording them subventions and artificially fixed prices, but by assisting them to adapt to new markets and attain new expertise. International trade should be as free as possible, based on sound currencies with stable exchange rates. The weaker members of society should be helped by a willingness to tax wealth, provided that this did not undermine individual self-reliance or overstrain the economy. "Laissez-faire" capitalism of a nineteenth-century type was strongly rejected. The neoliberals were by no means a united or even a well-coordinated group, but both inside and outside the Third Reich their leading advocates, Wilhelm Röpke, Alexander Rüstow, Walter Eucken, and Franz Böhm, kept in touch with each other or at least were informed about each other's writings. As for Erhard, although he was aware of the viewpoints of the neoliberals and remained sympathetic to their ideas, he was not part of any "school" of economic thought.[28]

Erhard indeed was not a natural party man, a fact that presented him with some difficulties in Hitler's Germany. His refusal even to join the German Labor Front, let alone any more dedicated Nazi organization, is supposed to have been one of the factors leading to his break with Vershoven in 1942 and his establishment of his own miniscule research "institute." His

27. Cf. Wünsche, *Erhards Gesellschaftskonzeption*, pp. 138–42; and V. Berghahn, "Ideas into Politics: The Case of Ludwig Erhard," in Bullen et al., eds., *Ideas into Politics*, p. 183.

28. A. Müller-Armack remarked that "it was not in Erhard's nature to be a committed member of any school of economists," even though he admired Eucken and his colleagues. Müller-Armack, "Wirtschaftspolitiker zwischen Wissenschaft und Politik," in Schröder, ed., *Erhard Festschrift*, p. 473. Cf. Berghahn, "The Case of Ludwig Erhard," pp. 179–80.

self-appointed task in this institute was to draw up his now-famous memorandum on the tasks of postwar reconstruction in Germany. The memorandum was remarkable for its lack of nationalist illusions about Germany's position in the postwar world; it not only impressed Carl Goerdeler, the doomed leader of the July 1944 attempt to overthrow Hitler, but was also communicated to a senior Nazi official in the Ministry of Economics, Otto Ohlendorf, and, more importantly, to the industrialists and bankers who had financed the study.[29] None of these groups could really be described as liberal, unless one assumes that hostility to Marxism and a willingness to consider the free price mechanism as an alternative to a state-controlled economy is an adequate definition of liberalism.

Nevertheless, the memorandum itself was important because it contained many of the central principles that were to inform Erhard's policy after the Second World War. First of all, there was the determination to restore free prices and to ensure a stable currency liberated from the burden of suppressed inflation (*zurückgestaute Inflation*) that price and wage controls of the Nazi era had brought with it. To deal with this, measures of a drastic kind would have to be taken to eliminate the excess purchasing power (*Kaufkraftüberhang*) that had been built up since the introduction of the Nazi Four-Year Plan in 1936. At the same time, competitive market forces should replace the command economy, which, Erhard admitted, had been necessary during the war, but which was quite inappropriate to peacetime production.[30] In practice the memorandum remained a dead letter, and Erhard was indeed fortunate not to be implicated in the purge of anti-Nazi oppositionists that followed the failure of 20 July 1944.

When the end of the war came, he was available to be recruited by the Americans as director of economic affairs at Fürth. They then pressed him on Bavaria's minister-president, the Social Democrat Wilhelm Hoegner, as economics minister, a post Erhard held until December 1946. Hoegner thought the

29. L. Erhard, *Kriegsfinanzierung und Schuldenkonsolidierung: Faksimiledruck der Denkschrift von 1943/4* (Frankfurt a.M., Berlin, and Vienna, 1977), p. xii. See also L. Herbst, *Der totale Krieg und die Ordnung der Wirtschaft: Die Kriegswirtschaft im Spannungsfeld von Politik, Ideologie und Propaganda, 1935–1945* (Stuttgart, 1982), p. 390.

30. Erhard, *Kriegsfinanzierung*, pp. 105ff., 137–38, 154–56, and 232–44.

Americans saw in Erhard an obstacle to possible tendencies towards socialization by his government.[31] Erhard certainly described himself as an "American invention." But Erhard was not the product of any political party.

He did, however, have some political friends. In the northern part of Bavaria where he still lived at the end of the war, he came to know Thomas Dehler, who was one of the founding members of the Liberal Democratic Party (Liberale-Demokratische Partei or LDP) – later to be part of the Free Democrats (Freie Demokratische Partei or FDP). Although he was not himself in the party, Erhard stood close to the liberals. He was certainly not attracted to the Bavarian equivalent of the Christian Democrats (Christlich-Demokratische Union or CDU), the CSU (Christlich-Soziale Union – Christian Social Union), who were bitterly critical of his efforts as Bavarian economics minister and even tried to censure him on the grounds of incompetence after he had left office.[32]

What, then, was the situation for a liberal economist in Germany after the Second World War? In many ways it seemed even less favorable than in November 1918. The great depression, perhaps unfairly, had been blamed on the anarchic workings of the free market. The economic militarization that characterized the war efforts of all developed countries had created large and self-confident planning organizations possessed of an itch to interfere in the economic process. The threat from Bolshevism appeared – and indeed was – far more serious in the period 1945–48 than it had been in the early years of Weimar. With the demise of National Socialism there was a real fear in Western Germany, a fear shared by occupiers and conquered subjects alike, that Stalinist Soviet Communism might prove attractive to a demoralized and disillusioned population. The fact that this was far from the truth was perceived only gradually.

There was therefore an understandable tendency to accept some form of planning, and even the socialization of major industries, as long as this did not involve Marxist class war or expropriation. Such measures were seen as a prophylactic against communism and as a way of meeting the genuine need

---

31. W. Hoegner, "Erhard als bayerischer Wirtschaftsminister," in Gerhard Schröder, ed., *Erhard Festschrift*, p. 128.
32. Laitenberger, *Ludwig Erhard*, pp. 52–54.

to prevent massive unemployment. The newly burgeoning Christian Democratic movement was not immune to such tendencies. In February 1947, for example, the Ahlen program of the CDU in the British zone announced that the postwar social order could no longer be based on the "capitalist striving for profit and power." Planning and controls would be necessary to a certain extent even in normal times to ensure that the economy met the needs of the population as a whole.[33]

If the CDU was ambivalent about free enterprise capitalism, the situation was hardly any clearer in the camp of political liberalism. At least the liberals had managed to achieve some sense of unity in the occupation period, with the emergence of the FDP. The troublesome split that had weakened the liberals in the Weimar Republic had been overcome. Yet in the early years of its existence, the FDP, like the CDU, did not express itself with great clarity or conviction on the subject of economic liberalism. The one party that might have been expected to jump at neoliberal ideas was apparently half-hearted about them.

Hesitations about free enterprise capitalism took various forms. For example, one influential group centered on Essen in the British Zone was highly critical of old-style capitalism and accepted that centralized planning would have to be an essential part of the future economy. In November 1945 this group, of which the future FDP leader Franz Blücher was a member, published a program containing an economic section beginning with words reminiscent of Hitler: "The economy is there for the people and not the people for the economy." It went on to state that "central planning is indispensable in order to bring production and material needs into harmony with each other."[34]

These notions certainly did not go unchallenged, and the program of the British Zone's FDP, adopted in January 1946,

---

33. Printed in *Konrad Adenauer und die CDU der britischen Besatzungszone, 1946–1949: Dokumente zur Grundungsgeschichte der CDU Deutschlands,* edited for the Konrad Adenauer Stiftung by H. Pütz (Bonn, 1975), pp. 280 and 285.

34. H.J. Ungeheuer, *Die Wirtschaftsprogrammatik und Wirtschaftspolitik der liberalen Parteien Deutschlands unter besonderen Berücksichtigung der Entwicklung in der SBZ und in der britischen Zone* (M.A. thesis, Bonn, 1982), pp. 134–35. See also K. Schröder, *Die FDP in der britischen Besatzungszone, 1946–1948: Ein Beitrag zur Organisationsstruktur der Liberalen im Nachkriegsdeutschland* (Düsseldorf, 1984), p. 157; and E. Lange, "Politischer Liberalismus und Verfassungspolitische Grundentscheidungen nach dem Kriege," in L. Albertin, ed., *Politischer Liberalismus in der Bundesrepublik* (Göttingen, 1980), p. 50.

was a much more liberal document. It argued that planning should only be used as necessary and should not become an end in itself.[35] Yet enthusiasm for the market mechanism was by no means unbridled. The controversy rumbled on for nearly two years, with Blücher having to play a mediating role, in spite of the fact that he himself was more inclined to freedom than to planning.[36]

At this time the FDP was as much concerned with national and religious issues as with economic ones. Following in the footsteps of the Weimar liberal parties, the DDP and the DVP, the Free Democrats tended to regard themselves as appealing to the interests of the business community without having a very clear concept of what their socioeconomic principles ought to be. Thomas Dehler expressed this attitude with exemplary frankness when he remarked: "The FPD stands for a policy that also interests business circles and for which the latter are therefore also ready to make a contribution [*Opfer*]. We should approach such circles."[37] The fact that the liberals were not so numerous as the Social Democrats or the Christian Democrats meant that financial support from interest groups was of more crucial importance for them.[38] This made the FDP a less than suitable vehicle for the propagation of neoliberal ideas, as they involved measures – the abolition of cartels, for example – that Free Democratic backers might not find to their taste.

Certainly the FDP did not itself seem very attractive to neoliberal theorists. Hardly any of them joined, and several, including Franz Böhm, became Christian Democrats.[39] It is difficult not to share the judgment of one distinguished historian of German liberalism that the FDP avoided serious discussion of neoliberal

35. Ungeheuer, *Wirtschaftsprogrammatik*, p. 138.

36. Schröder, *FDP in der britischen Besatzungszone*. See, for example, pp. 168–71.

37. Cited by H. Vorländer, "Der soziale Liberalismus der FDP," in Karl Holl et al., eds., *Sozialer Liberalismus* (Göttingen, 1986), p. 197.

38. This problem remained with the FDP. See H. Kaack, "Das Volksparteiensystem der Bundesrepublik Deutschland und die Situation der FDP," in L. Albertin, *Politischer Liberalismus in der Bundesrepublik*, p. 40.

39. Max-Gustav Lange could only find one of the contributors to the neoliberal journal *ORDO* who had joined the FDP. This was Hans Ilau, and even he had left the party by 1955. M.-G. Lange, "Die FDP – Versuch einer Erneuerung des Liberalismus," in *Studien zur Entwicklung der deutschen Parteien bis zur Bundestagswahl, 1955*, Schriften des Instituts für Politische Wissenschaft (Stuttgart and Düsseldorf, 1955) pp. 312–13.

viewpoints, and apart from occasional academic discussions at conferences it kept its distance from the new economic theories expounded by Müller-Armack, Rüstow, Böhm, and even Erhard himself. "A genuine discussion," wrote Lothar Albertin in *Politischer Liberalismus in der Bundesrepublik*, "would have required [the FDP] to make the effort to achieve a coherent and comprehensive social and economic policy; this seemed to be inconvenient, and even risky, in view of the interests of the party's potential electorate."[40]

It was not only in the economic sphere that neoliberal attitudes did not sit squarely with the views of the FDP. The party was committed to German reunification and a strong central government. Neoliberals tended to prefer checks and balances on state power and did not reject decentralization. In 1945 Wilhelm Röpke even produced a controversial book, *Die Deutsche Frage*, in which he urged that the Eastern parts of the Reich should be jettisoned and a free and liberal Germany should be established West of the Elbe.[41] He sought thereby to eradicate the legacy of Prussian etatism and militarism. It was not a message that appealed to most supporters of the FDP.

Nevertheless, in the crucial period between the summer of 1947 and the currency reform of June 1948 it was the role of the market and the free price mechanism rather than the anti-cartel or social welfare aspects of neoliberalism that lay at the heart of the struggle for the future of Germany's economy. It therefore proved important that at precisely this time the FDP gave up its early support for the public planning and administration of major enterprises. By January 1948 Blücher and his colleagues in the British Zone FDP were willing to commit themselves more decisively to the free market. On the North Sea Island of Wangerooge they drew up an economic program that began with the slogan "Freedom is indivisible" and stated that they expected a future German government to restrict its interference

---

40. L. Albertin, "Politischer Liberalismus zwischen Tradition und Reform: Eine Problemskizze," in L. Albertin, ed., *Politischer Liberalismus in der Bundesrepublik*, p. 17.

41. W. Röpke, *Die Deutsche Frage*, 2d ed. (Erlenbach and Zürich, 1945), pp. 249–50. Views in the FDP about the constitutional question were divided, which left the liberals seeking compromise between the centralizing SPD and the federalistic CDU. In the important matter of financial administration, however, their influence favored centralization. See Lange, "Politischer Liberalismus und Verfassungspolitische Grundentscheidungen," pp. 64–67.

in the economy to what was "necessary." This "necessary" was evidently going to be interpreted in a very restricted fashion: the program also called for "the liberation of the economy from state direction."[42]

Once again, it is difficult to equate this program with a commitment to the principles of the social market economy as it was being developed by people like Alfred Müller-Armack up to 1948 and as it was proclaimed by Erhard in 1949. Historians of the FDP regard the neoliberal element in the program with scepticism. One refers to a speech given in June 1947 by Friedrich Middelhauve, the FDP economics spokesman in North-Rhine-Westphalia, as "characteristic for the future relationship of the FDP with neoliberalism, in that neoliberal theories were in no way taken over en bloc as party ideology, but only insofar as they strengthened the case against socialist tendencies."[43] This view is reinforced by a marked disinclination to tackle the cartel question. The Wangerooge program spoke piously of preventing the abuse of property and of opposing monopolies, but specifically provided for market regulation agreements as long as they were supervised, claiming that a ban on such agreements was "untenable for economic reasons."[44]

As far as the social aspect of neoliberal thought was concerned, it may have impressed individual liberals, including possibly Blücher himself, who read and evidently appreciated Müller-Armack's views on the social market economy.[45] But in general there does not seem to have been widespread enthusiasm for tackling the evils of industrial society. It may be unfair to suggest, as one writer has done, that social policy was "terra incognita" for liberals until the 1960s, but the FDP certainly did not make that issue a high priority and always put the interests

42. See copy in Blücher papers, BA: NL Blücher, p. 230. Also referred to in Schröder, *FDP in der britischen Besatzungszone*, pp. 182–83.

43. Ungeheuer, *Wirtschaftsprogrammatik*, p. 165.

44. Wangerooger Programm, "Wirtschaftsprogramm," point 5, in BA: NL Blücher, p. 230.

45. On 27 March 1948 Blücher wrote to Müller-Armack thanking him for his book, *Wirtschaftslenkung und Marktwirtschaft*, which had arrived on Blücher's birthday. He claimed that he had started to read it three weeks earlier at the suggestion of a colleague Theodor Blank. There is little reason to suppose, however, that Müller-Armack, the self-styled inventor of the social market economy, had any close personal links with Blücher. See Blücher papers in Theodor Heuß Akademie, Gummersbach, A3 NL Blücher, 14, f. 113.

of its rather narrow, middle-class electorate before general concepts of social responsibility.[46]

However cautious the FDP might have been in relation to neoliberal theories as a package, it proved altogether more positive in its attitude towards one of their most successful protagonists, Ludwig Erhard. After he had been forced to give up the Bavarian economics ministry, Erhard remained in Munich, where he had been given the title of professor, and tried to propagate his view of a free market economy that did not exhibit the nastier characteristics of laissez-faire capitalism. "The real contradistinction," he wrote in October 1946, "is not between free and planned economic systems, nor between capitalist and socialist systems, but between a market economy with a free price level adjustment on the one hand and an authoritarian economy with state controls extending into the sphere of distribution on the other."[47]

State interference was actually necessary, according to Erhard, but its function should be to protect free competition. Six months later he was again stressing the incompatibility between state planning and the free price mechanism, but added: "Today social and economic policy faces the task of providing all individuals in the economic process with the greatest possible equality of opportunity [*Startbedingungen*]." It was also the duty of policymakers to eliminate economic privilege and power concentration and to work against the proletarianization of the people by the conscious cultivation of craft industries and small businesses.[48]

Erhard himself was less concerned about the social aspects of

46. The "terra incognita" suggestion is made by H. Vorländer in "Sozialer Liberalismus der FDP," p. 198, citing R. Zundel, *Die Erben des Liberalismus* (Freudenstadt, 1971), p. 23. To be fair to Zundel, it seems that he is talking about classical liberalism in the early nineteenth century rather than the policy of the FDP, but he, too, characterizes the party's policies in the 1960s as being socially conservative. Cf. Zundel, p. 163. In fact the FDP in the British Zone did manage – after great pressure from Blücher – to produce drafts for a social program, but it remained a minor aspect of the party's policy. See Schröder, *FDP in der britischen Besatzungszone*, pp. 200–204.

47. *Die Neue Zeitung*, 14 October 1946, cited in L. Erhard, *The Economics of Success* (London 1963), p. 8.

48. "Freie Wirtschaft oder Planwirtschaft," in *Die Neue Zeitung*, 7 April 1947. Berghahn questions Erhard's enthusiasm for small business, pointing out that he himself was used to dealing with large firms as clients. See Berghahn, "Ideas into Politics," pp. 183–84. Erhard was certainly no unsophisticated advocate of the "small man," but he was prepared to use the rhetoric of small business when presenting his views to the public.

the new economic liberalism than with the productive advantages of the free market. His eloquently expounded views were certainly incompatible with the concept of a planned and directed economy, and as such they made him attractive to liberals, whatever their attitude towards social problems might otherwise have been.

By the summer of 1947 Franz Blücher had become chairman of the finance committee of the bizonal Economic Council (Wirtschaftsrat) in Frankfurt. He was extremely concerned that the Allies should not introduce a currency reform without consulting the Germans, and therefore persuaded his committee to establish a special bureau to study the issue. On 23 July this was endorsed by the Economic Council.[49] The question of who should run the new bureau then arose. One FDP member of the Economic Council, a businessman from Munich, suggested Erhard as somebody with a "liberal conception of economics."[50] In September 1947 Erhard was duly appointed to run the "Special Bureau for Monetary and Credit Matters" with its headquarters in Bad Homburg. Although the report it duly produced was not of much consequence as far as Allied policy was concerned, Erhard's role as director brought him into close touch with Blücher himself and with the head of the Finance Administration at Frankfurt, Alfred Hartmann. Erhard's views on currency reform and the reduction of excess purchasing power can only have strengthened their impression of him as a clear-headed, optimistic exponent of liberal economic views.[51] Here was an academically trained economist with practical experience of government who was a robust opponent of socialization, planning, and cheap money. Such people were not all that easy to find in West Germany in 1948.

Despite the anti-Marxist character of the Christian Democratic movement, it was by no means committed to the "jump into the cold water" of the free market advocated by liberal economists. The CDU agricultural director in Frankfurt, Hans Schlange-Schöningen, was a strong *dirigist*, and the first economics director, Johannes Semler, was also willing to accept a

49. Notes by Köhler, 17–18 July 1947, BA: NL Blücher, 352, ff. 104–5.
50. Ungeheuer, *Wirtschaftsprogrammatik*, pp. 192–93.
51. Records of the Sonderstelle Geld und Kredit, 1–16 October 1947. Hartmann attended most of the meetings in early October, and their proceedings were reported to Blücher. BA: NL Blücher, 354.

regime of controls, even if he opposed socialization.[52] Erhard was therefore a more attractive option as far as liberals were concerned.

When Semler was dismissed by the Anglo-American authorities in January 1948, Erhard could not have been confident that his own candidacy would be supported by the CDU. In fact the Christian Democrats first wanted to reinstate Semler and only when that proved impossible did they turn toward a number of other candidates, including Hans-Christoph Seebohm and Erhard himself. It was the liberal FDP, led by Franz Blücher, that championed Erhard's cause. As the result of hard bargaining with the much larger Christian block, the FDP pushed through a compromise whereby it accepted Hermann Pünder, the CDU candidate for *Oberdirektor* of the Frankfurt administration – formally the senior position, but in practice one with little power – in return for the appointment of the apparently nonpolitical but market-oriented Erhard to the post as economics director.[53]

Blücher was anxious to prevent the Western Zones from settling down into a planned and controlled economy, as seemed quite likely in the spring of 1948. There were rumors of a currency reform, but the association of that reform with the abolition of controls was anything but certain. An advisory council of academic economists, among them Eucken, Böhm, and Müller-Armack, had recommended a restoration of the free price mechanism with only major necessities remaining rationed, but such expert advice was not unchallenged within the administration itself and would be ferociously opposed by the Social Democrats. Blücher urged Erhard to stand firm against attempts to extend price-fixing and rationing arrangements, supported as they were by the official empires responsible for their implementation.[54] Erhard certainly fulfilled the hopes of his sponsors. When the new currency was introduced

52. Semler was certainly no enthusiast for planning, but he seems to have fought shy of root-and-branch reform of the control system. See *Bericht des Direktors der Verwaltung für Wirtschaft Dr. J. Semler: Vorgetragen in der Sitzung des Wirtschaftsrats, 5 September 1947*, BA: Z8 1325, pp. 24–26. For Schlange-Schöningen's views, see J. Farquharson, *The Western Allies and the Politics of Food: Agrarian Management in Postwar Germany* (Leamington Spa, 1985), pp. 208–21.

53. Ungeheuer, *Wirtschaftsprogrammatik*, pp. 194–99; and Laitenberger, *Ludwig Erhard*, p. 63.

54. Blücher to Erhard, 6 March 1948, BA: NL Blücher, 93.

in the Western Zones on the weekend of 20 June 1948, he told the citizens of the Bizone that controls on most manufactured goods had been abolished and that the market was free to fix its own prices. He had already paved the way for this procedure by persuading the Economic Council in Frankfurt to pass a guidelines law giving him power to make consequential changes to regulations once the currency reform had been carried through. He was warmly supported by the FDP in this debate, but the votes that really counted were those of the CDU/CSU.[55]

Blücher was delighted with Erhard's leadership in economic affairs and urged his lieutenants in North Germany to support the new policy as strongly as possible. He assumed that this policy was a liberal rather than a Christian Democratic achievement. By the time the constitution of the Federal Republic, the modestly named Grundgesetz (Basic Law), had been ratified in May 1949, Erhard was one of the most popular politicians in Germany, but his political allegiance was still not clear. The FDP evidently had hopes of attracting him as one of their candidates in the forthcoming Bundestag elections, and he was offered at least one parliamentary constituency. His reply was vague about his intentions, but he stressed the need for a common front to defend his economic policies against Social Democracy.[56]

The FDP's hopes of party advantage from Erhard were to prove vain. Once he was established as economics director in Frankfurt, he attracted the attention of Adenauer, who had never been enamored of the economic principles enshrined in the Ahlen program. In August 1948 Erhard made a guest appearance at the British Zone CDU party conference, and his speech on the "modern form of market economy" was a great success. From February 1949 on contacts grew closer. Adenauer and Franz Etzel persuaded their somewhat reluctant Christian Democratic colleagues to adopt Erhard's policies as their own, a decision made easier month by month in 1949 as the success of liberalization became more apparent. In July the CDU in the

---

55. Among those casting their votes was Franz-Josef Strauss, who looked back on the occasion with considerable pride. F.-J. Strauss, "Die Weichenstellungen 1948 und unsere Verantwortung für die Zukunft," *Orientierungen*, no. 36 (June 1988): 10.

56. Correspondence with the mayor of Göttingen, 14 and 24 May 1949. Ludwig Erhard Stiftung, Bonn, Erhard papers.

British Zone announced its new economic platform, the Düsseldorfer Leitsätze, which incorporated Erhard's theory of the social market economy. Although claiming to build on the Ahlen program, the Düsseldorf principles actually jettisoned the remnants of Christian Socialism and uncompromisingly enthroned the consumer at the center of economic life, served by fierce, but state-protected, competition. Although the principles rejected a "so-called free economy of liberalistic stamp," by this they chiefly meant that private individuals should be prevented from undermining competition and market freedom for others. On the other hand, the new program did recognize the state's responsibility to combat unemployment by a sensible use of credit, taxation, tariff, and public investment policies.[57]

It was therefore the Christian Democratic camp and not the liberal one that benefited from Erhard's electoral locomotive power in the 1949 Bundestag elections, even though during the campaign Erhard was at great pains not to come into conflict with leading Free Democrats such as Theodor Heuß. It is clear that he wanted the election fought by both FDP and CDU as a defense of liberal economic policies against the collectivism of the SPD.[58] In this way he helped prepare the ground for Adenauer's "small coalition" of September 1949. Erhard's political choices were by no means unimportant for the future of Germany – in the summer of 1949 public opinion polls showed that he had more support than any other political leader apart from Schumacher.[59] The election was only won for the antisocialist coalition by a whisker, and so Erhard's popularity must be counted as a significant factor in establishing a market-oriented government in 1949.

Why did Erhard choose to stand for the CDU as a candidate – even though he was still not a member of the party? One obvious reason is that of political calculation; the Christian Democrats were already building up a large, socially conservative *Volkspartei*, whereas the liberals remained a relatively small

57. Pütz, *Konrad Adenauer und die CDU*, pp. 866–80. For the CDU negotiations with Erhard, ibid., pp. 46–50, 838–64; Koerfer, *Kampf ums Kanzleramt*, pp. 52–54; and A.J. Heidenheimer, *Adenauer and the CDU: The Rise of the Leader and the Integration of the Party* (The Hague, 1960), pp. 174–76.

58. Erhard to Blücher, 14 July 1949. Ludwig Erhard Stiftung, Bonn, Ludwig Erhard papers, *Schriftwechsel*, I–3/1948–9 Band 27. See also Blücher papers, BA: NL Blücher, 93.

59. See fn. 1, above.

group in the political spectrum. Nevertheless, Erhard could have expected that a continuation of the antisocialist coalition in the new Bundestag might have included him as a liberal economics minister. This outcome was open to doubt, however, and support from the CDU – and above all from Adenauer – would mean greater security. Nevertheless, there were other reasons why the CDU/CSU became the bearers of the social market economy rather than the FDP. These reasons are not without significance for an assessment of German liberalism both before and during the early years of the Federal Republic. They reflect the characteristics that had already become so marked in the German liberal movement before 1933: the overriding priority given to German nationalism, a tendency to distrust the masses, and a dependence on business pressure groups that limited policy options. When one added to this one cultural limitation, that the FDP appealed overwhelmingly to Protestants in a country where Roman Catholics were no longer in a minority, Erhard's choice may well have been a wise one. Had he joined the FDP, economic liberalism would have been clearly associated with a Protestant, nationalist party that – in some North German areas, at least – seemed suspiciously hospitable to former Nazis. Furthermore, its well-earned reputation for close links with business interests meant that for many trade unionists it might be seen as a bosses' party.

Erhard told Blücher at the time that he made his choice in order to put the necessary liberal backbone into the CDU and that only the influence of a strong personality could ensure that the Christian Democrats would stick to the social market economy.[60] This should not be seen simply as an excuse to mollify the FDP leader, even though Erhard may well have been embarrassed by his own apparent ingratitude to the FDP. Nevertheless, his priorities were genuine and important. The injection of a clear-cut liberal economic philosophy with a sensible social component into the program of the new mass conservative party in Western Germany, the CDU/CSU, was to have very positive consequences for both Germany's economic well-being and its political culture. It is not this paper's task to address the question of how economically effective Erhard's liberalization policies were in 1948 and later, in the 1950s and

60. See fn. 58, above.

1960s. Certainly by July 1949 the CDU could feel confident enough to claim in its Düsseldorf program that the return to market principles had been responsible for an upswing that had not occurred in the Soviet Zone, even though a currency reform had also taken place there.[61] Perhaps understandably, it did not make the same point about the French Zone, even though it could have strengthened its case by doing so. The judgment of historians has been mixed, but, after a period of skepticism, contemporary scholarship seems to be swinging back toward a positive view of Erhard's achievements, and the liberalization measures of June 1948 are now recognized as a major contribution to West Germany's economic recovery.[62]

Erhard's importance, however, was as much political as economic. His formulation of a market system based on competition (*Wettbewerbsordnung*), free prices, and the sovereignty of consumer choice was by no means obviously attractive when it was first adumbrated in the 1940s. Public opinion surveys in the early years of the Federal Republic showed that Germans were not inclined to take the laws of supply and demand for granted. Many of them felt happier with "just prices" fixed by the state.[63] Open competition was as likely to be perceived as a form of anarchy as it was to be approved for satisfying consumer needs. Erhard and his academic supporters of the neoliberal persuasion thus deserve credit for convincing a majority of their fellow-countrymen that the market mechanism was the best way of achieving prosperity for all and that it could be combined with socially responsible policies towards the weaker members of society.

To be sure, Erhard and his supporters were helped by a favorable international climate. The influence of the Americans was important, not only in the occupation administration but also as an example of a free market success that even Germany's

---

61. Pütz, *Konrad Adenauer und die CDU*, p. 867.

62. For more critical judgments, see the works of W. Abelshauser, esp. *Wirtschaft in Westdeutschland 1945 bis 1948: Rekonstruktion und Wachstumsbegingungen in der amerikanischen und britischen Zone* (Stuttgart, 1975). For a more positive assessment of liberalization policies in 1948–49, see C. Buchheim, "Die Währungsreform 1948 in Westdeutschland," *Vierteljahreshefte für Zeitgeschichte* 36 (1988): 189–231.

63. H. Wellmann, *Die soziale Marktwirtschaft im Spiegel von Meinungsumfragen* (Ph.D. diss., Cologne, 1962), p. 90. Also E. Noelle and E.P. Neumann, *Jahrbuch der öffentlichen Meinung, 1947–1955* (Allensbach am Bodensee, 1956), p. 233.

corporatistically inclined entrepreneurs could not fail to admire.[64] Yet the American example was not an inspiration for all other Western European countries; France and Britain, for example, chose different economic routes. Erhard's skill as an advocate for free market principles should not be underestimated. Nor should his genuine commitment to the "social market economy." On 24 November 1949, for example, he wrote to Adenauer expressing concern about the political situation:

> I was and still am convinced that a free economy can only be realized by the CDU. But this can be kept going along the lines envisaged only if the concept of the "social market economy" is really seriously and honestly accepted and is clearly recognizable in the implementation of our economic policy. The social market economy means much more than the return to liberalistic economic methods; it does not mean *laissez-aller*, but [rather] implies a very alert and sensitive economic leadership that leaves the principle of freedom undamaged, and indeed emphasizes it more strongly than was the case in the inherently interventionist abuses of the old capitalist system. The path of the social market economy, with its constant pressure for higher levels of achievement and a fairer distribution of income cannot always . . . reckon with the wholehearted applause of special interest groups [*Interessenten*].

Erhard's warning proved particularly true with respect to the vitally important questions of liberalization of foreign trade and decartellization. As he put it: "The ranks of organized business and the inherently protectionist agricultural lobby are arming themselves for the offensive, whilst on my side stand only the efficient and far-sighted entrepreneurs."[65]

This comment did indeed presage Erhard's struggles with Germany's industrial leaders, and in particular with Fritz Berg, the head of the industrialists' pressure group, the Federation of German Industry (Bundesverband der Deutschen Industrie or BDI), over such matters as decartellization and trade policy. In the conflict that followed, Erhard showed himself to be as tough

64. Although they took a long time to accept American ideas; see V. Berghahn, *The Americanisation of West German Industry, 1945–1973*, (Leamington Spa and New York, 1986), pp. 256–57.

65. Erhard to Adenauer, 24 November 1949, Ludwig Erhard Stiftung, Erhard papers, Adenauer *Schriftwechsel*, 1949–50.

and as determined as his opponents, but he needed all the allies he could get. He complained bitterly to Adenauer in July 1954 about Berg's demands, which, he claimed, would reduce the social market economy to a farce.[66] For their part, the industrialists tended to see Erhard as a utopian idealist, more the product of professorial theorizing than of practical experience in the business world.

Here again it is important to note that Erhard derived benefits from his curious position in the government as a CDU minister who presented an appeal to those outside the ranks of Christian Democracy. He maintained his own public relations organization within a ministry that associated him personally with Germany's economic progress in the public mind. It was a facility that did not please Adenauer.[67] He could also usually rely on the support of the FDP, who regarded him as a friend in the Christian camp. Had Erhard formally belonged to the FDP, his position would have been much weaker. Not only would it have been easier for pressure group interests within the CDU to disown him, but he would then have had to face up to the influence of business interests within the liberal party itself. It is significant that in June 1948, when Blücher was supporting Erhard's liberalization measures, he himself expected that distribution and allocation functions would be taken over by business associations and seems to have approved of such a development.[68] Erhard himself preferred to keep aloof from corporatist bodies.

On the key issue of the law against cartels, the FDP did indeed support the measure passed in 1957, but, as is well known, this was a much weaker instrument than anti-cartel purists such as Franz Böhm would have liked. When it came to toughening up the law in the 1960s, the FDP did not show itself willing to overrule business interests.[69] Even in the case of

66. Erhard to Adenauer, 1 July 1954, Ludwig Erhard Stiftung, Erhard papers, Adenauer *Schriftwechsel*, 1952–55. For a good account of Erhard's struggles with the BDI, see Berghahn, *Americanisation of West German Industry*, pp. 155–81.

67. F. Greiss, "Erhards soziale Marktwirtschaft und die WAAGE," in Schröder, ed., *Erhard Festschrift*, p. 98; and Koerfer, *Kampf ums Kanzleramt*, pp. 148–50, 157–58.

68. Blücher to FDP leaders in the British Zone, 5 June 1948, BA: NL, Blücher, 378.

69. Vorländer, "Sozialer Liberalismus der FDP," p. 198. For FDP policy in the 1960s see also H. Kaack, *Die FDP: Grundriß und Materialien zu Geschichte, Struktur und Programmatik*, 3d ed. (Meisenheim am Glan, 1979), pp. 22–28.

Erhard's elevation to the chancellorship, his friendly nonmembership in the FDP was an enormous advantage. On the one hand, they needed to support him because he was the alternative to Gaullists in the CDU who might even contemplate altering the electoral laws to the disadvantage of the FDP. On the other hand, the FDP could not dally with alternative coalition partners like the SPD as long as they were supporting Erhard's struggle against "collectivism." In 1966, however, they proved a broken reed and contributed to Erhard's fall from power. How much less would he have been able to achieve had he been forced to rely upon them entirely!

To sum up, Erhard was of importance for German liberalism because his influence, and that of the neoliberal economists who supported him, managed to permeate the political culture of West Germany in a manner unknown during the Weimar Republic or even the Wilhelmine Empire. Doubtless the international situation had something to do with this, but not everything. Had Seebohm been elected economics director of Bizone in March 1948, or had Schumacher won the first Bundestag elections in the summer of 1949, there might have been an entirely different outcome. As it was, by 1959 the Social Democratic Party was trying its best to produce a left-wing version of the social market economy with Karl Schiller's formula "As much competition as possible, as much planning as necessary," while by 1971 the FDP had finally established an imposing-looking, if not very convincing, social policy as part of its "Freiburg Theses."[70] In contributing to this important development in his compatriots' thinking about socioeconomic affairs, Erhard was helped by a long-standing left-liberal tradition and by important acts of support from the Free Democrats. But in politics, as in his career as an economist, he remained his own man. Insofar as he was a success in implementing his ideas, this was probably the reason.

70. Cf. A.J. Nicholls, "Political Parties and Party Government," in C.C. Schweitzer, ed., *Politics and Government in the Federal Republic of Germany* (Leamington Spa, 1984), pp. 218–22.

Select Bibliography on the History of German Liberalism

The following bibliography provides a brief survey of the most important secondary literature in English and German on the history of
German liberalism. No attempt has been made to include all of the
specialized monographs, essays, and dissertations that have been
written on the subject. Only works of major significance have been
listed. Scholars who would like a more comprehensive and detailed
bibliography on the history of German liberalism should consult J.C.
Heß and E. van Steensel van der Aa, *Bibliographie zum deutschen Liberalismus* (Göttingen, 1981). For the more recent literature, see the bibli-
ographies in the monographs by K.H. Jarausch, L.E. Jones, and D.
Langewiesche listed below.

Albertin, L. "Liberalismus in der Weimarer Republik." *Neue politische
Literatur* 19 (1974): 220–34.
——. *Liberalismus und Demokratie am Anfang der Weimarer Republik: Eine
vergleichende Analyse der Deutschen Demokratischen Partei und Deutschen
Volkspartei.* Düsseldorf, 1972.
——. "Die Verantwortung der liberalen Parteien für das Scheitern der
großen Koalition im Herbst 1921." *Historische Zeitschrift* 205 (1967):
566–627.
——, ed. *Politischer Liberalismus in der Bundesrepublik.* Göttingen, 1980.
Albertin, L., and Link, W., eds. *Politische Parteien auf dem Weg zur
parlamentarischen Demokratie in Deutschland: Entwicklungslinien bis zur
Gegenwart.* Düsseldorf, 1982.
Aldendorff, R. *Schulze-Delitzsch: Ein Beitrag zur Geschichte des Liberalis-
mus zwischen Revolution und Reichsgründung.* Baden-Baden, 1984.
Anderson, E.N. *The Social and Political Conflict in Prussia, 1858–1864.*
Lincoln, Nebr., 1954.
Anderson, M.L., and Barkin, K. "The Myth of the Puttkamer Purge
and the Reality of the Kulturkampf: Some Reflections on the Historio-
graphy of Imperial Germany." *Journal of Modern History* 53 (1982):
647–86.
Batscha, Z. *Studien zur politischen Theorie des deutschen Frühliberalismus.*
Frankfurt a.M., 1981.
Bazillion, R.J. *Modernizing Germany: Karl Biedermann's Career in the
Kingdom of Saxony, 1835–1901.* New York and Zurich, 1989.

417

Becker, J. *Liberaler Staat und Kirche in der Ära von Reichsgründung und Kulturkampf: Geschichte und Strukturen ihres Verhältnisses in Baden, 1860–1876.* Mainz, 1973.

Beeck, K.-H. "Die Gründung der Deutschen Staatspartei im Jahre 1930 im Zusammenhang der Neuordnungsversuche des Liberalismus." Unpublished Ph.D. thesis, Cologne, 1957.

Berghahn, V.R. "Ideas into Politics: The Case of Ludwig Erhard." In R.J. Bullen, H. Pogge von Strandmann, and A. Polonsky, eds., *Ideas into Politics: Aspects of European History, 1880–1950*, pp. 178–92. London and Sydney, 1984.

Blackbourn, D., and Eley, G. *The Peculiarities of German History: Bourgeois Society and Politics in Nineteenth-Century Germany.* New York and Oxford, 1984.

Block, H. *Die parlamentarische Krisis der Nationalliberalen Partei, 1879–80.* Hamburg, 1930.

Bowers, P.M. "The Failure of the German Democratic Party, 1918–1930." Unpublished Ph.D. thesis, University of Pittsburgh, 1973.

Boyer, J.W. *Political Radicalism in Late Imperial Vienna: Origins of the Christian Social Movement, 1848–1897.* Chicago, 1981.

Brantz, R.W. "Anton Erkelenz, the Hirsch-Duncker Trade Unions, and the German Democratic Party." Unpublished Ph.D. thesis, Ohio State University, 1973.

Bußmann, W. "Zur Geschichte des deutschen Liberalismus im 19. Jahrhundert." *Historische Zeitschrift* 186 (1958): 527–57.

Büttner, U. "Vereinigte Liberale und Deutsche Demokraten in Hamburg, 1906–1930." *Zeitschrift des Vereins für Hamburgische Geschichte* 63 (1977): 1–34.

Cecil, L. *Albert Ballin: Business and Politics in Imperial Germany, 1888–1918.* Princeton, N.J., 1967.

Chanady, A.A. "The Dissolution of the German Democratic Party in 1930." *American Historical Review* 70 (1968): 1433–53.

Childers, T. *The Nazi Voter: The Social Foundations of Fascism in Germany, 1924–1933.* Chapel Hill, N.C., 1983.

Conze, W. "Friedrich Naumann: Grundlagen und Ansatz seiner Politik in der nationalsozialen Zeit (1895–1903)." In W. Hubatsch, ed., *Schicksalswege deutscher Vergangenheit: Beiträge zur geschichtlichen Deutung der letzten hundertfünfzig Jahre*, pp. 355–86. Düsseldorf, 1950.

——. "Die Krise des Parteienstaates in Deutschland, 1929/30." *Historische Zeitschrift* 178 (1954): 47–83.

——. *Möglichkeiten und Grenzen der liberalen Arbeiterbewegung in Deutschland: Das Beispiel Schulze-Delitzschs.* Heidelberg, 1965.

——, ed. *Staat und Gesellschaft im deutschen Vormärz, 1815–1848.* Stuttgart, 1962.

Craig, G.A. *Germany, 1866–1945.* New York, 1978.

——. *The Triumph of Liberalism: Zurich in the Golden Age, 1830–1869.* New York, 1988.

Dahrendorf, R. *Society and Democracy in Germany.* New York, 1967.

Döhn, L. *Politik und Interesse: Die Interessenstruktur der Deutschen Volkspartei.* Meisenheim, 1970.

Düding, D. *Der Nationalsoziale Verein, 1896–1903: Der gescheiterte Versuch einer parteipolitischen Synthese von Nationalismus, Sozialismus und Liberalismus.* Munich, 1972.

Eichmeier, J.P. *Anfänge liberaler Parteibildung (1947–1854).* Göttingen, 1948.

Eisfeld, G. *Die Entstehung der liberalen Parteien in Deutschland, 1858–70: Studien zu den Organisationen und Programmen der Liberalen und Demokraten.* Hanover, 1969.

Eksteins, M. *The Limits of Reason: The German Democratic Press and the Collapse of Weimar Democracy.* Oxford, 1975.

——. *Theodor Heuß und die Weimarer Republik: Ein Beitrag zur Geschichte des deutschen Liberalismus.* Stuttgart, 1969.

Elm, L. *Zwischen Fortschritt und Reaktion: Geschichte der Parteien der liberalen Bourgeoisie in Deutschland, 1893–1918.* [East] Berlin, 1968.

Eschenburg, T. *Das Kaiserreich am Scheideweg: Bassermann, Bülow und der Block.* Berlin, 1929.

Evans, R.J. *Death in Hamburg: Society and Politics in the Cholera Years, 1830–1910.* Oxford, 1987.

——. *The Feminist Movement in Germany, 1894–1933.* London, 1976.

Faber, K.G. "Strukturprobleme des deutschen Liberalismus im 19. Jahrhundert." *Der Staat* 14 (1975): 201–28.

Fenske, H. *Der liberale Südwesten: Freiheitliche und demokratische Traditionen in Baden und Württemberg, 1790–1933.* Stuttgart, 1981.

Frevert, U. *Women in German History: From Bourgeois Emancipation to Sexual Liberation.* Translated by S.M. Evans. Oxford, 1989.

Fricke, D. et al., eds. *Die bürgerlichen Parteien in Deutschland: Handbuch der Geschichte der bürgerlichen Parteien und anderer bürgerlicher Interessenorganisationen vom Vormärz bis zum Jahre 1945.* 2 vols. Leipzig, 1968 and Berlin, 1970.

——. *Lexikon zur Parteiengeschichte: Die bürgerlichen und kleinbürgerlichen Parteien und Verbände in Deutschland (1789–1945).* 4 vols. Leipzig, 1983–86.

Frye, B.B. "The German Democratic Party and the 'Jewish Problem' in the Weimar Republic." *Year Book of the Leo Baeck Institute* 21 (1976): 143–72.

——. *Liberal Democrats in the Weimar Republic: The History of the German Democratic Party and the German State Party.* Carbondale, Ill., 1985.

Gagel, W. *Die Wahlrechtsfrage in der Geschichte der deutschen liberalen*

Parteien. Düsseldorf, 1958.

Gall, L. "Der deutsche Liberalismus zwischen Revolution und Reichsgründung." *Historische Zeitschrift* 228 (1979): 98–108.

——. *Der Liberalismus als regierende Partei: Das Großherzogtum Baden zwischen Restauration und Reichsgründung.* Wiesbaden, 1968.

——. "Liberalismus und 'bürgerliche Gesellschaft': Zu Charakter und Entwicklung der liberalen Bewegung in Deutschland." *Historische Zeitschrift* 220 (1975): 324–56.

——, ed. *Liberalismus.* Cologne, 1976.

Gilg, P. *Die Erneuerung des demokratischen Denkens im Wilhelminischen Deutschland.* Wiesbaden, 1965.

Grathwohl, R. *Stresemann and the DNVP: Reconciliation or Revenge in German Foreign Policy.* Lawrence, Kans., 1980.

Gutscher, J.M. *Die Entwicklung der FDP von ihren Anfängen bis 1961.* Meisenheim, 1984.

Hallowell, J.H. *The Decline of Liberalism as an Ideology with Particular Reference to German Politico-Legal Thought.* Berkeley, 1943.

Hamerow, T.S. *Restoration, Revolution, Reaction: Economics and Politics in Germany, 1815–1871.* Princeton, N.J., 1958.

——. *The Social Foundations of German Unification, 1858–1871.* 2 vols. Princeton, N.J., 1969–72.

Harris, J.F. *A Study in the Theory and Practice of German Liberalism: Eduard Lasker, 1829–1884.* Lanham, Md., 1984.

Hartenstein, W. *Die Anfänge der Deutschen Volkspartei, 1918–1920.* Düsseldorf, 1962.

Heckart, B. *From Bassermann to Bebel: The Grand Bloc's Quest for Reform in the Kaiserreich, 1900–1914.* New Haven, Conn., 1974.

Hein, D. *Zwischen liberaler Milieupartei und nationaler Sammlungsbewegung: Gründung, Entwicklung und Struktur der Freien Demokratischen Partei, 1945–1949.* Düsseldorf, 1985.

Herzfeld, H. *Johannes von Miquel.* 2 vols. Detmold, 1938.

Heß, J.C. "Die Desintegration des Liberalismus in der Weimarer Republik." In H.W. von der Dunk and H. Lademacher, eds., *Auf dem Weg zum modernen Parteienstaat: Zur Entstehung, Organisation und Struktur politischer Parteien in Deutschland und den Niederlanden,* pp. 259–72. Kassel, 1986.

——. *"Das ganze Deutschland soll es sein": Demokratischer Nationalismus in der Weimarer Republik am Beispiel der Deutschen Demokratischen Partei.* Stuttgart, 1978.

Hock, W. *Liberales Denken im Zeitalter der Paulskirche: Droysen und die Frankfurter Mitte.* Münster, 1957.

Holborn, H. *A History of Modern Germany.* 3 vols. New York, 1959–67.

Holl, K., and List, G., eds. *Liberalismus und imperialistischer Staat: Der Imperialismus als Problem liberaler Parteien in Deutschland, 1890–1914.*

Göttingen, 1975.

Holl, K.; Trautmann, G.; and Vorländer, H., eds. *Sozialer Liberalismus.* Göttingen, 1986.

Hunt, J.C. "The Bourgeois Middle in German Politics, 1871–1933." *Central European History* 19 (1978): 83–106.

———. *The People's Party in Württemberg and Southern Germany, 1890–1914.* Stuttgart, 1975.

Jarausch, K.H. *Students, Society, and Politics in Imperial Germany: The Rise of Academic Illiberalism.* Princeton, N.J., 1982.

———. "Illiberalism and Beyond: German History in Search of a Paradigm." *Journal of Modern History* 55 (1983): 268–84.

———. *The Unfree Professions: German Lawyers, Teachers, and Engineers, 1900–1950.* New York, 1990.

John, M. "Liberalism and Society in Germany, 1850–1880: The Case of Hanover." *English Historical Review* 102 (1987): 579–98.

———. *Politics and the Law in Late Nineteenth-Century Germany: The Origins of the Civil Code.* Oxford, 1989.

Jones, L.E. "Democracy and Liberalism in the German Inflation: The Crisis of a Political Movement, 1918–1924." In G.D. Feldman, C.-L. Holtfrerich, and P.-C. Witt, eds., *Die Konsequenzen der Inflation – The Consequences of Inflation,* pp. 3–43. Berlin, 1989.

———. *German Liberalism and the Dissolution of the Weimar Party System, 1918–1933.* Chapel Hill, N.C., 1988.

———. "Gustav Stresemann and the Crisis of German Liberalism." *European Studies Review* 4 (1974): 141–63.

———. "In the Shadow of Stabilization: German Liberalism and the Legitimacy Crisis of the Weimar Party System, 1924–30." In G.D. Feldman, ed., *Die Nachwirkungen der Inflation auf die deutsche Geschichte, 1924–1933,* pp. 21–41. Munich, 1985.

Judson, P.M. "German Liberalism in Nineteenth-Century Austria: Clubs, Parties, and the Rise of Bourgeois Politics." Unpublished Ph.D. dissertation, Columbia University, 1987.

Kocka, J., ed. *Das Bürgertum im 19. Jahrhundert: Deutschland im europäischen Vergleich.* 3 vols. Munich, 1988.

Koselleck, R. *Preußen zwischen Reform und Revolution: Allgemeines Landrecht, Verwaltung und soziale Bewegung von 1791 bis 1848.* Stuttgart, 1967.

Krieger, L. *The German Idea of Freedom: History of a Political Tradition.* Chicago, 1957.

Kunst, H. *Politischer Liberalismus und evangelische Kirche.* Cologne and Opladen, 1967.

Langewiesche, D. "Die Anfänge der deutschen Parteien – Partei, Fraktion und Verein in der Revolution von 1848/49." *Geschichte und Gesellschaft* 4 (1978): 325–61.

———. *Liberalismus in Deutschland*. Frankfurt a.M., 1988.

———. *Liberalismus und Demokratie in Württemberg zwischen Revolution und Reichsgründung*. Düsseldorf, 1974.

———, ed. *Liberalismus im 19. Jahrhundert: Deutschland im europäischen Vergleich*. Göttingen, 1988.

Link, W. "Der Nationalverein für das liberale Deutschland (1907–1918)." *Politische Vierteljahresschrift* 5 (1964): 422–44.

Lorenz, I.S. *Eugen Richter: Der entscheidende Liberalismus in Wilhelminischer Zeit, 1871–1906*. Husum, 1981.

Luchtenberg, P., and Erbe, W., eds. *Geschichte des deutschen Liberalismus*. Cologne and Opladen, 1966.

Mauch, B. *Die bayerische FDP: Portrait einer Landespartei, 1945–1949*. Munich, 1981.

Methfessel, W. "Die Deutsche Volkspartei am Ende der Weimarer Republik." Unpublished Ph.D. thesis, Jena, 1966.

Mielke, S. *Der Hansa-Bund für Gewerbe, Handel und Industrie, 1909–1914: Der gescheiterte Versuch einer antifeudalen Sammlungspolitik*. Göttingen, 1976.

Milatz, A. "Die linksliberalen Parteien und Gruppen in den Reichstagswahlen, 1871–1912." *Archiv für Sozialgeschichte* 12 (1972): 273–92.

Mitzman, A. *The Iron Cage: An Historical Interpretation of Max Weber*. New York, 1970.

Mommsen, W.J. *The Age of Bureaucracy: Perspectives on the Political Sociology of Max Weber*. Oxford, 1974.

———. "Der deutsche Liberalismus zwischen 'klassenloser Bürgergesellschaft' und 'organisiertem Kapitalismus': Zu einigen neuen Liberalismus-Interpretationen." *Geschichte und Gesellschaft* 4 (1978): 77–90.

———. *Max Weber and German Politics, 1890–1920*. Translated by M.S. Steinberg. Chicago and London, 1984.

Mosse, G.L. *The Crisis of the German Ideology: The Intellectual Origins of the Third Reich*. New York, 1964.

Mundle, G.F. "The German National Liberal Party, 1900–1914." Unpublished Ph.D. thesis, University of Illinois, 1975.

Na'aman, S. *Der Deutsche Nationalverein: Die politische Konstitutierung des deutschen Bürgertums, 1859–1867*. Düsseldorf, 1987.

Neumann, S. *Die Parteien der Weimarer Republik*. Stuttgart, 1970.

Neumüller, M. *Liberalismus und Revolution: Das Problem der Revolution in der deutschen liberalen Geschichtsschreibung des neunzehnten Jahrhunderts*. Düsseldorf, 1973.

Nicholls, A.J. "The Other Germany – The Neoliberals." In R.J. Bullen, H. Pogge von Strandmann, and A. Polonsky, eds., *Ideas into Politics: Aspects of European History, 1880–1950*, pp. 164–77. London and Sydney, 1984.

Nipperdey, T. *Deutsche Geschichte, 1800–1866: Bürgerwelt und starker Staat*. Munich, 1984.

——. *Die Organisation der deutschen Parteien vor 1918*. Düsseldorf, 1961.

Obenaus, H. "Gutbesitzerliberalismus: Zur regionalen Sonderentwicklung der liberalen Partei in Ost- und Westpreußen während des Vormärz." *Geschichte und Gesellschaft* 14 (1988): 304–28.

O'Boyle, L. "The Democratic Left in Germany, 1848." *Journal of Modern History* 33 (1961): 374–83.

——. "The German Nationalverein." *Journal of Central European Affairs* 16 (1957): 333–52.

——. "Liberal Political Leadership in Germany, 1867–1884." *Journal of Modern History* 28 (1956): 338–52.

O'Donnell, A.J. "National Liberalism and the Mass Politics of the German Right, 1890–1907." Unpublished Ph.D. thesis, Princeton University, 1973.

Offermann, T. *Arbeiterbewegung und liberales Bürgertum in Deutschland, 1850–1863*. Bonn, 1979.

Peterson, W.F. *The Berlin Liberal Press in Exile: A History of the "Pariser Tageblatt – Pariser Tageszeitung," 1933–1940*. Tübingen, 1987.

Pinson, K.S. *Modern Germany: Its History and Civilization*. New York, 1954.

Portner, E. *Der Verfassungspolitik der Liberalen, 1919: Ein Beitrag zur Deutung der Weimarer Verfassung*. Bonn, 1973.

Priamus, H.-J. *Angestellte und Demokratie: Die nationalliberale Angestelltenbewegung in der Weimarer Republik*. Stuttgart, 1979.

Puhle, H.-J. "Parlament, Parteien und Interessenverbände, 1890–1914." In M. Stürmer, ed., *Das kaiserliche Deutschland: Politik und Gesellschaft, 1870–1918*, pp. 340–77. Düsseldorf, 1970.

Rachfahl, F. "Eugen Richter und der Linksliberalismus im neuen Reiche." *Zeitschrift für Politik* 5 (1912): 261–374.

Real, W. *Der Deutsche Reformverein: Großdeutsche Kräfte zwischen Villafranca und Königgrätz*. Lübeck and Hamburg, 1966.

Riemann, J. *Ernst Müller-Meiningen senior und der Linksliberalismus in seiner Zeit: Zur Biographie eines bayerischen und deutschen Politikers (1866–1944)*. Munich, 1968.

——. "Der politische Liberalismus in der Krise der Revolution." In Karl Bosl, ed., *Bayern im Umbruch: Die Revolution von 1918, ihre Voraussetzungen, ihr Verlauf und ihre Folgen*, pp. 165–99. Munich, 1969.

Ritter, G.A. "Kontinuität und Umformung des deutschen Parteiensystems, 1918–1920." In G.A. Ritter, ed., *Entstehung und Wandel der modernen Gesellschaft: Festschrift für Hans Rosenberg zum 65. Geburtstag*, pp. 342–84. Berlin, 1970.

——, ed. *Die deutschen Parteien vor 1918*. Cologne, 1973.

Robson, S.T. "German Left Liberals and the First World War." In

Canadian Historical Association, *Historical Papers Presented at the Annual Meeting Held at Ottawa, June 7–10, 1967*, pp. 216–34.

——. "Left-wing Liberalism in Germany, 1900–1919." Unpublished Ph.D. thesis, Oxford University, 1966.

Rohr, D. *The Origins of Social Liberalism in Germany*. Chicago, 1963.

Rosenberg, H. *Politische Denkströmungen im deutschen Vormärz*. Göttingen, 1972.

——. *Rudolf Haym und die Anfänge des klassischen Liberalismus*. Munich and Berlin, 1933.

Rothmund, R., and Wiehn, E.R., eds. *Die F.D.P./DVP in Baden-Württemberg und ihre Geschichte*. Stuttgart, 1979.

Ruggiero, G. de. *The History of European Liberalism*. Translated by R.G. Collingwood. Oxford, 1927.

Runge, G. *Die Volkspartei in Württemberg von 1864 bis 1871: Die Erben der 48er Revolution im Kampf gegen die preußisch-kleindeutsche Lösung der nationalen Frage*. Stuttgart, 1892.

Runge, G. "Linksliberale Emigranten in Großbritannien: Überlegungen zu Gesellschaft und Demokratie im Nachkriegsdeutschland." *Vierteljahrshefte für Zeitgeschichte* 37 (1989): 57–83.

Rütten, T. *Der deutsche Liberalismus 1945 bis 1955: Deutschlands- und Gesellschaftspolitik der ost- und westdeutschen Liberalen in der Entstehungsgeschichte der beiden deutschen Staaten*. Baden-Baden, 1984.

Scaff, L. *Fleeing the Iron Cage: Culture, Politics, and Modernity in the Thought of Max Weber*. Berkeley, 1989.

Schieder, T. *The State and Society in Our Times: Studies in the History of the Nineteenth and Twentieth Centuries*. Translated by C.A.M. Sym. Toronto and New York, 1962.

Schieder, W. ed. *Liberalismus in der Gesellschaft des deutschen Vormärz*. Göttingen, 1983.

Schmidt, G. "Die Nationalliberalen – Eine regierungsfähige Partei? Zur Problematik der inneren Reichsgründung, 1870–1878." In G.A. Ritter, ed., *Die deutschen Parteien vor 1918*, pp. 208–23. Cologne, 1973.

Schmidt, S. "Liberale Parteibewegung and Volksmassen während der bürgerlichen Umwälzung in Deutschland, 1789–1871." *Zeitschrift für Geschichtswissenschaft* 26 (1978): 2–43.

Schneider, W. *Die Deutsche Demokratische Partei in der Weimarer Republik, 1924–1930*. Munich, 1978.

Schorske, C. *Fin-de-Siècle Vienna: Politics and Culture*. New York, 1979.

Schröder, K. *Die FDP in der britischen Besatzungszone, 1946–1948: Ein Beitrag zur Organisationsstruktur der Liberalen im Nachkriegsdeutschland*. Düsseldorf, 1985.

Schuchardt, H., and Verheugen, G., eds. *Das liberale Gewissen*. Berlin, 1982.

Schustereit, H. *Linksliberalismus und Sozialdemokratie in der Weimarer*

Republik: Eine vergleichende Betrachtung der Politik von DDP und SPD, 1919–1930. Düsseldorf, 1975.

Schwarz, G. *Theodor Wolff und das "Berliner Tageblatt": Eine liberale Stimme in der deutschen Politik, 1906–1933.* Tübingen, 1968.

Sedatis, H. *Liberalismus und Handwerk in Südwestdeutschland: Wirtschafts- und Gesellschaftskonzeptionen des Liberalismus und die Krise des Handwerks im 19. Jahrhundert.* Stuttgart, 1979.

Seeber, G. *Zwischen Bebel und Bismarck: Zur Geschichte des Linksliberalismus in Deutschland, 1871–1893.* (East) Berlin, 1965.

Sell, F.C. *Die Tragödie des deutschen Liberalismus.* Stuttgart, 1953.

Sheehan, J.J. *The Career of Lujo Brentano: A Study of Liberalism and Social Reform in Imperial Germany.* Chicago and London, 1966.

———. *German Liberalism in the Nineteenth Century.* Chicago, 1978.

———. "Liberalism and Society in Germany, 1815–1848." *Journal of Modern History* 4 (1973): 583–604.

———. "Liberalism and the City in Nineteenth-Century Germany." *Past and Present,* no. 51 (1971): 116–37.

———. "Partei, Volk, and Staat: Some Reflections on the Relationship between Liberal Thought and Action in Vormärz." In H.-U. Wehler, ed., *Sozialgeschichte Heute: Festschrift für Hans Rosenberg zum 70. Geburtstag,* pp. 162–74. Göttingen, 1974.

Simons, K. *Die württembergischen Demokraten: Ihre Stellung und Arbeit im Parteien- und Verfassungssystem in Württemberg und im Deutschen Reich, 1890–1920.* Stuttgart, 1969.

Smith, S. *Hegel's Critique of Liberalism: Rights in Context.* Chicago, 1989.

Snell, J.L. *The Democratic Movement in Germany, 1789–1914.* Edited and completed by Hans Schmitt. Chapel Hill, N.C., 1976.

Sontheimer, K., ed. *Möglichkeiten und Grenzen liberaler Politik.* Düsseldorf, 1975.

Stegmann, D. *Die Erben Bismarcks, Parteien und Verbände in der Spätphase des Wilheminischen Deutschlands: Sammlungspolitik, 1897–1918.* Cologne, 1970.

Stern, F. *The Failure of Illiberalism: Essays on the Political Culture of Modern Germany.* New York, 1972.

———. *The Politics of Cultural Despair: A Study in the Rise of the Germanic Ideology.* Berkeley, 1961.

Struve, W. *Elites against Democracy: Leadership Ideals in Bourgeois Political Thought in Germany, 1890–1933.* Princeton, N.J., 1973.

Stürmer, M. *Regierung und Reichstag im Bismarckstaat, 1871–1880.* Düsseldorf, 1974.

Suval, S. *Electoral Politics in Wilhelmine Germany.* Chapel Hill, N.C., 1985.

Thadden, R., ed. *Die Krise des Liberalismus zwischen den Weltkriegen.* Göttingen, 1978.

425

Theiner, P. *Sozialer Liberalismus und deutsche Weltpolitik: Friedrich Naumann im Wilhelminischen Deutschland (1860–1919)*. Baden-Baden, 1983.

Thiel, J. *Die Großblockpolitik der Nationalliberalen Partei Badens, 1905–1914*. Stuttgart, 1976.

Thieme, H. *Nationaler Liberalismus in der Krise: Die nationalliberale Fraktion des preußischen Abgeordnetenhauses, 1914–1918*. Boppard am Rhein, 1963.

Thimme, R. *Stresemann und die Deutsche Volkspartei, 1923–25*. Lübeck and Hamburg, 1961.

Thomas, R.H. *Liberalism, Nationalism, and the German Intellectuals, 1822–1847: An Analysis of the Academic and Scientific Conferences of the Period*. Cambridge, 1951.

Turner, H.A., Jr. *Stresemann and the Politics of the Weimar Republic*. Princeton, N.J., 1963.

Vascik, G. "Rural Politics and Sugar in Germany: A Comparative Study of the National Liberal Party in Hannover and Prussian Saxony, 1871–1914." Unpublished Ph.D. dissertation, University of Michigan, 1988.

Veblen, T. *Imperial Germany and the Industrial Revolution*. New York, 1915.

Vogel, B. *Allgemeine Gewerbefreiheit: Die Reformpolitik des preußischen Staatskanzlers Hardenberg (1810–1820)*. Göttingen, 1983.

Vorländer, H., ed. *Verfall oder Renaissance des Liberalismus? Beiträge zum deutschen und internationalen Liberalismus*. Munich, 1987.

Walker, M. *German Homes Towns: Community, State, and General Estate, 1648–1871*. Ithaca, N.Y., and London, 1971.

Warren, D. *The Red Kingdom of Saxony: Lobbying Grounds for Gustav Stresemann, 1901–1909*. The Hague, 1964.

Wegner, K. "Linksliberalismus in Wilhelminischen Deutschland und in der Weimarer Republik." *Geschichte und Gesellschaft* 4 (1978): 120–38.

———. *Theodor Barth und die Freisinnige Vereinigung: Studien zur Geschichte des Linksliberalismus im Wilhelminischen Deutschland (1893–1910)*. Tübingen, 1968.

Wehler, H.-U. *Deutsche Gesellschaftsgeschichte*. 2 vols. Munich, 1987.

———. *The German Empire, 1871–1918*. Translated by K. Traynor. Leamington Spa, 1985.

———. *Krisenherde des Kaiserreichs: Studien zur deutschen Sozial- und Verfassungsgeschichte*. Göttingen, 1970.

Wentzcke, P., ed. *Deutscher Staat und deutsche Parteien: Beiträge zur deutschen Partei- und Ideengeschichte*. Munich and Berlin, 1922.

White, D. *The Splintered Party: National Liberalism in Hessen and the Reich, 1867–1918*. Cambridge, Mass., 1976.

Winkler, H.A. *Liberalismus und Antiliberalismus: Studien zur politischen Sozialgeschichte des 19. und 20. Jahrhunderts*. Göttingen, 1979.

426

——. *Mittelstand, Demokratie und Nationalsozialismus: Die politische Entwicklung vom Handwerk und Kleinhandel in der Weimarer Republik.* Cologne, 1972.

——. *Preußischer Liberalismus und deutscher Nationalstaat: Studien zur Geschichte der Deutschen Fortschrittspartei, 1861–1866.* Tübingen, 1964.

Wulf, P. *Hugo Stinnes: Wirtschaft und Politik, 1918–1924.* Stuttgart, 1979.

Zucker, S. *Ludwig Bamberger: German Liberal Politician and Social Critic, 1823–1899.* Pittsburgh, Pa., 1975.

Notes on Contributors

RICHARD J. BAZILLION is director of library services at Brandon University in Brandon, Manitoba. He is author of the recent monograph entitled *Modernizing Germany: Karl Biedermann's Career in the Kingdom of Saxony, 1835–1901* (New York: Peter Lang, 1989). His current research entails a comparison of the *Zollverein* and the Canada-United States Free Trade Agreement of 1989 with respect to the influence of economic integration on political sovereignty.

REBECCA BOEHLING is assistant professor of history at the University of Maryland-Baltimore County. She has published articles on the reestablishment of political democracy in the U.S. zone of occupation after World War II in the *Archiv für Sozialgeschichte* (1985) and the *Archiv für Frankfurts Geschichte und Kunst* (1985). She is currently working on the process of German democratization from 1945 to 1955 and on the status of women in postwar Germany.

THOMAS CHILDERS is professor of history and director of the Center for European Studies at the University of Pennsylvania. He is author of *The Nazi Voter: The Social Foundations of Fascism in Germany, 1919–1933* (Chapel Hill: University of North Carolina Press, 1983) and editor of *The Formation of the Nazi Constituency, 1919–1933* (Totowa, N.J.: Barnes and Noble, 1986). He is currently working on a book-length manuscript on propaganda and the mobilization of the Nazi electorate in the Weimar Republic.

GEOFF ELEY is professor of history at the University of Michigan in Ann Arbor, Michigan. He is author of *Reshaping the German Right: Radical Nationalism and Political Change after Bismarck* (New Haven: Yale University Press, 1980) and, with David Blackbourn, coauthored *The Peculiarities of German History: Bourgeois Society and Politics in Nineteenth-Century Germany* (Oxford: Oxford University Press, 1984). He is finishing a book on the European Left in the nineteenth and twentieth centuries and is doing research on German liberalism between the 1860s and 1920s.

MARION W. GRAY is professor of history at Kansas State University in Manhattan, Kansas. His various publications on German social and political history in the era of the French Revolution include a monograph on *Prussia in Transition: Society and Politics during the Stein Reform Ministry of 1808* (Philadelphia: American Philosophical Society, 1986).

He is currently completing a book on changing gender norms in Germany between 1780 and 1830.

JAMES F. HARRIS is associate professor of history at the University of Maryland in College Park, Maryland. He is author of *A Study in the Theory and Practice of German Liberalism: Eduard Lasker, 1829–1884* (Lanham, Md.: University Press of America, 1984) and has edited a collection of essays entitled *Heritage and Challenge – German American Interrelations* (Tübingen: Attempto Verlag, 1986). He has just completed a manuscript on opposition to Jewish emancipation in Bavaria and is currently working on the emergence of grassroots political activity in Germany during the revolution of 1848–49.

DAGMAR HERZOG is a doctoral candidate in modern German history and European women's history at Brown University and held a DAAD fellowship at the University of Heidelberg in 1987–88. Her dissertation is entitled "Jews and Christians, Women and Men: Religious Dissent and Conflicts over Difference in Pre-Revolutionary Baden."

KONRAD H. JARAUSCH is Lurcy Professor of European Civilization at the University of North Carolina-Chapel Hill. He is the author of *The Enigmatic Chancellor: Bethmann-Hollweg and the Hubris of Imperial Germany* (New Haven: Yale University Press, 1972) and *Students, Society, and Politics in Imperial Germany: The Rise of Academic Illiberalism* (Princeton: Princeton University Press, 1982). He is currently working on the history of the German professions and has just finished a study entitled *The Unfree Professions: German Lawyers, Teachers, and Engineers, 1900–1950* (New York: Oxford University Press, 1990).

MICHAEL JOHN is a fellow and tutor in modern history at Magdalen College at Oxford University. He is author of *Politics and the Law in Late Nineteenth-Century Germany: The Origins of the Civil Code* (Oxford: Oxford University Press, 1989) and has published a number of articles on the history of nineteenth-century German liberalism. He is currently working on the history of liberalism in Hanover between 1848 and 1914 and on a social history of the German legal profession from 1800 to 1914.

LARRY EUGENE JONES is professor of history at Canisius College in Buffalo, New York, and is a specialist on the history of the German party system during the Weimar Republic. He is author of *German Liberalism and the Dissolution of the Weimar Party System, 1918–1933* (Chapel Hill: University of North Carolina Press, 1988). He is currently working on a book-length monograph on the German Right and the Nazi seizure of power from 1928 to 1934.

JONATHAN KNUDSEN is associate professor of history at Wellesley College in Wellesley, Massachusetts, and is the author of *Justus Moser and the German Enlightenment* (New York: Cambridge University Press, 1986). He also translated Rudolf Vierhaus, *Germany in the Age of Absolutism* (New York: Cambridge University Press, 1989). His current work is on the emergence of political liberalism in Berlin in the first half of the nineteenth century.

DIETER LANGEWIESCHE holds the chair of modern history at the University of Tübingen and is a specialist on the social and political history of German liberalism. He recently published *Europa zwischen Restauration und Revolution, 1815–1849* (Munich: Oldenbourg Verlag, 1985) and *Liberalismus in Deutschland* (Frankfurt a.M.: Suhrkamp Verlag, 1988) and has edited *Liberalismus im 19. Jahrhundert: Deutschland im europäischen Vergleich* (Göttingen: Vandenhoeck und Ruprecht Verlag, 1989).

A.J. NICHOLLS is an official fellow and university lecturer at St. Antony's College at Oxford University. He is the author of *Weimar and the Rise of Hitler* (New York: St. Martin's Press, 1968) and, with Sir John Wheeler-Bennett, coauthored *The Semblance of Peace: The Political Settlement after the Second World War* (New York: St. Martin's Press, 1972). His current area of research is the Federal Republic of Germany, with special attention to the social market economy.

ELEANOR L. TURK is associate professor of history at Indiana University East in Richmond, Indiana. Her publications include articles on the political press and pressure groups in Wilhelmine Germany and on German emigration in the nineteenth century. She is currently completing a monograph on civil liberty in Wilhelmine Germany.

Index

Index